Sensation & Perception

Sensation & Perception

Bennett L. Schwartz | John H. Krantz

Florida International University   Hanover College

SAGE

Los Angeles | London | New Delhi
Singapore | Washington DC | Boston

Los Angeles | London | New Delhi
Singapore | Washington DC | Boston

FOR INFORMATION:

SAGE Publications, Inc.
2455 Teller Road
Thousand Oaks, California 91320
E-mail: order@sagepub.com

SAGE Publications Ltd.
1 Oliver's Yard
55 City Road
London EC1Y 1SP
United Kingdom

SAGE Publications India Pvt. Ltd.
B 1/I 1 Mohan Cooperative Industrial Area
Mathura Road, New Delhi 110 044
India

SAGE Publications Asia-Pacific Pte. Ltd.
3 Church Street
#10-04 Samsung Hub
Singapore 049483

Printed in Canada

Cataloging-in-publication data is available for this title from the Library of Congress.

ISBN 978-1-4833-0810-4

Illustrations provided by Auburn Associates and Body Scientific International, LLC. Special thanks to Carolina Hrejsa, Senior Medical Illustrator of Body Scientific International.

Executive Editor: Reid Hester
Development Editor: Nathan Davidson
Digital Content Editor: Lucy Berbeo
Editorial Assistant: Morgan McCardell
Production Editor: Laura Barrett
Copy Editor: Jim Kelly
Typesetter: C&M Digitals (P) Ltd.
Proofreader: Scott Oney
Indexer: Wendy Allex
Interior & Cover Designer: Scott Van Atta
Marketing Manager: Shari Countryman

This book is printed on acid-free paper.

MIX
Paper from
responsible sources
FSC® C011825

15 16 17 18 19 10 9 8 7 6 5 4 3 2 1

BRIEF CONTENTS

DETAILED CONTENTS

PREFACE

Everything we do as human beings starts with our ability to perceive the world. We wake up in the morning to the jarring sound of an alarm clock, prompting us to turn on the light in the room in order to see. A few minutes later, the aroma of the coffee lifts our mood and gets us ready to face the day. We feel inside our pocketbooks and briefcases to make sure we have our keys. Then we listen to the radio as we watch for traffic on the busy streets in our cars. Thus, nearly everything one does over the course of one's waking hours involves sensation and perception. Moreover, think of the obstacles faced by a person missing one or more of these sensory systems. The famous Helen Keller was completely dependent on her senses of touch in the absence of vision and hearing. For this reason, the study of sensation and perception has been important to psychologists from the very beginnings of psychology.

Sensation and Perception is written to be a primary textbook for undergraduate courses in sensation and perception or, as in some universities, simply perception. We have written it primarily with students in mind, but also written it in a way that professors will find it useful as a supplement and guide to their teaching. The two authors come from very different settings; one is a professor at a large public state university, the other at a small private college. We have tried to meld our experiences into a textbook that will be useful in the large lecture typical of the public university and the small seminar of the private college.

When we teach sensation and perception, one of the most common questions that we receive from students is the following: How is this material relevant to my life and to my future as a psychologist? However, sensation and perception textbooks seldom address this topic. Students learn about theories, physiology, anatomy, and experiments, and they get to see some curious illusions. These are all important if one is to understand sensation and perception, and these issues are well covered in our book. But *Sensation and Perception* also instructs students in how to apply these concepts to their everyday lives and how sensation and perception research is valuable in the real world. For example, we discuss applications of sensation and perception research to driving cars, to playing sports, and to evaluating risk in the military. Moreover, we discuss numerous medical applications including extended discussion of such topics as macular degeneration, retinitis pigmentosa, color blindness, hearing aids, and cochlear implants, as well as neuropsychological conditions such as prosopagnosia. For each chapter, we finish with an "in depth" section. Many of these "in depth" sections deal directly with applications of sensation and perception research.

The higher-education classroom itself has changed dramatically in the past decade. Many students take some, if not all of their classes online without ever having to come to a university building. Classes now usually have companion Web sites and students have been "googling" interesting topics since they first could read. A modern textbook needs to adjust to the easy availability of information. What a modern textbook offers that distinguishes it from online sources of information is its accuracy at presenting the most relevant information in an engaging well-written manner. Of course, we wrote our textbook to be approachable and readable, but fundamentally what we offer our students is the guarantee that what they read here is an accurate reflection of what is relevant in the field of sensation and perception.

Having said that, *Sensation and Perception* is written with the current state of technology in mind. First and foremost, we have prepared the ISLE Web site, the companion Web site for the textbook. ISLE provides opportunities to view and hear many of the phenomena we discuss in the book including anatomical diagrams, visual illusions, auditory illusions, and musical selections. It provides simulations of experiments as well as neurological processes, and it provides exercises to understand how models such as signal detection actually work. A book cannot present sound or motion, important components of sensation and perception. But a click on an ISLE link will bridge the gap, bringing these phenomena to your attention. Both teacher and student will find ISLE an invaluable resource.

We also hope that student and professor alike will find our pedagogical resources to be helpful. To help students learn, we start each chapter with a list of learning objectives, which should help the reader organize the material and therefore learn it better. After each major section, we have a "test your knowledge" question. This question is an open-ended one that promotes thinking about the material broadly and linking concepts together. Must-be-learned definitions are clearly marked off in the margins, and illustrations throughout the text reinforce what is written in the text. At the end of each chapter is a carefully organized chapter summary, a set of review questions, a list of key terms, and a list of the ISLE (Interactive Sensation Laboratory Exercises) exercises for that chapter.

Sensation and Perception emphasizes science. It describes experiments, patients with neurological disorders, the areas of the brain involved in sensation and perception, and the theory that links this research together. We wrote this book with students in mind—their concerns, interests, and curiosity. We hope that—at the same time that this book emphasizes the science of sensation and perception—it also tells a story about our search to understand our own minds and how we can benefit from that understanding.

ANAGLYPH GLASSES

ISLE P.1 Obtaining or Creating Anaglyph Glasses.

Some of the photographic figures in the text and on ISLE are anaglyphic stereograms, and they will require special glasses to be seen properly. See chapter 7 for more information about stereograms. While these glasses are not provided with the book, they are easy to make, or, if you prefer, cheap to buy, individually or in bulk. Please not that you will need Red/Cyan anaglyph glasses. Consult ISLE P.1 for specific information about either making or ordering these glasses.

ANCILLARIES

SAGE edge offers a robust online environment featuring an impressive array of tools and resources for review, study, and further exploration, keeping both instructors and students on the cutting edge of teaching and learning. Go to **edge.sagepub.com/schwartz** to access the companion site.

SAGE edge for Instructors

<u>SAGE edge for Instructors</u>, a password-protected instructor resource site, supports teaching by making it easy to integrate quality content and create a rich learning environment for students. The following chapter-specific assets are available on the teaching site:

- **Author-created test banks** provide a diverse range of questions as well as the opportunity to edit any question and/or insert personalized questions to effectively assess students' progress and understanding.
- **Lecture notes** summarize key concepts by chapter to assist in the preparation of lectures and class discussions.

- **Sample course syllabi** for semester and quarter courses provide suggested models for structuring a course.
- Editable, chapter-specific **PowerPoint slides** offer complete flexibility for creating a multimedia presentation for the course.
- Lively and stimulating **ideas for class assignments** that can be used in class to reinforce active learning. The creative assignments apply to individual or group projects.
- Chapter-specific **discussion questions** help launch classroom interaction by prompting students to engage with the material and by reinforcing important content.
- **Multimedia content** includes audio and video resources that appeal to students with different learning styles.

SAGE edge for Students

<u>**SAGE edge for Students**</u> provides a personalized approach to help students accomplish their coursework goals in an easy-to-use learning environment. The open-access study site includes:

- **Interactive Sensation Laboratory Exercises (ISLE)** provide opportunities to view and hear many of the phenomena discussed in the book including anatomical diagrams, visual illusions, auditory illusions, and musical selections.
- A customized online **action plan** includes tips and feedback on progress through the course and materials, allowing students to individualize their learning experience.
- **Learning objectives** reinforce the most important material.
- Mobile-friendly **eFlashcards** strengthen understanding of key terms and concepts.
- **Multimedia content** includes audio and video resources that appeal to students with different learning styles.
- EXCLUSIVE! Access to full-text **SAGE journal articles** that have been carefully selected to support and expand on the concepts presented in each chapter.

ACKNOWLEDGMENTS

We need to thank many people for their contributions to making this book come together. Although the cover lists Bennett and John as the authors, there are a multitude of people who made invaluable contributions to ensuring that this book came together. First, we must thank many people at SAGE Publications for their contribution to the development, art program, and production of *Sensation and Perception*. We thank Reid Hester for initiating the project, bringing us together, guiding this book to the finish line, and seeing it published in a timely manner. We thank Lucy Berbeo for her tireless work in getting everything right from writing to the illustrations to the photographs to the permissions. We thank Nathan Davidson for his work, especially on the pedagogy. We thank Laura Barrett and her staff in Production. We thank Sarita Sarak for her work at the beginning of the project. We thank copy editor Jim Kelly for his hard work.

We also thank the people who reviewed earlier drafts of chapters or the whole book and generously gave us their feedback. These people people are listed under the Publisher's Acknowledgements.

We also need to thank many colleagues and students who read drafts of chapters or who gave us advice on what the important questions are in a particular topic. These people include, but are not limited to, Matthew Schulkind, Pat Delucia, Zehra Peynircioglu, Scott Pearl, Randy Blake, Adrien Chopin, Thomas Sanocki, Brian Pasley, and Todd Kahan. And thanks to Julia Overton, who sent us information on chili pepper eating contests.

We thank Hanover College for hosting the ISLE Web site.

We also need to thank various individuals who helped out with the art program for this textbook. Photographs, musical contributions, and likenesses were freely contributed by Margaret Krantz, Leslie Frazier, Sarina Schwartz, Erin Hunter, Jonathan Altman, Scott Pearl, Robert Kirkpatrick, and Todd Kahan.

Bennett L. Schwartz & John H. Krantz
September 24, 2014

PUBLISHER'S ACKNOWLEDGMENTS

SAGE Publications would like to acknowledge the following reviewers for their contributions to the manuscript:

Benoit-Antoine Bacon, Bishop's University

Mark E. Berg, The Richard Stockton College of New Jersey

Michael D. Biderman, The University of Tennessee at Chattanooga

Bryan R. Burnham, The University of Scranton

Beatrice M. de Oca, California State University Channel Islands

Robert Dippner, University of Nevada, Las Vegas

Susan E. Dutch, Westfield State University

Jim Dykes, University of Texas at San Antonio

John H. Flowers, University of Nebraska–Lincoln

Gina A. Glanc, Ph.D., Texas A&M University Corpus Christi

Paula Goolkasian, UNC Charlotte

Billy R. Hammond, Jr., The University of Georgia

Cheryl-Ann Hardy, Columbia College

C. Eric Jones, Regent University

Eric Laws, Longwood University

Fabio Leite, The Ohio State University at Lima

Poornima Madhavan, Old Dominion University

Sara J. Margolin, Ph.D., The College at Brockport, State University of New York

Daniel S. McConnell, University of Central Florida

John Philbeck, The George Washington University

Elisabeth J. Ploran, Hofstra University

Jamie Prowse Turner, Red Deer College

Jennifer S. Queen, Rollins College

Jason A. Rogers, State University of New York Institute of Technology

Tom Sanocki, University of South Florida

Matthew Schlesinger, Southern Illinois University Carbondale

Carl W. Scott, University of St. Thomas

T. C. Sim, Sam Houston State University

Sherril M. Stone, Northwestern Oklahoma State University

Albert K. Toh, Ph.D., University of Arkansas–Pine Bluff

Erik C. Tracy, University of North Carolina Pembroke

Emily A. Wickelgren, California State University, Sacramento

Robert J. Woll, Siena College

Takashi Yamauchi, Texas A&M University

Lonnie Yandell, Belmont University

Diana L. Young, Georgia College & State University

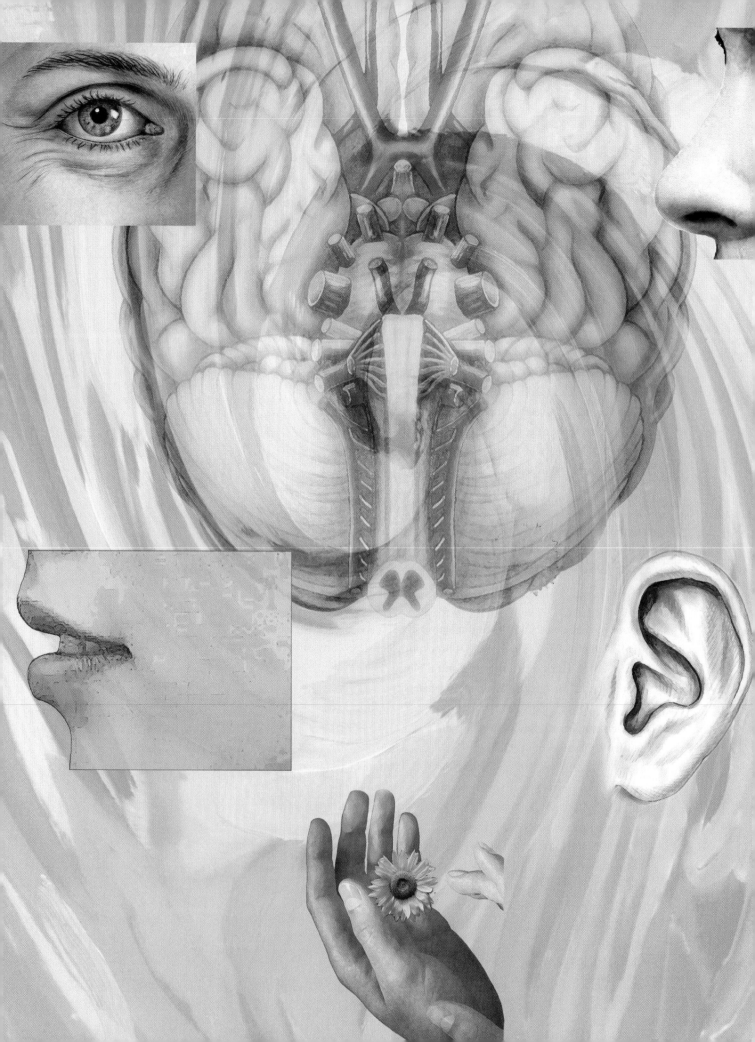

What Is Perception?

INTRODUCTION

Try to imagine the last concert you attended. It does not matter what kind of music you like—rap, country, even the opera. Most likely, your experience at the concert was thrilling—an experience initiated by the pleasure that auditory perception can bring. The sounds of the singer's voice and the guitarist's riffs stir your emotions. The music pulses into your ears. Despite your distance from the stage, and the assortment of voices and instruments, you correctly sort out the lead singer's voice from the guitar, the bass, the keyboard, and the drums. Moreover, even though there is a disconnect between the source of the sound (the loudspeakers) and the location of the musicians (the stage), you correctly attribute the sound to the stage. But in almost all cases, in all varieties of music, a concert is more than just sound. The flashy clothes and the elaborate video screens fill your eyes with color and movement. Most pop concerts are designed as much for the eyes as they are for the ears. The same is true for opera (see Figure 1.1). Because it incorporates drama as well as music, costumes and visual appearance are as much a part of the art form as is the music itself. Our enjoyment of a live concert comes from this symphony of sensory stimulation.

We tend to take our amazing sensory abilities for granted, even when we are specifically engaging in activities such as concerts or visits to art museums, in which we are deliberately challenging our sensory systems. In general, we think about the manner in which we see, hear, touch, taste, and smell the world, and how we become aware of our own internal states as well. Perceptual abilities work fast, and they provide us during every waking moment with an ongoing update as to the state of the world around us. We may attend to only certain aspects of the world at any given moment, but a wealth of potential information exists around us. Consider the simple act of reading this paragraph. Unless you are blind and using either touch or audition to read these words, you are looking at a pattern of black squiggles on a white background. Your attentional focus is on decoding these squiggles from an intricate pattern of visual stimulation into meaningful concepts. However, even if you are in a quiet room, you are surrounded by myriad other sources of sensory stimulation. Just a slight break of concentration, and you may become aware of the slight hum of the heating system, voices from upstairs chatting about campus events, the pulse of the refrigerator, the Hummer with the deafening bass line driving by outside, and maybe the plaintive cooing of a mourning dove in a tree outside the window. Look up from your text and you can see the flowers your mother sent you, the leftover dinner that needs to be

LEARNING OBJECTIVES

1.1 Explain why understanding sensation and perception is important.

1.2 Explain why there are actually more than five senses.

1.3 Describe how transduction transforms a physical signal into a neural signal.

1.4 Explore the history of the study of sensation and perception.

1.5 Apply sensation and perception research to collisions.

■ **FIGURE 1.1** Chinese opera.

In Chinese opera, elaborate and colorful costumes make the performance as much a visual experience as it is a musical one.

BILL HATCHER/National Geographic Creative

■ **FIGURE 1.2   Chocolate chip cookies.**

Just seeing chocolate chip cookies may make you hungry. However, most people cannot make a taste image—that is, try to imagine what chocolate chip cookies actually taste like (not look like) with nothing actual to taste. However, when we smell the cookies, we get a sensation very distinct from what they look like.

cleaned up, or your relaxed cat sleeping by your feet. An inadvertent sniff, smelling the cookies baking in the kitchen, breaks your concentration (see Figure 1.2). Feel free to put "Schwartz and Krantz" down for a moment and have one of those cookies before you continue reading. And don't worry about the vase.

The fact of the matter is that each of these sensory processes, from reading words in a book to smelling cookies baking in an oven, is incredibly complicated; each one is completed by exquisitely fine-tuned processes in our brains. By and large, however, we become conscious only of the finished product—the words on the screen, the music of the Black Eyed Peas gradually getting louder, then softer, as the car with the loud stereo passes by outside, the brush of your cat's soft fur against your skin, and the taste of the warm chocolate mixing with the sugary cookie dough. The incredible computing power of the human brain is focused on processing each of these sensory inputs and allowing your conscious mind to pick and choose among them. Indeed, sensory systems have evolved to accomplish these processes quickly and efficiently.

This textbook is an introduction to the science of sensory processes. We will address the issue of sensation and perception from the perspectives of both psychology and neuroscience. That is, we will discuss both the neural underpinnings of sensation and perception and the psychological processes based on those neural processes. Given that the study of sensation and perception initiated the very beginning of scientific psychology, science has made progress on how these processes work. Granted, there are many questions still unanswered about how sensory experience occurs, but there is a broad consensus on the general pattern, from how information is perceived by sensory neurons to the areas of the brain responsible for each sensory system to the cognitive processes whereby we recognize common objects. This textbook is written to help you, the beginning scientist, understand the complex processes that go into sensory perception. We hold that the study of sensation and perception is a fascinating area that sheds light on the basic nature of what it is to be human. We hope you find this journey interesting.

However, at the outset, we find it necessary to inform the reader: Understanding sensory processes is not easy. No matter how clearly we describe each topic in this book or how well your professor explains the material, understanding this material takes hard work and patience. The human mind and brain are complex, and therefore, to understand how they work and create our ability to sense and perceive is also a complex task. Thus, read your text slowly and repeatedly, consult the online resources, experience the illusions and demonstrations provided on ISLE, answer the review questions, test yourself repeatedly, and give yourself the time to learn about sensation and perception. Moreover, the terminology is often complex and certainly requires ample memorizing. Make sure to learn the key terms, because they are important in understanding the concepts (and presumably doing well in your class). Do not get frustrated—it is likely that other students need just as much time to learn the terms and help understanding sensation and perception as you do. We think it is worth the time—we hope you will find the incredible designs and abilities nature has evolved in our sensory systems to be inspiring, interesting, and important.

WHY IS THIS PSYCHOLOGY?

 1.1   Explain why understanding sensation and perception is important.

When each of your authors teaches this course, one of the questions he is occasionally asked is why sensation and perception are part of the psychology curriculum and not, say, the biology curriculum. This is a fair question given that much of what you will read in this book concerns anatomy and physiology, with a little bit of cognitive science thrown in. The answer, however, is simple: The goal is to understand perceptual experience, that is, how our brains make sense of the sensory world around us. This is an inherently psychological goal: understanding how our minds, though our brains, interpret the world around us. We will see, as well, that psychological processes, such as attention, intention, emotion, and biases, influence the ways in which we perceive the world. Consider the sensory experience of pain. Every marathon runner, whether an amateur or an Olympic medalist, crosses the finish line in intense bodily discomfort (see Figure 1.3). Body temperature is at fever levels, muscles are filled with lactic acid, sunburn covers the skin, dehydration is present, and sores are opening on the feet. But despite the pain and discomfort, the marathon runner is ecstatic—he or she has completed an incredibly challenging goal. The pain is interpreted in the context of competing a long-sought objective—to demonstrate that the marathon can be run. Duplicate the same physical conditions with an inmate at the Guantanamo Bay prison, and you have torture.

■ FIGURE 1.3　**Runners overcome pain.**

Marathon runners must overcome intense pain by the end of the race. Our bodies have a number of ways of easing the pain, and the social situation helps us endure it. The marathon runner may value the sense of accomplishment of finishing the race. But pain is still an intense sensory experience.

Consider too how our personal biases can influence perception. Think about two friends from Los Angeles watching a basketball game between the Los Angeles Clippers and the Los Angeles Lakers. Each person is watching the same game from the same vantage point in the stands. That is, both friends are receiving the same perceptual input. However, each person perceives different things. The Clippers fan sees Lakers all-star Kobe Bryant "charging," that is, committing an offensive foul. The Lakers fan sees the same play as a blocking foul on Clippers point guard Chris Paul, maybe even a flagrant foul. The same sensory input results in two different perceptual outputs. Research has shown that even when participants are instructed to be totally objective, they cannot overcome the kinds of biases that are created by being a fan of one team or another (e.g., Hastorf & Cantril, 1954). That is, even when trying to be totally objective, Lakers fans cannot see the game from a Clippers perspective, and Clippers fans cannot see the game from a Lakers perspective. For this reason, referees who grew up as Lakers fans are seldom assigned the job of refereeing games involving Los Angeles teams. The hope is that a referee from Seattle can see a game in an unbiased way (or at least a less biased way) compared with a referee from Los Angeles. However, because of the biases of the Clippers fans and the Lakers fans, they will never see what the referee sees. Thus, the most fair of referees may often be scolded by fans of both teams as being biased toward one or the other team—in the very same game.

Knowledge can influence perception in more subtle ways than occur among biased sports fans. Consider seeing a small dot on the horizon of the ocean. Because you know that it is a cruise ship out there, you tend to see it as such. That the object could be an alien spaceship is considered far less likely, so you do not see it as such. Indeed, we use our knowledge of objects to help us perceive them even in relatively simple and static scenes. Consider the horses in Figure 1.4. This painting by the artist Bev Doolittle uses the same color brown for both the horses and the rocks, and the same color white for both the horses and the snow. She makes the white slightly darker and bluer around the horses' knees, but in many places in the painting, only the imagined form of the horse separates it from the background. Yet we still see the horses, despite the camouflage.

Pintos © Bev Doolittle, The Greenwich Workshop, Inc.

■ FIGURE 1.4   **Knowledge influences perception.**

We see borders between snow and horses because we have knowledge that horses are complete beings not broken up by snowy patches, as are the rocks behind.

TEST YOUR KNOWLEDGE

Why are sensation and perception studied by psychologists?

THE MYTH OF FIVE SENSES

1.2   Explain why there are actually more than five senses.

Most of us were taught in elementary school about the five senses—vision, hearing, touch, smell, and taste. This standard taxonomy is not a simplified classification system, though it goes all the way back to Aristotle. It is wrong! We certainly have more than five senses. For example, in addition to these sensory systems, we have a vestibular system to help keep our balance and a proprioception system to allow us to monitor the position of our bodies. Our sense of touch is composed of multiple systems designed to sense different features of the environment. Heat, cold, pain, itchiness, and soft touch are all implemented by separable sensory systems. Indeed, the receptors for the "itch" experience are a unique kind of receptor different from those that sense touch and those that sense pain. Thus, depending on how the different touch systems are counted, it is more realistic to say that human beings have anywhere from 7 to 12 different sensory systems (see Table 1.1). Indeed, some have even argued that hunger and thirst should be counted as senses. We leave them out, as they deal strictly with internal states that are not directly linked to specific receptors.

    The standard five-sense approach also fails if you think of the sensory systems as hierarchically organized. For example, our perception of the flavors of foods is a complex interaction of smell and taste, and is something we feel is quite different from smell itself. Flavor may also take into account other sensory modalities. Indeed, flavor is influenced by vision as well. If you have ever tried to eat green eggs and ham, you know what we are saying. However, because smell and taste are so bound together, it makes sense to group these two senses in the same way that soft touch, pain, and temperature are grouped together as the sense of touch or as a somatosensory system. Nonetheless, old habits are hard to break, and this book is roughly organized according to the traditional five-sense taxonomy. This is merely a bow to convention, not an endorsement of any scientific truth behind it. In Chapter 12, we cover the skin senses (touch, pain, and temperature). You will see that the various senses that make up this group are different both perceptually and anatomically. Indeed, even the sensation of "hotness" and the sensation of "coldness" are brought about by different receptors, not a differential response from a "temperature" receptor. The classic "burn" sensation of feeling liquid nitrogen on one's skin is an example of this (burning off warts and moles with freezing liquid nitrogen is a common dermatological procedure).

It does make scientific sense to discuss the visual system and the auditory system as discrete sensory systems. And given the centrality of these two systems to human sensory processing, much of this book is devoted to them. Indeed, all but the last two chapters are about vision and audition. Increasingly, however, how sensory systems interact is becoming an important topic of study known as multisensory processing, studies of which address how one sense can affect perception in another (Alvarado, Vaughan, Stanford, & Stein, 2007).

Function	Organ	External or Internal Stimuli
Vision	Eyes	External
Hearing	Ears	External
Smell	Nose	External
Taste	Tongue	External
Light touch	Skin	External
Pressure	Skin	External
Cold	Skin	External
Heat	Skin	External
Pain	Skin/viscera	External/internal
Itch	Skin	External
Vestibular	Inner ear	External
Proprioception	Muscles	Internal

■ TABLE 1.1   Senses of the Human Body

This table shows that there are more sensory systems than the traditional five.

TEST YOUR KNOWLEDGE

What is meant by the myth of five senses?

THE BASICS OF PERCEPTION

 1.3   Describe how transduction transforms a physical signal into a neural signal.

Sensation refers to the registering of a physical **stimulus** on our sensory receptors. That is, sensation is the earliest stages of a process that starts off in the eyes, ears, or skin and ends in the higher centers of the brain. Sensation changes physical stimuli, such as light, sound waves, and mechanical vibrations, into information in our nervous systems. **Perception**, by contrast, refers to the later aspects of the perceptual process. To be specific, perception involves turning the sensory input into meaningful conscious experience. In this sense, perception means the translation of that neural signal into usable information.

Sensation and perception are usually thought of as distinct processes, one referring to the basic process of converting external information into a neural signal and the other concerned with interpreting what that signal means. Other researchers think that the dichotomy between sensation and perception is a false one (e.g., Gibson, 1979). We will begin with the standard model, in which sensation occurs in the sensory organs. That is, for audition, sensation occurs in the ear,

Sensation: the registration of physical stimuli on sensory receptors

Stimulus: an element of the world around us that impinges on our sensory systems

Perception: the process of creating conscious perceptual experience from sensory input

ISLE 1.1 Sequence of Sensory Events

■ **FIGURE 1.5   Seeing is a complex process.**

To understand this photograph, you must sense the colors and images, but cognitive processes aid in understanding what it is you are looking at. Without some cultural knowledge, the sensation makes little sense. However, to our conscious selves, the process of perceiving the Russian dolls is seamless.

■ **FIGURE 1.6   The smell of coffee.**

The smell of coffee comes from molecules in the air that rise from the coffee. Special cells in our noses must convert the presence of those molecules into neural signals, which we interpret as the wonderful aroma of coffee.

in particular the hair cells of the cochlea. For our sense of touch, sensation occurs along the surface of the skin. Perception occurs after cognitive processing begins, typically in the cerebral cortex of the brain. Sensation is about stimuli; perception is about interpretation. To perceive the world, we need both. We cannot perceive the Russian doll on the coffee table as a Russian doll on the coffee table without both ends of the process (see Figure 1.5). The image of the doll must fall on the retina in order for us to perceive, but equally important is the parsing of the perceptual environment, that is, knowing where the doll ends and the table begins. Perception also involves knowing what you are looking at.

So let's take a look at the perceptual process, that is, the sequence of mental operations that bring us from the initial sensory input to our understanding of our conscious experience (see ISLE 1.1).

Stimuli reflect light, produce sounds and vibrations, have surface texture, and produce volatile chemicals (which we can smell). The job of our perceptual processes is to determine what is out there in the world around us. We want our perceptual processes to produce a veridical (truthful) representation of what surrounds us and allow us to focus on those stimuli that are most important to us. Veridicality is important because we want our sensory systems to be guiding us in adaptive ways. For example, if we perceive an object as being farther away than it actually is, we may bump into it and injure ourselves.

Because there are many potential stimuli in our world, we must be able to focus on potential stimuli that are important or interesting. Such stimuli are called the attended stimuli. When most of us listen to a song, our attention is drawn to the voice of the singer or the melody of an instrumental tune. We can pick out different parts of the music, say, the drums or the bass, by switching the attended stimulus from the lead singer to the bass line, but usually our attention is focused on the melody. With vision, we may be looking at a beautiful beach, but our attended stimulus maybe the beer bottle a previous beachgoer forgot to clean up.

Through our senses, we are presented with an incredibly rich and varied experience of the world, including the aroma of roasting coffee, the texture of fine silk, the taste of dark chocolate, the sound of our favorite musician, and the sight of a glorious sunset. Not all sensory experiences are pleasant and lovely, of course. We have all smelled rotting garbage, felt a painful pinprick, placed our fingers on a hot stovetop, tasted foods we detest, heard fingernails screeching on the blackboard, and seen images in movies that have made us close our eyes. The senses unflinchingly bring to us an immense range of experiences from the world around us, positive and negative alike.

Yet the next question we can ask is, How do stimuli in the outside world become perceptual experiences? How do our sensory systems, such as our eyes, ears, and skin, translate light, sound, and surface textures into perceptions? For example, How does our nose turn the volatile chemicals of coffee into the tantalizing aroma of coffee (Figure 1.6)? We need to explore how physical stimuli are converted into a sensory representation. So we now introduce the concepts of **transduction** and neural responses.

For each of our sensory systems, we have specialized neural cells called **receptors**, which transduce (transform) a physical stimulus into an electrochemical signal, called a **neural response**, which then can be sent to the brain. For vision, these specialized cells are called rods and cones, and they are located on the retina of the eye. For hearing, these specialized cells are called the hair

(a)

(b)

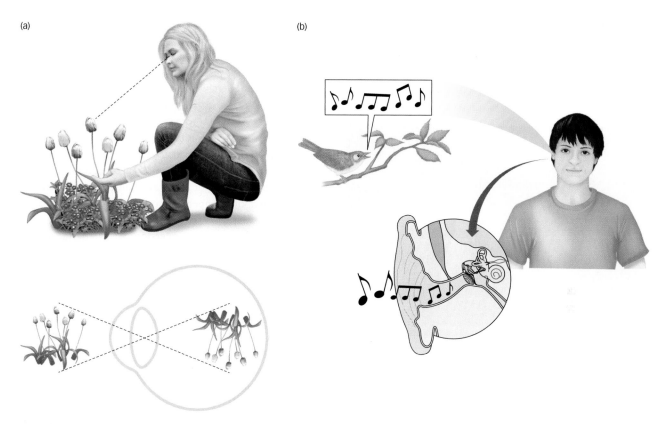

■ FIGURE 1.7 Converting energy into a neural signal.

Perception is the process of converting physical stimuli, such as light and sound energy, into neural signals within our sensory organs. (a) Light is reflected off the petals of the flowers and into the eyes. The eyes then transduce this light into a neural signal to be sent to the brain. (b) Sound is produced by the bird and reaches our ears. Special hair cells in the cochlea of the ear transduce the sound into a neural signal to be sent to the brain.

cells, and they are found in the cochlea in the inner ear. For our sense of taste, we have cells in our taste buds, which create neural signals when they come into contact with certain chemicals in our food. Rods and cones transduce the physical energy of light into an electrochemical signal, which is then transmitted to the brain via the optic nerve. Hair cells convert the vibrating of the cochlear membrane (which vibrates in response to physical sound) into a neural response, which is then transmitted to the brain via the auditory (or cochlear) nerve. Taste bud cells convert the presence of a particular chemical (such as sugars) into a neural response transmitted to the brain by gustatory nerves (see Figure 1.7).

Once a neural signal is transduced by the receptors, it is transmitted to the brain for processing. Though the neural signal contains much information, it is necessary for the brain to process that information in order to extract relevant information, such as color for vision and pitch for sound. It is for this reason that we find it useful to distinguish between sensation and perception. *Sensation* refers to the process of transduction, in which receptors convert physical signals into neural responses, and *perception* refers to the process of taking that signal and processing it into a usable image or experience. For example, when we hear orchestral music, the hair cells in our cochleae convert the sound waves into neural signals, but it is our brains that convert that neural signal into the experience of the music we hear, the rich sound of the violins contrasting with the sharp tones of the trumpets, and the underlying low tones of the basses and bassoons. Sensation takes in the sounds, but perception appreciates the music.

Transduction: the process of converting a physical stimulus into an electrochemical signal

Receptors: specialized sensory neurons that convert physical stimuli into neural responses

Neural response: the signal produced by receptor cells that can then be sent to the brain

Action

The goal of sensation and perception is to guide us through our environment. We use visual information to avoid obstacles while walking around campus or driving on the highway. When it is completely dark, we avoid obstacles by touch. We feel our way by touching the obstacles in front of us. In this way, most of us can negotiate our own homes at night with the lights off just using touch. We use auditory information to determine what people are saying and whether the phone is ringing. We use olfactory (smell) information to determine if we want to eat something or avoid any contact with it. We use information about temperature on our skin to determine if we want to wear a sweater or a T-shirt. Thus, perceiving what is around us guides us to action. We can define **action** as any motor activity. Thus, action includes moving one's eyes along the page of a book as well as a baseball player's swinging his bat at an incoming fastball (see Figure 1.8). It includes turning your head when you hear the voice of a friend or a concert pianist's fingers darting across her piano keyboard. Thus, any movement we make can qualify as action. If that movement is directed by something we perceive in the environment, then we can see that it is perception-guided action. In sum, one of the chief goals, if not the goal itself, is to guide functional action. (There are some interesting illustrations of this on ISLE; see ISLE 1.2).

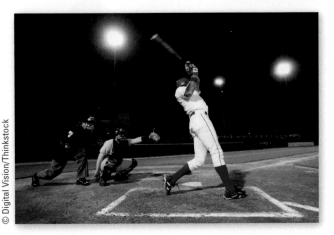

■ FIGURE 1.8   **Perception and action.**

The baseball player's swing is guided by the perception of the approaching baseball. Opposing pitchers may throw curveballs, which change direction at the last moment, to confuse batters' perceptions.

ISLE 1.2 Illustration of Action

ISLE 1.3 Bach's Violin Partita #2 in D minor

The Nature of Experience and Phenomenology

Think about the experience of listening to very beautiful music. For example, think of a violin virtuoso playing Bach's Violin Partita No. 2 in D minor. If you are not familiar with this piece of music, you can listen to an excerpt of it (ISLE 1.3). If you do not like this style of music, imagine a piece of music that you think is very sad but also very beautiful. In the example we provide, listening to the Bach partita, our ears are responding to differences in frequency, tempo, rhythm, and loudness as we hear the sound of the lone violin. Our toes may move in time to the music, and our eyes may cloud with tears at the poignancy of the music. These movements may be considered action. But why does the piece affect us emotionally? Why do we find music beautiful in the first place? How is it that we feel Bach's grief at losing his wife through his music nearly 300 years after the piece was written? If you are a music theorist, this speaks to the power of Bach's music. But for our purposes, it introduces us to the issue of phenomenology. Phenomenology is our subjective experience of perception. **Phenomenology** refers to our internal experience of the world around us. Phenomenology is the beauty of the lone violin, the aromatic smell of coffee in the morning, and the wonder of seeing the colors of the sunset in the west of an evening sky (see Figure 1.9). By the same token, *phenomenology* can refer to the annoying cacophony of the neighbor's lawnmower, the stink of an airplane bathroom, and an up-close look at a stranger's nose hairs. Regardless of the effects they induce in us, perception induces these internal mental experiences in each of us.

Phenomenology distinguishes us from computer-driven robots. Robots have microphones to capture sound, and internal computer processing units to decode the messages into something that can drive the robots to follow certain courses of action. But computer devices do not have internal experiences (as best we know). Phenomenology appears to be a unique creation of the living brain. Philosophers have argued about what purpose it serves, whether people share common phenomenology, how widespread it is among nonhuman animals, and if it is

Action: any motor activity

Phenomenology: our subjective experience of perception

possible in nonliving systems. The discussion of these questions is largely outside the scope of this book, but there is a lively debate in philosophy concerning how we would know if animals or artificially intelligent devices experience phenomenology when they process the external world.

An interesting issue in phenomenology is that it is a private experience. Each of us has sensory experiences, and we agree on common terminology for them, but because phenomenology is private, philosophers often wonder if this means that we share phenomenology. For example, scientists know what frequencies of light elicit an experience of blue, and people all across the world agree on what constitutes blue (regardless of language). We may also share common cultural referents to blue, which we all

■ FIGURE 1.9   **Phenomenology.**

When we see a beautiful sunset, we notice the colors and the landscape. The experience of all this is considered its phenomenology. Issues of phenomenology interest psychologists and philosophers alike.

agree on (blue jeans, blue moods, blue states, etc.). However, is our internal experience of blue the same? Do you and I have the same experience of blue? This conundrum is often referred to as the inverted-rainbow question. We all agree on the relation of frequency to color name when we see a rainbow, but what if our internal experiences were different? By and large, this question takes us out of the domain of scientific psychology, as it cannot be answered empirically. But philosophers take these questions quite seriously. At sagepub.com, you can find some approachable readings on the philosophy of phenomenology.

TEST YOUR KNOWLEDGE

What is transduction? How might it differ from one sensory system to the next?

THE HISTORY OF SENSATION AND PERCEPTION

1.4   Explore the history of the study of sensation and perception.

To understand any field of study, it is helpful to understand its history. Often the questions asked in the past and the way they were posed influence modern research. Therefore, knowing the history can often help us understand why issues are framed the way they are and why our knowledge has both the strengths and weaknesses that it does. It can also help us understand our own assumptions about the nature of the world by seeing ideas from different epochs, when ideas and technology were different. Sometimes a field does not even make sense until its history is considered. In this section, a short history of the field of the study of sensation and perception is covered to give some context to the material in this chapter and throughout the book.

The Beginnings

Thinking about our senses probably predates any written record. We would like to think that even in prehistoric times, people marveled at the beauty of a rainbow or a sunset. The formal study of sensation and perception goes nearly as far back as written records exist. The Ramesseum medical papyri date back to approximately 1800 BCE. That's nearly 4,000 years ago! The unknown authors describe disruptions in visual perception and their connection to diseases of the eye (Weitzmann, 1970). Interestingly, the papyri recommend hemp as a treatment for eye disorders, much as doctors now prescribe medical marijuana for glaucoma. In ancient Greece (some 1,500 years after the Ramesseum medical papyri), Greek architects were aware of how perception could be distorted by visual illusions (Coren & Girgus, 1978). Indeed, the Parthenon was built to appear as if it had straight columns, though in order to do so, the architects had to design columns that were not perfectly vertical. Elsewhere, Greek architects built perfectly straight columns, but these appear bent (see ISLE 1.4).

Aristotle (384–322 BCE) conducted conceptual work and observations in the field of sensation and perception. He clearly distinguished between sensory and motor functions; he described the sensory organs and their functions; he even gave us our prototypical list of five senses: sight, hearing, smell, taste, and touch (Murphy & Kovach, 1972). In addition to these basic ideas, Aristotle was a keen observer and is the first to record two very interesting sensory phenomena, which we describe here, as they are relevant to topics we discuss in later chapters.

The first is an illusion of touch that still bears his name, the Aristotle illusion (Benedetti, 1985). In this illusion, a single touch between the tips of two crossed fingers, say with a pen, will be experienced as if there were two touches, as if there were two pens and not a single one (see ISLE 1.5). You can experience the illusion very simply by crossing your index and middle finger (see Figure 1.10). Then pick up a pencil and touch the place just where the two fingers meet. You probably experience two touches (as there is one touch to each finger) that feel like two pencils. The Aristotle illusion is relevant to material discussed in Chapter 13.

The second illusion discussed by Aristotle is known as the motion aftereffect, also known as the waterfall illusion (Verstraten, 1996; Wade, 1996). A motion **aftereffect** is a sensory experience that occurs after prolonged experience of visual motion in one particular direction (see ISLE 1.6). So if we think of a waterfall, the water is all moving in the same direction: down. That is the only way real waterfalls actually occur. After staring at a waterfall for some time, if you move your eyes to a solid stationary object, you may get the sense that the stationary object is moving upward, that is, in the opposite direction the waterfall was moving. This is the waterfall illusion first written about by Aristotle. Another way to observe this illusion at home is to watch the credits at the end of a movie without taking your eyes off the television screen. After watching the credits for 2 minutes, have a friend or family member hit the pause button. You will see an illusion of the movie credits' moving up the screen, even though you know the video is now stopped. Aristotle observed this by looking at nonmoving surfaces after watching the downward motion of waterfalls (see Figure 1.11).

Many philosophers and scientists prior to the 19th century developed ideas about perception, some of which still influence our thinking today. For example, the astronomer Robert Hooke (1635–1703) developed the first acuity test for vision (Grüsser, 1993). However, it is with the 19th century that we see the beginnings

ISLE 1.4 Column Taper Illusion

ISLE 1.5 Aristotle's Illusion

ISLE 1.6 Motion Aftereffect

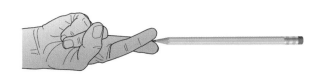

■ **FIGURE 1.10**   **The Aristotle illusion.**

In the illustration, we see two crossed fingers and a pencil touching in the middle. In this illusion, we feel as if we have been touched by two pencils rather than one.

Aftereffect: a sensory experience that occurs after prolonged experience of visual motion in one particular direction

of a real science of sensation and perception. The contributions came from people in many different disciplines. Physicist Thomas Young (1773–1829) argued that light is a wave and that color is detected by three kinds of nerve fibers, an idea elaborated on later by Hermann von Helmholtz. Biologist Johannes Mueller (1801–1858) developed the doctrine of the specific nerve energies. The **doctrine of specific nerve energies** argues that it is the specific neurons activated that determine the particular type of experience. That is, activation of the optic nerve leads to visual experiences, whereas activation of the auditory nerve leads to auditory experiences. This seemingly obvious conception was controversial at the time because one of the confusing findings of that time period was how similar the electrical activity was in all of the neurons, regardless of the sensory modality. This led Mueller and others to wonder how the brain could distinguish between seeing an apple and hearing a song, for example. Those neurons involved in seeing will cause the impression of seeing regardless of how they are stimulated. So if a sound stimulates the neurons involved in vision, you will still have a visual experience. Some early evidence for this view is the visual experience we have when we manually stimulate the retina. Try pushing at the side of your eye, and you will see that pushing on the eye can causes shifts of color and shading.

Helmholtz Versus Hering

One of Mueller's students was Hermann von Helmholtz (1821–1894) (see Figure 1.12). Helmholtz was born in Potsdam in what was then the Kingdom of Prussia (now part of Germany). He was a professor for many years at the University of Berlin. Helmholtz was trained in medicine and physiology but became famous for both his work in sensory perception and his work in physics. His work in physics includes the formulation of the law of the conservation of energy, an important landmark in physics. He was also a pioneer in thermodynamics and electrodynamics. In biology, Helmholtz was the first person to determine the speed of the neural impulse (or action potential). He also contributed greatly to the beginnings of sensory physiology and the scientific study of perception. Indeed, Helmholtz wrote a three-volume study of physiological optics and also wrote a book on music perception. In particular, he elaborated on the work of Thomas Young and developed the concept of the trichromatic theory of color vision. For this reason, the trichromatic theory of color vision is often called the Young-Helmholtz theory of color perception. Helmholtz thought of our color vision as being based on the perception of three primary colors, red, green, and blue, even though he was not certain that there were three cone types in the retina (this was not known for certain until much later). By and large, his color theory is still relevant today.

Helmholtz developed a general theory of how our senses work, which is mostly still held today by most researchers within the field of sensation and perception. In his **constructivist approach**, Helmholtz argued that the information from the sensory signal itself is inadequate to explain the richness of our experiences. That is, the sensory signal needs to be interpreted by active cognitive processes. For example, recognizing the face or voice of a loved one is more than basic sensations. Your auditory system must integrate the sound of the voice with your

■ FIGURE 1.11   Waterfall illusion.

After watching the constant downward motion of a waterfall, the motion detectors in our brains adapt or tire in response to the downward motion. When we look away from the waterfall, upward motion detectors become active, and we experience the illusion that whatever stationary object we are looking at is moving upward.

Doctrine of specific nerve energies: the argument that it is the specific neurons activated that determine the particular type of experience

Constructivist approach: the idea that perceptions are constructed using information from our senses and cognitive processes

© GL Archive / Alamy

■ FIGURE 1.12   Hermann von Helmholtz.

Hermann Ludwig Ferdinand von Helmholtz (1821–1894) was a German physician, physicist, and sensory physiologist. He is credited with developing a theory of color vision and promoting the constructivist view of sensory perception.

U.S. National Library of Medicine, History of Medicine Division

■ FIGURE 1.13   Ewald Hering.

Ewald Hering (1834–1918) was a German physiologist who introduced the opponent theory of color vision. He was also interested in binocular vision. He also disagreed with Helmholtz on constructivism. Hering argued that stimuli themselves had sufficient information to allow for direct perception.

knowledge of your sister and the knowledge of what she usually talks about to fully perceive the speech directed at you. Thus, we must incorporate information from our existing knowledge to completely perceive the world around us. According to Helmholtz, because our senses do not produce sufficient information about the world, we must use a form of reason, unconsciously, to make an educated guess about what we actually perceive. Helmholtz called this an **unconscious inference** (Turner, 1977). This type of theory is useful for explaining the occurrences of auditory and visual illusions, such as the waterfall illusion. In this way, Helmholtz's work foreshadowed the cognitive approaches known as information processing and the computational approach.

Helmholtz's colleague and rival was Ewald Hering (1834–1918) (see Figure 1.13). Hering was born in Saxony, in what is now Germany, but he was a professor in Prague in what is now the Czech Republic and Leipzig in Germany. Hering disagreed with Helmholtz both on the specifics of color vision and on a general model of how sensory processes worked. With respect to color vision, Hering did not see color vision as being based on three primary colors but as being based on color opponency (Turner, 1993). He saw two major pairs of color opponents, green-red and blue-yellow. Any receptor excited by green turns off red, and any receptor excited by red turns off green. Modern research suggests that both Helmholtz and Hering were correct to some extent. Trichromacy seems to best explain the workings of the retina, whereas opponency can account for how areas of the visual brain (occipital cortex) treat color. That they were both right would have displeased both of these proud scientists. This controversy is discussed at length in the chapter on color perception. Look ahead to the demonstration on this issue in that chapter.

Hering also disagreed with Helmholtz's theory of unconscious inference. Hering viewed environmental inputs and our sensory apparatus as sufficient for us to grasp the structure of the perceived world, without the need for internal unconscious inferences. That is, stimuli themselves contain adequate information for the viewer to perceive the world. In Hering's view, the perceptual processes in the brain do not need to make sense of the perceptual world; the brain simply needs to register it. Whereas Helmholtz's view is more popular with most experimental psychologists as well as physiologists, Hering's view influenced the development of gestalt psychology and later direct perception theory (also known as the Gibsonian view).

Weber, Fechner, and the Birth of Psychophysics

Helmholtz and Hering both approached sensation and perception from the perspective of physiology. Around the same time as Helmholtz and Hering were looking at the relation of physiology and perception, other German scientists were

Unconscious inference: perception is not adequately determined by sensory information, so an inference or educated guess is part of the process; this inference is not the result of active problem solving but rather a nonconscious cognitive process

doing work with a more psychological perspective. Ernst Heinrich Weber (1795–1878) discovered Weber's law (though it was Gustav Fechner, another German scientist, who named the law after Weber). **Weber's law** concerns the perception of difference between two stimuli. For example, do we hear the difference between a 1,000-Hz tone and one of 1,005 Hz? Another example is whether we see the difference in length between a line 466 mm long and one that is 467 mm long. Weber's law states that a "just-noticeable difference" (JND) between two stimuli is related to the magnitude or strength of the stimuli. What does this mean? Well, in our example, it means that we might not be able to detect a 1-mm difference when we are looking at lines 466 and 467 mm in length, but we may be able to detect a 1-mm difference when we are comparing a line 2 mm long with one 3 mm long. Another example of this principle is that we can detect 1 candle when it is lit in an otherwise dark room. But when 1 candle is lit in a room in which 100 candles are already burning, we may not notice the light from this candle. The JND is greater for very loud noises than it is for much more quiet sounds. When a sound is very weak, we can tell that another sound is louder, even if it is barely louder. When a sound is very loud, to tell that another sound is even louder, it has to be much louder. Thus, Weber's law means that it is harder to distinguish between two samples when those samples are larger or stronger levels of the stimuli.

Gustav Fechner (1801–1887) is generally considered the founder of **psychophysics**, the study of the relation between physical stimuli and perception (see Figure 1.14). Fechner's (1860/1966) book *Elements of Psychophysics* is often considered the beginning of the psychological study of sensation and perception. Fechner discovered the illusion known as the Fechner color effect, whereby moving black-and-white figures create an illusion of color (see ISLE 1.7). This illusion is also known as Benham's disk (see Figure 1.15). Fechner also developed Fechner's law, which states that sensation is a logarithmic function of physical intensity. This means that our sensory experience changes at a lower rate than does the physical intensity. That is, our perception of the intensity of a stimulus increases at a lower rate than does the actual intensity of the stimulus. For example, his law is captured in the decibel scale that we use to measure loudness, on which 20 dB is 100 times louder than 10 dB in terms of the physical stimulus. But in psychological studies, we hear 20 dB as only twice as loud as 10 dB, not 100 times. In vision, the psychological concept of brightness is a function of the intensity of a light. But to perceive a doubling of brightness, the intensity of the light must increase 10-fold. Fechner's book and his view on the relation between physical stimuli and psychological perception influenced many early psychological scientists, including Wilhelm Wundt, Hermann Ebbinghaus, and William James.

■ **FIGURE 1.14 Gustav Fechner.**

Gustav Fechner (1801–1887) is considered the "father of psychophysics." His landmark work on the relation between physical stimuli and perception established sensory psychology as a unique discipline separate from physiology. His work inspired the beginning of scientific psychology.

ISLE 1.7 Fechner Colors and Benham's Top

The 20th Century and the Study of Perception: Cognitive Psychology Approaches

The 20th century brought a burst of interest and research in the study of sensation and perception. First, sensation and perception research spread from Germany to many other countries across the world, and a number of perspectives emerged, including gestalt psychology, direct perception (or the Gibsonian approach), the information-processing approach, and the computational approach. These latter two, information processing and the computational approach, can both be considered cognitive psychology approaches. We briefly describe each approach here.

Gestalt Psychology

Gestalt psychology in general and sensation and perception in particular argued that we view the world in terms of general patterns and well-organized structures rather

Weber's law: a just-noticeable difference between two stimuli is related to the magnitude or strength of the stimuli

Psychophysics: the study of the relation between physical stimuli and perception events

Gestalt psychology: a school of thought claiming that we view the world in terms of general patterns and well-organized structures rather than separable individual elements

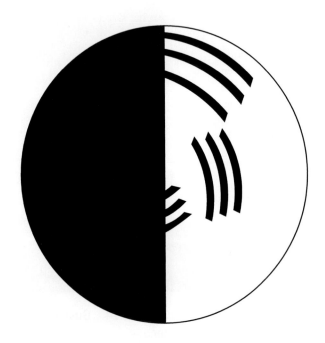

■ FIGURE 1.15 Benham's disk.

This illusion was discovered by Fechner. Copy the image shown here. Or look up Benham's disks on the Internet and print out a copy of the above image. Put a pin or needle through the very center of the image. Then spin the image as fast as you can. While the image is moving, you may see colors. Stop the movement and look at the image again. The colors will be gone.

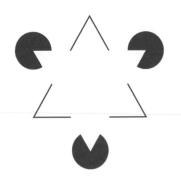

■ FIGURE 1.17 Kanizsa's triangle.

When most people look at this figure, they see a bright white triangle lying on top of a background consisting of a less bright triangle and some odd-shaped "Pac-Man" figures. The bright white triangle is illusory. The triangle is suggested by the pattern of figures, and our perceptual systems enhance the perceived brightness of the figure, but close inspection of the figure will convince you that there is no actual change in brightness.

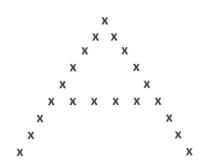

■ FIGURE 1.16 Gestalt psychology.

To see the A, one must order the individual elements into a pattern. Just by examining the individual elements, we would never see the A. Gestalt psychologists considered patterns such as these the rule rather than the exception.

than separable individual elements (Schultz & Schultz, 1992). Consider Figure 1.16. In this figure, we see the A only when we order the smaller elements together. In another example, gestalt psychologists were interested in apparent motion, which can be explained only by reference to the interaction between parts, not the individual parts themselves. Gestalt psychologists were also interested in how edges are perceived, an interest that has continued in both computational and neuroscience approaches to sensation and perception. Gestalt psychologists considered the perception of edges as critical to determining what objects were in visual perception. They also identified several situations in which we see illusory edges on the basis of gestalt principles. One of these is the famous Kanizsa triangle, depicted in Figure 1.17. In the Kanizsa triangle, we see illusory contours, which are suggested by the overall pattern of the figure but are not physically there. The gestalt psychologists established a number of laws, which they argued were constants in visual perception. These laws were devised to explain how patterns are seen from individual elements (see Figure 1.18).

Gestalt psychology flourished in Europe in the early 20th century. However, during the same time period, American psychology was under the influence of behaviorism, which had a very different perspective than did gestalt psychology. Behaviorists were firm believers in the importance of "nurture" when it came to developmental issues in psychology, whereas gestalt psychologists were firmly in the "nature" camp; that is, they believed that these perceptual laws and other principles of human behavior were genetically wired. Thus, gestalt psychology did not take hold in the United States. However, when the Nazis came to power in Germany, many gestalt psychologists came to the United States and Canada, where they influenced the development of the direct perception view of perception, which we discuss shortly.

One prominent gestalt psychologist was Wolfgang Köhler (1887–1967). Köhler was a patriotic, aristocratic German, who nonetheless vehemently opposed the Nazis (Figure 1.19). In 1933, he was the last person in Germany to publish an article critical of the Nazis during their regime. Soon afterward, he escaped to the United States. Once there, he became a successful professor first at Swarthmore College in Pennsylvania and then at Dartmouth College in New Hampshire. While

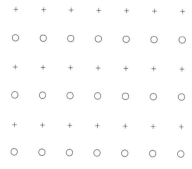

a. **The law of proximity.** You will see this arrangement as a set of columns–not a set of rows. Items that are near each other are grouped together. Now notice the typing in this book. You see rows of letters rather than columns because a letter is closer to the letters to the right and left than it is to the letters above and below.

b. **The law of similarity.** You will see this arrangement as a set of rows rather than columns. Items that are similar to each other are grouped together. Now look at the two words at the end of this sentence that are in **boldface type**. Notice how these two words in heavier print cling together in a group, whereas the words in regular, lighter print form their own separate groups.

c. **The law of good continuation.** You will see a zigzag line with a curved line running through it, so that each line continues in the same direction it was going prior to intersection. Notice that you do not see the figures as being composed of the two elements below.

Look out the window at the branches of a tree, and focus on two branches that form a cross. You clearly perceive two staight lines, rather than two right angles touching each other.

d. **The law of closure.** You will see a circle here, even though it is not perfectly closed. A complete figure is simply more tempting than a curved line! Now close this book and put your finger across one edge, focusing on the shape of the outline of your book. You should still see your book as complete, but with a finger in front of it.

e. **The law of common fate.** If dots 1, 3, and 5 suddenly move up and dots 2, 4, and 6—at the same time—suddenly move down, the dots moving in the same direction will be perceived as belonging together. The next time you look at automobile traffic on a moderately busy street, notice how clearly the cars moving in one direction form one group and the cars moving in the opposite direction form another group.

■ FIGURE 1.18   The laws of gestalt psychology.

at Dartmouth, he was also president of the American Psychological Association. Early in his career, Köhler applied gestalt psychology to auditory perception but then expanded gestalt psychology into other domains of psychology, including his famous study of problem solving in chimpanzees.

Direct Perception (The Gibsonian Approach)

The direct perception view was developed by the American husband-and-wife team J. J. and Eleanor Gibson, who were both professors at Smith College in Northampton, Massachusetts (Gibson, 2001). The Gibsons emphasized that the information in the sensory world is complex and abundant, and therefore the perceptual systems need only directly perceive such complexity. In this view, the senses do not send to the brain incomplete and inaccurate information about the world that needs to be reasoned about to generate a perception. Thus, the direct perception view is diametrically opposed to Helmholtz's concept of unconscious inference. Rather, in the **direct perception** view (**Gibsonian approach**), the world generates rich sources of information that the senses merely need to pick up directly.

Direct perception (Gibsonian approach): the approach to perception that claims that information in the sensory world is complex and abundant, and therefore the perceptual systems need only directly perceive such complexity

The direct perception view also emphasized ecological realism in experiments. This means that rather than showing simple displays to participants in experiments, direct perception theorists advocated using more naturalistic stimuli. Indeed, J. J. Gibson (1979) criticized much work in perception because the stimuli used by researchers were just points of light, tones, or stimuli that otherwise would not normally be encountered in everyday life. He emphasized that researchers should study real-world stimuli. For this reason, the direct perception view is often called the **ecological approach to perception**. For a demonstration of optic flow, one of the key contributions of this approach, see ISLE 1.8.

Information-Processing Approach

The **information-processing approach** postulates that perceptual and cognitive systems can be viewed as the flow of information from one process to another. Information is collected by sensory processes and then flows to a variety of modules that decode the information, interpret it, and then allow the organism to act on it. Consider the processing of visual information. Information flows from the eyes to various units in the brain that extract color, motion, figure-ground, and object information and then pass that information to cognitive systems that extract meaning and then pass it to other cognitive systems that determine actions that should be implemented on the basis of the visual information. The information-processing view stipulates that each of these stages or processes takes a finite amount of time, even if they are very fast, and therefore these processes can be observed or measured by recording reaction times as observers do various tasks (see Figure 1.20).

The information-processing view greatly influenced cognitive psychology. During the 1960s and 1970s, information-processing models were used in both perception research and memory research. The approach continues to influence both of these fields, thought contemporary researchers realize that the brain is massively "parallel," and many processes can be occurring simultaneously.

The information-processing view is different from Gibson's direct perception view because, like Helmholtz's view, the information-processing view requires internal cognitive processes to interpret the perceptual image, whereas the direct perception view asserts that the sensory input is sufficient in and of itself. The information-processing view is similar to the gestalt view in the specification of internal processes that extract information. However, the gestalt view emphasizes patterns and organization, whereas the information-processing view emphasizes the analysis of information and its flow from one system to another.

Computational Approaches

The **computational approach** studies perception by trying to specify the necessary computations the brain would need to carry out to perceive the world. Originally developed by David Marr (1982), it was heavily influenced by the growth of computer science and, in particular, early theory in artificial intelligence. Marr attempted to specify perception in terms of what computations the brain would need to perform the task of perception. He conceived of the brain as an incredibly complicated computer and sought a mathematical explanation for perceptual processes, especially vision. The computational approach built on the information-processing approach but acknowledged from the beginning that many perceptual processes may occur in parallel in the brain. In its modern form, researchers attempt to develop mathematical models that predict perceptual phenomena. Many of these mathematical models are based on neural networks, computer simulations of how nervous systems work (Venrooij et al., 2013).

Many who value the computational approach try to get computers to "see" in ways that make sense given our knowledge of the brain. In this way, the computational approach is often more theoretical, focusing on modeling perception in

ISLE 1.8 Optic Flow

© INTERFOTO / Alamy

■ **FIGURE 1.19   Wolfgang Köhler.**

Wolfgang Köhler (1887–1967) was a major theorist in the gestalt psychology movement. Köhler immigrated to the United States prior to World War II. He expanded the use of gestalt psychology beyond its traditional domain of sensation and perception to other areas of psychology, such as problem solving.

Ecological approach to perception: another name for the direct perception view

Information-processing approach: the view that perceptual and cognitive systems can be viewed as the flow of information from one process to another

Computational approach: an approach to the study of perception in which the necessary computations the brain would need to carry out to perceive the world are specified

nonhuman systems, whereas the information-processing approach is more directly linked to observations in behavioral experiments. In computational models, if the computer can "see," theoretically so should the brain, and it is quite possible that the brain will also use many of the same computations as the computer. Studies using this approach often attempt to simulate perception on computers. A researcher will give a computer some visual task. The task may be to see a real object, and the computer has some form of electronic "eye," such as a video camera, attached. It might also involve simply a computer-generated world. In either case, the computer may be give the task of identifying an object, perhaps partially hidden by another object (e.g., Doerschner, Kersten, & Schrater, 2009). If the computer can do the task and also tends to make the same types of mistakes humans do, then those doing research according to the computational approach have some confidence that they have made progress in their goal.

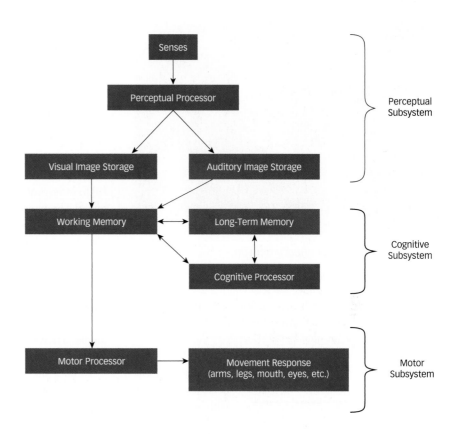

■ **FIGURE 1.20**   **An information-processing model.**

Information processing means that information flows from one process or stage to another during perception. Thus, in the diagram, we see an early sensory stage in which transduction takes place. Information then flows to a series of perceptual modules, eventually leading to final percept, which drives action.

Neuroscience in Sensation and Perception

The goal of **neuroscience** is to understand sensation and perception in terms of the structures and processes in the nervous system that produce it. Thus, the neuroscience approach starts with examining the physiological processes whereby a physical signal is transduced into a neural signal. Neuroscience then continues to investigate sensation and perception by looking at connections from the sensory organs to the brain and then at regions in the brain itself that are involved in perceptual processes. Neuroscience research can span the gamut from work on single cells within the brain to examining connections among differing regions in the brain.

Neuroscience is interested in the cellular level, necessary to understand how individual neurons convert physical stimuli into electrochemical signals (see Figure 1.21). At the cellular level, neuroscientists can look at the actions of individual cells and how they respond to particular signals. Neuroscience is also interested in what processes occur in the brain to process and interpret sensory information. Here, neuroscientists can look at larger units in the brain and attempt to correlate those regions with particular perceptual functions. For example, neuroimaging studies show activity in an area of the brain, in the occipital lobe, known as MT (middle temporal) or V5 when people are watching moving stimuli.

One of the most important developments in neuroscience was the development of the microelectrode in the 1940s and 1950s. A **microelectrode** is a device so small that it can penetrate a single neuron in the mammalian central nervous system without destroying the cell. Once in the cell, it can record the electrical activity there or even

Neuroscience: the study of the structures and processes in the nervous system and brain

Microelectrode: a device so small that it can penetrate a single neuron in the mammalian central nervous system without destroying the cell

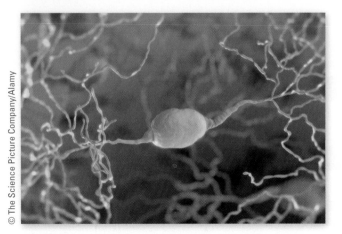

■ **FIGURE 1.21** **A sensory neuron.**

Bipolar cells, such as the one depicted in this image, connect the receptor cells to the tracts that lead information from the sensory organ to the brain. Bipolar cells in vision, for example, connect rods and cones to the cells that lead information out of the eye and through the optic nerve.

ISLE 1.9 Kuffler and Single Cell Recording

stimulate the cell by carrying electrical current to the cell from an electrical source at the command of the scientist. Thus, this method allows the recording of the behavior of single neurons in the mammalian brain. It was first used in the sensory systems by Kuffler (1953) (see ISLE 1.9). In this way, it can be used to determine what kind of stimuli a particular cell responds to. Thus, for example, a cell in Area V1 (also known as the primary visual cortex) of the brain may respond to visually seen lines of different orientations. Another cell might respond only to stimuli in the left visual field. This technique led to some profound breakthroughs in our understanding of how the brain processes sensory information.

Hubel and Wiesel (1959, 1962, 1965) are probably the names most associated with this technique. Their Nobel Prize–winning work not only helped us understand the behavior of individual cells but uncovered unexpected levels of organization in the brain (Hubel & Wiesel, 1965) and information on how the brain develops (e.g., Hubel & Wiesel, 1962). For example, they found cells in the brains of cats and monkeys that were selective to one eye or the other and other cells that responded only when both eyes were able to see the same objects in the visual world. Single-cell recording made major contributions to neuroscience with animal models but is used less nowadays because it is difficult to do with humans, and we have increased concerns about animal welfare.

The neuroscience approach also includes the field of neuropsychology. **Neuropsychology** is the study of the relation of brain damage to changes in behavior. In neuropsychological research, scientists know what part of a person's brain is damaged and then look for behavioral changes in that individual. Behavioral changes may include problems with language, memory, or perception. They may also include difficulties in decision making, action, or emotion. Brain damage may arise from a variety of tragedies and accidents, including strokes, tumors, aneurysms, loss of blood during surgery, blows to the head, bullet wounds, concussions, and near drowning. Indeed, the study of neuropsychology began in earnest in the 1870s in Europe, as antiseptic procedures allowed Franco-Prussian soldiers to survive gunshot wounds that would previously have been fatal. This was just a bit late for American soldiers in the Civil War, many of whom died from infections. Neuropsychology continues to learn from and help individuals returning from war to this day (Vasterling et al., 2006).

Consider a particular case in which the brain damage resulted from lifesaving surgery. A patient called D.B. had part of his occipital lobe removed as treatment for a malignant tumor growing on the visual portion of his brain. The tumor was causing seizures and could have threatened his life, were it to have spread to other regions of his brain and body. Thus, surgeons removed it as carefully as possible but also had to excise a great deal of tissue within this V1 area of his occipital lobe. Medically, the operation was a tremendous success. The tumor removal allowed D.B. to return to his job as a computer programmer and lead a normal life, with few or no side effects. However, as a result of the resulting loss of Area V1 tissue, D.B. developed partial blindness in one area of his visual field (Weiskrantz, 1996). This sounds more serious than it actually was. D.B. had no difficulties moving his eyes, so his eye movements quickly compensated for this patch of blindness. However, it allowed D.B. to be an interesting research participant. The researchers could correlate the brain damage (known to be in a particular area of the occipital lobe) and the behavioral deficits (partial blindness). As such, it was possible to correlate the area of the occipital lobe that was removed with being responsible for seeing in a certain part of the visual field. D.B. was also an important patient in the study of the phenomenon of blindsight, a topic that is covered in depth in Chapter 4.

Neuropsychology: the study of the relation of brain damage to changes in behavior

One form of brain damage affecting perception is known as agnosia. **Agnosia** is a deficit in some aspect of perception as a result of brain damage. For example, there is a form of agnosia caused by damage to an area of the temporal lobe known as the fusiform face area (**prosopagnosia**, or face agnosia). Damage to this area results in a deficit in perceiving faces. Damage to certain areas of the right temporal lobe can result in a person's loss of appreciation of music. This condition, known as amusia, a form of agnosia, is covered in Chapter 13. Thus, neuropsychological methods are effective at relating areas of the brain to particular perceptual functions.

Neuroscience research also includes the neuroimaging techniques. **Neuroimaging** involves technologies that allow us to map living intact brains as they engage in ongoing tasks. Neuroimaging allows us to observe an intact living brain as it perceives, learns, and thinks. This is the newest technology used in neuroscience, with the first magnetic resonance imaging (MRI) research not beginning until the 1990s. Since then, however, neuroimaging research has become a major force in understanding both the brain and cognition and perception. One method is **functional MRI (fMRI)**. This technique can image the blood levels in different areas of the brain, which correlate with activity levels in those regions, allowing activity in the human brain to be correlated with our actual sensory abilities (Tremblay, Dick, & Small, 2011). See Figure 1.22 for an illustration of what an fMRI scan looks like.

The fMRI technique is thought of as a hemodynamic technique because it measures the blood flow to the brain. The technique starts with the reasonable assumption that because the brain is a biological organ, it requires oxygen. Moreover, the areas of the brain that are active require more oxygen and therefore blood than other areas of the brain. Thus, a person talking will need oxygen delivered to the parts of his or her brain that are responsible for speech production. A person listening to music will require a greater oxygen supply to areas that are responsible for music perception. Thus, if you can trace the flow of blood in the brain, you will know what areas of the brain are currently in use. For example, Kau et al. (2013) recorded the neural activity in the brains of participants tracking moving dots across a screen. When the participants were attending to the motion, there was activity in an area of the brain known as V3, located in the occipital lobe. Other studies also associate Area V3 with movement perception.

Neuroimaging may very well be the fastest growing area in scientific psychology. It offers us the opportunity to watch the human brain as it does its work, certainly a fascinating proposition. In this way, it can tell us a great deal about the structure and function of the human brain and the nature of sensation and perception. But neuroimaging can also be misleading. For example, small differences in methodology between studies can sometimes lead to big differences in the neural patterns. Moreover, because fMRI researchers may do many statistical tests per scan, there is a risk that neural activity in some regions may exceed a criterion level simply by chance (Bennett, Wolford, & Miller, 2009). It is also true that neuroimaging, at present, is still looking at vast groupings of cells. So neuroimaging technology still cannot bridge the gap from gross anatomy to the fine-tuned results of single-cell studies. Thus, it is still worthwhile to cast a critical eye at data that come from fMRI studies, as they are not immune to such methodological problems. Nonetheless, neuroimaging is a useful tool and one that has definitely broadened the scope of the neuroscience of perception.

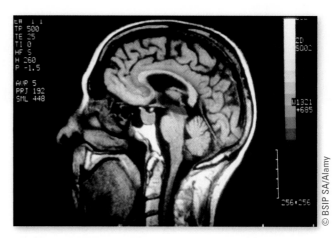

© BSIP SA/Alamy

■ FIGURE 1.22   fMRI.

This functional magnetic resonance image shows the areas of the brain that are active when an odor is presented to an individual. The areas depicted in color include areas of the brain critical in odor perception, such as the piriform cortex in the temporal lobe.

Agnosia: a deficit in some aspect of perception as a result of brain damage

Prosopagnosia: face agnosia, resulting in a deficit in perceiving faces

Neuroimaging: technologies that allow us to map living intact brains as they engage in ongoing tasks

Functional magnetic resonance imaging (fMRI): a neuroimaging technique that generates an image of the brain on the basis of the blood levels in different areas of the brain, which correlate with activity levels in those regions

TEST YOUR KNOWLEDGE

What is the difference between the views of gestalt psychology, direct perception, the information-processing view, and the computational approach?

IN DEPTH: *Applications of Sensation and Perception and Avoiding Collisions*

1.5 Apply sensation and perception research to collisions

There is probably no field of psychology in which there have been greater applications of psychological work than the area of sensation and perception. It also likely that applications of this research area will only grow in the future. That is because we use our perceptions of the world around us in nearly everything we do in our lives, with the possible exception of daydreaming. Every practical aspect of life involves looking, listening, touching, and tasting. Thus, if you are considering a career in applied psychology, you should pay very close attention to the topics in this book and to your course in sensation and perception. Understanding the basics of sensation and perception is critical for any human factors psychologist working in industry or government. Understanding the basics of sensation and perception is important for civil engineers designing safer roads.

Just consider a few of our technological horizons. Think of designing the face of a modern smart phone. The size of text and icons must be large enough for the human eye to distinguish, buttons must be positioned so that human fingers can distinguish between the button for the phone and the button for the music player. Companies such as Apple and Samsung hire many human factors psychologists to help them design these products in ways that are consistent with human perception. Moreover, consider the console of a modern jet plane. Warning lights and controls must be positioned so that they quickly demand the attention of the pilot if there is a problem with a particular system in the airplane.

Sensory systems are also important in developing new technologies. A major technological innovation that many car companies are working toward is functional self-driving cars. What goes into engineering such a system? Cameras and computers have to be wired like eyes and brains (only without blinking, falling asleep, and road rage). Understanding the cues the human eye attends to while driving is critical in designing safe self-driving cars (Arthur, 2013). Consider also computerized voice recognition systems. The engineers who design these systems must first understand the processes by which humans recognize one another's voices and interpret meaning. Thus, several of our major technological fronts involve a role for understanding human perception.

Returning to cars, it may be many years before self-driving cars are widespread, but road safety is a major issue both in the United States and throughout the world. According to U.S. government statistics, there are more than 32,000 fatalities per year in car accidents in the United States alone. This translates into more than 2,600 deaths per month on American roads. That means that approximately the same number of Americans die in car accidents every month as did in the tragic attacks of September 11, 2001. It is estimated that there were 5.5 million automobile accidents in the United States in 2010 (Keane, 2011). Thus, there is still much that can be done to improve road safety outcomes. Sensation and perception research has much to offer here.

Many sensation and perception researchers study the visually guided action associated with driving cars or flying planes. Some of this research concerns the effects of distraction on driving, a topic we discuss in depth later (Chapter 5). Other research considers the effect of fatigue on perception and driving ability. In this in-depth section, we consider the perceptual processes that drivers use to avoid automobile accidents.

Think about driving (assuming that you are a driver). It is a visual task: We look in front of us to see where we are going, and we check our rearview mirrors often for potential dangers coming from behind us. We use this visual information for simple tasks, such as noticing when our exit is coming and moving to the right, to seeing a swerving car and quickly applying the brakes. In this way, avoiding impending collisions involves perceptually guided action. When people see approaching objects, their visual systems rely on their perception of depth, that is, how far away the oncoming objects are and judgments of time to collision. These judgments need to be very accurate in order to make good driving decisions.

However, research shows that people have systematic biases in making these decisions. People estimate that a large but farther away approaching object will collide with them sooner than a smaller but closer approaching object (DeLucia, 2013). That is, people estimate accurately the likelihood that a truck will strike them but underestimate the likelihood that a smaller object such as a motorcycle will strike them. Motorcyclists often complain about how cars "cut them off." This may not be the result of recklessness or rudeness but rather a poor estimate on the part of the car's driver of how close the motorcycle actually is (see Figure 1.23). We now consider the research of Dr. Patricia DeLucia of Texas Tech University, who has devoted her career to understanding the factors that affect our perceptual decisions in collision situations (DeLucia, 2011, 2013).

Why is this? Research shows that the human visual system uses two cues to make judgments about impending collisions. The first is called **time to collision**. This means that, in theory, your visual system estimates the time an object will collide with you by dividing the object's optical size at a given point in time by the object's rate of expansion within the visual field. That is, time to collision is given by the object's optical size per unit time. In simpler language, approaching objects increase in size, and more rapidly approaching objects increase in size more as they approach you. Think of a baseball player judging when to swing his bat. A fastball increases in optical size as it approaches him more so than does a changeup (a pitch thrown deliberately slow). Or think of a pilot guiding a plane to touchdown on a runway. As the plane approaches the ground, the runway increases in optical size for the pilot. There is ample evidence that people attend to this aspect of looming objects in a variety of situations (Hecht & Savelsbergh, 2004).

However, people also use another cue to determine time to collision. The second cue is the size of the object. Larger objects are judged to be closer than smaller objects. This is known as the **size-arrival effect** (DeLucia, 2013). Numerous studies have shown that perception of collision is affected by the relative sizes of objects (Brendel, DeLucia, Hecht, Stacy, & Larsen, 2012; DeLucia, 2013; Hahnel & Hecht, 2012). You can see an illustration of this effect in ISLE 1.10.

The size-arrival effect results in the illusion that smaller objects are less likely collide with the viewer. This has a number of unfortunate consequences for driving and transportation safety. For example, drivers may underestimate the likelihood of collision when turning when a smaller oncoming vehicle is approaching because it is perceived as being farther away. Indeed, data from both actual accidents and experimental simulations show that a crash between a motorcycle and a car can occur when the car intrudes on the motorcycle's path, with the car's driver thinking the motorcycle is farther away (Brendel et al., 2012; DeLucia, 2013). In one simulated study, participants were asked to press a button when they thought an approaching vehicle would arrive

■ **FIGURE 1.23   Avoid collisions.**

The automobile driver must estimate the time to collision with the bicyclist. If the driver determines that a collision is imminent, he or she must apply the brakes immediately, in this case, to spare the bicyclist major injury.

at a particular location (Horswill, Helman, Ardiles, & Wann, 2005). The experimenters varied the sizes of the vehicles (motorcycle, car, or van) and their speeds (30 or 40 mph). Time-to-collision estimates were greater for motorcycles than for cars and vans, consistent with the size-arrival effect.

ISLE 1.10 Size-Arrival Effect

Thus, DeLucia and others have recommended that roads and motorcycle design should consider this factor in order to make transportation safer. It is also possible that education can be directed at drivers to help them realize that they often underestimate the likelihood of collision with smaller objects. Motorcycles designed to look bigger may also be safer to ride for motorcyclists. Thus, this first in-depth section introduces the concept of applications of sensation and perception research and describes a particular area, research on time to collision and its implications.

Time to collision: the estimate that an approaching object will contact another

Size-arrival effect: bigger approaching objects are seen as being more likely to collide with the viewer than smaller approaching objects

CHAPTER SUMMARY

1.1 Explain why understanding sensation and perception is important.

The study of sensation and perception sheds light on the basic nature of what it is to be human. Sensation is the registration of physical stimuli on sensory receptors, and perception is the process of creating conscious perceptual experience from sensory input. In this textbook, we discuss the science and applications of research on sensation and perception. In this chapter, we have discussed the nature of physical stimuli, whether they be light for vision on the retina or sound waves for the auditory system.

1.2   Explain why there are actually more than five senses.

In addition to vision, hearing, touch, smell, and taste, we have a vestibulatory system to help keep our balance, and a proprioception system to allow us to monitor the position of our bodies. Our sense of touch is composed of multiple systems designed to sense different features of the environment. Heat, coldness, pain, itchiness, and soft touch are all implemented by separable sensory systems.

1.3   Describe how transduction transforms a physical signal into a neural signal.

Sensory systems transduce physical signals into neural responses, which are sent to the brain for processing. The brain processes the signals, determines their meaning, and decides on appropriate actions. Perception also produces a characteristic phenomenology, which is the purely subjective experience we get when perceiving the world.

1.4   Explore the history of the study of sensation and perception.

Writings on disorders of sensation and perception go back all the way to the ancient Egyptians. Aristotle theorized extensively about perception and its causes. Later, in the 19th century, German physiologists began experimenting on the neural processes that underlie sensation, and others started the field of psychophysics, which studies the relation of physical stimuli to the psychological experience. Later influences in the development of sensation and perception research include gestalt psychology, Gibsonian direct perception, information processing, and the computational approach. Neuroscience also addresses issues of sensation and perception. Neuroscience research includes single-cell recording, neuropsychology, and neuroimaging.

1.5   Apply sensation and perception research to collisions

In the last section, we took one topic in depth as a case study in applications of sensation and perception research. This research concerns the visual perception of imminent collisions. The research shows that people use both the rates of expansion of approaching objects and the sizes of the objects to estimate time to collision. The use of the sizes of objects to estimate time to collision results in errors, in that smaller objects are judged to impact later than they actually do.

REVIEW QUESTIONS

1. What is the myth of five senses? Can you list eight different human sensory systems?

2. What do the terms *sensation* and *perception* mean? What is the difference between the two?

3. What is the process of transduction? Why is it important to perception?

4. What is phenomenology? Why is it so difficult to address in science?

5. Who was Hermann von Helmholtz? What was his view of color vision? How did it differ from that of Ewald Hering?

6. What is an unconscious inference in perception? Why is it important to the constructivist approach?

7. What is a JND? Can you give a real-world example of a JND?

8. What is the direct perception view? How does it differ from the information-processing view?

9. What is neuropsychology? How can we use agnosia to study the relation between brain region and perception?

10. What is meant by the term *time to collision*? How is it that the size-arrival effect changes our judgments of collision times? What practical suggestions could you make to improve transportation safety on the basis of these findings?

KEY TERMS

Action, 8

Aftereffect, 10

Agnosia, 19

Computational approach, 16

Constructivist approach, 11

Direct perception (Gibsonian approach), 15

Doctrine of specific nerve energies ,11

Ecological approach to perception, 16

Functional magnetic resonance imaging (fMRI), 19

Gestalt psychology, 13

INTERACTIVE SENSATION LABORATORY EXERCISES (ISLE)

Experience chapter concepts at edge.sagepub.com/schwartz

Sharpen your skills with SAGE edge at edge.sagepub.com/schwartz

SAGE edge for students provides a personalized approach to help you accomplish
your coursework goals in an easy-to-use learning environment.

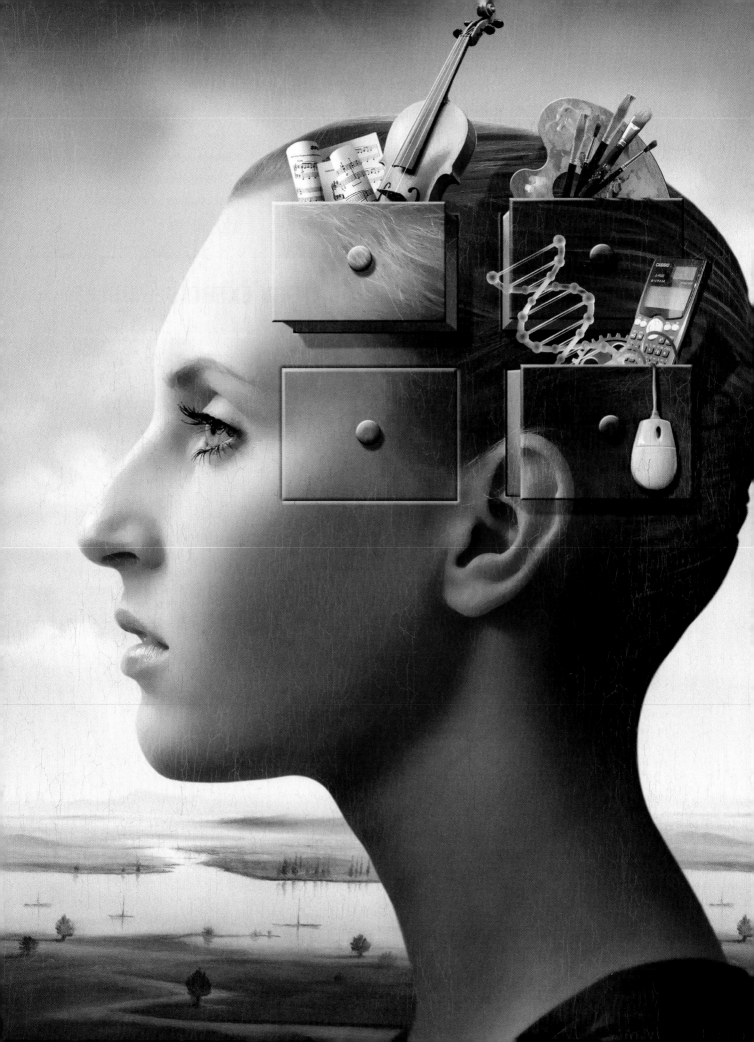

Research Methodology

2

INTRODUCTION

In 2012, the Trinidad Moruga Scorpion blend was ranked the world's hottest chili pepper (Bryan, 2012). According to the Chile Pepper Institute at New Mexico State University, the Trinidad Moruga Scorpion rates over 2 million on the Scoville scale. That puts this pepper in roughly the same range on the Scoville scale as law enforcement–grade pepper spray. By contrast, scotch bonnet peppers and habanero peppers score from 100,000 to 300,000 Scoville units. Scotch bonnets and habaneros are usually the hottest peppers most people eat. The first question we can ask is, Why would anyone ever want to eat a Trinidad Moruga Scorpion? And the next question we can ask is, How do we determine hotness and how people experience it?

The **Scoville scale** measures our detection of the amount of an ingredient called **capsaicin** in chili peppers. Capsaicin is a chemical present in peppers that directly stimulates the somatosensory system, especially heat and pain receptors in our mouths or other wet surfaces on our bodies (which is why pepper spray irritates the eyes). It presumably evolved to be present in wild chili peppers to prevent mammals from consuming their fruit. Capsaicin, in general, repels mammals but does not affect birds, as the birds are necessary to disperse the seeds. However, many people acquire a taste for capsaicin, as the heat and pain felt in the mouth interact with smell and taste to create interesting, if acquired, flavors, known as piquancy. Indeed, worldwide, the chili pepper has become an important ingredient in cooking. Moreover, some chili pepper enthusiasts "compete" in competitions to see who can eat the hottest pepper. For example, there is a chili pepper–eating contest at the North Carolina Hot Sauce Contest. In order to win, a contestant must eat an entire orange habanero chili (300,000 Scoville units; see Figure 2.1). In the competition, one starts off with milder peppers and then works one's way up to the really spicy stuff. In order to find out more about this competition, see the link on ISLE 2.1.

The Scoville scale is a psychophysical scale, meaning that it relates psychological experience to some aspect of the physical world. A **psychophysical scale** is one in which people rate their psychological experiences as a function of the level of a physical stimulus. In this case, the Scoville scale measures our experience of piquancy or "hotness" at different concentrations of capsaicin. Thus, the concentration of capsaicin in a particular food or drink is the physical dimension, whereas our experience of piquancy is the psychological correlate of that physical dimension. We will encounter numerous instances of psychophysical scales throughout this textbook. For example, the decibel scale measures the psychological construct of loudness as a function of the intensity of a sound stimulus.

The Scoville scale is named after a chemist named William Scoville, who developed the scale more than 100 years ago, in 1912. He derived the scale before chemists could accurately measure the amount of capsaicin in a particular pepper, which

LEARNING OBJECTIVES

2.1 Explain the nature of psychophysical scales and how they measure the relation of stimuli in the world and our perceptions of them.

2.2 Explain signal detection theory.

2.3 Examine how audiologists and optometrists use psychophysical assessment tools to measure patients' hearing and visual abilities and, in some cases, help them find appropriate corrective measures.

ISLE 2.1 North Carolina Hot Sauce Contest Link

Scoville scale: a measure of our detection of the amount of an ingredient called capsaicin in chili peppers

Capsaicin: the active ingredient in chili peppers that provides the experience of hotness, piquancy, or spiciness

Psychophysical scale: a scale on which people rate their psychological experiences as a function of the level of a physical stimulus

■ FIGURE 2.1   Eat at your own risk.

These are orange habaneros, which rate about 300,000 on the Scoville scale. The Scoville scale is a psychophysical scale that measures our experience of piquancy or "hotness." The more capsaicin is present in a particular food, the spicier it will taste.

labs can do routinely now. In Scoville's time, having a reliable scale to measure how "hot" foods were was important in the development of commercial foods. To measure the piquancy, Scoville recruited brave volunteers from the company he worked for to evaluate chili peppers. Once he had willing volunteers, Scoville adjusted the level of chili peppers in a liquid solution that he had his observers taste. Obviously, the greater the concentration of chili peppers, the hotter would be the taster's experience, but Scoville wanted to quantify this relation. He measured when the observers first starting experiencing heat when tasting the pepper solution and how much more capsaicin he needed to add to get people to notice a difference in the hotness of the solution. If a taster did not notice any difference as a function of more chili peppers, Scoville added more until that taster did notice the difference. In this way, Scoville was measuring a characteristic known in psychophysics as the just-noticeable difference (JND). A JND is the smallest amount of physical change observers notice as a perceptual change.

The Scoville scale, then, measures people's perceived sense of hotness as a function of the amount of capsaicin in the sample solution. This scale was critical for the development of commercial products that contained capsaicin. The scale is now widely used in the food industry. The production of commercial hot sauces is a worldwide business, and companies will report the Scoville ratings of their sauces. Tabasco sauce, spicy to many of us, rates only about 2,000 on the Scoville scale, far less than the piquancy of a Scotch bonnet pepper, let alone a Trinidad Moruga Scorpion. So if you know that Tabasco sauce is relatively mild on the Scoville scale, you might try it on your tofu. However, if someone is offering you Trinidad Moruga Scorpion sauce, you might want to think twice before dousing your dinner. For our purposes here, the perception of piquancy and the Scoville scale serve as an excellent introduction to the research methods used in sensation and perception and in understanding the concepts of psychophysics.

This chapter covers basic questions, techniques, and research methods used by researchers to discover how human sensory systems work. This information will set the stage for later chapters that cover specific sensory systems, how they work, and what we perceive. In terms of methods, in some cases, participants are asked to rate a stimulus on a numerical scale, whereas in other situations, they may be asked to decide only whether a stimulus is present (see the various demonstrations on ISLE). In the latter case, a researcher can quantify on the basis of the percentage of correct responses at each level of the stimulus.

The study of human sensory systems starts with psychophysics, the study of the relation between physical stimuli and perception events, much as we just saw with the Scoville scale for chili pepper hotness. Psychophysical methods involve presenting a carefully controlled stimulus to a participant and asking a question directly of the participant that allows the answer to be quantified, that is, turned into a number. From these direct questions, we hope to understand the way the mind works to accomplish sensation and perception. Thus, the psychophysical approach focuses on the relation between physical properties (e.g., the amount of capsaicin present) and perception (the experience of hotness).

However, the actual questions asked of participants may vary depending on what the research concerns. Participants may be asked to do a detection task ("Is there any hotness in the taste?"), a comparison task ("Which is hotter, Stimulus A or Stimulus B?"), or a magnitude task ("How hot is the stimulus?"). Moreover, the scale might be a preference scale ("Which level of hotness is preferable?"). Researchers need to be clear about which methods they use, because sometimes different methods may reveal different patterns, which lend complexity to the understanding. As such, it is important to detail the research methods of sensation and perception in this chapter, before we delve into individual sensory systems in the remaining chapters.

THE MEASURES AND METHODS OF PSYCHOPHYSICS

2.1 Explain the nature of psychophysical scales and how they measure the relation of stimuli in the world and our perceptions of them.

When you go to an optometrist to get your vision tested or to an audiologist to get your hearing tested, you essentially perform a series of psychophysical tests. At the optometrist, you are asked questions such as "Can you distinguish the *d*'s from the *b*'s and the *o*'s from the *q*'s?" If you can, great; if you cannot, you may need to start wearing glasses (see Figure 2.2). At the audiologist, you are asked questions such as "In which ear do you hear the tone?" If you can't identify whether the sound is coming from the left or the right, it may be time to consider hearing aids. But for our purposes, it is the basic methods of psychophysics that allow us to start studying the processes of perception. Many of the methods go back to Gustav Fechner in the 19th century.

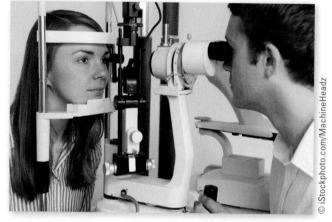

■ **FIGURE 2.2   A woman undergoing a routine optometrist's exam.**

People should have these exams annually to determine the health of their eyes. Many of the tests an optometrist runs are similar to psychophysical tests.

Method of Limits

In the **method of limits**, stimuli are presented on a graduated scale, and participants must judge the stimuli along a certain property that goes up or down. For example, a participant may be presented with an increasingly dimmer set of lights. The participant is asked to tell the experimenter when the lights are no longer visible. The researcher will then present the participant with lights so dim that they cannot be seen and present increasingly intense lights until the participant detects them (see Figure 2.3). Similarly, one could present a series of tones, starting at a volume so soft that one cannot hear them and gradually increasing the loudness until the participant can hear the tones. We illustrate the method-of-limits with ISLE 2.2. In the first screen of this experiment, you will find a window in which you can set up the values that will adjust how your method of limits experiment will run. The first item asks you to determine the number of levels to test. The number of levels refers to the number of intensity steps in the independent variable that will be tested. In the method of limits, the researcher hopes to pick an extreme value that is readily detected and a level that is never detected and then several levels between these.

The method of limits is often used to determine both absolute and difference thresholds. An **absolute threshold** is the smallest amount of a stimulus necessary to allow an observer to detect its presence. For example, the smallest amount of light energy at any particular wavelength of light that we can detect is its absolute threshold. Similarly, the least amount of sound that we can hear at any particular frequency is its absolute threshold. The smallest amount of capsaicin that we can detect as hotness is its absolute threshold. Indeed, a bell pepper has such a small amount of capsaicin that it earns a zero on the Scoville scale. For a final example, the smallest amount of salt that your taste buds can detect is also its absolute threshold.

ISLE 2.2 Method of Limits

Method of limits: stimuli are presented in a graduated scale, and participants must judge the stimuli along a certain property that goes up or down

Absolute threshold: the smallest amount of a stimulus necessary to allow an observer to detect its presence

Intensity	Trial Number								
10	Y		Y		Y		Y		Y
9	Y		Y		Y		Y		Y
8	Y		Y		Y		Y		Y
7	Y		Y		Y		Y		Y
6	Y		Y		N		Y		Y
5	Y		N	Y		Y	Y		Y
4	N	Y		N		N	Y	Y	N
3		N		N		N	N	N	
2		N		N		N		N	
1		N		N		N		N	
Crossover	4.5	3.5	5.5	4.5	6.5	4.5	3.5	3.5	4.5

Threshold = mean crossover = 4.5

■ FIGURE 2.3   The method of limits.

The participant must decide if a stimulus is present at a number of different levels of intensity. The stimulus is increased in even trials and decreased in odd trials. A *Y* indicates that the participant detects the stimulus, whereas an *N* indicates that the participant does not detect the stimulus. The estimate of the threshold is considered to be the mean crossover point.

The method of limits can also be used to determine the **difference threshold** (the **JND** mentioned earlier), which is the smallest difference between two stimuli that can be detected. Thus, one might hold two weights and attempt to determine if their masses are the same or different. The smallest difference in weight that can be detected is the difference threshold, equal to 1 JND. Similarly, an observer might see two green lights and be asked if the lights are the same or not. The smallest difference in the wavelengths of the lights that can be detected is the difference threshold, or 1 JND. Similarly, the smallest increase of capsaicin that can be detected as a difference in piquancy is also a 1 JND difference.

Returning to the concept of absolute thresholds, it turns out that detecting absolute thresholds is harder than simply finding the softest sound a person can hear or the dimmest light a person can see. For example, if you are just leaving the firing range and have been hearing loud percussions for the past hour, detecting a very soft tone might be difficult. If you have been studying in the library for the past hour, that same tone might be quite audible. Similarly, it may be easier to detect a dim light in the dark of night than it is to detect the same light on a bright summer day. If you have just eaten a large and satisfying meal, the taste of another piece of lasagna may not be as satisfying as the first. That is, absolute thresholds are not so absolute—they depend on many internal and external conditions. In other words, our sensory systems are constantly adapting to local conditions. On one hand, this makes assessing absolute thresholds difficult, but on the other hand, it is an adaptive feature of our sensory systems, as it allows us to perceive under a wide range of conditions. On a bright sunny day at the beach, we want our sensitivity to light to be less than when we are trying to find our way around a forest campground on a dark, moonless night.

In assessing thresholds, we often need to estimate the threshold and try to compensate for any sensory adaptation that is occurring, such as whether a person has

Difference threshold (JND): the smallest difference between two stimuli that can be detected just eaten. Thus, to determine an absolute threshold with method of limits, a researcher must use both an ascending series and a descending series. An **ascending series** (or an ascending staircase) is one in which a stimulus gets increasingly larger along a physical dimension. Thus, the intensity of light might increase, the amplitude of sound might increase, or the amount of capsaicin in a taste capsule might increase. By contrast, a **descending series** (or a descending staircase) is one in which the stimulus gets increasingly smaller along a physical dimension. Thus, the researcher starts with a clearly visible light and lowers the amount of light on each successive trial (see Figure 2.4).

■ FIGURE 2.4   **Absolute threshold.**

Illustration of the detection of absolute thresholds through the method of descending limits. Each light is more dim than the one to its left.

Consider a light detection experiment. We want to determine a person's absolute threshold for a red light in an otherwise dark environment. In the ascending method, we start off with a level of red light that is known to be below the threshold. The participant should respond that he or she does not see it. The experimenter then gradually increases the intensity of the light until the person can detect the light. In the descending method, we start off with a bright level of red light that the person can obviously detect and then lower the intensity of the light until the person can no longer see it. The point at which people change from detecting to not detecting or vice versa is known as the **crossover point**. Typically, the threshold will be different when measured by the ascending method and by the descending method. In general, with ascending series, people are likely to claim that they can detect a stimulus when in fact the stimulus is below the threshold. With descending series, people are likely to claim that they cannot detect a stimulus when it actually is above the threshold. Researchers will typically average over several descending and ascending series to get their best estimate of the absolute threshold (see ISLE 2.2).

Consider some common absolute thresholds in the natural world. Think of looking up at the stars on a clear night (see Figure 2.5). Think of the faintest star you can possibly see—this star may be at or around your visual threshold. And for the auditory system, consider hearing the faintest drone of a conversation from the upstairs dorm room. You cannot make out the content of what they are saying, but you can just barely hear their voices. In the domain of taste, consider how much sugar you must put in your iced tea before it has the slightest hint of sweet. And think of the faintest hint of a distant odor—perhaps a faraway smell of coffee. Thus, in real life, we do encounter at-threshold stimuli from time to time.

In Chapter 1, we mentioned the work of Ernst Heinrich Weber, who did some of the earliest work on thresholds in the 19th century. One area he investigated was threshold in touch along the surface of the skin. He was interested in the **two-point touch threshold**, which is the minimum distance at which two touches are perceived as two touches and not one. In this case, two needles can be brought gently to touch a person's skin close to one another. If a person only feels one touch, then it is below the threshold, but if the person feels two touches, then they are above the threshold. Our two-point touch thresholds vary across our skin. Our fingers can detect two touches even when the needles are extremely close to each other. However, the skin of our backs requires greater distance to feel two touches. Areas on the face and mouth have small two-point thresholds, but not as good as the fingers. Other areas, such as the arms and legs, require larger distances to perceive two touches, but not as great distances as the skin of the back. The two-point threshold is an absolute threshold. The size of the absolute threshold differs on different parts of the body, just as acuity changes across the surface of the eye's retina. Table 2.1 lists a few everyday absolute thresholds.

Ascending series: a series in which a stimulus gets increasingly larger along a physical dimension

Descending series: a series in which a stimulus gets increasingly smaller along a physical dimension

Crossover point: the point at which a person changes from detecting to not detecting a stimulus or vice versa

Two-point touch threshold: the minimum distance at which two touches are perceived as two touches and not one

© iStockphoto.com/Baltskars

■ FIGURE 2.5   Stars on a clear night.

Many stars are easy to see, but some may lie just at our thresholds. When we look at these starts straight on, we may miss them, but we see them again "out of the corner of our eye," or at our periphery, which is more light sensitive.

Sense	Threshold
Vision	A candle 30 miles away on a dark night
Audition	A ticking watch 20 feet away in an otherwise silent location
Taste	A teaspoon of sugar in 2 gallons of water
Smell	A drop of perfume in three rooms

■ TABLE 2.1   Everyday Absolute Thresholds

SOURCE: Adapted from Galanter (1962).

ISLE 2.3 Method of Constant Stimuli

Method of constant stimuli: a method whereby the threshold is determined by presenting the observer with a set of stimuli, some above threshold and some below it, in a random order

Method of Constant Stimuli

In the **method of constant stimuli**, the threshold is determined by presenting the observer with a set of stimuli, some of which are above the threshold and some of which are below it; the stimuli are presented in a random order. This differs from the method of limits. In the method of limits, the stimuli are changed to home in on a particular observer's threshold. In the method of constant stimuli, all stimuli are always presented, and all are selected beforehand. In the method of constant stimuli, the presentation of stimuli is given in a random order rather than zeroing in on the threshold. This technique prevents the observer from being able to predict or anticipate what the next stimulus will be. This reduces errors that may result from habituation or fluctuations in perception due to attention or other factors. However, the method of constant stimuli is often quite time-consuming, as it requires pretesting to gauge the general region of the threshold for each participant. Moreover, it requires many trials to home in on a statistically determined threshold. In the method of constant stimuli, the stimulus that is detected 50% of the time and not detected 50% of the time is considered to be the threshold (see Figure 2.6). You can see a demonstration of the method of constant stimuli on ISLE 2.3.

These graphs illustrate how we measure the threshold in psychophysical experiments. In Figure 2.6a, we see a hypothetical cutoff at a particular level of intensity that separates the stimulus level at which we see the stimulus and the stimulus level at which we do not see the stimulus. Figure 2.6b illustrates that in most cases, thresholds vary from trial to trial, and we must estimate the threshold from the point at which participants are 50% likely to say "saw it" and 50% likely to say "didn't see it."

The method of constant stimuli is used by audiologists when testing patients for hearing thresholds (Gelfand, 2009). For each frequency of sound, the audiologist will present the patient with an assortment of louder and softer tones to detect (see ISLE 2.3b). In this way, the audiologist can determine the threshold of hearing at each frequency and, in some cases, if that threshold is higher than it should be,

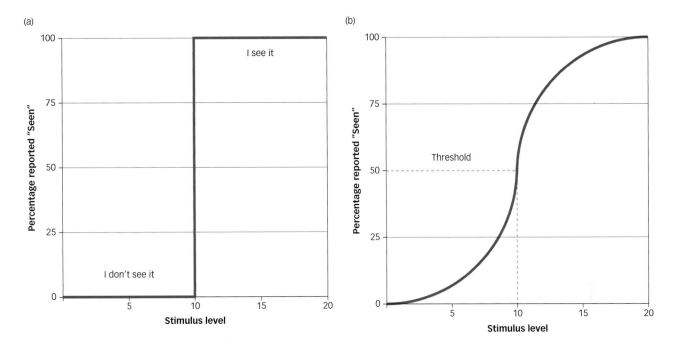

■ FIGURE 2.6   Measuring threshold.

whether the person might be a candidate for hearing aids. Typically, hearing loss varies as a function of sound frequency, meaning that for some sound frequencies, a person may be impaired but for others have normal hearing. An audiologist needs to know the profile of hearing loss to properly program a patient's hearing aids. For this reason, as we will see later in the chapter, audiology starts with psychophysics.

Method of Adjustment

In the **method of adjustment**, the observer controls the level of the stimulus and "adjusts" it to be at the perceptual threshold. The participant does so by increasing or decreasing the level of the stimulus until it feels like it is just at the detectable level. Typically, the participant will do so by continuously adjusting a knob to control the level of the stimulus. This is an intuitive measure for most participants because it mirrors many normal activities, such as adjusting the volume control on a radio or a dimmer switch on a light. In a light threshold study, the method of adjustment would require the observer to adjust the light source to the dimmest light the participant can detect. Adjusting the knob any lower would render the stimulus invisible. The advantage of this technique is that it can quickly yield a threshold for each participant, but a disadvantage is that it leads to great variance from one participant to the next and between successive trials for each participant.

The method of adjustment is very useful for matching one stimulus to another to determine the **point of subjective equality (PSE)**. The PSE is the settings of two stimuli at which the observer experiences them as identical. For example, consider a researcher who is interested in the JND in the detection of pitch differences as a function of sound frequency. The observer hears a constant sample tone at, for example, 1,000 Hz. The observer would then adjust a

Method of adjustment: a method whereby the observer controls the level of the stimulus and "adjusts" it to be at the perceptual threshold

Point of subjective equality (PSE): the settings of two stimuli at which the observer experiences them as identical

ISLE 2.4 Method of Adjustment

ISLE 2.5 Point of Subjective Equality

second tone until it matched perceptually the sample tone. The experimenter could then look at the frequency selected by the observer and see just how closely he or she actually matched the sample tone. In vision research, the experimenter may present a stimulus of particular brightness. The participant would have to adjust another stimulus to be equally bright to the first one. And, returning to our chili pepper example, an experimenter might present a chili pepper sauce as the sample taste. Then a participant would have to adjust the level of capsaicin in a second sample to match the level of hotness in the first. To see and experience an auditory example of the method of adjustment, see ISLE 2.4 and try a PSE in ISLE 2.5.

Closely related to the concept of threshold is the concept of sensitivity. **Sensitivity** is the ability to perceive a particular stimulus. It is inversely related to threshold. As the threshold goes down, the observer is deemed to be more sensitive. That is, lower thresholds mean higher sensitivity. This makes sense when one considers that *threshold* refers to the ability to perceive a stimulus at smaller and smaller levels of that quantity. Thus, a person who can hear a sound at 10 decibels (dB) is more sensitive than a person who can hear the sound only at 15 dB. A person who can smell a perfume at smaller concentrations in the air is more sensitive to that odor than someone who requires larger concentrations. Sensitivity may vary across situations. For example, one may be more sensitive to changes in the intensity of light in a room when one has just been in a dark room than when one has just come out of the brilliant sunshine.

Magnitude Estimation

Magnitude estimation is a psychophysical method in which participants judge and assign numerical estimates to the perceived strength of a stimulus. This technique was developed by S. S. Stevens in the 1950s (e.g., Stevens, 1956). Magnitude estimation usually works in the following way. An experimenter presents a standard tone and assigns it a particular loudness value, say 20. Then the participant must judge subsequent tones and give them numerical values, in comparison to the standard. So if the participant thinks the new tone is twice as loud as the standard, it should be assigned a 40. If the next tone is just a bit softer than the standard, it may be assigned a 15. If the tone is heard to be much softer than the standard, it might receive a 5 on this hypothetical scale of loudness.

ISLE 2.6 Magnitude Estimation

Magnitude estimation can also be used for visual experiments. It follows the same principle: In brightness estimation, a sample light might be given a standard value, and then other samples are judged in relation to the standard. Magnitude estimation can be adapted to just about any perceptual dimension. Participants may be asked to judge the brightness of light, the lengths of lines, or the sizes of circles on a numerical scale. For visual and auditory examples of the method of adjustment, go to ISLE 2.6.

As experimenters in a psychophysics experiment, we can control the stimulus. For example, we can have people taste and make judgments of the sweetness of a sample with a known quantity of sugar, say 1 teaspoon per gallon. We then present them with a sample of a solution of sugar water calibrated to 2 teaspoons per gallon. The new stimulus has twice as much sugar in it per unit of water, but is it perceived as twice as sweet? In all sensory systems, there is a phenomenon called response compression. **Response compression** means that as the strength of a stimulus increases, so too does the perceptual response, but the perceptual response does not increase by as much as the strength of the stimulus increases. That is, if you judge the first sugar-water solution as a 5 on

Sensitivity: the ability to perceive a particular stimulus; it is inversely related to threshold

Magnitude estimation: a psychophysical method in which participants judge and assign numerical estimates to the perceived strength of a stimulus

Response compression: as the strength of a stimulus increases, so does the perceptual response, but the perceptual response does not increase by as much as the stimulus increases

the sweetness scale, doubling the sugar in the solution will cause an increase in your sweetness judgment but not a doubling of the perceived sweetness. In fact, you will likely judge the 2-teaspoon solution as a 7 or an 8 on the sweetness scale.

There is an exception to the response compression rule for sensory perception, and that involves pain perception. In pain perception, as well as a few other perceptual characteristics, there is response expansion instead of response compression. **Response expansion** means that as the strength of a stimulus increases, the perceptual response increases even more. In this case, if a person receives an electric shock of physical intensity 10 and judges it to be 5 on a pain scale, increasing the physical intensity to 20 will lead to a more than doubling of the judgment, to perhaps 15 on the pain scale. That is, smaller increments of increase in the physical dimension (e.g., electric shock) lead to greater increments in the perception of the perceptual characteristic (e.g., the perception of pain).

Stevens (1957, 1961) developed an equation to try to encapsulate both types of data sets (this is one of just a few mathematical equations that will be presented in this book). It is called **Stevens' power law**, and it is as follows:

$$P = cI^b$$

In this equation, P is equal to the perceived magnitude of a stimulus, that is, how bright we perceive a light to be or how sweet we perceive a sugar solution to be. I is equal to the intensity of the actual stimulus. Thus, at the simplest level, our perception is a function of the physical intensity of the stimulus. However, there two other parts of the equation that explain the relation between perception and the physical stimulus. The letter c represents a constant, which will be different for each sensory modality or for each sensory dimension. The constant also allows you to scale your measure appropriately. For example, both the Fahrenheit and Celsius temperature scales measure the same underlying property, but do so with different scales. The exponent b equals the power to which the intensity is raised. It is this exponent b that allows response compression and response expansion. Response compression occurs when b is less than 1, and response expansion occurs when b is greater than 1. Thus, Stevens' power law equation can account for both types of subjective responses. This is depicted in Figure 2.7. For a graphical demonstration of how this works, go to ISLE 2.7.

To give an example, let us return to the Scoville scale. We could present a chili sauce with 1 milligram of capsaicin per kilogram of other substances. We tell people that this is a 1 on the piquancy scale. We then increase the dosage to 2 mg/kg. Thus, we have doubled the active "hot" ingredient. Applying Stevens' law, we need to know the constant and the exponent to determine a person's perceptual response. Because capsaicin stimulates pain receptors, we can expect an exponent of greater than 1 (and hence response expansion). Thus, the hotness judgment should be more than double the baseline, leading to a hotness judgment of greater than 2. We must know the psychological response in order to

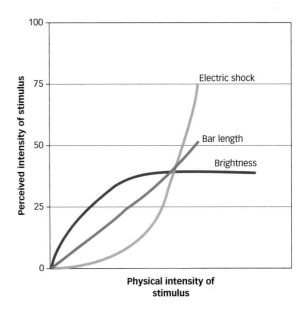

■ FIGURE 2.7 Comparison of the physical intensity of a stimulus and its perceptual correlate.

In response compression, as the physical intensity of a stimulus increases, its perceptual correlate increases as well, but not by as much. In response expansion, as the physical intensity of a stimulus increases, its perceptual correlate increases by even more so. The curve for brightness illustrates response compression, whereas the curve for electric shock illustrates response expansion.

ISLE 2.7 Stevens' Power Law

Response expansion: as the strength of a stimulus increases, the perceptual response increases even more

Stevens' power law: a mathematical formula that describes the relationship between stimulus intensity and our perception; it allows for both response compression and expansion

Sense	Perception	Exponent
Vision	Brightness	0.3
Audition	Loudness	0.5
Taste	Sweetness	0.8
Vision	Apparent length	1.0
Touch	Pain	3.5

■ TABLE 2.2   Stevens' Power Law Exponents

SOURCE: Adapted from Stevens (1961).

apply Stevens' law. That is, knowing the amount of capsaicin in a food would not have allowed Scoville to measure piquancy. He needed the psychophysical measure to map response expansion. A few exponents for Stevens' power law are given for different sensory domains in Table 2.2. A value greater than 1 indicates response expansion, whereas a value less than 1 indicates response compression.

Catch Trials and Their Use

One of the potential difficulties that arise with the traditional methods of limits, constant stimuli, and adjustment is that the participant might be willingly or unwillingly misinforming the experimenter about perceptual experience. For example, a participant may indicate that he heard a sound when he was not sure or perhaps because he thinks a sound should have occurred even though he did not perceive one. Or worse, perhaps the participant wants to impress the experimenter with his extraordinary sensory abilities. In all of the methods described so far, it would be easy to do; you could simply report that you see or hear the stimulus when you do not. Because the stimulus is always present, even at a very soft volume or at a very low brightness, the experimenter cannot know if the participant is being truthful or not. One technique to counter this strategy is to use catch trials. A **catch trial** is a trial in which the stimulus is not presented. It is easy to insert these trials as checks on the participant's accuracy and honesty. Thus, in catch trials, the correct answer is "No, I didn't hear it" or "No, I didn't see it." If a participant reliably says that she saw the stimulus in a catch trial, we can dismiss this participant as an unreliable observer.

Another method that circumvents problems of false reporting is the **forced-choice method** (Blackwell, 1953; Jones, 1956). In every trial, the subject is asked to report either when the stimulus occurred or where it occurred. Thus, instead of determining whether a light was present or not, the participant must decide if a light was present in one location or another or at one time slot or another time slot. Instead of determining whether the participant heard a sound or not, the participant must determine in which of two time intervals there was a sound or not. This technique prevents the need for catch trials because the observer cannot simply say "yes" in every trial, regardless of the presence of a stimulus in that trial. But it also allows the determination of thresholds, because if a stimulus cannot be detected, performance will be at chance (50% if there are two choices). Threshold can be determined by finding a level of performance that is significantly above chance. See ISLE 2.8 for an illustration of the forced-choice method (also see Figure 2.8).

ISLE 2.8 Forced-Choice

Catch trial: a trial in which the stimulus is not presented

Forced-choice method: a psychophysical method in which a participant is required to report when or where a stimulus occurs instead of whether it was perceived

Signal Detection Theory

2.2 Explain signal detection theory.

On July 3, 1988, Iran Air Flight 655 was shot down by a U.S. missile from the Navy vessel U.S.S. *Vincennes* (see Figure 2.9). All 290 passengers and crew, including 66 children, were killed. Although the United States has never apologized to Iran, the U.S. government gave $61 million to the relatives of the victims of the attack. The incident took place at a time when there was heavy tension between the United States and Iran, and Iranian jets had previously attacked U.S. Navy vessels. However, in this case, the radar operators on the *Vincennes* mistakenly judged the civilian airplane, an Airbus 300, to be an incoming Iranian F-14 fighter, with the horrifying consequences described here. How had the Navy made such a terrible mistake? We will couch an explanation of how this disaster occurred in terms of one of the most influential theories in the history of sensation and perception research, namely, **signal detection theory**.

Consider the radar specialist examining the screen that depicted incoming objects. He or she had to decide, on the basis of the information available on the radar screen, whether the incoming object was an enemy warplane (an Iranian F-14) or a harmless jetliner (an Airbus 300). In 1988, this involved examining a radar screen and making a judgment as to the nature of the incoming airplane. The United States had (and has) complicated procedures to differentiate military and civilian airplanes on incoming radar. But in a war zone with an object approaching you at 600 mph, decisions must be made quickly.

From the U.S. Navy's standpoint, there are two types of errors. The Navy could mistake a civilian airplane for a military jet, or it could mistake a military jet for a civilian airplane. Both of these errors could have fatal consequences for innocent people, as indeed they did in this case. In the *Vincennes* case, the mistake that arose is called a **false alarm**. A false alarm, in psychophysical terms, occurs when the observer mistakes a harmless or null signal for a dangerous or an active signal. The other type of error is called a **miss**, in which a harmful signal is perceived as harmless. In one case, the danger is to innocent civilians aboard the aircraft, whereas in the other case, the danger is to equally innocent personnel aboard the Navy vessel. Thus, in this situation, everything must be done to avoid both errors (Table 2.3).

In such a situation, there are also two potential correct responses. A **correct rejection** occurs when a harmless signal is perceived as harmless, and a **hit** occurs when a harmful signal is correctly perceived as harmful. In the case of the *Vincennes*, the correct response should have been a correct rejection. The plane was a civilian jetliner that offered no threat to the Navy. In this example, a hit would have occurred if the radar had correctly identified an incoming military warplane as a threat. Military action must optimize hits and correct rejections in order to achieve strategic objectives and minimize civilian casualties. Thus, one of the goals of any military surveillance equipment is to maximize hits and correct rejections while minimizing false alarms and misses.

■ **FIGURE 2.8** **Illustration of the forced-choice method.**

The participant in this experiment is engaged in a psychophysical task using the forced-choice method. The participant must press the button on the left or the right to indicate in which area of the computer screen a light was displayed.

Signal detection theory: the theory that in every sensory detection or discrimination, there is both sensory sensitivity to the stimulus and a criterion used to make a cognitive decision

False alarm: in signal detection analysis, a false alarm is an error that occurs when a nonsignal is mistaken for a target signal

Miss: in signal detection analysis, a miss is an error that occurs when an incoming signal is not detected

Correct rejection: in signal detection analysis, a correct rejection occurs when a nonsignal is dismissed as not present

Hit: in signal detection analysis, a hit occurs when a signal is detected when the signal is present

■ FIGURE 2.9 The U.S.S. *Vincennes.*

The U.S.S. *Vincennes*, seen here in 2005, was a guided-missile cruiser. In 1988, its crew mistakenly shot down a civilian aircraft. This error, called a false alarm in psychophysical terminology, had devastating consequences.

Response	Incoming Signal	
	Is a Fighter Jet	**Is a Civilian Plane**
Think it is a fighter jet	Shoot down enemy plane	Innocent civilians killed
Think it is a civilian plane	Innocent sailors killed	No hostile interactions

■ TABLE 2.3 Signal Detection Theory: Is It a Threat?

ISLE 2.9 Signal Detection Experiment

Criterion: an internal cutoff, determined by the observer, above which the observer makes one response and below which the observer makes another response

Consider a radar operator examining the signal on his or her radar screen. Such an operator may be more likely to define a signal as "dangerous" if the signal is coming from an aircraft over the Strait of Hormuz, especially after recent attacks on the U.S. Navy, than if he or she is monitoring aircraft flying over the skies of central Nebraska. This differing judgment on the basis of situation is called the **criterion**. In Nebraska, the radar specialist will select a very high criterion, so as to avoid false alarms, and misses are less of a concern. However, when a Navy vessel is patrolling the Strait of Hormuz, near a highly hostile Iranian government, which has recently launched attacks against U.S. ships, the criterion will be lower, as there are more risks in the environment and the Navy does not want to miss an actual attack; thus, there is greater risk for more false alarms. This is exactly what happened off the coast of Iran in 1988. Thus, this military tragedy fits into the logic of signal detection theory, as we will shortly see (Green & Swets, 1966). See ISLE 2.9 to play such a war game yourself.

Here's another way of thinking about signal detection theory (see Figure 2.10). Consider the following situation: You are driving down the road, and you think you hear an noise from the engine that sounds like a clunk. However, with your stereo playing and the sounds of the road, you are not sure exactly what the clunk is. If your car is relatively new and has a history of smooth running, perhaps you will decide that you didn't really hear anything (high criterion). Your hearing is "playing tricks" on you. However, if you are driving an old car that has a history of spending nearly as much time in the shop as on the road, you might decide that you did hear something and head to the nearest service center (low criterion). What is important in this example is that even in this very basic sensory discrimination, there is a cognitive decision-making element that needs to be taken in to account. This is another practical example of the situations for which signal detection accounts (see Table 2.4).

So let us look at a model of signal detection starting with a visual detection example (see Table 2.4b). Signal detection assumes that there is "noise" in any system. On occasion, this noise may be mistaken for an actual signal. In these examples, what should have been seen as noise, in the military sense, was mistaken for a military signal by the crew of the *Vincennes*. This noise may occur because of distortion on the screen or a wobble on the radar caused by atmospheric

(a)

(b)

© iStockphoto.com/nwinter

© iStockphoto.com/Rawpixel

■ FIGURE 2.10   Old car/new car.

When we think we hear a noise associated with an engine malfunction, we adopt different criteria, depending on the situation. If we are driving the old clunker (a), we may adopt a more liberal criterion for hearing an engine problem. This will help us catch engine trouble (hits) but may also increase the rate of bringing the car to the shop when there is no problem (false alarm). If we are driving the shiny new sports car (b), we may adopt a more conservative criterion for hearing an engine problem. This will increase the likelihood of correctly dismissing a sound as noise rather than a mechanical problem (correct rejection), but may increase the likelihood that we do not hear a problem when there is one (miss).

Response	The Clunk	
	Actual	Did Not Happen
Think it happened	You get needed service	You make an unneeded service visit
Think it did not happen	You break down	You go happily on your way

■ TABLE 2.4A   Signal Detection Theory: Possible Situations

Response	The Signal Is	
	Present	Absent
Perceived it	Hit	False alarm
Did not perceive it	Miss	Correct rejection

■ TABLE 2.4B   Signal Detection Theory: Possible Situations

conditions. Similarly, if we have an old car, we may hear "clunks" even when the car is operating effectively. This noise in the system may be other sounds from the road, tinnitus in our ear, or something rustling in the trunk. Thus, the task for the observer is to distinguish an actual signal from the background noise. In a vision threshold experiment, this might be the actual dim light in the noise produced by random firing of retinal receptors.

So consider first the case in which there is a faint signal. We can detect it (hit) or not detect it (miss). But there is also the case in which the signal is absent. In that case, we may detect something (false alarm) or correctly realize that there is no signal (correct rejection). Signal detection theory states that we must consider all four possibilities to successfully measure thresholds.

Consider a situation in which there is little noise in the system. Imagine if the captain of the *Vincennes* in 1988 had access to 2015 satellite imaging (perhaps courtesy of Dr. Who, the fictional time-traveling British superhero). In this case, there is little noise in the system. He could watch the video feed from the satellite and see that the incoming plane is an Airbus rather than an F-14. In this case, there would be few false alarms and few misses, only hits and correct rejections. But in 1988, the radar technology had noise in the system, presumably generated by a number of atmospheric conditions. Thus, the noise introduces the potential for error in the system.

These differences are represented graphically in Figure 2.11. In the figure, we consider a common psychophysical task, detecting a soft sound in a quiet environment. Noise here can be defined as random neuronal firing—think of the odd "sound" you experience but are not sure if it is for real. Thus, a hit occurs when we detect a soft light when present, and a false alarm represents when we think we heard a soft sound when one was not present. A correct rejection occurs when we say that no sound was present when no sound was present, but a miss occurs when we say that no sound was present when in fact there was a soft sound. Each of these situations is represented in the figure.

Let's return now to an idea introduced in comparing the threat in the Strait of Hormuz and the threat in Nebraska, that is, the idea of a criterion in signal detection theory. The criterion is an internal cutoff determined by the observer, above which the observer makes one response and below which the observer makes another response. Thus, in the Strait of Hormuz, we adopt a criterion or an internal cutoff to respond at a lower threat level than we do in Nebraska. After all, we assume that the danger of an incoming enemy aircraft is much higher off the coast of a hostile nation than in the safety of the middle of our own. In our other example, if the clunking sound is above a certain level of loudness, we decide that there really is a clunk, and there is a problem with the car. If it is below that level of loudness, we decide that there is no reason to worry. This cutoff point may be

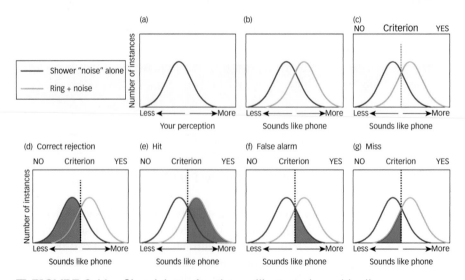

■ FIGURE 2.11   Signal detection theory illustrated graphically.

Figure 2.11a shows the continuum of neurons firing in response to a soft or an absent sound. Figure 2.11b shows a potential distribution for perceiving the soft sound or misperceiving the absent sound. Figure 2.11c adds the criterion. Figures 2.11d through 2.11g show correct rejections, hits, false alarms, and misses.

different depending on whether we have a new car or that old clunker. Similarly, in a psychophysical study, the criterion determines the level of stimulation above which we decide a light is present and below which we decide not to indicate the presence of the light.

However, criteria vary depending on the situation. You might adopt a lax criterion for hearing the clunk if your car is old and has a history of engine problems. That is, you are more likely to attribute the clunk to the car than to random road sounds. This means you will risk more false alarms to catch all hits—you don't want your car to fall apart at 70 mph on the highway. But there is little cost to taking it the shop one more time. Alternatively, if your car is new and has just been checked by a mechanic, you may adopt a more strict strategy. This means that you are more likely to attribute the noise to the road and not to the car. In signal detection terms, this means a greater desire to avoid false alarms (not paying extra money to the mechanic) and risking missing hits (i.e., a breakdown, which you think is unlikely).

Thus, a criterion is a value set by the observer depending on circumstances that only he or she knows. If the stimulus is above the criterion, the observer will say "yes" or "present," but if the stimulus is below the criterion, the observer will say "no" or "absent." Consider how the concept of a criterion might apply to real-world decisions. A radiologist screening for breast cancer must weigh the risks of unnecessary testing against the risk for cancer in evaluating a mammogram. If the women is young and has no family history of breast cancer, the radiologist might adopt a stricter criterion, not wanting to raise a false alarm and put the woman through the pain of taking a tissue sample. However, if the woman is older or has a family history of breast cancer, the radiologist may adopt a more lax criterion, not wanting to make a miss, and recommend further testing. Mammographic screening is very effective, but there are still misses and false alarms to be concerned about.

There is one last piece to understand in signal detection theory. **Sensitivity**, as used in signal detection theory, is the ease or difficulty with which the observer can distinguish the signal from noise. That is, sensitivity measures how easy it is to tell if a signal is present or absent (see Figure 2.12). Thus, one can imagine a radar operator with 1948 technology and one with 2015 technology. The older system has lower sensitivity, so it is harder to determine the nature of the incoming threat. The 2015 version has higher sensitivity, so it is easier to

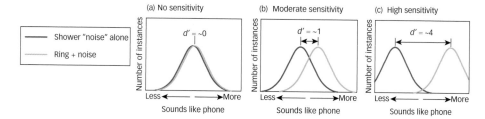

■ FIGURE 2.12   Sensitivity.

Sensitivity is the ability to distinguish a noise signal from an actual signal, such as the difference between random noise from the clunking sound in your car. Figure 2.12a shows an example of when the perceiver has no sensitivity—it is impossible to tell the difference between signal and noise. Figure 2.12b shows when the perceiver is somewhat better at distinguishing signal from noise, and Figure 2.12c shows much higher sensitivity.

Sensitivity (signal detection theory): the ease or difficulty with which an observer can distinguish signal from noise

tell the difference between a harmless passenger plane and a dangerous enemy fighter jet. Similarly, if you have had a "clunking" problem before, you may know exactly what to listen for. Therefore, it will be easy to distinguish between noise and the clunk.

An observer with high sensitivity will be able to make mostly hits and correct rejections. But, as you can see in Figure 2.12, as sensitivity decreases, more false alarms and misses occur. As sensitivity increases, the observer has more hits and correct rejections. Thus, when you know what distinguishes between noise and clunks, you will make few mistakes and catch the car if it is on the brink of breaking down and ignore the sound if you know that it is just random noise. In psychophysics, if you know the relation of hits to false alarms, you can determine d' (*d*-prime), which is a mathematical measure of sensitivity.

Sensitivity and criterion interact in interesting ways. Sensitivity may be high, but if the criterion is also very lax, there still might be many false alarms. Even if sensitivity is high, if the criterion is very loose, there still might be many false alarms. That is, even if our radar system is very good at detecting enemy aircraft, a trigger-happy officer might still be making too many false alarms. This is illustrated in Figure 2.13. You can also review all of the issues related to signal detection theory in ISLE 2.10.

For any given sensitivity, d', there is a range of possible outcomes according to signal detection theory. To simplify seeing all of the possible outcomes for a given signal strength, researchers have developed a way to summarize all of the possible outcomes for this situation across all possible criteria. This summary is called the **receiver-operating characteristic (ROC) curve** (see Figure 2.14). The ROC curve is a graphical plot of how often false alarms occur versus how often hits occur for any level of sensitivity. See ISLE 2.11, in which you can adjust the criterion and the sensitivity and see what the ROC curve looks like.

The advantage of ROC curves is that they capture all aspects of signal detection theory in one graph. Sensitivity or d' is captured by the "bow" in the curve. The more the curve bends up to the right, the better the sensitivity. Moving along the bow captures the criterion. As one moves up any individual level of sensitivity, the higher you go, the more loosely you are setting your criterion, thus opening the possibility of more hits but also more false alarms. Regarding Figure 2.14, the blue line indicates the highest d'. This observer can set her criterion low and still catch many hits while minimizing false alarms. For the

ISLE 2.10 Signal Detection Theory

ISLE 2.11 Signal Detection Theory and Receiver Operating Characteristic

d' (*d*-prime): a mathematical measure of sensitivity

Receiver-operating characteristic (ROC) curve: in signal detection theory, a plot of false alarms versus hits for any given sensitivity, indicating all possible outcomes for a given sensitivity

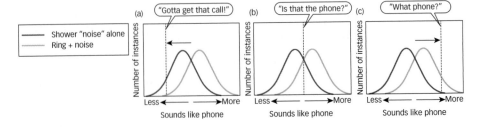

■ **FIGURE 2.13   Hits and false alarms.**

When sensitivity is kept constant, there can still be differences in the ratio of hits to false alarms, depending on the criterion. Figure 2.13a shows a lax criterion, which allows many false alarms but maximizes hits. Figure 2.13b shows a medium criterion, and Figure 2.13c shows a strict criterion, which minimizes false alarms but also reduces the detection of hits.

observer represented by the green line to make as many hits, he risks more false alarms. If the blue line and green line were radar operators, we would prefer to have Blue line making decisions, as she has a higher sensitivity. Depending on circumstances, she can set her criterion low or high and achieve the accuracies indicated on the ROC curve.

ROC curves are also important in evaluating medical decision making. Consider radiologists evaluating computed tomographic (CT) scans looking for brain tumors. They want to be able detect as many brain tumors as possible but also minimize the risk for false alarms, as false alarms can be quite dangerous here—one does not want to initiate brain surgery if there is nothing wrong with the patient's brain. So in evaluating radiologists, we want those with the highest values of d', that is, those who can best distinguish real tumors from false alarms in the CT scans. And we may also want them to set intermediate criteria, because false alarms also come with risk (Xue, Peng, Yang, Ding, & Cheng, 2013).

TEST YOUR KNOWLEDGE

What is signal detection theory? How does it differentiate between accurate perception and errors?

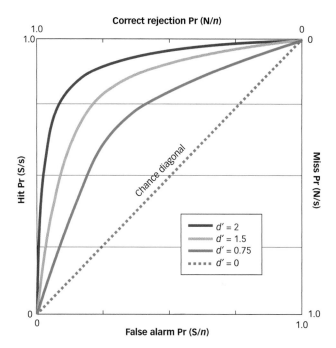

■ FIGURE 2.14   Receiver-operating characteristic (ROC) curves for different values of d' (sensitivity).

When $d' = 0$, sensitivity is zero, and the perceiver cannot discriminate between signal and noise. As d' increases, hits and correct rejections increase, and misses and false alarms decrease. If d' were perfect, we would get only hits and correct rejections, but in the real world, d' is never perfect.

IN DEPTH: *Psychophysics in Assessment: Hearing Tests and Vision Tests*

2.3   Examine how audiologists and optometrists use psychophysical assessment tools to measure patients' hearing and visual abilities and, in some cases, help them find appropriate corrective measures.

Our sensory capabilities are critical to living our lives in the manner that we choose. One's ability to make a livelihood, attend school, and enjoy various recreational opportunities is directly related to one's ability to perceive the world accurately. Take, for example, the everyday activity of driving a car. Most of us have to drive to work or school. Driving is completely dependent on being visually competent—if you become visually impaired, your ability to drive safely decreases, and if you lose your eyesight, driving is no longer an option. Once you get to school, you are also dependent

on your senses. You have to read a textbook and listen to lectures. These require both vision and audition. Having a conversation with anyone requires that your hearing allow you to understand what others are saying. Even pain allows us to recognize health issues that threaten us. Many people will endorse the statement that eating delicious food is one of life's great pleasures.

But now, consider a student who is visually impaired or has a hearing deficit. If you do not think you know any, you are not paying attention. These impairments can range from mild nearsightedness, requiring glasses or contact lenses, to much more severe impairments. Being visually impaired presents a number of obstacles that a sighted person cannot even imagine. Even in a technological world that can offer the visually impaired many ways of compensating for their deficit and competing against normally sighted individuals, being blind obviously creates obstacles. Blind students now can use technology that automatically reads text aloud, but text readers proceed more slowly than sighted people can typically read while looking at text. Blind readers who use Braille type can read silently, but this process is also typically slower than reading by vision. So even with the best technology, blind students work much harder and longer to keep up with their sighted classmates. Auditory impairment can be equally challenging. Those of us with normal hearing take spoken language for granted. But deaf individuals rely on sign language to communicate, which renders reading and writing essentially the same as learning a second language. Even less severe auditory impairment can be challenging. Hearing aids may amplify sounds, but it is often tricky to get them to amplify the sounds you want to hear (e.g., voices) and not the sounds you do not want to hear (e.g., traffic noise).

Assessing vision and hearing loss is an important task, and one fulfilled by professional optometrists and audiologists with great competence. At the heart of each of these professions is applying the ideas of psychophysics to diagnosing visual and auditory problems. In this section, we take an in-depth look at this aspect of applied psychophysics, that is, focusing on the psychophysics tests optometrists and audiologists typically perform.

According to the National Institute on Deafness and Other Communication Disorders, there are 35 million people in the United States alone with some form of hearing impairment. That's roughly 10% of the nation's population. In adults 65 years and older, the percentage exceeds 33% (National Institutes of Health, n.d.). Hearing loss can be caused by any number of factors, including genetic dispositions, but also age, disease, and exposure to noise. Hearing loss in children and younger adults is usually due to genetic conditions. But among older adults, hearing loss is just as likely to be caused by environmental conditions. Hearing loss is particularly common among those who work in professions in which exposure to loud noise (or music) is chronic. This includes airport employees, police officers, DJs and bartenders at nightclubs, and, yes, rock musicians. Indeed many older rock musicians have serious hearing loss issues, including Ozzy Osbourne, Phil Collins, and Pete Townshend.

Hearing loss can be divided into two broad categories, sensorineural hearing loss and conductive hearing loss. **Sensorineural hearing loss** refers to permanent hearing loss caused by damage to the cochlea or auditory nerve. This means that the hearing loss is due to problems in the transduction of the physical sound waves into a neural signal. Sensorineural hearing loss can result either from genetic causes or from damage to hair cells or auditory nerve fibers. **Conductive hearing loss** refers to the inability of sound to be transmitted to the cochlea. This means that the problem is that inadequate levels of sound reach the cochlea to be transduced into a neural signal. Some conductive hearing loss may be as simple as clogged pathways, but conductive hearing loss may also be permanent. In many cases, medical treatment can restore hearing loss caused by conductive causes, which may include earwax buildup or a punctured eardrum (tympanic membrane). Sensorineural hearing loss is seldom treatable, although in extreme cases, cochlear implants can restore some hearing lost through sensorineural damage.

The first step in assessing hearing loss is visiting a professional audiologist. An **audiologist** is a trained professional who specializes in diagnosing hearing impairments. Audiologists usually train to the doctoral level and obtain a degree known as a doctorate in audiology (AuD). This qualifies them to diagnose and treat hearing impairment (see Figure 2.15). An audiologist can fit a patient with the appropriate hearing aids or refer the patient to a medical doctor if the audiologist thinks the situation requires medical intervention.

The audiologist uses a device called an audiometer to assess hearing loss. An **audiometer** can present tones of different frequencies, from low in pitch to high in pitch, at different volumes from soft to loud. A patient will listen on headphones in a soundproof room to a series of tones

Sensorineural hearing loss: permanent hearing loss caused by damage to the cochlea or auditory nerve

Conductive hearing loss: the inability of sound to be transmitted to the cochlea

Audiologist: a trained professional who specializes in diagnosing hearing impairments

Audiometer: a device that can present tones of different frequencies, from low in pitch to high in pitch, at different volumes from soft to loud

■ FIGURE 2.15   **Audiologists.**

Audiologists are trained to treat hearing loss. They assess hearing loss and help fit people with hearing aids. If medical issues arise, they will forward patients to medical doctors who specialize in auditory issues.

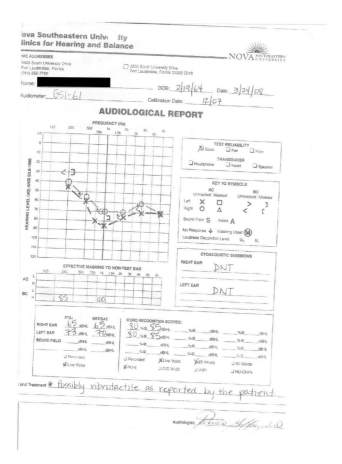

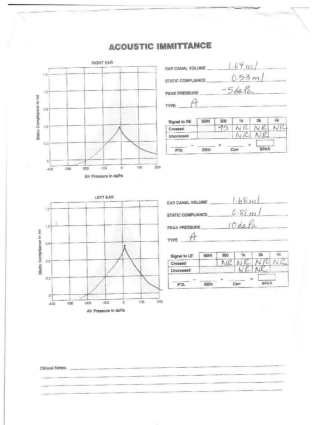

■ FIGURE 2.16   Audiology report.

This audiology report concerns a middle-aged woman with moderate sensorineural hearing loss. In the left graph, the y-axis indicates how loud in decibel units a tone must be presented in order for the patient to hear it. The x-axis indicates frequency, from low frequency (low notes) to high frequency (high notes). This patient shows maximum hearing loss for medium frequencies, unfortunately in the range of human voices.

presented by the audiometer. Tones are presented to one ear at a time, so as to determine if there is hearing loss in each ear. Typically, an audiologist will use the method of constant stimuli combined with a touch of the forced-choice method and vary the loudness of the tone among trials. The patient will typically indicate if he or she heard the tone in the left or the right ear. If the patient cannot hear the tone, this will be obvious from chance performance for that frequency at that sound level. Usually, the audiologist includes catch trials in which tones are not presented. This allows the audiologist to determine the criterion at which the patient is indicating hearing a sound.

After the test is complete, the audiologist will plot the threshold for each frequency as a function of decibels. That is, the audiologist makes a graph indicating how loud each frequency needs to be in order for the patient to hear it. The

audiogram is the graph that illustrates the threshold for the frequencies as measured by the audiometer (see Figure 2.16). The y-axis represents intensity, measured in decibels, and the x-axis represents frequency, measured in Hertz. The threshold is then compared with a standardized curve, which represents normal or average hearing. This graph can then be used to determine if there is hearing loss at any frequency. If there is, the audiologist can help the patient with choosing hearing aids or other remedies.

Particularly important for human hearing is the ability to hear human speech sounds. Many hearing-impaired people can detect sounds but have difficulty hearing words, especially if there is background noise. A deficit in hearing the voices of family members is often what brings a patient to an audiologist in the first place. Thus, audiologists will assess patients' ability to hear speech sounds against background noise. Specialized tests have been developed to allow audiologists to check for speech recognition in hearing-impaired individuals in many different languages (Zokoll,

Audiogram: a graph that illustrates the thresholds for the frequencies as measured by the audiometer

Wagener, Brand, Buschermöhle, & Kollmeier, 2012). In setting up hearing aids for patients, audiologists can program the hearing aids to filter out sounds that are not likely to be voices and amplify sounds that are likely to be human voices. When programmed correctly, hearing aids can selectively filter out noise and increase the volume of human voices.

Turning now to vision, most of us may be more experienced with optometry, as minor visual problems are more frequently corrected with eyeglasses than minor auditory problems are corrected with hearing aids. Optometrists have a similar job to audiologists, but with respect to vision. **Optometrists** provide most people's primary eye care. Optometrists have doctoral degrees in optometry and are licensed to diagnose and give prescriptions for many eye-related problems. But the most common task they do is an eye examination, in which they run a patient through a battery of tests, some to look for diseases of the eye and others to look at basic psychophysical properties of the vision of each patient. Like audiologists, if an optometrist detects a medical problem, that patient will be directed to an ophthalmologist, that is, a medical doctor who specializes in care and diseases of the eye.

Included in the eye exam is a test of visual acuity. The test of visual acuity measures a person's ability to resolve an object in focus at a particular distance. An individual person's acuity is then compared with a "standard" or normal reference. The most common form of the test of visual acuity is the ubiquitous Snellen chart (see Figure 2.17). Using a Snellen chart, an optometrist will ask a patient to read off the chart each line until the letters become difficult to resolve. Typically, this is done one eye at a time, as one eye may be normal but the other may need to be corrected. Results from the Snellen chart yield the typical measure of visual acuity that most people are familiar with. A person of normal vision is said to have 20/20 vision, as he or she can see what a normal person can distinguish at 20 feet. If a person sees at 20 feet what a

ISLE 2.12 Seeing With Myopia and Presbyopia

Optometrist: a trained professional who specializes in diagnosing visual impairments and diseases

Myopia: a condition causing an inability to focus clearly on far objects, also called nearsightedness; occurs because accommodation cannot make the lens thin enough

Presbyopia: a condition in which incoming light focuses behind the retina, leading to difficulty focusing on close-up objects; common in older adults, in whom the lens becomes less elastic

normal person sees at 60 feet, then that person has 20/60 vision. If so, the optometrist would prescribe corrective lenses, either glasses or contact lenses. In other countries, these tests are done in meters, so 6/6 would be the standard for 6 meters (6 meters = 19.7 feet).

Someone who has trouble seeing distant objects is said to have myopia. **Myopia** is a condition in which incoming light does not focus directly on the retina but in front of it. An optometrist can easily treat myopia by prescribing glasses or contact lenses. In older adults, presbyopia becomes more frequent. **Presbyopia** is a condition in which incoming light focuses behind the retina, leading to difficulty focusing on close-up objects. People with presbyopia need glasses to read small print. Even adults who have had 20/20 vision their entire lives are likely to develop presbyopia as they age into their 40s and 50s. To see what it would be like to have these conditions, go to ISLE 2.12.

Optometrists serve as initial screeners and diagnosticians of a number of diseases that affect the eye, including glaucoma, macular degeneration, diabetic retinopathy, and conjunctivitis. However, these diagnoses do not require psychophysical testing, and therefore we do not consider them here. The American Optometric Association has valuable educational resources on its Web site. If you are interested, go to http://www.aoa.org/patients-and-public/eye-and-vision-problems?sso=y.

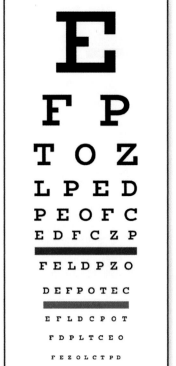

© iStockphoto.com/alfabravoalfaromeo

■ FIGURE 2.17   The Snellen chart.

A patient is asked to read the lowest line that he or she can. This measures visual acuity and is the first test for myopia (nearsightedness). Normal vision is considered 20/20. Anyone who cannot see what a normal person can see at 20 feet may be myopic.

CHAPTER SUMMARY

 2.1 Explain the nature of psychophysical scales and how they measure the relation of stimuli in the world and our perceptions of them.

In this chapter, we covered the basics of psychophysics. The method of limits, the method of constant stimuli, and the method of adjustment are used to determine psychophysical properties of the observer, including the observer's thresholds, or ability to detect differences between stimuli along a particular dimension. Absolute thresholds are the smallest amount of a stimulus necessary for an observer to detect its presence, whereas a difference threshold (also known as a JND) is the smallest difference between two stimuli that can be detected. Closely and inversely related to the concept of threshold is the idea of sensitivity. Sensitivity is the ability to perceive a stimulus. Magnitude estimation is a psychophysical method in which participants judge and assign numerical estimates to the perceived strength of a stimulus. Magnitude estimation fits Stevens' power law, a mathematical formula that describes the relation between the intensity of physical stimuli and the magnitude of the perceptual response

2.2 Explain signal detection theory.

Signal detection theory is the theory that in every sensory detection or discrimination, there is both sensory sensitivity to the stimulus and a criterion used to make a cognitive decision. In signal detection theory, there is a trade-off between successful detection of the target (e.g., a hit) and a detection response when there is no stimulus (e.g., a false alarm). An observer wants to maximize his or her hits and correct rejections (saying "no stimulus" when none is present) and minimize his or her false alarms and misses (saying "no stimulus" when a stimulus is actually present).

Critical in signal detection theory is the idea of sensitivity but also criterion, an internal threshold, determined by the observer, above which the observer makes one response and below which the observer makes another response. Mathematically using signal detection theory allows researchers to determine the ROC curve, which is usually a plot of hits as a function of false alarms.

2.3 Examine how audiologists and optometrists use psychophysical assessment tools to measure patients' hearing and visual abilities and help them find appropriate corrective measures.

Audiologists and optometrists apply the ideas of psychophysics to diagnosing visual and auditory problems. An audiologist is a trained professional who specializes in diagnosing hearing impairments. An audiologist uses an audiometer to assess hearing loss. An audiometer can present tones of different frequencies from low in pitch to high in pitch at different volumes from soft to loud. The audiologist will plot the threshold for each frequency as a function of decibels. If hearing loss is detected, an audiologist can help the patient with choosing hearing aids or other remedies. Optometrists are trained professionals who specialize in diagnosing visual impairments and diseases. The most common task they do is an eye examination, in which they run a patient through a battery of tests, some to look for diseases of the eye, but others to look at basic psychophysical properties of the vision of each patient. Optometrists prescribe corrective lenses to patients with imperfect vision. If an optometrist detects a medical problem, that patient will be directed to an ophthalmologist, that is, a medical doctor who specializes in care and diseases of the eye.

REVIEW QUESTIONS

1. What does the Scoville scale measure? Why is it considered to be a psychophysical scale?

2. What is the method of limits? How is it used to determine absolute thresholds?

3. What is the method of adjustment? How is it used to determine the point of subjective equality?

4. What is the two-point touch threshold? How does it illustrate the concept of a JND? How do two-point touch thresholds differ across the human body?

5. What is the difference between response expansion and response compression? How do both relate to Stevens' power law?

6. What is signal detection theory? How is it used to predict performance on perception tests?

7. Define the terms *criterion* and *sensitivity*. How do they interact in signal detection theory?

8. What is the ROC curve? What does it tell us about criterion and sensitivity?

9. What is the difference between an audiologist and an optometrist? What does each measure?

10. How is an audiogram used to assess hearing loss? How might an audiogram help an audiologist program a hearing aid?

KEY TERMS

Absolute threshold, 27

Ascending series, 29

Audiogram, 43

Audiologist, 42

Audiometer, 42

Capsaicin, 25

Catch trial, 34

Conductive hearing loss, 42

Correct rejection, 35

Criterion, 36

Crossover point, 29

d' (d-prime), 40

Descending series, 29

Difference threshold (JND), 28

False alarm, 35

Forced-choice method, 34

Hit, 35

Magnitude estimation, 32

Method of adjustment, 31

Method of constant stimuli, 30

Method of limits, 27

Miss, 35

Myopia, 44

Optometrist, 44

Point of subjective equality (PSE), 31

Presbyopia, 44

Psychophysical scale, 25

Receiver-operating characteristic (ROC) curve, 40

Response compression, 32

Response expansion, 33

Scoville scale, 25

Sensitivity, 32

Sensitivity (signal detection theory), 39

Sensorineural hearing loss, 42

Signal detection theory, 35

Stevens' power law, 33

Two-point touch threshold, 29

INTERACTIVE SENSATION LABORATORY EXERCISES (ISLE)

Experience chapter concepts at edge.sagepub.com/schwartz

ISLE 2.1 North Carolina Hot Sauce Contest Link, 25

ISLE 2.2 Method of Limits, 27

ISLE 2.3 Method of Constant Stimuli, 30

ISLE 2.4 Method of Adjustment, 32

ISLE 2.5 Point of Subjective Equality, 32

ISLE 2.6 Magnitude Estimation, 32

ISLE 2.7 Stevens' Power Law, 33

ISLE 2.8 Forced-Choice, 34

ISLE 2.9 Signal Detection Experiment, 36

ISLE 2.10 Signal Detection Theory, 40

ISLE 2.11 Signal Detection Theory and the Receiver Operating Characteristic (ROC) Curve, 40

ISLE 2.12 Seeing With Myopia and Presbyopia, 44

Sharpen your skills with SAGE edge at edge.sagepub.com/schwartz

SAGE edge for students provides a personalized approach to help you accomplish your coursework goals in an easy-to-use learning environment.

E
200 FT. 61 m
F P
100 FT. 30.5 m
T O Z
70 FT. 21.3 m
L P E D
50 FT. 15.2 m
P E C F D
40 FT. 12.2 m
E D F C Z P
30 FT. 9.14 m
F E L O P Z D
25 FT. 7.62 m
D E F P O T E C
20 FT. 6.10 m
E F O D P C T
15 FT 4.57 m
F D P L T C E O
P E Z O L C F T D

Visual System: The Eye

3

INTRODUCTION

We live in a visual world. As human beings, we typically first seek out information around us with our amazing eyes and the visual system behind them. Indeed, our ability to see affects so much of our lives. Before you read on, pause for a minute and think of all the reasons for which we need to see. We use vision to read, to look at photographs on Instagram, and to ponder the stars at night by observing them. We need to see to drive our cars, to cook our meals, to mow our lawns, and to sew our clothes. Despite all the ways seeing is vital to us, we often take vision for granted. But all it takes is one scare with an eye injury, such as a detached retina or the onset of a disease such as glaucoma, to make us realize how critical our vision is to our everyday well-being.

Vision can also be a source of much joy to us. Imagine looking across a field at a bright red rose in full bloom against the green foliage of its leaves. The texture, color, and contrast all create an experience of beauty. Consider further being at the Louvre museum in Paris, patiently waiting for your chance to see the Mona Lisa. You've paid thousands of dollars and traveled thousands of miles to wait uncomfortably in a long line, just to get a glimpse of this famous Leonardo da Vinci painting, a distinctly visual experience. Think about watching a movie and how much excitement and relaxation you may get from watching, that is, seeing, the adventure unfold before you. And perhaps imagine looking at the face of one's significant other. The sight of this person's face should also bring joy to us (see Figure 3.1).

To summarize, our visual system provides us with useful practical information all the time, so we can find our way, not bump into walls, and obtain information from the landscape. It also transcends these practical aspects by providing us with a sense of beauty and wonder. Whether mundane or majestic, most of all visual experiences start with a light source, which is where this chapter starts. Before we can talk about the eye, we need to introduce light as a scientific concept. So we start with light.

LIGHT

3.1 Explain the nature of light as electromagnetic energy and the relation of wavelength to perception.

Vision is the system that allows us to perceive light. Thus, before we begin describing the visual system, it is important to know just a little bit about the physics of light. We live in a world bathed in light, sunshine by day, artificial light by night, and the constant omnipresence of glowing screens, big and small,

■ FIGURE 3.1   Visual images can be beautiful.

We often find great beauty and emotional comfort in merely looking at visual images. Do these images make you smile?

Electromagnetic energy: a form of energy that includes light that is simultaneously both a wave and a particle

but what exactly is light? Visible light is an example of **electromagnetic energy** (Feynman, 1985, 1995). As most of us know, light, like other forms of electromagnetic radiation, moves very fast—approximately 186,000 miles per second (300 million meters per second) in a vacuum. Visible light is one part of the electromagnetic spectrum, which also includes radio waves, infrared radiation, ultraviolet radiation, and gamma rays. They differ in their frequencies, which we discuss shortly. According to modern physics, light is made up of particles called photons that also behave in a wavelike manner (see Feynman, 1985, for a more thorough explanation of our current understanding of light in lay terms). The wavelike behavior of light is important to vision, as we see different wavelengths (or frequencies, wavelengths' inverse) as different colors. So, in this chapter, we are concerned with light more as a wave phenomenon than as discrete photons.

Consider waves at the beach before they break on the shore. The waves are up-and-down undulations of the water's surface. As a result, waves are usually drawn as going up and down (see ISLE 3.1). If you watch the waves coming in, you can tell that not all waves are the same. Some are taller than others, and some peaks are closer together, and other peaks are farther apart. Surfers look for "sets" of waves that come in with higher peaks, though these higher peaked waves also often come close together, so that a surfer may be able to ride only one per set. We can quantify differences among waves, in terms of both how high they are (amplitude) and how close they are to adjacent waves (wavelength). Thus, the distance between the peaks of a wave is called the **wavelength**, and the height of the wave is called its **intensity**. The number of waves per unit of time is called the **frequency**, which is equal to 1/wavelength. In perceptual terms, wavelength correlates with color, and intensity correlates with brightness. To make matters confusing for students everywhere, the tradition is to refer to light waves by their wavelengths, but sound waves by their frequencies. Because this is the tradition throughout the field, we respect it here.

Visible light represents a tiny slice of the **electromagnetic spectrum**. The electromagnetic spectrum is the complete range of wavelengths of light and other electromagnetic energy. Visible light represents wavelengths between 400 and 700 nm, but electromagnetic radiation extends in both directions beyond those boundaries (see Figure 3.2). Wavelength is also related to energy. The shorter the wavelength, the higher the energy. The longer the wavelength, the lower the energy. Thus, wavelengths shorter than visible light come with higher energy, such as gamma rays, x-rays, and ultraviolet rays. With longer wavelengths than those of visible light comes lower energy radiation, such as infrared radiation, microwaves, and radio waves.

Consider an old-fashioned candle (Figure 3.3). The burning wick creates electromagnetic radiation at many wavelengths. We see the light emitted in the visible range as the pretty yellow glow of the flame, with the darker (higher energy) blue by the wick itself and the less energetic yellow light toward the top. The light is being emitted by burning of the wick, which heats up the air around it, emitting electromagnetic radiation. We also feel some of the energy in the form of heat, energy being emitted in the infrared range.

Wavelengths are usually measured in nanometers. A nanometer is equal to 1 billionth of a meter. The shortest wavelengths we see are about 400 nm, and we perceive these as violet. Blue has a wavelength of about 470 nm, and green has a wavelength of about 500 nm. Red has a wavelength approaching 700 nm, the longest wavelengths that we can perceive. Other animals have different sensitivities to wavelength of light. Bees, for example, can see shorter wavelengths than we can (ultraviolet) (Horridge, 2012). Flowers are colorful to us, but bees and hummingbirds may use ultraviolet coloring of flowers to determine when they can obtain nectar from those flowers. Some birds use ultraviolet coloration to attract mates. For example, male blue tits have ultraviolet crowns on their heads, which they display during mating courtships. A human observing the birds would

ISLE 3.1 The Basics of Waves

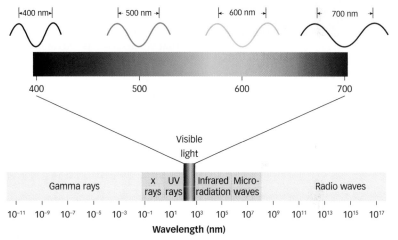

■ **FIGURE 3.2**   **The electromagnetic spectrum.**

Electromagnetic radiation varies in wavelength from very low-energy, long-wavelength waves (shown to the right of the visible spectrum) to very high-energy, short-wavelength waves (shown to the left of the visible spectrum). Visible light is just a tiny segment of this continuum. Within the visible spectrum, we see shorter wavelengths as bluish and longer wavelengths as reddish.

Wavelength: the distance between two adjacent peaks in a repeating wave; different forms of electromagnetic energy are classified by their wavelengths

Intensity: when referring to waves, the height of a wave

Frequency: the number of waves per unit of time; frequency is the inverse of wavelength

Electromagnetic spectrum: the complete range of wavelengths of light and other electromagnetic energy

■ FIGURE 3.3   Light in the visible spectrum.

A burning candle emits light in the visible spectrum. We can use this light to illuminate a room when the electricity is off and we cannot use our electric lights.

■ FIGURE 3.4   Blue tits.

Blue tits are pretty birds, with beautiful colorations. However, there are colors present in the ultraviolet range that we cannot see, but other blue tits can. Blue tit females prefer males with shiny ultraviolet crowns.

Photon: a single particle of light

not see any differences, but female blue tits prefer more shiny ultraviolet colorings (see Figure 3.4). Even some mammals such as bats and rodents see shorter wavelengths than we do (Beran, 2012).

Recall that in physics terms, light can be thought of as either a wave phenomenon or a particle phenomenon. When physicists are thinking of light as a wave, they refer to wavelength, but when they are thinking of light as a particle phenomenon, they refer to **photons**. Photons are single particles of light. Photons are useful for thinking about the amount of light. A very bright light has many more photons than a dim light, regardless of its wavelength. So bright sunshine sends many more photons your way than does a single candle burning at night. As psychophysicists, we use the terminology of wavelength when discussing color but the terminology of photons when discussing intensity and brightness. We also use the concept of light as particles when talking about the process of transduction.

Most light reaches our eyes indirectly, after bouncing off objects in our world. We see the rose in the garden because its surface reflects the light of the sun (or your flashlight, if you are prowling around the garden after dark). Surfaces, such as the rose petals, tend to absorb some wavelengths and reflect others. We see the rose as red because it absorbs most wavelengths but reflects the long wavelengths that we perceive as red. Similarly, the grass is green because the plant is absorbing most wavelengths, but reflecting green light back into the world.

TEST YOUR KNOWLEDGE

What is the electromagnetic spectrum? What part is considered light?

THE EYE AND ITS ROLE IN THE VISUAL SYSTEM

3.2   Describe the anatomy of the eye and how it makes vision possible.

It will not come as a surprise to most readers that the eye is the primary organ of visual perception. However, how the eye converts light into colors, objects, motion, and a third dimension is a fascinating topic, which this and the next several chapters cover. The eye is a finely tuned instrument, with many integrated parts working together to create our visual perception. To understand visual perception, it is necessary to understand the anatomy and the physiology of the eye. Thus, our first task will be to consider the structure of the human eye, its physiology, and how it relates to seeing.

The human eye is a fairly typical mammalian eye. Like most primate eyes, our eyes are located at the front of our heads and are slightly spaced. This gives us good depth perception. Relative to other mammals, human beings have excellent visual acuity, but are fairly poor at seeing in dim light relative to familiar animals such as cats and dogs. Cats are especially good at seeing in dim light. Because of the structure of the receptors in the retina, humans are good at color vision. Dogs can see in color, but are similar to humans with red-green color deficiency. Other animals seem to have better color vision than us, though. Indeed, goldfish see many more colors than we do. It is interesting to think that compared with your pet goldfish, swimming in its bowl, you are seemingly color-blind.

The basic story is as follows. Light emanates from a light source, such as the sun or an overhead light in an indoor location. Light falls on objects in the environment, and in turn, some wavelengths are reflected by those objects. It is this reflected light from objects that we actually see. The reflected light enters the eye through the pupil and is focused on the retina by the cornea and lens. The retina contains specialized cells called rods and cones, which transduce the light energy into an electrochemical signal, which is then sent to the brain for processing through the optic nerve. Of course, humans, like most animals, have two eyes, so coordinating the slightly different view of each eye is critical to vision, especially depth perception. So let's look at each of the events in greater detail.

Field of View

Human eyes are located approximately 6 cm (2.4 inches) apart from each other. Of course, there is variation depending on genetics and how big one's head actually is. In humans, as in other primates, the eyes have evolved to be adjacent to each other to allow for accurate depth perception. Frontally placed eyes allow us to see in stereo, as each eye has a slightly different view of the world. By computationally comparing the two images, our visual systems can estimate distance from the offset of the two images. Such depth perception is useful for animals that must hunt for food or that live in trees and must judge distances from branch to branch. The drawback of this arrangement is that such animals can only see in front of themselves (see Figure 3.5). Large herbivores, such as deer and antelope, are often subject to predation. For these animals, detecting incoming predators is paramount. For this reason, these species have evolved eyes placed on the sides of the head rather than in front. Animals with eyes positioned on the sides of their head such as antelope have a greater field of view but weaker depth perception (Figure 3.6). This allows them to detect predators coming from almost any position relative to them, except

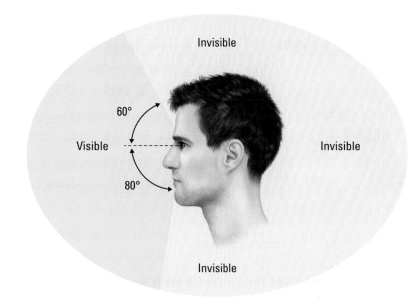

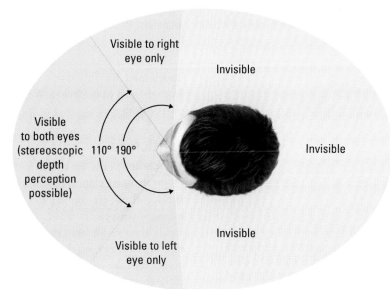

■ FIGURE 3.5   Field of view.

Our eyes give us a large zone of binocular vision, that is, an area we can see with both eyes. Beyond that is a region in which we only see with one of our eyes. However, we cannot see the world behind us. If you think of the world as a circle around you, you can see approximately 190° in front of you, but you cannot see the 170° behind you.

usually a small area directly behind their heads. Your **field of view** is the part of the world you can see without eye movements. For humans, that is approximately 190° horizontally (side to side) and 140° vertically (up and down).

Anatomy of the Eye

The complexity of the human eye has often led to debates as to how it got that way. Before Darwin, the eye was often held up as a marvel of intelligent design. Indeed, the naturalist William Paley labeled the design of the eye a "miracle."

Field of view: the part of the world you can see without eye movements

■ FIGURE 3.6   **Pronghorn antelope.**

The pronghorn antelope can be found in the American West, such as this one in Montana. The pronghorn antelope has eyes on the sides of its head. This limits its depth perception but allows it to see behind its head as well as in front. This allows the pronghorn antelope to detect incoming predators, such as mountain lions.

Cornea: the clear front surface of the eye that allows light in; it also is a major focusing element of the eye

Sclera: the outside surface of the eye; it is a protective membrane covering the eye that gives the eye its characteristic white appearance

Anterior chamber: the fluid-filled space between the cornea and the iris

Iris: the colored part of the eye; it is really a muscle that controls the amount of light entering through the pupil

Pupil: an opening in the middle of the iris

Pupillary reflex: an automatic process by which the iris contracts or relaxes in response to the amount of light entering the eye; the reflex controls the size of the pupil

For Paley, he could not see how such a complex piece of biological machinery could have just happened. He reasoned that because it was so complex, it must have been designed. Perhaps because of this challenge, many evolutionary biologists have studied the evolution of complex eyes in great detail. Biologists have carefully mapped out how nature has selected for complex eyes and have investigated various intermediaries. Indeed, complex eyes have evolved independently. For example, the octopus is a mollusk more related to clams and barnacles than it is to us. However, the octopus has a complex eye, but one that evolved along a very different pathway than our human eye. Our concern here is not how eyes evolved in the distant past, but how humans use them now. In human evolution, the end product of evolution is a remarkably complex apparatus designed for transforming light energy into perceptual information.

In this section, we describe the anatomy and physiology of the parts of the eye, with an emphasis on their function in vision (review Figure 3.7 first). Make sure you learn both the vocabulary and the concepts. That is, memorize the technical terms, but also make sure you understand the function of each part of the eye and how information moves from the eye to the brain. We start now with the cornea and iris, the outermost parts of the eye.

The Cornea

The **cornea** is the clear front surface of the eye that allows light in. It is also a major focusing element of the eye. The cornea is transparent and is the outermost surface of the eye (see Figure 3.8). It begins the process of refracting or bending the light to come into focus on the retina of the eye, which is the back surface inside the eye. Indeed, the cornea does most of the focusing of images toward the retina. However, the cornea is rigid, and therefore changes in refraction must come from the adjustable lens, which brings images into sharp focus. The cornea is the transparent part of the **sclera**, a tough membrane, which provides a protective covering for the eye. The sclera is the "white" of the eye as well. Between the cornea and the iris is the fluid-filled **anterior chamber**.

Just behind the cornea is a part of the eye called the **iris**. The iris is really a muscle with an opening in the middle. Light enters through this opening. The opening itself is called the **pupil**. In dim light, the iris relaxes control, and the pupil expands (or dilates) to allow more light into the eye. In bright light, the iris contracts and the pupil narrows, allowing less light into the eye. This is a process that is not directly under conscious control and is known as the **pupillary reflex**. Shine a bright light into someone's eyes, and his or her pupil will immediately contract. When you enter a dim room after being outside in the sunshine, your pupils will quickly dilate. The two eyes coordinate their pupillary reflexes, so that each dilates and contracts simultaneously. In this way, the pupil can range from a diameter of about 2 mm to about 8 mm, depending on lighting conditions (see Figure 3.8). Interestingly, it is the iris that gives individual eyes (or pairs of eyes) their characteristic colors, whereas the pupil appears dark or black (see Figure 3.9). The amount of melanin in the iris is a major factor in whether one has blue eyes or brown eyes, though other factors contribute as well. **Heterochromia** is the term that describes the condition in which a person has two irises of different colors. It is rare in people (but not in Siberian huskies) and is often a sign of ocular disease. The **posterior chamber** is the space between the iris and the lens. It is also filled with fluid, known aqueous humor.

The Lens

The **lens** (also called the crystalline lens) is the adjustable focusing element of the eye. It is located just behind the iris. This process of adjusting the focus for different distances by changing the shape of the lens is called accommodation. **Accommodation** is the process of adjusting the lens of the eye so that you can see both near and far objects clearly. This process is very rapid, although changing accommodation from a near object to a far object is faster than from a far object to a near object (Kirchhof, 1950). Accommodation is controlled by muscles connected to the lens, called **ciliary muscles**. The ciliary muscles work in concert with the **zonule fibers**, which connect the lens to the choroid membrane. As with the control of the iris, the ciliary muscles work automatically, without conscious control. Indeed, we seldom need to think about whether what we are looking at is in focus. The ciliary muscles

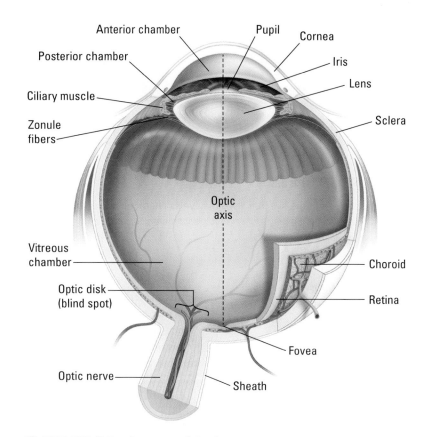

■ FIGURE 3.7   Anatomy of the human eye.

Light enters the eye through the pupil, an opening in the outer layer of the eye, surrounded by the iris, the colored area that gives eyes their characteristic color (brown, blue, green, etc.). Ciliary muscles control the zonule fibers that pull on the lens, allowing light to focus on the retina at the back of the eye. The fovea is a little pit at the center of the retina that picks up light from the point in space the eye is looking at. Information leaves the eye via the optic nerve through a part of the eye called the optic disc.

Heterochromia: a condition in which a person has irises of two different colors

Posterior chamber: the space between the iris and the lens; it is also filled with fluid, known as aqueous humor

Lens: the adjustable focusing element of the eye, located right behind the iris of the eye; also called the crystalline lens

Accommodation: the process of adjusting the lens of the eye so that both near and far objects can be seen clearly

Ciliary muscles: the small muscles that change the curvature of the lens, allowing accommodation

Zonule fibers: fibers that connect the lens to the choroid membrane

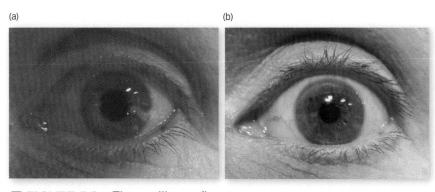

■ FIGURE 3.8   The pupillary reflex.

In dim light, the iris relaxes control, and the pupil expands (or dilates) to allow more light into the eye (a). However, when a bright light is shined into the eye, the iris contacts and the pupil narrows, allowing less light into the eye (b).

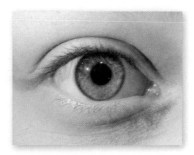

■ FIGURE 3.9   **Irises.**

The iris is the part of the eye that gives the eye its characteristic color. Those eyes containing the most melanin will appear brown. Those with less melanin may appear blue or sometimes green.

ISLE 3.2 Accommodation

ISLE 3.3 Presbyopia

Near point: the closest distance at which an eye can focus

Presbyopia: a condition in which incoming light focuses behind the retina, leading to difficulty focusing on close-up objects; common in older adults, in whom the lens becomes less elastic

can contract and increase the curvature of the lens so that the lens thickens. The increased curvature of the lens allows the eye to focus on a close object. When the person then looks at a faraway object, the muscles relax, and the focus of the lens changes to an object farther away (see Figure 3.10). Look at an object close to you, such as the text of this book. Then look up and look out the window and across the street. As you do, the process of accommodation automatically adjusts your focus. For a demonstration of how this works, go to ISLE 3.2. You can also see a demonstration there of how the lens and pupil differ in the ways they contribute to the accommodation.

The process of accommodation allows us to focus on near objects and far objects and switch between them effortlessly. Look up from your textbook now and look out the window. As you do, your lens relaxes and allows you to focus on a distant object. Look back at the text and your lens contracts, allowing you to focus on the words on the page or screen. But accommodation has limits. Close one eye and with the other look at your index finger at arm's length and then slowly bring it toward your eye. At some distance, probably close to your nose, you will no longer be able to focus on your finger, and it will start to look a bit blurry. If you can bring your finger right up to your nose and still focus on it, switch to a smaller object. When you can no longer focus on the object, you have reached your **near point**. The near point is the closest distance at which an eye can focus.

As people age, the near point shifts farther away from the eyes. For younger adults, say, around 20 years of age, the near point is usually about 10 cm from the eyes. However, it averages about 100 cm for people around 60 (Rutstein & Daum, 1998). This condition in older adults is called **presbyopia**. Because of the decreased elasticity of the lens, accommodation does not occur to the extent it does in younger eyes. This relative failure of accommodation increases the near point of the eye. Presbyopia usually starts to become noticeable in adults in their 40s and accelerates after that (see Figure 3.11). When presbyopia first becomes noticeable, people may simply hold their reading material farther from their eyes. But as it progresses, reading glasses, which help bring near images into focus, become necessary. For a demonstration of how this works, go to ISLE 3.3.

TEST YOUR KNOWLEDGE

What is accommodation? Explain how it produces a focused image on the retina.

THE RETINA

3.3 Explain how the retinae transduce light energy into a neural signal.

In English, the word *retina* is singular, referring to one eye. The words *retinae* and *retinas* are both acceptable as the plural form of the word *retina*. To be more formal, we will use *retinae* when talking about both retinae. Before we discuss the retina, perhaps the most complex part of a complex eye, let us review what we have covered so far. The iris and the lens direct light and focus that light. The pupil allows more or less light in, depending on ambient conditions. The goal of these processes is to focus an image on the **retina**, which is the eye's photosensitive surface. This image is known as the **retinal image**. Receptor cells on the retina transform the light image into a neural signal to be sent to the brain. The intricacy and precision of the arrangement of the retina is very complex, but at the same time fascinating (see Figure 3.12). Although very thin, the retina is composed of several interconnected layers. Let's see how this process takes place.

Anatomy of the Retina

The retina is the third and innermost of the three membranes in the eye. Retinal anatomy is quite complicated, but it can be understood when one thinks of the functions of the retina. First, the retina is the location in the eye where transduction takes place. Photoreceptors convert light into a neural signal. Thus, part of retinal anatomy is designed to help the photoreceptors capture light. Second, the retina starts the process of transmitting

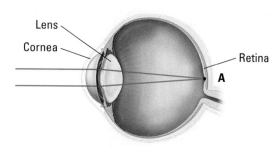

Focus on retina

(a) Object far – eye relaxed

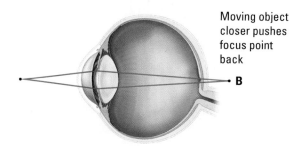

Moving object closer pushes focus point back

Focus behind retina

(b) Object near – eye relaxed

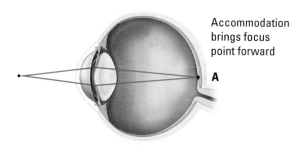

Accommodation brings focus point forward

Focus on retina

(c) Object near – accommodation

■ **FIGURE 3.10** **Curvature of the lens.**

The increased curvature of the lens allows the eye to focus on a close object (a). When the person then looks at a faraway object, the muscles relax and the focus of the lens changes to an object farther away (b).

■ **FIGURE 3.11** **Presbyopia and the near point.**

In this graph, the x-axis represents age, and the y-axis represents the near point in centimeters from the eye. As you can see in the graph, the near point is closest when we are young and then accelerates after we reach the age of approximately 50. There are very few among us who do not need reading glasses by the time they are in their 50s. This presbyopia ("old vision") is the result of the fact that the lens becomes less flexible as we age.

Retina: the paper-thin layer of cells at the back of the eye where transduction takes place

Retinal image: the light projected onto the retina

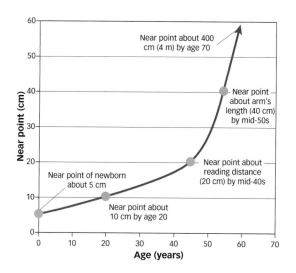

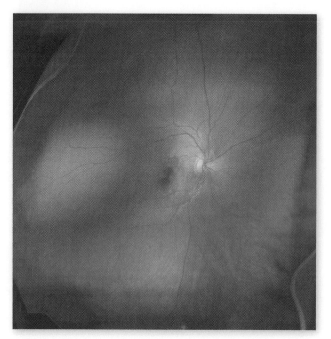

■ FIGURE 3.12   An optometrist's view of the retina of one of the authors.

This is an image of the fundus, or the back surface of the right retina. The bright yellow spot is the optic disc, where the optic nerve leaves the eye to head into the brain. This also corresponds to the blind spot of the eye. The dark patch just to the right of the yellow disc is the macula or fovea, the part of the eye designed for visual acuity. The eye depicted belongs to Dr. Bennett Schwartz.

visual information to the brain. Thus, part of the retinal anatomy is designed to allow the retina to send accurate signals to the brain. Figure 3.13 illustrates this complex anatomy, and Table 3.1 lists the functions of different neural cells in the retina.

The Receptors: Rods and Cones

There are two types of receptors (or photoreceptors), the **rods** and the **cones**. These are the cells that transform light energy into an electrochemical signal. Rods predominate at the periphery (away from the center) of the retina, whereas cones cluster in and near the fovea of the retina. The **fovea** is a small pit at the center of the retina (indeed, the word *fovea* means "small pit" in Latin). The fovea and the area around it are called the **macula**. Beyond that is the periphery of the retina. There are about 120 million rods and only about 7 million cones in each eye. There is only one type of rod, whereas there are three classes of cones (Nathans, Piantanida, Eddy, Shows, & Hogness, 1986; Neitz & Jacobs, 1986, 1990). We return to these cone types a bit later in the chapter, as each is important in detecting different frequencies of light and perceiving color. Because there is only one type of rod, these receptors see only in shades of gray (from black to white). The rods and cones are not spread evenly across the eye. If you examine Figure 3.14, you will see that the cones are most centrally located in the fovea. There are no rods in the fovea. The rods are mostly at the periphery, starting about 20° off the fovea away from your nose and toward your temples. In one region, however, the two receptor types mix. This is in the outer areas of the fovea, or where the fovea blends into the periphery, sometimes called the parafoveal region. Here, both kinds of cells can be found (Curcio, Sloan, Kalina, & Hendrickson, 1990).

The human fovea is densely packed with cones. It looks like a little pit on the retina because the cells that are above the retinal surface, such as retinal ganglion cells, horizontal cells, and amacrine cells, are swept away so that the cones are at

Rods: photoreceptors at the periphery of the retina; they are very light sensitive and specialized for night vision

Cones: photoreceptors in the fovea of the retina; they are responsible for color vision and our high visual acuity

Fovea: an area on the retina that is dense in cones but lacks rods; when we look directly at an object, its image falls on the fovea (also referred to as the macula)

Macula: the center of the retina; the macula includes the fovea but is larger than it

Neuron Type	Function
Receptors	Transduce light into a neural signal
Rods	Night vision, light detection, grayscale vision
Cones	High visual acuity, color vision, daytime vision
Horizontal cells	Receive information from photoreceptors and other horizontal cells; cross talk across photoreceptors
Bipolar cells	Receive information from photoreceptors; send signals to retinal ganglion cells
Amacrine cells	Receive information from bipolar cells and other amacrine cells; cross talk function
Retinal ganglia	Receive information from bipolar cells; send signal to brain via the optic nerve

■ TABLE 3.1   Neurons in the Retina

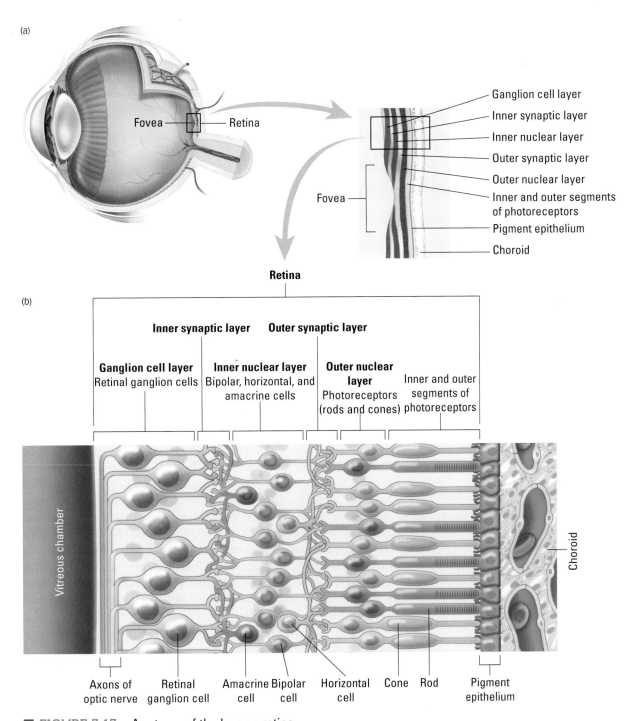

(a)

Fovea — Retina

Ganglion cell layer
Inner synaptic layer
Inner nuclear layer
Outer synaptic layer
Outer nuclear layer
Inner and outer segments of photoreceptors
Pigment epithelium
Choroid

Fovea

Retina

(b)

Inner synaptic layer   **Outer synaptic layer**

Ganglion cell layer   **Inner nuclear layer**   **Outer nuclear layer**   Inner and outer segments of photoreceptors
Retinal ganglion cells   Bipolar, horizontal, and amacrine cells   Photoreceptors (rods and cones)

Vitreous chamber

Choroid

Axons of optic nerve   Retinal ganglion cell   Amacrine cell   Bipolar cell   Horizontal cell   Cone   Rod   Pigment epithelium

■ **FIGURE 3.13**   Anatomy of the human retina.

In Figure 3.13a, we see the location of the retina relative to other anatomical structures in the eye. As you can see in this figure, the foveal region looks like a pit, as the top layers of the retina are swept aside so that there is no scatter of light reaching the receptor cells, that is, the cones. In Figure 3.13b, we see a schematic of what the retina would look like if it were stretched out to reveal the layers. Oddly, the rods and cones form the back layer of the retina, even though they are the light-sensitive portion of the retina. The horizontal, amacrine, and bipolar cells serve as a middle layer and connect the photoreceptors to the retinal ganglion cells, which exit the retina and bring visual information to the brain.

the surface. Because of the layers that are swept away, there is less scattering of light in the fovea, allowing visual acuity to be higher in the fovea. It is the foveae of the retinae that give humans our excellent color vision and our excellent visual acuity.

■ FIGURE 3.14   Receptor density in the retina.

The graph shows the density of cones and rods in the retina. The density of cones is highest in the fovea, whereas cones become very sparse as one moves away from the fovea. Rods become more common at the periphery.

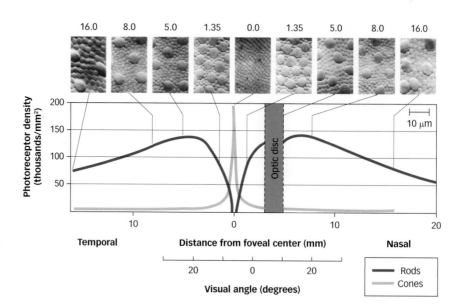

ISLE 3.4 Letters and the Fovea

By *visual acuity*, we mean clarity of vision. Thus, the visual image of the words you are reading right now is falling on the foveae of your retinae. Words you have just read or have not yet read are tailing off into the periphery of the retinae. When you move your eyes to look at something new, say, a family member walking into the room, it is your foveae that are directed toward the new stimulus. This is why it is said that the foveae represent the direction of your gaze. For a demonstration of how much space on the retina is occupied by one letter, go to ISLE 3.4.

The fovea is unique anatomically. First, it is the location on the retina with the highest density of cones. Second, other retinal cells are brushed away from the surface of the retina. This allows light to reach the surface of the fovea with minimal scatter of that light. Both of these factors evolved to enhance our visual acuity.

Interestingly, other animals have different arrangements of rods and cones in their eyes. Many birds, for example, have a fovea in the middle of the retina for good central vision, but have a second, cone-rich fovea along the edge of the retina. Birds with this visual arrangement include such diverse species as birds of prey, hummingbirds, and swallows (Ruggeri et al., 2010). This second fovea gives these birds accurate vision to their sides as well as in front of them, useful to birds that must perform complex aerial movements. Other animals, including many mammals such as dogs, have no foveae at all (Walls, 1963). The lack of a fovea is characteristic of animals that tend to be nocturnal or rely primarily on senses other than vision. These animals are more concerned about detecting moving objects than pinpointing an exact location. Thus, rod vision is more critical than foveal vision.

In Figure 3.12, you can see a part of the retina called the optic disc. The **optic disc** is the part of the retina where the optic nerve leaves the eye and heads to the brain. Along the optic disc, there are no receptor cells. Axons of the retinal ganglion cells gather at the optic disc and form the optic nerve, which carries the neural signal into the brain. Because there are no receptors at the site of the optic disc, this location is also called the blind spot. Because the blind spot in the left eye does not correspond to the same region in space as the blind spot in the right eye, humans really do not have a blind spot in their visual field. Even when viewing the world with only one eye, we are not aware of our blind spot. Higher areas of visual processing "fill in" the blind spot (Ramachandran, 1992). To observe your blind spot, see Figure 3.15. For an interactive look at the blind spot, go to ISLE 3.5.

ISLE 3.5 Map Your Blind Spot

Optic disc: the part of the retina where the optic nerve leaves the eye and heads to the brain; along the optic disc, there are no receptor cells

Retinal Physiology

Retinal anatomy concerns the structures of the retina. This refers to where cells are located and how they connect with one another. *Retinal physiology* refers to the functions of these structures—how they accomplish the processes that allow us to see. Because we have reviewed the structures of the eye, we can now turn to how the eye converts light into a neural signal at a physiological level. Retinal physiology is difficult, so read carefully, review, and test yourself. Once you understand the physiology of transduction in vision, the transduction processes for other senses will be more straightforward too.

Transduction of Light

The rods and cones of the retina are equipped with the ability to convert light into a neural signal. They accomplish this task by using chemicals known as photopigments. **Photopigments** are molecules that absorb light and by doing so release an electric potential by altering the voltage in the cell. When a photopigment absorbs a photon of light, it changes shape. This change in shape initiates a series of biochemical processes, which result in a change in electric potential, which allows a signal to exit the photoreceptor. In this way, a neural signal leaves the photoreceptor and is transmitted to the optic nerve to be sent to the brain. After sending a signal, other biochemical processes reset the photopigment to its original shape so that it can detect more light. Photopigments are contained in discs within the rods and cones. Each photoreceptor may contain about 100 to 200 of these discs, and in each disc, there may be billions of photopigment molecules (Fain, 2003). The many biochemical steps necessary to convert photopigments from one form to another have been heavily investigated (see Rodieck, 1998).

Photopigments are composed of two molecules, which are bound together, a protein called an **opsin** in rods (and chromodopsin in cones) and a form of vitamin A called **retinal**. The photopigment in the rods is called rhodopsin. The photopigments in the cones are similar to rhodopsin, but there are three classes of these cone photopigments (Bowmaker, 1998). The nature of the photopigment is central to determining how the receptor behaves with regard to light. These different receptors tend to absorb different wavelengths of light, and it is the differences in the opsins that are key to these differences (see Figure 3.9).

The role of retinal in the rhodopsin explains one piece of folk knowledge you may have heard about. You may have been told that eating carrots will help your night vision. Carrots are very rich in vitamin A, which is the source of retinal. If you have a healthy diet, you will probably not improve your vision by eating more carrots, but diets that are deficient in vitamin A can result in night blindness, that is, an inability to see under dim-light conditions (Wald, 1968).

In the photopigment that is ready to respond to light, retinal is in a bent form, called 11-*cis*, that fits into the opsin. When a photon of light is absorbed by the photopigment, the rhodopsin straightens out and the photopigment breaks apart (Wang, Schoenlein, Peteanu, Marthies, & Shank, 1994). This straightening of the bond takes place during a very short time period (Schoenlein, Peteanu, Mathies, & Shank, 1991). The effect of this absorption of the photon by the photopigment causes the receptor to have a more negative voltage inside relative to outside the receptor (Tomita, 1970). This is called **hyperpolarization**, referring to the polarization of electric charge increase. This hyperpolarization causes the receptor to

■ FIGURE 3.15   **Finding your blind spot.**

Close one of your eyes and hold the book or your laptop at arm's length. Slowly move the book toward you while looking at the orange circle. At some point, the plus sign will disappear. The plus sign disappears when its image lands on the optic disk, where there are no receptor cells.

Photopigment: a molecule that absorbs light and by doing so releases an electric potential by altering the voltage in the cell

Opsin: the protein portion of a photopigment that captures the photon of light and begins the process of transduction; it is the variation in opsin that determines the type of visual receptor

Retinal: a derivative of vitamin A that is part of a photopigment

Hyperpolarization: a change in the voltage of a neuron whereby the inside of the cell becomes more negative than it is in its resting state

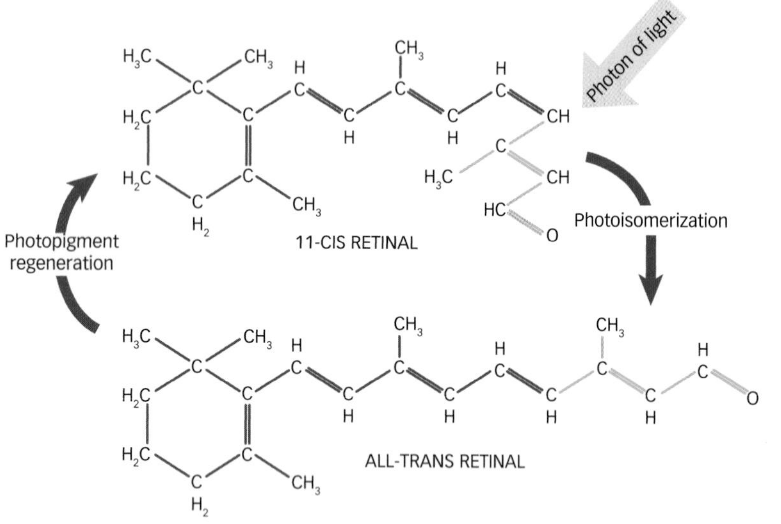

FIGURE 3.16 Transduction at the molecular level.

The photopigment molecule has one of two shapes, each called an isomer of the other. In the photopigment that is ready to respond to light, retinal is in a bent form, called 11-*cis*, that fits into the opsin. When a photon of light is absorbed by the photopigment, the rhodopsin straightens out and the photopigment breaks apart. This straightening of the bond takes place during a very short time period. The effect of this absorption of the photon by the photopigment causes the receptor to have a more negative voltage inside relative to outside the receptor.

Receptor Type	Peak Sensitivity (Nanometers)
Rods	496
S-cones	420
M-cones	530
L-cones	560

TABLE 3.2 Receptor Types

NOTE: Each receptor type shows a peak sensitivity to light at a particular wavelength. The receptor type is shown on the left, and the peak sensitivity (in nanometers) is shown on the right. These peak sensitivities are approximate and may vary among people with normal vision.

release less of the neurotransmitter, which the receptor uses to communicate with the rest of the retina (see Figure 3.16). Thus, oddly, light is inhibitory. So the question naturally arises, How does light act to stimulate the visual system so that we can see? It turns out that the neurotransmitter of the rods, probably glutamate, is inhibitory to the other cells of the retina; that is, it stops the responses of these bipolar and horizontal cells (Schiells & Falk, 1987). Thus, light inhibits the release of an inhibitory neurotransmitter and, ultimately, excites the visual system. There is no good explanation why the visual system evolved this seemingly illogical system.

Given that one photon of light can change a photopigment molecule in one receptor and induce a neural signal, a natural question to ask is, How many photopigment molecules must be activated to create a perception of light? In particular, because we know that rods are sensitive to small amounts of light, we will look to the photoreceptors at the periphery to answer this question. In fact, if you optimize the conditions for light detection, a single rod may start a signal in response to as little as one photon of light, and a person may actually see a light with as few as seven photopigment molecules activated (Hecht, Schlaer, & Pirenne, 1942).

Classes of Receptors

The human eye uses four different photopigments, one for the rods and three in different cone classes in the retina (see Figure 3.17). Each of these photopigments is maximally sensitive to a particular frequency of light (see Table 3.2). It is the interaction of these three photopigments and subsequent perceptual processing that provides for us our complex color vision. This classification system is actually a simplification, as each class of cone photopigment has many subtypes, especially in the cones that respond to red and green.

In rare cases, some people (most often women) have a fourth cone class with a fourth photopigment. There is some evidence that these people see a greater range of colors than do normal people (Jameson, Highnote, & Wasserman, 2001).

TEST YOUR KNOWLEDGE

Why do our retinae need more rods than cones? And why are cones concentrated in one area?

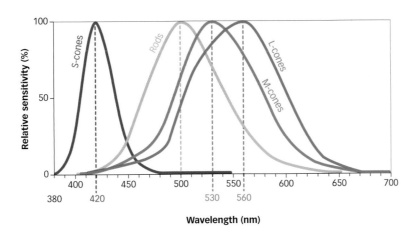

■ FIGURE 3.17   **Wavelength sensitivity of cones and rods.**

The photopigments in each cone and in the rods vary with respect to their ability to absorb light at different wavelengths. Rods show a peak sensitivity at just shy of 500 nm, which would be seen as dark green by the color system. With respect to the cones, the S-cones' peak sensitivity is at 420 nm, the M-cones' at 530 nm, and the L-cones' at 560 nm. Note that each photoreceptor responds to a broad band of wavelengths, but at less strength than to the peak. We determine color by a complex comparison of the responses from each of the cone photoreceptors.

THE DUPLEX THEORY OF VISION

 Examine how the visual system adapts to the dark and then adapts again to the light.

The **duplex theory of vision** is the idea that there are functionally two distinct ways in which our eyes work. The first system is called the photopic system, and the second is the scotopic system. The **photopic** system is associated with the cones, and the other, the **scotopic** system, is associated with the rods. The duplex theory is the idea that our visual system can operate in fundamentally different ways, depending on the conditions in the environment. Daytime is the domain of photopic vision, but nighttime is when our scotopic vision comes to the forefront. These hypothesized differences in visual function derive from the following observations. First, rods are more sensitive to light overall than cones. Second, rods are most sensitive to different wavelengths than cones are. That is, they have a different spectral sensitivity. Third, rods and cones have different spatial and summation properties, which we discuss shortly. And finally, cones support color vision, but rods do not. In general, the photopic system is associated with daytime vision, and the scotopic system is our night vision system. However, there is a range of intermediate ambient light intensity within which both systems work. This intermediate zone is said to be mesopic vision. See ISLE 3.6 to see differences between photopic vision and scotopic vision. Table 3.3 also illustrates the differences between these two parts of the duplex system.

Spectral Sensitivity and the Purkinje Shift

Spectral sensitivity refers to the relative sensitivity of a receptor type to all of the wavelengths. Rods are relatively more sensitive to the shorter wavelengths,

ISLE 3.6 Photopic vs. Scotopic Vision

Duplex theory of vision: the doctrine that there are functionally two distinct ways in which our eyes work, the photopic, associated with the cones, and the scotopic, associated with the rods

Photopic vision: the vision associated with the cones; it is used in the daytime, has good acuity in the fovea, and has color vision

Scotopic vision: the operation of the visual system associated with the rods; it has relatively poor acuity and no color ability but is very sensitive to light

Characteristic	Photopic	Scotopic
Color vision	Yes (three cone classes)	No (only one type of rod)
Peak spectral sensitivity	~550mm	~505 nm
Acuity	Good	Poor
Temporal resolution	Good	Relatively poor
Regions of greatest sensitivity	Fovea	~20° at the periphery
Relative sensitivity	1,000,000	1

■ TABLE 3.3   Photopic Versus Scotopic Vision

ISLE 3.7 Purkinje Shift

whereas cones are relatively more sensitive to the longer wavelengths. Indeed, cones are most sensitive to about 555 nm, and rods are most sensitive to just under 500 nm. This difference in spectral sensitivity is named the **Purkinje shift**. This shift occurs as we transition from day vision to night vision and back again. We have simulated these differences in the relative sensitivity of rods and cones to long- and short-wavelength light in ISLE 3.7.

An interesting practical implication of the Purkinje effect is that, as night-time conditions appear, longer wavelengths of light will appear darker, whereas shorter wavelengths will appear relatively brighter. This means that red objects become more difficult to see at night than blue or green objects with similar reflectance values. It is for this reason that, some years ago, fire departments started shifting away from traditionally red vehicles. Because red is harder to see at night, fast-moving red fire trucks will be more difficult for other drivers to see than fast-moving blue fire trucks. Nonetheless, tradition is often hard to break, and many fire departments still opt for the traditional fire-engine red, even though it puts both firefighters and other drivers at more risk. However, another driving convention does have perceptual validity. Red light is less likely to affect our dark adaptation than other colors. This validates the decision to make taillights on cars red. Drivers will see red taillights at night, but the red light will not affect their dark adaptation as much as taillights of other colors would. You may have noticed how distracting a white (or broken) taillight can be at night, as it interferes with your ability to see well in the dark. This is also why the little screens of cell phones can be so distracting in an otherwise dark movie theater.

Spatial Summation and Acuity

The next difference between photopic and scotopic vision is the relative acuity of the two systems. *Acuity* refers to the ability to see or resolve fine details. The reason for the acuity difference is partially that rods and cones have different spatial summation characteristics. *Spatial summation* refers to the ability to pool light across different regions of space. At night, you want to detect as much light as possible, even if spatial summation causes things to be a bit blurry. During the day, there is ample light, so acuity becomes the important issue. As you know by now, rods are more sensitive to dim light than cones are. Part of this light sensitivity occurs because many rods connect to one retinal ganglion cell. This allows the scotopic system to pool responses across different rods in order to maximize sensitivity to light. However, by pooling across rods,

Purkinje shift: the observation that short wavelengths tend to be relatively brighter than long wavelengths in scotopic vision versus photopic vision

the scotopic system loses some ability to resolve light to particular sources in the visual world. This pooling of information is called **convergence**, and it is much greater for rods than for cones. Each one in the fovea typically connects to one and only one retinal ganglion cell, thus maximizing the ability to pinpoint the source of the light in space, even if it does not allow sensitivity to dim lights. See ISLE 3.8.

To illustrate this concept with an example, consider admiring the fine coat of a Bengal cat (see Figure 3.18). You want to be able to make out the intricate patterns on the coat and see them in fine detail. To do this, you cannot confuse one location along the cat's fur with another. Thus, neutrally, you want as little spatial summation as possible. This is what the cones provide. The cones pick up light in one very small area and project that through one ganglion cell, so as not to cause spatial confusion. Thus, cones allow us to see with greater visual acuity, whereas rods are more sensitive to low levels of light.

Dark and Light Adaptation

Imagine waking up in the middle of the night. It is dark, and there are other people still asleep in your house, so you do not want to turn the lights on and alarm them. But you are hungry, and you want a snack. You know that there are still some delicious brownies in the kitchen. You feel your way along the wall into the kitchen and enjoy the chocolate brownies in the middle of the night. With your late-night craving satisfied, you are ready to return to sleep. But before you return to bed, you may notice that after you have been up for a little while, you can see in the dark. What before was obscured you can now discern. This is the process of dark adaptation. It takes nearly 30 minutes for the process to be completed, but the shift from photopic to scotopic vision allows people to see much better in the dark. See ISLE 3.9 and 3.9a.

What is going on during dark adaptation? First, a definition: **dark adaptation** is the process in the visual system whereby its sensitivity to low light levels is increased. During the first 8 minutes of trying to see in the dark, it is still the cones that are doing most of your seeing. Then, your sensitivity to low levels of light increases, as your scotopic-system rods come online and start taking over. Part of the explanation for dark adaptation has to do with the properties of the photopigments themselves. Dark-adapted eyes have a higher concentration of rhodopsin, the active pigment in the rods. In the darkness, the levels of rhodopsin increase. Thus, one factor in dark adaptation is the concentration of photopigment (Rushton, 1965). Other factors include dilatation of the pupil, which happens rapidly in lower light levels (see Figure 3.19).

Light adaptation occurs when light returns, such as when electric lights are turned on in an otherwise dark room. It is acceptable to think of light adaptation as being like dark adaptation, but in reverse. However, there is one major difference: Light adaptation will be completed in about 5 minutes, or even less, as the visual system switches back to relying on cones rather than rods. Dark adaptation is therefore much slower. It seems that this difference is due partly to the fact that light adaptation is driven actively by the light entering the eye, whereas dark adaptation is a more passive response to the lack of light. Of course, under natural conditions, in which the only source of light is the sun, dark adaptation is sufficiently fast to adjust to changing light conditions, and light adaptation might be mostly gradual as well. The change from afternoon sun, through dusk, to evening is about the time it takes dark adaptation to complete its total swing.

There are some interesting implications of the shift from light adaptation to dark adaptation and back again, especially in our constructed world, in which a

© iStockphoto.com/photodeti

■ FIGURE 3.18   **The fine coat of a Bengal cat.**

Our photopic system allows us to see the fine detail of patterns and colors in the coats of these beautiful cats.

ISLE 3.8 Convergence

ISLE 3.9 Dark Adaptation Function

Convergence: the number of photoreceptors that connect to each ganglion cell; more convergence occurs for rods than for cones

Dark adaptation: the process in the visual system whereby its sensitivity to low light levels is increased

Light adaptation: the process whereby the visual system's sensitivity is reduced so that it can operate in higher light levels

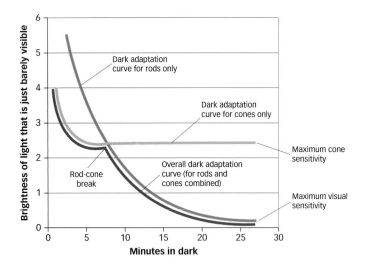

■ **FIGURE 3.19**   The process of dark adaptation.

As a dark period extends in time, sensitivity to light increases. In the graph, the blue line shows the overall increase in sensitivity to light. The orange line shows the change in sensitivity for cones in the fovea.

person may go back and forth from lit rooms to dark ones every few minutes. Think about a police officer, patrolling at night. He or she should be dark adapted to survey the nighttime scene, but may need to shift to photopic vision to read the computer in the patrol car. If a task requires a person to go quickly from a lighted area to a dark area in a short period of time, such as our police officer, then the period required for full dark adaptation may present problems. If the officer, after checking his or her computer, must enter a dark alley in pursuit of a suspect, his or her vision may not be optimized. This dark adaptation period delays how fast the person can begin functioning in the dark. However, this limitation can be overcome by having the person work in an environment with only red lights. The red light will not be absorbed by the rods as well as other wavelengths, allowing the dark adaptation process to begin. Then, when the light is removed, the person is dark adapted to a large degree and can operate immediately in the dark, an advantage for a police officer in the field. This works because the cones are relatively more sensitive to long-wavelength light than the rods. The greater sensitivity of cones than rods to the long wavelengths is so significant that cones are actually more sensitive to these wavelengths than rods are in an absolute sense, not just a relative sense (Cornsweet, 1970).

A common example of this technique is the use of red flashlights when observing with a telescope at night. An observer can look at a star chart or other information using the red flashlight. This will give her the ability to use her photopic vision to read the details of the star chart. Then, when the light is turned off, she still has her scotopic rod vision to see the subtle detail in the night sky, such as a faint galaxy or nebula. In modern smart phones, apps are available to help you determine which star is which when you stargaze. Smart phone apps, such as Google Sky Map, can be put into night mode, in which the display is in red.

Another application of the knowledge of dark adaptation takes place in the modern aircraft cockpit. There are a lot of visual situations that can alter a person's ability to read a cockpit display. Think of a pilot flying with the sun directly in his or her face. The pilot may light-adapt to the sun and then not have sufficient sensitivity to read the electronic display when needed. The opposite problem occurs at night, when it is desirable to not have the displays so bright that the pilot will light-adapt to the display and not be able to see the runway clearly. To avoid these problems, researchers determined the light levels needed to see the sky in front of the airplane and also to see the displays inside the cockpit in situations with high light intensity and low light intensity. From these data, Krantz, Silverstein, and Yeh (1992) developed automatic adjustments so that pilots do not have to spend time adjusting the luminance of their displays when the lighting conditions change. When it is dark outside, the displays inside the cockpit will switch to a red light that allows the pilots to dark-adapt for seeing outside the plane but also allows them to read their instruments inside the plane. See ISLE 3.10.

ISLE 3.10 Automatic Light Adjustment in Cockpits

TEST YOUR KNOWLEDGE

How do rods and cones relate to photopic and scotopic vision?

RETINAL GANGLION CELLS AND RECEPTIVE FIELDS

3.5 Describe what retinal ganglion cells do and how receptive fields are constructed.

Each photoreceptor is connected to several different retinal ganglion cells, which convey the signal into the optic nerve and toward the brain. There are only about 1.1 million ganglion cells, many fewer than the total number of rods and cones. Therefore, most ganglion cells receive inputs from many different photoreceptors (called convergence; see Figure 3.20). A ganglion cell receives

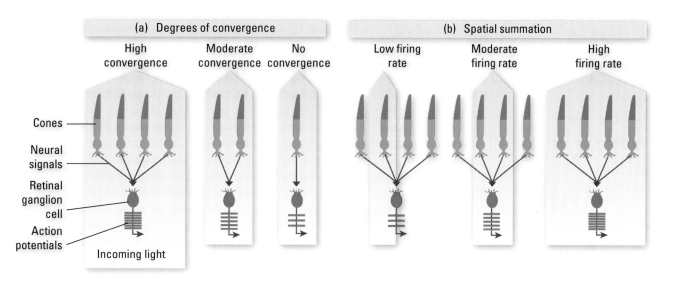

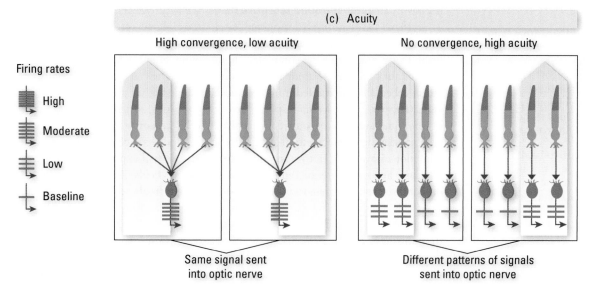

■ **FIGURE 3.20**   Convergence of photoreceptors onto ganglion cells.

In the fovea, there is little convergence or no convergence, as one receptor cell matches onto one ganglion cell. However, as one moves into the periphery, there is more convergence, as multiple photoreceptors match onto the same ganglion cell. The more convergence, the greater the light sensitivity, whereas the less convergence, the greater the acuity.

input from receptors that are next to each other on the retina, which form a grouping of adjacent receptors. This grouping is called a receptive field. A **receptive field** is the area in the visual world that a particular vision neuron responds to. But in this case, it also refers to the array of photoreceptors from which each retinal ganglion cell receives input. In the retina, the first receptive fields studied were the receptive fields of the ganglion cells. Kuffler (1953) was the first researcher to study these remarkable cells. A particular ganglion cell that receives input from the fovea might have a receptive field that corresponds to exactly the point you are looking at. A ganglion cell that receives input from the far periphery might have a receptive field that corresponds to a point in space just at the edge of your visual field, away from your point of central fixation. Receptive fields are illustrated in Figure 3.17.

In the fovea, each cone (or, more often, just a few cones) maps onto one retinal ganglion cell. Therefore, the receptive fields of these ganglion cells are quite small and correspond to small regions in visual space, consistent with the idea that the fovea is designed for high visual acuity. At the periphery, however, many rods, in some cases hundreds of them, will map onto a single ganglion cell. As you move away from the fovea, ganglion receptive fields get progressively larger (Watanabe & Rodieck, 1989). These greater receptive fields allow greater convergence and greater sensitivity to dim light. This summation across adjacent rods is called convergence (reviewed earlier in the section on spatial summation and different from the meaning of *convergence* as applied to the lens). Thus, retinal ganglion cells are processing for acuity in the fovea and light detection at the periphery.

Retinal ganglion cells also start the process of edge detection. Critical to vision, **edge detection** involves determining the location at which one object ends and the next object begins. This is important in discriminating objects, detecting camouflage, and many other important visual functions. We focus on edge detection in terms of perception later. But for now, it is important to know that the visual system searches for these edges and enhances them, so that we can clearly see them. The earliest stage of edge detection occurs in the retinal ganglion cells and is known as **center-surround receptive fields** (see Figure 3.21).

Kuffler (1953) noticed during single-cell recording of retinal ganglion cells that he could stimulate the center of a visual field, resulting in a different response from the cell than when he stimulated the surrounding area of the visual field of that cell. In some cases, stimulating the center of the field resulted in excitation, but in other cells, it resulted in inhibition. Note that both a positive (excitation) and a negative (inhibition) response are still responses, just of different kinds. If you stimulate an area outside a particular cell's receptive field, you will get no response, neither activation nor inhibition. This difference in activation and inhibition allows the cell to start coding for edges. We will explain why shortly.

There are two kinds of center-surround receptive fields. They are known as **on-center receptive fields** and **off-center receptive fields**. In on-center receptive fields, the cell's center produces activation, whereas the surround produces inhibition. In off-center receptive fields, the center produces inhibition, whereas the surround produces activation. In either case, if you present light that covers the entire receptive field of the cell, the response will be small, as the excitation and inhibition will cancel each other out. However, if you present a pattern with edges (contrasting light and dark), the cell may respond maximally. That is, these cells respond to luminance contrast, or differences in light intensity across the field. To make sense of this, think of the following: A uniform field in the visual world is usually not interesting or important (think of a blank wall or a uniformly blue sky). Contrast, however, is important—whether it be the change of lightness where the wall meets the door or the roiling patterns of clouds of an impending

Receptive field: a region of adjacent receptors that will alter the firing rate of a cell that is higher up in the sensory system; the term can also apply to the region of space in the world to which a particular neuron responds

Edge detection: the process of distinguishing where one object ends and the next begins, making edges as clear as possible

Center-surround receptive field: a receptive field in which the center of the receptive field responds opposite to how the surround of the receptive field responds; if the center responds with an increase of activity to light in its area, the surround responds with a decrease in activity to light in its area

On-center receptive fields: retinal ganglion cells that increase their firing rate (excitation) when light is presented in the middle of the receptive field and decrease (inhibition) their firing rate when light is presented in the outside or surround of the receptive field

Off-center receptive fields: retinal ganglion cells that decrease their firing rate (inhibition) when light is presented in the middle of the receptive field and increase (excitation) their firing rate when light is presented in the outside or surround of the receptive field

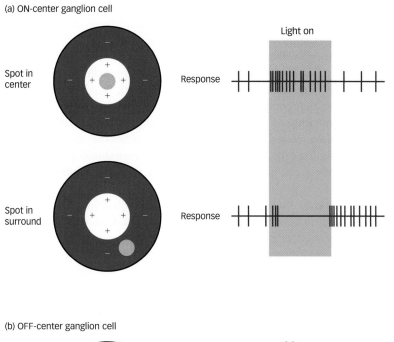

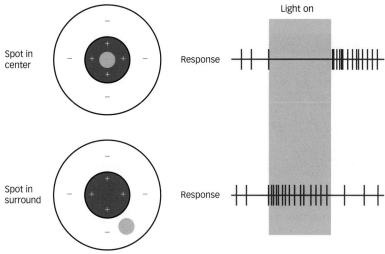

■ FIGURE 3.21 Center-surround receptive fields.

(a) An on-center ganglion cell. The image shows a receptive field for an on-center ganglion cell. When a light is shined in the center, the ganglion cell becomes more active than its base-rate state. However, when a light is shined at the periphery of the receptive field, the ganglion cell is inhibited below base rate. (b) An off-center ganglion cell. The image shows a receptive field for an off-center ganglion cell. When a light is shined in the center, the ganglion cell becomes less active or inhibited relative to its base-rate state. However, when a light is shined at the periphery of the receptive field, the ganglion cell becomes more active than base rate.

thunderstorm. Or think about our police officer on patrol at night. She wants to be able to make out the dim form of a prowler as distinguished from the background night. Thus, the visual system should be looking for these contrasts, as they indicate interesting features of the visual world. Indeed, it appears that edge detection, such as what is seen in center-surround organization, starts early in visual processing, already occurring in the retinae themselves. For an illustration of this, go to ISLE 3.11.

The physiological mechanism that creates center-surround receptive fields is quite complex. To understand how it works, one must consider the roles of horizontal cells and bipolar cells, as well as the rods, cones, and retinal ganglion cells. Consider the receptive field of retinal ganglion cells in the foveal region of the retina. A person directs his or her gaze to an object, such as a cup of coffee on a table. The image of the coffee cup is now projecting directly onto the fovea. Cones in the fovea will initiate an excitatory signal in response to the light reflecting off the coffee cup. This signal will move to both the bipolar cells and

ISLE 3.11 Center-Surround Receptive Fields

the horizontal cells. In response to the signal from the cones, horizontal cells send inhibitory signals back to the cones (and to adjacent cones). Horizontal cells also send excitatory signals across to other horizontal cells, thus increasing the inhibitory feedback on the cones. That is, these cells act to minimize the responses to uniform fields (an empty table) and maximize the response to changing fields (a coffee cup on that table). However, this inhibition decreases across space, so that cones farther from the source of the image are less inhibited. The combination of the positive signals coming from bipolar cells and the inhibition coming from the horizontal cells determines the strength of a signal to a retinal ganglion cell, which then has its own center-surround characteristics. The result of these complex processes is known as **lateral inhibition** (Hartline & Ratliff, 1958).

The goal of lateral inhibition is to facilitate edge detection. Edge detection is the process of distinguishing where one object ends and the next begins. That is, it works to make edges as clear as possible. Edge detection is important—think about trying to see a camouflaged predator, perhaps a lioness, in the tall dry grass. The lioness's fur and the grass are roughly the same color, important for the lioness as she slowly stalks her prey (you, in this case). However, the fur and the grass are not identical, and you want your visual system to pick up where the grass ends and where the lion begins (so you can jump back into your Land Rover and speed away and have stories to tell for a long time). This involves edge detection and gestalt figure-ground discrimination. But if we think of it in terms of figuring out where one object ends and the next begins, we have the basic function of edge detection (see Figure 3.22). It is for this reason that edge detection evolved; as we will see throughout our discussion of the visual system, it is built in at every level.

(a)   (b)

© Anup Shah/ Digital Vision / Thinkstock

■ FIGURE 3.22   **Edge enhancement.**

These Thomson's gazelles are alert for the possibility of approaching predators. (a) A normal photograph. (b) The edges are enhanced. This kind of enhancement allows better detection of objects against a uniform background.

Lateral inhibition explains a famous visual illusion known as *Mach bands*, named after their discoverer, Ernst Mach (1838–1916). Mach bands are illustrated in Figure 3.23. Examining the pattern in the figure, you see bands of dark gray on the left and progressively lighter bands of gray to the right. If you look at each band, it looks as if it is slightly lighter on the left side than on the right side. This is an illusion. The reflectance of each band is uniform. That is, the perceived intensity appears to take a big step at the border of each band and then gradually declines until you get to the next edge. This is edge enhancement. Lateral inhibition accentuates the edges of the stimulus, so that you see the borders of reflectance more clearly. However, it is also an illusion, as each band has the same reflectance across its space. In the Mach bands, the enhanced edges are illusory. But the system has functional value—in the real world, perceiving shape is critical, and lateral inhibition helps us do so. See Interactive Illustration 3.12 on ISLE.

ISLE 3.12 Mach Bands

....

Lateral inhibition: the reduction of a response of the eye to light stimulating one receptor by stimulation of nearby receptors, caused by inhibitory signals in horizontal cells

TEST YOUR KNOWLEDGE

What is the difference between on-center center-surround receptive fields and off-center center-surround receptive fields?

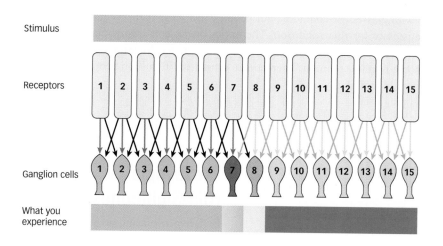

Stimulus

Receptors

Ganglion cells

What you experience

■ FIGURE 3.23 **Mach bands.**

Each bar in this picture is uniform in lightness. However, we see a different level of lightness in each bar from left to right. For each bar, the left edge looks more black than the right edge, which looks lighter or whiter. This illusion is the result of processes of edge detection, such as lateral inhibition. When cells with receptive fields that straddle the bars detect the lightness contrast, they act to enhance the edges.

REFRACTIVE ERRORS AND DISEASES OF THE EYE

3.6 Examine the nature of refractive errors and how they affect the ability of the eye to see.

As you can tell from reading this chapter, the human eye is an extremely complicated organ, and vision is a very complex process. The result, seeing, is remarkable when you consider all the eye and brain must do in such a short time to allow us to see as we do. Nonetheless, problems can arise that interfere with clear visual perception. Undoubtedly, you know people who wear eyeglasses or contact lenses, and you may wear them yourself. The origin of these minor problems is interesting and is discussed below. You may also know someone with more serious visual problems, such as cataracts or macular degeneration. We discuss these as well.

Myopia (Nearsightedness)

Myopia is a common form of mild visual impairment, often called nearsightedness because people with myopia can focus well on near objects, but faraway objects appear blurry. There is usually a parallel problem with both eyes, but a person can potentially be myopic in one eye but not the other. Moreover, it is typical that each eye has a different level of myopia. With myopia, the eye tends to be too long from front to back for the lens. The process of accommodation does not make the lens thin enough to focus the light from more distant objects onto the retina. Because these distant objects are focused in front of the retina instead of onto it, the objects appear blurry. Another way to state this is that the lens is too strong for the length of the eye. To correct the problem, the lens must be weakened. To weaken the lens, a diverging or negative artificial lens is used, that is, typical eyeglasses. A diverging lens is wider at the edges than at the middle, the opposite of the eye's own lens and the lenses that have been used in the figures. As a result, light spreads out even more after it has passed through the lens than it would otherwise. Eyeglasses or contact lenses refract or bend light just enough so that the image can be focused onto a person's retinae, allowing a focused image. However, once the glasses or contacts are removed, light comes into focus in front of the lens, and objects at a distance will appear blurry, though objects up close will be in focus. Thus, myopia is readily compensated

Myopia: a condition causing an inability to focus clearly on far objects, also called nearsightedness; occurs because accommodation cannot make the lens thin enough

for with glasses (or contacts), but people must wear their eyeglasses in order to compensate for this condition. The optics of the lens in myopia are illustrated in Figure 3.24. For a dynamic demonstration, see Illustration 3.13 on ISLE. Myopia is quite common. There are an estimated 70 million people in the United States alone with myopia.

ISLE 3.13 Correcting
Myopia and Hyperopia

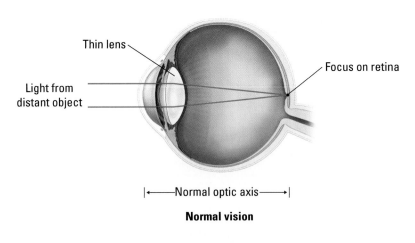

Normal vision

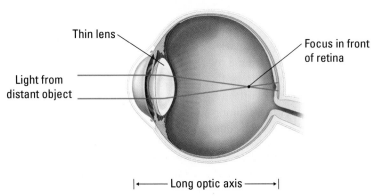

Myopia (Nearsightedness)

■ FIGURE 3.24   Myopia.

If the eye is too long internally, the lens cannot become thin enough to focus an image on the retina. Instead, the image focuses in front of the retina, making the image on the retina blurry. Myopia is correctable with eyeglasses.

Hyperopia: a condition causing an inability to focus on near objects, also called farsightedness; occurs because accommodation cannot make the lens thick enough

Astigmatism: a condition that develops from an irregular shape of the cornea or the lens, which makes it impossible for the lens to accommodate a fully focused image

Hyperopia (Farsightedness) and Presbyopia (Old-Sightedness)

Both hyperopia and presbyopia are common forms of mild visual impairment, often called farsightedness because people with these impairments can focus well on faraway objects, but near objects may appear blurry. With **hyperopia**, the eye tends to be too short for the lens (see Figure 3.25). The process of accommodation does not make the lens thick enough to focus the light from closer objects onto the retinae. Because these close objects are focused behind the retinae instead of on them, the objects will appear blurry. Distant objects, however, are seen just fine. As with myopia, eyeglasses can be fitted that will allow near objects to be imaged on the retinae.

Presbyopia is a condition associated with older eyes (or older people). As we age, the lens hardens, and the ciliary muscles lose power. This makes it harder for older eyes to accommodate to nearby objects. Presbyopia increases the distance of the near point, which is the closest object we can bring into focus. As with hyperopia, the lens now focuses objects behind the retina, requiring eyeglasses to be fitted to allow magnification, which will focus objects onto the retinae. Presbyopia is a seemingly universal condition. It is seldom noticed before the age of roughly 40. But by the age of 50, there are very few people who do not need reading glasses to correct presbyopia. Indeed, after 50 years of age, the rate at which presbyopia advances might be quite steep, requiring further magnification in order for individuals to see small objects close to their eyes.

Astigmatism

Astigmatism develops from an irregular shape of the cornea or an irregular shape of the lens, which makes it impossible for the lens to accommodate a fully focused image, usually in a relatively small area of the visual world.

In the case of the cornea, the surface of the cornea may be unsymmetrical, and in the case of the lens, the shape of the lens may not be sufficiently spherical. In astigmatism, the cornea bends the light more strongly in one direction, say in the vertical direction, than it does in the direction that is at a right angle to the first direction, say the horizontal direction. Thus, no matter how the lens changes shape, an object in a particular location and orientation will not be in focus (see Figure 3.26). Astigmatism makes seeing some orientations blurry, whereas others are still relatively clear. To correct this problem, a complex, conelike lens is used to offset the differences, though it is often difficult to correct an astigmatism with eyeglasses alone. Sometimes contact lenses are used to directly correct the problem. More recently, LASIK (laser-assisted in situ keratomileusis) surgery is used to reshape the cornea to bend the light in the correct fashion.

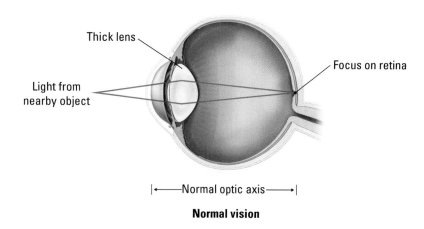

Normal vision

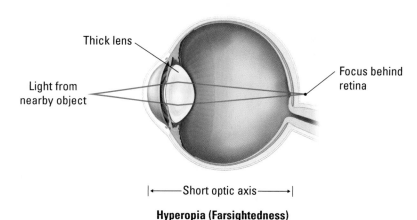

Hyperopia (Farsightedness)

■ FIGURE 3.25　Hyperopia, or farsightedness.

If the eye is too short internally, the lens cannot become thick enough to focus an image on the retina. Instead, the image focuses behind the retina, making the image on the retina blurry. Hyperopia is correctable with eyeglasses. Similar to hyperopia is presbyopia, in which a hardened lens tends to focus images behind the retina. Presbyopia is very common as people age into their 40s and 50s.

Cataracts

Cataracts result from the clouding of the lens. Cataracts affect older adults more than they do younger adults, but they can occur in anyone at any age. With cataracts, over time, the clear appearance of the lens becomes cloudy because of water buildup, eventually leading to blindness unless there is surgical intervention. Cataracts may result from complications of diabetes, exposure to ultraviolet radiation, or simply natural aging. Cataracts can now be fixed surgically. The biological lens is removed and replaced by an artificial lens. After surgery, patients will need glasses to focus at particular distances, but they can see normally with glasses.

The conditions we have discussed so far arise from problems with the lens or cornea. However, there are also some conditions that affect the retina itself. These problems tend to be far more tragic than most problems with the lens, which are now treatable with eyeglasses or, in the case of cataracts, with a relatively straightforward surgical procedure.

Macular Degeneration

Macular degeneration is a disease that destroys the fovea and the area around it. The medical term *macula* refers to the center of the retina. The macula includes the fovea but is larger than it. The destruction of the macular region causes a blind spot in central vision. A patient will direct his or her point of gaze to a

Cataract: a condition that results from a darkening of the lens

Macular degeneration: a disease that destroys the fovea and the area around it

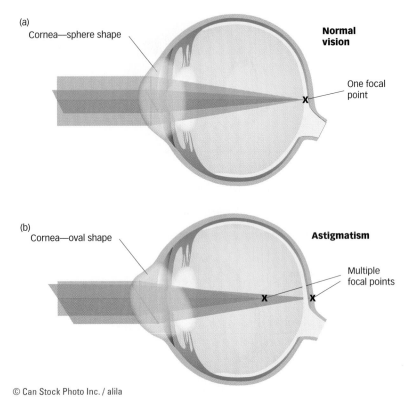

(a) Cornea—sphere shape

Normal vision

One focal point

(b) Cornea—oval shape

Astigmatism

Multiple focal points

© Can Stock Photo Inc. / alila

■ FIGURE 3.26   Astigmatism.

(a) A normal cornea. (b) A cornea with an irregular shape, allowing astigmatism to develop.

particular point in space and then promptly lose sight of it. Macular degeneration can occur in younger adults but is more common in older adults. Macular degeneration occurs in two forms, known as wet and dry. Wet macular degeneration has a very fast onset but is partially treatable. Dry macular degeneration may take years to develop, but no treatment is available at present. Wet macular degeneration occurs because of abnormal growth of blood vessels, leading to the leaking of blood below the retina. This leakage leads to scarring of the macula. Wet macular degeneration can be treated with a variety of medicines that shrink the damaged blood vessels, leading to some improvement of vision. However, injections must be given frequently to maintain this improved visual function (Arroyo, 2006). Wet macular degeneration is the less common form of macular degeneration (Bressler, 2004). Dry macular degeneration, the more common form, results from degeneration of the cells that produce photopigments (pigment epithelium) for the cones (and rods) in the macular region of the retina. This results in impaired function of those photoreceptors (Stone, 2007). No treatment is yet available for the dry form of macular degeneration. Figure 3.27 illustrates what the visual world looks like to patients with macular degeneration. Figure 3.28a is an ophthalmoscopic fundus photograph of a patient with macular degeneration.

■ FIGURE 3.27   Macular degeneration and retinitis pigmentosa.

Cordelia Molloy / Science Source

Macular degeneration affects central vision, blurring our perception of whatever it is we are trying to look at. Retinitis pigmentosa affects peripheral vision, creating a "tunnel" vision effect in which we see what we are looking at with normal acuity but cannot see what surrounds our focus.

Retinitis Pigmentosa

Retinitis pigmentosa is an inherited progressive degenerative disease of the retina that may lead to blindness. Over a long period of time, retinitis pigmentosa leads to degeneration and destruction of the photoreceptors, particularly rods at the periphery. Indeed, some patients will exhibit symptoms such as night blindness as children, whereas in other patients, the condition might not develop until adulthood (Hartong, Berson, & Dryja, 2006). In many cases, the rods are affected first, particularly those midway through the periphery. This results in tunnel vision (see Figure 3.27b), in which a person can see only in a small area in the middle of the visual field. Retinitis pigmentosa may progress and cause complete blindness as the destruction of photoreceptors spreads to the cones (Figure 3.28b). At present, there is no treatment for this condition. However, some recent research suggests that gene therapy might be useful in the near future (Wert, Davis, Sancho-Pelluz, Nishina, & Tsang, 2012).

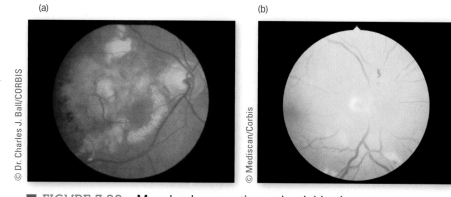

(a)   (b)

© Dr. Charles J. Ball/CORBIS

© Mediscan/Corbis

■ **FIGURE 3.28**   Macular degeneration and retinitis pigmentosa.

(a) The retina of a person with advanced dry macular degeneration. (b) The retina of a person with retinitis pigmentosa.

TEST YOUR KNOWLEDGE

What is the difference in terms of the structure of the lens between myopia and hyperopia?

Retinitis pigmentosa: an inherited progressive degenerative disease of the retina that may lead to blindness

IN DEPTH: *Vision Prostheses*

3.7   Describe how vision prostheses can restore visual function to blind individuals.

Vision prostheses are mechanical devices intended to restore visual function to blind individuals. They are sometimes referred to as bionic eyes. Unlike the Bionic Woman of television fame, vision prostheses are real and are being developed to restore vision to those who have become blind for a number of reasons. In particular, they may have use in people with macular degeneration and retinitis pigmentosa, diseases that affect transduction in the eye. Blindness due to brain damage will not be improved by vision prostheses. Moreover, although vision prostheses are potentially useful to people who have lost vision, at present, they are not helpful to congenitally blind individuals.

In the Western world, macular degeneration and retinitis pigmentosa are the most common forms of blindness. In both conditions, the photoreceptors are damaged, but the underlying retinal ganglion cells and the optic nerve remain intact. Therefore the goal of vision prostheses is to replace the missing photoreceptors with essentially an artificial layer of photoreceptors, sometimes called an "artificial retina." There are a number of developments in artificial retinae, but only one company has marketing approval for its device from the U.S. Food and Drug Administration, granted in 2013, having previously received approval in Europe in 2011. It is called the Argus II, developed by California-based Second Sight Medical Products (McKeegan, 2013). At present, it is approved only for patients with profound retinitis pigmentosa. See Figure 3.29 for an illustration.

Unlike the Bionic Woman, the Argus II is still a bit bulky. A small video camera is mounted on a pair of eyeglasses the patient wears. Images from the video camera are relayed wirelessly to a chip placed directly (via surgery) on the patient's retina or retinae. The chip's electrodes then stimulate the retinal ganglion neurons in a pattern that roughly approximates the image the camera

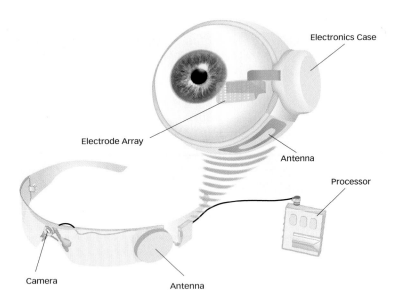

Electronics Case

Electrode Array

Antenna

Processor

Camera

Antenna

■ FIGURE 3.29   Vision prostheses.

In the Argus II, images are created by a video camera mounted on eyeglasses worn by the patient. The images are then sent to a computer processor on the eyeglasses themselves. The signal is then sent wirelessly to a chip embedded on the retina, which then stimulates the retinal ganglion cells.

is detecting. In its current form, the Argus II creates a visual field approximately 20° wide, thus allowing some central vision, though with only limited peripheral vision. In the current version of the Argus II, there are only 200 electrodes in the chip. It is estimated that it would take 1,000 of these to allow the patient to see clearly enough to recognize individual faces (Humayun et al., 2012). Thus, at present, this system also has limited visual acuity. It is likely that at present, reading is also still not an option. But as the technology improves, more electrodes may be loaded onto the chip, allowing enhanced acuity.

Interestingly, patients don't immediately "see" again. They have to be trained to interpret the signals they are receiving. However, with just a few hours' worth of training, patients can avoid obstacles, locate objects, recognize colors, and even recognize very large letters. Obviously, it is far from perfect. Although patients can localize objects, tests of visual acuity show that they improve to, at best, only approximately 20/1,000. Nonetheless, many patients are pleased to have some vision restored.

The Argus II is not the only device being built that uses remote cameras to directly stimulate the optic nerve. A number of other companies are developing similar devices. One device, the artificial silicon retina, implants the visual sensors directly into the damaged retina (Chow et al., 2004). It then electrically stimulates the retinal ganglion cells (DeMarco et al., 2007). This device has the advantage of not requiring cameras and external electronics. However, at present, clinical trials are still ongoing, and the device is not yet approved for general use. Another interesting approach to restoring eyesight in those with retinal disease involves regrowing photoreceptor cells using stem cell therapy. This research is still in its beginning stages but is showing some progress. Other researchers are using fetal retinal tissue to regrow photoreceptors in patients with retinitis pigmentosa. One study found improvements in patients' vision up to 5 years later. One patient improved from 20/800 to 20/200 acuity after tissue implants (Radtke et al., 2008). Like other techniques, this one is still in the clinical trials stage.

CHAPTER SUMMARY

3.1   Explain the nature of light as electromagnetic energy and the relation of wavelength to perception.

Visible light is a small slice of the electromagnetic spectrum. The electromagnetic spectrum is the complete range of wavelengths of light and other electromagnetic energy. Light from a light source such as the sun or a reading lamp reflects off objects in the environment and enters our eyes. The pattern of light enters our eye, and then our visual processes start decoding it. Light is made up of particles called photons that also behave in a wavelike manner. We see differences in wavelengths as different colors.

3.2   Describe the anatomy of the eye and how it makes vision possible.

The cornea and the pupil control the amount of light that enters the eye. The cornea adjusts the size of the pupil to control the amount of light entering the eye, and then the lens focuses that light on the retina. The retina contains photoreceptors, which convert the light energy into a neural signal.

3.3 Explain how the retinae transduce light energy into a neural signal.

The rods and cones of the retina are able to convert light into a neural signal through chemicals known as photopigments. Photopigments are molecules that absorb light and by doing so release an electric potential by altering the voltage in the cell. When a photopigment absorbs a photon of light, it changes shape. This change of shape initiates a series of biochemical processes, which result in a change of electric potential, which allows for a signal to exit the photoreceptor. In this way, a neural signal leaves the photoreceptor and is transmitted to the optic nerve to be sent to the brain. Opsin is the protein portion of a photopigment that captures the photon of light and begins the process of transduction. It is the variation in this opsin that determines the type of visual receptor.

3.4 Examine how the visual system adapts to the dark and then adapts again to the light.

The retina has two types of photoreceptors, rods and cones. The rods are specialized for night vision (scotopic) and light detection, whereas the cones are specialized for visual acuity (photopic) and color vision. The duplex theory of vision states that there are functionally two distinct ways that our eyes work, one, the photopic, associated with the cones, and the other, the scotopic, associated with our rods. Dark adaptation takes about 15 minutes. Technologies have been developed to allow people to see visual displays, such as computers with red light that do not interfere with dark adaptation. The rods and cones project to the retinal ganglion cells, the next topic covered.

3.5 Describe what retinal ganglion cells do and how receptive fields are constructed.

The rods and cones project to cells called the retinal ganglion cells, whose axons exit the eye through the optic nerve. Retinal ganglion cells have receptive fields. Receptive fields are regions of adjacent receptors that will alter the firing rate of cells that are higher up in the sensory system. The term can also apply to the region of space in the world to which a particular neuron responds. These receptive fields have a characteristic shape known as center-surround. Center-surround receptive fields occur when the center of the receptive field responds opposite to how the surround of the receptive field responds. If the center responds with an increase of activity to light in its area, the surround will respond with a decrease in activity to light in its area (on-center). If the center responds with a decrease of activity to light in its area, the surround will respond with an increase in activity to light in its area (off-center). This creates the phenomenon of lateral inhibition. Lateral inhibition is the reduction of a response of the eye to light stimulating one receptor by stimulation of nearby receptors. It is caused by inhibitory signals in horizontal cells and creates the Mach band illusion. It is responsible for enhanced edge detection by our visual system.

3.6 Examine the nature of refractive errors and how they affect the ability of the eye to see.

We also described a number of diseases and problems with the eye. Myopia, presbyopia, and hyperopia are common problems in the refracting power of the lens. Astigmatism is a problem in the shape of the lens or cornea. They are all correctible with eyeglasses. Cataracts occur when the lens gets cloudy and allows less or no light to pass through. Macular degeneration and retinitis pigmentosa are diseases of the retina that can lead to serious visual impairment. Macular degeneration leaves a blind spot right at the location we are trying to look at. Retinitis pigmentosa can cause tunnel vision in its early and middle phases and lead to total blindness later on.

3.7 Describe how vision prostheses can restore visual function to blind individuals.

There are several approaches to helping patients with retinitis pigmentosa and macular degeneration. Vision prostheses are devises that bypass the damaged photoreceptors by linking a camera directly to the optic nerve, leading to some improvement in visual functioning.

REVIEW QUESTIONS

1. What is light? Why is it considered both a wave and a particle?

2. What are the roles of the cornea, the iris, the pupil, and the lens in human vision?

3. What is accommodation? Explain how it produces a focused image on the retina.

4. What are the different classes and subclasses of photoreceptors? How do they convert light into a neural signal?

5. What is the difference between photopic vision and scotopic vision? What is each used for, and what physiological mechanism underlies each?

6. What is the Purkinje shift? What does it tell us about photopic vision and scotopic vision? How does it relate to dark adaptation?

7. What are retinal ganglion cells? What do they do in visual processing?

8. What are center-surround receptive fields? What is the difference between on-center and off-center center-surround receptive fields? How do these explain lateral inhibition?

9. Distinguish between myopia, presbyopia, and hyperopia. What are the differences between macular degeneration and retinitis pigmentosa?

10. What are vision prostheses? How do they restore vision to people with retinal disease?

KEY TERMS

Accommodation, 55

Anterior chamber, 54

Astigmatism, 72

Cataracts, 73

Center-surround receptive field, 68

Ciliary muscles, 55

Cones, 58

Convergence, 65

Cornea, 54

Dark adaptation, 65

Duplex theory of vision, 63

Edge detection, 68

Electromagnetic energy, 50

Electromagnetic spectrum, 51

Field of view, 53

Fovea, 58

Frequency, 51

Heterochromia, 55

Hyperopia, 72

Hyperpolarization, 61

Intensity, 51

Iris, 54

Lateral inhibition, 70

Lens, 55

Light adaptation, 65

Macula, 58

Macular degeneration, 73

Myopia, 71

Near point, 56

Off-center receptive fields, 68

On-center receptive fields, 68

Opsin, 61

Optic disc, 60

Photon, 52

Photopic vision, 63

Photopigment, 61

Posterior chamber, 55

Presbyopia, 56

Pupil, 54

Pupillary reflex, 54

Purkinje shift, 64

Receptive field, 68

Retina, 57

Retinal, 61

Retinal image, 57

Retinitis pigmentosa, 75

Rods, 58

Sclera, 54

Scotopic vision, 63

Wavelength, 51

Zonule fibers, 55

INTERACTIVE SENSATION LABORATORY EXERCISES (ISLE)

Experience chapter concepts at edge.sagepub.com/schwartz

ISLE 3.1 The Basics of Waves, 51

ISLE 3.2 Accommodation, 56

ISLE 3.3 Presbyopia, 56

ISLE 3.4 Letters and the Fovea, 60

ISLE 3.5 Map Your Blind Spot, 60

ISLE 3.6 Photopic vs. Scotopic Vision, 63

ISLE 3.7 Purkinje Shift, 64

ISLE 3.8 Convergence, 65

ISLE 3.9 Dark Adaptation Function, 65

ISLE 3.10 Automatic Light Adjustment in Cockpits, 66

ISLE 3.11 Center-Surround Receptive Fields, 69

ISLE 3.12 Mach Bands, 70

ISLE 3.13 Correcting Myopia and Hyperopia, 72

$SAGE edge™

Sharpen your skills with SAGE edge at edge.sagepub.com/schwartz

SAGE edge for students provides a personalized approach to help you accomplish your coursework goals in an easy-to-use learning environment.

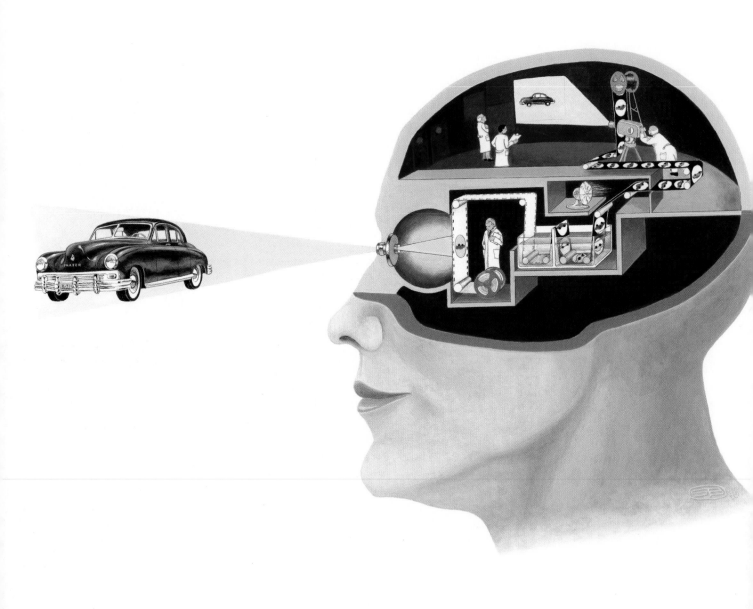

Visual System: The Brain

4

INTRODUCTION

In 1981, two Harvard professors won the Nobel Prize in Physiology or Medicine for their work on the anatomy and physiology of the visual cortex (Figure 4.1). The two men, Torsten Wiesel (born 1924) and David Hubel (1926–2013), collaborated for more than 20 years on research that has revolutionized our understanding of the mammalian visual cortex, including the human visual cortex. Dr. Wiesel, originally from Sweden, and Dr. Hubel, born in Canada to American parents, started their collaboration as postdoctoral fellows with Stephen Kuffler (whose work was discussed in Chapter 3). A postdoctoral fellow, or postdoc, is someone who has earned his or her PhD but is learning new techniques in a senior researcher's laboratory. Later, they both moved to Harvard and continued working together as they rose through the ranks at Harvard. Their contribution to the field of sensation and perception cannot be overstated. We refer to work they did 50 years ago, and it is just as relevant today as it was when it was first done. Both men continued to be active professionally well into their 80s. Indeed, in 2005, they published a book together outlining their collaborative research over the decades, including much work done after their Nobel Prize was awarded (Hubel & Wiesel, 2005). Wiesel also has been active in promoting global human rights and in promoting collaboration between Israeli and Palestinian scientists.

Among their amazing discoveries is that areas of the visual brain, including areas in the thalamus and areas in the occipital cortex, are specifically sensitive to certain kinds of stimuli, and that this sensitivity can be mapped into predictable patterns (Hubel & Wiesel, 1965). That is, they discovered neurons in the brain that have specific visual fields; the cells respond to some patterns of stimuli but not others. They also found that these stimulus-specific cells are organized into complex but predictable columns. In related research, they also pioneered how environmental input affects the development of the mammalian nervous system, that is, how these systems grow and change as mammalian babies get older.

In this chapter, we consider the visual brain, namely, the networks in the lateral geniculate nucleus (LGN) of the thalamus and the networks in the occipital cortex that allow us to see in the way we do. It is these areas of the brain that allow us to perceive beautiful sunsets, drive very fast cars at racetracks, and quietly read at night by the glow of our tablet computers. However, at the outset, we issue our readers a warning: Do not read this chapter once and think you understand the material. The organization of the visual system is complex, and our derived naming system for it can tax our mnemonic abilities—you will encounter *parasol retinal ganglion cells*, *parvocellular layers*, *hypercolumns*, and one area of the brain referred to by five different names. So our advice is to review repeatedly, do all of the online demonstrations, and self-test as you go through the material in this chapter. You will be glad you did—the organization of the human

LEARNING OBJECTIVES

4.1 Describe the anatomy of the optic chiasm and how that affects the lateralization of vision in the brain.

4.2 Describe the anatomy of the lateral geniculate nucleus and the role of this area in visual processing.

4.3 Explain the role of the superior colliculus in visual processing.

4.4 Explain the nature of the retinotopic organization of V1.

4.5 Explore the anatomy of the V2 area of the visual cortex.

4.6 Compare the difference between the dorsal pathway and the ventral pathway.

4.7 Discuss the current problem in determining where the dorsal and ventral pathways reunite to form a common perception.

4.8 Describe the concept of "nature versus nurture" as it applies to the visual system.

4.9 Explain the concept of blindsight.

© Ira Wyman/Sygma/Corbis

■ FIGURE 4.1   David Hubel and Torsten Wiesel.

David Hubel and Torsten Wiesel in 1982, shortly after winning the Nobel Prize in 1981 for their work on the visual system.

visual system is a wonder of the natural world, one to which science has paid particularly close attention.

In Chapter 3, we discussed how light is transduced by the retinae of the eyes and converted into a neural signal. The retinae begin the processing of the visual signal, already looking for edges and coding for color. This process intensifies when the optic nerves leave the eyes and head for their first synapses in the brain. In this chapter, we follow the neural signal as it leaves the eye and travels first to the LGN of the thalamus and from there to the visual cortex in the occipital lobe. We also consider other pathways of visual information after it leaves the eye. Much of the information we consider in this chapter comes from research on nonhuman eyes and brains, as most of the electrophysiological research was done on rats, cats, and monkeys. However, much of what we know about mammalian visual systems generalizes to our own. At the end of this chapter, we also consider a neuropsychological condition called blindsight, which results from damage to the visual regions of the brain without damage to the eyes. This peculiar condition underlines the critical nature of the brain in our ability to see.

ISLE 4.1 From Eye to LGN

Optic chiasm: the location in the optic tract where the optic nerve from each eye splits in half, with nasal retinae crossing over and temporal retinae staying on the same side of the optic tract

Optic tract: the optic nerve starting at the optic chiasm and continuing into the brain

Contralateral representation of visual space: the arrangement whereby the left visual world goes to the right side of the brain, and the right visual world goes to the left side of the brain

Ipsilateral organization: same-side organization; in the visual system, the temporal retina projects to the same side of the brain

THE OPTIC NERVE AND CHIASM

> 4.1   Describe the anatomy of the optic chiasm and how that affects the lateralization of vision in the brain.

Approximately 1 million retinal ganglion cells form the optic nerve of each eye. The optic nerve of the left eye and the optic nerve of the right eye meet just a couple of centimeters behind the eyes, in an area called the **optic chiasm**. Here at the optic chiasm, your visual system does one of its most interesting tricks, which is also one of the most difficult aspects of visual anatomy for people new to the area to keep straight (see Figure 4.2). So again, we warn you to pay close attention and review this information multiple times.

The optic nerve from each eye splits in half at the optic chiasm. The axons from the ganglion cells from the right half of the right retina and the ganglion cells from the right half of the left retina combine, forming the right **optic tract**, which then proceeds to the right hemisphere of the brain. Axons from the ganglion cells in the left half of the right retina and the left half of the left retina combine, forming the left optic tract, which then proceeds to the left hemisphere of the brain. For an illustration of how the optic nerve divides in the optic chiasm, see ISLE 4.1.

Why is this organization important for the visual system? Consider the right optic tract. It combines retinal signals from the temporal side (near the temple or toward the forehead) of your right retina with retinal signals of the nasal side (toward the nose) of your left retina. If you examine Figure 4.2, you will see that these two retinal areas receive input from the left visual world. Similarly, the left optic tract receives information from the right visual world. Thus, initially, the brain is respecting the outside visual world in terms of its representation in the brain. The left world goes to the right hemisphere, and the right world goes to the left hemisphere. This organization is known as **contralateral representation of visual space**.

We wish to reiterate this point, as it serves to dispel some myths about the eyes and the brain. Here's the main point of this paragraph: (a) Information from each eye goes to both hemispheres, and (b) each hemisphere of the brain receives input from the contralateral visual field. So the left eye sends information to both the left and right hemisphere. However, the left visual field of the world is initially sent to the right hemisphere. For example, if you consider the left eye only, the left temporal retina receives information from the right visual world, which stays on the same side of the brain and goes to the left hemisphere (**ipsilateral organization**, or same-side organization). The left nasal retina receives information from the left visual world, which crosses over and goes to the right hemisphere (**contralateral organization**). Thus, each eye sends a signal to each hemisphere. And it is the visual world that projects to the contralateral side of the brain. We know: It sounds confusing. Study Figure 4.2 closely, as in this case, the picture better conveys this organization.

Once the optic tract has left the chiasm, 90% of the axons make their way to the LGN of the thalamus. Here, the organization continues to respect the left-field/right-field distinction. This pathway then leads to the visual cortex. However, 10% of the axons from the optic tract go to other locations in the brain. Many of these axons that do not go to the thalamus go instead to a locus in the brain known as the superior colliculus, a midbrain structure that sits below the LGN. The superior colliculus is an important structure in eye movements. A small number of these axons also head to the frontal eye field region—an area in the frontal lobe also instrumental in eye movements. Some fibers also go to the pineal gland, which regulates our circadian rhythms. It is for this reason that exposure to bright lights can help "reset" our internal clocks. We will first consider the main pathway from the retinae to the brain.

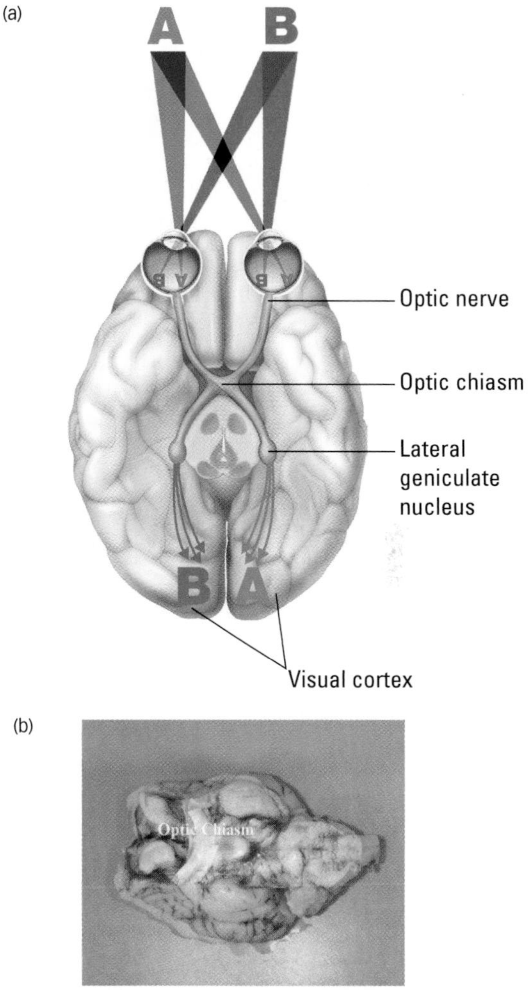

■ **FIGURE 4.2** **The optic chiasm and visual space in the brain.**

(a) The optic nerves leave the eyes and travel toward the brain. At the optic chiasm, each optic nerve splits apart. Information from the left visual world first travels toward the right side of the brain, whereas information from the right visual world first travels toward the left side of the brain. Information from each eye, however, goes to both sides of the brain. For example, the left temporal retina receives information from the right visual world, which stays on the same side of the brain and goes to the left hemisphere (ipsilateral or same-side organization). The left nasal retina receives information from the left visual world, which crosses over and goes to the right hemisphere (contralateral organization). (b) Use your anaglyph glasses to see the optic chiasm as it appears in the sheep brain. It is nearly identical to how it appears in the human brain.

TEST YOUR KNOWLEDGE

Describe how information moves through the optic chiasm. How does this lead to left and right field organization in the brain?

Contralateral organization: opposite-side organization; in the visual system, the nasal retina projects to the opposite side of the brain

THE LATERAL GENICULATE NUCLEUS

4.2 Describe the anatomy of the lateral geniculate nucleus and the role of this area in visual processing.

The **lateral geniculate nucleus** is a bilateral structure (one is present in each hemisphere) in the thalamus that relays information from the optic nerve to the visual cortex. The thalamus is a large structure that serves as a relay station for a number of sensory systems, including both vision and audition (we discuss the medial geniculate nucleus, critical in hearing, in Chapter 11). The LGN is the critical locus in the thalamus for vision. We now know that the LGN has complex functions and is not simply a relay station but is already doing visual processing. However, it is often thought of as a relay center because it holds an intermediate position between the retinae of the eyes and the visual cortices.

Anatomically, the LGN is divided into six layers (see Figure 4.3). Layers 1 and 2 are called the **magnocellular layers** because the cells in these layers are large. Layers 3 through 6 are called the **parvocellular layers** because the cells are somewhat smaller. There are also very thin layers between each of the two magnocellular levels and the four parvocellular layers. These are called **koniocellular layers** and consist of very small cells. Thus, there are six koniocellular layers, one under each of the six parvocellular and magnocellular layers.

LGN anatomy gets complicated very quickly. So read carefully, review what you just read, and then write it down, so you can be confident that you have understood and retained this material. You should also study the figures to reinforce your understanding of the organization of the LGN.

First, keep in mind that we have two LGNs, one in each hemisphere. The left LGN receives input primarily from the right visual world, and the right LGN receives input primarily from the left visual world. Also remember that each eye projects inputs to both the left and right LGNs when half of the retinal axons cross over in the optic chiasm. Once in the brain, it is the representation of the visual world that is more important than which eye this information came from (except when considering depth perception). This is important to repeat, because it is often misrepresented outside of scientific publications.

So here are some important facts about the LGN. First, each LGN layer receives input from only one eye. Magnocellular Layer 1 and Parvocellular Layers 4 and 6 receive input from the contralateral eye (i.e., the eye on the opposite side of the head). This is also true for the koniocellular layers underneath each of these layers. Magnocellular Layer 2 and Parvocellular Layers 3 and 5 receive input from the ipsilateral eye. This is also true for the koniocellular layers underneath each of these layers (Hendry & Reid, 2000). This means that the LGN preserves information about both where in the visual world information is coming from and which eye is detecting that information. Obviously, it is critical to know where in the world objects are, but knowing which eye an image comes from is important in constructing a three-dimensional image.

It is also critical that particular retinal ganglion cells are projecting to particular layers in the LGN. The magnocellular layers of the LGN receive input from the **parasol retinal ganglion cells (M cells)**. The parvocellular layers of the LGN receive input from the **midget retinal ganglion cells (P cells)**. And the koniocellular layers of the LGN receive input from the **bistratified retinal ganglion cells (K cells)**.

The last general feature of the LGN that is important to understand is that the neurons in each layer of the LGN show retinotopic organization. This means that

Lateral geniculate nucleus: a bilateral structure (one is present in each hemisphere) in the thalamus that relays information from the optic nerve to the visual cortex

Magnocellular layers: layers of the lateral geniculate nucleus with large cells that receive input from M ganglion cells (parasol retinal ganglion cells)

Parvocellular layers: layers of the lateral geniculate nucleus with small cells that receive input from P ganglion cells (midget retinal ganglion cells)

Koniocellular layers: layers of the lateral geniculate nucleus with very small cells that receive input from K ganglion cells (bistratified retinal ganglion cells)

Parasol retinal ganglion cells (M cells): retinal ganglion cells that project to the magnocellular layer of the LGN; they represent 10% of ganglion cells and possess high sensitivity to light

Midget retinal ganglion cells (P cells): retinal ganglion cells that project to the parvocellular layer of the LGN; they represent 80% of ganglion cells, possess low sensitivity to light, and are sensitive to wavelength

Bistratified retinal ganglion cells (K cells): retinal ganglion cells that project to the koniocellular layer of the LGN; they represent 10% of ganglion cells, possess low sensitivity to light, and are sensitive to wavelength

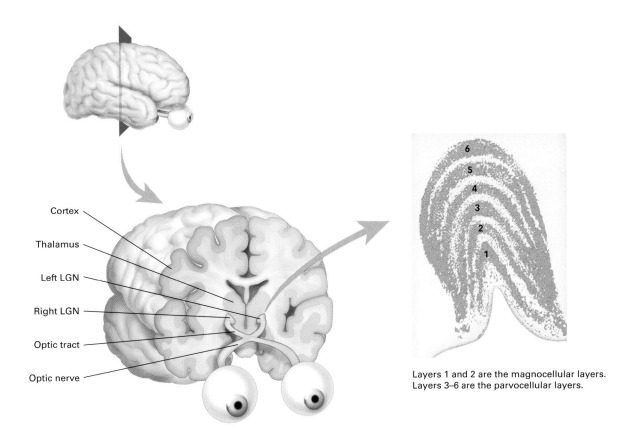

Cortex

Thalamus

Left LGN

Right LGN

Optic tract

Optic nerve

6
5
4
3
2
1

Layers 1 and 2 are the magnocellular layers.
Layers 3–6 are the parvocellular layers.

■ FIGURE 4.3   The lateral geniculate nucleus (LGN).

The LGN is a six-layered structure. Layers 1 and 2 are called the magnocellular layers because the cells in these layers are large. Layers 3 through 6 are called parvocellular layers because the cells are somewhat smaller.

retinal ganglion cells from adjacent regions of the retina connect to cells in adjacent areas of the LGN. This also means that the LGN has an organization oriented to the visual world, as adjacent areas in the visual world are picked up by adjacent areas of the retina, which are in turn projected to adjacent areas of the LGN. To see all this information graphically, examine Figure 4.4.

To understand the functional significance of this complex anatomy, it is necessary to backtrack a bit and examine the different kinds of retinal ganglion cells that have been shown to exist. Remember that the retinal ganglion cells emerge from specific locations along the retina. Those close to the fovea receive input from few or just one receptor cell, and those at the periphery may be collecting input from many more receptor cells. We now know, however, that not all retinal ganglion cells are the same. Indeed, we see the beginning of three unique pathways that start in the retinae and continue to the visual cortex. We consider each of these pathways now.

The **parvocellular pathway** (or simply **P pathway**) is characterized by the retinal ganglion cells known as midget retinal ganglion cells (so named because of their small size). Midget retinal ganglion cells usually receive input from a single cone in the fovea of the retina, thus carrying detailed information necessary for visual acuity. When stimulated, these cells show a sustained response; that is, they continue to fire throughout the time period when a stimulus is present. These retinal ganglion cells are sensitive to wavelength (the basis for color perception). The **koniocellular pathway** (or simply **K pathway**) starts with bistratified retinal ganglion cells and

Parvocellular pathway (P pathway): a pathway characterized by the retinal ganglion cells known as midget retinal ganglion cells

Koniocellular pathway (K pathway): a pathway that starts with bistratified retinal ganglion cells and projects to the koniocellular layers of the lateral geniculate nucleus

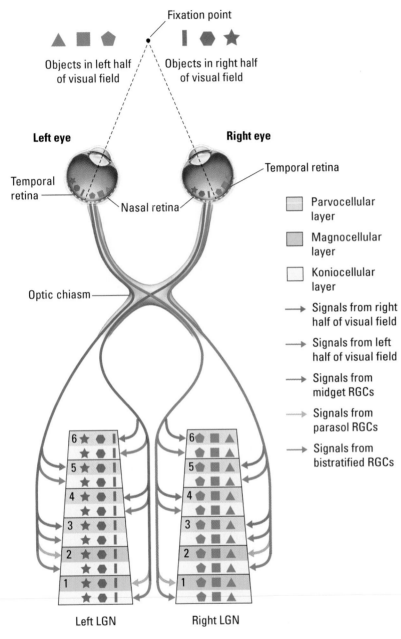

Fixation point

Objects in left half
of visual field

Objects in right half
of visual field

Left eye

Right eye

Temporal retina

Temporal
retina

Nasal retina

Parvocellular
layer

Magnocellular
layer

Koniocellular
layer

Optic chiasm

Signals from right
half of visual field

Signals from left
half of visual field

Signals from
midget RGCs

Signals from
parasol RGCs

Signals from
bistratified RGCs

6   5   4   3   2   1

6   5   4   3   2   1

Left LGN   Right LGN

■ FIGURE 4.4   Organization within the LGN.

Objects in the left visual world initially go to the right hemisphere, whereas
objects in the right visual world initially go the left hemisphere. This is
represented here in both the eye and the optic chiasm with color coding.
Different types of ganglion cells project to different layers of the LGN. The
parvocellular layers receive input from the midget retinal ganglion cells, whereas
the magnocellular levels receive input from the parasol retinal ganglion cells. The
koniocellular layers receive input from the bistratified retinal ganglion cells.

**Magnocellular pathway (M
pathway):** a pathway that starts with
the parasol retinal ganglion cells
and projects to the magnocellular layers
of the LGN

projects to the koniocellular layers of the
LGN. These retinal ganglion cells also
receive input from cones. However, there
is more convergence among these cells,
so that they show lower acuity than the
P-pathway cells. But they do show some
role in color vision.

The **magnocellular pathway** (or simply **M pathway**) starts with the parasol
retinal ganglion cells and projects to the
magnocellular layers of the LGN. These
retinal ganglion cells receive input from
many photoreceptors, including both
rods and cones. As such, they have large
receptive fields and are sensitive to light,
but not to color. They have lower acuity
relative to the K-pathway or P-pathway
cells. For this reason, the M system is usually associated with visual functions such
as light detection and motion detection.

Processing in the LGN

The LGN also maintains a retinotopic
map of the left or right visual world in each
of its layers (see Figure 4.5). Interestingly,
each of these layers emphasizes different
aspects of visual processing. We know
this from single-cell studies that found
adjacent cells in the LGN that respond
to visual stimuli that excite adjacent
cells in the retina. However, the receptive
fields of LGN cells are more like retinal
ganglion cells than receptors. LGN neurons have receptive fields that are similar
in characteristics to the retinal ganglion
cells, with center-surround organization
(Xu, Bonds, & Casagrande, 2002). That
is, some LGN cells respond maximally to
stimuli that are present in the center of the
cell's receptive field but absent outside the
center (or reversed). Thus, like the retinal
ganglion cells, LGN neurons show specific
responding to edges, spots, and gratings.
As we have discussed earlier, edge detection is critical to perception, as it allows
the visual system to determine where one
object ends and the next object begins.

Originally, the LGN was thought of as a relay point—a synapse between
the retina and the visual cortex, where the complex processing occurred. But,
as with much with the human brain, the LGN turns out to be much more complex than that. There are many feedback loops from the cortex back to the LGN
and many connections from the LGN to other areas of the brain (Babadi, Casti,

Xiao, Kaplan, & Paninski, 2010). The LGN receives input from the cortex, from the brainstem, from other loci in the thalamus, and from within the LGN itself. Indeed, there are more connections from the cortex back to the LGN than there are from the LGN to the cortex. Many of these pathways are only now being investigated. Thus, much remains to be discovered about the complex function of the LGN.

As indicated earlier, studies suggest that the different layers of the LGN have different functions. The magnocellular layers are sensitive to motion, light detection, and sudden changes in the visual image. The parvocellular level specializes in foveal functions—color, acuity, texture, and depth. The koniocellular layers also seem to specialize in color. One obvious question is, How do we know this? Most of what we know about these functions comes from single-cell recording experiments using nonhuman mammalian models. We turn to those now.

Many of the single-cell recording experiments on the LGN use rhesus macaques as the research participants. Their visual brains are very similar to our own. Because the visual system does not require the animal to be conscious while it is looking at stimuli, the monkey does not experience pain or discomfort, as it is fully anesthetized during the procedure. In a typical physiological study, a monkey is trained to examine visual displays. Then, using single-cell recording on particular neurons, different stimuli can be presented to the monkey. For example, a cell in the magnocellular layer may be sensitive to movement in a particular area of the visual world. A cell in the parvocellular layer may be maximally sensitive to light of a particular wavelength in a particular region in central vision. In this way, we can map which cells respond to which kinds of stimuli (Nassi & Callaway, 2009).

We end our discussion of the LGN with one interesting fact. As mentioned earlier, the LGN is part of the thalamus. During sleep, the thalamus is inhibited by complex neural circuitry in the brain. Thus, unless very bright lights are shined directly into the eye, a person's eyes can be open during sleep, but they will not see, because information does not leave the LGN. Information would be registered on the retina and would be sent to the LGN, but stop there, as the inhibition prevents it from being sent on to visual areas of the cortex.

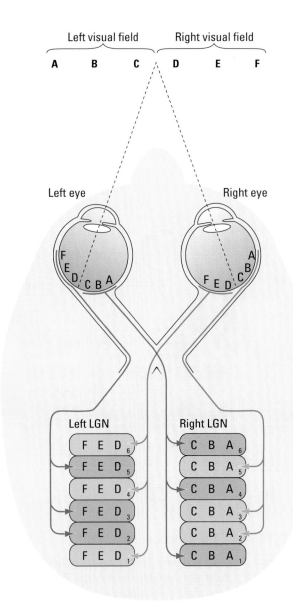

■ FIGURE 4.5   Organization in the LGN.

Stimuli in the world are mapped in a consistent fashion onto each layer of the LGN. Input from the left visual field goes to the right LGN, and input from the right visual field goes to the left LGN. Layers 1 and 2 are the magnocellular layers receiving input, whereas Layers 3 to 6 are parvocellular. The koniocellular layers, not pictured, are in between.

TEST YOUR KNOWLEDGE

Describe the neuroanatomy of the lateral geniculate nucleus. How do the different ganglion cells project to the different layers of the LGN?

THE SUPERIOR COLLICULUS

4.3   Explain the role of the superior colliculus in visual processing.

We have two superior colliculi, one on each side of the brain. The **superior colliculus** is at the top of the brainstem, anatomically just beneath the thalamus (see Figure 4.6). Like the LGN, the left superior colliculus receives input from the right visual world, and the right superior colliculus receives input from the left visual world. Its main function in mammals (including humans) is the control of rapid eye movements. The superior colliculus is part of a largely nonconscious system that helps us direct our eyes toward new or approaching objects.

Approximately 90% of retinal ganglion cells synapse in the LGN, but about 10% go to the superior colliculus. It is unclear still which retinal ganglion cells innervate the superior colliculus, but it is likely that they are bistratified retinal ganglion cells (the K pathway). Like the LGN, the superior colliculus receives feedback from the visual cortex, and the superior colliculus also projects to the koniocellular levels of the LGN (May, 2006). The superior colliculus also projects to areas of the visual cortex beyond the primary visual cortex. As with the LGN, one can find a retinotopic map of the visual world in cells inside the superior colliculus. Nonetheless, the main pathway is directly from the retinal ganglion cells to the superior colliculus, allowing the superior colliculus to produce quick eye movements. The superior colliculus is often implicated in the phenomenon of blindsight, a phenomenon we examine in depth at the end of the chapter.

To understand the role of the superior colliculus, we must first discuss the nature of human eye movements. In general, human eyes can make two kinds of voluntary eye movements, **smooth pursuit** and **saccades**. We will start with smooth-pursuit movements. Think about watching a bird fly across the sky: Your eyes slowly and smoothly move as the bird moves across your field of vision. These smooth-pursuit eye movements can be made only when we are watching a moving object. If you don't believe it, try it. Try to slowly move your eyes across a stationary landscape. Have someone watch you. You will find that you cannot slowly move your eyes. Rather, your eyes jump from one point to another.

The superior colliculus is vital in making smooth-pursuit movements. Consider that when we are looking directly at an object without moving our eyes (fixation), activity can be registered in the region of the superior colliculus that responds to the fovea. When the object begins to move, cells adjacent to the foveal area in the superior colliculus become active. This helps guide our smooth-pursuit movement, which we can do only in response to a moving object. There are also close connections between the superior colliculus and the innervation of the muscles that control our eyes.

The rapid movement of the eye from one stationary object to another is called a saccade. We make saccades when we move our eyes from one stationary object, such as a sleeping cat, to another, such as a clock on the wall. We also make saccades as we read, moving our fixation from one word to the next. If an object

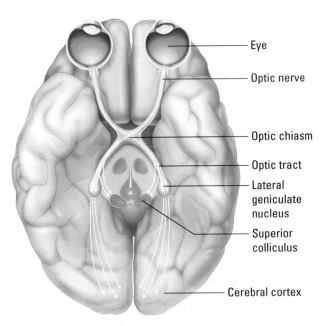

— Eye

— Optic nerve

— Optic chiasm

— Optic tract

— Lateral geniculate nucleus

— Superior colliculus

— Cerebral cortex

■ **FIGURE 4.6   The superior colliculus.**

This illustration shows the location of the superior colliculi relative to other brain structures relevant for vision. The superior colliculus is involved in controlling eye movements.

Superior colliculus: a structure located at the top of the brainstem, just beneath the thalamus, whose main function in mammals (including humans) is the control of rapid eye movements

Smooth-pursuit eye movements: voluntary tracking eye movements

Saccades: the most common and rapid of eye movements; they are sudden eye movements and are used to look from one object to another

abruptly appears at our periphery, activity in the area of the superior colliculus responsible for that area in visual space becomes active, leading to a saccade, that is, a sudden movement directly from our fixation to the new point in space. Think of a light going on in an adjacent room. The light surprises you, and you make a sudden eye movement toward the source of the light. Saccades are also the responsibility of the superior colliculus.

Another interesting feature of the superior colliculus is that it receives input from other sensory systems, most noticeably the auditory system and the somatosensory system. This allows our eyes to be directed quickly to the location of a sound or a touch. Thus, when someone taps our shoulder, we quickly move our eyes in that direction. This is adaptive—we want to be able to orient our visual system to any surprising stimulus, regardless of how it is detected. We feel a strange tug on our arm, and we want to be able to look at what is happening. We hear a loud sound off to our side, and we want to be able to see what caused the noise. Interestingly, these responses in the superior colliculus are additive. If we visually detect something at the periphery and hear a loud sound off to the same side, our superior collicular response will be larger than for either stimulus alone. In this way, the superior colliculus is thought to be an area of multisensory integration (Stein & Meredith, 1993).

TEST YOUR KNOWLEDGE

How does the superior colliculus control eye movements?

THE PRIMARY VISUAL CORTEX

| 4.4 | Explain the nature of the retinotopic organization of V1. |

We now return to the main visual pathway. After leaving the LGN, the next synapse in the visual pathway is in the primary visual cortex, in the occipital lobe of the brain. The primary visual cortex, unfortunately, is referred to by a number of names. In different contexts, you may hear different nomenclature, but all refer to the same area of the brain. So get ready—there is about to be a list of terms that all refer to the same area of the brain: **primary visual cortex**, **V1**, striate cortex, Area 17, and BA 17. Here's the significance of each term. The terms *primary visual cortex* and *V1* refer to its position along the flow of information in the visual system—the first area in the cortex to receive visual information. *Striate cortex* refers to the way the brain cells in this area look under certain staining conditions. They appear striated, whereas other adjacent areas of the occipital cortex are "extrastriate." *Area 17* and *BA 17* refer to the area's position on Brodmann charts. We use the terms *primary visual cortex* and *V1* in this text, but it is important to be aware of the other terms, as they are used just as frequently in other discussions of the human visual system. When V1 is the specific topic being discussed, we will use the term *V1* for brevity. When the primary visual cortex is secondary to the main discussion, we will switch to the term *primary visual cortex* to avoid excessive jargon.

The cerebral cortex is the outer surface of the brain. Indeed, the word *cortex* comes from a Latin term for a tree's bark. The cerebral cortex is only 2 mm thick, but it is essential for all higher perception and cognition in humans and other mammals. The cerebral cortex is divided into four lobes (see Figure 4.7). The frontal lobe, located behind the forehead, is the seat of higher cognition—thinking, planning, speaking, as well as a variety of motor functions. The temporal lobe

Primary visual cortex (V1): the area of the cerebral cortex that receives input from the LGN, located in the occipital lobe and responsible for early visual processing

■ FIGURE 4.7   **The four lobes of the brain.**

There are four lobes of the brain, including the frontal, temporal, parietal, and occipital. The occipital lobe is the visual area of the brain. This figure shows the location of V1 within the occipital lobe. V1 is the first area in the cortex that receives input from the retinae.

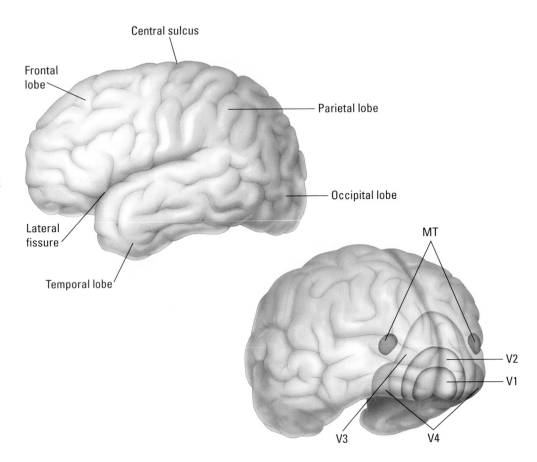

is responsible for memory, language comprehension, and auditory perception. The parietal lobe is involved in attention and somatosensory perception. The occipital lobe, at the back of the brain, is the visual cortex. This large area is responsible for vision and nothing else. At the very back of the visual cortex is the area known as V1.

You can easily locate your own V1. Run your hand along the back of your head, just above the neck. At the very back of your head is a slight bump, known as the inion, on the occipital bone. Press your finger against that bone. Underneath the inion is V1. Because your inion is right at the center or your head, your finger will be above both the left and right V1s. You can also see its position in the diagram in Figure 4.8.

Mapping the Eye on the Brain

One of the important characteristics of the visual cortex is that it is highly organized. This means that its anatomical structure can be correlated directly with its function. That is, if we know where a neuron is, we know what it does for the visual system. This knowledge has come about from more than 50 years of intensive study, starting with the work of Hubel and Wiesel (see Hubel & Wiesel, 2005). We now take a look at this exquisite organization.

The primary visual cortex is a bilateral structure—there is one in the left hemisphere that receives input from the right visual world, and there is one in the right hemisphere that receives input from the left visual world. The left and right V1s meet in the middle of the brain (see Figure 4.9). The area where they meet in the center is the area responsible for representing the fovea, or the area in space we are looking at.

© James Woodson/Digital Vision/Thinkstock

■ FIGURE 4.8   **The inion marks the occipital lobe.**

On this bald person's skull, you can see a prominent inion. Right underneath that bone at the back of the skull is V1 in the occipital cortex.

The left V1 receives input from the left LGN, and the right V1 receives input from the right LGN. As we saw above, this means that each V1 will receive input from the opposite half of the visual world. The left V1 receives input from the left half of each retina, which corresponds to the right half of the world. More than that, adjacent locations on the retina project to adjacent points on V1. Think of the retina as a terrain and the V1 as a map of that terrain. There is a point-by-point relation between the retina and the V1, as seen on a topographic map. As a result, V1 is said to have a **retinotopic map** of the retina (see Figure 4.9).

Just as maps of the world are not exactly the same as the original terrain, neither is V1 a precisely exact map of the retina. Some regions of the retina get to take up a much greater proportion of V1 than others. This feature is called **cortical magnification**. Cortical magnification means that there is more space in the cortex devoted to some sensory receptors than to others. In this case,

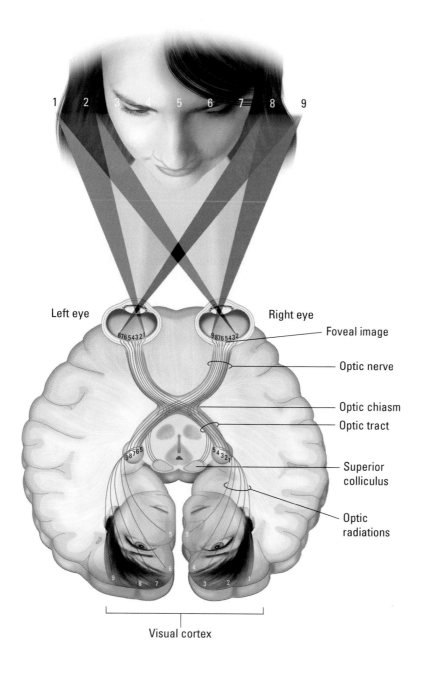

Left eye

Right eye

Foveal image

Optic nerve

Optic chiasm

Optic tract

Superior colliculus

Optic radiations

Visual cortex

■ FIGURE 4.9   Organization of the visual world in V1.

As in earlier areas in visual processing, the right V1 represents the left visual world, and the left V1 represents the right visual world. Note that the representation of the point of fixation, or the foveae of the retinae, is toward the middle of V1, with the left and right V1s adjacent to each other.

Retinotopic map: a point-by-point relation between the retina and V1

Cortical magnification: the allocation of more space in the cortex to some sensory receptors than to others; the fovea has a larger cortical area than the periphery

the fovea has a larger cortical area than the periphery. In particular, the fovea takes up a huge proportion of V1 and the rest of the visual cortex. Indeed, the fovea is less than 1% of the retina in terms of size, but its representation takes up over 50% of V1 (Mason & Kandel, 1991). That is a lot of the brain's real estate in the cortex dedicated to a small portion of the retina. Of course, it is the fovea that is specialized for color vision and visual acuity, and these features are often the important features we need to determine what an object is. So it is not surprising that representation of the fovea of the retina takes up so much space in the cortex.

V1 is a six-layered structure, like all of the cerebral cortex. Each layer is numbered 1 through 6. However, in V1, most anatomists divide Layer 4 into at least three separate sublevels, and one of these sublevels is typically also divided into still smaller sublevels. Layer 4 is the critical layer that receives input from the LGN. As we discussed earlier, there are three distinct pathways coming from the retina through the LGN to V1. Two of these arrive at V1 in Layer 4, the magnocellular synapses in Sublayer 4cα and the parvocellular layer synapses in Sublayer 4cβ (Yabuta & Callaway, 1988) (see Figure 4.10).

Receptive Fields of V1 Cells

When Hubel and Wiesel set out to do research on the anatomy and physiology of V1, they expected to find receptive fields in V1 similar to those that were found in retinal ganglion cells and in the LGN—that is, the basic center-surround organization. What they found was much more complicated. They found a host of different types of cells that had differing sensitivities to objects in their receptive fields. For example, they found that V1 cells in cats were most sensitive to bars of different orientations in different locations in the visual world. Thus, a particular neuron in V1 might respond maximally to a vertical bar at 3° off the fovea on the left. An adjacent neuron in V1 might respond maximally to a bar 2° off vertical bar at 3° off the fovea to the left. And this pattern would continue from one cell to the next. They had not expected the organization to be so logical, but cells seem to line up in columns sensitive to the orientation of objects in particular areas in the visual field.

They also discovered two distinct kinds of cells in V1, which they called simple and complex cells. We turn to them next.

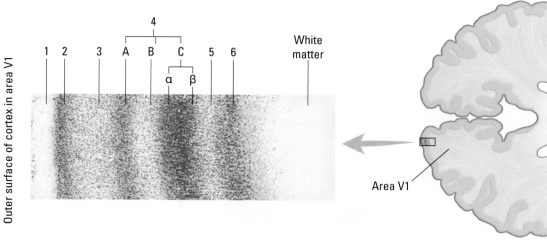

■ FIGURE 4.10   **V1 layers.**

This illustration shows the multiple layers of V1. Layer 4 has been subdivided into three sublayers.

Simple Cells

Simple cells are V1 neurons that respond to stimuli with particular orientations to objects within their receptive field. Simple cells are found in Layer 4B of V1 and receive input primarily from Layer 4C of V1. Like cells in the LGN, they have clear excitatory and inhibitory regions. But unlike LGN cells, they have orientation selectivity rather than center-surround visual fields. Hubel and Wiesel (1959) found that elongated stimuli that looked like bars seemed to be particularly effective stimuli for these cells. Indeed, they found that some cells wanted dark bars on a light background, and others responded to white bars on a dark background. The bars may also occur at varying angles of orientation, and these vary in a predictable pattern (see Figure 4.11). This selective firing rate to the orientation shows the selectivity of the cell to orientation. You can find an interactive illustration of simple cells on ISLE 4.2.

The preferred orientation of a simple cell is the stimulus orientation that produces the strongest response from the simple cell. Experiments using single-cell recordings demonstrate **orienting tuning curves** for any particular simple cell in V1. These orienting tuning curves are graphs that demonstrate the typical response of a simple cell to stimuli of different orientations. Such a curve can be seen in Figure 4.12. As you can see in the curves in Figure 4.12, simple cells respond best to a stimulus with a particular orientation; as the orientation gets larger or smaller, the response of the cell decreases. If the orientation is greatly off, the cell will not respond at all. Other cells have different peak sensitivities. Thus, V1 indicates the orientation of lines in the visual world by having select cells respond to different angles of orientation.

ISLE 4.2 Simple Cells

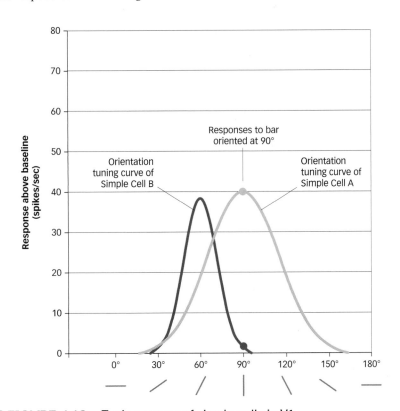

■ FIGURE 4.12   Tuning curves of simple cells in V1.

You can see here the response patterns of two simple cells. One is tuned best to a perpendicular 90° bar, whereas the other one is tuned to a 60° bar. You can see that the cells will respond to other orientations, but they peak for one orientation.

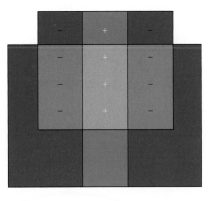

■ FIGURE 4.11   A bar detector.

This cell's receptive field allows it to respond to a bar of light at a particular orientation. It is best stimulated by a light bar surrounded by a dark field.

Simple cells: V1 neurons that respond to stimuli with particular orientations to objects within their receptive field; the preferred orientation of a simple cell is the stimulus orientation that produces the strongest response

Orienting tuning curve: a graph that demonstrates the typical response of a simple cell to stimuli or different orientations

Complex Cells and V1 Responses to Visual Features

Complex cells are also neurons in V1 that respond optimally to stimuli with particular orientations. But, unlike simple cells, they respond to a variety of stimuli across different locations. For example, a complex cell will respond to a dark bar on a light background and a light bar on a dark background. In contrast, a simple cell responds to one but not the other. Moreover, complex cells do not have peak location sensitivity, as simple cells do. That is, they will respond equally well to an optimal orientation regardless of where it is within their receptive field. Some complex cells also receive input from both eyes and may be involved in depth perception (Read, 2005). Complex cells also respond best to moving stimuli. For moving stimuli, some complex cells are responsive to movement in one direction, whereas other complex cells are responsible for movement in the other direction. Complex cells are found in Layers 2, 3, 5, and 6 of V1, but not Layer 4. You can find an interactive illustration of complex cells in ISLE 4.3.

We have focused on the observation that simple and complex cells are particularly sensitive to edges and bars with specific orientations. But it is also important to keep in mind that neurons in V1 are tuned to many different features, including color, motion, depth, direction, length, and size. This is particularly true of the complex cells. There are also neurons in V1 called **end-stopped neurons**. End-stopped neurons respond to stimuli that end within the cell's receptive field. If the pattern continues beyond the receptive field, these cells do not respond as greatly. Because of this pattern, end-stopped cells are considered to be involved in the detection of corners and the boundaries of shapes.

The Organization of V1

When Hubel and Wiesel were recording from single cells, they recorded from several cells in a single penetration of the electrode into the brain. They recorded from one cell, and then they moved the electrode slowly further into the brain until they found another cell (see Figure 4.13). Then Hubel and Wiesel would record from that cell and determine its receptive field, and repeat the procedure again. If their electrode entered the brain perfectly perpendicular to the brain's surface, they found an interesting pattern. All of the cells in the perpendicular column responded to a bar in the same location on the retina, thus demonstrating the same receptive field (see Hubel & Wiesel, 1979). This is consistent with the idea of a retinotopic map.

Hubel and Wiesel also discovered that some cells prefer to respond to inputs from one eye, and other cells prefer to respond to the other eye. This is called the ocular dominance of the cell. These were also organized in columns, with some cells responding more to stimuli from the right eye and some to stimuli from the left eye (see Figure 4.14).

Moreover, Hubel and Wiesel also found that simple cells all selected for bars at particular locations. If they inserted their electrode at a different angle, they could find cells that all responded to the same location, but for different orientations. At a different angle, the electrode might find cells that responded to the same orientation along an adjacent column. Thus, this vertical arrangement of cells that all responded to cells in the same orientation in the same retinal location Hubel and Wiesel called a column. Next, they noticed that adjacent

ISLE 4.3 Complex Cells

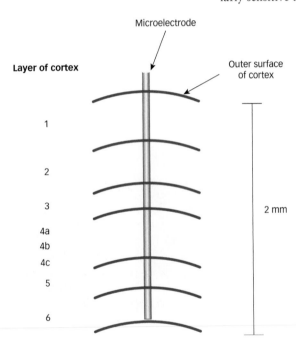

■ FIGURE 4.13   Orientation in V1.

When an electrode is inserted into a column of cells in V1, all respond to a specific orientation of bars.

Complex cells: neurons in V1 that respond optimally to stimuli with particular orientations; unlike simple cells, they respond to a variety of stimuli across different locations, particularly to moving stimuli

End-stopped neurons: neurons that respond to stimuli that end within the cell's receptive field

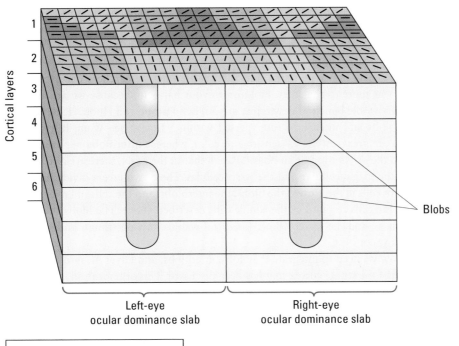

■ FIGURE 4.14   Ocular dominance columns in V1.

Alternating columns in V1 receive signals from either the left eye or the right eye through the LGN.

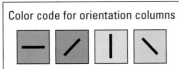

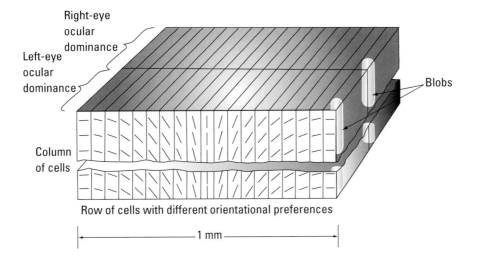

■ FIGURE 4.15 Hypercolumns in V1.

The hypercolumns organize the orientation columns, the location columns, and the ocular dominance columns into a predictable pattern. The image here is a schematic showing everything at right angles. In real mammalian brains, the pattern may be curved or folded in on itself. In this figure, you can also see the "blobs," which are designed to detect color.

columns responded to lines that were tilted only slightly differently from one another. In fact, the columns formed an organized pattern according to their orientation. It was later discovered that orientational selectivity goes in one direction in V1, whereas the input from the two eyes goes in the other direction in V1 (see Figure 4.15).

Thus, Hubel and Wiesel found both ocular dominance columns and orientation columns. The **ocular dominance columns** are made up of neurons that respond only to one eye, and these columns are perpendicular to **orientation columns**, which selectively respond to small variations in orientation. Ocular dominance columns alternate systematically between left-eye and right-eye dominance. Orientation columns change systematically across orientations (Hubel & Wiesel, 1962).

Ocular dominance column: a column within V1 that is made up of neurons that receive input from only the left eye or only the right eye

Orientation column: a column within V1 that is made up of neurons with similar responses to the orientation of a shape presented to those neurons

When ocular dominance columns and orientation columns are combined, they form something Hubel and Wiesel called a hypercolumn. A **hypercolumn** is a 1-mm block of V1 containing both the ocular dominance and orientation columns for a particular region in visual space.

This view of V1 persisted into the 1980s, when researchers discovered that there was more to the story. Hold on to your hat here, because we are about to throw a whole bunch of new terms at you. Livingstone and Hubel (1984) discovered blobs and interblobs interspersed within V1 (also see Wong-Riley, 1979). **Blobs** are areas within V1 sensitive to color, whereas **interblobs** are areas sensitive to the orientation of an object. Recall that in the LGN, there are two types of cells, the magnocellular and the parvocellular. These two layers divide into three types of cells in the cortex: the blobs, the interblobs, and the cells in Layer 4B. The interblob cells respond as the simple cells described above. The blobs show color responses, and the Layer 4B cells respond well to moving stimuli and stimuli of very low contrast.

Now we need to integrate the blobs, interblobs, and Layer 4B into the organization of the striate cortex that has been discussed. This organization is seen in the hypercolumn. The orientational selectivity goes in one direction, and the ocular dominance goes at right angles. In each set of orientation columns for each eye, there are two blobs. Layer 4B runs throughout all of the cortex and cuts across all of the columns. This hypercolumn is one functional unit, processing all of the information from one region of the cortex. Adjacent hypercolumns process information from adjacent regions of the cortex, and it is these hypercolumns that make up the topographical map discussed above. The portions of the hypercolumns that are active at any point in time will indicate the features of what is stimulating that region of the retina. Figure 4.15 gives you a sense of what all this would look like in the brain if everything were all straightened out. For an interactive illustration of hypercolumns in V1, examine ISLE 4.4.

We understand that we are advancing a very complicated picture of the brain. Many researchers have spent their careers investigating this so that we can understand the visual system. But in other ways, it is remarkable that nature could have designed such an incredible mechanism for decoding visual information and that it does so in such a systematic fashion. We think that the organization of V1 is one of the great accomplishments of nature and the work to understand it one of the great feats of science.

ISLE 4.4 Hypercolumns

TEST YOUR KNOWLEDGE

Describe the relation of retinotopic organization to representation in the external world.

V2 AND BEYOND

4.5   Explore the anatomy of the V2 area of the visual cortex.

You might wonder how the visual system goes from detecting edges and bars at particular angles to perceiving waving palm trees, skittering dragonflies, and smiling people. This question has also motivated researchers for some time. This is probably a question that cannot be adequately answered as of now. Nonetheless, some progress can be made. To begin to answer this question, V1 is not the end of visual processing. Indeed, it is more the beginning. Information leaves V1 and proceeds to a number of other areas within the occipital lobe. Many of

Hypercolumn: a 1-mm block of V1 containing both the ocular dominance and orientation columns for a particular region in visual space

Blobs: groups of neurons within V1 that are sensitive to color

Interblobs: groups of neurons that are sensitive to orientation

these areas eventually project to sites in the temporal lobe or to sites in the parietal lobe. The number of such distinct regions identified in the occipital lobe grows as more research continues, but we will touch on a few of the important areas and also describe the two critical pathways that emanate from V1.

V2

After information leaves V1, it travels to other areas in the occipital cortex. These areas are collectively called the **extrastriate cortex** or **secondary visual cortex**. The visual signals that leave V1 go in many different directions. One of the major pathways is from V1 to the adjacent **V2** region (see Figure 4.16). There are three distinct regions within V2, which match directly up with the three different types of cells in V1. The blobs connect

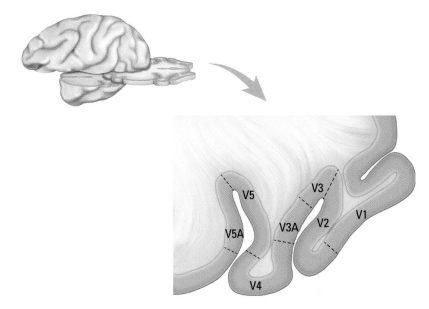

■ FIGURE 4.16 **Visual areas of rhesus macaque brain.**

This illustration shows a rhesus macaque brain. These monkeys have occipital lobes very similar to those of humans. You can see the relative locations of V2 and V1, as well as other areas of the occipital cortex.

to the thin stripes. Layer 4B connects to the thick stripes, and the interblobs connect to the interstripes (Zeki, 1993). It is possible to deduce something of how these regions of V2 respond on the basis of their inputs from V1. Thin stripes will have color responses, thick stripes will be sensitive to motion, and interstripes will be sensitive to shape and position. V2 cells also combine input from both eyes (Pasternak, Bisley, & Calkins, 2003).

Other regions, such as V3, V4 (color processing), and V5 (also known as MT, a motion detection area) receive input from only some of the cell types in V1 and V2. V1 and V2 send information in parallel to these regions. We return to these higher areas of visual processing later, after we discuss the dorsal and ventral pathways. V2, however, still seems to be involved in representing what is out there rather than making sense of it.

TEST YOUR KNOWLEDGE

What is meant by the term *extrastriate cortex*? How does it differ from the striate cortex?

FUNCTIONAL PATHWAYS IN THE VISUAL CORTEX

4.6 Compare the difference between the dorsal pathway and the ventral pathway.

We know the final goal of the visual system because most of us, except for those with extreme visual impairment, know the end result: fluent perception of the visual world around us. Because we mostly take the act of seeing for granted, we seldom consider how complex visual perception is. We have seen

Extrastriate cortex (secondary visual cortex): the collective term for visual areas in the occipital lobe other than V1

V2: the second area in the visual cortex that receives input; often considered the area that starts with visual associations rather than processing the input (sometimes called the prestriate cortex)

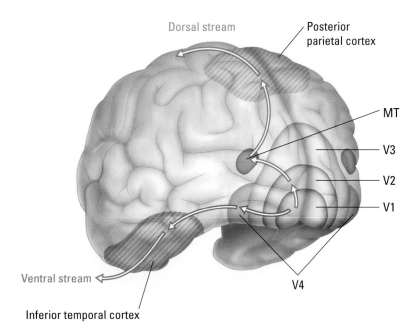

■ FIGURE 4.17   The ventral and dorsal pathways in the brain.

This illustration shows the important visual areas of the occipital lobe and the flow of information in both the ventral and dorsal pathways. The ventral pathway flows through V2 and eventually into the temporal lobe and is concerned with object identification, as well as color perception. The dorsal pathway flows through V2 to area MT and then to the parietal lobe. It is concerned with where objects are in visual space as well as motion.

Ventral pathway: starts with midget and bistratified retinal ganglion cells and continues through the visual cortex into the inferotemporal cortex in the temporal lobe; often called the "what" pathway, as it codes for object identification as well as color vision

Dorsal pathway: starts with parasol retinal ganglion cells and continues through the visual cortex into the parietal lobe; often called the "where" pathway, as it codes for the locations of objects and their movement

the complexity of the eye and the intricacy of visual processing in V1. We next consider two essentially parallel pathways that have been discovered within the visual system. We have begun to discuss these pathways, as we have already introduced the terms *P pathway* (and *K pathway*) and *M pathway* as they relate to the retinal ganglion cells. However, in V1, these pathways show very distinct organization, and even more so, as these pathways leave V1 toward other regions of the cortex. The P pathway has been described as the "what" or **ventral pathway** and the M pathway as the "where" or **dorsal pathway** (DeYoe & Van Essen, 1988; Mishkin, Ungerleider, & Macko, 1983). You can see the anatomy of this system in Figure 4.17. Let us take a closer look at each of these systems.

The most straightforward way of learning these pathways is to examine Figure 4.18. This figure shows the flow of information from the retinal ganglion cells through the LGN and occipital lobe and into other areas of the brain, including the temporal and parietal lobes. What is striking about these pathways is that (a) very early in the visual system, information is being sorted and channeled into different directions, and (b) these pathways are both anatomically distinct and functionally separate. The ventral pathway starts with bistratified and midget retinal ganglion cells. These retinal ganglion cells connect with the koniocellular and parvocellular layers of the LGN, respectively, which in turn project to V1 Layers 2 and 3 and Layer 4cβ, respectively. From V1, the signal is sent to other visual areas in the occipital cortex, which we discuss shortly, and then to an area in the temporal lobe known as the inferotemporal cortex. This area is known from a great deal of research to be involved in object recognition. Hence, the ventral system is often called the "what" system. The dorsal system starts with the parasol retinal ganglion cells, which project to the magnocellular cells in the LGN. From there, the pathway leads to Layer 4cα in V1. The pathway then projects to V2 and from there to such areas as MT, ending up in the parietal cortex. This pathway codes for place and movement, hence its nickname, the "where" system. Ultimately, what remains unclear is where in the brain the systems rejoin so that we see a unified perception of the world.

We consider an experiment that was done to establish the reality of the dorsal and ventral pathways. Keep in mind that all the knowledge we have been presenting is the result of careful experimentation, like the study we are about to describe. In this study, Mishkin et al. (1983) trained rhesus monkeys (*Macaca mulatta*) to do two different tasks. One task was called a landmark task, which required the monkeys to remember the location of an event, and the other task was called an object task, which required the monkeys to learn a particular object. In the study, monkeys saw two containers, one of which contained food. In the landmark task, the monkey was required to select the container that was closer to a specific landmark in the room. In the object task, the monkey was required

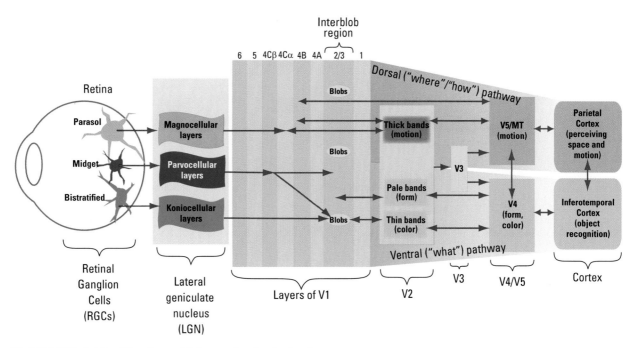

Interblob
region

6   5   4Cβ 4Cα 4B 4A   2/3   1

Dorsal ("where"/"how") pathway

Retina

Parasol

Magnocellular
layers

Blobs

Thick bands
(motion)

V5/MT
(motion)

Parietal
Cortex
(perceiving
space and
motion)

Midget

Parvocellular
layers

Blobs

V3

Bistratified

Koniocellular
layers

Blobs

Pale bands
(form)

Thin bands
(color)

V4
(form,
color)

Inferotemporal
Cortex
(object
recognition)

Ventral ("what") pathway

Retinal
Ganglion
Cells
(RGCs)

Lateral
geniculate
nucleus
(LGN)

Layers of V1   V2   V3   V4/V5   Cortex

■ FIGURE 4.18   The flow of information in the brain.

This figure illustrates the flow of information schematically from retinal ganglion cells to higher areas in the cortex of the human brain. Note that the ventral and dorsal pathways are defined very early, starting in the retinal ganglion cells. Thus, from early in visual processing, the "what" and the "where" pathways are distinct.

to select the container that was covered by a particular object. Rhesus monkeys learn these tasks quickly and then seldom make errors. Note that for each task, the monkey is expected to do something that emphasizes a different system. In the landmark task, the monkey is focusing on where an object is (the dorsal stream), whereas in the object task, the monkey must remember what the object is (the ventral stream).

Mishkin et al. (1983) then created damaged areas in parts of the monkeys' brains (see Figure 4.19), a process known as lesioning. In some monkeys, they lesioned the inferotemporal cortex, an important area in the dorsal or "what" pathway. In other monkeys, they lesioned the parietal lobe, part of the ventral or "where" pathway. After recovering from surgery, the monkeys were again presented with the landmark task and the object task. The monkeys with damage to the inferotemporal cortex showed normal performance on the landmark task but were impaired on the object task, consistent with the contention that the inferotemporal cortex is involved in establishing the "what" of an object. In contrast, the monkeys with parietal lobe lesions showed normal performance on the object task but were impaired on the landmark task, consistent with the contention that the parietal lobe is involved in establishing where an object is. Thus, damaging the inferotemporal cortex interferes with visual object recognition, but damaging the parietal lobe interferes with seeing the spatial relation of objects.

Although it is unethical to do such an experiment with human beings (and many would argue the above experiment was unethical as well), accidents have resulted in damage that approximates what Mishkin et al. (1983) did to the monkeys. In one case, a patient known as D.F. suffered carbon monoxide poisoning, which damaged her ventral pathway (Goodale, Milner, Jakobsen, & Carey, 1991). As a consequence of the brain damage, D.F. showed severe deficits in her ability

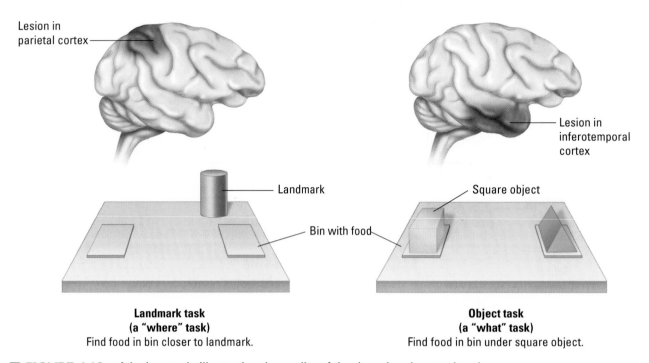

Landmark task
(a "where" task)
Find food in bin closer to landmark.

Object task
(a "what" task)
Find food in bin under square object.

■ FIGURE 4.19   A lesion study illustrating the reality of the dorsal and ventral pathways.

Monkeys learned one of two tasks, a landmark task and an object task. Lesions to the parietal lobe interfered with the landmark task, and lesions to the inferotemporal lobe interfered with the object task. This study provides support for the view that the dorsal and ventral streams are separate.

to perceive and therefore name objects (a condition known as **object agnosia**). Despite her inability to perceive objects, which is a function of her ventral system, she was able to grasp and manipulate them, presumably because of her intact dorsal system. For example, when asked to estimate the length of an object, her accuracy was severely impaired relative to a normal person. However, when asked to lift the object, her hands adjusted appropriately to the size of the object.

The Ventral Pathway

The ventral pathway starts with midget and bistratified retinal ganglion cells and continues through the visual cortex into the inferotemporal cortex in the temporal lobe. The ventral pathway is often called the "what" pathway, as it codes for object identification as well as color vision. After being processed in Layers 2, 3, and 4cβ of V1, information is sent to V2 and from there to areas such as V3 and V4 in the extrastriate cortex. V4 then sends information to the inferotemporal cortex. V4 has some interesting properties. V4 neurons are sensitive to **binocular disparity**, helpful in recognizing three-dimensional objects in space. Thus, V4 is seen as primarily involved in shape recognition (Pasupathy & Connor, 2002). However, V4 also seems critical in color vision as well. Patients with damage to V4 have disorders of color vision (Zeki, 1993). We return to V4 and disorders of color vision in Chapter 6.

From V4, information flows out the occipital lobe and into the temporal lobe to an area of the cortex known as the inferotemporal cortex. The **inferotemporal cortex** is the region in the temporal lobe that receives input from the ventral visual pathway. One of its major functions is object identification. Early studies of

Object agnosia: an acquired deficit in identifying and recognizing objects even though vision remains intact

Binocular disparity: the binocular depth cue that arises from the fact that the images of most objects that are in the visual scene do not fall on the same location of the retinae of the two eyes; disparity is actually the measure of this difference in the position of the images on the two retinae

Inferotemporal cortex: the region in the temporal lobe that receives input from the ventral visual pathway; one of its functions is object identification

the inferotemporal cortex showed that its neurons are sensitive to highly specific kinds of shapes (Bruce, Desimone, & Gross, 1981). Although some neurons in the inferotemporal cortex are sensitive to basic visual features such as size, shape, color, and orientation, the studies that attracted interest found neurons with specific responses to such complex features as hands, paws, and faces. Indeed, research has now demonstrated a region within the inferotemporal cortex called the fusiform face area (FFA). The FFA seems to be a region specifically dedicated to recognizing familiar faces (Kanwisher & Yovel, 2006). Single-cell recording studies with monkeys show that neurons in the FFA are maximally responsive to the faces of other same-species monkeys. Neuropsychological studies with brain-damaged patients show that patients with damage to the FFA have deficits in identifying familiar faces (Schwartz, 2014; Susilo & Duchaine, 2013). We return to the topic of face recognition in Chapter 5. Other areas of the inferotemporal cortex appear to be sensitive to other kinds of object recognition. Indeed, one study showed that a particular area of the inferotemporal cortex is sensitive to the perception of individual persons. Cells in this area become active when particular individuals are presented—either pictures of them or the spelling of their names (Quiroga, Reddy, Kreiman, Koch, & Fried, 2005). Thus, the ventral or "what" pathway is the neural pathway that allows us to perceive and recognize the objects in our environment, regardless of whether they are the faces of our family members or the books, cups, kettles, smart phones, and eyeglasses that populate our visual world.

The Dorsal Pathway

The dorsal pathway starts with parasol retinal ganglion cells and continues through the visual cortex into the parietal lobe. The dorsal pathway is often called the "where" pathway, as it codes for the locations of objects and their movement. After information leaves V2 in the dorsal pathway, it is sent to an area in the occipital lobe known as **MT** (for middle temporal, its location in the occipital lobe). MT is also known as **V5**. MT is also connected to noncortical visual movement areas, such as the superior colliculus (Born & Bradley, 2005). Single-cell studies with monkeys show that neurons within MT are sensitive to the direction and speed of motion (Albright, 1984). These data have been confirmed in human studies using functional magnetic resonance imaging (fMRI) (Born & Bradley, 2005). Transcranial magnetic stimulation studies, which render an area of the brain temporarily disrupted, have also been used to probe human MT function. These studies show that interfering with MT functioning results in a disruption of motion perception (Schenk, Ellison, Rice, & Milner, 2005). Finally, patients with damage to MT have difficulties perceiving motion. We return to these issues in Chapter 8.

After the signal leaves MT, it is sent across the occipitoparietal junction into the parietal lobe. There are a variety of specific regions in the parietal lobe that are part of the dorsal pathway. These include the anterior intraparietal, the lateral intraparietal, and the medial intraparietal areas. These areas are involved in the visual guidance of action. Research in both humans and monkeys suggests that these areas are involved in the visual guidance of reaching and of grasping at objects (Culham, Cavina-Pratesi, & Singhal, 2006). We return to these topics in Chapter 8.

TEST YOUR KNOWLEDGE

What are the functions of the dorsal and ventral pathways?

MT (V5): an area of the occipital lobe in the dorsal pathway, specific to motion detection and perception

WHERE DOES VISION COME TOGETHER?

4.7 Discuss the current problem in determining where the dorsal and ventral pathways reunite to form a common perception.

So, we know that object perception comes through the ventral pathway and that movement and object location come through the dorsal pathway. But what we perceptually experience are moving objects—a unified world. Thus, as a result of our discussions of brain regions and visual pathways, you might be wondering where all of vision comes together, that is, what region of the brain is responsible for giving us a unified and common perception of the world. After all, when we look at the world, we see talking people, running cats, and airplanes moving across the sky, rather than the objects and their movement separately, as might be inferred from our discussion of pathways. One can simplify the question: Where in the brain do these pathways come together to give us this common perception? At present, such a region has not been found, and many researchers think it does not exist. In fact, nowhere in the brain has a single location been found where all visual information converges (Dennett, 1991; Zeki, 1993). Remember, V1 and V2 are the last areas to have all of the visual information, and that is only for the central visual pathway (Zeki, 1993). It now appears that vision happens with simultaneous or approximately simultaneous activation across all visual areas. Perhaps important to this neurologically are the feedback loops that exist in the brain. At every level, there is return feedback to earlier levels in the pathways from higher levels in the pathways. Forward and backward connections are thought to play a role in synchronizing a response in the brain, so that our perceptual experiences are of whole objects and not fragmented parts. Thus, our experience of vision is distributed at least across the areas of the visual cortex. So one answer to why we experience the world as a unified whole is that the constant feedback loops from higher to lower levels integrate our perceptions.

TEST YOUR KNOWLEDGE

In your view, will the search for an area of the brain that unifies visual processes into a common perception be successful? Why or why not?

DEVELOPMENT OF THE VISUAL SYSTEM

4.8 Describe the concept of "nature versus nurture" as it applies to the visual system.

We have seen that the brain organization involved in vision is complex, highly structured, and supremely well adapted. However, regardless of whether we have been discussing the visual systems of cats, monkeys, or people, we have so far been considering mature individuals. An important question pertains to how our visual systems mature and develop. In this section, we take up the issue of development. Often critical in discussions of development is whether a particular ability requires practice and experience or whether it will develop innately, regardless of experience. In other words, is the organization of our visual system hardwired? That is, is it set specifically by our DNA, does it follow a set course of development, and is this unchangeable? Or are environmental inputs necessary for the visual system to develop normally? If so, how flexible is our visual system, depending on that environmental change? As we will see shortly, there is much flexibility in the development of the visual system. Certain patterns appear to be fixed, but much can be altered by the organism's early environment.

Is it nature (our genetics) or nurture (our experiences) that is more important in how our sensory systems operate? Texts usually present the two extreme positions and contrast them. At one extreme, there is the genetic position, that all that is needed for our sensory systems, or whatever biological or psychological factor is being discussed, is coded in our genes. Sensory operation is thus essentially "preordained." On the other side is the tabula rasa position, that we are blank slates at birth, and experience writes on these slates to determine who we are going to be. The fact is, however, that genes and the environment interact in incredibly complex ways to allow development to occur, and pretty much all scientists agree that this interaction is inevitable and complex. Indeed, it may not be possible in many cases to specify what is innate and what is learned when it comes to something as complex as the mammalian visual system. Certainly the interaction position fits all the data and studies we discuss here.

One landmark research study on the development of the visual brain comes from work by Held and Hein (Held, 1965, 1980; Held & Hein, 1963). These studies, which some of you may find distasteful, concerned the development of the visual system in young cats. The researchers carefully showed how important environmental input is to the development of the visual brain. Held and Hein raised kittens in complete darkness for a few weeks. After the initial period of darkness, the kittens were divided into two groups. Both groups were still kept in darkness most of the day, but now spent an hour a day on a "kitten carousel" (see Figure 4.20). The kittens in one group were free to move themselves. As they moved, the visual environment moved around them. Thus, they could correlate their movement with the movement around them. The second group of kittens

■ FIGURE 4.20   **The kitten carousel experiment.**

The illustration shows two kittens, both reared in an all-dark environment, seeing vertical stripes in the experimental setup. The kitten on the left is active in its exploration, whereas the kitten on the right is yoked to the first. Because of its lack of active experience, the yoked kitten shows slowed visual development (Held & Hein, 1963).

were kept in little baskets and were moved by the movements of the other kittens. Thus, their movement was passive—tied not to their own motor systems but to those of the other kittens.

Later, the kittens were tested on a variety of visual tasks. In all cases, the active kittens performed better than the passive kittens, despite their identical visual experience. For instance, in a test of visually guided paw placement, the active kittens were better able to extend a paw to touch a point on a flat surface than were the passive kittens. In another test, the active kittens were more likely to avoid a "visual cliff," that is, an illusion that a sharp drop-off is present where they are walking. In yet another test, the active kittens were better at the visual pursuit of a moving object, which is important for carnivorous cats, which must chase fast-moving prey. Indeed, the active kittens showed no differences from cats raised normally with full visual experience. It was only the control-deprived passive kittens that did poorly on the visual tests. These results suggest that there is flexibility in the development of the visual system, that early visual-motor experience can later influence perceptual abilities (Held & Hein, 1963).

At the same time that Held and Hein were doing pioneering work with the kitten carousel, Hubel and Wiesel were also examining developmental issues in the visual brain (Wiesel & Hubel, 1965). Like Held and Hein, they also focused on deprivation studies, that is, studies in which young organisms (usually cats) were deprived of visual experience of one form or another. In Hubel and Wiesel's research, the goal was to examine the receptive fields of individual neurons rather than the cats' behavior in general. They found, consistent with the "nature" view of the brain, that some organization already existed at birth in the cats' visual system. Even with no visual experience, there was some organizational structure in the cats' visual cortices (Daw, 2009; Hubel & Wiesel, 2005).

Wiesel and Hubel (1963) also showed that there is degeneration in the cortex if an organism is denied visual experience. For example, in one study, kittens were deprived of visual experience in one eye (monocular deprivation). The other eye allowed the kittens to interact normally with their environment. Later, Wiesel and Hubel looked at the receptive fields of neurons in the kittens' V1s. They found clear evidence that monocular deprivation resulted in a reduction in the number of cells that responded to the deprived eye and fewer cells that responded to both eyes. However, such changes occurred only if the kittens were deprived of visual experience during the first 3 months of life. Visual deprivation after 3 months had no effect on neural organization. Thus, Wiesel and Hubel's studies suggest that both innate organization and environmental inputs are important to the developing visual system (Daw, 2009).

Conducting such a deprivation experiment with human infants would be highly unethical. So experiments cannot be applied to young human visual systems. But correlational research can be done, examining changes in the visual cortex as infants begin to mature. In one such study, Huttenlocher and de Courten (1987) found that during early infancy (2 to 4 months), there is rapid growth of synapses within V1 of the cortex. This is followed by a loss of synapses later in childhood (8 to 11 years). This suggests that early visual experience is necessary for establishing the parameters of vision, but unnecessary connections will later be pared down. Thus, it is likely that human visual development follows a similar trajectory in terms of some innate patterns elaborated on by experience.

TEST YOUR KNOWLEDGE

Describe the "kitten carousel" experiment. What does it tell us about visual development?

IN DEPTH: *Blindsight*

4.9   Explain the concept of blindsight.

Patient T.N. is a doctor, born in Burundi, Africa, but living in Switzerland. Before his strokes, he was a doctor for the World Health Organization. In 2003, while in his mid-50s, T.N. had two serious and successive strokes over a period of 5 weeks, each stroke causing lesions on one side of his visual cortex. The first stroke affected his left visual cortex, and the second stroke, 5 weeks later, destroyed his right visual cortex (de Gelder, 2010). Subsequent anatomical testing showed that T.N.'s entire primary visual cortex (V1) was compromised (de Gelder et al., 2008). As a consequence of these strokes, T.N. is now completely blind. He reports no visual experience, though his overall intelligence and verbal abilities remain completely intact. Not relying solely on these subjective reports, de Gelder and her team ran a series of routine tests of vision. The tests turned up nothing—T.N. showed no evidence of seeing in these standard tests. Moreover, MRI revealed extensive structural damage to V1, and functional MRI revealed no activity in this region of the brain when T.N. was shown visual stimuli (de Gelder et al., 2008). However, because the strokes affected his visual cortex, his eyes themselves were undamaged.

What makes T.N.'s case fascinating is that despite his complete perceptual blindness, he still makes visual responses. Indeed, in 2008, de Gelder et al. staged a stunning demonstration of this. T.N. was told that a cluttered corridor was empty and that he would not need his cane to walk down the corridor. Reluctantly, T.N. agreed. As he walked down the corridor, he was followed by another person (a prominent researcher in this area) to ensure that he would not stumble. When you watch the video, you can see that despite his total blindness, T.N. avoided the obstacles placed in front of him. He sidesteps a box and avoids a tripod. After completing the trip down the hallway, T.N. does not know what he has avoided or whether there was anything in his way at all. In other words, he made visually guided movements in the absence of conscious sight. This is a phenomenon known as blindsight. **Blindsight** is the presence of visual abilities in the absence of the visual cortex. The patient claims to be blind but makes visual responses.

To see T.N. walking down the corridor, you can watch a video at the *Scientific American* Web site (http://www.youtube.com/watch?v=ACkxe_5Ubq8, see also ISLE 5.4).

The researcher who followed him down the hallway reported that T.N. did not make vocalizations for which he might listen for slight echoes, the way a bat or dolphin uses echolocation. However, they had no sound-monitoring equipment, so this could not be completely ruled out. Amazingly, in your textbook authors' opinion, the researchers

failed to do a simple control—to have T.N. negotiate an obstacle course with a blindfold on. If blindsight were the explanation for his avoiding the obstacles, then cutting off input to the retinae would render him unable to negotiate the course. Indeed, they did only one trial with T.N., and they did not perform appropriate control investigations. Nonetheless, this demonstration is now a well-cited example of the abilities of blindsight patients (de Gelder, 2010). Luckily, other research has been done both on T.N. and on other patients with similar conditions that have used the necessary experimental controls.

T.N.'s case is unique in that his entire V1 was compromised (see Figure 4.21). In other cases of blindsight, the patient has damage in some areas of V1 but not all. The result is a **scotoma**, an area of partial or completely destroyed cells, resulting in a blind spot in a particular region of the visual field. In these patients, vision may be normal in most regions of the visual field, allowing them to see normally under most circumstances. However, when a patient keeps his or her eyes still, there will be a blind spot (the scotoma) where the patient cannot see or cannot see normally. In a number of patients tested, blindsight may exist within the scotoma region (Weiskrantz, 1996). Such patients have been yielding an understanding and exploration of blindsight for many years, but T.N.'s case is unique in that the scotoma consists of his entire visual field.

The first studies of blindsight go back to the 1970s. At the time, Lawrence Weiskrantz, an English neurophysiologist, was examining the visual responses of monkeys with lesioned V1s. He found that monkeys were still able to make visually guided responses even without this region. He then focused his research on the superior colliculus, the part of the brain described earlier that guides eye movements. Weiskrantz reasoned that intact colliculi allowed the monkeys to respond to visual stimuli in the absence of V1 (see Weiskrantz, 1996). Indeed, despite their missing V1 regions, these monkeys appeared to be behaving normally and responding appropriately to visual stimuli. However, he knew from neuropsychological research that humans with damaged V1 regions had visual problems known as scotomas, that is, areas in the visual field in which they could not see. The blind field in the visual world corresponds to

ISLE 5.4. Video of Navigation in Blindsight

Blindsight: the presence of visual abilities in the absence of the visual cortex; the patient claims to be blind but makes visual responses

Scotoma: an area of partially or completely destroyed cells, resulting in a blind spot in a particular region of the visual field

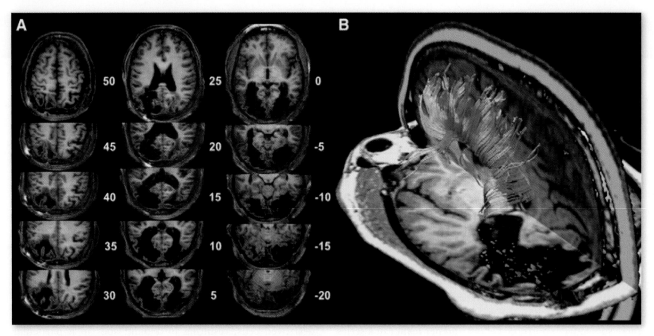

■ FIGURE 4.21   Damage to blindsight patient's brain.

An MRI study of patient T.N.'s brain, showing the bilateral destruction of the V1 region of his brain. This damage means that his V1 does not process visual information. As such, T.N. is blind. However, other areas of the brain, such as the superior colliculus, allow him to make visual responses.

the damaged area in V1, which is responsible for that region in space.

Then Weiskrantz discovered patient D.B., and the two began a long collaborative investigation of D.B.'s blindsight (Weiskrantz, Warrington, Sanders, & Marshall, 1974). D.B. was a 34-year-old British man, working as a computer programmer. He was married with young children. He was also an amateur musician and an amateur rugby player. He started developing headaches, and his doctor sent him to a neurologist. The neurologist discovered a large tumor located in the primary visual cortex of his right hemisphere. To ensure his long-term health, much of D.B.'s right V1 was removed surgically along with the tumor, leaving him with a large left-field scotoma. Nonetheless, his vision was still fine in his right visual field, and D.B. was able to return to his normal life. However, he agreed to continue having his scotoma investigated by Weiskrantz and his colleagues (Weiskrantz, 1986). Note that D.B., unlike T.N., still has much of his V1 intact, meaning that he can still see much of the world. His left V1, responsible for his right visual field, was just fine. He could see normally in this region. His scotoma (blind spot), however, extended through much of his left visual field.

When shown objects in his intact right visual field, D.B. was able to identify and describe them as sighted person would. However, when objects were presented in the scotoma in his left visual field, D.B. reported not being able to see them, nor could he identify them. To D.B., he simply could not see in this field, and like T.N., D.B. was subjectively

blind in the scotoma region. To test for blindsight, Weiskrantz used a forced-choice procedure in which D.B. had to guess at what he saw. In this procedure, D.B. might feel as if he had not seen anything, but he had to make a response anyway. In one study, Weiskrantz presented either a square shape or a diamond shape, and D.B. had to guess at which was presented. Even though the image was presented to his scotoma and the only difference between the two images was orientation, D.B. guessed at the correct shape at a rate significantly higher than chance. In another study, D.B. could discriminate between X's and O's at above-chance rates. In yet another study, D.B. had to determine whether an image in his scotoma was stationary or moving. Again, D.B. reported no conscious seeing of the movement, but his guesses were significantly greater than chance (Weiskrantz, 1986). Since then, this phenomenon has been observed in many patients and continues with D.B. today as well (Tamietto et al., 2010).

Having established that patients with blindsight (a) are truly without visual experience in their scotoma fields, and (b) are able to make visual responses, the term *blindsight* may seem slightly less paradoxical. Starting with Weiskrantz et al. (1974), the predominant view is that blindsight is mediated by mechanisms in the superior colliculus that continue to get input from the retina even when the pathways to the visual cortex have been damaged. Here is the basis of Weiskrantz's view.

Patients such as T.N. and D.B. have extensive damage to the visual cortex, which creates the experience of blindness.

However, their retinae continue to project axons, which reach the superior colliculus and other noncortical areas of the brain. In people without brain damage, the superior colliculus is an area of the brain involved in the rapid movement of the eyes and the head toward the source of an incoming visual stimulus. These mechanisms appear to be intact in patients with blindsight, as they may move their heads toward incoming stimuli even though they cannot see the stimuli. Consider T.N.—he cannot see the obstacles placed in front of him, but as he moves toward them, he slowly but surely avoids them. His actions are consistent with the explanation that blindsight is caused by spared noncortical routes from the retina to the brain.

Given that there are several routes from the retinae to noncortical areas of the brain, one might expect to find other kinds of blindsight in addition to object avoidance and forced-choice discrimination. Indeed, research with T.N. demonstrates a form of emotional blindsight (Pegna, Khateb, Lazeyras, & Seghier, 2005). When presented with images of fearful faces, T.N. made cringing expressions himself and showed activity in his amygdala (an area of the brain associated with emotion), even though he could not report what the stimuli were that he was seeing. Remember that T.N. shows no activity in his V1 during these studies. Thus, it is likely that the responses are mediated by the superior colliculus route. Interestingly, some research now demonstrates that the superior colliculus projects to higher order areas in the visual cortex (Ptito & Leh, 2007). This may account for T.N.'s emotional responses.

Over the years, blindsight has drawn significant interest from philosophers. For them, the intriguing phenomenon is that someone is blind but is making responses to visual stimuli. This seeming paradox is resolved when we think of conscious seeing as being a function of V1 in the cortex. When V1 is damaged, we lose conscious vision. However, intact retinae continue to project to noncortical areas, which allow us to respond to visual stimuli, despite the lack of visual seeing.

CHAPTER SUMMARY

4.1 Describe the anatomy of the optic chiasm and how that affects the lateralization of vision in the brain.

When information from the optic nerve enters the optic chiasm, information crosses over, so that the axons from the ganglion cells from the right half of the right retina and the ganglion cells from the right half of the left retina combine, forming the right optic tract, which then proceeds to the right hemisphere of the brain (and similarly for the other half of the system).

4.2 Describe the anatomy of the lateral geniculate nucleus and the role of this area in visual processing.

The optic nerve projects to the LGN (lateral geniculate nucleus). The LGN is a six-layered structure in the thalamus that serves as a relay point for the transmission of visual information, although processing of information also occurs in the LGN. Each of the three types of retinal ganglion cells (parasol, midget, and bistratified) projects to a particular layer of the LGN. The parasol retinal ganglion cells project to the magnocellular layer of the LGN (forming the M pathway). The midget retinal ganglion cells project to the parvocellular layer of the LGN (forming the P pathway), and the bistratified retinal ganglion cells project to the koniocellular layer of the LGN (forming the K pathway).

4.3 Explain the role of the superior colliculus in visual processing.

The superior colliculus can be found at the top of the brainstem, just beneath the thalamus. Its main function is the control of rapid eye movements.

4.4 Explain the nature of the retinotopic organization of V1.

After leaving the LGN, the next synapse in the visual pathway is in the primary visual cortex in the occipital lobe of the brain. The primary visual cortex is also known as V1 (and Area 17). The cerebral cortex is the outer surface of the brain. It consists of four lobes; the frontal, the temporal, the parietal, and the occipital. The occipital lobe is the visual brain. V1 is in the occipital lobe right toward the back of the head. It is a six-layered structure with different layers receiving input from different regions of the LGN. V1 is organized in retinotopic coordinates, which also refer to the spatial organization of the external world. One of the features in V1 is cortical magnification. Cortical magnification means that there is more space in the cortex devoted to some sensory receptors than to others. In this case, the fovea has a larger cortical area than the periphery.

The Nobel prize–winning scientists Hubel and Wiesel discovered both simple cells and complex cells in V1, which are sensitive to different properties of the visual stimulus. Simple Cells are V1 neurons that respond to stimuli with particular orientations to objects within their receptive field. The preferred orientation of a simple cell is the stimulus orientation that produces the strongest response from the simple cell. Complex cells are also neurons in V1 that respond optimally to a stimulus with a particular orientation. But, unlike simple cells, they respond to a variety of stimuli across different locations. In particular, they also respond best to moving stimuli. End-stopped neurons respond to stimuli that end within the cell's receptive field. V1 is organized into columns, which are sensitive to orientation and ocular dominance. A hypercolumn is a 1-mm block of V1 containing both the ocular dominance and orientation columns for a particular region in visual space. Hypercolumns also include information about where in space those columns are. Blobs are groups of neurons within V1 that are sensitive to color whereas interblobs are the groups of neurons that are sensitive to orientation. The M pathway, K pathway, and P pathway all enter the cortex through V1.

4.5 Explore the anatomy of the V2 area of the visual cortex.

There are three distinct regions within V2, which match directly up with the three different types of cells in V1. Thin stripes have color responses, thick stripes will be sensitive to motion, and interstripes will be sensitive to shape and position.

4.6 Compare the difference between the dorsal pathway and the ventral pathway.

Starting with V1, we can see two distinct pathways, the dorsal and ventral pathways. The dorsal pathway is responsible for information about movement and continues through MT in the occipital lobe and then into the parietal lobe. The ventral pathway is responsible for object and color recognition. It goes through areas such as V2 and V4 before heading into the inferotemporal cortex in the temporal lobe.

4.7 Discuss the current problem in determining where the dorsal and ventral pathways reunite to form a common perception.

Nowhere in the brain has it been found where all of the visual information converges to a single location. It now appears that vision happens with the simultaneous or approximately simultaneous activation across all of the visual areas. Forward and backward connections are thought to play a role in synchronizing a response in the brain, so that our perceptual experiences are of whole objects and not fragmented parts.

4.8 Describe the concept of "nature versus nurture" as it applies to the visual system.

Research shows that some aspects of visual organization are present at birth whereas others require experience to develop. Studies with kittens demonstrate the necessity of early visual experience for visual systems to develop normally.

4.9 Explain the concept of blindsight.

In the "in depth" section, we discussed blindsight, the neuropsychological condition in which damage to V1 causes a blind spot or scotoma. However, because of noncortical areas such as the superior colliculus, the patient can still make visual responses, in the absence of conscious seeing.

REVIEW QUESTIONS

1. What is the optic chiasm? Describe how retinal ganglion cells cross over in the optic chiasm. How does this crossing over affect the representation of the visual world in the LGN?

2. What are the three types of layers in the LGN? What kind of retinal ganglion cell innervates each? What is the functional significance of each layer?

3. What is the function of the superior colliculus? Where in the brain is it found?

4. What is meant by the term *cortical magnification*? How does it explain the retinotopic organization of V1 of the visual cortex?

5. Describe the receptive fields of simple and complex cells in V1. What is the function of each type of cell?

6. What are ocular dominance columns? How were they discovered by Hubel and Wiesel? What role do they play in the hypercolumns of V1?

7. What are V2 and V3? Where are they found in the brain, and what is their functional role in vision?

8. What is the dorsal pathway? What is the ventral pathway? What is the functional significance of each pathway?

9. What does *visual deprivation* mean? How has it been used to study the development of V1 neurons?

10. What is blindsight? Describe its expression in neuropsychological patients. What is the likely anatomical cause of blindsight?

KEY TERMS

Binocular disparity, 100

Bistratified retinal ganglion cells (K cells), 84

Blindsight, 105

Blobs, 96

Complex cells, 94

Contralateral organization, 83

Contralateral representation of visual space, 83

Cortical magnification, 91

Dorsal pathway, 98

End-stopped neurons, 94

Extrastriate cortex (secondary visual cortex), 97

Hypercolumn, 96

Inferotemporal cortex, 100

Interblobs, 96

Ipsilateral organization, 83

Koniocellular layers, 84

Koniocellular pathway (K pathway), 85

Lateral geniculate nucleus, 84

Magnocellular layers, 84

Magnocellular pathway (M pathway), 86

Midget retinal ganglion cells (P cells), 84

MT (V5), 101

Object agnosia, 100

Ocular dominance column, 95

Optic chiasm, 82

Optic tract, 82

Orientation column, 95

Orienting tuning curve, 93

Parasol retinal ganglion cells (M cells), 84

Parvocellular layers, 84

Parvocellular pathway (P pathway), 85

Primary visual cortex (V1), 89

Retinotopic map, 91

Saccades, 88

Scotoma, 105

Simple cells, 93

Smooth pursuit, 88

Superior colliculus, 88

Ventral pathway, 98

V2, 97

INTERACTIVE SENSATION LABORATORY EXERCISES (ISLE)

Experience chapter concepts at edge.sagepub.com/schwartz

ISLE 4.1 From Eye to LGN, 82

ISLE 4.2 Simple Cells, 93

ISLE 4.3 Complex Cells, 94

ISLE 4.4 Hypercolumns, 96

ISLE 4.5. Video of Navigation in Blindsight, 105

Sharpen your skills with SAGE edge at edge.sagepub.com/schwartz

SAGE edge for students provides a personalized approach to help you accomplish your coursework goals in an easy-to-use learning environment.

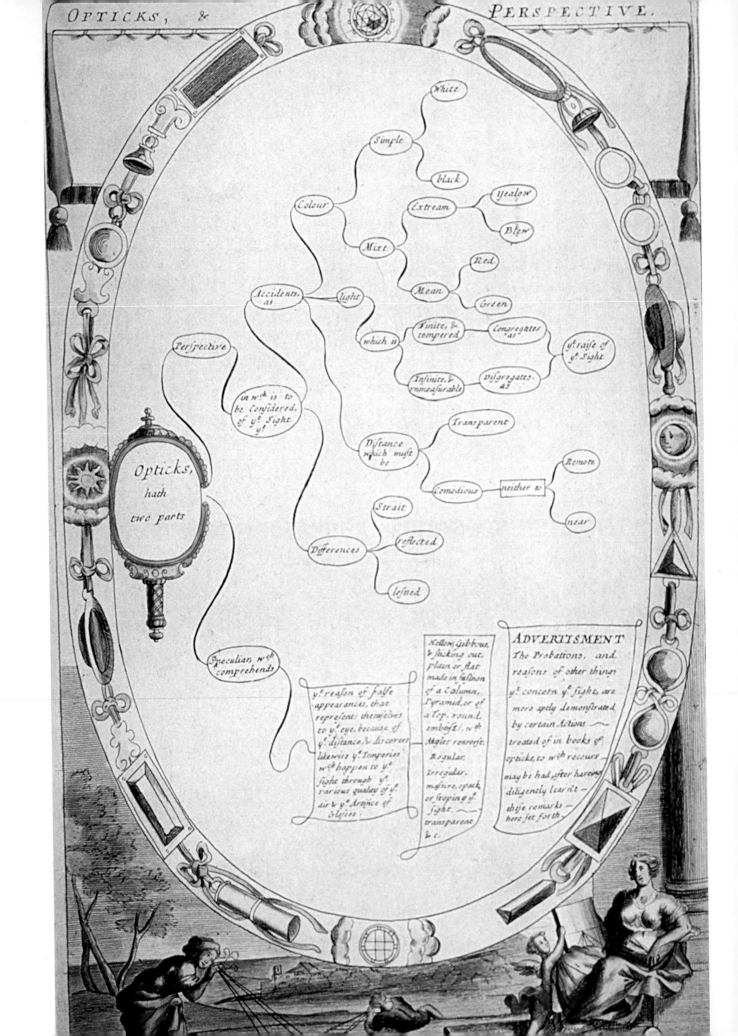

OPTICKS,   PERSPECTIVE.

Opticks, hath two parts

Colour
Simple — White, black
Mixt — Extream — Yealow, Blew
Mean — Red, Green

Accidents, as
light — which is — Finite, & tempered — Congregates as — yᵗ raise of yᵉ Sight
Infinite, & vnmeasurable — Disgregates, as

Perspective
in wᶜʰ is to be Considered, of yᵉ Sight, yᵗ

Distance which must be — Transparent
Comodious — neither to — Remote, near

Differences — Strait, reflected, lesned

Speculian, wᶜʰ comprehends

yᵗ reason of false appearances, that represent themselves to yᵉ eye, because of yᵉ distance, & discovers likewise yᵉ Imperies wᶜʰ happen to yᵉ sight through yᵉ various quality of yᵉ air & yᵉ Artifice of Glasses

Hollow, Gibbous, & sticking out. plain or flat made in fashion of a Column, Pyramid, or of a Top, round, embosst, wᵗʰ Angles renveryt. Regular, Irregular, mastive, opack, or scoping yᵉ sight, transparent &c.

ADVERTISMENT
The Probations, and reasons of other things yᵗ concern yᵉ sight, are more aptly demonstrated by certain Actions treated of in books of opticks, to wᵗʰ recours may be had, after having diligently learnt these remarks here set forth.

Object Perception

5

INTRODUCTION

Dr. P was a professor of music at a college in New York City (Sacks, 1985). His wife and his colleagues were concerned that he was having problems seeing, though not the ordinary problems, like presbyopia, that eyeglasses correct. Dr. P failed to recognize both long-time colleagues and new students. Only when his acquaintances spoke did he know who they were. In the street, he might stop to talk to a fire hydrant and be surprised when it did not reply. Finally, his wife had him visit Oliver Sacks, the noted neurologist and writer, and Sacks wrote of this case in his famous book *The Man Who Mistook His Wife for a Hat* (Sacks, 1985). Sacks determined that Dr. P had lost none of his intelligence or any of his musical ability. However, he had a form of agnosia we now know as **object agnosia**. Agnosias are acquired sensory deficits that occur without any loss of sensation. Dr. P could not identify simple objects, despite the fact that he could see them. For example, Dr. Sacks handed Dr. P a rose, and Dr. P responded by telling him that it was "about six inches in length, a convoluted red form with a linear green attachment" (p. 13). When given a glove to inspect, Dr. P responded by describing it as "a continuous surface, infolded on itself. It appears to have five outpouchings . . . it could be a change purse" (p. 14). In each case, Dr. P demonstrated that he saw the object and could describe it accurately, but he had lost the ability to identify it, despite what would be to us the obvious nature of each object. Whereas a normal person might not be able to describe these objects in such eloquent terms, a normal person would instantly see a rose and a glove. Although Sacks's interests lie in the philosophical interpretations of such a condition, we now know that such descriptions mark a case of object agnosia, which is likely the result of damage to the inferotemporal cortex (see Figure 4.19).

What object agnosia shows is that we have specialized areas in the brain to identify specific objects. Dr. P sees the shape of the flower, but he cannot identify it as such. His color perception is accurate, his shape perception is accurate, but he cannot put them together to see the rose, something any normal verbal person does effortlessly (see Figure 5.1). This suggests that perceptual processes we take for granted are actually quite complicated. Although it may be difficult to imagine what it is like to be agnosic, we hope to show you how complex the processes are that allow us to effortlessly visualize objects. Examine the two photographs in Figure 5.2. Both depict the same TV remote, each from a different angle. The representation of the remote is very different on the retina in each photograph. In Figure 5.2a, we are looking directly down on the remote. It is flat against the surface, and we can see only one side. In Figure 5.2b, the remote is on its side, and we are viewing straight on rather than from above. Yet most of us will have no difficulty seeing the same object. This is an example of shape constancy, the concept that an object remains the same despite changes to its retinal image. How the visual system recognizes objects despite such changes is one of the topics we explore in this chapter.

LEARNING OBJECTIVES

5.1 Explain the computational difficulties the visual system must overcome in recognizing objects as themselves under a multitude of situations and angles.

5.2 Examine the difference between top-down processing and bottom-up processing and how they affect object perception.

5.3 Describe the gestalt laws of perceptual grouping.

5.4 Define the concept of a geon.

5.5 Explain why the ventral pathway is critical for object perception.

5.6 Explain how we can distinguish human faces from doll and mannequin faces.

Object agnosia: an acquired deficit in identifying and recognizing objects even though vision remains intact

INTRODUCTION TO OBJECT PERCEPTION

■ FIGURE 5.1   Roses.

Convoluted red forms or roses? What do you see?

5.1 Explain the computational difficulties the visual system must overcome in recognizing objects as themselves under a multitude of situations and angles.

Despite Dr. P's intelligence and musical ability, he probably would not be able to function in everyday life if he did not have his wife to guide him through it. Think of trying to prepare a meal for oneself when one mistakes one's newspaper for the frying pan, and one's telephone for the spatula. It would be a real disaster and quite dangerous. Indeed, under such circumstances, it might be wiser for Dr. P to blindfold himself and rely exclusively on his other senses, rather than trust his distorted vision. Dr. Sacks never followed up on his patient, so we never learned what happened to him after their initial meeting. Nonetheless, Dr. P's dilemma illustrates an important concept for the rest of us. Being able to recognize quickly the objects in our environment is critical.

Consider the environment you are in now. Surrounding you are many objects. Most likely you have a book or laptop (or tablet device) in front of you. If you have come this far in the course, this textbook has already become a familiar if hefty companion. If you are reading it on your tablet computer, that object was already familiar to you before you started the course. Perhaps you are drinking coffee from your favorite mug. Your eyeglasses and phone rest on the table near you. You are sitting in the comfortable chair that your aunt purchased for you last year. You are surrounded by the familiar objects that you recognize instantly. However, our ability to recognize objects goes far beyond that with which we are immediately familiar. A friend comes in with a new mug, and we recognize the mug instantly as a mug, and we do not have to ask what such an object is. Another friend enters with the latest cellular phone, and we recognize it as a cell phone even if we have never seen that particular model before. In fact, we recognize individual unfamiliar examples of familiar categories all the time—a new species of tree, a paper clip shaped like a musical note, or a lava lamp. Only occasionally do we come across a genuinely unfamiliar object—one about which we have no knowledge of what it is made of, what its function is, and where it came from (see Figure 5.3). We see here how much knowledge influences our perception. When we see a genuinely unfamiliar object like this, even its size may not be clear.

However, even recognizing a familiar object is an enormously difficult computational problem (however effortless it feels to us). Consider Figure 5.4. In order to recognize the television remote in this picture (and yes, it is the same as in Figure 5.2), our visual systems must do a great deal of computation. Consider first that the top half of the remote is being illuminated by the light from a nearby window and, as a consequence, is reflecting significantly more light than the bottom half, which is in the shadow of the wall. Nonetheless, we see the remote as a continuous object.

(a)   (b)

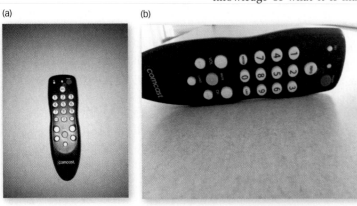

■ FIGURE 5.2   Two perspectives of the same object.

The same object looks very different from different angles and creates very different images on the retina. But those of us with normal visual perception have no difficulty deciding that these photographs depict the same object.

The pen in the glass bowl is obscuring part of the remote. Finally, the glass bowl is distorting the image of the far upper corner of the remote. But what we see is a standard TV remote, not some odd space-age object. The point here is that our visual system has to make a lot of complex inferences for us to see even an ordinary object in a familiar scene.

Our ability to detect objects must overcome three aspects of the environment: image clutter, object variety, and variable views. To overcome image clutter, we must discern the object despite the overlapping presence of nearby objects, such as coasters, other remotes, and glass bowls. Although detection of objects is normally easy, increased clutter can make it difficult, as in the *Where's Waldo?* series of children's books. In object variety, we must recognize a particular object as a member of a particular class or category despite small or large differences from our general prototype of that category. That is, the remote in Figure 5.4 is likely one that you have never seen before. However, because of its similarity to other remotes, chances are you had no difficulty assigning it to the correct category. Finally, in variable views, we must recognize an object despite its being placed in very different orientations relative to ourselves and casting different images onto our retinae. That is, we must be able to identify the same object from different vantage points (as in Figure 5.2). This is particularly important when it comes to face recognition. You want to be able to recognize your friend regardless of the angle at which you are looking at him or her. The point here is that object recognition is actually a computationally difficult task for our visual systems.

Another way of examining the idea that object recognition is a hard problem is to look at the current state of affairs in self-driving cars (see Cain Miller & Wald, 2013). Although self-driving cars have come a long way, no state allows them unless there is also a human driver sitting at the wheel. Why is it that self-driving cars are still not to be trusted? One reason is the difficulty of object recognition. The computer that responds to the video input must be able to quickly and accurately recognize many thousands of objects from any number of angles. More important than distinguishing between two views of a remote, the self-driving car must distinguish between discarded dolls, which may not require swerving, and children on the street, which must be avoided at all costs. At present, according to Cain Miller and Wald (2013), the technology is almost there, though issues of legal responsibility for accidents remain wide open. Self-driving cars, of course, have certain advantages over human drivers—they do not get tired, they do not get angry or get road rage, they do not drink alcohol, they can be programmed not to tailgate, and they do not need to text while driving. Thus, as object recognition software improves, it is likely that self-driving cars will ultimately become much safer than human driving (see Figure 5.5).

© iStockphoto.com/apomares

■ **FIGURE 5.3   A genuinely unfamiliar object.**

Can you tell what this object is? Can you judge its approximate size? What function might this object have? What is it made of? When you do not have knowledge about the object, these questions may be very tricky to answer.

■ **FIGURE 5.4   A complex scene.**

Despite the presence of odd lighting, obstructions, and a clutter of other objects, we can still recognize the remote behind the glass bowl. Our visual systems are tuned to identify objects across a wide range of transformations.

■ FIGURE 5.5   A self-driving car.

This is a photo of Google's prototype of a self-driving car. The computer that navigates the car must make real-time computations on a dizzying amount of data to negotiate the road and avoid obstacles. These computations are done routinely in the human brain but are difficult to program into a computer.

TEST YOUR KNOWLEDGE

What computational difficulties does the visual system face in recognizing objects? How is this related to the difficulty in building self-driving cars?

TOP-DOWN PROCESSING AND BOTTOM-UP PROCESSING

5.2   Examine the difference between top-down processing and bottom-up processing and how they affect object perception.

In sensation and perception research, we seek explanations both at the neurological level and at the psychological level. We need to understand what is going on in the sensory organs and with the brain in order to make sense of sensory processes, but we also need to understand psychological processes in order to determine how we go from sensation of a pattern of light to the recognition of objects, such as individual people, roses, and self-driving cars. To this point, we have mostly been discussing the physiology and anatomy of sensation, but in this chapter, we begin discussing the more psychological issues of perception. One way to view this distinction is in the cognitive psychology logic of top-down and bottom-up processing. **Bottom-up processing** means that physical stimuli influence how we perceive them. This is relatively straightforward—our eyes detect reflected long-wavelength light when we examine the object depicted in Figure 5.1, and therefore, we see it as red. **Top-down processing** means that our existing knowledge of objects influences how we perceive them. Thus, we perceive a "rose" because we already know that roses are bright red and have this particular pattern of shape and shadow. If we did not know about roses, we might give a description of one similar to the one given by Dr. P.

Look back again at the object depicted in Figure 5.3. Because we do not know what the object in Figure 5.3 is, we have a hard time perceiving many of its important aspects, such as its size. Could you fit this object in your hand, or could you fit yourself inside the object? It is hard to tell. As you read through this chapter, think about when the issue at hand is bottom-up processing and when it is top-down processing.

Recognition and Representation

Although the focus of this chapter is object perception, the issues discussed here dovetail with issues of memory, in this case our knowledge base of visual objects. As we just discussed, our existing knowledge of the world is important in identifying individual objects in it. Because existing knowledge is important to perceiving objects, it is necessary to have a memory system capable of storing this knowledge. Thus, memory and perception are integral to understanding object perception. As a result, we need to define two memory terms here. **Recognition** refers to the ability to match a presented item with an item in memory. In more technical terms, it refers to the perceptual matching of something currently present to our visual system with a stored representation in memory. We can think of recognition as being

Bottom-up processing: a process whereby physical stimuli influence how we perceive them

Top-down processing: a process whereby our existing knowledge of objects influences how we perceive them

Recognition: the ability to match a presented item with an item in memory equivalent to a police lineup. A witness is shown several possible suspects and must pick out the one who was seen at the crime. In perceptual terms, recognition implies that we know something about what we are seeing—that is, we are able to match the object we see with a stored memory. Obviously, recognizing objects is an important part of our visual perception. In the case of Dr. P, he sees objects but does not recognize them as members of learned categories, such as gloves or flowers. In normal vision, we must recognize two classes of objects. We must recognize specific objects as members of larger classes. For example, we must recognize the object on the shelf as a screwdriver. But we also must recognize objects as specific instances of that category. For example, that screwdriver on the shelf is my screwdriver. Being able to recognize specific instances of a particular category is vital in face recognition, in which you must recognize a person as, for example, your uncle, rather than as a member of a category, such as men (Schwartz, 2014).

Representation refers to the storage and/or reconstruction of information in memory when that information is not in use. Those objects that are familiar to us must be stored in our memory system. We add in the term *reconstruction* because in some cases, the information comes from our imagination, or, in fact, we may make mistakes storing what we see. **Representation** is the technical term concerning how information is stored in memory. It can be applied at a number of levels. In neuroscience, *representation* refers to how neurons code for information, such as the shapes and colors of objects. It can also denote how networks of neurons across the brain store the information we will need to retrieve at some point. In cognitive psychology, a representation is the form in which information itself is stored. If you consider a class of objects, such as familiar faces, we need to be able to represent information about them. We need to be able to represent the general form of human faces and the specific forms of particular human faces (e.g., your mother, your brother, your landlord). In cognitive representation, one of the questions has been whether visual information is stored in a visual code or a descriptive language-like code (Farah, 2006). The process by which we match a particular face to that which we have represented is the process of recognition, which we also cover in this chapter.

TEST YOUR KNOWLEDGE

What is figure-ground organization? What rules dictate what is figure and what is background?

Perceptual Organization

Perceptual organization is the process by which multiple objects in the environment are grouped, allowing us to identify those objects in complex scenes. Look about you—it is likely that anywhere you are likely to be is a complex scene. Books, computer equipment, pens, and pencils as well as other personal possessions probably surround you if you are reading this book at home. Other people, bookshelves, paintings, and other objects are likely to surround you if you are reading this at the library. Perceptual organization is necessary, as almost any scene will be complex, with overlapping objects, occluding objects, and sometimes ambiguous objects. Perceptual organization permits us to group what we see into coherent perceptions. That is, it is necessary to group some objects together (e.g., books) and separate other objects even if they have similar shapes (books from bricks, for example).

Two important processes in perceptual organization are grouping and segregation. **Grouping** is the process by which elements in a figure are brought together into a common unit or object. In Figure 5.4, we see the remote as one object or grouped together, even though the glass bowl occludes part of the remote. **Segregation** is the process of distinguishing two objects as being distinct or discrete.

Representation: the storage and/or reconstruction of information in memory when that information is not in use

Perceptual organization: the process by which multiple objects in the environment are grouped, allowing us to identify multiple objects in complex scenes

Grouping: the process by which elements in a figure are brought together into a common unit or object

Segregation: the process of distinguishing two objects as being distinct or discrete

■ FIGURE 5.6   Fancy dinner.

How many distinct candles are there on the table? You probably have no difficulty determining the number of candles, despite the visual obstruction of some of the candles. Moreover, it is trivial for you to determine where one object ends, such as the chairs in the front, and where the table begins. Although easy in practice, this is a complex process computationally and relies on stored representations of objects.

ISLE 5.1 Segregation and Grouping

Thus, in Figure 5.4, we need to segregate where behind the glass bowl the end of the first remote is located and where the beginning of the second remote starts. In the Thanksgiving table scene depicted in Figure 5.6, a perceiver will group the plates together, the chairs together, and the squares on the tablecloth together. However, segregation will be used to distinguish those plates that will contain people's individual meals and the serving dishes that will be spared. You can see an illustration of these principles on ISLE 5.1.

GESTALT PSYCHOLOGY AND PERCEPTUAL ORGANIZATION

5.3   Describe the gestalt laws of perceptual grouping.

In the early 20th century, while behaviorists were ascendant in the United States, a school of psychology known as gestalt psychology pursued a different path in research, largely in Western Europe, particularly Germany. The gestalt psychologists were led by such psychological greats as Max Wertheimer, Kurt Koffka, and Wolfgang Kohler. In a general sense, the gestalt theorists claimed that the brain is holistic, with self-organizing tendencies. That is, the higher levels of organization take precedence over the lower levels. This differs to some extent from current research trends, which are often reductionist, in the sense that we try to build our models from the lowest levels upward. In terms of vision, gestalt psychology argues that what we see is greater than its individual parts. That is, the processes of perception are designed to see the scene rather than bits of light here and there. In this way, gestalt psychologists thought that stimuli were sufficiently rich in structure to allow the perceptual system to extract meaning directly from the stimuli, rather than building it up from image to thought. As such, it was important for them to establish the rules that governed the building of bigger perceptual units.

The gestalt psychologists were structuralists who thought that conscious perception rested upon the building blocks of sensation. However, unlike Helmholtz, gestalt psychologists thought that stimuli were rich enough for meaning to be interpreted directly rather than through unconscious inference. Thus, we sense incoming stimuli, but perception is an active process that interprets perceptions out of these sensory building blocks. Gestalt psychology also maintained that the whole is often different from the sum of its parts. That is, the perception that emerges from a physical scene may not be directly predicted by the sensory components that it is composed of, but emerges when we integrate the components into a whole. Think of the standard way in which comic books used to be created—the images were composed of many colored dots. Each dot was just a little speck of red, but when put together, one saw Spiderman. Examine Figure 5.7. The eye in Figure 5.7 is composed of many dots. To gestalt psychologists, the dots make up the sensory components of the stimuli, but seeing the eye emerges from perception. Moreover, the stimulus makes no sense unless we see it as an eye. It is just dots otherwise. So this immediate perception of higher level interpretations is necessary in any visual system.

For these reasons, gestalt psychologists were interested in understanding the rules by which perception picked out the whole from its parts. In particular, they investigated three principles concerning how our perceptual systems do this. These principles are figure-ground relations, the laws of Prägnanz or good fit, and the laws of grouping. Although these ideas were developed approximately 100 years ago, they still apply to the science of vision in important ways. We start with figure-ground organization.

Figure-Ground Organization

Figure-ground organization refers to the experience viewers have as to which part of an image is in the foreground and which part is in the background of a particular scene. In essence, we divide the world into two elements: the figure that is the object of regard and the rest, which is ground or background. In many cases, we can choose what will be the figure. For example, if you are giving a public lecture, you can look at one person's face in the audience. As you look at that face, that face is the figure—everyone else at that moment is ground. When you look at a new face, the last person's face is now ground. Consider Figure 5.8. When you look at this photograph, when you direct your gaze toward the oranges, the cat is ground and the oranges are figures. However, when you look at the cat, figure-ground reverses. In other situations, figure and ground may be determined by other components of the stimulus. Look around you—you will see objects close to you and those farther around. Objects close to you tend to be lower in your visual field and less obstructed by other objects than those farther away. Is such information useful to your visual system? Indeed it is, as normally, figure-ground determinations are relatively easy, as is apparent in Figure 5.9. In this figure, we tend to see the puffins as the foreground and the sea as the background.

However, there are exceptions in which the bottom of an image may not represent what is close, and the top of an image may not represent what is far away. Consider the photograph in Figure 5.10. Here we are looking down and across at a pond in the Everglades. Here the foreground circles the background. There are branches hanging down from the top of the image that are close to the observer in addition to the vegetation at the bottom, which is also in the foreground. The background of the photograph is the stuff in the middle, which is farthest from the observer. Because of this, this photograph takes a moment or two to figure out, because it does not conform to ordinary rules of figure-ground. Note the turtle swimming just beneath the surface of the pond at the center of the photograph.

There are other situations in which figure-ground can be highly ambiguous, and it may not be possible to determine which part of the image is the front and which is the back. This is true of many classic visual illusions. One such classic example is the face-vase figure, first introduced into the literature by psychologist Edgar Rubin in 1915 (see Figure 5.11). In this figure, the border between the orange and white regions is seen as being part of one or the other, not both. Thus, either the orange vase at the middle stands out as the foreground

■ **FIGURE 5.7**   **Eye or dots?**

All that is really present physically in this image is a series of black dots on a white background. However, the arrangement of the dots creates the image of an eye. Gestalt psychologists argue that the process behind seeing the eye instead of the dots is fundamental to perception. Our visual systems extract this higher meaning from the array of stimuli in the world.

Figure-ground organization: the experience viewers have as to which part of an image is in front and which part of an image is in the background of a particular scene

and the white faces are in the background, or the white faces stand out as the foreground and the orange space is the background. Interestingly, in these ambiguous figures, people see either one interpretation or the other, and although they can flip back and forth, they cannot see both at the same time. You can see a demonstration of this illusion on ISLE 5.2.

One of the useful aspects of such illusions is that we can make systematic changes in the way the images are presented and see how those changes affect the perception of the figure. Consider Figure 5.12. In this figure, we see that the field representing the faces and the vase are offset. When the vase is lowered and moved to a corner, it stands out as the figure, and it is nearly impossible to see the faces. When the faces are lowered and moved to the corner, they stand out as the figure, and the vase is no longer visible in the background. This illustrates the point that figures tend to be in the front, and the background on top.

A Few Rules That Govern What We See as Figure and What We See as Ground

We have already seen that the top of an image is more likely to be seen as the background and that what is in the front of an image is likely to be seen as the figure. But there are other rules as well that apply to the figure-ground relation. We outline them here (also see ISLE 5.3).

■ **FIGURE 5.8**   **Figure-ground.**

If you are looking at the cat, other aspects of the stimulus become ground or background. However, if you switch your focus from the cat to the oranges, the cat becomes background.

ISLE 5.2 Ambiguous
Figure-Ground Perception

ISLE 5.3 Figure-Ground Symmetry

■ **FIGURE 5.9**   **Figure-ground.**

In this figure, we tend to see the resting puffins as the figure, as they are closer to us, and the distant sea as background.

■ FIGURE 5.10   Figure-ground.

In this photograph of an Everglades alligator hole, the construction of the scene leads one to see the middle as foreground and a the top, bottom, and sides as background.

■ FIGURE 5.11   More on figure-ground.

Do you see two faces looking at each other in front of a orange background? Or do you see a orange vase in front of a white background? You may see either one or the other and switch between the two, but you cannot see both at the same time.

(a)

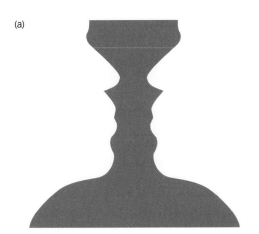

(b)

■ FIGURE 5.12   The face-vase figure-ground illusion.

(a) With the shifting down of the position of the orange area, we are more likely to see the vase. (b) With the shifting down of the position of the white area, we are more likely to see the faces.

We can identify another environmental feature that influences our perception of figure-ground. As we have seen already, perceived depth is one feature. The figure that appears in the foreground is often below the figure that appears in the background. Another feature is symmetry. A figure with symmetrical borders is more likely to be judged as being in the foreground than in the background (see Figure 5.13).

Another feature that affects figure-ground perception is that a figure is more likely to be perceived as being in the foreground if it is perceived to be on the convex side of a border. That is, the figure that appears to be in the foreground is the one with outward bulging (convex) borders, not the one with inward-facing (concave) borders. This point is illustrated nicely in an ambiguous figure taken from research by Stevens and Brookes (1988). In Figure 5.14, you can see either

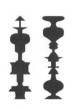

■ FIGURE 5.13   **Symmetry affects figure-ground organization.**

Images that are symmetrical are more likely to be seen as figure and therefore in the foreground, whereas less symmetrical images are more likely to be perceived as background.

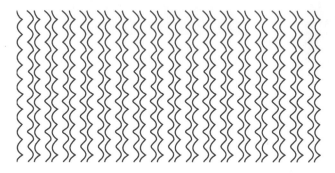

■ FIGURE 5.14   **Convexity affects figure-ground organization.**

Images with convex borders are more likely to be seen as figure, whereas those with concave borders are more likely to be seen as ground. Adapted from Stevens and Brookes (1988).

swirly ropes descending or a thorny branch descending. Most perceivers, though, see the swirly ropes, as these are the convex figures.

That convex images are perceived as figure and concave images as ground was also illustrated in an experiment by Peterson and Salvagio (2008). These researchers presented figures like those depicted in Figure 5.15. In Figure 5.15, one can see convex black bands and concave white bands. According to the ideas concerning convexity and figure-ground relations, we should see the black bands as the figure and the white bands as the background. Peterson and Salvagio placed a small red square at some point on the figure and had participants make judgments of front or back. When the square landed on a convex band, participants indicated that it was in the front, but when the square was on a concave band, they indicated that it was in the background.

In summary, there are a number of rules that govern figure-ground relations. These rules allow us to make sense of complex scenes because we use our existing knowledge of the world to help us interpret what is visually in front of us. For example, we know from experience that heavy objects do not usually float 3 feet above the ground. Thus, even though we cannot see the bottom of a chest of drawers, we infer that there must be a bottom, and that the couch we see in its entirety is in front of the chest of drawers. Thus, the couch becomes the figure and the chest is ground behind it. We next turn to more of these rules developed by the gestalt psychologists.

Gestalt Laws of Perceptual Grouping

The process by which visual systems combine figures within an image into wholes is called perceptual grouping. Perceptual grouping involves using existing knowledge to place similar items together or to group images in different parts of the visual field into a perception of the same object. Consider Figure 5.4 once more. When you view this image, you immediately group figures into coherent wholes. Thus, even though the blue on the two coasters is the same, you see these as two different objects because they are not continuous; one blue pattern is associated with the "pig" coaster, whereas the other blue pattern is associated with the "rooster" coaster. This

■ FIGURE 5.15   **Figure-ground judgments.**

The participants' task was to decide if the red square was on the figure or in the background. When the square landed on a convex band, participants indicated that it was in the front, but when the square was on a concave band, they indicated that it was in the background. Based on stimuli from Peterson and Salvagio's (2008) experiment.

is also why we see a complete glass bowl even though it is possible that the bowl is broken, as the reflection of sunlight makes it difficult to see the complete bowl.

The gestalt psychologists, especially Max Wertheimer, developed a number of "laws" that predict how perceptual grouping occurs under a variety of circumstances (Wertheimer, 1923/1938). Technically, in sciences, "laws" are predictions that are always true, no matter the conditions. In reality, these laws are better classified as principles, which are true most of the time. However, the term *laws* has stuck with these principles because they were established so long ago. So we will continue to refer to them as laws, even though technically, they are not scientific laws.

The **law of good continuation** means that figures that have edges that are smooth are more likely to be seen as continuous than those with edges that have abrupt or sharp angles. This law is best seen rather than described. Examining Figure 5.16a, most people see a horizontal orange bar behind a blue vertical bar. This is because the two orange rectangles would meet if each was extended. So we see them as continuous behind the blue vertical bar. However, in Figure 5.16b, the two orange rectangles would not be continuous behind the blue vertical bar. Therefore, we see them as two separate entities.

The **law of proximity** is the gestalt grouping law that states that elements that are close together tend to be perceived as a unified group. This straightforward law states that items close to one another tend to be grouped together, whereas items farther apart are less likely to be grouped together. In Figure 5.17, we tend to see five groups of 3 letters rather than one group of 15 letters.

The **law of similarity** is the gestalt grouping law that states that elements that are similar to one another tend to be perceived as a unified group. Similarity can refer to any number of features, including color, orientation, size, or indeed motion. This is illustrated in Figure 5.18.

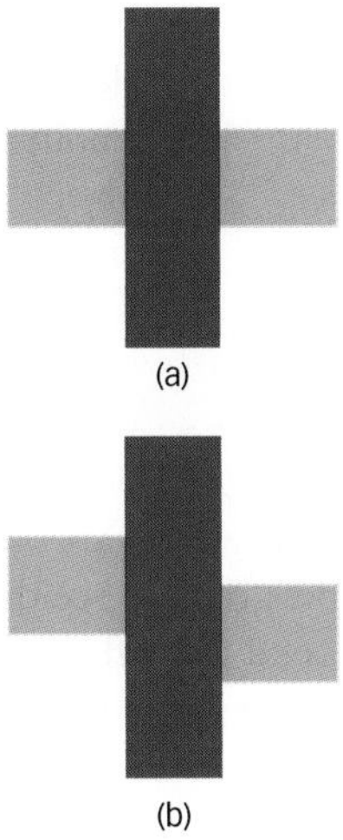

■ FIGURE 5.16

In (a), we see one bar on top of another bar. The good continuation of the bar in the back suggests its presence. In (b), we see two separate bars behind the front bar because good continuation does not suggest continuity.

LKS AJC QWE PKX JPB

■ FIGURE 5.17   Proximity.

When we see these letters, we see five groups of three letters because of the proximity of the three letters together. That is, elements that are close together tend to be grouped together.

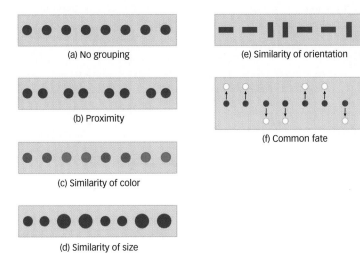

(a) No grouping

(b) Proximity

(c) Similarity of color

(d) Similarity of size

(e) Similarity of orientation

(f) Common fate

■ FIGURE 5.18   The law of similarity.

We tend to group together objects that look similar. Thus, we see objects grouped together by color (c), and objects grouped together by size in (d).

Law of good continuation: the gestalt grouping law stating that edges that are smooth are more likely to be seen as continuous than edges that have abrupt or sharp angles

Law of proximity: the gestalt grouping law stating that elements that are close together tend to be perceived as a unified group

Law of similarity: the gestalt grouping law stating that elements that are similar to one another tend to be perceived as a unified group

Symmetry

■ FIGURE 5.19   The law of symmetry.

In this figure, the figures that are symmetrical are grouped together.

ISLE 5.4 Gestalt Laws

Law of symmetry: the gestalt grouping law that states that elements that are symmetrical to each other tend to be perceived as a unified group

Law of common fate: the gestalt grouping law that states that elements that are moving together tend to be perceived as a unified group

Edge completion: the perception of a physically absent but inferred edge, allowing us to complete the perception of a partially hidden object

The **law of symmetry** is the gestalt grouping law that states that elements that are symmetrical to one another tend to be perceived as a unified group. Similar to the law of similarity, this rule suggests that objects that are symmetrical to one another will be more likely to be grouped together than objects not symmetrical to one another. This is illustrated in Figure 5.19.

The **law of common fate** is the gestalt grouping law that states that elements that are moving together tend to be perceived as a unified group. Think of watching a flock of geese moving across a fall sky. The geese are all flying in the same direction at approximately the same speed. Therefore, we see them as a gestalt group or, in this case, a flock. We might see a second flock flying in a different direction in a different pattern. You can see an illustration of each of the gestalt principles on ISLE 5.4.

Perceptual Interpolation

In real-world scenes, as we have already mentioned, particular objects are often partially occluded. That is, a particular object may be blocked by another object, rendering the physical image of the first object disjointed. Yet our perceptual systems see objects as continuous wholes despite that blocking. In Figure 5.20a, for example, the leaves of the tree do not impede our perception of a single koala, even though parts of the koala are not visible. In Figure 5.20b, the iron gate breaks up our view of the grass field beyond, but we see a continuous field of grass rather than a series of smaller ones divided by some unseen fence that coincides exactly with the grates of the gate. Look around you. Many of the objects around you are occluded by other objects, yet you see each object as a whole rather than a set of disjointed parts. Thus, filling in edges and completing surfaces are important jobs of our object recognition system.

One important process used in perceptual interpolation is edge completion. **Edge completion** is the perception of a physically absent but inferred edge,

(a)   (b)

© iStockphoto.com/ViktorCap

© iStockphoto.com/Pixel-Productions

■ FIGURE 5.20   Perceptual interpolation.

We infer the continuation of objects even when they are partially occluded by other objects. In Figure 5.20a, for example, the leaves of the tree do not impede our perception of a single koala, even though parts of the koala are not visible. It could be that the koala is terribly disfigured and the leaves are arranged so that we cannot notice it. But it is more likely that this is a normal super-cute koala. In Figure 5.20b, the iron gate breaks up our view of the grass field beyond, but we see a continuous field of grass rather than a series of smaller ones divided by some unseen fence that coincides exactly with the grates of the gate.

allowing us complete the perception of a partially hidden object. A stunning example of edge completion comes from illusory contours, as illustrated by the famous Kanizsa triangle (see Kanizsa, 1979; Petry & Meyer, 1987). Kanizsa developed these illusions explicitly working in the tradition of gestalt psychology, and you can apply many of the principles of gestalt psychology to interpret or predict the presence of illusory contours. **Illusory contours** (or subjective contours) are perceptual edges that exist because of edge completion but are not actually physically present. In Figure 5.21, we see a bright white triangle imposed on a background of blue circles. However, looking closer, there is no real difference in brightness between the white of the triangle and the white of the background. In fact, if you can force yourself to see three blue Pac-Man figures rather than three occluded triangles, the illusion of the bright triangle may disappear. Important to note here is that most people really do see a brightness difference. Only when you block out the figure and compare the brightness of the center of the triangle with the brightness of the background do you perceive them as being identical. And to really "mess with your mind," examine the illusory Necker cube in Figure 5.22. You can try ISLE 5.5 to control the parameters yourself and see how they affect the perception of illusory contours.

ISLE 5.5 Necker Cube

Illusory contours have interested perception researchers for a long time (see Petry & Meyer, 1987). This includes neuroscientists as well as gestalt psychologists. Neuroscience data suggest that illusory contours are processed at a very early level in vision, consistent with the illusory brightness differences. The physiological explanation for illusory contours arises from studies on V2 neurons in the brains of monkeys (von der Heydt, Peterhans, & Baumgartner, 1984). In these studies, von der Heydt et al. (1984) showed that edge detection cells responded to illusory edges as strongly as they did to real ones when the stimuli were aligned to create perceptual illusions of edges. However, the cells did not fire when stimuli without implied edges were presented. Other research shows that cells in V1 are

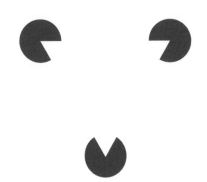

■ FIGURE 5.21   Kanisza triangles.

These illusory contours illustrate the principle of edge completion. The arrangement of the circles with the bites taken out of them suggest that a white triangle overlaps three blue circles. Because we unconsciously infer this, we see the triangle as slightly brighter in color than the white background, even though it is not.

■ FIGURE 5.22   An illusory Necker cube.

Perceptual interpretation here creates the appearance of a white-barred cube resting on top of a number of blue circles. The bars that appear to define the cube seem brighter than the surrounding background. This is due to the nonconscious inference of the cube. Moreover, the cube created is ambiguous and can be seen in one of two orientations.

Illusory contours: perceptual edges that exist because of edge completion but are not actually physically present

activated by illusory contours in the same way that they are activated by actual contours (Maertens & Pollmann, 2005). Thus, illusory contours appear to be a relatively low-level feature of object identification. This reinforces the notion that the gestalt principles are based on low-level features of perception, consistent with the gestalt view that we pick up these features in the stimulus rather than as a function of nonconscious processing.

> **TEST YOUR KNOWLEDGE**
>
> What are the laws of perceptual grouping? What do they account for?

RECOGNITION BY COMPONENTS

5.4   Define the concept of a geon.

Whereas the gestalt psychologists emphasized organization, that is, how we use implicit knowledge to help us perceive objects in the environment, other research has emphasized the bottom-up approach, that is, how we use the information in the world to construct a perception of what we see. One of the most influential bottom-up theories advanced to account for object recognition was developed by Irving Biederman in the 1980s (see Biederman, 1987). In this view, the complexity of object recognition is solved when the visual system breaks down objects in the environment into what Biederman called geometric ions, or geons. **Geons** represent the basic units of objects and consist of simple shapes, such as cylinders and pyramids. **Recognition by components** theory states that object recognition occurs by representing each object as a combination of basic units (geons) that make up that object. We recognize an object by the relation of its geons. Biederman tentatively proposed that there were roughly 40 independent geons and that just about any object could be represented by some combination of these geons. Figure 5.23 shows a few sample geons, and Figure 5.24 shows simple objects made up of geons. You can also do an interactive version of building shapes from geons on ISLE 5.6.

One of the advantages of this model is that if any object is a combination of a few basic geons, then the object is specified by those components, and its position relative to the observer should not matter. Thus, this model accounts

---

ISLE 5.6 Illusory Contours

Geons: the basic units of objects, consisting of simple shapes such as cylinders and pyramids

Recognition by components: a theory stating that object recognition occurs by representing each object as a combination of basic units (geons) that make up that object; we recognize an object by the relation of its geons

---

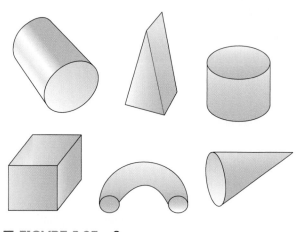

■ FIGURE 5.23   **Geons.**

These basic shapes, or geons, were thought by Biederman (1987) to be the basic building blocks of object perception.

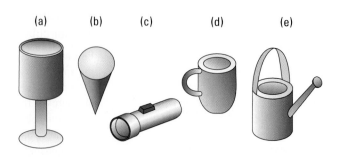

■ FIGURE 5.24   **Objects from geons.**

When we put various geons together, we can create various recognizable objects.

for the **viewpoint invariance** of objects, that is, that objects are seen as the same regardless of the vantage point relative to a viewer (see Figure 5.4 again). However, recently recognition-by-components theory has fallen into disfavor, largely because of its limits in accounting for some phenomena, such as letter recognition and face recognition, two big categories of object recognition in humans.

> **TEST YOUR KNOWLEDGE**
>
> What are geons, and why are they considered the building blocks of object perception?

THE NEUROANATOMY AND PHYSIOLOGY OF OBJECT PERCEPTION

5.5 Explain why the ventral pathway is critical for object perception.

We start this section with a brief review of some of the material covered in the last chapter. Remember that two pathways emerge from area V1 of the occipital cortex. One of these pathways is known as the "where" pathway or the dorsal pathway. This pathway works its way through the extrastriate cortex and then continues on to the parietal lobe. The dorsal pathway is concerned mainly with locating objects in space and perceiving motion. We focus on this pathway in Chapter 8. The second pathway that emerges from V1 is known as the "what" pathway or ventral pathway. This pathway works its way through the extrastriate cortex and then continues on to the temporal lobe. One of its main functions is object recognition. We focus on this pathway in this section.

Representation of Shapes in Area V4

After information leaves V1 and heads toward the extrastriate cortex along the ventral pathway, one of the important loci is area **V4** in the occipital cortex (see Figure 5.25). V4 has been linked to color vision but also to shape perception. V4 neurons seem to have a clear preference for edges, but a more complex analysis of edges than seen in V1 or V2. For example, V4 neurons can respond to edges that are either straight or curved, whereas V1 neurons show a strong preference for straight edges (Pasupathy & Connor, 2002). Also, like V1 neurons, V4 neurons respond to contours (Pasupathy & Connor, 2002). However, V4 neurons respond to either convex or concave contours. Thus, this area is involved in delineating shapes, necessary for object recognition.

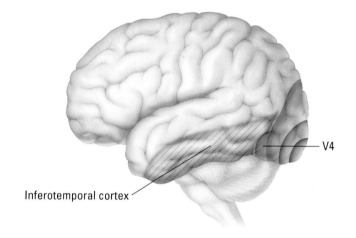

V4

Inferotemporal cortex

■ **FIGURE 5.25**   **Object recognition in the brain.**

Area V4 and the inferotemporal area are two critical areas in the neural substrate of object recognition.

Viewpoint invariance: the perception that an object does not change when an observer sees the object from a new vantage point

V4: an area of the brain involved in both color vision and shape perception

Inferotemporal (IT) area: the region in the temporal lobe that receives input from the ventral visual pathway; one of its functions is object identification

Object Recognition in the Inferotemporal Area

Information in the ventral pathway leaves the occipital lobe and heads into the **inferotemporal (IT) area** of the temporal lobe (see Figure 5.14). Neurons in the IT area have much larger receptive fields than those in V1 and V4 and seem to be

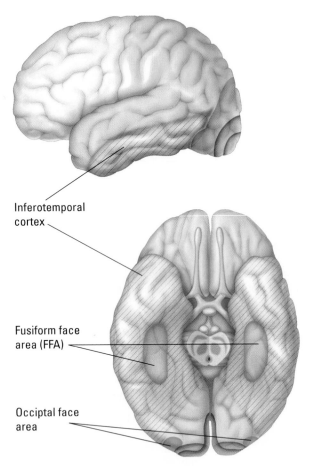

Inferotemporal cortex

Fusiform face area (FFA)

Occiptal face area

■ FIGURE 5.26   The fusiform face area (FFA) and the occipital face area (OFA).

Within the IT cortex is an area known as the fusiform face area or FFA. It is associated with the recognition of familiar faces in humans. The OFA is located within the occipital lobe and is associated with recognizing any face as a face.

ISLE 5.7 Geons

Fusiform face area: an area in the inferotemporal area of the temporal lobe that specializes in recognizing familiar faces

Occipital face area: an area of the brain in the occipital lobe, associated with recognizing faces as distinct from other objects

devoted to detecting particular kinds of objects anywhere in the visual field rather than specific features in specific places. Indeed, some areas in the IT area seem to be very specific to particular kinds of shapes or forms (Brincat & Connor, 2004). That is, rather than detecting edges or contours, the IT area seems to specialize in detecting specific objects from chairs to bears to faces.

Neuroscience researchers have known for a long time of the relation between the IT cortex and object recognition. Back in the 1930s, Klüver and Bucy (1939) lesioned the temporal lobes of monkeys in their lab. After creating these lesions, Klüver and Bucy observed what they called "psychic blindness" but what we now call object agnosia. The monkeys were able to demonstrate that they could see, but they could not discriminate among different objects. For example, the monkeys could press a button when a light flashed, thus indicating that they could see, but they could not discriminate among shapes. Later research pinpointed these symptoms to disruption of the IT area (Barlow, 1995).

Other lesion studies in monkeys found cells that appeared to be specific for face recognition. For example, Rolls and Tovee (1995) presented monkeys with pictures of faces and other images. Recording from single cells within the IT area, Rolls and Tovee identified a class of cells that responded strongly to faces, both monkey and human, but barely responded to nonface stimuli. As we will see in the next section, this finding is consistent with what we see in the human IT area as well (see ISLE 5.7).

The Fusiform Face Area and Face Recognition

One important area within the IT cortex is known as the **fusiform face area** (FFA). The FFA appears to be a specific region in the brain designed for a specific kind of object recognition, that is, the recognition of familiar faces (Kanwisher, McDermott, & Chun, 1997; Kanwisher & Dilks, 2013). The FFA is located on the ventral surface of the temporal lobe. This area can be seen in Figure 5.26. Although there is some debate as to how specific the FFA is to face recognition, most research now suggests that the area is involved in the recognition of familiar faces after an object has already been perceived as a face (Liu, Harris, & Kanwisher, 2010). That is, we use the FFA to distinguish Aunt Sally's face from Aunt Mary's face, rather than to identify a strange array of colors and textures as a face in the first place. Another area of the brain known as the **occipital face area** (OFA) appears to be responsible for making the initial identification of a face as being a face, regardless of its familiarity. That is, the OFA is an area associated with recognizing faces as distinct from other objects. The OFA is located in the extrastriate cortex and is strongly connected to the FFA (Liu et al., 2010).

Grill-Spector, Knouf, and Kanwisher (2004) examined the role of the FFA in face recognition using functional magnetic resonance imaging (fMRI) technology. In one condition of their experiment, they used photographs of the face of the actor Harrison Ford as their face stimulus. In control conditions, participants saw another face, or they simply saw a texture gradient with no face. They saw these stimuli for only 50 ms, followed immediately by a masking stimulus, which made it difficult to identify the stimulus they had just seen. The participants' task was to identify the briefly presented photo as Harrison Ford, another face, or nothing at all. The participants did the task while the fMRI machine was monitoring activity in the FFA.

Grill-Spector et al. (2004) found strong activity in the FFA when participants identified Harrison Ford in the stimulus. Interestingly, they got strong, though not as strong, activity in the FFA when the participants thought they saw Ford in the stimulus, but it had actually been a control stimulus. When participants saw the other face or the texture pattern and identified it as such, there was much less activity in the FFA. Importantly, the response in the FFA was greatest when the participants recognized Harrison Ford and not the nonfamous face (see Figure 5.27). The FFA shows a selective response to seeing faces already known rather than all faces. Thus, this study shows a strong relation between the recognition of familiar faces and activity in the FFA.

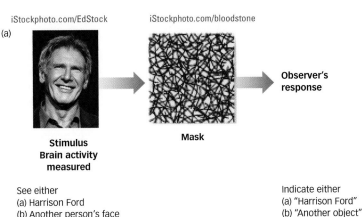

See either
(a) Harrison Ford
(b) Another person's face
(c) A random texture

Indicate either
(a) "Harrison Ford"
(b) "Another object"
(c) "Nothing"

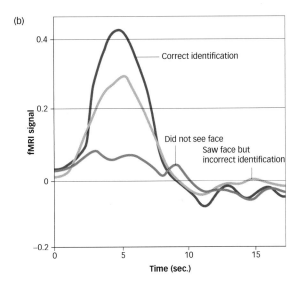

Prosopagnosia

Damage to the FFA results in a condition known as prosopagnosia. The term *prosopagnosia* comes from two Greek words, one meaning "face" and one meaning "knowledge." **Prosopagnosia** is a selective deficit in recognizing faces. Prosopagnosia is a neurological condition in which face recognition is impaired, but other forms of visual object recognition are relatively intact. Thus, a patient with prosopagnosia will have difficulty recognizing particular people, but will not have difficulty identifying roses or gloves. It usually occurs in patients who have had strokes, but there are some cases of people born with prosopagnosia (Duchaine & Nakayama, 2006). Patients with prosopagnosia recognize faces as faces but fail to recognize specific faces, even of close family members. For example, when a prosopagnosic patient is presented with a photograph of the face of a family member or a celebrity, the patient will be able to identify the object as a face but will not be able to identify the specific person. However, prosopagnosic patients can recognize familiar people by other cues, such as their voices, their particular ways of walking, and even distinctive features such as a big nose or a large facial scar.

One question researchers have debated is whether prosopagnosia occurs on its own or whether it is always associated with a more general object agnosia. Most of this research suggests that, in some cases, a person can have impairment of face

■ **FIGURE 5.27**   **The Grill-Spector experiment.**

Participants briefly saw Harrison Ford's face followed by a mask or a control stimulus followed by a mask (a). In (b), we can see the activity in the FFA when the participant recognized the photo as Harrison Ford and when he or she did not. Note that the highest response in the FFA is for correct recognition.

Prosopagnosia: face agnosia, resulting in a deficit in perceiving faces recognition but intact recognition of other objects. For example, Moscovitch and Moscovitch (2000) compared prosopagnosic patients and object-agnosic patients. Patients with object agnosia were normal at face recognition but showed deficits in object recognition. In contrast, the prosopagnosic patients showed deficits in facial recognition but not object recognition. That is, the prosopagnosic patients, relative to control patients, were just as able to recognize common objects, such as spoons, pianos, slippers, and candles. However, these patients could not recognize the faces of people who were otherwise familiar to them. The object agnosic patients were able to recognize familiar faces, but they had difficulty recognizing the common objects. This pattern has now been found in many studies (Busigny & Rossion, 2011).

There is also a condition known as developmental prosopagnosia, which occurs in individuals who have normal vision and normal social functioning but show a selective deficit in face recognition (Duchaine & Nakayama, 2006). Although this condition is very rare, recent fMRI research shows less activity in the FFA in patients with developmental prosopagnosia than in normal controls when identifying familiar faces than when viewing other objects (Furl, Garrido, Dolan, Driver, & Duchaine, 2011). Thus, the evidence with developmental prosopagnosics also supports the view that the FFA is an area unique to face recognition. Oliver Sacks described what he thinks of as his own developmental prosopagnosia in his 2010 book *The Mind's Eye* (Sacks, 2010).

Other IT Cortex Areas With Specific Object Recognition Functions

The parahippocampal place area (PPA) is an area within the IT cortex that appears to have the specific function of scene recognition. This area seems to be selectively tuned for the recognition of spatial landscapes, both indoor and outdoor scenes (Epstein, 2005; Epstein & Kanwisher, 1998). This area is responsive to photographs of spatial landscapes but shows no additional activity when images of people are present in those landscapes. As with the FFA, there is a form of agnosia that accompanies damage to the PPA. **Topographic agnosia** involves a deficit in recognizing spatial landscapes and is related to damage to the PPA (Mendez & Cherrier, 2003).

Another area in the IT cortex with a specific function is the extrastriate body area. The **extrastriate body area** is activated when its cells view bodies or body parts, but not faces (Downing, Jiang, Shuman, & Kanwisher, 2001). This interesting area appears to be responsible for visual recognition of body areas other than the face. It may be that other areas of the IT cortex are also sensitive to particular stimuli as well. These areas can be seen in Figure 5.28.

Grandmother Cells and Specific Coding in the IT Cortex

An early issue in the history of neuroscience was how specific brain regions are to function and to particular stimuli. This debate often centered on whether the brain worked as a whole or was composed of the many separate areas we know it to be composed of now. But part of the debate concerned where memories were stored in the brain. Thus, early neuroscientists wanted to know where in the brain was the memory of your cat. When your cat enters the room, you recognize the cat not just as any cat, but as your cat. Clearly, areas in the IT cortex are helping you recognize this animal as a cat and as your good friend Whiskers. The question

Parahippocampal place area (PPA): an area within the inferotemporal cortex that appears to have the specific function of scene recognition

Topographic agnosia: a deficit in recognizing spatial landscapes, related to damage to the parahippocampal place area

Extrastriate body area: an area within the inferotemporal cortex that is activated when its cells view bodies or body parts, but not faces

addressed in this section is whether there is an area of the brain that is specific to Whiskers but not to your other cat, Fluffball, or any other cat. In the past, this question has been phrased not in terms of cats, but rather another equally cute category, grandmothers (see Figure 5.29). Is there an area in the brain or, more specifically, in the IT cortex, that codes for your grandmother, but no other person?

In memory research, this quest has been labeled the search for the engram. The engram is the specific location of a specific memory, such as the visual identity of your cat or your grandmother (Schacter, 2001). Note that the FFA is responsive to familiar faces but does not necessarily discriminate between the face of your grandmother and that of your aunt. For many years, the general wisdom was that such "grandmother" cells would not be found. Identifying an individual requires the coordination of networks of cells and communications among them. However, one remarkable demonstration suggests that grandmother cells may in fact exist. This study examined famous landmarks and celebrities rather than grandmothers, but the investigators found remarkable characteristics of specific object recognition in IT neurons (Quiroga, Reddy, Kreiman, Koch, & Fried, 2005).

Quiroga et al. (2005) were able to conduct a very unusual study because of particular circumstances of their participants. Their participants were all people about to undergo elective brain surgery to treat epilepsy. During this procedure, neurosurgeons need to be very careful about the function of brain regions on which they are about to operate. As such, as a matter of course, single-cell recordings are taken in some areas of the brain in these patients. Normally, single-cell recording in live people is not permitted, but in this case, electrodes were to be implanted in the brains of the patients anyway, and thus the patients themselves were under no additional risk from Quiroga et al.'s experimental procedure. Although the results of this study are remarkable, there has been some controversy over whether these results can be replicated in other studies.

Quiroga et al. (2005) asked their patients to look at a series of pictures presented on a computer screen while individual neurons were being monitored. The cells that were monitored were in the medial temporal lobe, adjacent to but not identical to the IT cortex. They found cells that appeared to be specific to individual people. For example, one cell was selectively responsive to photographs of the basketball player Kobe Bryant but did not respond to photographs of the actor Mark Hamill (i.e., Luke Skywalker). Another cell was responsive to photographs of Mark Hamill but not to Kobe Bryant. The cell responded to Kobe Bryant's photo with different hairstyles, to a photo of Mr. Bryant and a teammate, and to his printed name. Different cells in this area appeared to make stronger responses to Mark Hamill, as Luke Skywalker, to other photos of him, and to his name in print. Similarly, Quiroga et al. found a cell in the medial temporal lobe that was responsive to images of the leaning tower of Pisa but not to the Golden Gate Bridge, and another cell that was responsive to the Golden Gate Bridge but not the leaning tower of Pisa. Thus, these cells are astonishingly like the grandmother cells, responding to a particular person or landmark from different angles and in different contexts, but not to other people or other famous landmarks (see Figure 5.30).

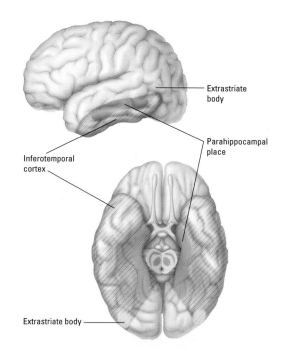

■ FIGURE 5.28   **The parahippocampal place area and the extrastriate body area.**

The parahippocampal place area (PPA) is an area within the inferotemporal cortex involved in scene recognition. The extrastriate body area is associated with recognizing parts of the body other than the face.

■ FIGURE 5.29   **Grandma and her cat.**

Where in the brain is the representation of the memory of your grandmother and her favorite cat?

■ FIGURE 5.30   The results of Quiroga et al.'s (2005) study.

These data are from single cells within the human temporal cortex. One cell responded to the image of Kobe Bryant but not to images of other people. Similarly, one cell responded to the image of the Golden Gate Bridge but not to images of other landmarks.

There are some problems, however, with Quiroga et al.'s (2005) study, some of which the researchers themselves have discussed (Quiroga, Reddy, Kreiman, Koch, & Fried, 2008). First, they did not have much time to test each patient. Thus, they were not able to test related stimuli. For example, would the "Kobe Bryant" cell also respond to his fellow Laker star Shaquille O'Neal? Would the "Golden Gate Bridge" cell also respond to a photograph of the San Francisco–Oakland Bay Bridge? These were questions the investigators were not able to answer, given the time constraints before the patients' surgeries. It is also possible, given that the medial temporal lobe is more involved in memory than visual perception, that the cells were involved in the retrieval of photograph-related information rather than recognizing specific objects or people, although such a result would still be surprising. Finally, this study has proved difficult to replicate, though there has now been at least one conceptual replication (Gelbard-Sagiv, Mukamel, Harel, Malach, & Fried, 2008). Nonetheless, these studies show that areas in the temporal lobe may be highly specialized in recognizing particular objects in the visual world. Thus, Quiroga et al.'s findings are consistent with the goals of the ventral system—identifying objects in the environment.

TEST YOUR KNOWLEDGE

What is the IT area? What does it do, and what happens when it is damaged?

IN DEPTH: *Vision and Animacy: How Do We Tell a Who From a What?*

5.6 Explain how we can distinguish human faces from doll and mannequin faces.

Creepy dolls are almost a cliché in horror movies. Every couple of years, we see another movie about Chucky, the crazed doll who terrorizes all who come into contact with him in the *Child's Play* and *Chucky* movies. Creepy dolls are a staple of other horror movies, including *The Woman in Black* (2012) and one movie aptly named *The Creepy Doll* (2011). But dolls are supposed to be playthings for very young children. How could we give to young children objects that produce terror in adults? Store mannequins are also often the stuff of horror fantasies, from *The Twilight Zone* to *Dr. Who*. But mannequins are supposed to inspire us to buy particular cloths. So why do we see dolls both as cute and harmless toys for our children and as representations of our deepest fears? And why do seemingly harmless mannequins also bring our fears to the forefront? Well, we think there is an interesting answer. Recent research by Thalia Wheatley and her colleagues at Dartmouth College shed some light on this issue (e.g., Looser & Wheatley, 2010).

In Wheatley's view, what draws us to dolls and repels us at the same time is that they have faces (see Figure 5.31). Humans are drawn to see and seek out faces. Presumably, this was important in human evolution. Adults need to be able to recognize familiar kin and distinguish them from potentially dangerous strangers. Young infants must be able to recognize their mothers and distinguish them from other women. Thus, it is likely that strong evolutionary pressures led to the special module for face recognition that exists in the FFA of the IT lobe, which allows us to quickly recognize and identify familiar faces. However, a module that is designed to seek out faces wherever they are may seek out faces where none actually exist. It is perhaps for this reason that we see faces where none actually exist, such as in clouds, mountains, constellations, and various inanimate objects (see Figure 5.32). For many years, for example, the symbol of the state of New Hampshire was a rock formation on a mountain that bore a passing resemblance to a human face. Dolls and mannequins are an interesting case, as they are deliberately designed to strongly resemble people, but are clearly not people. Dolls have faces, but they are inanimate objects. Thus, we are drawn to them, but at the same time, we must recognize that they are not real human faces. The question that Wheatley's group was interested

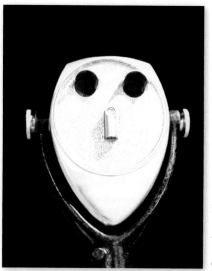

© wanderworldimages / Alamy

■ **FIGURE 5.32   A smiley face?**

We are tuned to see faces and often see them in objects that do not really have eyes, noses, and mouths. We often see faces in clouds, on the sides of mountains, and in tortillas. This is likely due to an evolutionary disposition to detect human faces.

© iStockphoto.com/mitza

■ **FIGURE 5.31   Dolls have faces.**

A doll has human features but is decidedly not human.

in was what differences might exist in the perception of real and simulated faces. For a fascinating take (albeit in a commercial) on our detection of human faces in odd stimuli, watch this YouTube video: http://www.youtube .com/watch?v=TQk7Zh-dXCk.

Looser and Wheatley (2010) pointed out that all human minds have faces, but not all faces have human minds. Dolls and mannequins are not the only mindless faces—we have masks, sculptures, even photographs and painted portraits. So why are dolls and mannequins potentially creepy, but not photographs? Dolls and mannequins are not exact duplications of faces (as in photographs) or clearly iconic representations, as are masks and sculptures. The better the doll, the more closely it resembles a real human baby or other human figure. However, it does not move, it does not speak, and there are usually telltale signs of nonanimacy. Whereas most of the research we have discussed so far examines how we detect faces, Wheatley's research goes a bit further and asks how we detect faces that have minds attached. When we see a face, it instantly activates face-sensitive areas of the brain, such as the FFA. However, animate face recognition requires an additional step: to associate the face with a moving, living, animate being. Thus, we must make an additional step to go from face to mind.

This is supported by Wheatley's research. Wheatley, Weinberg, Looser, Moran, and Hajcak (2011) used electroencephalographic (EEG) technology to look at responses to photographs of real faces and photographs of dolls and mannequins. The EEG responses were averaged to look at characteristic wave patterns, known as event-related potentials, in response to these face stimuli. Wheatley et al. found that they could identify an event-related potential wave that occurred after recognizing faces, real or inanimate, but not other stimuli, presumably emanating from the FFA. When dolls and mannequins were presented to participants, the face response on the EEG decreased about 200 ms after presentation. However, for real faces, the EEG response continued. Wheatley's team could therefore tell what kind of face, animate or inanimate, a person had examined by looking at the EEG response. Thus, human visual systems can quickly distinguish between human faces and inanimate replicas.

In another experiment, Looser and Wheatley (2010) combined the images of real faces and inanimate faces, as can be seen in Figure 5.33. They found images of statues and dolls that matched the faces of

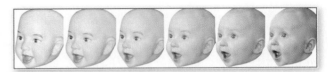

■ **FIGURE 5.33** Transformation from real baby to doll.

Consider the middle two faces—are they of a doll or a person?

actual people and, using a computer program, morphed the images together. Looser and Wheatley then varied the level at which each image contained more human or more mannequin in the face, with some being all doll and some being all human, as well as various in-between levels. Participants then made a number of different judgments concerning the faces, including alive or not alive, realistic or unrealistic, has a mind or does not have a mind, and able to feel pain or not able to feel pain. Regardless of the particular judgment, Looser and Wheatley found a tipping point at about 65% human. That is, if the combined image was at 65% human face or higher (i.e., 35% doll), it was judged to be

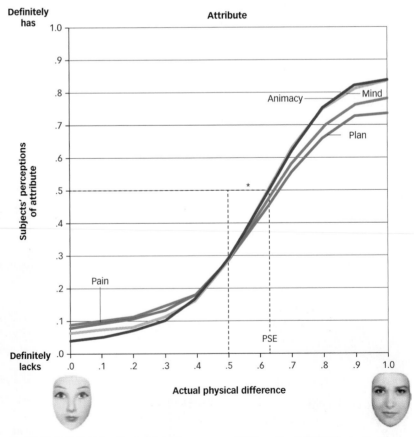

■ **FIGURE 5.34** Results of Looser and Wheatley's (2010) study of animacy.

These data show participants' perceptions of whether the figures were animate or not. The colored lines indicate the ratings for attributes of animacy, such as animacy itself, having a mind, the ability to plan, and the ability to feel pain.

alive, to be realistic, to have a mind, and to feel pain. At less than 65%, the animacy ratings tailed off quickly (see Figure 5.34). Looser and Wheatley found it significant that this tipping point was higher than 50%. They think it is important that we have a high criterion for recognizing animacy in a human face.

Looser and Wheatley (2010) compared their results with earlier social-psychological data on object perception that showed that, in many situations, we find facelike inanimate objects to be likable (e.g., a rock with eyes drawn on it), but we are often suspicious of or revolted by clearly inanimate objects that look too human (e.g., mannequins, dolls). It may be for this reason that many children's cartoons use anthropomorphic animals or caricature images of children to portray their characters rather than more lifelike representations.

In another experiment, Looser and Wheatley (2010) examined individual features of faces, including the eye, the mouth, the nose, and the skin, and then compared the judgments of animacy from just these facial features with those from whole faces. Overall, they found lower animacy judgments for parts of a face than for a whole face, but they also found that animate-looking eyes were the biggest predictor of animacy. Seeing an eye by itself allowed participants to judge animacy in a way in which mouths and noses did not. In evaluating inanimate faces, it may be that the other features of the face activate the brain's face detectors, but the lack of animate eyes may give a doll or mannequin its "creepy" look (see Figure 5.35).

© iStockphoto.com/sqback

■ **FIGURE 5.35**   **The perception of creepiness.**

Is this creepy or what?

To summarize this research, human visual systems are extremely sensitive to stimuli that look like human faces. This means that we may often get "false alarms," that is, stimuli that look like human faces but are actually not. We can quickly reject faces in stones and clouds as not being really human, but dolls and mannequins give us pause. In most cases, we reject dolls as being human, but perhaps every so often, they tweak our "mind" detectors. This causes us to wonder, if only for a second, if they are watching us and observing our actions. This leads to a creepy feeling that the old unused doll gathering dust in the closet is really plotting its revenge on us.

CHAPTER SUMMARY

5.1 Explain the computational difficulties the visual system must overcome in recognizing objects as themselves under a multitude of situations and angles.

Object perception concerns our ability to visually identify the world around us, from socks to bird feeders to our Aunt Sally. Object agnosia is an acquired deficit in identifying and recognizing objects even though vision remains intact.

5.2 Examine the difference between top-down processing and bottom-up processing and how they affect object perception.

Object perception requires both bottom-up processing, from stimulus to perception, and top-down processing, from knowledge to perception, in order to function efficiently. Object perception requires a memory representation system that allows us to recognize familiar objects when we see them.

5.3 Describe the gestalt laws of perceptual grouping.

Perceptual organization is the process by which multiple objects in the environment are grouped, allowing us to identify those objects in complex scenes. Two important processes in perceptual organization are grouping and segregation. Gestalt psychology argues that what we see is greater than the sum of its individual parts, and as such emphasizes the rules that govern how objects in scenes are determined from background noise. One set of these rules concerns figure-ground organization, which refers to the inference viewers must make as to which part of an image is in front and which part of an image is in the background of a particular scene. Gestalt psychologists also emphasized the laws of perceptual grouping, which allow us to infer which parts of an image go with which other parts. One such illustration of these principles comes from illusory contours, in which we see figures present that are not part of the physical stimulus.

5.4 Define the concept of a geon.

Recognition by components is a theory that states that object recognition occurs by representing each object as a combination of basic units (geons) that make up that object. We recognize an object by the relation of its geons.

5.5 Explain why the ventral pathway is critical for object perception.

Object perception occurs along the ventral pathway in the brain, which leads from V1 in the occipital lobe to the inferotemporal (IT) area of the temporal lobe. V4 is an area in the extrastriate cortex involved in shape perception. The IT area is the area of the temporal lobe involved in object perception. It receives input from V4 and other areas in the occipital lobe. Part of the IT lobe is known as the fusiform face area (FFA). The FFA is an area in the IT cortex of the temporal lobe that specializes in recognizing familiar faces. There is also a region known as the occipital face area (OFA), which is an area of the brain in the occipital lobe that is associated with recognizing faces as distinct from other objects. Damage to the FFA results in a condition known as prosopagnosia. The term

prosopagnosia comes from two ancient Greek words, one meaning "face" and one meaning "knowledge." Prosopagnosia is a selective deficit in recognizing faces. The parahippocampal place area (PPA) is an area within the IT cortex that appears to have the specific function of scene recognition. Topographic agnosia involves a deficit in recognizing spatial landscapes, related to damage to the PPA. Quiroga et al. (2005) conducted a study that found cells in the temporal lobe that responded to specific people, regardless of the whether a photograph or a name was presented. Some people regard this study as evidence for neural areas that code for very specific information about individual objects or people.

5.6 Explain how we can distinguish human faces from doll and mannequin faces.

When we see a face, it instantly activates face-sensitive areas of the brain, such as the FFA. However, animate face recognition requires an additional step: to associate the face with a moving living animate being. Research by Wheatley and her colleagues shows that faces are recognized rapidly, but an extra step exists to distinguish real human faces from facsimiles, such as dolls.

REVIEW QUESTIONS

1. What is object agnosia? What areas of the brain likely cause it, and what are its symptoms?

2. Define object perception. What are some of the obstacles programmers must overcome to design a computer system with object perception?

3. What is the difference between top-down and bottom-up processing?

4. What is meant by perceptual organization? What is the difference between grouping and segregation?

5. Who were the gestalt psychologists? How did they contribute to our understanding of figure-ground perception?

6. What is edge completion? How does it account for illusory contours?

7. Describe the neural pathway that leads from V1 to the temporal lobe that is responsible for object perception.

8. What is the difference between the FFA and the OFA in perceiving faces? Which area is damaged in prosopagnosia?

9. Several experiments have demonstrated the role of the FFA in face perception. Describe one of these experiments and how it confirms this area's function.

10. Why is judging animacy in a face important? Why do dolls and mannequins elicit "creepy" responses, but pictures of real faces do not? What difference do we see in EEG scans when people view photographs of real faces and those of dolls?

KEY TERMS

Bottom-up processing, 114

Edge completion, 122

Extrastriate body area, 128

Figure-ground organization, 117

Fusiform face area, 126

Geons, 124

Grouping, 115

Illusory contours, 123

Inferotemporal (IT) area, 125

INTERACTIVE SENSATION LABORATORY EXERCISES (ISLE)

Experience chapter concepts at edge.sagepub.com/schwartz

Sharpen your skills with SAGE edge at edge.sagepub.com/schwartz

SAGE edge for students provides a personalized approach to help you accomplish your coursework goals in an easy-to-use learning environment.

Color Perception

INTRODUCTION

If you live in South Florida, seeing rainbows is a frequent occurrence. In the summer, rainbows are quite common after a late afternoon thunderstorm. Driving along Route 1 in the Florida Keys in the summer, one can often see layer upon layer of rainbows as one heads east in the late afternoon (see Figure 6.1). Many people find rainbows to be beautiful, partly because they appear to be pure color—just color, not attached to a particular object, seemingly magically suspended in the air. The physical explanation for rainbows, millions of water droplets acting as prisms, just makes the phenomenon more mysterious. We know it has to be true, but for many, the physical explanation just does not connect with their perceptual experience. When most of us look at rainbows, we see seven distinct bands: red, orange, yellow, green, blue, indigo (a dark blue), and violet (a reddish blue resembling purple). However, there is actually a continuous band of wavelengths there—the seven bands are a function of our eyes and brains. As we will see in this chapter, colors are usually properties of objects, but in a rainbow, we do not see the raindrops that create the rainbows.

Many of you may have heard that your cat is colorblind. This is not quite true—cats do have some ability to see in color, but much less than we do (Buzás et al., 2013). Cats are actually "color deficient," meaning that they have a two-cone color system, compared with our three-cone system. Cats also have fewer cones in total than humans, but they can see colors. Cats' eyes are better adapted than ours for nocturnal vision, and their eyes are more specialized for detecting low levels of light at night. Nonetheless, because cats are active during the day, they also have some color vision. Dogs are also color deficient relative to us, but they do see in color as well. It turns out that their retinae resemble those of color-deficient people, in having a two-cone system. You probably know a person who is red-green colorblind (really color deficient). Whereas you see a green light or a red light at a traffic signal, she sees both the green and the red lights as the same color. Luckily, she knows that the red light is always above the green light, so red-green color deficiency is not a risk for driving. Are there animals with better color vision than ours? You may have heard that goldfish have a four-cone system, compared with our three-cone system. On the basis of research on goldfish, it is known that they can see color differences that look the same to us.

Interestingly, it turns out that some people may also have functional four-cone systems that allow them to see more colors than normal people do. Gabriele Jordan, a researcher at the University of Newcastle in the United Kingdom, recently identified a woman with a functional four-cone system, who seemingly can see different colors where most of us would just see one color (Greenwood, 2012; Jordan, Deeb, Bosten, & Mollon, 2010). However, Jordan and her colleagues think functional four-cone vision is extremely rare in people. In their study, they looked at the genetics that cause some women to have four-cone systems and

Fred Burrell / Science Source

LEARNING OBJECTIVES

6.1 Examine the relation of the wavelength of light to perceived color.

6.2 Identify the perceptual principles of hue, saturation, and brightness.

6.3 Summarize the idea of a metamer and what color-matching experiments show.

6.4 Explain how the three cones interact to influence color perception.

6.5 Describe the trichromatic theory of color vision.

6.6 Illustrate the opponent theory of color vision.

6.7 Describe the concept of color deficiency and why it is a better term than *color blindness*.

6.8 Define the term *constancy* and how it applies to color vision.

6.9 Explain how purple is distinguished from violet.

REUTERS/Marc Serota

■ FIGURE 6.1   **Rainbow.**

Rainbows are a continuous band of wavelengths that we see as seven colors blending into one another. In addition to being a beautiful sight, a rainbow can tell us a bit about color perception.

then tested behaviorally whether women with four-cone systems could actually discriminate more colors. Because many of the genes for color vision are on the X chromosome, men are more likely to be color deficient and less likely to have the extra cone system. Jordan et al. examined many people (all women) who have a genetic mutation that gives them what looks like an extra cone system in their retinae. The question was whether this would be expressed in terms of extra color vision. Only one of these women actually was able to discriminate colors that looked identical to the other participants or to normal controls. Jordan et al. estimated that this woman may see millions more hues than other people do. Current research by Jordan's group aims to understand what this woman sees, how it differs from normal color vision, and whether it really gives her abilities the rest of us do not possess.

WAVELENGTHS OF LIGHT AND COLOR

6.1   Examine the relation of the wavelength of light to perceived color.

In Chapter 3, we introduced the idea of the wavelength of light and its relation to the perception of color. Humans can see wavelengths of light that vary between 400 and 700 nm, often known as the **visual spectrum** (or **visible spectrum**). Within the visual spectrum, we see different wavelengths as different colors. It is important to keep in mind that the physical stimulus is the wavelength of the light entering our eye. Color is a perceptual attribute. The term *wavelength* refers to the distance between two peaks of light energy. It is the inverse of frequency. As frequency increases, wavelength decreases. In color vision, the wavelength of light is usually referred to, and as we will see, with sound waves, we tend to use frequency instead of wavelength (just to keep students on their toes).

Sunlight is a mix of many different wavelengths, which blend together to form white light. Because the wavelengths are bunched together, we cannot discriminate the different wavelengths in white light. But because sunlight is composed of so many wavelengths, raindrops can diffract (i.e., spread out) the light into the multiple wavelengths that make up the rainbow. The raindrops act as a prism and separate the many wavelengths that are mixed together. Once they are separated, we can see the individual bands of wavelengths as colors. Natural sunlight, however, varies in the distribution of wavelengths during the course of a day. At noon,

Visual spectrum (visible spectrum): the band of wavelengths from 400 to 700 nm that people with normal vision can detect

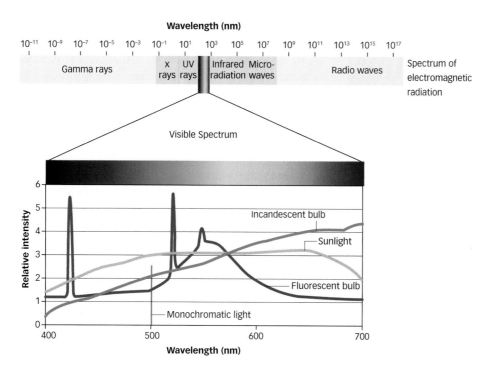

FIGURE 6.2 The distribution of wavelengths in natural and artificial light.

The top part of the figure shows the visible spectrum of light on a continuum of electromagnetic radiation. The figure makes it clear that visible light is just a small range on this continuum. The bottom part of the graph shows the distribution of wavelengths across natural sunlight, incandescent light-bulbs, and fluorescent bulbs. Note the interesting peaks in the fluorescent bulbs, which are very strong in the blue and green range, whereas incandescent light-bulbs show a gradual increase, peaking in the longer red wavelengths.

there is more blue light than in the morning, and evening is well known for its lingering red light. Artificial sources of light tend to be mixes of multiple wavelengths as well and therefore can also be classified as white light. Normal incandescent light-bulbs tend to emit more long-wavelength light than short-wavelength light. This gives incandescent light-bulbs their characteristic yellow color. Fluorescent light-bulbs tend to have the opposite pattern, giving them their slightly blue hue (Figure 6.2). All of these are variants of white light, that is, **heterochromatic light** consisting of many wavelengths. In contrast, **monochromatic light**, which can be produced by special lightbulbs, is light of only one wavelength or a very narrow band of wavelengths. When monochromatic light reflects off of a white surface, we see that surface as the color associated with that wavelength.

Another important feature in the perception of color is the spectral reflectance of objects in the world. **Spectral reflectance** is the ratio of light reflected by an object at each wavelength. This means that every object has particular characteristics that permit it to absorb some wavelengths of light and reflect other wavelengths of light. Thus, white clothes reflect wavelengths equally, whereas blue jeans absorb most wavelengths but reflect light at about 450 nm, which we perceive as blue. Thus, the color of any object is determined by what wavelengths it reflects the most. Leaves are green because their surfaces absorb most light but reflect green light. Carrots are orange because they absorb most wavelengths, but reflect light at about 650 nm, which we perceive as orange (see Figure 6.3).

Surfaces that reflect all light equally can be said to be achromatic (which means "without color") because we do not see them as containing color.

FIGURE 6.3 Familiar colors.

Objects with their familiar characteristic colors, and the same objects but with odd colors. Object get their characteristic colors because they reflect light at particular wavelengths. Ripe bananas absorb most light, but reflect light at about 550 nm, giving them their yellow color.

Heterochromatic light: white light, consisting of many wavelengths

Monochromatic light: light consisting of one wavelength

Spectral reflectance: the ratio of light reflected by an object at each wavelength

■ FIGURE 6.4   **Achromatic lightness.**

When objects reflect all light wavelengths equally, they are said to be achromatic. The three squares depicted here do not show any differences in the reflectivity of wavelengths. However, the white square reflects most light that shines on it, the gray square reflects about half of the light that shines on it, and the black square absorbs most of the light that shines on it.

Achromatic surfaces are judged to be white to gray to black (see Figure 6.4). With such surfaces, what matters is the proportion of ambient light they reflect. Surfaces that reflect most of the light that hits them will be seen as white surfaces (e.g., 90% or higher reflectance). Surfaces that reflect some but not all light will be seen as gray (e.g., 50% reflectance), and those that absorb most light will be seen as black (10% or lower reflectance). An important property of our visual system is that we respond to the percentage reflected rather than the total amount reflected. This allows us to see surfaces as the same level of grayness despite changes in the total amount of light. Thus, we still see a gray cat's fur as gray in bright sunlight or by a dim lamp in the evening, even though the fur is reflecting much more total light in broad daylight. With this background, we can now turn to perceptual features of color.

TEST YOUR KNOWLEDGE

How do the colors of the rainbow map onto wavelength as measured in nanometers?

HUE, SATURATION, LIGHTNESS, AND BRIGHTNESS

6.2   Identify the perceptual principles of hue, saturation, and brightness.

The perception of color is often described by referring to three dimensions of the color experience: hue, saturation, and brightness. We start with hue. **Hue** refers to the color quality of the light and corresponds to the color names that we use, such as orange, purple, green, indigo, yellow, cyan, aquamarine, and so on. In fact, hue is the quality of color. A **quality** is a value that changes, but it does not make the value larger or smaller. For example, when intensity (the amount of light present) changes, it gets larger or smaller. But when hue or color changes, it does not make sense to say, for example, that red has more or less hue than green. This is because color is a quality, not an amount. We see red and green as distinct units, even though some greens may seem darker or lighter, but this corresponds to the next dimension: saturation. But certainly red is very different from green. Many hues have direct correspondence to particular wavelengths, such as red (650 nm) and green (550 nm). Colors that are associated with particular wavelengths are called monochromatic colors, which include the basic colors or spectral colors, such as red, green, orange, yellow, and blue. There are also colors known as nonspectral, which are made of combinations of more than one monochromatic color. These are colors such as purple, brown, silver, and gold. Brown, for example, is a yellow or orange spectral color with very low saturation, that is, mixed with black. Purple is usually a mix of red and blue, though it can be combined in other ways as well.

Saturation refers to the purity of light. The more saturated the stimulus, the stronger the color experience, and the less saturated, the more it appears white or gray or black, that is, achromatic. The classic example of saturation differences concerns the continuum from red to pink. Pink is a combination of red light and white light. The more white light is added, the less "red" the pink is. A pastel pink

Hue: the color quality of light, corresponding to the color names we use, such as orange, green, indigo, and cyan; hue is the quality of color

Quality: a value that changes but does not make the value larger or smaller

Saturation: the purity of light

may contain just a bit of red light along with a lot of white light. Eventually, the red may be so overwhelmed by the white that we barely notice the pink at all. A solid blue becomes less saturated as we added more white, eventually becoming the "baby blue" we might paint a baby boy's room's walls (see Figure 6.5).

Hue and saturation can be represented as a color circle (see Figure 6.6). Along the perimeter of the circle, we find the monochromatic hues—red, orange, yellow, green, blue, indigo, and violet. As we head toward center of the circle, we get less and less saturated colors. Thus, a deep red and a deep blue exist on the perimeter, but pink and baby blue exist toward the center. You can explore an interactive illustration of these principles on ISLE 6.1.

Brightness refers to the amount of light present. The more bright an object it, the easier it is to see and the more noticeable the colors are. Brightness is the dimension that goes vertically through the color circle, now a color solid (see Figure 6.7). Brightness does have a relation to color—it is easier to see color at higher brightness values. Brightness is distinguished here from lightness. **Lightness** refers to the amount of light that gets reflected by a surface. This is a different property than the amount of light present. *Brightness* usually applies to colors, whereas *lightness* usually refers to the white-gray-black continuum.

TEST YOUR KNOWLEDGE

What is the relation between hue and wavelength? What is the relation between brightness and intensity?

■ FIGURE 6.5   Saturation.

On the left side are hues with strong saturation. We see these colors as very strong. On the right, we see hues with less saturation. The red becomes pink, and the blue becomes baby blue. The figures at the right have more white light mixed with the red or blue light in the shape.

ISLE 6.1 Dimensions of Color

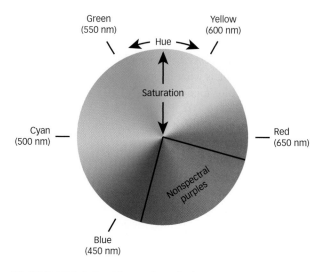

■ FIGURE 6.6   The color circle.

The color circle is a two-dimensional representation of how hue and saturation interact. Hue is represented around the perimeter, whereas saturation is represented as distance from the center (along the radius of the circle). The most saturated hues are along the perimeter, and saturation decreases as one moves toward the center.

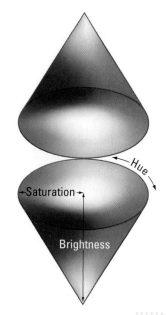

■ FIGURE 6.7   The color solid.

The color solid is a three-dimensional representation of the relations between brightness, saturation, and hue. As in the color circle, hue is represented around the perimeter, whereas saturation is represented as distance from the center (along the radius of the circle). The new dimension, brightness, is represented by the vertical dimension.

Brightness: the amount of light present

Lightness: the amount of light that gets reflected by a surface

ADDITIVE AND SUBTRACTIVE COLOR MIXING

6.3 Summarize the idea of a metamer and what color-matching experiments show.

Color has a very odd characteristic that is suggested by the color circle. Colors can be mixed. That may not seem odd, but that is because you have been doing it for so long—probably first during preschool art sessions. Usually, children in kindergarten have a pretty good intuitive sense about how to mix paints. But it is a relatively unique feature of color within the domain of visual perception, and the science is quite complex. To understand this statement, consider the following questions: Can you try to mix forms or motions? Can you mix size and depth? Most of our sensations and perceptions do not mix in the ways that colors do. Isaac Newton's classic experiments with prisms illustrate the profundity of the idea that colors mix. You can explore an interactive illustration of this principle on ISLE 6.2.

There are two main types of color mixing: subtractive color mixing and additive color mixing. **Additive color mixing** is the creation of a new color by a process that adds one set of wavelengths to another set of wavelengths. Additive color mixing is what happens when lights of different wavelengths are mixed. When we add all of the different wavelengths of sunlight, we see white light rather than many individual colors. This is called additive because all of the wavelengths still reach our eyes. It is the combination of different wavelengths that creates the diversity of colors. **Subtractive color mixing** is the creation of a new color by the removal of wavelengths from a light with a broad spectrum of wavelengths. Subtractive color mixing occurs when we mix paints, dyes, or pigments. When we mix paints, both paints still absorb all of the wavelengths they did previously, so what we are left with is only the wavelengths that both paints reflect. This is called subtractive mixing because when the paints mix, wavelengths are deleted from what we see because each paint will absorb some wavelengths that the other paint reflects, thus leaving us with a smaller number of wavelengths remaining afterward. The easy way to remember the difference between additive and subtractive color mixing is that additive color mixing is what happens when we mix lights of different colors, whereas subtractive color mixing occurs when we mix paints or other colored materials.

In the theater, lighting technicians use colored lights to create additive color mixing to illuminate the stage. When we look overhead at the lights, we may see a variety of colored lights projecting onto the stage, although the mix of these lights may create a different color than any present in the bank of lights overhead. Professional painters (and preschool children) can create a large of palette of colors by mixing different paints, thereby using subtractive color mixing. But if you do not know what you are doing when mixing paints, the result very often looks muddy and unappealing. We now look at the science of each form of color mixing a little more in depth.

Additive Color Mixing (Mixing Lights)

Additive color mixing occurs when lights of different wavelengths are mixed. This is what occurs in televisions. All of the colors one sees on a television screen are the result of the mix of three different light sources built into the television and controlled at different intensities. The same is true for our computer screens. What

ISLE 6.2 Newton's Prism Experiment

Additive color mixing: the creation of a new color by a process that adds one set of wavelengths to another set of wavelengths

Subtractive color mixing: color mixing in which a new color is made by the removal of wavelengths from a light with a broad spectrum of wavelengths

causes us to see colors such as chartreuse on our computer screens is a carefully balanced mix of three lights. When we shine equally bright green and red lights onto the same white surface, the lights add, as they do in sunlight, leaving us with a shade of gray. However, if the red light is brighter than the green light, you will still perceive color, most likely an orange hue. This is how televisions can create so many colors using just three dots. The principle of additive color mixing is illustrated in Figure 6.8. You can see a demonstration of additive color mixing on ISLE 6.3.

ISLE 6.3 Color Mixing

In Figure 6.8, you can see the color circle. It can be used to predict perceived colors in additive mixtures. The center of the circle represents the point at which any additive mixture contains equal amounts of the different wavelengths present. This center point is perceived as a gray. If you draw a line between two colors on the circle, say yellow and blue, the perceived color will fall on that line, depending on the relative intensities of the two lights. When you mix three lights, the color form is a function of a triangle between the three primary lights. Exactly what hue is perceived within that triangle is a function of the relative intensity of the three primary lights.

In the late 19th century, artists such as Georges Seurat, Paul Signac, and Vincent van Gogh invented a technique of painting that came to be known as pointillism (see Figure 6.9). In pointillism, an artist uses small distinct dots of simple primary colors as the basis of a painting. From a distance, the dots of colors blend together through a process similar to additive color mixing to form a rich array of colors. What makes pointillism relevant here is that it uses additive color mixing in painting rather than subtractive color mixing, the approach typically used in painting. The difference is that colors are created not by mixing paints but by keeping each dot a specific color, so that the dots blend together in a person's vision when viewed from a distance.

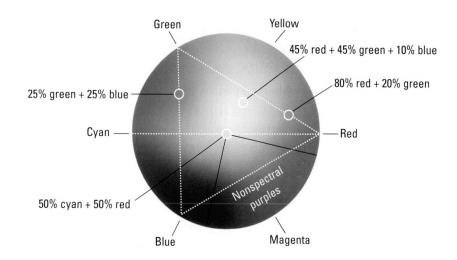

■ FIGURE 6.8   Additive color mixing.

Predicting what color will be created when mixing monochromatic lights involves using the color circle. If you are mixing two lights, you just draw a straight line from one color along the perimeter to the one you are mixing it with. The color you will create will lie somewhere along that line, depending on the brightness of each light. To predict what color will be created when mixing three monochromatic lights, you can connect the three colors along the perimeter to create a triangle as seen in the figure. The color created will fall somewhere inside that triangle. Where it falls will depend on the respective degrees of brightness of the three monochromatic lights.

Subtractive Color Mixing (Mixing Paints)

Subtractive color mixing is more common in the natural world, as there are many more situations in which pigments on the surfaces of objects interact than situations in which lights interact, as outside of artificial lighting, all lighting in nature comes from the sun and is therefore white light, not monochromatic light. Subtractive color mixing occurs when we mix substances with different absorption spectra. That is, when we mix substances, the mixture will absorb the wavelengths

■ **FIGURE 6.9** **A Sunday Afternoon on the Island of La Grande Jatte.**

This famous painting by Georges Seurat (1859–1891) illustrates the principles of pointillism. In pointillism, an artist uses small dots of color to form bigger images. With respect to color, the dots may be of very few primary colors, but when seen from a distance, the colors form an additive mixture, and we see a richer array of colors.

■ **FIGURE 6.10** **Subtractive color mixing.**

When light green paint is applied to the pink wall, the green paint continues to absorb most wavelengths other than green and, to some extent, close-by colors such as yellow. The pink paint continues to absorb most wavelengths other than red and, to some extent, close-by colors such as yellow. So when the first coat of green paint is put on the wall, the net result may be a yellow color.

both substances absorb, leaving only those wavelengths to reflect that both do not absorb. For example, consider repainting a room in your house. Perhaps as a young child, you wanted pink walls. Your parents may have painted your room with a very low saturation pink. Pink, as a low-saturation red, absorbs most wavelengths but reflects red light more than it does other wavelengths. As paints are likely to have a bit of spread in the wavelengths they reflect, there is also some yellow light that may be reflected (see Figure 6.10). Now you want your room to be a light shade of green. So when the first coat of paint is applied, you use a light green paint on top of the existing pink. To your dismay, when you look at the swath of color on your wall, you have a drab yellow wall instead of a light green one. How does this occur? Indeed, the green paint may include a little reflection of light in the yellow zone as well. So when the two paints are mixed, green pigment now absorbs the red wavelengths that were previously being reflected, and the old pink paint absorbs the green pigment from the new paint. What is left is the yellow in between. You can see a demonstration of subtractive color mixing on ISLE 6.3b.

Color-Matching Experiments

Color mixing and matching can be quite a complex phenomenon. Nonetheless, understanding how we match colors is critical to the development of theories of human color vision, which is the main focus of much of this chapter. Therefore, before we introduce the physiology of color vision, we briefly discuss color-matching experiments. Our contention here is that with a mix of three primary (monochromatic) colors, we can re-create any other monochromatic light. This is how televisions and computer monitors can reproduce any color: by mixing red, green, and blue lights. However, there are other possible primary colors that can be mixed to re-create other colors. For example, color printers, using a subtractive color mixing, employ cyan, magenta, and yellow to create a large array of colors.

Many psychophysical experiments have looked at the perceptual reality of color matching. These experiments are known as metameric color-matching experiments (Silverstein & Merrifield, 1985). A **metamer** is a psychophysical color match between two patches of light that have different sets of wavelengths. This means that a metamer consists of two patches of light that look identical to us in color, but are made up of different physical combinations of wavelengths. For example, a monochromatic light at 520 nm looks green. But we can create a color that looks identical by balancing the right amounts of light at 420, 480, and 620 nm.

In an experiment in metameric matching, an observer is shown two patches of light. One is called the test patch, and the other is called the comparison patch. The test patch is a single wavelength of an unchanging illumination or brightness (e.g., a monochromatic light at 520 nm at a set brightness). The comparison patch is composed of three primary colors, such as the red, green, and blue used in a television. The observer has control over the intensities of the three lights in the comparison patch. The observer's task is to adjust the level of each of the three primary colors in order to make the color of the comparison patch equal to that of the test patch. When the observer does this to his or her satisfaction, a metameric match is achieved for that individual. In general, a match that satisfies one individual will also satisfy other individuals of normal color-vision abilities. That is, most observers will see this match as identical unless they have some form of color deficiency. This is illustrated in Figure 6.11. You can try metameric matching for yourself on ISLE 6.4.

ISLE 6.4 Color Matching Experiment: Metameric Matches

In Figure 6.11, you can see the test patch with a wavelength of 550 nm (light green). The observer has control over three primary lights, with wavelengths of 440 (dark blue), 490 (dark green), and 650 (red) mm. These three primary lights are projected onto the comparison patch and combined through additive color mixing (they are lights, not pigments or paints). The observer has control over the intensities of the three primary lights making up the comparison patch and can change them until a metameric match is made. Even though none of the comparison patch primary lights are the same as the test patch light, we see the two patches as identical. This is the essence of metameric matching and, to some extent, the basis of much of the color vision we experience, given the amount of time modern people spend looking at computer screens, cell phone screens, and television screens.

TEST YOUR KNOWLEDGE

How do color-matching experiments illustrate the concept of a metamer?

THE RETINA AND COLOR

6.4   Explain how the three cones interact to influence color perception.

In Chapter 3, we introduced the cone systems in the retinae of the eyes (see Table 3.2). Cones are photoreceptors in the foveae of the retinae that are responsible for high acuity and color vision. Here we explain how cones allow us to code for color and how they transmit information about color to the occipital lobe. First, we review the function of the three cone systems and then describe how the presence of three cone types is important in developing the trichromatic theory of color vision.

Metamer: a psychophysical color match between two patches of light that have different sets of wavelengths

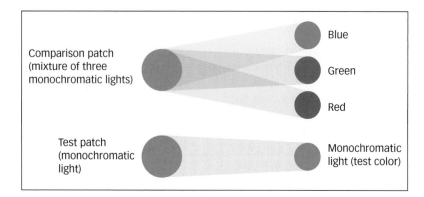

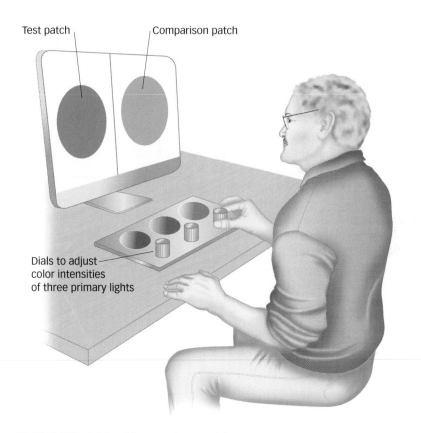

■ FIGURE 6.11   Metameric matching.

The participant in a metameric matching study is shown a test patch of monochromatic light. The participant has control over three primary lights in the comparison patch. He or she must adjust the intensity of each of the primary lights until the mix of the three lights looks subjectively identical to the monochromatic test patch.

S-cone: the cone with its peak sensitivity to short-wavelength light, around 420 nm (blue)

We have three classes of cone photoreceptors present in the foveae of the retinae. Each cone type has a different photopigment present and is therefore sensitive to a different band of wavelengths. The cone that has a maximum response to light at 420 nm is known as the **S-cone** (because it is sensitive to short-wavelength light). It is sometimes (and erroneously) called the blue cone because 420-nm light is perceived as blue. Calling it the blue cone is misleading because, as we discussed with metameric matches, all three cones are critical to perceiving all colors. The **M-cone** class has a maximum response to light at 535 nm, and the **L-cone** class has a maximum response to light at 565 nm. Here the *M* stands for *medium*, and the *L* stands for *long*, even though the two peaks are surprisingly close to each other. For the M-cone, 535-nm light is a yellowish green, and for the L-cone, 565-nm light is still to the yellow side of red. When these cone systems are combined together, we can see color over a range of 400 to 700 nm, from the S-cone's sensitivity to lower frequencies to the L-cone's sensitivity to higher frequencies. This range is approximate—there have been some studies suggesting that some people can detect very bright light at levels just below 400 nm. Nonetheless, the 400- to 700-nm range is a pretty good estimate. This is illustrated graphically in Figure 6.12.

The S-cones are distinctive for a number of reasons. First, there are many more M- and L-cones than there are S-cones. Indeed, S-cones make up only 5% of the total number of cones. Second, S-cones are less sensitive overall than are M- and L-cones. This means that they are less important in our perception of brightness, but they are still very important in our perception of color, especially when we consider their role in opponent processes. Interestingly, M- and L-cones are not all alike. There are subclasses of each (Mollon, 1992). These differences may result in subtle differences in color perception.

To understand how the cone systems relate to color perception, consider the following. A monochromatic light at 500 nm (green) is projected onto a white piece of paper. When the reflected light strikes the retina, there will be a very weak response in the S-cone, a strong response in the M-cone, and a relatively weak response in the L-cone (see Figure 6.13). It is this pattern of responses that induces the experience of the color green. In metameric matching, we can duplicate the pattern with other lights by simulating the pattern of light. Thus, we can dim the lowest wavelength light and strengthen the higher wavelength lights of three primary colors to match the same output of the retinal cones. You can try this for yourself on ISLE 6.5.

We have just reviewed the finding that each cone type has a wavelength to which it maximally responds. As we can see in Figures 6.12 and 6.13, each cone type responds to a swath of different frequencies as well. The M-cone, for example, responds weakly to light at 450 nm, greatly to light at 535 nm, and weakly to light at 650 nm. If this is the case, how can the M-cone distinguish between a very bright light at 450 nm and a dimmer light at 535 nm? The answer is that it cannot. If this were all the information V1 were provided with, a person could not see in color. Any cone system, by itself, cannot determine wavelength and therefore color. Furthermore, consider the response of the M-cone to a light equally intense at 500 and 630 nm. Given that the M-cone responds equally strongly to these wavelengths, equally intense lights at these frequencies cannot be distinguished by the M-cone. Thus, at least two cone types are necessary for any color vision to occur.

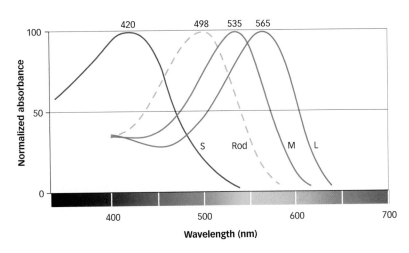

■ **FIGURE 6.12   Peak sensitivity of cones.**

The sensitivities of the S-, M-, and L-cones are given as a function of their response sensitivities to light of different wavelengths. The rod system's sensitivity is also shown for comparison. An object's color is determined by the joint response of each cone in response to that object's reflected wavelength pattern.

ISLE 6.5 Trichromatic Theory and Cone Responses

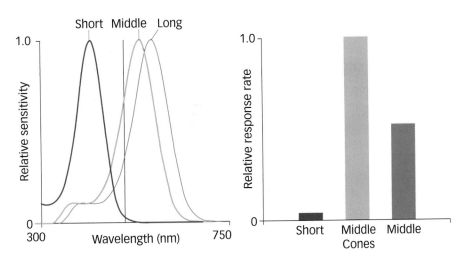

■ **FIGURE 6.13   The response of cones to a 500-nm light.**

Note that each cone system responds to this light but with a weaker or stronger response. Color is partially determined by this pattern of responses of each cone to any particular wavelength.

M-cone: the cone with its peak sensitivity to medium-wavelength light, around 535 nm (green)

L-cone: the cone with its peak sensitivity to long-wavelength light, around 565 nm (yellow)

Univariance, or Why More Than One Receptor Is Necessary to See in Color

The principle of **univariance** means that any single cone system is colorblind in the sense that different combinations of wavelength and intensity can result in the same response from the cone system. This implies that color vision depends critically on the comparative inputs of the different cone systems. Indeed, we can define the problem of univariance in the following way: The problem of univariance refers to the fact that many different wavelength and intensity combinations can elicit the same pattern of response from a single cone system. This means that any individual cone system cannot, by itself, distinguish colors.

The solution to this problem is that we have three cone systems that allow us to map any particular wavelength at any particular intensity onto a specific match among responses by the three cone systems. A monochromatic light, for example, will elicit a unique combination of outputs of the three cone systems that distinguishes it from other monochromatic light. However, we can still "trick" a three-cone system by adjusting the intensity of two or more lights so that they elicit the same overall response from the cone systems. This "trick" is the metameric match created by our television monitors. Recall that a metamer is the matching of a monochromatic color by manipulating the intensity of three lights so that their combination of wavelengths and intensities results in the same net output as that of the monochromatic light.

Recall the women whose retinae possess four cones, introduced at the beginning of the chapter. The reason these women can perceive more colors than the rest of us is that the fourth cone has a different spectral sensitivity than do the rest of the cones. Thus, any particular pattern of light will elicit a more complex response by the four cones. For these people, the intensity of four lights must be adjusted to match any particular wavelength. This leads them to have millions more combination of settings of their four-cone systems than do normal people with three-cone systems.

Finally, the problem of univariance explains why we do not see colors under nighttime lighting conditions. When we are under scotopic conditions (dim light), we use only our rod system. Because we have one class of rods, we do not see color under these conditions. You can see a dynamic illustration of viewing colored lights under one-cone or rod-only vision on ISLE 6.6.

ISLE 6.6 Color Matching in Monochromat or During Scotopic Vision

TEST YOUR KNOWLEDGE

Why are three cones necessary to see the colors we do? What evidence is there that some people have a four-cone system?

THE TRICHROMATIC THEORY OF COLOR VISION

6.5 Describe the trichromatic theory of color vision.

Although there have been many theories of color vision throughout history, the first modern theory was proposed by Thomas Young, the 19th-century philosopher and scientist, and later further developed by Hermann von Helmholtz, perhaps the 19th century's greatest scientist. Both of these scientists advanced a theory that is very similar to what we call today the trichromatic theory (and

Univariance: the principle whereby any single cone system is colorblind, in the sense that different combinations of wavelength and intensity can result in the same response from the cone system

sometimes the Young-Helmholtz trichromatic theory). Breaking down the word *trichromatic*, you have *tri*, which means "three," and *chromatic*, which means "colored." This theory proposes that color vision is based on there being three elements in our visual system that respond differently to different wavelengths. Young and Helmholtz did not know about cones; the theory was instead developed to explain how we make color matches. Now, however, it fits in squarely with the idea of a three-cone retina. The **trichromatic theory of color vision** states that the color of any light is determined by the output of the three cone systems in our retinae.

We have already reviewed much of the evidence that supports the trichromatic theory. First, color-matching experiments show that it takes a minimum of three primary colors to make a metameric match to a single monochromatic light. With people of normal vision, mixing two lights will not always yield a match to a pure monochromatic light, and four is not necessary (for nearly all people). That it takes three lights to make a match supports the trichromatic theory and was observed by Helmholtz, though he did not yet have a physiological explanation. Second, there is strong evidence for the trichromatic theory from the overwhelming data supporting the existence of three classes of cones in human retinae. Third, the trichromatic theory predicts what happens when individuals lose one of the cone classes in their retinae. These people—sometimes called colorblind, but more accurately called color deficient—still see in color, but they cannot distinguish between hues normal three-coned individuals cans. In the classic form, most color-deficient people cannot distinguish between reds and greens. There are now ample data showing that red-green color deficiency results from the loss of either the M-cones or the L-cones. There is also evidence that shows that blue-yellow color deficiency is the result of loss of the S-cones. Furthermore, a color-deficient individual with only two cones requires a match of only two light sources to match any one monochromatic light. The bottom line is that the trichromatic theory explains extremely well the relation of cones in the retinae and our perception of color.

National Portrait Gallery, London

© GL Archive / Alamy

■ FIGURE 6.14   **Thomas Young (1773–1829) and Hermann Von Helmholtz (1821–1894).**

Thomas Young and Hermann von Helmholtz developed the trichromatic theory of vision. This theory was a precursor of the modern view of color vision, in which the cones essentially serve as a trichromatic system.

TEST YOUR KNOWLEDGE

What is the peak sensitivity of each cone system?

THE OPPONENT THEORY OF COLOR PERCEPTION

6.6   Illustrate the opponent theory of color vision.

The traditional rival of trichromacy theory is the opponent theory of color perception. Opponent theory is based on a different set of observations and has a different underlying physiological basis. Of course, we now know that

Trichromatic theory of color vision: the theory that the color of any light is determined by the output of the three cone systems in our retinae

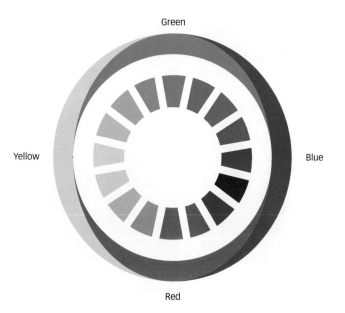

Green

Yellow

Blue

Red

■ **FIGURE 6.15**   **Hering's model of opponent processes.**

Hering's view was that all colors on the color circle (here the inner circle) can be represented by two pairs of opposing colors: blue-yellow and red-green. These opponents are represented along the outer circle.

the two theories are not mutually exclusive, and that both explain some aspects of color vision. But until relatively recently, they were considered rival theories. Certainly when the opponent theory was first developed, it challenged the Young-Helmholtz view.

The historical rival of Hermann von Helmholtz was Ewald Hering, as discussed in Chapter 1. Helmholtz proposed his version of trichromacy theory, and Hering proposed the **opponent theory of color perception** (see Figure 6.15). We know now that each theory explains certain aspects of color perception that the other theory cannot account for. We have already seen how trichromacy theory explains what the cones of the retinae are doing. We will see shortly how opponent theory explains color perception, starting in the ganglion cells and continuing to the lateral geniculate nucleus (LGN) and the occipital cortex. For many years, opponent theory was discredited, but the work of Russell DeValois on opponency cells in the LGN led to its revival (e.g., DeValois, 1960, 1965; DeValois, Abramov, & Jacobs, 1966). But before we discuss the physiological evidence for opponent theory, we will discuss the perceptual data.

Findings That Support Opponent Theory

Findings such as color-naming data and complementary color data led Hering to propose that color vision was not trichromatic but was organized with four primaries, or unique hues. These four primaries are organized in two sets of oppositional pairs (blue-yellow and red-green). Blue and yellow are opposite to each other, and red and green are also opposite to each other. In Hering's view, there were several observations that Helmholtz's trichromacy theory could not explain. Nonetheless, in their day, Helmholtz's view prevailed. But we now have physiological evidence to support opponent theory, in addition to Hering's perceptual data. Here are some of the important reasons advanced to support opponent processes in color perception:

a. Nonprimary colors can look like combinations of two primary colors. For example, purple looks like a combination of blue and red, and brown looks like a mix of yellow and black. But no colors look like a mix of blue and yellow or red and green. That is, our perception of colors supports the idea that red and green do not combine and that blue and yellow do not combine. It is hard to imagine what a yellowish blue might look like or what a reddish green might look like.

b. In color-sorting experiments, people tend to sort colors into four basic groups—green, red, yellow, and blue—rather than the three colors that might be predicted from trichromacy theory. This has been shown across Western and non-Western cultures (Rosch, 1973).

c. Color **afterimages** are visual images that are seen after an actual visual stimulus has been removed. If you stare at a bright incandescent light/bulb for even a short time and then close your eyes, you will continue to see an afterimage of that light/bulb for a relatively brief period of time. But you will notice

Opponent theory of color perception: the theory that color perception arises from three opponent mechanisms, for red-green, blue-yellow, and black-white

Afterimages: visual images that are seen after an actual visual stimulus has been removed

that although the light/bulb has a yellowish hue, your afterimage will appear somewhat blue. Afterimages are strong after seeing lights, but they work for reflected light as well. After staring at a patch of red light for 30 seconds or so, one can close one's eyes and see a vague patch of cyan (between green and blue, at about 485 nm). These afterimages have led to the amusing illustrations you can see in Figure 6.16. An afterimage is actually a complementary color, which is not the same as an opponent color. Red and green are opponent colors, but because together they also give the yellow input to the blue-yellow system, they are not complements. Thus, aftereffects lead to complementary colors, whose existence is nonetheless a problem for trichromatic theory. For a demonstration of afterimages, go to ISLE 6.7.

d. **Simultaneous color contrast** occurs when our perception of one color is affected by a color that surrounds it. The effect occurs when a color is surrounded by its opponent color and not by other colors or achromatic backgrounds. A green circle will seem more green if it is surrounded by a red background, and a red circle will seem more red if it is surrounded by a green background. Similarly, a blue circle will seem more blue if it is surrounded by a yellow background, and a yellow circle will appear more yellow if it is surrounded by a blue background (see Figure 6.17). You can explore an interactive illustration of simultaneous color contrast on ISLE 6.8.

In a series of important experiments, Hurvich and Jameson (1957) described the phenomenon of **hue cancellation**, which led to a rebirth in the idea that opponent processing does explain color vision. These experiments also support the opponent processes theory. We turn to this experiment next.

Hue Cancellation

In this classic experiment, the husband-and-wife team of Hurvich and Jameson redeveloped Hering's view on opponency. Hurvich and Jameson (1957) developed a new way to empirically examine this view. In this experiment, participants saw a monochromatic light at a wavelength between two particular primary colors. For example, a participant might see a cyan light with a wavelength at 485 nm. Then the participant was given control over the amount of a second light that could be added to the first, through additive color mixing. The instructions were to cancel out the blue so that the light appeared only as green. The participant could do this by adding a yellow-wavelength light, but if he tried to do it with red light, he could never succeed. Only yellow light could cancel out the blue light (and vice versa). However, if you have a light between red and yellow, green must be added to cancel out the red. You can see the procedure illustrated in Figure 6.18. You can do a dynamic illustration of this principle on ISLE 6.9.

We discuss one last bit of psychophysical data on opponent theory before turning to the underlying physiology. Most colors can be described in terms of combinations of other colors. Orange, for example, feels like a mix of yellow and red. Pink feels like a mix of red and white. However, four colors can be described only in terms of themselves. These four colors are the four opponent colors: blue,

ISLE 6.7 Color Aftereffect

ISLE 6.8 Simultaneous Color Contrast

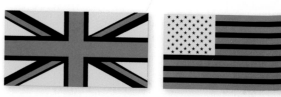

■ **FIGURE 6.16** **Color afterimages.**

Stare at one flag for roughly 30 seconds without moving your eyes. Then look at a blank space on the page. You should see the correct flag as an afterimage. Note that complementary colors of afterimages are not the same as opponents. In order to get the red in each flag, you need a cyan, not a green.

■ **FIGURE 6.17** **Simultaneous color contrast.**

Opponent colors can enhance the experience of each other. Thus, a green square surrounded by red looks more green than if surrounded by a neutral color. Similarly, a yellow square looks more yellow when surrounded by a blue background than a neutral background.

ISLE 6.9 Hue Cancellation

Simultaneous color contrast: a phenomenon that occurs when our perception of one color is affected by a color that surrounds it

Hue cancellation: an experiment in which observers cancel perception of a particular adding light of the oppo

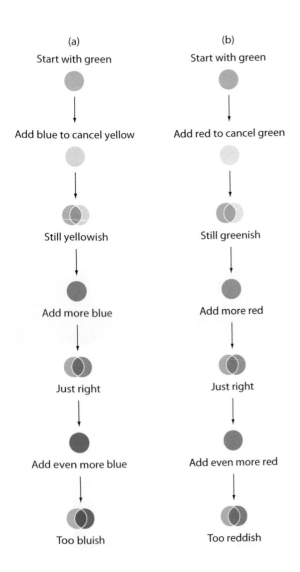

(a)
Start with green

↓

Add blue to cancel yellow

↓

Still yellowish

↓

Add more blue

↓

Just right

↓

Add even more blue

↓

Too bluish

(b)
Start with green

↓

Add red to cancel green

↓

Still greenish

↓

Add more red

↓

Just right

↓

Add even more red

↓

Too reddish

■ **FIGURE 6.18   Hue cancellation.**

In a hue cancellation experiment, a participant starts off with a given color (in the figure, a greenish blue). Then the participant must add another color to eliminate any experience of one of the colors (e.g., the blue). Thus, the participant must add yellow to eliminate blue (or red to eliminate green). In these studies, only the opponent theory predicts how participants match the colors.

colors: colors that can be
~~~ only with a single color
~~~ green, blue, and yellow

~~ cells: neurons that
~~ input from one
~~ er, but inhibited
~~ er cone type in

yellow, red, and green. In this way, these colors can be thought of as **unique colors**. Interestingly, these unique colors feel basic to us, but none of them reflects the peak sensitivity of one of our cones. Even the S-cone's peak wavelength sensitivity would not be described as an iconic blue. Rather, 420 nm appears violet, as if there were a bit of red to it. The peak sensitivity of the M-cone is a yellowish green, and the peak sensitivity of the L-cone is an orange-yellow. Thus, these unique colors must arise from a different level of the nervous system than the cones in the retinae.

Opponent Cells in the LGN and V1

In Chapter 4, we discussed center-surround cells in V1. These are cells that respond best to a spot of light in the center surrounded by a darker circle. There are also cells that respond to darkness in the center surrounded by an annulus of light. We discussed how such a system was important for edge detection and discriminating shapes. A similar system exists for color that also supports the opponent process view. Researchers have also found opponent cells in V1 that respond to a particular color in the center and respond best when that center color is surrounded by an annulus of its opponent color. We can see the first opponent cells in the retinal ganglion cells, but we focus here on opponent cells in the LGN and in V1.

In the LGN, one finds color-sensitive cells called **cone-opponent cells**. These cells respond best when they are excited by the input from one cone in the center, but inhibited by the input from another cone type in the surround. For example, in the LGN, one can find cells that are excited by L-cones in the center but inhibited by M-cones in the surround. There are also cells that are excited by S-cones in the center but inhibited by both L- and M-cones in the surround. These cone-opponent cells are likely the building blocks of the opponency system (DeValois, 2004).

In V1, we find cells that are specific not to cones but to colors themselves. These neurons are called color-opponent cells. **Color-opponent cells** are excited by one color in the center and inhibited by its opponent color in the surround. A color-opponent cell may also be inhibited by one color in the center and excited by its opponent color in the surround (see Figure 6.19). Color-opponent cells are red-green and blue-yellow, but never, for example, red-yellow or green-blue, consistent with Hering's opponent processes theory. That is, these cells work in opponent pairs. There will be a cell that responds to red in the center and inhibits green in the surround, the presumed basis of simultaneous color contras.

In V1, there is also a class of color-sensitive cells called double-opponent cells. **Double-opponent cells** have a center, which is excited by one color and inhibited by the other. In the surround, the pattern is reversed. Thus, if the center is

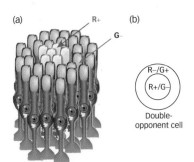
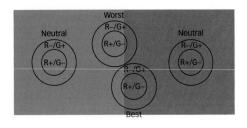

■ FIGURE 6.19   Color-opponent cells.

(a) A single-opponent cell's receptive field is shown. It responds best when one color (red) is seen in the middle and its opponent (green) surrounds it. (b) The center of each double-opponent cell is excited by one color (green) and inhibited by the opponent color (red). In the surround, the cell is excited by red and inhibited by green. When we put this cell just along the edge of a green-red barrier, it will respond maximally, whereas when it is in an open green or red field, the excitation and inhibition will cancel out. Thus, the cell along the edge will respond robustly, while the cell in the open field will not. Thus, opponent cells serve as color-edge detectors.

excited by green and inhibited by red, the surround will be excited by red and inhibited by green. Double-opponent cells are useful for detecting color edges, that is, where one colored object ends and a differently colored object begins, by enhancing color divisions at the edges of objects (Johnson, Hawken, & Shapley, 2001). Think of red berries surrounded by green leaves. Double-opponent cells sharpen the boundaries where the red berries end and the green leaves begin, making it easier for the observer to home in on some delicious raspberries. This type of information is useful to the visual system. For a demonstration of how single-opponent and double-opponent cells work, go to ISLE 6.10.

ISLE 6.10 Single and Double-Opponent Cells

TEST YOUR KNOWLEDGE

What are afterimages? What theory of color perception do they support?

COLOR DEFICIENCY

6.7   Describe the concept of color deficiency and why it is a better term than *color blindness*.

Color deficiency refers to the condition of individuals who are missing one or more of their cone systems. Color deficiency used to be called colorblindness, but the latter term is not appropriate. The vast majority of color-deficient individuals do see colors, just not as many colors as normal people do. Color deficiencies are usually the result of genetic defects that prevent the development of one or more cone systems. Thus, in general, color deficiencies are present at birth and seldom develop later in life. Interestingly, because of the nature of those genetic issues, color deficiencies are much more common in men than they are in women.

The genetic information for forming cones in fetal development travels on the X chromosome in a region of that chromosome disproportionately likely to have a mistake (Woods & Krantz, 2001). These genetic mistakes are of different

Color-opponent cells: neurons that are excited by one color in the center and inhibited by another color in the surround, or neurons that are inhibited by one color in the center and excited by another color in the surround

Double-opponent cells: cells that have a center, which is excited by one color and inhibited by the other; in the surround, the pattern is reversed

Color deficiency: the condition of individuals who are missing one or more of their cone system types, and it is the type of mistake that determines the type of color deficiency. It is important to remember that males have only one X chromosome and females have two. Because the genes that lead to color deficiency are on the X chromosome, males need only one of these defective genes to be color deficient, but females need two of these genes, one on each chromosome, to be color deficient. As a result, males are far more likely than females to have a color deficiency. Such types of traits are known as sex-linked traits. Other sex-linked traits include male pattern baldness and hemophilia, both much more common among men than women.

Color deficiency is quite common in humans. Usually, in a college class of 100 students or so, there is at least 1 young man who admits to being color deficient. Indeed, it is estimated to occur in as many as 8% of males and 0.4% of females (Birch, 2001). The most common diagnosed form is red-green color deficiency. These individuals see colors in a general spread from dark blues to light blues to dim yellows to bright yellows. The frequencies normal people see as green and red are just part of the blue-to-yellow continuum for individuals with this form of color deficiency. However, there are really two separable types of red-green color deficiency, one caused by the loss of the M-cone system and one caused by the loss of the L-cone system. In the past, a simple way to identify color deficiency was to show potential patients Ishihara plates (see Figure 6.20). In these plates, normal people can see the numbers created by the dots because they are different colors than the surrounding dots. The dots, however, are isoluminant dots; that is, they reflect light at the same intensity, even though the wavelengths are different for the dots that make up the number and the background. Because of this, normal people will see the number, because they can detect the color differences. But a red-green color-deficient individual will see only dots and not be able to tell them apart because of intensity differences. Because the dots are isoluminant and chosen to be metamers for color-deficient individuals, a red-green color-deficient person cannot see the number in an Ishihara plate. Thus, these plates allow for easy identification of color deficiency. Another way of identifying color-deficient individuals is to have them do metameric matching tasks. Their matches will be very different from those of people with normal vision.

We start by defining normal color vision and how color deficiency differs from it. People with normal color vision have three functioning cone systems. Such a normal person could match any pure wavelength by varying the intensity of three colors, such as red, green, and blue. Across normal people, these matches will be nearly identical. Then there are color-deficient people, who come in a number of varieties.

Rod Monochromacy

Rod monochromacy is a very rare form of color deficiency, affecting only 1 in every 30,000 people (Carroll, Neitz, Hofer, Neitz, & Williams, 2004). Rod monochromats have no functioning cones of any kind and therefore can be described as truly colorblind. As a results, they see the world in shades of gray—high-reflectance objects are white, low-reflectance objects are black, and intermediate-reflectance objects are various shades of gray. In metamer matching, only one color is required to match

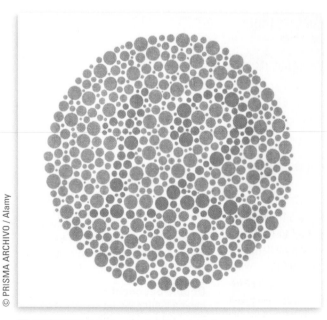

■ FIGURE 6.20   **An Ishihara plate.**

These figures are used as a quick test for color deficiencies. The dots are all isoluminant, regardless of color, so the number cannot be determined by differences in brightness. Only color allows you to see the number. For the plate shown, a red-green color-deficient individual would not be able to see the number.

another, as all a rod monochromat will be doing is adjusting the percentage of reflected light, that is, how gray the surface is.

Because they have no cones, rod monochromats have many other visual problems in addition to colorblindness. Rod monochromats are dependent on their rod vision in both bright and dim light. This has serious disadvantages during daylight conditions, as these individuals are highly sensitive to light but have poor visual acuity. Because they are using scotopic vision all the time, rod monochromats are extremely sensitive to bright lights. For example, in a room that would be considered normally illuminated for people with intact cone systems, a rod monochromat will find it too bright. As such, rod monochromats often must wear sunglasses indoors. Going outside on a bright sunny day can be overwhelming and requires very strong eye protection. In reality, most rod monochromats will avoid bright outdoor conditions even with very strong sunglasses. Moreover, because the rods do not support acuity, rod monochromats have very poor visual acuity and must wear very strong lenses in order to read. Even then, most rod monochromats require large typefaces in order to read normally. To summarize, unlike those with color deficiencies, rod monochromats are at a serious disadvantage relative to normally sighted people (you can see the world as a rod monochromat might on ISLE 6.11).

ISLE 6.11 Rod Monochromat Vision

Cone Monochromacy

There are extremely rare cases of individuals known as cone monochromats. These people lack two cone types but have one present. S-cone monochromats have been found; they have the S-cone system, but lack both the M- and L-cone systems (Alpern, Lee, Maaseidvaag, & Miller, 1971). S-cone monochromacy is an X-chromosome-linked trait and thus is more common in men than women, though it has been observed in women. However, S-cone monochromacy is still extremely rare in men, as only 1 in 100,000 men will exhibit it. Because of the low overall sensitivity of the S-cone system, cone monochromats exhibit many of the symptoms seen in rod monochromats, although the symptoms tend to be less severe in S-cone monochromats than in rod monochromats. Cone monochromats also have poor acuity and high sensitivity to bright light. Wavelength discrimination is poor in S-cone monochromats, and subjectively, the world appears in blacks, whites, and grays. Interestingly, in twilight conditions, in which both the rod and cone systems are at work, S-cone monochromats can distinguish some colors, essentially using the one cone system and the one rod system as might a dichromat.

Dichromacy

Dichromats have only two working cone systems. Thus, they can see colors, though a much lesser range of colors than do normal trichromats. There are three major forms of dichromacy: **protanopia**, **deuteranopia**, and **tritanopia** (see Table 6.1). Dichromats require only two colored lights to match any monochromatic light, compared with normal individuals, who require three. Dichromats see in color, but they cannot make some of the discriminations that are easy for trichromats. Protanopia and deuteranopia are linked to the X chromosome and are therefore inheritable and more common in men than women. Protanopia and deuteranopia are also more common than tritanopia.

Because men have only one X chromosome (and one Y chromosome), if they have a deficiency gene on the X chromosome, they will express the deficiency. However, women have two X chromosomes. The same deficiency gene must be present on both X chromosomes for a woman to be a protanope or a deuteranope. If a woman has only one deficient X chromosome, she will see colors normally,

Protanopia: a lack of L-cones, leading to red-green deficiency; this trait is sex linked and thus more common in men

Deuteranopia: a lack of M-cones, leading to red-green deficiency; this trait is sex linked and thus more common in men

Tritanopia: a lack of S-cones, leading to blue-yellow color deficiency; this trait is much rarer and is not sex-linked as the single normal X chromosome is enough to structure her retinae correctly. However, she is still a carrier, and there is thus a 50% chance that she will pass that gene on to an offspring. A son inheriting the carrier X chromosome would be color deficient, and a daughter would have a 50% chance of being a carrier. Thus, the only way a woman can be color deficient is if she has a color-deficient father and either a color-deficient mother or a mother who is a carrier.

Protanopia

Protanopes lack L-cones in their retinae, as a function of a deficient gene. Protanopia can occur in as many as 1% of males, but is very rare in females, roughly 0.02%. Because protanopes do not have L-cones, they are classified as red-green colorblind (the common name for the condition). An approximation of what they see as a function of wavelength is depicted in Figure 6.21a. At short wavelengths, protanopes see blue. As wavelength increases, the blue becomes less saturated until it eventually becomes gray (at 492 nm), and then as the wavelengths continue to increase, the color is perceived as a more and more saturated yellow. The yellow fades at the high end of the visual spectrum (Figure 6.22).

Deuteranopia

Deuteranopes lack M-cones in their retinae, as a function of a deficient gene. Deuteranopia has about the same frequency as protanopia, and in many contexts they are indistinguishable and are both referred to as red-green colorblindness. However, the crossover wavelength from blue to yellow occurs at a different wavelength (498 nm). For an approximation of how deuteranopes perceive color, inspect Figure 6.21b.

Tritanopia

Tritanopes lack S-cones in their retinae. This is the rarest form of dichromat color deficiency, occurring in just about 1 in 100,000 people. Because this deficiency is not sex linked, it is just about as common among women as it is among men. Tritanopes see blue at short wavelengths, which becomes less saturated as the wavelength increases. At higher wavelengths, tritanopes see red. The crossover point for tritanopes is 570 nm. For an approximation of how tritanopes perceive color, inspect Figure 6.21c. You can explore an interactive illustration of what the world looks like to dichromats and color matching in dichromats on ISLE 6.12.

ISLE 6.12 Dichromacy

(a)   (b)   (c)

■ FIGURE 6.21   **The world as it looks to color-deficient individuals.**

This is how these colored displays look to (a) protanopes, (b) deuteranopes, and (c) tritanopes.

There is also a form of color deficiency called **anomalous trichromacy**. In anomalous trichromats, all three cone systems are intact, but one or more of the cone systems has an altered absorption pattern, leading to different metameric matches than in normal individuals. The most common form of anomalous trichromacy is an abnormality in the M-cone system (Smith & Pokorny, 2003). However, it can also occur with the L- or the S-cone system. In general, anomalous trichromats are not as good at discriminating similar wavelengths as normal trichromats. You can see the different forms of anomalous trichromacy and their incidence in Table 6.2.

A question that may have occurred to you is, How can we be sure of the colors dichromats and anomalous trichromats are seeing? After all, because they have missing or abnormal cone systems, their perception of color may not be imaginable by people with normal color vision. If this were the case, the perceptual spectra in Figures 6.20 and 6.21 would not be accurate. In other words, when looking at the sky, a deuteranope may know to say "blue" as normal individuals do, but is the color-deficient person really seeing the same color?

The answer to this question comes from a very small class of color-deficient persons known as unilateral dichromats. A person with **unilateral dichromacy** has dichromacy in one eye but normal trichromatic vision in the other. This is an extremely rare condition. However, the existence of unilateral dichromacy allows researchers to discover the nature of the experience of dichromacy. A unilateral dichromat can observe a colored figure with one eye at a time and describe the color both as a person with normal color vision would and as a person with dichromacy would (Alpern, Kitahara, & Krantz, 1983; Graham & Hsia, 1958). When viewing objects with both eyes, they see color essentially normally, but when they close their trichromatic eye, they become dichromats. Thus, such a person would describe a 520-nm light as green with her trichromatic eye but as yellow with her dichromatic eye. When she reopens her trichromatic eye, she again

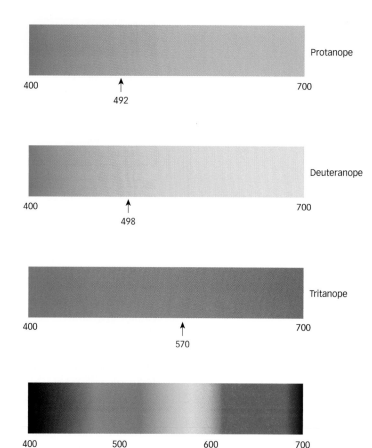

■ FIGURE 6.22　The visual spectrum as it appears to color-deficient individuals.

Type of Color Deficiency	Cone System Absent	Color Experience
Rod monochromacy	All	No color
Tritanopia	S	Lack green and yellow
Deuteranopia	M	Lack green and red
Protanopia	L	Lack green and red
Anomalous trichromacy		
Normal trichromacy	None	Normal color experience

■ TABLE 6.1　A Description of Different Types of Color Vision

Anomalous trichromacy: a condition in which all three cone systems are intact, but one or more has an altered absorption pattern, leading to different metameric matches than in normal individuals

Unilateral dichromacy: the presence of dichromacy in one eye but normal trichromatic vision in the other

Type of Anomalous Trichromacy	Males	Females
Protanomalous (L-abnormal)	1%	0.02%
Deuteranomalous (M-abnormal)	5%	0.04%
Tritanomalous (S-abnormal)	0.005%	0.01%

■ TABLE 6.2   Percentages of Different Anomalous Color Deficiencies

sees it as a normal person would. It is based on the experiences of these unilateral dichromats that we know the color experience of dichromats.

The most common question often asked of deuteranopes and protanopes when other people find out that they are "red-green color blind" is how they know to stop at a traffic signal when it is red or drive through when it is green, if they cannot discriminate between red and green. This is more of a practical question than one related to the nature of their visual experience. In the past, traffic signals were a major problem for color-deficient drivers. However, they are no longer a problem because it is now standard to put the red light at the top of the series of lights (three if there is a yellow light) and the green light at the bottom. So color-deficient individuals can stop and go by attending to vertical position rather than color. Those of us with normal trichromacy do not pay attention to this feature, but color-deficient people learn it quickly and use it to respond to traffic signals as well as people with normal vision.

As we discussed at the beginning of the chapter, some women seemingly have four-cone systems. Interestingly, these women are usually related to men with anomalous trichromacy, so one theory that accounts for the existence of this condition is that the same mutation that results in anomalous trichromacy in men can occasionally result in tetrachromacy in women (Jordan et al., 2010). According to this research, roughly 10% of women may carry the gene for anomalous trichromacy. But in Jordan et al.'s (2010) study, only 1 in 24 women with this gene showed any evidence of being a tetrachromat. Such women require four separate colors to match a monochromatic light and presumably sees countless shades of color that normal individuals do not (Jameson, Highnote, & Wasserman, 2001). To tetrachromats, all of us normal individuals are effectively color deficient. Tetrachromacy is extraordinarily rare, but it has been documented.

Cortical Achromatopsia

In **cortical achromatopsia**, loss of color vision occurs because of damage to the occipital lobe. Cortical achromatopsia is extremely rare, much less common than the color deficiencies caused by pigment problems in the retinae. Cortical achromatopsia usually comes about from damage to Area V4 (also involved in shape perception, as discussed in Chapter 5). Cortical achromatopsia usually involves a perceptual experience of seeing only in black and white (and shades of gray) or the impression that colors seem washed out. In some cases, the perception is of shades of gray, but patients can still discriminate by wavelength even though they do not experience the colors. These patients still have all their cone systems intact, and the problem is at a higher level of processing. This may be why they can discriminate wavelengths but still not see colors. In addition, in some cases, patients with achromatopsia lose the ability to remember color. That is, they do not remember what it was like to experience color. In contrast, a person who

Cortical achromatopsia: loss of color vision due to damage to the occipital lobe

becomes blind because of eye damage still remembers his or her experience of color. In some cases, patients with cortical achromatopsia can no longer put color into mental images and may fail to be able to remember objects by their colors. Thus, a banana is no longer yellow in memory, nor is a ripe tomato red. Even in memory, these objects lose their colors. Finally, in some cases, individuals may not even be aware that color vision has been lost (von Arx, Müri, Heinemann, Hess, & Nyffeler, 2010). Again, all of this symptomatology has been linked to damage in V4 (Wade, Augath, Logothetis, & Wandell, 2008).

> **TEST YOUR KNOWLEDGE**
>
> What is the difference between a rod monochromat and a cone monochromat? What differences are there in their vision?

CONSTANCY: LIGHTNESS AND COLOR CONSTANCY

6.8   Define the term *constancy* and how it applies to color vision.

Constancy refers to our ability to perceive an object as the same object under different conditions. That is, I want my visual system to recognize a barracuda whether it is swimming directly toward me or away from me, in murky water or clear water, or at an angle to me or coming straight at me. The image on the retinae may be quite different in each of these cases, but I still need to recognize the same object. This is an important goal of the visual system. We want to be able to tell if an object is the same object across changes in lighting, shading, distance, movement, and orientation. For another example, we want to be able to detect a banana as being a banana whether we are seeing it close up or from far away. We want to be able to judge if the banana is ripe regardless of whether we are viewing the fruit in broad daylight, by the light of a lightbulb, or even by twilight. For this reason, we have evolved many processes that enact constancy in different domains of perception. **Lightness constancy** refers to our ability to perceive the relative reflectance of objects despite changes in illumination. **Color constancy** refers to our ability to perceive the color of an object despite changes in the amount and nature of illumination. We will now unpack these definitions.

Before we delve into the science color and then lightness constancy in depth, consider Figure 6.23. We see a pleasant garden scene. Look at the grass. We see a light green field of grass with a few scattered small white flowers. In the background, some pretty yellow flowers adorn a bush. Across the foreground, a tree, which is not visible in the photograph, casts a shadow over the grass. The core idea of constancy is that we see the grass as green, and the same green, despite the changes in illumination caused by the shade. We perceive correctly that there is a shadow present and infer that there is differential illumination on the grass, but the grass's color does not change as a function of illumination. This is an illustration of color constancy, the fact that we see an object as the same color across changes in illumination.

■ FIGURE 6.23   Color constancy.

We want to be able to recognize the grass here as one continuous object of one continuous color, even though some of the grass is shaded by trees and therefore reflects less light back to the viewer. That we see the grass as one color despite the differences of illumination is an example of constancy.

Constancy: the ability to perceive an object as the same under different conditions

Lightness constancy: the ability to perceive the relative reflectance of objects despite changes in illumination

Color constancy: the ability to perceive the color of an object despite changes in the amount and nature of illumination

Color Constancy

We consider color constancy first. *Color constancy* refers to the observation that we see the same color despite changes in the composition of the wavelengths of light that is striking that object. Thus, a green mug appears to be the same color regardless of whether the light illuminating it is natural sunlight, a fluorescent light/bulb, or an incandescent light/bulb. This is true even though the object is now reflecting different absolute amounts of light at different wavelengths under each illumination condition. Color constancy serves an important perceptual function—the properties of objects seldom change as a function of changes in the source of illumination. Thus, a system that sees an object as a constant color across such changes leads to accurate perception. Interestingly, the distribution of wavelengths in sunlight changes across the day. Evening light has more long-wavelength light than light earlier in the day. Although we might enjoy the colors of twilight, we do not normally see objects as changing colors, though we are aware of general changes in illumination when we attend to them. We can see this in Figure 6.24. The statues of the presidents appear to be the same color despite the change from peak sunlight to twilight. You can explore an interactive illustration of these principles on ISLE 6.13.

Color constancy is not perfect. There are a number of situations in which color constancy fails. That is, we see the same object as being differently colored under different lighting conditions. One such situation is when we use a monochromatic light. Shining a monochromatic light on an object will allow that object to reflect only that wavelength. Thus, depending on how much of that wavelength is reflected by the object, the object will appear the color of the light regardless of its reflectance characteristics. What we will see is a different level of saturation, depending on how much the object reflects the wavelength being shined on it. Another situation occurs when an object is viewed in front of a pure black background. This makes it difficult for the visual system to get the context to see the object as the right color.

The mechanism whereby our visual systems control color constancy is not well understood. Seemingly, the visual system is able to compare the reflectance patterns of different wavelengths from one object to those from another to determine which object is reflecting more blue, yellow, and so on. However, because the visual system cannot intrinsically measure the wavelength distributions in the illuminant light, it must infer this as well (Foster, 2011). Data support the idea

ISLE 6.13 Illumination and Color Constancy

■ **FIGURE 6.24**   Color constancy on Mount Rushmore.

We see the monument as being the same color despite the change in illumination from day to night.

that the visual system automatically determines the ratio of wavelengths in a scene by comparing across many objects in that scene. That is, the color of an object is determined not just by the wavelengths coming off of that object, but also by the wavelengths of the light coming from neighboring objects.

One of the classic demonstrations of color constancy has been called Mondrian experiments by Edwin Land (1977), after the Dutch painter Piet Mondrian (see Figure 6.25). In these experiments, a surface with a random collection of rectangles of different sizes and colors of matte paper (much like Mondrian's paintings) is presented to participants. Each rectangle is surrounded by rectangles of different colors. The illumination of the surface is provided by three projectors, each of which projects a different narrow band of wavelengths. One projector emits long wavelengths, the second emits middle wavelengths, and the third emits short wavelengths. When all give light with the same level of illuminations, these three projectors are a match for white light.

The method for these experiments is complicated. First, a participant is asked to look at one square, say a red one. Once the participant is focused on the red square, the experimenter changes the illumination by adjusting the three projectors so that the light coming off of the red square reflects twice as much middle-wavelength light as long-wavelength light. The question for the participant is, What is the color now for this red square? The square itself reflects more long-wavelength light than others (hence its red color). But now, it is being differentially illuminated by more light lower in wavelength. After the adjustment of the projectors, the reverse is true; it is reflecting more middle-wavelength light than long-wavelength light. Still, participants say that the rectangle they have been focused on the whole time looks red. Within wide ranges of the bands of illumination, the wavelength coming off of the square does not change its color appearance. Once red, always red. And of course, the same is true for squares of other colors on the Mondrian image as well. This is important because the other squares have

■ FIGURE 6.25   **A building painted in the style of Piet Mondrian (1872–1944).**

This building painted in the style of Mondrian shows a pattern of color. Stimuli such as this have been used for experiments on color constancy. In the experiments, the wavelengths of the light illuminating the stimuli are altered. As long as viewers can see all the different boxes of color, they maintain color constancy. But if they only see one square, its color will change as a function of illumination.

© iStockphoto.com/hohl

changed their reflectance as a function of the incoming lights. The fact that each square is surrounded by squares of different colors is important to the outcome of this experiment. Thus, the comparison of each area with the varied colors around it is critical to maintaining color constancy. This supports the idea that color constancy is achieved by an implicit comparison across different objects in a scene, which each reflect different wavelengths, allowing the visual system to extract the illumination from known reflective properties.

Lightness Constancy

Lightness constancy refers to our ability to perceive the relative reflectance of objects despite changes in illumination. The easiest way to think of lightness constancy is to think of it along the continuum from black to gray to white. These achromatic colors simply refer to the amount of white light an object reflects. A black

Edward H. Adelson

■ **FIGURE 6.26   Lightness constancy.**

In this illustration, we see a checkerboard being shaded by a peculiar cylinder. Because we infer that there is less illumination on the shaded part of the checkerboard, we see Square A as being the same shade as Square B, even though objectively B is a darker gray than A.

ISLE 6.14 Lightness Constancy

ISLE 6.15 Gelb Effect

object absorbs most light, whereas a white object reflects most light, with gray objects being in between. *Lightness constancy* refers to the observation that we continue to see an object in terms of the proportion of light it reflects rather than the total amount of light it reflects. That is, a gray object will be seen as gray across wide changes in illumination. A white object remains white in a dim room, while a black object remains black in a well-lit room. In this sense, lightness constancy serves a similar function as color constancy in that it allows us to see properties of objects as being the same under different conditions of lighting (Adelson, 1993).

Consider an object that reflects 25% of the light that hits its surface. This object will be seen as a rather dark gray (see Figure 6.26). If we leave it in a dim room that receives only 100 units of light, it will reflect 25 units of light. However, if we place it a room that is better lit, it will still reflect the same 25%. If there are now 1,000 units of light, it will reflect 250 units of light. But we still see it as the same gray, despite the fact that the object is reflecting much more light. Similarly, an object that reflects 75% of ambient light will be seen as a light gray in the dim room, even though it reflects less total light than it does in the bright room. Thus, lightness constancy is the principle that we respond to the proportion of light reflected by an object rather than the total light reflected by an object. You can explore an interactive illustration of these principles on ISLE 6.14.

As with all constancies, there are conditions that create illusions that overwhelm the processes that create constancy. The Gelb effect is an exception to the principle of lightness constancy. The **Gelb effect** is a phenomenon whereby an intensely lit black object appears to be gray or white in a homogeneously dark space. Think of a cat caught in the headlights of a car at night. In your mind, hit the brakes quickly, so as not to hurt the cat. The headlights illuminate only a small space in front of the car, dark pavement in addition to the cat. Because there is nothing to compare the object to, the cat appears white, because it is reflecting a lot of light in an otherwise dark space. However, if we suddenly place a white object next to the cat, the cat now appears black, its actual color, as our visual systems now have something with which to compare it. For an illustration of the Gelb effect and related illusions, go to ISLE 6.15. The Gelb effect neatly shows the importance of the ratio principle in explaining lightness constancy (Gilchrist et al., 1999).

The ratio principle states that the perceived lightness of an object is explained by the ratio of light it reflects rather than the absolute amount of light it reflects, assuming even illumination across the visual scene. As long as illumination is constant across the field of view, the ratio captures the properties of reflectance. In an illusion such as the Gelb effect, the constant illumination requirement is violated—the cat is more illuminated than its surroundings, and lightness constancy is compromised. Of course, situations such as the Gelb effect are rare in the real world, and for the most part, the ratio principle allows us to correctly interpret the lightness of objects.

Gelb effect: a phenomenon whereby an intensely lit black object appears to be gray or white in a homogeneously dark space

TEST YOUR KNOWLEDGE

Why is it important to have color constancy in the real world? What function does it serve?

IN DEPTH: *The Color Purple*

6.9 Explain how purple is distinguished from violet.

Purple has, in the West, long been associated with royalty and religiosity. Perhaps because of its rarity in nature and the difficulty in generating purple dyes, purple has always been a regal and expensive color. We find this from our earliest recorded records to very recent history. In the Hebrew Bible, God tells Moses that the Israelites should bring Him offerings of purple cloth. In both ancient Greece and Rome, purple was the color worn by kings and royalty, a tradition that continued in Europe through the centuries. Roman Catholic bishops wear purple to this day. This regard for purple is also seen in other cultures—purple is a symbol of royalty in Japan and of piety in China. Even today, purple dyes made from murex snails can cost hundreds of dollars. Because purple pigments are also rare in nature, we value plants and flowers that are purple as well. Purple flowers are a staple of gardens everywhere (see Figure 6.27).

Following Livingstone (2002), we make a distinction between violet and purple. In practice, these colors are very similar perceptually, but technically, they refer to different kinds of color. Violet is a spectral color that we see at the very shortest wavelengths of the visual spectrum, shorter even than blue. We see violet from 400 to about 440 nm, at which point wavelengths become blue. Purple, by contrast, is a nonspectral color that cannot be generated by a single wavelength of light. Purple is a mix of red light and blue light. Most dyes and pigments are purple, reflecting both red and blue light, rather than violet (see Figure 6.28). We now describe why these colors look similar (see Monnier, 2008).

■ **FIGURE 6.27**   Purple flowers are especially valued by gardeners everywhere.

At 440 nm and under (i.e., until about 400 nm, below which we cannot see), colors look blue but also a little red. This is why these colors are called violet. Although they are spectral colors, they look like a mix of red and blue. There is a clear physiological explanation for this phenomenon. At 440 nm, our S-cones are nearly at their peak. However, the L-cone system is also active. Although these cones are sensitive mainly to long-wavelength light, they have this minor peak for short-wavelength light. Thus, these very short wavelengths activate both blue and red responses in our cones, resulting in the perception of violet.

Purple is a nonspectral color that results from the combination of red and blue light. A more bluish purple may be metameric to violet, but purple is a mixed color, not a spectral color. Thus, purple objects need to have an odd pattern

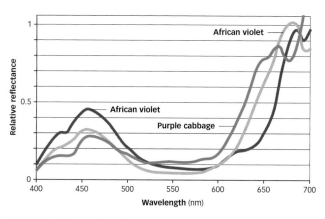

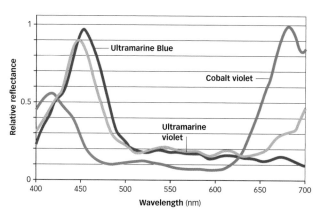

■ FIGURE 6.28   How to make purple.

In order to be purple, an object must absorb light in the central or green part of the visual spectrum but reflect light in the red and blue portions at the ends of the visual spectrum.

of reflectance. In order to be purple, an object must absorb light in the central or green part of the visual spectrum but reflect light in the red and blue portions at the ends of the visual spectrum. This particular arrangement—absorbing wavelengths in the middle of the spectrum but not at the endpoints—is particularly difficult for chemical compounds to achieve. Hence the rarity of purple in nature. You can see that for purple plants, the surface reflects the long and short wavelengths but absorbs the middle ones. Because purple is rare in nature, it also makes it more difficult for people to generate purple dyes. In the past, this resulted in purple dyes' and paints' being very expensive. Long live purple!

CHAPTER SUMMARY

6.1 Examine the relation of the wavelength of light to perceived color.

The visible spectrum is the band of wavelengths from 400 to 700 nm that people with normal vision can detect. We see different wavelengths as different colors. However, wavelength is not the only property that governs color vision.

6.2 Identify the perceptual principles of hue, saturation, and brightness.

Hue refers to the color quality of the light and corresponds to the color names we use. *Saturation* refers to the purity of the light or the amount of white light mixed with the colored light. And *brightness* refers to the amount of light present. Additive color mixing is the creation of a new color by a process that adds one set of wavelengths to another set of wavelengths. When we add all of the different wavelengths of sunlight, we see white light rather than many individual colors. Subtractive color mixing is the creation of a new color by the removal of wavelengths from a light with a broad spectrum of wavelengths.

6.3 Summarize the idea of a metamer and what color-matching experiments show.

A metamer is a psychophysical color match between two patches of light that have different sets of wavelengths. Any three wavelengths can be adjusted to match a single-wavelength light in people with normal color vision.

6.4 Explain how the three cones interact to influence color perception.

Color vision starts off with the cones of the retina. We have three cone systems, responsible for different parts of the visual spectrum. The S-cones have peak sensitivity to short-wavelength light, at around 420 nm (blue). The M-cones have peak sensitivity to medium-wavelength light, at around 535 nm (green), and the L-cones have peak sensitivity to long-wavelength light, at around 565 nm (yellow).

6.5 Describe the trichromatic theory of color vision.

The existence of these three cone types supports the trichromatic theory of color vision, which states that the color of any light is determined by the output of the three cone systems in our retinae.

6.6 Illustrate the opponent theory of color vision.

There is also evidence that supports the opponent theory of color vision, which states that color perception arises from three opponent mechanisms, for red-green, blue-yellow, and black-white. Four primaries are organized in two sets of oppositional pairs (blue-yellow and red-green). Blue and yellow are opposite to each other, and red and green are also opposite to each other. Evidence for this theory comes from color afterimages and hue cancellation studies. Neuroscience has also shown that there are cone-opponent cells in the LGN, and color-opponent cells in V1. In particular, double-opponent cells seem to be specialized for detecting edges, where one color ends and another color starts.

6.7 Describe the concept of color deficiency and why it is a better term than *color blindness*.

Color deficiency refers to the condition of individuals who are missing one or more of their cone systems. Rod monochromats have no functioning cones of any kind and therefore can be described as truly colorblind. Cone monochromats are people lacking two cone types but have one present in addition to their rod systems. Protanopia (red-green color deficiency) is a lack of L-cones that is sex linked and therefore more common in men. Deuteranopia (red-green color deficiency) is a lack of M-cones that is sex linked and more common in men. Tritanopia (blue-yellow color deficiency) is a lack of S-cones that is much rarer and is not sex linked. Anomalous trichromats have all three cone systems intact, but one or more has an altered absorption pattern, leading to different metameric matches than in normal individuals. A unilateral dichromat is a person with dichromacy in one eye but normal trichromatic vision in the other. And finally, cortical achromatopsia is a loss of color vision that occurs because of damage to the occipital lobe.

6.8 Define the term *constancy* and how it applies to color vision.

Constancy refers to our ability to perceive an object as the same object under different conditions. Lightness constancy refers to our ability to perceive the relative reflectance of objects despite changes in illumination.

Color constancy refers to our ability to perceive the color of an object despite changes in the amount and nature of illumination. The Gelb effect or Gelb illusion is an exception to lightness constancy in which we see as white a dark object when it alone is illuminated and we cannot see other objects.

6.9 Explain how purple is distinguished from violet.

Finally, we discussed purple and distinguished it from violet. Violet is a spectral color seen at very short wavelengths. Purple, however, is a nonspectral color made from combining red and blue light. In order for an object to appear purple, it must reflect light at short and long wavelengths and absorb light in the middle portion of the visible spectrum.

REVIEW QUESTIONS

1. What is the range in nanometers of the human visible spectrum? What is the difference between heterochromatic light and monochromatic light?

2. What is meant by the terms *hue*, *saturation*, and *brightness*? What does each contribute to our perception of color? Give an example of two colors that differ with respect to saturation.

3. What are additive and subtractive color mixing? How do the two processes differ? When would you use each one?

4. What are the three cone systems? What kind of monochromatic light is each cone sensitive to? Why do the cone systems support the trichromacy view of color vision?

5. What is the problem of univariance? How does it relate to metameric matching? How does it relate to colorblindness under scotopic conditions?

6. What is the opponent processes theory of color vision? Describe three perceptual phenomena that demonstrate the reality of opponent processing.

7. What is the difference between cone-opponent cells and color-opponent cells? Where do you find each kind of cell? Describe the visual field of a double-opponent cell.

8. What is meant by the term *color deficiency*? What is the difference between a rod monochromat and a cone monochromat? What are the three types of dichromats? Describe the physiological issue and the perceptual consequences for each kind of dichromat.

9. What is meant by the term *constancy*? What are lightness constancy and color constancy? How do we infer the nature of the illuminant in each case?

10. What is the difference between violet and purple? What is the physiological explanation for why purple looks like a mix of red and blue?

KEY TERMS

Additive color mixing, 142

Afterimages, 150

Anomalous trichromacy, 157

Brightness, 141

Color constancy, 159

Color deficiency, 153

Color-opponent cells, 152

Cone-opponent cells, 152

Constancy, 159

Cortical achromatopsia, 158

Deuteranopia, 155

Double-opponent cells, 152

Gelb effect, 162

Heterochromatic light, 139

Hue, 140

Hue cancellation, 151

L-cone, 146

Lightness, 141

INTERACTIVE SENSATION LABORATORY EXERCISES (ISLE)

Experience chapter concepts at edge.sagepub.com/schwartz

Sharpen your skills with SAGE edge at edge.sagepub.com/schwartz

SAGE edge for students provides a personalized approach to help you accomplish
your coursework goals in an easy-to-use learning environment.

Depth and Size Perception

7

INTRODUCTION

Our ability to see depth and distance is a skill we take for granted, as is the case for much of perception. Like other perceptual processes, it is an extremely complex process both computationally and physiologically. The problem our visual system starts off with is simple. How do you extract information about a three-dimensional (3D) world from the flat two-dimensional (2D) surface known as the retina (see Figure 7.1)? As we will see, our visual system uses a complex combination of various cues and clues to infer depth, which often results in vivid perceptual experiences, such as when the huge monster lunges out at you from the movie screen while watching that notoriously bad 3D movie *Godzilla* (2014). As most readers know, an important part of depth perception comes from the fact that we have two eyes that see the world from slightly different angles. We know that people blind in one eye may not see depth as well as others, but they can still judge distances quite well. In the course of this chapter, we discuss how single-eyed people perceive depth and explore the reasons why binocular vision (two eyes) enhances our depth perception.

Our visual system uses a number of features, including a comparison between what the two eyes see, to determine depth, but other animals' visual systems achieve depth perception in very different ways. What would it be like to see the world through a completely different visual system? We cannot necessarily experience what this would be like, but we can study the mechanisms involved and compare them with our own visual system. Consider spiders, a class of animals that have eight eyes in addition to their famous eight legs. Do eight eyes give spiders a more complex system to see depth, just as some of the four-coned animals we spoke of in the last chapter see more colors? Interestingly, there have been a few studies on how spiders see depth, and the system is incredibly different from our own. We'll consider one of these studies examining depth perception in spiders. Nagata et al. (2012) examined the use of depth information in jumping accuracy in a species of spiders known as Adanson's jumping spiders (*Hasarius adansoni*).

These spiders have eight eyes; the four frontal eyes are used for hunting (see Figure 7.2). As their name suggests, Adanson's jumping spiders catch their prey by jumping onto small insects and eating them. In order to be effective at this hunting strategy, their jumps must be accurate, which requires good depth perception. If they land in front or behind their insect prey, the prey is likely to escape. So good depth perception is necessary if the spider is going to eat and survive. Nagata et al. (2012) were interested in what neural mechanisms the spiders use for depth perception, given the large number of eyes but the small brain in these spiders. They focused on the two largest eyes, known as the principal eyes. They rendered the spiders' other eyes temporarily blind by dabbing them with black paint, allowing them to focus on the principal eyes. They then set out insects for the spiders to catch, allowing them to assess the accuracy of the spiders' jumps.

LEARNING OBJECTIVES

7.1 Explain oculomotor depth cues and how they work.

7.2 Explain monocular depth cues and how they work.

7.3 Summarize the principle of stereopsis and how it applies to human depth perception.

7.4 Describe the correspondence problem and how it relates to stereopsis.

7.5 Explain the concept of size perception and the inferential nature of its determination.

7.6 Discuss the concept of size constancy.

7.7 Explain the concept of illusions of size and depth and how they affect perception.

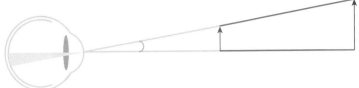

■ **FIGURE 7.1** Our visual systems must re-create the 3D world using an essentially flat, 2D retina.

This figure shows the equivalence of size of objects at different distances from the retina. Everything along this cone projects the same-size image onto a flat retina. The visual system must then determine relative size and relative distance (depth).

ISLE 7.1 Depth Perception and Adanson's Jumping Spider

■ **FIGURE 7.2** Adanson's jumping spiders.

These spiders have eight eyes but use the multiple layers in their retinae to determine depth. In this photograph, their four frontal eyes, used for hunting, are easily visible.

Unlike a human eye, which has only one layer of photosensitive cells on the retina, the retinae in the principal eyes of these jumping spiders have four distinct photosensitive layers. Each layer is sensitive to a different range of wavelengths, much as our cones are sensitive to different ranges of wavelengths. When an image is in focus on one layer of the spider's retina, it is out of focus on the other layers. Although you might think this would make their vision blurry, the spiders actually use the extent to which the second image is out of focus to determine the distance they are from objects. Nagata et al. (2012) showed that the spider's eyes focus a sharp image on the first layer of the retina, leaving blurred images on the subsequent layers. The spider then compares the sharpness of the first image to the blurriness of subsequent images to compute an estimate of depth. Thus, these spiders use information from different layers of each retina to compute depth. This fascinating way of determining depth is quite different from how our visual system determines depth (see ISLE 7.1 for a demonstration of how spiders use this system to determine depth). In our visual system, we use the comparison of images across two eyes given flat retinae.

Look around your current environment. You probably have your book (or e-book) about 12 to 20 inches away from your eyes. Beyond that, you may see a table, a window, and clouds drifting in the sky outside your room. It seems almost trivial that the book is closer to you than the window, and the window is closer to you than the clouds. All of these observations serve to hide a rather interesting feature of depth perception. The retina is essentially flat. Although it is curved along the back of the eye, it is all one layer and can be flattened out very easily. There is only one layer of receptors (unlike in those pesky spiders). Regardless of the distance an object is from the eye, light is imaged by the same receptors, so at this point in the visual system, there is no information about depth. In other words, which receptors actually serve to transduce the light into action potentials does not depend on how far an object is from the eye. Thus, other sources of information about distance must be used for 3D perception. This information must be found primarily in the visual scene itself. In addition, for the first time, the role of having two eyes will become apparent, in terms of both the advantages and the complications that having two eyes cause for us.

The solution that our visual system evolved is to rely on a system of cues and clues for depth perception. This view of how humans see depth is sometimes known as the cue approach to depth perception. This approach focuses on the observation that because information on the retina is 2D, we must infer the third dimension from other cues our visual system provides. As we discuss shortly, these cues include monocular cues such as occlusion and relative size, oculomotor cues such as convergence and accommodation, and, most famously, binocular cues from comparing images from each retina. In this chapter, we consider the three major factors in depth perception: oculomotor cues, monocular cues (including motion cues), and binocular cues. We start this survey with the oculomotor cues.

It is important to make explicit what we mean by a cue or a clue. In this discussion, we essentially use the terms *cue* and *clue* interchangeably. A cue is a factor that aids you in making a nonconscious and automatic decision. Cues tell us about which objects are closer and which are farther away. Thus, the **cue approach to depth perception** emphasizes that we combine information we can use to infer depth given that we cannot compute it directly.

OCULOMOTOR CUES

7.1   Explain oculomotor depth cues and how they work.

Rest your index finger on the tip of your nose and look at your finger. Then, without moving your head or the direction of your gaze, adjust your focus so that you are looking at an object farther away, such as the wall of the room in which you are reading. As you adjust your eyes, you can feel the movements involved in your focus. These adjustments that your eyes make as they look from objects near to objects far away or from objects far away to objects closer can serve as cues to depth in and of themselves. The movements involved come from two sets of muscles, one that controls the shape of the lens (**accommodation**) and one that controls the position of the eyes relative to each other (**vergence**). We look at each in turn.

Accommodation

Accommodation is the process of adjusting the lens of the eye so that you can see both near and far objects clearly. We discussed this process in Chapter 3. To focus on a more distant object, we relax the ciliary muscles that contract the lens, and to focus on an object close to our eyes, we contract the ciliary muscles. These contractions and relaxations take place automatically as we change our focus. However, we can sense these muscle movements. And it is the sensing of these movements that gives us information about depth. However, the narrowness of the pupil during the day makes accommodation imprecise in day vision, and the poor acuity at night makes accommodation imprecise then as well.

ISLE 7.2 Accomodation

Vergence (or Convergence)

Vergence (also known as convergence) occurs when the eyes bend inward to see a near object and then bend outward (diverge) when we look at a more distant object. When you are looking at your finger resting against your nose, your eyes are bent inward to focus on this very close object. Essentially, to see your finger, your gaze must become "crossed." When you shift your gaze to the window or wall beyond your eyes, your eyes move outward from each other (see Figure 7.3). As with accommodation, this process is automatic, but we can sense the movements, and this gives us information about the relative distance of objects. Convergence is probably the more useful cue than accommodation, and it can provide the visual system with reliable depth information to about 2 m in length, at which point there is no appreciable difference in eye angle (Schachar, 2006). You can explore an interactive illustration of convergence and accommodation on ISLE 7.2 and 7.3, respectively.

ISLE 7.3 Vergence

Cue approach to depth perception: the system whereby depth perception results from three sources of information, monocular cues to depth present in the image, binocular cues from the comparison of images in each eye, and cues from focusing the eyes, such as vergence and accommodation

Accommodation: the process of adjusting the lens of the eye so that both near and far objects can be seen clearly

Vergence: the inward bending of the eyes when looking at closer objects

TEST YOUR KNOWLEDGE

What is accommodation, and how can it be used to infer depth?

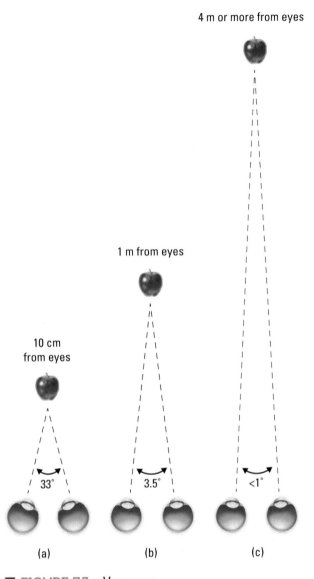

4 m or more from eyes

1 m from eyes

10 cm
from eyes

33°   3.5°   <1°

(a)   (b)   (c)

■ FIGURE 7.3   Vergence.

Your eyes cross to focus on a nearby object. People can "feel" this movement, and that gives them information that objects are close by. When looking at an object farther away (more than 4 m), there is no vergence at all. This too provides information about depth.

ISLE 7.4 Monocular Depth Cues

....

Monocular depth cues: depth cues that require only one eye

Pictorial cues: information about depth that can be inferred from a static picture

Movement-based cues: cues about depth that can be seen with a single eye in which the inference of distance comes from motion

MONOCULAR DEPTH CUES

7.2   Explain monocular depth cues and how they work.

Monocular depth cues are the information in the retinal image that gives us information about depth and distance but can be inferred from just a single retina (or eye). In everyday life, of course, we perceive these cues with both eyes, but they are just as usable with only one functioning eye. That is, these are cues that tell us about depth even if we are looking at the world with only one eye. Try it—close one eye. You can still use vision to distinguish between objects near and far. Some people describe the world as seeming a bit flatter when using only one eye than when using two, but we still judge distances accurately. Monocular cues include **pictorial cues**, those cues from which we can judge depth from static or nonmoving pictures, and **movement-based cues**, in which moving objects allow us to make inferences about depth and distance (see Table 7.1).

We start with the pictorial cues.

Occlusion (or Interposition)

Occlusion occurs when one object partially hides or obstructs the view of a second object. We infer that the hidden object is farther away from us than the object that obstructs it. Consider the whitewater kayakers in Figure 7.4. In the photograph, the blue helmet of one kayaker partially occludes the view of the other kayaker's boat. From this, we know that the blue-helmeted kayaker must be in front of the black-helmeted kayaker. Similarly, the blue-helmeted kayaker's paddle occludes the view of his own lifejacket. From this, we infer that the paddle is in front of the lifejacket. Such a scene as this makes the cue of occlusion look obvious. However, it is still an inference, based on knowledge we bring to the act of viewing scenes. Occlusion provides information about only relative position, not absolute distance. In the kayaking photograph, we cannot determine with much accuracy how far apart are the two kayakers. You can explore an interactive illustration of occlusion and all other monocular cues on ISLE 7.4.

Relative Height

Relative height means that objects closer to the horizon are seen as more distant. In a picture, this means that objects below the horizon are seen as more near the viewer if they are closer to the bottom of the picture, but objects above the horizon are seen as more near if they are closer to the top of the picture. To understand relative height, think of the horizon dividing the world into two roughly equal portions, the ground below and the sky above. Think about paintings you may have seen. Usually, the horizon is somewhere near the middle in Western perspective painting. The distant part of the sky is painted near the middle of the picture, near where the sky and ground meet at the horizon. The part of the ground and sky near the viewpoint of the painter, then, occurs at the extremes of the painting, the close part of the ground near the bottom and the close part of the sky near the top of the painting. Examine the photograph in Figure 7.5a. The horizon here is where the ocean meets the sky and is very clear in this photograph. This places the conch shell and the coral rocks in front of the ocean, relatively close to the viewer (or camera). The rocks closest to the bottom of the photograph are closest to the viewer. However, look at the clouds above the horizon. The clouds nearest to the top of the photograph are viewed as closest to the viewer.

We see the same pattern in the painting depicted in Figure 7.5c. The water in the river is close to us and is depicted as such by being at the bottom of the painting. At the top of the painting are clouds looming over us. The horizon is in the center of the painting, where the blue sky and white clouds meet the distant green hills and more distant buildings.

Relative Size

Relative size refers to the fact that the more distant an object, the smaller its image will be on the retina. Therefore, if there are two identical objects, the one that is farther away will be the one that has a smaller image on the retina. For example, if we assume that the two kayakers in Figure 7.4 are approximately the same size (the one in the front is actually slightly shorter than his companion), then the one who has a smaller image on the retina must be farther away from the viewer. As the image of the blue-helmeted kayaker is larger in the picture than that of his companion, we assume that he is closer to the viewer. Note that the kayaker in the background does not look abnormal in any way. Despite creating a smaller image on the retina, the person does not look oddly small. The normal size of the more distant person is due to a mechanism called size constancy, which we discuss later, when more of the depth cues have been covered. Because we infer that this person is farther away, we do not mistake his smaller size on the retina for his being a smaller person. You can explore an interactive illustration of relative size on ISLE 7.4a.

Familiar Size

Related to relative size is the cue of **familiar size**. Familiar size comes into play when we judge distance on the basis of our existing knowledge of the sizes of objects. Thus, if we know that a particular object is smaller than another object, but it is taking up more space on our retina, we assume that the smaller object must be more near to us and that the larger object is farther away (see Figure 7.6). Thus, in

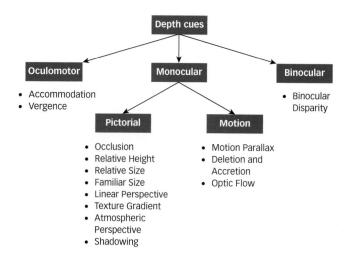

■ TABLE 7.1   **A Graphical Depiction of the Different Types of Depth Cues**

Note: Each class of depth cues is labeled in a box, with the specific depth cues listed below.

■ FIGURE 7.4   **Occlusion.**

We know that the kayaker in the yellow boat is in front of the kayaker in the red boat because the head of the closer kayaker occludes the boat of the kayaker farther away. What other cues for depth are present in this photograph?

Occlusion: a visual cue that occurs when one object partially hides or obstructs the view of a second object; we infer that the hidden object is farther away from us than the object that obstructs it

Relative height: a visual cue in which objects closer to the horizon are seen as more distant

Relative size: the fact that the more distant an object, the smaller the image will be on the retina

■ FIGURE 7.5 **Relative height.**

(a) The horizon here is where the ocean meets the sky and is very clear in this photograph. This places the conch shell and the coral rocks along the bottom of the image as relatively close to the viewer. However, above the horizon, objects closer to the horizon are judged as farther away, and objects toward the top of the image are judged to be closer. (b) A more complex illustration of relative height. Again, though, we see that objects closer to the horizon are judged as being farther away, leading to their being judged as close if they are along the bottom or along the top of the image. (c) An illustration of how an artist uses this rule to create depth in a painting.

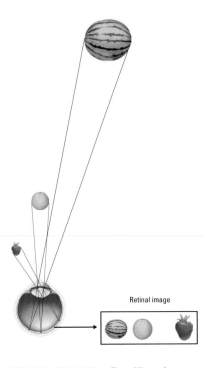

Retinal image

■ FIGURE 7.6 **Familiar size.**

Familiarity can be used as a cue for distance of depth. In this image, there are three objects that are familiar to most of us, all of which take up the same space on the retinae. But because we know that strawberries are smaller than oranges and oranges are smaller than watermelons, we unconsciously infer that the strawberry is closest and the watermelon is farthest.

Familiar size: the cue whereby knowing the retinal size of a familiar object at a familiar distance allows us to use that retinal size to infer distance

Linear perspective: the pictorial depth cue that arises from the fact that parallel lines appear to converge as they recede into the distance

the figure, each object occupies the same amount of space on the retinae, but the watermelon is judged to be farthest away because we know that this is the largest fruit.

The cue of familiar size is often eclipsed by other cues. For example, in Figure 7.7a, the presence of children climbing on the lobster informs us that the lobster in this figure is no ordinary lobster. In Figure 7.7b, we find a gift shop inside a lobster trap, and finally, in Figure 7.7c, the building in the background informs us that this is no ordinary boot. We might well wonder whether people in Maine and eastern Canada don't have better things to do.

Linear Perspective

Linear perspective is the pictorial depth cue that arises from the fact that parallel lines appear to converge as they recede into the distance. From the point of view of a human observer, parallel lines seem to get closer and closer to each other as they recede into the distance. Of course, you may remember from your high school geometry class that parallel lines never meet. But perceptually they do, at the edge of the horizon. To see what this cue looks like, examine the photograph in Figure 7.8a. The railroad tracks are parallel, and in this scene, they go straight through the desert landscape. The linear perspective cue is that the parallel lines of the railroad tracks seem farther apart close up, as they take up more space in the

(a)

(b)

(c)

© David R. Frazier Photolibrary, Inc. / Alamy

© Visions of America, LLC / Alamy

■ **FIGURE 7.7**   **When familiar size is unhelpful.**

(a) The presence of children informs us that this is an abnormally large lobster. It is possible that the lobster is normal size, and the children are the size of shrimp, but this is a less likely scenario, so the presence of the children immediately informs us of the nature of the lobster. (b) Note the normal lobster traps in front of the building. Various cues here tell us that restaurant is normal size, and the lobster trap that surrounds it is unusually large. (c) The famous L.L. Bean boot, with various amounts of context that tell us about the boot's size.

image and on our retinae. They get smaller and closer together higher in this image, and we extract from this information that the tracks go off into the distance. This linear perspective serves as a cue to depth. The larger the distance between parallel lines (the tracks), the closer those lines must be. Of course, in Figure 7.8a, there are other monocular depth cues in addition to linear perspective. In Figure 7.8b, we have a good example of linear perspective. The numbers all look the same size to us, even though the lower numbers are much smaller in terms of their retinal image size, but because they are farther away, they do not look smaller.

Linear perspective is an important technique for painters who wish to convey a 3D scene on a 2D canvas. Look at the painting in Figure 7.9, which is called *Paris Street: A Rainy Day*, by Gustave Caillebotte (1848–1894). Look at the building in the background. The separation between the floors is clearly indicated. The lines appear to diverge and give the indication that the building is angled and larger toward the back, and that the surfaces recede in depth. In fact, the lines that make up this building are essentially parallel. Thus, parallel lines indicate a flat surface, and converging lines that we see as parallel indicate a surface that recedes in depth. Note also that we assume that the people are roughly the same size. Thus, the smaller images of people serve as a cue that those people are farther from the point of the viewer.

© Digital Vision/ Photodisc / Thinkstock

© iStockphoto.com/ murengstockphoto

■ **FIGURE 7.8**   **Linear perspective.**

In these images, parallel lines appear to converge in the distance. With the train tracks, we infer that the tracks are parallel and thus must be getting more distant as they converge toward the top of the photo. In the photo of the finish line, how many depth cues can you see?

Texture Gradients

Texture gradients are a monocular depth cue that occur because textures become finer as they recede in the distance. Texture gradients as a monocular cue are clearly related to relative size. In both cases, we use existing knowledge about sizes or patterns of objects and assume that smaller images closer to the horizon are the same size, but farther away. Most surfaces, such as walls and roads and a field of flowers in bloom, have texture. As the surface gets farther away

Texture gradient: a monocular depth cue that occurs because textures become finer as they recede in the distance

Google Cultural Institute

■ FIGURE 7.9   **Linear perspective in art.**

This painting by Gustave Caillebotte (1848–1894), titled *Paris Street: A Rainy Day,* was painted in 1877. Notice how Caillebotte used linear perspective to show depth and distance in the painting. There is a progression of people painted large and up close toward the bottom of the painting and smaller and farther toward the top of the canvas to indicate their distance from the painter. Notice also the odd building in the distance. The lines appear to diverge and give the indication that the building is angled and larger toward the back, and that the surfaces recede in depth. In fact, the lines that make up this building are essentially parallel.

© iStockphoto.com/KarenMassier

■ FIGURE 7.10   **Texture gradients.**

This field of tulips demonstrates how texture gradients show depth. As with apparent size, as the tulips get farther away from us, their size on the retinae becomes smaller. This helps create the experience of depth.

Atmospheric perspective: a pictorial depth cue that arises from the fact that objects in the distance appear blurred and tinged with blue

from us, this texture gets finer and appears smoother (Gibson, 1950). Another way of saying this is that common elements that are evenly spaced in an image appear more close together in the distance than they do in the foreground. For example, the tulips in Figure 7.10 represent a texture gradient. We assume that the flowers are about the same size and the same distance apart in the field. That the images are smaller and closer together toward the top of the image suggests that these tulips are farther away. We can also see texture gradients in the cobblestones in the painting depicted in Figure 7.9. The cobblestones get progressively smaller as the road recedes in depth, until the stones are not clearly distinguishable from one another. In the distance, only the general roughness of the street is noticeable.

Atmospheric Perspective

Atmospheric perspective is a pictorial depth cue that arises from the fact that objects in the distance appear blurred and tinged with blue. When we look at a visual image, close objects are clear and well defined, and objects farther away are more blurred. Moreover, because the atmosphere scatters light, more distant objects will also have a blue tinge. This feature of depth perception can be seen in Figure 7.11. In the photograph in Figure 7.11a, the road in the foreground is clear and sharp. The distant mountains at the horizon have a clear blue tinge. The photograph in Figure 7.11b was taken along the Blue Ridge Parkway in North Carolina. Dr. Krantz swears that the blue on the horizon is natural and not "PhotoShopped in."

If we were standing on the moon, which has no atmosphere, faraway objects would appear neither blurred nor blue. But our atmosphere scatters light, and it scatters blue light more than other wavelengths (which is why our sky appears blue). Indeed, that the atmosphere scatters light also plays a role in our depth perception. The short or blue wavelengths of light are most easily scattered by the particles in the atmosphere. In addition, the scattering occurs for all light, regardless of the direction it comes from. Thus, light coming from a distant object should have some of its light scattered. That will have two effects on the light reaching our eyes: (a) because blue is scattered more, more distant objects should appear bluish, and

(a)

(b)

■ FIGURE 7.11   Atmospheric perspective.

Very distant objects tend to have a blue tinge to them. (a) The mountains in the Chilcotin region of British Columbia, Canada, take on a blue tinge. (b) The mountains in the distance along the Blue Ridge Parkway in North Carolina also take on a distinct blue tinge. Because the atmosphere scatters light, more distant objects will also have a blue tinge.

(a)

(b)

■ FIGURE 7.12   Shadows and shading.

We see two views of the same image. (a) The lighting appears to be coming from above and to the right. (b) The picture is merely flipped, so that the light appears to be coming from below and to the left. Note how this changes our perception of whether the circles in the rock art are bumps or indentations.

(b) because not all of the light is traveling in a straight line to us, more distant objects should appear a bit fuzzy.

Shadows and Shading

Shadows may also enhance the perception of depth in images. **Shadows** provide a depth cue because the object is in front of the shadow, and the angle of the shadow can provide some information about how far the object is in front of the background. Objects that are in shadow must be farther from the light than objects that are not in shadow. In particular, on a curved surface, light falling on an object will create a pattern of light and shadow. This gives us information about the relative depths of different parts of a surface. In Figure 7.12, we see two different views of what really is the same image. In the first image, in Figure 7.12a, the lighting appears to be coming from above and to the right. In the second image, in Figure 7.12b, the picture is upside down, so that the light appears to be coming from below and to the left. Note how this changes our perception of whether the circles in the rock art are bumps or indentations. In Figure 7.12a, we see the circles

Shadows: a depth cue arising because an object is in front of its shadow, and the angle of the shadow can provide some information about how far the object is in front of the background

as indentations in the rock, but in Figure 7.12b, we see the circles as bumps. In this way, shadows can cause different perceptions of the 3D structure of an object.

Motion Cues

The monocular cues we have been discussing so far can be extracted from stationary images. These are the pictorial cues to depth. However, once objects are set in motion, a number of other monocular cues to depth emerge; these are the motion-based cues. From an observer's point of view, objects moving at different speeds can reveal information about relative distance. We discuss three motion cues to depth here: (a) motion parallax, (b) accretion and deletion, and (c) optic flow. Each of these motion cues is considered monocular because it can be seen with only one eye. However, motion parallax and optic flow can create visual experiences that are similar to those produced by the binocular cue of stereopsis.

Motion Parallax

Motion parallax is a monocular depth cue arising from the relative velocities of objects moving across the retinae of a moving person. The term *parallax* refers to a change in position. Thus, motion parallax is a change in position caused by the movement of the viewer. Motion parallax arises from the motion of the observer in the environment. In this way, it is similar to the binocular cues, because binocular cues rely on two images across space (one to each eye), whereas motion parallax depends on multiple images across time (i.e., multiple images to each eye). It is perhaps easier to think of what motion parallax is by imagining yourself as a passenger in a car looking out the side window. The car is moving very fast down the highway. The objects very close to the window, such as the small trees planted by the highway, seem to rush by. Beyond the small trees, you can see a distant farmhouse. The farmhouse appears to move more slowly relative to you in the car. You know that the trees and the farmhouse are standing still; you are the object that is moving. But your constant speed (of, say, 60 mph) creates the illusion that the trees are rushing by but the farmhouse is not. Farther off, you see the tiny image of a commercial jet airplane moving across the sky. Although you know this plane is moving in excess of 500 mph, it does not look nearly as fast as the trees whizzing close by. Thus, we can use this movement relative to the viewer as a cue for depth. Faster moving objects are closer to us. More slowly moving objects are farther away. This is illustrated in Figure 7.13. We also highly recommend that you view the interactive animations of motion parallax on ISLE 7.5a.

■ FIGURE 7.13   Motion parallax.

As you move, objects closer to you appear to move faster, whereas objects farther away appear to move slower. This is because the closer objects move a greater amount on your retinae from Time 1 to Time 2 than do the more distant objects.

ISLE 7.5 Motion Depth Cues

Motion parallax: a monocular depth cue arising from the relative velocities of objects moving across the retinae of a moving person

A more technical description of motion parallax involves considering one's fixation point. If you are looking directly at the farmhouse from your car window, that farmhouse can be said to be your fixation point (fixation points are also important when discussing stereopsis). We can then divide the world into points closer to you than your fixation point, such as the trees, and objects farther away from your fixation point, such as the parked tractor beyond the farmhouse or the more distant airplane. Objects closer to your position on the highway will appear to move in a

(a)

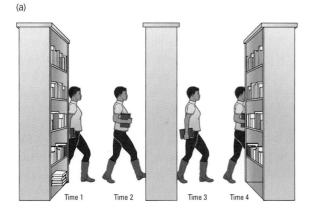

(b)

■ FIGURE 7.14   Deletion and accretion.

(a) As we watch an object move relative to another object, we judge the object that disappears (deletion) and reappears (accretion) as being farther away from us than the object that is continually visible. (b) You can experience motion parallax a bit in an anaglyph stereogram. Put on your anaglyph glasses and move your head from side to side while looking at the image. You will see the finger of the front figure move more that the faces in the background.

direction opposite to your motion. Thus, even though the trees are stationary, and it is the car you are in that is moving, the trees appear to move very quickly in the opposite direction. In contrast, objects farther than the point of fixation, such as the parked tractor beyond the farmhouse, appear to move in the same direction as you do. This movement opposite to your own by near objects and the in same direction as your own by far objects is motion parallax. You can examine this effect in motion by watching the interactive animation of motion parallax on ISLE 7.5a2.

Deletion and Accretion

Deletion is the gradual occlusion of a moving object as it passes behind another object. **Accretion** is the gradual reappearance of a moving object as it emerges from behind another object. Think about being in a library. You watch someone emerge from behind one bookshelf and then disappear behind another bookshelf. When the person first becomes visible, you note that the bookshelf was not moving, but the person suddenly emerged. This provides information about relative depth. The person must be behind the shelf. Similarly when the person is "deleted" as she moves behind the next shelf, you again see from her movement the relative positions of her and the furniture. Thus, we can formalize this in the following way. The object that is being deleted and then later accreted is the object that is farther away than the object we can see continuously, which is therefore closer. This can be seen in Figure 7.14. You can also examine this effect in motion by watching the interactive animation of deletion and accretion on ISLE 7.5b.

Optic Flow

Optic flow is the motion depth cue that refers to the relative motions of objects as the observer moves forward or backward in a scene. Optic flow is related to motion parallax. However, *optic flow* refers to our perception of objects as we move forward or backward in a scene (Gibson, 1950) (see Figure 7.15). Imagine now that you are driving down a straight country road. As you move forward, the world rushes by you in the opposite direction. In front of you, however, the world is still coming toward you and getting larger as it does. We can determine depth from optic flow because faraway objects appear to move more slowly relative to more close objects, which appear to rush toward us more quickly. Indeed, extremely large

Deletion: the gradual occlusion of a moving object as it passes behind another object

Accretion: the gradual reappearance of a moving object as it emerges from behind another object

Optic flow: a motion depth cue that involves the relative motion of objects as an observer moves forward or backward in a scene

Focus of expansion

■ FIGURE 7.15 Optic flow.

Consider being in the driver's seat and seeing the view in front of you. As you move forward, the world moves toward you and then disappears behind you. Your fixation point remains constant in the distance, but objects flow toward you and spread out as they do, relative to your position. The arrows in the figure represent this relative movement as you drive down the road.

faraway objects may appear essentially fixed in position. And the objects that are most close in front of you rush by you at high speeds. Optic flow is often used to convey depth information in movies. Think of the words flowing through space that give you the background for a *Star Wars* movie. The moving words create an optic flow, which allows you to judge the relative distance of different words. Car chases in movies also use optic flow to get you to feel as if you are in the car chasing the bad guys at high speed. You can also examine an interactive animation of optic flow on ISLE 7.5c.

Now imagine you are driving a car on a winding country road. The motion cues for depth are a combination of optic flow, relative movement coming directly at you, and motion parallax, relative movement at a 90° angle from you. Add in hills for up-and-down motion, and even more depth cues become available. The amazing thing about our visual system is that it computes all these relative distances and speeds fast enough for us to make sense of the world, even at 65 mph.

TEST YOUR KNOWLEDGE

What is occlusion? How does it give us information about depth?

BINOCULAR CUES TO DEPTH

7.3　Summarize the principle of stereopsis and how it applies to human depth perception.

At the beginning of the chapter, we introduced jumping spiders, amazing creatures with eight eyes (and eight legs). Human beings are not fortunate enough to have eyes at both the front and back of our heads. But we do have two eyes, located adjacent to each other at the front of our heads. Because our eyes are next to each other at the front of our head, each eye sees mostly the same objects in the visual world as does the other eye, but from slightly different angles. This contrasts with animals such as horses, which have eyes on the opposite sides of their heads, such that there is almost no overlap in what each eye sees. This gives horses a greater ability to see completely around them—a horse essentially has a panoramic view around it. However, because the fields of view of the eyes do not overlap, horses cannot take advantage of the binocular cues that we do. That we humans have two eyes that see the world from slightly different angles provides us with an important cue to depth. The reason our two eyes both look in the same ways is that we pick up information about depth perception from the overlap of the two visual fields. In the area where both eyes see the same part of the world, we have binocular vision. We define **stereopsis** as the

Stereopsis: the sense of depth we perceive from the visual system's processing of the comparison of the two different images from each retina

sense of depth that we perceive from the visual system's processing of the comparison of the two different images from each retina.

Focus your gaze on some nearby object. If there is nothing readily available, hold one hand out at arm's length and look at your own thumb. First look at that thumb with your left eye and then with your right eye. You get an illusion that your hand has shifted somewhat as you go back and forth from one eye to the other. This quick test allows us to see the slightly different perspective on the world that each eye gives us. If you have an object to look at just beyond your thumb, you can see that the object may appear closer to your thumb through one eye than through the other (see Figure 7.16). What is important to binocular vision is this area of overlap. We see the same objects in the area of overlap, but it is not the same image. Binocular vision involves comparing the two images.

The sense in which stereopsis changes the experience of depth perception is apparent to anyone who has seen a 3D movie, which recently have become quite popular again (this technology also relies on vergence). In 2014, movies as varied as *How to Train Your Dragon 2*, *The Amazing Spider-Man 2*, and *Godzilla* all were available in theaters in 3D format. The sense of objects coming out of the screen toward you in the audience can often distract from plot development and good acting, but it is a perceptually unmistakable phenomenon. The sense of Spider-Man flying out of the screen toward you in three dimensions is a perceptually very different experience than watching the same movie in standard format. We see both 2D and 3D movies on flat screens, whether they are movie screens or smaller television screens. But the 3D glasses one wears while watching a 3D film create a situation in which a slightly different image is sent to each eye. This allows the use of binocular cues to extract depth from the images. To see how 3D movies work, refer to Figure 7.17. You can also examine a demonstration of 3D movies on ISLE 7.6.

Binocular Disparity

Disparity arises because our two eyes are in different locations in our head and therefore have slightly different views of the world. The explanation of how disparity allows us to extract depth information is quite complex. So read through this section slowly, make sure you understand the diagrams, and review it until you know it well. After you are certain that you know it well, draw yourself a diagram of how the two eyes perceive through stereopsis and explain it to someone who is not taking your sensation and perception class. Only after you have done that can you be sure that you understand the explanation of stereopsis. You can see a demonstration of binocular disparity on ISLE 7.7.

View from right eye   View from left eye

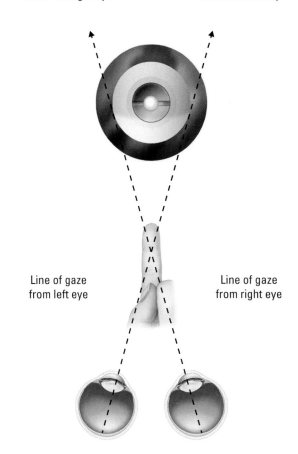

Line of gaze   Line of gaze
from left eye   from right eye

■ FIGURE 7.16 **Binocular disparity.**

Each eye has a slightly different view of the world. If you hold your finger out at arm's length and then look at it alternately with your left eye only and then your right eye only, the image of your finger relative to the world behind it will shift somewhat. This is binocular disparity, which helps provide the basis for the determination of depth.

ISLE 7.6 Stereopsis

ISLE 7.6 Binocular Disparity

■ **FIGURE 7.17**

Three-dimensional movies.

(a) A traditional 2D movie. In these movies, each eye sees the same information, and depth is inferred from monocular and motion cues. (b) A 3D movie. In this situation, each eye receives different images, allowing stereoscopic vision to occur.

2D image on flat screen

3D information on flat screen

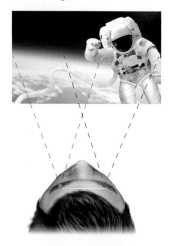
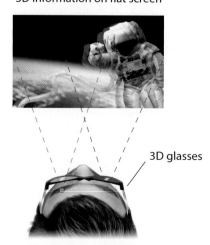

3D glasses

Left eye image   Right eye image   Left eye image   Right eye image

Perception = 2D   Perception = 3D

(a)   Same image to left and right eyes   (b)   Different images to left and right eyes

Corresponding and Noncorresponding Points

Look around you and find some reference points to use when following this argument. If you are in a room in your house, a dorm room, or a library, there is likely a lamp nearby. Position yourself so that you are about 10 feet (3 m) from that lamp. Hold your thumb out in front of you. Notice how you can use convergence and accommodation to change your focus from looking at your thumb to looking at the lamp. When you focus on the lamp, you may also notice that you may see a double image of your thumb. When you focus on your thumb, you may notice two images of the lamp in the background. So let us see what is going on with your visual system as you do this.

Corresponding points refers to a situation in which a point on the left retina and a point on the right retina would coincide if the two retinae were superimposed. In contrast, *noncorresponding points* refers to a situation in which a point on the left retina and a point on the right retina would not coincide if the two retinae were superimposed. For example, when looking at your thumb with your hand held out at arm's length, the image of your thumb falls on corresponding points on your left and right retinae. The lamp beyond it does not. This is why you have the illusion of seeing two lamps (see Figure 7.18). Now imagine a semicircle in front of you, with all the points at the same distance from your eyes as your thumb. This imaginary line is the horopter. Thus, if you stretch out your other arm alongside the one you are fixated on, your other thumb is not your fixation point, but lies along the horopter. Technically, the **horopter** is the region in space where the two images from an object fall on corresponding locations on the two retinae. If you switch your focus from your thumb to the lamp, you now have established a new horopter. Because you are now fixating on the lamp, the horopter is now an imaginary semicircle of points that is the same distance

ISLE 7.8 The Construction of Visual Depth With Binocular Disparity

Horopter: the region in space where the two images from an object fall on corresponding locations on the two retinae

from your eyes as is the lamp. Please go to ISLE 7.8 for a demonstration of this phenomenon.

Objects that lie along the horopter are perceived as single unified objects when viewed with both eyes. We can also fuse the images from the left and right eyes for objects that fall inside **Panum's area of fusion**. Inside Panum's area, including the horopter, we see images as singles. Outside Panum's area, either in front or behind, we see double images. As we move in front of the horopter, we are looking at objects closer and closer to ourselves. At some point, we lose the perception of these objects as being single unified objects and we see instead two images of the same object. Thus, when looking at the lamp 3 m away, the image of your thumb appears as a double. This double vision is known as **diplopia**.

Examine Figure 7.19. We can see schematically the retinae of the left and right eyes. In the diagram, the eyes are fixated on Object A, depicted in red in the diagram. The image of A falls on Points A and A′ on the left and right retinae, respectively. Because we are fixated on Image A, it defines the horopter for our visual world. Object B, for example, lies along the horopter. Thus, Object B falls along Points B and B′ on the retinae. We perceive Object B as being in the same plane or the same distance from us as Object A. Now consider Object C. Object C lies closer to us than does Object A and falls on Points C and E′ on the retina. Because it does not lie along the horopter, its image falls on noncorresponding points. Object D lies farther from us than Object A and falls on Points D and F′ on the retinae. Because it does not lie along the horopter, its image falls on noncorresponding points.

Points that are closer to us than the horopter have crossed disparity, and points farther away have uncrossed disparity. You can see this in the diagram.

Bear with this example, as we introduce a little more terminology necessary to understanding binocular vision. Consider Object C. Object C is closer to the observer than the horopter line. Its image falls on Points C and E′ on the retina. Look closely at these points. You see Object C to the right of the fixated Object A with the left eye, but to the left of the fixated Object A with the right eye. Because of this differential position along the retina, we call this crossed disparity. **Crossed disparity** refers to the direction of disparity for objects in front of the horopter (the image in the left eye is to the right of the image of the object in the right eye). This disparity is often given a positive sign. You can also see this interactively on ISLE 7.8b.

Next consider Object D. Object D is farther from the viewer than the horopter line. The image of Object D falls on Points D and F′ of their respective retinae. Note that the image of Object D falls to the left of Object A (the fixated object) on the left retina, but to the right of Object A on the right retina. Because of this positioning along the retina, we call this uncrossed disparity. **Uncrossed disparity** is the name given to the direction of disparity for objects that are behind the horopter (the image of the object in the left eye is to the left of the position of the

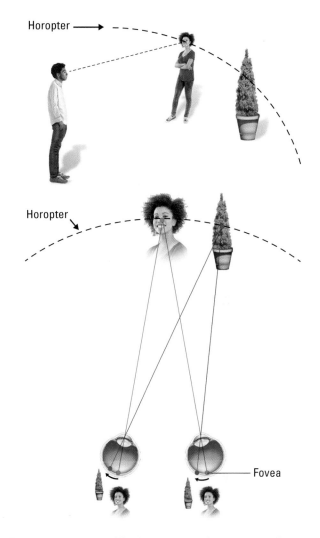

■ **FIGURE 7.18**   **The horopter and corresponding points.**

When we look at an object, that object defines our horopter—all points equally distant from us form the horopter. Technically, the horopter is the region in space where the two images from an object fall on corresponding locations on the two retinae. Points that are closer to us than the horopter have crossed disparity, and points farther away have uncrossed disparity.

Panum's area of fusion: the region of small disparity around the horopter where the two images can be fused into a single perception

Diplopia: double images, or seeing two copies of the same image; usually results from the images of an object having too much disparity to lead to fusion

Crossed disparity: the direction of disparity for objects in front of the horopter (the image in the left eye is to the right of the image of the object in the right eye)

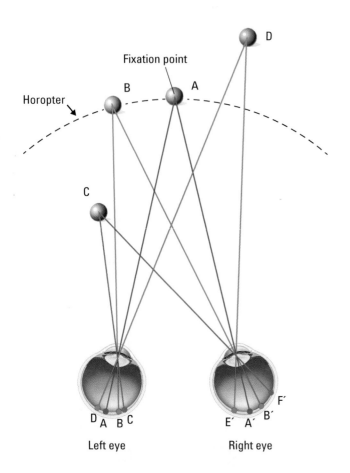

■ FIGURE 7.19 Corresponding and noncorresponding points and the horopter.

image of the object in the right eye). This type of disparity is often given as a negative value.

Finally, consider Object A itself. Its image falls on corresponding points on the left and right retinae. Similarly, Object B, though not the focus of our fixation, also falls along the horopter, so its image falls on corresponding points on the left and right retinae. Points along the horopter are said to have zero disparity. **Zero disparity** means that retinal images fall along corresponding points.

So, now let us examine Figure 7.20. We now consider the magnitude of retinal disparity between the two images. We can see here that the amount or magnitude of disparity increases as the distance of an object from the horopter increases. Consider Figure 7.20a. This figure shows two objects with crossed disparity, that is, two objects that are closer to the viewer than the object being fixated on. You can see that Object C is closer to the viewer than Object B. Therefore, Object C has a greater crossed disparity than Object B. Now consider Figure 7.20b. This figure shows two objects with an uncrossed disparity, that is, two objects that are farther from the viewer than the object being fixated on. You can see that Object D is farther from the viewer than Object E. Therefore, Object D has a greater uncrossed disparity than Object E.

We now have the cue people use to determine relative distance of objects by comparing the relative positions of the images of objects on the two eyes. The degree of retinal disparity gives us information about objects near and far. Indeed, retinal disparity can give us information about depth distances as small as 4 mm at a distance of 5 m. It is also useful up to distances of up to 200 m (roughly an eighth of a mile) (Howard & Rogers, 2002).

Think again about 3D movies. The plane of the screen becomes the horopter. The manipulation of images to the left and right eyes allows the filmmaker to create images that go to noncorresponding points along the retinae of the left and right eyes. If the filmmaker creates an image with uncrossed disparity, we see that image as being behind the plane of the screen. If the filmmaker creates an image with crossed disparity, we see that object as being in front of the screen. Indeed, if we perceive an object with increasing crossed disparity, this object appears to come out of the screen toward us. Think of the shark in the 1983 movie *Jaws 3-D*. The expanding image of the deadly shark is caused by increasing crossed disparity. If you have not seen this movie, don't bother. It is awful, but the image of a giant shark coming out of the screen to attack you is a powerful illustration of stereopsis.

In everyday vision, our brain automatically uses binocular disparity as a cue for depth. Although the monocular cues provide good estimates of depth and distance, binocular disparity provides strong subjective cues. When watching a regular movie, we have no problem judging distances between characters and objects. However, the binocular cues available in 3D movies create a strong experiential boost to our perception of three dimensions. Seeing objects move into and out of the screen, much as they do in real life, reinforces the importance of binocular disparity in creating the perception of a 3D world.

Uncrossed disparity: the direction of disparity for objects that are behind the horopter (the image of the object in the left eye is to the left of the position of the image of the object in the right eye)

Zero disparity: the situation in which retinal images fall along corresponding points, which means that the object is along the horopter

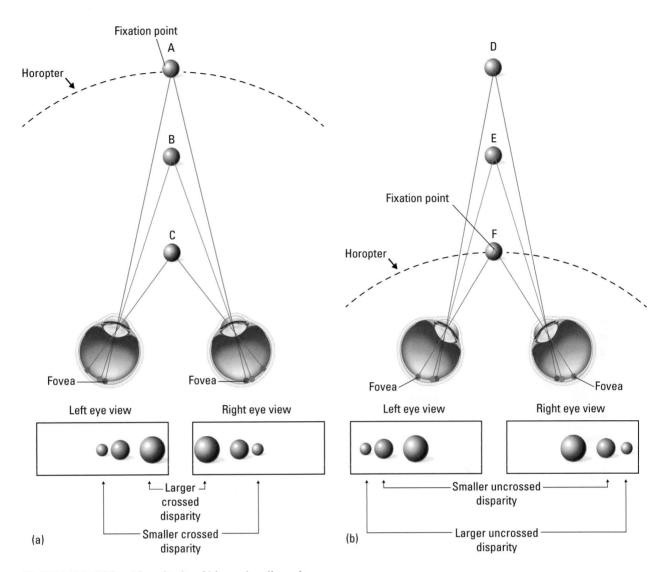

■ FIGURE 7.20   Magnitude of binocular disparity.

The farther away an object is from the horopter, the larger the disparity will be. Consider Figure 7.20a. This figure shows two objects with crossed disparity, that is, two objects that are closer to the viewer than the object being fixated on. You can see that Object C is closer to the viewer than Object B. Therefore, Object C has a greater crossed disparity than Object B. Now consider Figure 7.20b. This figure shows two objects with an uncrossed disparity, that is, two objects that are farther from the viewer than the object being fixated on. You can see that Object D is farther from the viewer than Object E. Therefore, Object D has a greater uncrossed disparity than Object E.

The Correspondence Problem

As we just described, the brain uses crossed and uncrossed disparity to determine if objects are in front of or behind the horopter. But there is an important assumption our visual system makes that must be questioned. How does our visual system know which image in the left eye matches up with which image in the right eye? In simple scenes, this may be relatively obvious. Because we know a lot about objects, in some cases, matching the image in the left and right eyes should be easy. For example, when looking at the lamp, that the "thumb-shaped object" about a meter away from your eyes is your thumb in both your left and right eyes is not surprising. But in many complex scenes, matching images to the left and right eyes may be more difficult. Real scenes often involve complex textures, similar objects in motion, and many other variations that may cloud an easy linking of an image in one eye to an image in the other. Imagine watching a raft of ducks swimming by. Some ducks are closer than others, but they all look identical to the untrained eye. How do our eyes match up the correct image of ducks in the left and right eyes? What happens if we match the wrong ducks together across eyes? This is the correspondence problem. The **correspondence problem** is the problem of determining which image in one eye matches the correct image in the other eye. How our visual system solves the correspondence problem has been an area of some fascinating research, which we discuss shortly. But in order to understand how our visual system solves the correspondence problem, we must describe the techniques researchers have used to investigate the issue. This means we will have to take a quick look at the nature of stereograms so that we can discuss how random-dot stereograms help us solve the correspondence problem.

TEST YOUR KNOWLEDGE

What is the difference between crossed and uncrossed disparity? Which corresponds to points closer than the horopter, and which corresponds to points farther away than the horopter?

STEREOGRAMS

 Describe the correspondence problem and how it relates to stereopsis.

Charles Wheatstone (1802–1875) was an English inventor during the 19th century. Among his inventions were a concertina (a small handheld accordion-like instrument), devices necessary for the creation of the first telegraph networks, and his famous Wheatstone stereoscope, invented before the first photographs. The stereoscope is a small instrument (see Figure 7.21) that presents one image to one eye and a second image to the other eye. The pictures presented to each eye are images slightly offset from each other in order to replicate the phenomena of crossed and uncrossed disparity. When one looks through a stereoscope, one sees a single 3D image of the scene. Originally, Wheatstone used drawings for his stereograms, as photography was still a year away from being invented and thereafter was expensive.

It is fairly easy to take stereographic pictures. A photographic stereogram can be made by taking a photograph of a scene. First, select a "still-life" type scene, perhaps a bowl of fruit. Take a photograph and then move the camera 4 inches (6 cm) to the right and take a second photograph. Keep in mind that the first photograph is the left-eye photo and the second photograph is the right-eye photograph. Print out the photographs and place them in an object like the stereograph above. Such an image is presented in Figure 7.22. When we look at the stereogram through a stereoscope, one image goes only to the left eye, and one image goes only to the right eye. Because the images are so similar, they are combined by the visual system, and the result is the illusion of depth.

Some people can examine stereograms without the use of a stereoscope, a skill known as free fusion. The way to do so is to control the convergence movements of one's eyes. If one relaxes one's gaze and imagines that one is looking at a distant point, the left and right eyes may diverge sufficiently such that the left eye is seeing only the left-eye image, and the right eye is seeing only the right-eye image. If this is difficult, you may be able to free-fuse the images by crossing your eyes. This means maximally converging your eyes as if you were looking at an object very close. This usually involves reversing the photos, because when you cross your eyes, you will be seeing the left-eye image with your right eye and the right-eye image with your

(a)

(b)

■ FIGURE 7.21 Wheatstone stereograph.

(a) This simple device projects one image to each eye. If there is disparity in the images, a 3D image will jump out at the viewer. (b) A stereoscope as an anaglyph stereogram. Use your anaglyph glasses.

Correspondence problem (depth perception): the problem of determining which image in one eye matches the correct image in the other eye

left eye. So if you copy, cut out, and reverse the photos as usually depicted, you can see the correct depth relationship with a crossed-eye approach. In both forms of free fusion, one is usually left with the odd perception of seeing three pictures. You can still see each of the original pictures, but you now see a third picture in the middle from the combination of your two eyes. It is this third (and essentially illusory) picture in which you can see the depth relations. In Figure 7.22, we see a stereogram of British coal miners on their way to work in a mine. When we fuse the two images, some of the miners should stand out in depth (see ISLE 7.9 for some really fun examples of stereograms).

ISLE 7.9 Anaglyph Stereograms

The anaglyph is another form of stereogram and the technique generally used in older 3D movies. Like traditional Wheatstone stereograms, anaglyphs are made by taking two photographs of a scene from cameras separated by about 6 cm. However, one photograph is then printed in a shade of one color, such as blue, whereas the other photograph is printed in a shade of another color, such as red. The two photographs are then integrated into a common image. The common image looks a bit fuzzy under normal viewing. However, when viewed through special color-coded anaglyph glasses, each of the two images goes to one eye, allowing for the stereoscopic image to emerge. The current convention is for the red lens to cover the left eye, and the cyan (blue) lens to cover the right eye. If you look at Figure 7.23 first without anaglyph glasses, you see a fuzzy image. But then put on a pair of anaglyph glasses and look at Figure 7.23 again. As with the stereograms, your left eye now sees one image and your

■ FIGURE 7.22   **An old-fashioned stereogram.**

© Photos.com/Thinkstock

■ FIGURE 7.23   **Anaglyph.**

This is another form of stereogram and the technique generally used in recent 3D movies. Use a pair of anaglyph glasses to look at these images.

right eye another image, and your visual cortex extracts the 3D information from the photograph. In one photograph, we see two students studying in their science classroom, but the anaglyph glasses gives us a stunning illusion of depth. Similarly, the masks seem to pop out of the book when you look at them through the glasses. Make sure to keep your anaglyph glasses handy. Go to ISLE 7.9 if you want to see more of these.

Random-Dot Stereograms

Earlier, we introduced the correspondence problem, that is, how the visual system determines which object's image in one eye matches the same object's image in the other eye. Here we explain how stereograms can be used to study the correspondence problem and potentially derive some solutions. How the visual system is able to solve the correspondence problem is quite complex computationally.

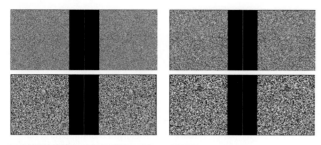

■ FIGURE 7.24   Random-dot stereograms.

When these images are viewed through a stereograph, you can see patterns floating in front of the black and white dots.

■ FIGURE 7.25   Random-dot stereograms as anaglyphs.

Use a pair of anaglyph glasses to examine the image. You should see patterns floating in front of the pattern of black and white dots.

ISLE 7.10 Random Dot Stereograms

The specifics of this computation were the subject of a debate that took place about the nature of stereopsis. On one side was the view that the visual system must bring to bear knowledge of objects and use that knowledge to match images. The other view was that the visual system matches the left and right images before bringing knowledge to bear on the situation.

In order to distinguish these hypotheses, Hungarian American vision researcher Béla Julesz invented random-dot stereograms (Julesz, 1971). **Random-dot stereograms** are stereograms in which the images consist of a randomly arranged set of black and white dots. The left-eye and right-eye image are arranged identically, except that a portion of the dots is moved to the left or the right in one of the images to create either a crossed or an uncrossed disparity. This creates the experience that part of the image is either in front of or behind the rest of the dots. Such a stereogram is seen in Figure 7.24. Figure 7.25 shows random-dot stereograms as anaglyphs. A graphic on how random-dot stereograms are made can be seen in Figure 7.26. You can explore an interactive illustration of random-dot stereograms on ISLE 7.10.

When you view a random-dot stereogram without a stereoscope or without free fusing, all you see is a grid of white and black dots. There is no shape apparent other than this uninteresting field of dots. Thus, if we can extract depth information from such images, it must come from depth perception processes that precede object recognition, because there are simply no objects to perceive in such figures until after stereopsis has occurred. Thus, the argument Julesz (1971) made is the following. Correspondence between points in the left image and right image is necessary for the perception of binocular disparity. If object recognition is necessary for matching correspondence, then random-dot stereograms will not result in a 3D perception.

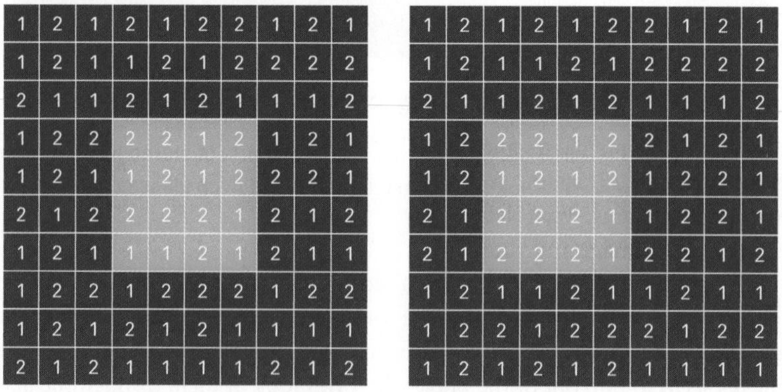

Random-dot stereograms: stereograms in which the images consist of a randomly arranged set of black and white dots, with the left-eye and right-eye images arranged identically except that some of the dots are moved to the left or the right in one of the images, creating either a crossed or an uncrossed disparity

■ FIGURE 7.26   How random-dot stereograms are made.

To make a random-dot stereogram, you make a random grid of black and white dots. Each number in the figure represents either a black (1) or white (2) dot. You then copy the image to make two such images. But in the second image, you shift a central section of the first image to the right or left. Thus, the same pattern is represented in each image, but part of it is shifted. When we look at this through a stereograph, the shifted part will appear either in front of or behind of the rest of the dots, depending on which direction it was shifted.

However, if correspondence matching occurs before object recognition, then it should be possible for people to extract binocular depth cues from random-dot stereograms. Inspect Figure 7.24 through a stereoscope or Figure 7.25 with a pair of 3D glasses. What do you see? Do any patterns jump out of the page at you? The majority of people with normal stereopsis will see these patterns in front of the page. If you are free fusing by crossing your eyes, the figure will appear behind the plane of the page. Thus, because people do see depth information in random-dot stereograms, we know that correspondence precedes object recognition.

The Anatomy and Physiology of Binocular Perception

The next question we can ask about stereopsis is how it is achieved in the human visual cortex. We already touched on the answer to this question in Chapter 4. We review these issues and expand on them here. As discussed in Chapter 4, there are binocular cells in V1 of the occipital cortex (Hubel & Wiesel, 1962). Binocular cells have two receptive fields, one for each eye. These cells are also usually similar with respect to their preferred orientation and motion sensitivity, suggesting that the main function of these cells is to match the images coming to each eye. Moreover, many binocular cells in the cortex respond optimally when the images are on corresponding points on each retina. Interestingly, there are also binocular cells that respond best to varying degrees of disparity, that is, when similar images lie in front of or behind the horopter (Barlow, Blakemore, & Pettigrew, 1967).

This arrangement is depicted in Figure 7.27. Indeed, different binocular cells are tuned to different disparities. For example, a neuron may be tuned to crossed disparity of a particular magnitude, whereas another cell might be tuned to an uncrossed disparity of another magnitude. Moreover, such disparity-tuned cells are found through the visual cortex, including along both the ventral pathway (what) and the dorsal pathway (where and when). For both systems, depth information can play an important role in visual perception (Parker, 2007).

Development of Stereopsis

Are human beings born with stereopsis, or is it a visual skill that requires experience in the environment to learn? If it does develop, what are the perceptual and physiological processes that allow infants to learn stereopsis? Research suggests that

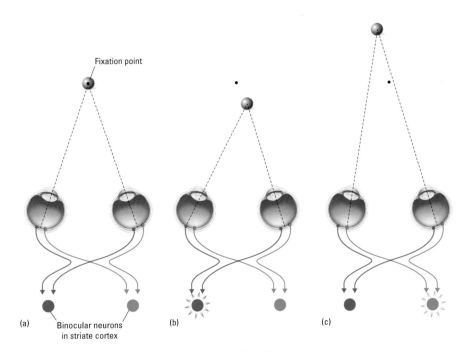

■ FIGURE 7.27 Binocular cell receptive fields.

These are simplified illustrations of what a receptive field for disparity-tuned neurons in the occipital cortex look like. In Figure 7.27a, both the red cell and the blue cell are not responding, as the only object is the fixation point, to which disparity-tuned neurons do not respond. In Figure 7.27b, there is an object closer than the fixation point. A crossed disparity neuron (red) is firing in response to this object. In Figure 7.27c, there is an object farther away than the fixation point. A blue uncrossed disparity neuron is firing in response to this object.

newborn infants are blind to binocular depth information and continue to show no stereopsis until the age of about 4 months. At about 4 months of age, stereopsis develops rapidly in human infants (Teller, 1983). Indeed, a number of studies have found that 3-month-old infants do not detect disparity at all, but by 5 months of age, infants perceive depth from disparity as well as normal adults (Birch, 1993).

Testing infants at this age is tricky because they cannot make verbal responses, nor are they yet in control of all their muscular movements. Thus, researchers must be clever in designing tasks on which infants can provide measurable responses. It turns out that most infants like novel stimuli. When presented with an image they have seen before or a completely new one, infants will direct their gaze toward the new stimulus. This is often called a novelty preference. Gaze direction and novelty preference can be measured by researchers. Thus, we can habituate an infant to a 2D stimulus. Once the stimulus is no longer novel, we can show the infant an alternative stimulus that has the same structure in two dimensions but has a 3D interpretation if the infant can use binocular cues. Thus, if the infant prefers the 3D image to the 2D image, it demonstrates stereopsis, as only with the 3D information is the image novel. Preferential looking tasks show that infants start becoming sensitive to disparity at about 5 months of age (Birch, 1993).

One explanation for this phenomenon is that binocular cells in the cortex are not mature and not yet functioning (it also could be acuity and lack of vergence). The current research suggests that the area in the brain that is not yet mature is found not in V1 but in higher areas of the occipital cortex. Chino, Smith, Hatta, and Cheng (1997), for example, found that binocular cells of 1-week-old monkeys were responding to disparity in the same way that binocular cells of older monkeys were doing. Ocular dominance columns also appear to be mature at birth. At this point, it is not clear where the locus of origin emerges from, but some evidence points to Area V2 (Zheng et al., 2007). Nonetheless, as of yet, there is no ready explanation for the sudden development of stereopsis at around 4 months of age.

TEST YOUR KNOWLEDGE

What is a random dot stereogram? How is it made? And what issue does its study address?

SIZE PERCEPTION

| 7.5 | Explain the concept of size perception and the inferential nature of its determination. |

Size and depth are deeply intertwined. Think of watching a professional basketball game from the seats at the top of the coliseum. One knows the players are taller than normal people, but at that distance, it is hard to perceptually distinguish just how tall they are. Contrast this with the experience of finding yourself next to Shaquille O'Neal at the deli counter of your supermarket. At close range, his extreme tallness is apparent, whereas at a distance, we use familiar size cues to perceive people, any people, and thus, the basketball players' height is underestimated. This is similar to the experience we have looking at the ground from airplanes. Intellectually, we understand that we are 2 miles above the surface of the earth and the cars and houses we see are really quite large. But at that vertical distance, our sense of size is problematic, and we perceptually experience what look like toy cars and houses. In both of these cases, we misjudge size because we are at unfamiliar distances. We are more familiar with interacting with people, houses, and cars at closer distances. At these familiar distances, we can scale size better. Indeed, at most distances, we can judge the sizes of objects quite well, despite the changes in size these objects make on our retinae as they approach us or recede from us. Think of watching your friends leave your house. As you watch their car speed away down the street, you do not see your friends' car getting smaller. You perceive the car at the same size, but moving farther away from you. This leads us to the concept of size-distance invariance.

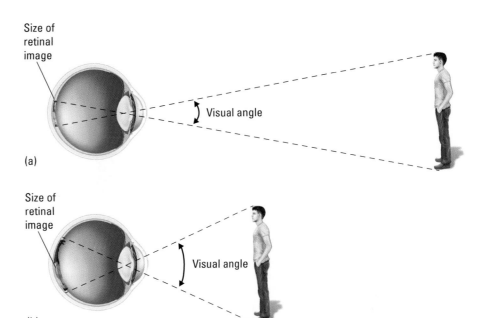

Size of retinal image

Visual angle

(a)

Size of retinal image

Visual angle

(b)

■ FIGURE 7.28   Visual angle and size.

Visual angle is a function of the size of an object and its distance from the observer. When the object moves closer, its visual angle on the retina increases. When the object moves more distant, its visual angle decreases. If we know the object, we will see this difference not as changes in size but as changes in distance.

Size-distance invariance refers to the relation between perceived size and perceived distance and simply states that the perceived size of an object depends on its perceived distance, and the perceived distance of an object may depend on its perceived size. In a classic experiment, Holway and Boring (1941) looked at this relation. (College students may not make jokes about the second author's name. He was a famous psychologist.) They placed disks at various distances from the observers in such a way that the disks all took up the same amount of space on the observers' retinae. If there were no depth cues, the observers judged the objects to be of the same size, a natural judgment given that the objects were equivalent on the retinae. But when depth cues were provided, the observers correctly distinguished the smaller objects up close from the larger objects farther away. That is, as soon as distance was clear, the observers' visual systems used the size-distance invariance principle to scale the sizes of the objects consistent with their distance.

Important to studying size-distance invariance is the concept of a visual angle. **Visual angles** are the angles of objects relative to an individual's eyes. That is, if we drew lines from the top and bottom of an object and extended those lines to your eyes, we would have the visual angle of that object (see Figure 7.28). Smaller objects close up can have the same visual angles as larger objects farther away. Classic examples of this are the sun and the moon. Each appears approximately the same size in the sky and makes a similar visual angle to our eyes (by sheer coincidence). However, the moon is much smaller than the sun, and the moon is also much closer to Earth than the Sun is. Similarly, a thumb held at arm's length also makes approximately the same visual angle as do the sun and the moon (although again, your thumb is obviously much smaller and closer than either the sun or the moon). We perceive the thumb as smaller than these faraway objects

Size-distance invariance: the relation between perceived size and perceived distance, whereby the perceived size of an object depends on its perceived distance, and the perceived distance of an object may depend on its perceived size

Visual angle: the angle of an object relative to the observer's eye

(a)   (b)

Margaret Krantz   REUTERS/Jamal Saidi

■ FIGURE 7.29   Size and visual angle illusions.

(a) Is the author (JHK) really a giant and as tall at the pyramid in front of the Louvre? The lack of cues for distance suggest that he's as tall as the pyramid and standing right next to it. (b) The effect is similar in the picture of the woman "kissing" the sphinx. She is really much closer to the camera than the sphinx but the lack of depth cues makes it appear that she is even with the sphinx and big enough to kiss it.

because of size-distance invariance. However, we cannot perceptually determine the distances or the sizes of objects as massive and as distant as the sun and the moon, and therefore, we do not see the size differences between the sun and the moon. For another example, the actor Danny DeVito standing close to you might make the same visual angle as Shaquille O'Neal would standing some distance from you. Similar visual angles from objects of different sizes and different distances is also the point of Figure 7.29. The point of Holway and Boring's (1941) experiment was that depth provides information that allows us to appropriately scale the size of an object. Go to ISLE 7.11 for a demonstration of the relation of visual angles and size perception.

ISLE 7.11 Retinal Image Size and Distance

TEST YOUR KNOWLEDGE

What is size-distance invariance? How is it used by the visual system to determine size?

SIZE CONSTANCY

7.6   Discuss the concept of size constancy.

Size constancy is the perception of an object as having a fixed size, despite the change in the size of the visual angle that accompanies changes in distance. That is, we have a tendency to see an object as the same size regardless of the size of its image on our retinae. As we have seen, there are limits to size constancy. Shaquille O'Neal does not look so tall when we see him from far away. However, at the range of normal viewing, size constancy allows us to see objects as the "right" size even as they move away from or toward us. For example, consider talking to a friend. You see her as the same size if she is standing 6 feet away from you or if she is standing 3 feet away from you. If she is standing 6 feet away and suddenly takes a step closer to you, you do not see her grow, even though her visual angle is now twice as large on your retina. Thus, size constancy usually allows us to see objects as not changing in size, but

Size constancy: the perception of an object as having a fixed size, despite the change in the size of the visual angle that accompanies changes in distance

there are also exceptions to it. Consider the boot in Figure 7.7. If we saw this boot in isolation, we might think it was an ordinary boot. Only in the context of all the cues that tell us that it is an enormous boot do we see it as such. We now turn to a set of illusions that occur when depth and size information are not well specified in a visual image.

TEST YOUR KNOWLEDGE

Under what circumstances might size constancy result in illusions rather than the perception of reality?

VISUAL ILLUSIONS OF SIZE AND DEPTH

7.7 Explain the concept of illusions of size and depth and how they affect perception.

Visual illusions fascinate us because they cause us to see that which is not really there. We see colors when no colors exist, we see spots of light where no such spots exist, and we see shapes that cannot be. Illusions of size and depth are no exception. By manipulating the cues we have discussed in this chapter, it is possible to get viewers to see depth relations that are really not present in an image.

The Müller-Lyer Illusion

In the Müller-Lyer illusion (Figure 7.30), we see the left line as longer than the right line, even though both lines are exactly the same length. If you do not believe this assertion, measure the two lines with a ruler. They are the same length. We will not distort illusions in this textbook, but please do not trust us. Measure our illusions objectively, and you will discover how your perception can be tricked. With respect to the Müller-Lyer illusion, it is the smaller lines that split off from the main line that create the illusion that the main line is longer or shorter. An obvious question is, Why would these additional lines affect our perception of the length of the longest line? Most explanations of the Müller-Lyer illusion focus on the relation of size and depth. For example, Gregory (1966) advanced the view that the Müller-Lyer illusion is the result of misapplied size constancy. What this means is that the visual system wants to keep objects of the same size looking the same size, but in the case of the Müller-Lyer illusion, we mistakenly see size differences when the size is actually the same.

The argument works as follows. Consider the left image in the Müller-Lyer illusion. Think about what this might look like in three dimensions. We may see the image as a corner in a wall. The corner is close to us and the little projections at the top and bottom point away from us, as they might if the corner were near us, and the walls led away. In the image on the right, we see the corner as being farther away, and the little projections that mark the corner are coming toward us. Here we see the corner as being at a distance and the walls coming toward us. Because we see the line as being farther away in the right-hand image than we do in the left-hand image, we see the line in the right-hand image as longer. Why? Because it takes up the same space as the left-hand line on our retina, but we perceive it as being more distant. Objects that take up the same amount of space on our retina, but are more distant, are necessarily larger. Hence, we see the line as longer. You can see how this looks in real life by examining the corners in Figure 7.31.

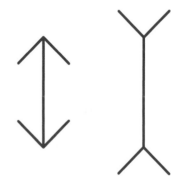

■ **FIGURE 7.30**   **The Müller-Lyer illusion.**

We see the vertical line as longer in the right figure than the left figure even though the vertical lines are the same length in both.

■ FIGURE 7.31 **The Müller-Lyer illusion in the real world.**

Note in the first picture that the angled lines indicate an outside corner, whereas the angled lines in the second picture indicate an inside corner. The inside corner with the walls coming toward us suggests that the straight line is farther away from us, and thus we perceive it as bigger.

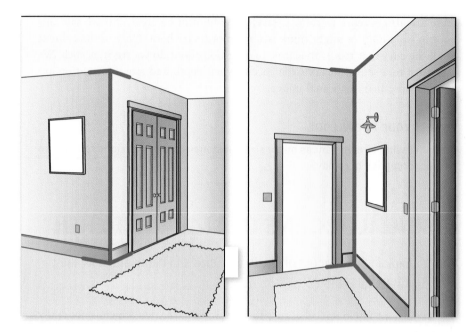

However, the above explanation stemming from Gregory's (1966) work is not the only explanation for the Müller-Lyer illusion. Some researchers have questioned whether an implicit assumption of depth is required to see the Müller-Lyer illusion. Day (1990) proposed a more simple explanation of the Müller-Lyer illusion. Day claimed that because the extending lines reach up and out in the right-hand image of Figure 7.30, the overall figure is longer in that image than the one on the left-hand side. Thus, we perceive components as longer as well. Thus, this view accounts for the Müller-Lyer illusion without recourse to a depth illusion. Go to ISLE 7.12, for interesting variants on the Müller-Lyer illusion.

ISLE 7.12 Müller-Lyer Illusion

■ FIGURE 7.32 **The Ponzo illusion.**

Even though both cows take up the exact same space on the retina, the one higher on the image looks bigger because it appears farther away.

The Ponzo Illusion

The Ponzo illusion is a strong example of misapplied size constancy as well as the influence of linear perspective (a monocular cue to depth) on size perception. The Ponzo illusion is illustrated in Figure 7.32. The two cows are the identical size (indeed, the identical animal). They take up exactly the same amount of size on the page or screen. If you do not believe this, you can measure them. However, the cow closer to the top of the page looks bigger. This is because there are a number of cues in the photograph that give clear indications of depth relations. We see the roughly parallel lines of the side of the road receding into the distance. We see a texture gradient of flowers and grasses. We see that the trees at the top of the photo are a bit hazy. Familiar size cues suggest that the trees, despite their smaller retinal image than the grass, must be larger but more distant. As a function of all this, we see the upper cow as farther away from the viewer than the lower cow. Because the cows take up the same amount of space on the retina, and the upper cow is farther away, the visual system makes the inference that the upper cow must be larger, leaving us with the strong perception of a big cow and tiny cow in front of her. The Ponzo illusion is so called because it was discovered by the Italian psychologist Mario Ponzo (1882–1960). For more on the Ponzo illusion, go to ISLE 7.13.

ISLE 7.13 Ponzo Illusion

The Ames Room Illusion

The Ames room is a neat illusion because it can be instantiated in real space, as has been done in numerous science museums, such as those in Melbourne, Australia; Keswick, England; and Jerusalem, Israel. It also works on paper (see Figures 7.33 and 7.34). In the Ames room, we put two people of normal size into a room that is anything but normal. When viewed through a peephole on the side of one of the walls, the perception is of a very large person in one corner and a very small person in the other corner. The room, however, looks normal. But the room is not normal. Indeed, it defies almost all conventional rules of rooms. Its walls (except the one people are looking through) are trapezoids, as are the windows in the room. In versions in which there are floor tiles in the room, these are also trapezoids (see Figure 7.33). However, when we look through the viewing hole, we cannot distinguish the trapezoids, and we use our cues of familiar sizes and shapes to infer a normal room. Our visual systems convert the trapezoids into squares, so that we can perceive the room itself as normal. Because we perceive a normal room, we must therefore infer that the people are abnormally short or tall. To make the illusion fun, you can find twins who are dressed alike and put one at each end of the room, making for a very tall twin and a very short twin.

The Moon Illusion

The moon illusion is another powerful illusion related to size-depth relations. What is interesting about this illusion is that we can see it in the night sky several times each month. Find out when the next full moon is, or a day before or after the full moon. Then find out when sunset will occur, and watch the moon rise at sunset and then look at it again a few hours later. When we see the full moon on the horizon (such as when it rises at sunset and sets at sunrise), we perceive it as being larger than when it is higher up in the sky. This perceptual fact is seen in countless romantic movies, in which a love-struck couple stares at an abnormally large full moon. The moon illusion is depicted in Figure 7.35. As you can see, in Figure 7.35, the moon looks bigger at the horizon than at zenith. However, the moon does not change size across the night. Its size remains constant, and its distance from the Earth remains constant. If you do not believe this, take a photograph of the full moon as it rises and then again a few hours later. Print out the photograph and cut out the image of the moon. You will see that the zenith moon fits perfectly on top of the horizon moon. The moon does not change size; only our perception of it does.

The explanation for the moon illusion is similar to other size-depth illusions: a misperception of distance causes a change in the perception of size. We see the sky as a giant dome overhead, and objects in the sky as all at the same distance, that is, "painted" on the dome (though intellectually we know this to be untrue). As such,

STEPHANIE PILICK / Staff / Getty Images

■ FIGURE 7.33 **The Ames room illusion.**

The people in the photo are the same size, but the person on the left appears much larger than the others because of the shape of the room. Note that the person on the left in one photograph is the person on the right in the other photograph. Has she shrank while her friend grew?

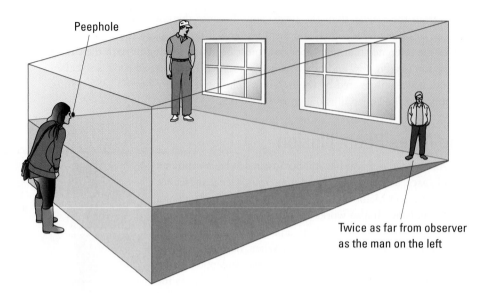

Peephole

Twice as far from observer
as the man on the left

■ FIGURE 7.34 The Ames room revealed.

You can see in this drawing what an Ames room looks like. When you look through the peephole, as the observer is doing, it looks like Figure 7.33, but you can see here that the person on the right is approximately twice as far away from the observer as the person on the left. But for the observer, this difference is not seen, and instead the person on the left is seen as much bigger.

ISLE 7.14 Moon Illusion

on this dome, the horizon is farther away from you than is the zenith, directly overhead. Because we perceive the horizon as being farther away than the zenith overhead, an object that takes up the same amount of space on our retina must be larger. At zenith, the moon looks smaller because the same-size object is now thought to be closer. This explanation is illustrated in Figure 7.36. You can explore an interactive illustration of the moon illusion on ISLE 7.14.

TEST YOUR KNOWLEDGE

What is the Ames room? How does it illustrate the cue approach to depth and size perception?

(a)

(b)

■ FIGURE 7.35 Moon illusion.

You can see here that the moon looks bigger (a) when we see it on the horizon than when it is higher in the sky (b). But if you match the moons, you will see that they are the same size.

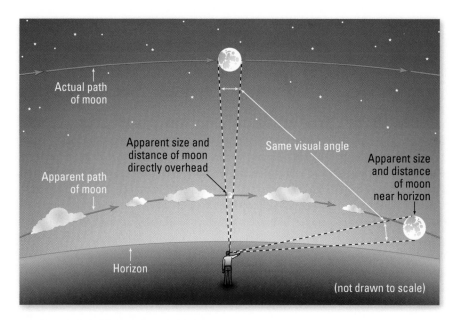

■ **FIGURE 7.36   The moon illusion explained.**

We view the sky as a dome, and the moon and stars as "painted" on the dome, even though we know intellectually that this is not true. Thus, because the horizon is perceived as farther away than the zenith, the same-size object is viewed as larger on the horizon than at the zenith.

IN DEPTH: *Stereopsis and Sports: Do We Need Binocular Vision in Sports?*

In everyday life, we can get by with monocular cues, but the binocular cues add to our perception of depth and give us additional invaluable cues, which in some cases may help us perceive depth. But are there situations in which having binocular vision is absolutely essential, and are there situations in which binocular vision gets in the way? Sports provide one of these situations—competing in sports requires finely honed senses and close coordination between what one is seeing and what one is doing. Think of the coordination between quarterback and wide receiver in football. The quarterback must time his pass at just the right time to avoid the hands of oncoming defenders and in such a way as to bring the football into contact with the wide receiver's hands at just the right moment. Similarly, the wide receiver must be aware of the positions of defenders, the pattern he is supposed to run, and the exact arrival of the football at a particular point in time. Moreover, the wide receiver must do this while running nearly 20 mph (32 km/h). One would think that such activities require excellent depth perception (and peripheral vision), and yet the former football player Wesley Walker succeeded at being a wide receiver despite being legally blind in one eye. However, Walker was a runner as fast as Olympic sprinters, which gave him an advantage despite his monocular vision.

However, in target sports, the conventional wisdom is that it is desirable to eliminate binocular cues. Archers and target shooters are usually instructed to close one eye. The thinking here is that good shooting means focusing on lining up a close point, such as your gun's sight, and a far point, the target. Because the close point may be on noncorresponding points on your left and right retinae, it may not be possible to line up the sight using both eyes, especially if firing a handgun. Given that shooters in competitions are usually aiming at targets that are largely out of the range of binocular depth cues anyway, there is no real advantage to using both eyes, but there is this one big disadvantage. Unfortunately, there has been no published empirical research on the advantages or disadvantages of stereopsis in target sports.

But are there any empirical data athletes could rely on? Do we know that quarterbacks, for example, use binocular cues of depth to judge distance, and do we know if archers would shoot better if they kept both eyes open? In this section, we discuss some of the existing literature on stereopsis and sports.

Much of the research has been done with respect to the batter in baseball. Consider the perceptual-motor task a baseball batter is confronted with. A pitcher is throwing a ball with a 9-inch circumference (230 mm) at over 90 mph (145 km/h) from a distance of 60 feet (18 m). Baseball hitters must react extremely quickly; indeed, they often initiate their swing even before the pitcher has released the ball. As the ball approaches the batter, there are a number of depth cues that the batter may attend to, including familiar and relative size, linear perspective, shading, optic flow, and binocular disparity. So our question is, To what extent do baseball batters use binocular disparity information?

In one study, Hofeldt and Hoefle (1993) compared professional baseball players in the highest professional league (the major leagues) with professional baseball players who had not made the highest professional league (the minor leagues) (see Figure 7.37). Hofeldt and Hoefle looked at the players' ability to do a stereo matching task that measured individual differences in the ability to use stereopic cues. The researchers found that the major league players were more accurate at the stereopic task than the minor league players and that ability in the task predicted batting average (a measure of baseball performance) in the major leaguers. This suggests that baseball batters do use stereo cues to time their swings. However, this study is still correlational in nature. We do not know if batters are better because they have better stereopsis, or if better stereopsis is the result of working harder to be good at baseball. So Hofeldt and his colleagues next designed an experimental procedure to look at baseball batting and depth perception.

Hofeldt, Hoefle, and Bonafede (1996) examined amateur baseball players hitting in batting cages under controlled conditions, including a constant speed of pitches. Again, they were interested in the interaction of the two eyes in timing the swing of a baseball bat. Baseball batting success was measured by looking at the rate of hits (contact with the ball into play), fouls (contact with the ball, but out of play), and misses (not making contact with the ball). They then used filters to impair one eye or the other during swinging. These filters reduced the amount of light reaching the filtered eye. When one eye receives less light than the other, that eye essentially perceives more slowly, making it harder to match corresponding points. They found that when both eyes were filtered, the decrease in hitting success was negligible and nonsignificant. However, when one eye was filtered, but not the other, motion-for-depth cues were interrupted, and hitting success decreased dramatically, from 87% hits to 36% hits. However, this was when the dominant eye was filtered. The effect was smaller (80%) when the nondominant eye was filtered. Scott, van der Kamp, Savelsbergh, Oudejans, and Davids (2004) also found that participants were better able to hit a foam object thrown at them if they had access to binocular cues than when they only had monocular cues. Hofeldt et al. concluded that

(a) binocular information is important for baseball batting and (b) baseball batters really do have a dominant eye, consistent with the conventional sports wisdom.

In baseball, players must be able to catch balls as well as hit them. Outfielders must judge the distance and direction a ball is going to go after the batter hits it, and they must also time their running speed to meet the ball in an anticipated location. We can ask the question, To what extent do baseball players use stereopsis to judge where they must run to in order to intercept the ball? Mazyn, Lenoir, Montagne, and Savelsbergh (2004) looked at the ability of people to catch a tennis ball with one hand. They compared performance under binocular viewing conditions as well as monocular viewing conditions at a variety of ball speeds. People with normal stereo vision caught more balls under binocular conditions than under monocular conditions, and this effect was more pronounced the faster the ball was thrown at them. Thus, binocular cues are used in catching balls, contrary to some earlier notions of how baseball players intercept fly balls (see Mazyn et al., 2004). Mazyn et al. also looked at people who do not see well in stereo. These individuals were no better in the binocular condition than the monocular condition and were somewhat lower in their overall ability to catch tennis balls. Along similar lines, Isaacs (1981) found that people with better stereo vision were also better at shooting foul shots in basketball than people with weaker stereo vision. Thus, across an assortment of athletic tasks, we see that stereo vision is useful in performing athletic tasks.

■ FIGURE 7.37   Binocular vision in baseball.

A batter must be able to accurately time an incoming baseball in a fraction of a second in order to hit it. Batters hit better with binocular vision than with monocular vision.

CHAPTER SUMMARY

7.1 Explain oculomotor depth cues and how they work.

The problem our visual systems must solve is that we represent the world on flat, 2D retinae. However, we live in and therefore must perceive a 3D world. Our visual system seems to do this in classic Helmholtzian fashion—by using unconscious inference from myriad clues that inform us of relative depth. We divide these cues into three groups—the oculomotor cues, the monocular cues, and the binocular cues. The oculomotor cues are convergence (or vergence) and accommodation. Convergence means that the eyes bend inward when looking at closer objects. We sense this motion, and it informs us about whether we are looking at a near or a far object. Accommodation is the process of adjusting the lens of the eye so that both near and far objects can be seen clearly. Again, we can sense the muscles that make this adjustment, and this informs us about the proximity of the objects that we are looking at.

7.2 Explain monocular depth cues and how they work.

The monocular cues include information about depth that we can infer with just one eye. These tend to be characteristics of the scene itself or motion-based cues. Monocular cues include occlusion, relative height, relative size, familiar size, texture gradients, linear perspective, atmospheric perspective, shading, and shadows. Included in the monocular cues are the motion-based cues of motion parallax, accretion and deletion, and optic flow.

7.3 Summarize the principle of stereopsis and how it applies to human depth perception.

Stereopsis is the strong sense of depth we perceive from the visual system's processing of the comparison of the two different images from each retina. Stereopsis arises from binocular disparity. Binocular disparity occurs because our two eyes are in different locations in our head and therefore have slightly different views of the world. In order for stereopsis to work, the visual system must match the image on the left retina to that on the right retina.

7.4 Describe the correspondence problem and how it relates to stereopsis.

Corresponding points refers to a situation in which a point on the left retina and a point on the right retina would coincide if the two retinae were superimposed. In contrast, *noncorresponding points* refers to a situation in which a point on the left retina and a point on the right retina would not coincide if the two retinae were superimposed. Corresponding points lie along the horopter, the region in space where the two images from an object fall on corresponding locations on the two retinae. We use disparity information to determine if an image is in front of the horopter or behind it. Crossed disparity means that an object is in front of the horopter, whereas uncrossed disparity means that an object is behind the horopter. The correspondence problem is the problem of determining which image in one eye matches the correct image in the other eye. Stereograms and anaglyphs are specially designed pictures in which the photograph or film replicates the binocular disparity and therefore creates a pop-out phenomenon that we see as depth. Random-dot stereograms have been used to show that object recognition is not necessary for disparity cues, thus placing the solution to the correspondence problem as something that occurs prior to object recognition. Physiological studies demonstrate that there are binocular cells in the visual cortex. These cells are tuned to disparity information, thus allowing the neurons to extract information about depth. Infants do not develop stereopsis until the age of about 4 months, though the physiological reasons for this are unclear.

7.5 Explain the concept of size perception and the inferential nature of its determination.

Size and depth are deeply intertwined. Size-distance invariance refers to the relation between perceived size and perceived distance, and simply states that the perceived size of an object depends on its perceived distance, and the perceived distance of an object may depend on its perceived size.

7.6 Discuss the concept of size constancy.

Size constancy is the perception of an object as having a fixed size, despite the change in the size of the visual angle that accompanies changes in distance.

7.7 Explain the concept of illusions of size and depth and how they affect perception.

A number of illusions demonstrate violations of size-distance invariance and size constancy. In the Müller-Lyer illusion, we see a line that looks longer than an identical-length line because the ends of one line suggest a corner moving away in depth. The Ponzo illusion is a strong example of misapplied size constancy as well as the influence of linear perspective (a monocular cue to depth) on size perception. In the Ponzo illusion, we see two objects that take up the same amount of space on our retinae as different in size because of their perceived differences in depth. In the Ames room, we put two people of normal size into a room that is anything but normal. When viewed through a peephole on the side of one of the walls, the perception is of a very large person in one corner and a very small person in the other corner. The room, however, looks normal. The moon illusion is another powerful illusion related to size-depth relations. When we see the full moon on the horizon (such as when it rises at sunset and sets at sunrise), we perceive it as being larger than when it is higher up in the sky.

REVIEW QUESTIONS

1. How do jumping spiders use their multilayered retinae to perceive depth? How is this different from mammalian depth perception?

2. What are the oculomotor cues to depth? How do they work, and how do they give us depth information?

3. Describe three pictorial monocular depth cues. How does each one provide us information about depth or distance?

4. What is motion parallax? How is it used as a cue for depth?

5. What is meant by the term *stereopsis*? Why does stereopsis require two frontally placed eyes?

6. What is the horopter? How do crossed and uncrossed disparity relate to the horopter? What is meant by *zero disparity*? Where would such a point lie along the horopter?

7. What is the correspondence problem? How do random-dot stereograms address the theoretical issues raised by the correspondence problem?

8. What evidence suggests that stereopsis is not innate? What areas of the brain appear to be involved in stereopsis?

9. What is meant by *size-distance invariance*? What is size constancy? Describe one illusion that illustrates each principle.

10. What data exist to support the idea that stereopsis can help athletic performance? Choose a sport not considered in this chapter (e.g., volleyball) and describe how depth perception might be critical to perform well in that sport.

KEY TERMS

Accommodation, 171

Accretion, 179

Atmospheric perspective, 176

Correspondence problem (depth perception), 186

Crossed disparity, 183

Cue approach to depth perception, 171

Deletion, 179

Diplopia, 183

Familiar size, 173

Horopter, 182

Linear perspective, 174

Monocular depth cues, 172

Motion parallax, 178

Movement-based cues, 172

Occlusion, 172

Optic flow, 179

Panum's area of fusion, 183

Pictorial cues, 172

Random-dot stereograms, 188

Relative height, 172

Relative size, 173

Shadows, 177

Size constancy, 192

Size-distance invariance, 191

Stereopsis, 180

Texture gradient, 175

Uncrossed disparity, 183

Vergence, 171

Visual angle, 191

Zero disparity, 184

INTERACTIVE SENSATION LABORATORY EXERCISES (ISLE)

Experience chapter concepts at edge.sagepub.com/schwartz

Sharpen your skills with SAGE edge at edge.sagepub.com/schwartz

SAGE edge for students provides a personalized approach to help you accomplish
your coursework goals in an easy-to-use learning environment.

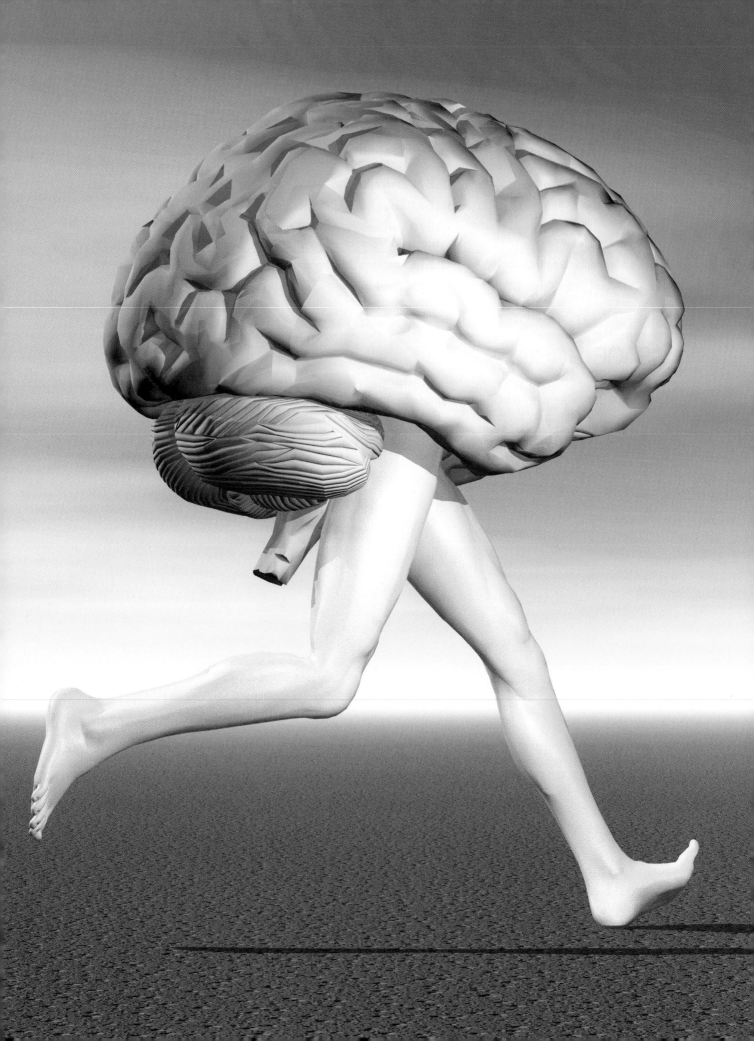

Movement and Action

8

INTRODUCTION

A number of major world cities, such as Los Angeles, San Francisco, Port-au-Prince (Haiti), Tokyo (Japan), Reykjavik (Iceland), Ankara (Turkey), and Wellington (New Zealand), to name just a few, lie in earthquake zones. Anyone who has ever lived through an earthquake understands how motion can induce fear. Once the earthquake starts, things that are not supposed to move, like walls and floors, may start shaking, undulating, and cracking. Other things start falling—books, jars, glasses, and televisions. People outside their homes may see bridges sway and roads crumble. Cities heavily fortified against earthquakes (e.g., San Francisco, Tokyo) design their buildings to sway in an earthquake, so as to avoid cracking and crumbling. However unnerving this may be for residents of these cities, it saves countless lives when these highly populated cities are struck by earthquakes. But simply watching swaying buildings is rather unnerving. Only when all this motion subsides can people relax. What many find striking about perceiving motion during an earthquake is that objects we generally perceive as stable—walls, roads, and buildings—move. This type of motion induces fear. Clearly, perceiving motion is important and vital for human beings.

Imagine now that you are on an airplane, perhaps one bound from San Francisco to Tokyo on your way to a conference on sensation and perception research. You are 7 miles above the Pacific Ocean, traveling at nearly 1,000 km/h (621 mph). A serendipitous error on the airline's part bumped you up into first class. Therefore, you are sitting in a comfortable reclining chair, eating warmed nuts and drinking champagne, completely unaware that you are moving at nearly the speed of sound (which is 1,236 km/h). Why is it that you are not perceiving the incredible motion that is occurring in this situation? With the shades drawn shut, you do not see your motion relative to the ground below. You see only the tranquil scene of people relaxing in their first-class seats, feeling smug that they are comfortable while the rabble behind them is not. Your world is stable and not moving.

You may remember from physics class that all motion is relative. In the case of the airline passenger, everything around her is moving at the same speed. The comfortable chair, the champagne glass, the overhead television projector, the magazines, and the passenger are all moving together at the exact same speed. We may feel the rumbling of the engines and the rumbling in our stomachs when the plane encounters turbulence. But we feel this motion rather than seeing it. Unless you look out the window, you will not perceive motion visually under these circumstances. It is not all that dissimilar to why we do not perceive the rotation of the earth itself (see ISLE 8.1). Everything around us, including us, is rotating with the earth, so we do not perceive the motion. In this sense, we can define **motion** as a relative change in position over time. If I start running to the west, I am now going faster than the speed of the earth's rotation (though not by very much). Now, a viewer can observe my motion against the backdrop of a stable ground.

LEARNING OBJECTIVES

8.1 Explain the concept of a motion threshold and what variables influence that threshold.

8.2 Describe the anatomy of the visual system dedicated to motion perception.

8.3 Discuss how we infer form from the perception of biological motion.

8.4 Summarize the concept of an affordance.

ISLE 8.1 Relative Motion

Motion: a change in position over time

(a)

(b)

© iStockphoto.com/monkeybusinessimages

© iStockphoto.com/mevans

■ FIGURE 8.1   Motion is relevant.

(a) We see this woman and her child approaching us. Their speed, however, probably does not cause concern. (b) These race cars bearing down on us would cause concern and, hopefully, a sudden leap off the road.

Our visual systems must be able to attend to motion. Perceiving motion allows us to move ourselves as well as to time the arrival of incoming objects, whether they are cars, baseballs, cheetahs, or falling coconuts. One can imagine that motion perception evolved to help our distant ancestors perceive incoming predators and fleeing prey. Nowadays, motion detection is important in driving cars, crossing city streets, playing sports, and watching movies. Thus, at its very basic level, there are a number of features our visual system must be able to perceive. First, we need to know if moving objects are approaching us or heading away from us. In many cases, such as a fast moving train, we need to know if an object is heading toward us so that we can get out of its way. In other cases, we need to know if an object is moving away from us, so that we can slow it down, as in the case of a child trying to catch an ice cream truck. Thus, the direction of motion, toward us or away from us, is critical. But we must be able to perceive this motion across three dimensions—directly ahead of us, to our sides, and above (or below) us. An object going straight up may not represent a danger, but an object coming down, and being accelerated by gravity as it does so, may represent a danger. Finally, we must also be able to estimate the speed of moving objects. A woman and child walking may not constitute a danger, but speeding race cars may very well be a danger (see Figure 8.1). You can work with an interactive illustration of relative motion and frame of reference on ISLE 8.1a.

HOW DO WE PERCEIVE MOTION?

 8.1   Explain the concept of a motion threshold and what variables influence that threshold.

Perceiving Motion: Motion Thresholds— How Slow and How Fast?

Think about watching a spinning bicycle wheel. When the rider first starts peddling, we see the motion of the spokes of the wheel. As the bicyclist pedals faster, the spokes start spinning faster and faster. We can see this motion, but eventually, the wheel is moving so fast that we can no longer track the individual spokes. Instead, we see a blur of motion. There are two points to be made here. First, some motion is so slow that we cannot perceive it, and other motion is so fast that we cannot perceive it. Think of a plant bending its leaves toward the direction of sunlight. Most plants move their leaves extremely slowly, so slowly in fact that human eyes do not perceive the motion. Only when we view a plant through time-lapse photography do we know that it is actually moving. Similarly, movements that are extremely fast, such as the spinning of an automobile's wheel, may simply be too fast for us to perceive. Similarly, many sources of light flicker, such as our computer screens, but they do so at so rapid a rate that we do not perceive the change.

Motion thresholds are a function of what parts of the retinae are seeing the motion. Interestingly, we have rather poor motion thresholds in the foveal regions of our retinae. But our motion thresholds are much lower (i.e., better) at the periphery of our retinae. You may occasionally become aware of this, when you detect motion to your side and move your eyes and head to engage with the oncoming motion. Motion thresholds also nicely illustrate the importance of peripheral vision. Most of the functions of the visual system discussed have involved the region of the visual field near and around the fovea. Color and much of the discussion of form relate to the fovea and near it. Yet motion is a function that does very well at the periphery. It is tempting to think of our peripheral vision as merely poor vision, or a poor version of how vision operates in the fovea. However, that would be a mistake. Vision at the periphery is not so much poorer as different. The relative importance of acuity and motion in the fovea and at the periphery gives some insight into this difference. A moving stimulus at the periphery seems to grab the attention, and may even direct the fovea over to this stimulus.

As with any other perceptual feature of vision, we can ask a few basic psychophysical questions about motion thresholds. For example, how slow can motion be if we are to still perceive it as motion? Do we see snails moving or plants shifting their leaves toward the sunlight? The answer may be yes for the snails, but no for the plants. Because snails are small objects that move slowly, their motion has few consequences for us, so we may not ordinarily attend to snails in motion. But if we do, we can probably detect their motion as they slime their way up the sides of our houses. We know that to detect movement, an object must move at least 1 minute of 1° across the retina to be detected (that's 1/60 of 1° of visual angle). Thus, our absolute threshold for motion detection will be a function of the speed of the moving object and its distance from us.

At the other end of the spectrum, we can ask, At what high speed do we lose the ability to track motion? Can we follow the motion of a supersonic jet? Can we follow the individual rotations of a car's wheels spinning when the car is moving at 70 mph? Of course, we know that such thresholds will be context dependent, so specific answers cannot be given. The brightness of an object, the size of the object, and the amount of time the object is visible all will influence motion thresholds. In general, we can usually perceive fast motion, even if we cannot track it. Nonetheless, some objects move at such high speeds that we just cannot see them (a bullet shot at 1,000 feet per second, for example). You can examine your own motion thresholds on ISLE 8.2.

ISLE 8.2 Motion Thresholds

Real and Apparent Motion

Motion in the world is created by the continual change in position of an object relative to some frame of reference. That is, we watch the cat run across the kitchen tiles. We watch the leaves of the trees bend back and forth in the wind. We watch the ducks swim across the pond. This is **real motion**. However, human beings also perceive a number of forms of illusory motion, that is, situations in which we perceive motion when none actually occurs. One form of this illusory motion is apparent motion. **Apparent motion** is the appearance of real motion from a sequence of still images (see Figure 8.2; also see ISLE 8.3 to see these in motion). Apparent motion occurs whenever stimuli separated by time and location are actually perceived as a single stimulus moving from one location to another. Apparent motion is the basis of our sense of motion in watching videography and animation, and forms the basis for much of our entertainment in the form of television, movies, and computer games. When we watch Iron Man flying across the sky in the movies, what we are seeing is apparent motion. The pattern of lights on your screen creates an illusion that an object is moving.

ISLE 8.3 Apparent Motion

Real motion: motion in the world created by continual change in the position of an object relative to some frame of reference

Apparent motion: the appearance of real motion from a sequence of still images

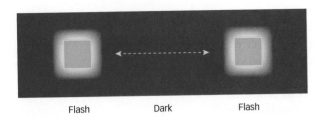

Flash   Dark   Flash

■ **FIGURE 8.2   Apparent motion illustrated (beta motion).**

When Light 1 and Light 2 are flickered on and off at just the right rate, it will look like a single light is jumping from one location to the other.

Apparent motion includes beta motion (optimal motion), in which an object is perceived as moving on the basis of what is actually a series of stationary images being presented sequentially. Beta motion is the basis of motion seen in movies. It is similar to but different from phi motion, the basis of motion in the displays in Las Vegas. In beta motion, the perceived motion is indistinguishable from real motion, while in phi motion, you perceive motion but can see that the elements, like the individual bulbs in the Las Vegas displays, do not move. In both beta motion and phi motion, the images are turned on and off quickly to induce the perception of motion, and you can see both in ISLE 8.3 by changing how fast the dots go on and off.

Phi motion forms the basis of billboard displays, such as the famous Times Square signs that depict stock market information. You can work with an interactive illustration of apparent motion, both beta and phi, on ISLE 8.3. Indeed, all the motion illustrations on ISLE make use of apparent motion. This is true for any movement one perceives on a television or computer screen.

If you recall from the last chapter, we discussed the correspondence problem with respect to depth perception. In that case, the correspondence problem pertains to how the visual system knows how to match objects perceived in the left eye with objects perceived in the right eye. We discussed how the visual system matches objects in the left and right eyes before object recognition, as indicated by successful depth perception in random-dot stereograms. In this chapter, we briefly describe the correspondence problem as it applies to motion perception.

In motion perception, the **correspondence problem** refers to how the visual system knows if an object seen at Time 1 is the same object at Time 2. In most normal vision settings, we know that an object is the same because most objects do not go through rapid changes across time when they are in motion. Moreover, we may use eye movements to track that motion across time. But consider watching a flock of birds move across the sky. In this case, it may be difficult to track a particular bird, but we do not see some birds flying out of existence and others coming into existence. We see a pattern of birds flying. This means that there must be a way in which we keep coherence in motion perception. The correspondence problem is illustrated in Figure 8.3. You can see an illustration of the issues involved in the correspondence problem on ISLE 8.4, which shows the wagon-wheel effect. In the wagon-wheel effect, we perceive the direction of motion in the opposite direction of the actual motion.

Another motion-based illusion is induced motion. **Induced motion** means that one moving object may cause another object to look like it is moving. The classic

ISLE 8.4 Correspondence Problem in Motion

Correspondence problem (motion perception): how the visual system knows if an object seen at Time 1 is the same object at Time 2

Induced motion: an illusion whereby one moving object may cause another object to look like it is moving

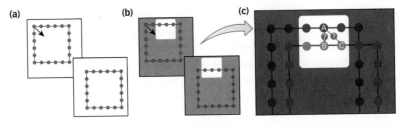

■ **FIGURE 8.3   The correspondence problem.**

How do we know that what we see at Time 1 corresponds to what we see at Time 2? The pictured square moves up and to the left. To detect the motion, the visual system must match points along the square at Time 1 with points along the square at Time 2.

example of induced motion is the movement of clouds at night, which may make it seem as if the moon is moving. The clouds moving in one direction induce a perception that the moon is moving in the opposite direction. Similarly, the movement of your car makes it look as if the world is rushing by you, when in fact it is you in the car who is rushing by the world, and the surroundings are relatively motionless. Induced motion is illusory because we misperceive what is moving relative to the other object. Your car is really moving relative to the surface of the road, but you perceive the road as moving relative to your stable position in the car (see ISLE 8.5).

ISLE 8.5 Induced Motion

How different is apparent motion from real motion? When we watch a movie, we suspend our knowledge that we are just looking at a screen. But it sure looks like we are watching speeding planes and talking people. How close is it to real motion?

One question we can ask is whether there are different neurocognitive systems involved in the perception of real and apparent motion. That is, does apparent motion look like motion because it activates the same neural networks as real motion does? This question was put to the test by Larsen and his colleagues (Larsen, Madsen, Lund, & Bundesen, 2006). Larsen et al. (2006) compared the neural responses to real and apparent motion by recording brain activity with functional magnetic resonance imaging (fMRI) technology. In the apparent motion condition, participants watched a standard apparent motion display of lights flashing back and forth such that it looked like one light was moving from one location to the other. In the real motion condition, participants watched an actual light move from one location to the other. And in a control condition, participants also saw two lights flashing, but the lights did not appear to be moving. Larsen et al. then compared the areas of the brain that were active during each stimulus. The fMRI brain scans found that the areas of the primary visual cortex that were responsive to apparent motion were the same as those responsive to real motion. These areas within the visual cortex were active during both forms of motion, but not during the control condition. So the region in the cortex was responding to movement, not to flashing lights. For this reason, we can be reasonably certain that the apparent motion participants view in experiments generalizes to motion perception of actual moving objects.

TEST YOUR KNOWLEDGE

What is the correspondence problem as it applies to motion? How is it best solved?

THE NEUROSCIENCE OF VISION AND MOTION

8.2 Describe the anatomy of the visual system dedicated to motion perception.

Motion Detection in the Retina

The retinae play an important role in early motion detection. We know that some types of amacrine cells in the retina are sensitive to motion (Masland, 2012). Thus, the beginnings of analyzing motion occur quite early in the human retinae. We also see, in the optic nerve that leaves the retina, the beginning of the M pathway, which codes for motion in V1 and along the dorsal stream of vision (Tapia

& Breitmeyer, 2011). The P pathway also contributes to motion perception, as we see moving objects in color. So both pathways at the level of the retina contribute to motion perception.

Some studies have looked at motion perception in other animals. In a series of classic papers, Barlow and his colleagues investigated motion perception in the retinae of frogs. Barlow (1953), for example, found cells in the retina of frogs that responded to the transition from light to dark and then to the opposite transition. Later, Lettvin, Maturana, McCulloch, and Pitts (1968) called these cells bug detectors because they were particularly good at identifying the movements of flies, a primary food of frogs.

The Complexity of Motion

As we often repeat in this book, perceptual processes are complex, even if we do them effortlessly. The neuroscience of the perception of motion is no exception. First of all, our bodies are constantly in motion—we must be able to discriminate our own motion, both intended and unintended, from the motion of other people, animals, and objects. Consider an eye blink—every so often we mistake our own eye blinks for moving objects, but not very often. Usually, our visual systems take into account our own motions and do not project them onto the perception of other objects. Even when we are perfectly still and watching a moving object, such as a bird flying across the sky, our visual system has a complex task. Think of a simple case of motion—a single object moving in a straight line across the visual field. This might be a bird flying across the sky or a person walking down the street. As we mentioned earlier, we must be able to judge the direction, in each of the three dimensions, and the speed of this object. As we discussed in the opening chapter, we must also be able to judge the time to impact, that is, how long it will take before the moving object smashes into us. A bird flying fast directly at you is not usually a desirable state of affairs, whereas a bird flying past you is harmless. So the two elements of motion detection, direction and speed, must be coded at the neural level.

Now consider how this might be done in the visual system. We start off with the simplest case—your eyes are not moving. They are looking straight ahead and not tracking a moving object. The object is passing in front of you, moving from left to right in a straight line, without dipping or wobbling (see Figure 8.4). The visual system must be able to correlate an object at one time (T1) in one position (P1) with the same object at another time (T2) in another position (P2). It must also be able to distinguish this motion from motion going in the opposite direction, that is, starting at P2 at T1 and reaching P1 at T2. And to reiterate, we also want to know the approximate speed of the moving object.

Now think about this in terms of a neural circuit. We need to have neurons that have receptive fields that include the points P1 and P2 in the visual world. But we need these neurons to respond temporally as well. That is, we want neurons that are sensitive to an object at P1 at T1 and then at P2 at T2, some specific later time point. We need other neurons that fire when objects are at P1 at T1 and at P2 at T2 at a range of differences in (T2 − T1), that is, different speeds. We also need neurons sensitive to movement in the other direction, that is, if an object moves from P2 to P1 at a particular speed. This allows us to track motion in the other direction. One possible model for motion detection in neurons is shown in Figure 8.5. The neurons in this model have been called **Reichardt detectors** after the German psychophysicist who first hypothesized them (Reichardt, 1969).

If you inspect Figure 8.5 carefully, you will notice a few important features of Reichardt detectors. In the model, you can see motion-sensitive neurons (labeled *M* for *motion*). These M neurons are tuned to activity first in Receptive

Moving spot of light

Motion in retinal image

■ **FIGURE 8.4**   **Motion on the retina.**

A moving object (here moving from left to right) moves a certain distance across the visual field. The distance correlates with a distance across the retina.

....

Reichardt detectors: neural circuits that enable the determination of direction and speed of motion by delaying input from one receptive field, to determine speed, to match the input of another receptive field, to determine direction

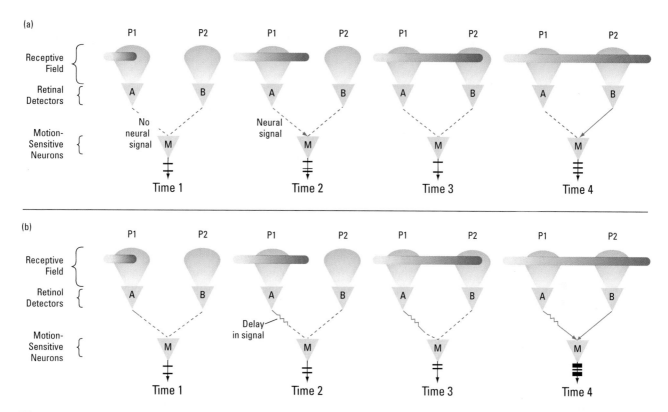

FIGURE 8.5   Reichardt detectors.

A simple neural network for detecting motion. The signals arrive at Neuron M (lower line) at the same time, from a neuron with a receptive field at P1 and then from a neuron with a receptive field at P2. Depending on the time course of arrival, Neuron M will determine motion and speed.

Field P1 and then in Receptive Field P2, if there is a specific delay between the activity in the two receptive fields. The delay specifies the speed to which this neuron is sensitive. If the delay is too short or too long, the M neuron will not make as large a response. Similarly, if the moving object is going the other way, this neuron will not respond. Thus, this simple model can account for both speed (as measured by delay) and direction (as measured by which receptive field is activated first). Of course, there will be other motion-sensitive neurons that will respond to different delays and different directions of motion. Motion-sensitive neurons with longer delay times are sensitive to slower motion, whereas motion-sensitive neurons with shorter delay times are sensitive to faster motion. We find these cells in the magnocellular tract. You can work with an interactive illustration of Reichardt detectors on ISLE 8.6.

ISLE 8.6 Reichardt Detectors

Are there neurons like this in the human visual system? It turns out that there are many neurons in V1 that show these characteristics. V1 neurons, in addition to the features already discussed, seem to be tuned to specific directions and speeds of motion (Orban, Kennedy, & Butler, 1986; Wang & Yao, 2011). In nonprimate species, such as cats, there are also motion-sensitive neurons in the lateral geniculate nucleus (Wang & Yao, 2011).

Corollary Discharge Theory

Reichardt detectors work well when the eyes are stationary, but consider a situation in which the viewer is tracking motion across a scene. What happens when our eyes are moving? Think about watching that bird fly across the sky. Perhaps it is

■ FIGURE 8.6 Smooth pursuit eye movements.

As the bird soars across the sky, smooth-pursuit eye movements allow you to track the motion of the bird. Smooth-pursuit movements are possible only in the presence of movement.

■ FIGURE 8.7 Using smooth-pursuit eye movements.

While playing a sport such a tennis, our eyes and head move to track the movement of the ball using smooth-pursuit eye movements.

ISLE 8.7 Corrollary Discharge

....

Corollary discharge theory: the theory that the feedback we get from our eye muscles as our eyes track an object is important to the perception of motion

an eagle, and you want to watch it soar on the wind. As you follow its motion, your eyes and head move as the eagle flies. Indeed, while tracking motion, your eyes make small movements (called smooth-pursuit movements) to keep the image of the eagle on the foveae of your retinae (see Figure 8.6). In another setting, consider a tennis player tracking a tennis ball as it approaches her racket. Her eyes track the movement of the ball from the moment her opponent hits the ball as it approaches her side of the court. Her eyes, head, and body must be in continual movement to maintain alignment with the speeding tennis ball (see Figure 8.7). This continual tracking of movement allows another method of detecting direction and speed of motion.

This brings us to the corollary discharge theory, an important concept in understanding how our visual system detects and tracks motion. The **corollary discharge theory** states that the feedback we get from our eye muscles as our eyes track an object is important to the perception of motion. Corollary discharge theory starts off quite similar to the Reichardt detector model, with neurons that are sensitive to movement across the retina. However, when we wish to track an object such as a tennis ball, a command signal must be sent from the brain to the muscles that control eye movements. Corollary discharge theory states that, in addition to the muscles of the eye, this signal will be sent to areas of the brain responsible for motion detection. This signal, or corollary discharge, provides the brain with updated information about the locations and speeds of moving objects (Sommer & Wurtz, 2008). In other words, we use the fact that we are moving our eyes and heads as a means to detect motion in the world. It is as if our visual systems were interpreting the situation as follows: We are making smooth-pursuit movements with our eyes, and therefore, we must be tracking motion. This logic then allows the feedback from the eye movements to assist our visual system in seeing and timing the motion.

Evidence for the corollary discharge theory comes from the movement of afterimages. If you look directly at a bright light and then close your eyes, you will see an afterimage of that light. When you move your eyes, the afterimage stays on the exact same part of the retina. However, you sense motion. Why is this the case, if the afterimage has not moved across your visual field? It must be because of feedback from a corollary discharge loop. Similarly, experiments have shown that people can keep their eyes fixated on a central point even when their eyes are being physically pushed. Here too, even though there is no movement of objects across the visual field, we sense motion, stemming from a corollary discharge feedback system (Bridgeman & Stark, 1991). For a demonstration of corollary discharge, see ISLE 8.7.

Physiological evidence for this theory comes from the discovery of real motion neurons, which respond only to movements of objects but not movements of eyes. To determine the difference, these neurons must first get feedback from eye movement signals so that they can "know" the difference. Experiments with monkeys show that these real motion neurons in the extrastriate cortex respond when an object is moving across the monkeys' visual field but not when their eyes are moving and the object is stationary (Galletti & Fattori, 2003). Corollary discharge, therefore, allows our visual system to integrate the movements of objects with our own basic motility.

The corollary discharge theory means that one of the cues to detecting motion is the movement of our own eyes. Thus, it is important to understand how and why our eyes move in order to understand the nature of motion perception. We turn our attention next to eye movements.

Eye Movements

Our visual system can perceive objects in the world that move, but, of course, we move as well. We can move our eyes, our heads, and our bodies. We can track motion just by moving our eyes, or we can follow the direction of a moving object by walking or running. In this section, we are concerned with eye movements that direct our eyes from one location to another in the visual world. This contrasts this discussion of eye movements with vergence, which we discussed in the last chapter. *Vergence* refers to the eye movements that cause our eyes to resolve a particular object or bring it into focus. Here we are concerned with changing our gaze from one object to another or tracking a moving object. We have already discussed how feedback from eye movements helps our visual system sort out different forms of motion. Eye movements serve a great many other functions as well, the most significant being the ability to direct the gaze of our foveae on whatever stimulus in the world attracts our attention. Eye movements allow us, for example, to read. We make small discrete movements along the page to ensure that our foveae are directed at whatever it is we want to read right now. When we watch moving print, such as the credits at the end of a movie, we make small eye movements from left to right and up and down. There is a simulation of eye movements on ISLE 8.8.

ISLE 8.8 Eye Movements

Saccades

Saccades are the most common and rapid of eye movements. They are used to look from one object to another. Saccades are very rapid—we make them in less than 50 ms, and we can make approximately three saccades each second. In other circumstances, we may need up to 1 second to plan a saccade, but once initiated, the movement is very rapid. What characterizes saccades is the quick jump from the focus on one object to another. When you read, you make a series of saccades along the page. When you look up from what you are reading to see who is looking in the window, you make a saccade from your book to the window. Then, when you change your gaze from looking at a stationary tree to your car parked outside your house, you are also making a saccade. Interestingly, vision is suppressed during the actual movement. That is, during the 50 ms it takes to make the eye movement, we essentially cannot see anything new. Only when our saccade lands at the new location do we again see.

Smooth-Pursuit Eye Movements

Smooth-pursuit eye movements are the voluntary movements we use to track moving objects. We can make smooth-pursuit eye movements only when there is an actual moving object in the environment. In an environment without movement, we can make only saccades. Feedback from our visual system, however, allows our eyes to continuously follow motion. Thus, our eyes move gradually as we follow an airplane across the sky or a tennis ball back and forth across a tennis court.

Saccades: the most common and rapid of eye movements; they are sudden eye movements and are used to look from one object to another

Smooth-pursuit eye movements: voluntary tracking eye movements

MT: The Movement Area of the Brain

MT, also known as **V5**, is an area in the occipital cortex critical to motion perception. *MT* stands for "medial temporal," because MT is adjacent to the medial temporal lobe, although it is itself within the extrastriatal areas of the occipital lobe. Recall that *extrastriate* refers to an area in the occipital lobe, but not in V1. MT receives input from both V1 and V2, as well as from the superior colliculus, an important area in controlling eye movements. From the research we review shortly, we know that MT is sensitive to both direction of motion and speed of motion. In contrast, MT neurons are not tuned to other perceptual characteristics, such as color or orientation. We also know that it integrates motion-sensitive cells from across V1 to detect large-scale motion (such as a walking person). In Figure 8.8, you can see where MT and other important motion perception areas are located in the brain. Thus, we can consider MT a region of the brain critical to the visual perception of motion.

Some of the most important work on the function of MT was done by the neurophysiologist William Newsome and his colleagues (Hedges et al., 2011; Newsome, Shadlen, Zohary, Britten, & Movshon, 1995). They were interested in how and why neurons in MT respond to motion, particularly larger scale motion, such as a dog running in a park. So they set out to understand motion perception in rhesus monkeys, which have visual brains very similar to our own. We now describe some of their experimental work linking MT to motion perception in rhesus monkeys. The logic of the experiment is as follows. Newsome and his team trained rhesus monkeys to respond to particular forms of motion with specific behaviors. That is, if a visual pattern was moving in one direction, the monkeys made one response, but if the visual pattern was moving in the opposite direction, the monkeys made another response. Once the monkeys were trained, Newsome could lesion MT in the monkeys' brains and see what behavioral deficits the monkeys developed or, somewhat more humanely, conduct single-cell recordings of individual cells within MT while the monkeys were watching movement.

In an important first experiment, Newsome and Paré (1988) trained monkeys to respond to a pattern of dots all moving in the same direction (see Figure 8.9). However, they added an interesting manipulation. In some trials, all of the dots were moving in the same direction (100%), but in other conditions, only 50% or 20% of the dots were moving in sync, whereas the rest of the dots were moving randomly. As such, in these conditions, no dot, in and of itself, could determine the large-scale motion seen in the pattern, as any particular dot might just be going in the opposite direction. However, clearly our visual systems must be tuned to this kind of motion (fish swimming in a school or cattle in a herd provide real-world examples of this situation). In essence, this experiment was looking at the physiological basis of the gestalt principle of common fate—do we see motion

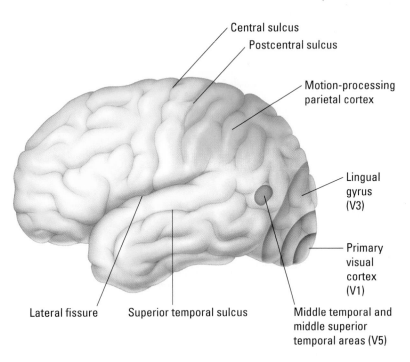

Central sulcus
Postcentral sulcus
Motion-processing parietal cortex
Lingual gyrus (V3)
Primary visual cortex (V1)
Lateral fissure   Superior temporal sulcus   Middle temporal and middle superior temporal areas (V5)

■ **FIGURE 8.8   Motion areas in the brain.**

In this map of the brain, you can see V1 at the back of the occipital lobe. MT (also known as V5) is anterior in the occipital lobe, located just above the temporal lobe. This map also shows motion-sensitive areas in the parietal lobe.

MT (V5): an area of the occipital lobe in the dorsal pathway, specific to motion detection and perception when a pattern of dots is moving in a particular direction, even if an individual dot is not? The visual system must pull information across many dots in order to determine the pattern of motion in the 50% and 20% conditions (see Figure 8.9). By the time the monkeys were fully trained, they could detect the general pattern of motion even when only 3% of the dots were moving in the same direction (and the rest were moving randomly). That is, MT neurons integrate across any number of local detectors to infer the general pattern of motion in the display. You can see these patterns in motion on ISLE 8.9.

Newsome and Paré (1988) then surgically lesioned MT in these monkeys. Following recovery from surgery, the monkeys' performance on the direction-of-motion task was severely impaired. However, the monkeys were not impaired at visual tasks that involved stationary objects—only motion tasks were affected. Thus, for example, color identification was fine, but the direction-of-motion task showed strong decrements in performance. Thus, because these monkeys had been able to do motion tasks prior to the lesioning, but were impaired afterward, Newsome and Paré concluded that MT is involved in this kind of motion discrimination.

In another experiment (Newsome, Britten, & Movshon, 1989), Newsome and his colleagues found through single-cell recording that MT neurons fired more strongly the more coherent or correlated the motion was. That is, there was more activity in MT when all the dots were moving in the same direction than when only 20% of the dots were moving in the same direction. This was the case even though the 20% motion is very salient when humans view it and presumably similarly salient to the monkeys. Thus, these studies provided strong evidence that MT is not just a motion area but one that is sensitive to larger scale motion.

There have also been studies using neuroimaging that confirmed the role of MT in humans. For example, fMRI studies with human participants have confirmed the role of MT in such large-scale movement, similar to Newsome's studies. In humans, as with monkeys, MT responds more to moving stimuli than to stationary stimuli, and more to complex movement than simple movement. For example, Weigelt, Singer, and Kohler (2013) looked at the human MT by recording activity with fMRI technology. Weigelt et al. showed participants moving stimuli. In some trials, participants attended to the locations of certain objects, whereas in other trials, participants attended to the direction of motion of certain objects. In this case, the stimuli were identical—the difference was what the person was attending to, either the locations of objects or the direction of motion. Weigelt et al. found that attention to motion resulted in a bigger response in MT than did attention to location. In contrast, they found no difference in the neural responses in V1 between the two attention conditions. Thus, as in monkeys, the human MT is responsive to large-scale motion. Weigelt et al.'s results can be seen in Figure 8.10.

Weigelt and her group have also found evidence that MT is active during visual imagery that involves motion (Kaas, Weigelt, Roebroeck, Kohler, & Muckli, 2010). That is, even when there is no actual movement present, but participants are imagining moving objects, MT may be active. In the study, participants were asked to imagine objects moving without actually seeing the motion of those objects. They compared this with a visual imagery condition that did not involve motion as well as an auditory imagery task. Relative

ISLE 8.9 Correlated Motion

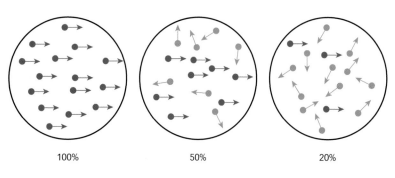

100%   50%   20%

■ FIGURE 8.9   Stimuli used in Newsome and Paré's (1988) experiment.

In the 100% condition, all the dots were moving in the same direction. In the 50% condition, half the dots were moving in a consistent direction. And in the 20% condition, only one fifth of the dots were moving in a consistent direction.

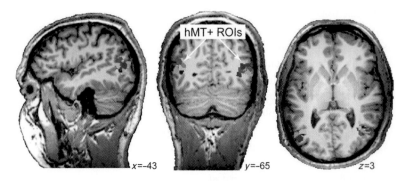

■ FIGURE 8.10   Weigelt et al.'s (2013) results.

In this fMRI study, Weigelt et al. found that activity in MT was associated with attention to movement. In these fMRI pictures, the activity in MT is highlighted in color. The results are averaged across 15 participants.

to the control conditions, when participants were engaged in motion visual imagery, larger responses were recorded from MT. These results can be seen in Figure 8.11. Here too, we can see how important MT is to higher order aspects of motion perception.

Last, we turn to neuropsychology and its role in understanding the function of Area MT. Neuropsychology provides us with some of the most convincing and, at the same time, bizarre evidence for the role of MT in motion perception. When MT is damaged, a condition can arise called **akinetopsia** or **motion blindness**. Akinetopsia is a rare condition in which a patient is unable to detect motion despite intact visual perception of stationary stimuli. Patients with this disorder no longer see objects in motion. Rather, their perception resembles a series of still photographs moving one to the next. It occurs without any loss of object recognition, color vision, or visual acuity, but nonetheless, it can have profound effects on a person's vision and ability to function in a visual world.

What would the world be like for someone with no perception of visual motion? A potential metaphor in normal experience is being in a dark room illuminated by a stroboscope, as might occur in some dance clubs. The room is dark except for brief flashes in which it is illuminated. Under these conditions, normal people may feel as if they have motion blindness.

Several patients have been tested and shown to have motion blindness. One of the most widely tested is a patient labeled L.M. (Zihl, von Cramon, & Mai, 1983). Patient L.M. described the difficulty of pouring water into a glass, because

a. Individual hMT/V5+ regions of interest

b. Regions influencing Left hMT/V5+ during motion imagery

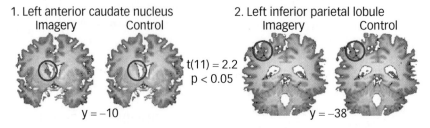

1. Left anterior caudate nucleus
   Imagery   Control

2. Left inferior parietal lobule
   Imagery   Control

$t(11) = 2.2$
$p < 0.05$

$y = -10$ $y = -38$

Akinetopsia (motion blindness): a rare condition in which a patient is unable to detect motion despite intact visual perception of stationary stimuli, caused by damage to Area MT

■ FIGURE 8.11   fMRI results from Kaas et al. (2010).

These diagrams illustrate how MT is activated when people imagine perceived motion, particularly, 8.11 (a).

she could not see the movement of the water from the pitcher into the glass and therefore could not tell exactly when the glass was full. Similarly, crossing a street is difficult for L.M., because she does not know if her current image of the world is recent and therefore how close the cars actually are to passing in front of her. From this testimony of L.M., we can see how important it is to be able to perceive motion as it is happening.

Schenk, Mai, Ditterich, and Zihl (2000) showed that a patient with akinetopsia had difficulties with simple action tasks as well. When instructed to grasp moving objects, the motion-blind patient took more time and was less accurate at grasping objects than age-matched controls. Thus, the deficit in motion blindness extends to control of the motor system as well as the profound perception deficits it causes. In another rare but documented case, epileptic seizures induced temporary akinetopsia in at least one patient (Sakurai, Kurita, Takeda, Shiraishi, & Kusumi, 2013). In summary, damage to MT in human patients can cause a terrible motion perception deficit.

Interestingly, akinetopsia can be simulated in normal human brains. A technique called TMS allows researchers to temporarily disable selective areas of the human brain. *TMS* stands for "transcranial magnetic stimulation." In some cases, it can increase activity in the area of the brain to which it is applied, but it also can decrease activity. It depends on the kind of stimulation that is applied and what behavior is being measured. Interestingly, when TMS is applied to area MT, temporary akinetopsia results (Beckers & Zeki, 1995). These participants will experience a temporary inability to perceive motion, which, fortunately, wears off shortly after the TMS is no longer being applied.

Motion Aftereffects

One of the illusions we see quite commonly in everyday life is the motion aftereffect. Motion aftereffects are also called the "waterfall illusion" because they occur when we stare at a waterfall (see Figure 8.12). After we have watched the falling of the water for about a minute, if we look at a blank surface, such as a white wall, we will get a sense of motion going upward, that is, in the opposite direction of the falling water. Perhaps today, the most common experience of motion aftereffects comes when we watch the credits at the end of a movie. If you want to know where the movie was filmed, for example, you may dutifully watch the names of the actors and actresses scroll up the screen (apparent motion, not real motion), the stunt staff, and the camera staff, until finally, the credits reach the spot where they tell what town and in what state or country the movie was filmed. At this point, you may pause your DVD player or your mobile device's video player to read the information about where the movie was filmed. When you pause the apparent motion, you may get a definite sense of the words on the screen moving downward after watching them scroll upward for a couple of minutes. This illusion a nonmoving surface moving opposite to the movement just watched is called the motion aftereffect or waterfall illusion. For a demonstration of motion aftereffects, go to ISLE 8.10.

We can define a **motion aftereffect** as a motion-based visual illusion in which a stationary object is seen as moving in the opposite direction of real or apparent motion just observed. Aristotle wrote about the waterfall illusion around 350 BCE. He described watching the water tumbling down the falls for several

© iStockphoto.com/BambiG

■ **FIGURE 8.12**   **The waterfall illusion: motion aftereffects.**

A beautiful waterfall in Tennessee. If we stare at the downward motion of a real waterfall, we can see the aftereffect when we look at another surface afterward.

ISLE 8.10 Motion Aftereffect

Motion aftereffect: a motion-based visual illusion in which a stationary object is seen as moving in the opposite direction of real or apparent motion just observed

entranced minutes. He then fixed his gaze on a stationary object and experienced the illusion of that object's moving upward, opposite the direction of the waterfall (see Figure 8.12).

The motion aftereffect suggests that motion neurons in the occipital cortex may have an opponent system, similar to that for color vision. Because we see movement opposite the direction of the motion we were just watching, the motion aftereffect suggests that movement in one direction is linked to movement in the opposite direction. Thus, upward and downward motion is an example of motion contrast, just as red and green are color contrasts. Consider two motion-sensitive neurons in Area MT of the occipital cortex. One neuron, N-l, is sensitive to motion in the upward direction, whereas N-r is sensitive to downward motion. Activity in N-l may prompt inhibition in N-r, but when N-l is no longer activated and the inhibition is turned off, we will sense the downward motion that has been inhibited. Of course, neurons are sensitive to many features in addition to the one under discussion. Thus, N-l might also have particular brightness, orientation, and speed preferences. For example, N-l might be stimulated by a dim object moving in the neuron's preferred direction or by a very bright object moving in a less than optimal direction for that neuron. On the basis of this cell's response alone, we cannot tell the difference between these two possibilities. However, if N-r is tuned to the opposite direction of motion, but perhaps other features, the inhibition it gets as a function of movement in the opposite direction is enough to disambiguate the N-l stimulation. Thus, motion aftereffects are an illusory consequence of a system that allows neurons to pick out specific directions of motion.

TEST YOUR KNOWLEDGE

What are Reichardt detectors? How have researchers looked for them in the brain?

© iStockphoto.com/photos_martYmage

■ FIGURE 8.13   A well-camouflaged arctic hare.

As long as it stays still, it is hard to detect.

ISLE 8.11 Structure From Motion

FORM PERCEPTION AND BIOLOGICAL MOTION

8.3   Discuss how we infer form from the perception of biological motion.

Scared animals instinctively know to stay perfectly still, especially those species that wear camouflage on their skin or fur. Think of an arctic hare hiding in the snow from wolves or polar bears (see Figure 8.13). Its white fur allows it to blend in perfectly with the winter snow. However, keeping still is also critical to an animal or a person attempting to hide via camouflage. Once prey is in motion, predators can detect the motion, despite the camouflage. Indeed, we demonstrate in this section that we are often able to detect form directly from the perception of motion when motion cues are the only cues to what an object is. See ISLE 8.11.

Motion perception provides us with information about what object we are observing. Think about someone you know with a distinctive style of walking. You may know someone who always appears to have a hop in his or her step, and you may know someone else who seems to be trudging around all the time. These motion cues may help you recognize that person. Consider running into one of these people at night, when you cannot get a good view of the person's face. Detecting the style of walking may allow you to recognize the person. An ingenious technique allows researchers to assess whether these assertions are true.

Johansson (1973) developed an ingenious method to examine this phenomenon. This method is called the point-light walker display. A **point-light walker display** is one in which small lights are attached to the body of a person or other animal, which is then filmed moving in an otherwise completely dark environment. In Johansson's experiment, small lights were placed on a person's body, including the wrists, elbows, shoulders, ankles, knees, and hips. He then video recorded the person walking, running, and dancing in total darkness. Thus, the only thing visible to viewers were the lights, and not the person's body (see Figure 8.14). It is absolutely necessary to view the demonstration and experiment on this topic on ISLE 8.12a. You can also go to http://www.biomotionlab.ca/Demos/BMLwalker.html to view a demonstration.

When Johansson (1973) showed participants still photographs of the light patterns, the participants were unable to extract any form information from the photographs. However, when participants viewed videos of the light patterns, they were able to detect the human form when it was walking or running. Moreover, the participants were able to distinguish between forms of motion, including walking and running. Other studies using similar methods have shown that human observers can distinguish between different animals on the basis of the patterns of their movements in point-light displays (Blake & Shiffrar, 2007). In addition, human participants can judge age, gender, and a person's emotional state solely on the basis of point-light displays (Blake & Shiffrar, 2007). Finally, human observers can learn distinctive walking patterns of individuals in point-light displays and later recognize those individuals when they see them moving in a normal video (Westhoff & Troje, 2007). Thus, these studies support the notion that patterns of motion can allow us to see or infer the presence of form.

It is also possible to disrupt our usual good perception in point-light displays. Troje and Westhoff (2006), for example, showed videos of biological motion through point-light displays of people walking, but the videos were inverted. Under these circumstances, it was very difficult for participants to detect the biological motion. Breaking down the coordination between the lights on various parts of the body can also interfere with perception under these circumstances (Troje, 2013). Interestingly, children with autism are impaired at inferring form in point-light displays relative to matched normal controls (Swettenham et al., 2013). Thus, variables or situations that affect our perception of patterns can render form-from-motion extraction more difficult. To see some of these exceptions, go to ISLE 8.12b.

As with most successful experimental paradigms in sensation and perception (and all of psychology), the point-light display procedure has now been used while participants are monitored by fMRI technology. The perception of biological motion in these point-light displays is associated with activity in the posterior superior temporal sulcus in the temporal lobe (Troje, 2013). In studies using point-light displays in which neural activities have been monitored by fMRI, there is more activity in the posterior superior temporal sulcus for biological motion than nonbiological motion. Thus, this region

ISLE 8.12 Biological Motion

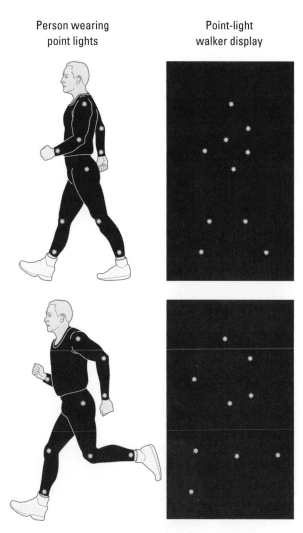

Person wearing point lights   Point-light walker display

■ FIGURE 8.14   **Point-light walker display.**

Lights are attached to a person's joints while walking or running in one direction or another. The person is filmed walking or running in a completely dark room except for the lights on his or her joints. Then the point-light displays are shown to participants. In general, most participants can determine the type of and direction of motion from these point-light displays alone. We can even determine the gender of the walker from the lights alone.

Point-light walker display: an experiment in which small lights are attached to the body of a person or an animal, which is then filmed moving in an otherwise completely dark environment is not motion specific—it does not rise above baseline activity for nonbiological motion. Rather, it seems to be involved in the recognition of particular forms of motion, consistent with the idea that we can use motion perception to infer forms. In another study, Grossman, Battelli, and Pascual-Leone (2005) interfered with the posterior superior temporal sulcus with a pulse from a TMS device. While under the influence of TMS, normal individuals showed a severe deficit in the perception of biological motion. As you can see, this methodology has been enormously successful in examining higher order levels of movement.

TEST YOUR KNOWLEDGE

What is a point-light walker display? What does it tell us about how motion contributes to form perception?

ACTION

8.4 Summarize the concept of an affordance.

Young cats existed for millions of years before the invention of the laser pointer. In those bygone days, kittens found lots of things to play with. But with the laser pointer, the young cat has found the ultimate human-cat interface. Even though laser pointers were invented for less exciting reasons, including allowing professors to point to overhead screens, laser pointers afford playing in young cats. And for lazy cat owners, laser pointers afford play sessions with their cats without their having to get off the couch (see Figure 8.15). We will see that the concept of an affordance is critical in understanding the theory of the interplay between perception and action that we are about to develop. If you are a bit tired of studying and need a laugh, you can watch Dr. Krantz playing the laser game with his cat on ISLE 8.13.

ISLE 8.13 Cat and Laser Pointer

© iStockphoto.com/borzywoj

■ **FIGURE 8.15** For a young cat, a laser pointer affords hours of fun.

Affordance: information in the visual world that specifies how that information can be used

An **affordance** is the information in the visual world that specifies how that information can be used. For example, seeing a piano affords playing music. Seeing an elevator affords being able to go up or down in a tall building. For a track athlete, seeing a hurdle affords jumping over it. And for a kitten, seeing the laser light of a laser pointer affords high-speed chases across the floor. According to the prominent vision theorist J. J. Gibson (1979), perception is about finding these affordances in the world. Perception, according to Gibson, is not about whether a person can detect a very dim spot in an otherwise completely dark room, but rather about perception in everyday life, and how we use perception to guide action. Animals, including people, see in an ever changing world, while constantly moving themselves. As such, Gibson argued, we should pay more attention to the complexity of stimuli in vision. Moreover, he argued, the goal of perception itself is to afford action, that is, movement of the organism.

Affordances mean that perception is determined partially by meaning or function. We see objects as stimuli with particular characteristics not just of color, depth, width, size, and shape, but also of function. An object that has no function may also not draw our attention, whereas we seek out objects we need at the moment. Not seeing where your eyeglasses are, for example, may elicit some search behavior, but you are not likely to search for an object with no apparent use. Similarly, we may judge beanbags to be more similar to regular chairs than we might expect on the basis of their similarity in shape. This is because beanbags and chairs share a common function—they afford sitting in comfort. Gibson (1979) emphasized that function drives perception.

One of Gibson's chief contributions was to the understanding of optic flow. We discussed optic flow in the last chapter as one of the motion cues to depth. We defined **optic flow** as a motion depth cue that refers to the relative motions of objects as the observer moves forward or backward in a scene. In this chapter, we focus our attention on how we perceive motion in optic flow patterns and how they influence our action in motion. To see an optic flow pattern of driving along a road or landing a plane, go to ISLE 8.14 (and see Figure 8.16).

ISLE 8.14 Optic Flow

Optic flow provides information about distance and consequently can be used to aid in our own movement. As we discussed in the previous chapter, objects closer to us seem to move faster past us, whereas more distant objects appear to move slowly as we move toward them. This pattern is called the **gradient of flow**. In simulations, if we increase the speed at which the observer is moving, this gradient of flow accelerates. If the speed of the observer decreases, the gradient of flow lessens. The

© Can Stock Photo Inc. / nacroba

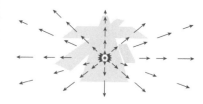

■ FIGURE 8.16   Optic flow

As we move in one direction, objects appear to get bigger as they approach us. In addition to this being a cue for depth, it also indicates motion. A driver can judge his or her speed by the rate at which objects are flowing toward him or her.

horizon or destination point is the distant point at which the gradient of flow comes to zero. This point is called the **focus of expansion**. As we voluntarily change directions in an optic flow pattern, this focus of expansion will shift.

In this section, we are interested in how action and perception interact. At a simple level, knowing where you are going means that you can assess if you are actually going in the intended direction. If your goal is to pilot your small Cessna plane from Fort Lauderdale, Florida, to Bimini, in the Bahamas, decisions about slight deviations in course will occur with respect to both the goal and your present position. A strong wind starts blowing out of the east, slowing your speed, and you may seek to fly at a different altitude. In a virtual reality experiment, Warren, Kay, Zosh, Duchon, and Sahuc (2001) controlled the optic flow pattern that participants were viewing while walking in a specially designed room. Participants were asked to walk toward a goal: a red line visible in the virtual reality setup. When Warren et al. slowed or sped up the optic flow pattern, participants adjusted their walking to be consistent with their goal of making it to the red line. Thus, optic flow patterns can change the actions we are engaged in. This result is consistent with many others demonstrating that optic flow plays an important role in adjusting our movements as well as allowing us to perceive depth (Chrastil, 2013).

In the modern world, driving a car is an important and frequent activity. Ensuring safe driving should be—even if it is not—a national concern. Thus, examining how drivers use optic flow is also relevant. Do drivers use optic flow patterns to ensure that they are driving safely and in the correct direction? Some research suggests that optic flow is one way in which drivers maintain their positions on the road. For example, Kandil, Rotter, and Lappe (2010) were interested in what information drivers use when driving on bends or turns. While rounding a turn, which is quite normal for drivers, the focus of expansion will not be obvious to

Optic flow: the relative motions of objects as an observer moves forward or backward in a scene

Gradient of flow: the difference in the perception of the speeds of objects moving past us in an optic flow display

Focus of expansion: the destination point in an optic flow display, from which point perceived motion derives

the driver's visual system. Thus, Kandil and his colleagues were interested in what other cues drivers use to keep their cars on the road and going in the correct direction while driving on curves. In their experiment, people drove real cars on real roads, while their eye movements were being recorded. The investigators recorded these eye movements as drivers drove through a series of bends. They found that drivers kept their eyes on the focus of expansion during straight-ahead driving. But as drivers approached bends, they took their eyes off the focus of expansion and instead directed their eyes to the straight road segments that were coming up. This focus on the goal of rounding the turn—the straight stretch of road ahead—allowed the drivers to direct their cars' movement in a smooth pattern around the bend. New drivers tend to focus on the curve itself rather than the straight stretch ahead, leading to more adjustments and less smooth driving. Thus, optic flow information is one source, but not the only source, of information drivers use to adjust their motion.

Visually Guided Eye Movements

The anatomical bases for the interaction between action and perception emerge from the parietal lobe. The parietal lobe appears to have critical networks for integrating muscle systems, somatosensory systems, and the visual system. This interaction allows the smooth transition from visual perception to guided action. The parietal lobe itself is divided by the postcentral sulcus, which divides the anterior parietal lobe from the posterior parietal lobe (see Figure 8.17). The anterior parietal lobe is concerned with the somatosensory system, a topic for a later chapter. However, the posterior parietal lobe contains regions that are specific to visually guided action (Snyder, Batista, & Anderson, 2000). Studies with monkeys reveal an area known as the **lateral intraparietal (LIP) area**, which is involved in the control of eye movements. There appears to be an equivalent area in human brains (you can see where this region is located in Figure 8.17).

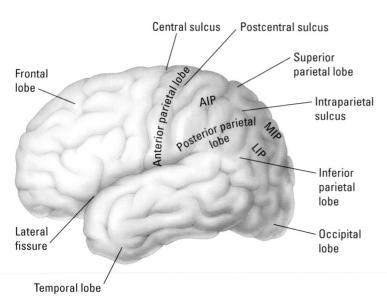

■ FIGURE 8.17　The parietal lobe serves important functions in the perception of action.

Studies with monkeys have revealed an area known as the lateral intraparietal (LIP) area, which is involved in the control of eye movements. This area is marked on the human brain shown here.

Colby, Duhamel, and Goldberg (1996) performed some interesting experiments on the role of the LIP area using single-cell recording with rhesus monkeys. In these experiments, a monkey is required to hold fixation on a central point (see Figure 8.18). Once the monkey has started to maintain fixation, the experimenters flash another point at the near periphery relative to the fixation point. The monkeys are trained to not move their eyes to this new point until after it disappears. When the point disappears, the monkeys make a saccade to this second point, even though the light is no longer present. The researchers were interested in what the LIP area was doing during the original appearance of the signal at the periphery and when the monkey actually made the eye movement. Colby et al. found that neurons within the LIP area, which had a receptive field corresponding to the area where the second spot appeared, became active as soon as the spot appeared on the screen. Activity in the LIP area

Lateral intraparietal (LIP) area: an area of the primate parietal cortex involved in the control of eye movements

then continued as the monkey made its saccade to this spot and then diminished afterward. Thus, the LIP area of the parietal lobe is involved with both the anticipation of the eye movement and the eye movement itself. Studies using fMRI with humans have found an equivalent area in the human brain that also shows activity that reflects intended eye movements (Quiroga, Snyder, Bastista, & Andersen, 2006).

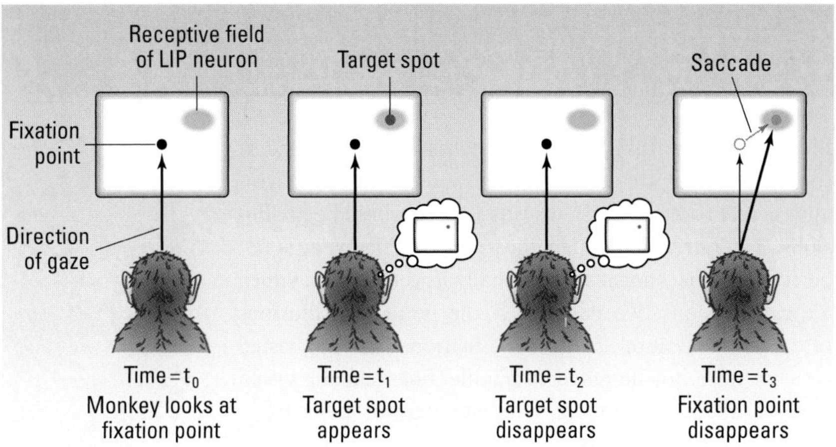

Visually Guided Grasping

As we have emphasized in this chapter, the visual system functions to provide us with information, which we can then use to guide our actions. Toward this end, our visual systems and our motor systems have coevolved to allow us precise control over movement on the basis of continual feedback from our visual system. This aspect of vision-action interaction can be seen in research on the control of grasping in humans and other primates. Primate hands, especially human primate hands, are instruments of fine motor control. Think of all the tasks you do that require fine motor control of your hands, from typing on your computer keyboard to knitting a sweater to changing the spark plugs on your car. Each of these tasks requires fine motor control of the hand combined with complex feedback from the visual system.

If you refer back to Figure 8.17, you will see an area of the posterior parietal lobe identified as the **medial intraparietal (MIP) area**. This area of the parietal lobe is involved in the planning and control of reaching movements of the arms. The MIP area seems to be critical in guiding the movement of the arms toward a visually selected location. MIP area neurons also seem to be involved in goal-directed arm movements (Swaminathan, Masse, & Freedman, 2013). Nearby is the **anterior intraparietal (AIP) area**, a region of the posterior parietal lobe involved in the act of grasping. Once your arms are close enough to an object that your fingers can start picking the item up or grasping it, activation shifts from MIP area neurons to AIP area neurons. Gallivan, McLean, Flanagan, and Culham (2013), using fMRI, showed that the AIP area was active during visually guided movements to grasp at specific objects. Moreover, like the LIP area, which controls eye movements, the AIP area was also active during the planning of grasping motions. Gallivan et al. had participants plan to grasp either small or large objects, which would require different hand movements. Activity occurred in the AIP area before the participants were given instructions to actually move their hands. These experiments elegantly demonstrate the interaction between visual and motor systems in subserving perceptually guided action.

■ FIGURE 8.18 An experiment showing the function of the LIP region of the parietal lobe.

Monkeys are expected to keep their eyes on a central fixation point. The researchers can then look at the receptive field of a particular neuron in the LIP area. A target then appears in the receptive field of that neuron. When the target disappears, the monkey must make a saccade to that location. Activity in the LIP area precedes the saccade.

TEST YOUR KNOWLEDGE

What is meant by the term *optic flow*? What does it tell us about how we use visual information to inform our own motion?

Medial intraparietal (MIP) area: an area of the posterior parietal lobe involved in the planning and control of reaching movements of the arms

Anterior intraparietal (AIP) area: a region of the posterior parietal lobe involved in the act of grasping

IN DEPTH: *Motion Illusions*

Illusions can be thought of as glitches in the system. At some level, they are errors—we misperceive what is actually there. In a perfect visual system, there would be no illusions. But, our visual system, however effective it is, is not perfect—its mechanisms occasionally lead to errors, which we call illusions. We have made the point that illusions often occur because of unusual situations that our visual systems were not designed to handle, but that our visual systems are very good at handling natural perception. While viewing an illusion, we do not see what is actually there, and we do see what is not. However, illusions can be fun. We often pay to see professional magicians entertain us with illusions. And more important, illusions can reveal to us how our perceptual systems work. By finding when and where these mechanisms fail, we can figure out how the perceptual system is working in the first place. Inspection of the various motion-based illusions is no exception to this rule.

We have already discussed the famous waterfall illusion or motion aftereffect. This adaptation effect tells us much about how neurons are organized in Area MT of the occipital cortex. It also tells us about the nature of saturation of motion channels. Watching movement at a particular speed exhausts the neurons tuned to motion at that speed, leading to the characteristic sense of motion going the opposite direction when we look away from a steadily moving object. In this in-depth section, we address several interesting and important motion illusions and discuss what they tell us about motion perception. Keep your access to the ISLE system handy. As with all illusions, seeing them is usually necessary to understand them, so reading this section without viewing the illusions is not advised. And because a static book cannot show movement, you will certainly need to access your electronic resources for this section.

Illusion 1: Rotating Snakes

This illusion was developed by Akiyoshi Kitaoka (2005), a psychologist in Kyoto, Japan (see Figure 8.19). Because this illusion creates an illusion of motion from a static display, you can see the motion in Figure 8.19. It is also in ISLE 8.15. You can also visit Dr. Kitaoka's Web site (http://www.ritsumei.ac.jp/~akitaoka/index-e.html) to view not only this illusion but many other striking motion illusions that occur with static displays. The rotating snakes illusion is based partially on the earlier Fraser-Wilcox spiral staircase illusion

ISLE 8.15 Rotating Snakes

ISLE 8.16 Spiral Staircase

■ **FIGURE 8.19**   **The rotating snakes illusion.**

There is no actual movement in this display—how could there be, especially if you are looking at a piece of paper in a textbook? Yet the illusion of movement is powerful. When you look at the center of one of the snakes, that snake appears stationary, but all the others in the figure appear to be rotating. Dr. Kitaoka's Web site (http://www.ritsumei.ac.jp/~akitaoka/index-e.html) shows many variations on this theme.

(Fraser & Wilcox, 1979), which you can see on ISLE 8.16, as well. Kitaoka, however, has multiplied the effect. If you look at the center of any particular "snake," you can see that the snake you are looking at is stationary. However, you will notice that the rest of the "snakes" are in motion. The motion is illusory—the figure is completely static. You can test this by changing your gaze and looking at another "snake." Now the new snake is stationary and the one you were just looking at appears to move. And if you are looking at the illusion on paper rather than on a computer screen, you know it is impossible for that paper to move in the way you are perceiving motion. If you are viewing the illusion on a computer screen, consider printing out the illusion to convince yourself that the motion is illusory.

The explanation of the motion induction revolves around eye movements. As we discussed earlier, saccades are eye movements we make in which we direct our gaze from one location to a new location. Some of these saccades may involve very small changes in focus. These micro-saccades are sometimes so small that we do not even notice them as we make them. A micro-saccade can be as small as changing one's focus from the first "hump" in the letter *m* to the second one. According to Otero-Millan, Macknik, and Martinez-Conde (2012), the explanation for the rotating snakes involves these micro-saccades. In their study, participants were shown the rotating snake illusion and asked to indicate when the perceived motion was at a maximum and to indicate when the figure appeared to be not rotating. The perception of motion was highly correlated with the micro-saccades, which they measured via eye tracking. Apparently, we make small saccades along the figure, but do not notice them. Instead, the change of position of our eyes relative to the figure induces an illusion of motion.

Knowing this, you can focus your gaze on the center of one snake and focus really hard on keeping your eyes still. What you will notice when you do this is that the motion tends to stop. Then move your eyes to a new location, and the snakes will start to spin again. Prior to Otero-Millan et al.'s (2012) work, it was assumed that the illusion was called by random drift movements of the eyes. But Otero-Millan et al. showed that it was saccade eye movements that induce the perceived motion.

Micro-saccades have an important function. They prevent visual fading during fixation. Visual fading refers to the loss of visual experience that occurs when neither the visual world nor our eyes are moving. What this means is that if an image were perfectly aligned with our retina for even a short time, there would be rapid adaptation, and the image would quickly fade. Although this never happens in the real world, in the lab, it is possible to create a stabilized image. In a stabilized image, whenever and however we move our eyes, the visual world moves with them. That is, no matter how we move our eyes, we are still looking at the exact same static picture. Under these conditions, unless the picture we are viewing changes, the image quickly fades (Troncoso, Macknik, & Martinez-Conde, 2008). Micro-saccades prevent this from happening in the real world, but also lead to the induction of these motion illusions from static stimuli.

Illusion 2: Illusory Rotation

As with most illusions, you must see this one first to appreciate the effect and then to understand its cause. Because it involves apparent motion, you must go to either ISLE 8.17 or the Web site of this illusion's creator, Dr. Stuart Anstis (http://psy2.ucsd.edu/~sanstis/Stuart_Anstis/Illusions.html). A static view of this illusion is shown in Figure 8.20. Anstis calls this one the "spoked wheel" illusion (Anstis & Rogers, 2011). When you watch the pattern in the illusion, you see what looks like a bicycle wheel. The spokes of the disk are thin gray lines. These lines do not move, nor do they change their brightness. The apparent movement comes from the wedges between the spokes. The movement comes from the clockwise rotation of the gray of the wedges. Once the illusion is set in motion, people see both the clockwise motion of the wedges and what looks like counterclockwise motion of the spokes. This motion is both apparent and illusory, because these lines do not move. That is, the spokes remain

absolutely immobile, whereas the gray wedges shift position from one frame to the next. Moreover, if you stare at the pattern long enough and then look at a clear white screen or sheet of paper, you will see a subtle counterclockwise motion aftereffect. Evidently, the apparent motion of the wedges interacts with the edge detection system to create the backward motion of the spokes (Anstis & Rogers, 2011).

ISLE 8.17 Illusory Rotation

The spoked wheel display likely arises from the interaction of edge contrasts that the visual system is tuned to perceive and the detection of motion in the apparent motion display. Because the motion system is very sensitive to time, when we introduce factors that influence the visual system's ability to discriminate stimuli quickly, we can see illusions. In this case, it is likely that the different grays are processed at different speeds, with lighter grays being processed more quickly. This creates differences in the speed of processing, which, in this case, we perceive as the counterclockwise movement of the spokes.

Illusion 3: The Furrow Illusion

This is another illusion developed and studied by Anstis (2012). You can view this illusion either on ISLE 8.18 or on Dr. Anstis's Web site. A static image of it appears

ISLE 8.18 The Furrow Illusion

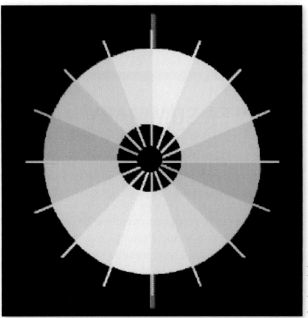

■ **FIGURE 8.20**   **The spoked wheel illusion.**

When you see the static image in the figure, you see what looks like a bicycle wheel. Once the illusion is set in motion, people see the clockwise motion of the wedges, but can also see what looks like counterclockwise motion of the spokes.

Antsis website

in Figure 8.21. Take a minute to view the illusion before continuing to read this section. When you are looking at the static image (Figure 8.21), you see a circle with an odd

■ FIGURE 8.21   The furrow illusion.

When the image is set in motion, the yellow circles move from left to right or right to left across the larger circle. When you look at the top yellow circle, it moves straight across the field from left to right and back again. However, when you look at the top yellow circle, the lower yellow circle appears to zigzag back and forth as it makes its way across the screen.

pattern of gray and white inside it. You also see a small yellow circle along the top and another yellow circle in the bottom half of the larger circle. When the image is set in motion, the yellow circles move from left to right or right to left across the larger circle. When you look at the top yellow circle, it moves straight across the field from left to right and back again. However, when you look at the top yellow circle, the lower yellow circle appears to zigzag back and forth as it makes its way across the screen. But if you shift your gaze and now look at the lower circle, that circle appears to move in a straight line, and it is the top yellow circle that appears to zigzag back and forth. Thus, the same image causes a different perception of motion depending on whether we are viewing it with the foveal vision or with the peripheral vision. Anstis argues that the intersections between the grating within the circle and the moving colored circles cause the illusion, revealing differences in the way in which motion is perceived in the fovea and at the periphery.

What do these illusions tell us about motion perception? In general, we could make the case that motion perception interacts with other aspects of visual processing. In these illusions, we have seen how motion can be seen in nonmoving displays (rotating snakes), and that motion can be induced by the interaction of apparent movement and edge detection (illusory rotation). We also saw how motion perception can be induced when what is actually moving is our eyes (rotating snakes). We also saw how motion perception may be different in the fovea and at the periphery. For this reason, it is clear that motion perception interacts with other aspects of visual perception. We also hope you found looking at these illusions to be a "wow" experience.

CHAPTER SUMMARY

8.1 Explain the concept of a motion threshold and what variables influence that threshold.

Motion is a change in position over time. We need to know if moving objects are approaching us or heading away from us. We must be able to perceive motion across three dimensions—directly ahead of us, to our sides, and above or below us. We must also be able to estimate the speeds of moving objects. Motion thresholds are a function of what part of the retinae are seeing the motion. We have rather poor motion thresholds in the foveal regions of our retinae. But our motion thresholds are better at the periphery of our retinae. Apparent motion is the appearance of

real motion from a sequence of still images. We see apparent motion every time we watch a movie. Induced motion means that one moving object may appear to make another object look like it is moving. Larsen et al. found that fMRI showed that the areas of the primary visual cortex that were responsive to apparent motion were the same as those responsive to real motion.

8.2 Describe the anatomy of the visual system dedicated to motion perception.

The retinae play an important role in early motion detection. We know that some types of amacrine cells in the retina are sensitive to motion. In frogs, we find motion detectors, known as bug detectors, built right into the retinae. Reichardt detectors are hypothetical neurons that are sensitive to motion. They respond to activity in one receptive field at Time 1 and in another receptive field at Time 2. The corollary discharge theory states that the feedback we get from our eye muscles as our eyes track an object is important to the perception of motion. Thus, in addition to being sensitive to motion in receptive fields, we use our own eye movements to help us perceive motion. Saccades are the most common and rapid of eye movements. They are used to look from one object to another. Smooth-pursuit eye movements are the voluntary tracking eye movements that allow us to slowly move our eyes in concert with the motion of an object. MT (V5) is an area in the occipital cortex critical to motion perception. Newsome and his colleagues have shown that the monkey's MT is responsive to large-scale movement, that is, the movement of many objects together. Weigelt et al. showed that the human MT is active when we are attending to motion in a moving display and even when we are just imagining movement. Akinetopsia or motion blindness is a rare condition in which a patient is unable to detect motion despite intact visual perception of stationary stimuli. It is caused by damage to Area MT. A motion aftereffect is a motion-based visual illusion in which a stationary object is seen as moving in the opposite direction of real or apparent motion just observed.

8.3 Discuss how we infer form from the perception of biological motion.

A point-light walker display is one in which small lights are attached to the body of a person or another animal, which is then filmed as it moves in an otherwise completely dark environment. Even when we can see only the lights, we can see the form of the human just from the pattern of movement. Thus, we can infer form from motion perception.

8.4 Summarize the concept of an affordance.

Affordances are the information in the visual world that specifies how that information can be used. One important aspect of visually guided action is optic flow. Optic flow is the relative motion of objects as an observer moves forward or backward in a scene. The gradient of flow is the difference in the perception of speed of objects moving past us in an optic flow display. The focus of expansion is the destination point in an optic flow display, from which point perceived motion derives. The lateral intraparietal (LIP) area is an area of the primate parietal cortex involved in the control of eye movements. The medial intraparietal (MIP) area is an area of the posterior parietal lobe involved in the planning and control of reaching movements of the arms. The anterior intraparietal (AIP) area is a region of the posterior parietal lobe involved in the act of grasping. Finally, we reviewed three motion-based illusions—rotating snakes, the spoked wheel, and the furrow illusion.

REVIEW QUESTIONS

1. What is meant by the term *motion threshold*? How would you go about measuring the speed threshold at which we perceive motion?

2. What is real motion? What is apparent motion? Why would a visual system evolve to perceive apparent motion as real motion? What common brain mechanisms underlie the perception of both forms of motion?

3. What is a Reichardt detector? How might the visual system use Reichardt detectors to perceive motion?

4. What is the corollary discharge theory? How does it link eye movements to the perception of motion?

5. What is MT or V5? What area of the brain is it in? Describe one study using single-cell recording and one study using fMRI that support the role of this area in motion processing.

6. What are motion aftereffects? How are they experienced? What areas of the brain are involved in producing them?

7. What are point-light displays? How have they been used to examine the relation of form and motion perception? Describe an experiment that supports that role.

8. What is an affordance? How does the concept of an affordance serve to bridge the gap between perception and action?

9. What is the lateral intraparietal area? Describe a study that links this area of the brain to its role in the relation of perception and action.

10. What is the rotating snakes illusion? Why are micro-saccades critical in perceiving this illusion? Why do we make micro-saccades?

KEY TERMS

INTERACTIVE SENSATION LABORATORY EXERCISES (ISLE)

Experience chapter concepts at edge.sagepub.com/schwartz

Sharpen your skills with SAGE edge at edge.sagepub.com/schwartz

SAGE edge for students provides a personalized approach to help you accomplish your coursework goals in an easy-to-use learning environment.

Visual Attention

9

INTRODUCTION

In 2008, the classical violinist Joshua Bell brought his $3 million, 300-year-old Stradivarius into a busy Metro station in Washington, D.C. Bell, a renowned soloist who has toured the world playing the most complex pieces in the classical repertoire, plays to packed concert halls. A front-row seat can cost upward of $200. But on that Friday morning, Mr. Bell took out his violin near an escalator in a busy station and played his finest pieces for 45 minutes (see Figure 9.1). Amazingly, few people stopped to listen, and only one person recognized him. Most people walked right by him, not realizing that a rock star of classical music was performing in a place where less talented street musicians often play. What had happened? People were busy rushing to work, making sure they caught their trains on time, and presumably were more focused on their own lives than the beautiful music emanating across the train station. It is reasonable to guess that what had occurred was not a failure of music appreciation, but rather an illustration of the critical nature of attention. Because no one was attending to the musician in their midst, no one realized who he was (see Chabris & Simons, 2009).

A major social concern in many countries is now the scourge of driving while texting. People lead busy lives, and in many places such as big cities, many people spend an inordinate amount of time stuck in traffic. The temptation to use that time to talk or text to friends, family, or colleagues is strong. But research shows that texting (and talking on cell phones) is a major distraction and strongly impairs the ability to drive, resulting in many accidents and many deaths. Drivers are slower to respond to dangers while texting and consequently get into more accidents. This has been demonstrated both on the road and in the lab (Strayer, Watson, & Drews, 2011). But why? Why can't we drive and text at the same time? Of course, part of the answer is that if you are looking at a small screen and not at the road, you can hardly make responses to objects on the road if you cannot see them. But even if you are looking out over your cell phone so that you can direct your vision back and forth, you are still putting yourself and others at risk, because you have only a limited amount of visual attention, which when directed to your small phone is not being directed to the potential hazards on the road. Thus, the reason why we cannot drive well and text at the same time revolves around the concept of attention. The question we concern ourselves with in this chapter is the nature of visual attention, how attention can be selected

LEARNING OBJECTIVES

9.1 Explain selective and divided attention.

9.2 Describe the nature of attentional capture and how it works in our visual system.

9.3 Explain the differences between the orienting attention network and the executive attention network.

9.4 Identify what factors lead to the development of visual attention.

■ FIGURE 9.1 Violinist Joshua Bell.

The violin soloist Joshua Bell played in a Washington, D.C., train station for 45 minutes, and most people passed by without attending to his artistry.

and divided, whether we are justified in thinking about attention as unified or whether it must be considered multiple phenomena, and finally the neurological underpinnings of visual attention.

It is also important to make an initial distinction among three psychological terms, which are all sometimes called attention in everyday life. We will see that each one has different psychological traits and different psychological functions. The terms are *alertness*, *attention*, and *awareness*. *Alertness* refers to a state of vigilance. When alert, we are awake, mindful, and likely scanning our surroundings. Alertness, however, implies that we are not attending to any particular stimulus—we are waiting to find out what we should be paying attention to. For example, we want a security guard to be alert—looking out for any kind of danger at any time. A security guard asleep in his patrol car is not providing much security. However, we do not want him focusing too much on one screen on his bank of monitors, because an intruder may be coming in through another entrance. We want our security guard to be alert, but not directing his attention too much to one source. Attention, the main focus of this chapter, is the allocation of our limited cognitive resources to one of many potential stimuli. Thus, while visiting the zoo, you may see many individual animals of many species within one enclosure. But you attend to the cute giraffe following its mother around. At a restaurant, there may be many people and voices, but you attend to the person with whom you are dining. Moreover, once the security guard detects an intruder on one camera, we want him to attend to what the intruder is doing, as he notifies the police. Finally, awareness is active thought about something, which can be either physically present or just in our imagination. Thus, you are aware that the bright blue sky outside indicates a pleasant day, but that does not mean that you are attending to that stimulus. In general, we are aware of our surroundings whenever we are awake, but there are also bizarre disturbances of awareness. In this chapter, we discuss patients who have lost their awareness of their visual world, even though their eyes are still functioning (blindsight). As issues of awareness are very close to issues of consciousness, we devote some time to visual awareness at the end of the chapter.

Reading a textbook on sensation and perception requires your complete attention. In order to understand psychophysical methods, neurophysiological techniques, and the terminology of brain anatomy, you must stay focused on your reading. If you let your attention wander, you may find that you do not remember or understand the last sentence you read. The lead pipe transformed into a feckless pecan. Did you catch that last sentence, or has your attention already drifted to the person sitting near you in the library or the chattering voice on the television? Distraction is the negative side of attention. When we are attending to an object in space, we gather much information about it, but it means that we are distracted from other stimuli in our world. In some cases, this distraction has interesting consequences. We will discuss inattentional blindness, which describes how we miss important stimuli when our attention is directed elsewhere. And worry not—neither the lead pipe nor the pecan will be on the exam.

Why is it that we cannot attend to more stimuli at any particular time? There is some evidence to suggest that the human brain just does not have the computing power to follow more than one possible incoming stream of information (Dewald, Sinnett, & Leonidas, 2013). To compensate for this inability, our visual systems (and cognitive systems) have evolved to pay attention to some stimuli, but not others. In this chapter, we use the term *attention* to refer to several mechanisms that allow us to direct our perceptual processes to those stimuli. That is, attention is not a single process but many (Chun, Golomb, & Turke-Browne, 2011). We start with the following definition of **attention**: a set of processes that allow us to select or focus on some stimuli.

Attention: a set of processes that allow us to select or focus on some stimuli

There are a few features of attention worth noting at the outset. First, our focus in this chapter is visual attention. But attention can be directed to auditory sources or somatosensory sources. Indeed, when we are enjoying a good meal, we can direct attention to our taste senses. Second, attention can be directed externally to perceptual features of the world, but we can also direct attention internally to our thought processes or imaginal processes. Thus, for example, when you think about the *Mona Lisa*, you may attend to your internal imagery, which conjures up a picture of the da Vinci painting. Can you see the landscape in the background of your mental image of the *Mona Lisa* (after conjuring up your image, have a look at Figure 9.3)? In this chapter, as in this book, our focus is on external attention, that is, our attention to stimuli in the perceptual world.

Attention can also be sustained or temporary. Sustained attention is required in many security-related jobs. An airport security official may spend 8 hours a day, 5 days a week, for years looking at x-rays of clothes, shoes, magazines, and computers. In most cases, the security official will never see anything but combs and toothpaste. But we all hope that he or she is paying attention when a weapon is present in a person's luggage. Indeed, a major subarea in attention research is how to get airport security personnel to be better at detecting contraband while screening luggage (Matthews et al., 2010).

Temporary attention is an everyday phenomenon as well. We may pay attention to some stimuli for short time periods and then direct our attention to other stimuli. For example, you may look up from your reading to see that your dog is not in need of food or a walk. For that moment, your attention is directed toward your dog rather than your book. You pat his head and then go back to the book. Now your attention is back on your reading. Attention can also be overt—when we are looking directly into someone's eyes, we are telling that person that we are paying attention to her. But attention may be covert as well. We may be looking at our conversational partner but attending to news coming from a distant radio. Our first topic is selective attention, the how and why of focusing attention processes on one, and only one, visual input.

■ FIGURE 9.2   **Divided attention.**

Modern life requires us to constantly divide our attention, as this family seems to be doing.

SELECTIVE ATTENTION: COVERT ATTENTION

9.1   Explain selective and divided attention.

Selective Attention

Consider the following situation. You are sitting in your family's living room. Your father is watching a baseball game on the television, your brother is playing a video game, your mother is talking on the telephone, and you are trying to study. Obviously, this is not an ideal scenario for you to concentrate on your studying (see Figure 9.2). However, what you are trying to do is engage in selective attention. You are trying to focus on your sensation and perception

■ **FIGURE 9.3**   **Attention to internal sources.**

How well were you able to focus on your internal representation of the *Mona Lisa*? Could you attend to the background in your visual image? It is harder to attend to stimuli in imagery than it is when we can actually see the stimuli.

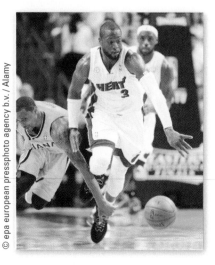

■ **FIGURE 9.4**   **Covert attention.**

Dwayne Wade of the Miami Heat may be looking left, but he may also make a no-look pass to the right. Thus, his attention is somewhere other than the direction of his gaze.

Selective attention: the processes of attention that allow us to focus on one source when many are present

Divided attention: the process of attending to multiple sources of information

textbook and block out the competing distractions. This is the essence of selective attention, in which we direct our perceptual resources to one stimulus among many potential stimuli. **Selective attention** can be defined as the processes of attention that allow us to focus on one source when many are present. Selective attention can be compared with divided attention. Divided attention occurs when we try to attend to competing sources of information. Thus, in the example, you may be trying to study and pay attention to the balls and strikes in the baseball game. To the extent that you are successful at this, your attention is divided. Thus, we can define **divided attention** as the process of attending to multiple sources of information.

Attention and the Direction of Gaze in Space

Typically, we attend to a particular location in space by directing our gaze to that location. Thus, when reading, you are directing your gaze at the words on the page, and when you glance up at the baseball game, you direct your gaze to the television screen. In almost all situations, what is being represented in our foveae is what we are attending to. If our attention shifts, so does our gaze. When one changes one's attention from the textbook to the baseball game, it is usually accompanied by a change in the direction of gaze. A question we can ask, however, is whether it is possible to attend to spatial locations other than the location we are looking at. That is, can I be looking at my textbook, but actually attending visually to the presence of the baseball slugger Miguel Cabrera at home plate? That is, is it possible to direct our attention to an object at our periphery?

The assumption in sports is that we are capable of directing our attention to places other than our direction of gaze. Think of the "no-look" pass in basketball. A basketball player may be running down the court looking to the left at a teammate ahead of him. Instead, he passes the ball to a player moving to his right. This may catch the opposing team off guard, and the no-look pass results in a score, thanks to covert attention (see Figure 9.4). The opposing player assumes that attention is directed toward the location at which the player with the ball is looking, but that player is actually attending to another location, allowing the recipient of the pass a better chance at making a basket.

Michael Posner and his colleagues investigated this phenomenon in a series of interesting experiments in the late 1970s and early 1980s (see Posner, 1980). In this paradigm, a participant is directed to look at a central fixation light. In many experiments, the participant's eyes are monitored to ensure that they are looking at the central fixation point. Trials will not start until the participant's eyes are still and focused on the fixation point (Hughes & Zimba, 1985). The participant then sees an arrow appearing either just to the left of the fixation mark or just to the right of the fixation mark. This arrow is a cue, which directs the participant's attention in visual space (see Figure 9.5). The task of the participant is to maintain fixation on the center point, but direct his or her covert attention in the direction of the arrow. Then a light appears on either the same side as the cue or the opposite side of the cue. When the light occurs on the same side as the cue, it is said to be a valid cue, but when it occurs opposite the cue, it is said to be an invalid cue. In Posner's original experiment, the cues were 80% valid and 20% invalid. Other experiments have used other ratios of valid to invalid trials. But the basic effect works as long as the arrow provides mostly accurate information to the participant. If there was an 80/20 mix, when the cue was given on the left, the target occurred on the left 80% of the time (valid), whereas it occurred 20% on the right (invalid). When the cue was given on the right, the target occurred on the left 80% of the time (valid), whereas it occurred 20% on the left (invalid). There were also neutral trials in which arrows occurred on both sides. In the neutral condition, the participant did not have a hint as to the side on which the target would occur. The task for the participant was to respond as quickly as possible when the target light came on. Posner's question was, Would covert attention to the cued location facilitate the response to that location, and would covert attention to the cued location inhibit the response in the opposite location? The investigators measured this by recording the reaction time to indicate that the participant had seen the target. In general, most young adults are quite fast at this task and can make their responses in about 250 ms (a quarter of a second) (see Figure 9.5 for an illustration of the procedure).

Posner (1980) varied one other feature in this experiment. Sometimes the cue appeared at the exact same time as the target, but in other conditions the cue occurred at set intervals, up to 400 ms before the target. Thus, Posner could also look at the time course of any cuing effect. This variable was called stimulus onset asynchrony. **Stimulus onset asynchrony** refers to the difference in time between the occurrence of one stimulus and the occurrence of another, in this case, the cue and the target. If the stimulus onset asynchrony is zero, there is no difference between the occurrence of the cue and the target; that is, they occur at the same time. If the stimulus onset asynchrony is 200 ms, the target occurs 200 ms after the cue was presented. This variable turned out to predict the results. First, when there is zero stimulus onset asynchrony, there is

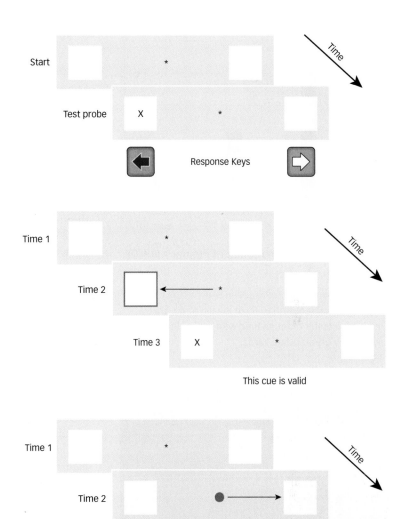

■ FIGURE 9.5   **The Posner cuing paradigm.**

The participant maintains fixation at the central point. Cues indicate whether the target will appear on the left or right. In most trials, the cue is valid; that is, the target appears on that side. But in some trials, the cue is invalid; that is, the target appears on the opposite side of the cue. The experimenters measure the reaction time to indicate that the target is present.

no difference in reaction time between the valid and invalid signals. However, if the cue occurs 200 ms before the target, there is a distinct advantage, with faster reaction times for targets in the valid location than targets in the invalid location. This is also true at longer stimulus onset asynchronies. Neutral trials were of intermediate speed (see Figure 9.6). Later work on this paradigm showed that relative to an appropriate neutral trial, most of the effect was inhibition of invalid trials rather than facilitation of valid trials (Hughes & Zimba, 1985). This means that, relative to the neutral trials, the disadvantage for invalid trials was bigger than the advantage for valid trials. You can see a demonstration of this experiment on ISLE 9.1.

ISLE 9.1 Spatial Cuing

Stimulus onset asynchrony: the difference in time between the occurrence of one stimulus and the occurrence of another, in this case, the cue and the target

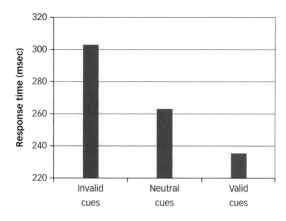

■ **FIGURE 9.6**   The results of Posner's (1980) experiment.

Valid cues result in faster reaction times to the target than do neutral (control) trials or invalid trials. This figure depicts the reaction time with a stimulus onset asynchrony greater than zero.

© Adam Taylor/Digital Vision/Thinkstock

■ **FIGURE 9.7**   The spotlight model of attention.

The spotlight model argues that, much like a spotlight on a stage, attention focuses on one location in visual space and allows us to process information better there.

What does this study tell us about attention? First, it tells us that we can devote attention covertly, that is, direct attention to a location in space that we are not looking at directly with our foveae. Thus, our intuition that we can be looking at our computer screen, but attending to the cute girl or boy at the other table in the library, is confirmed. Similarly, it confirms that athletes can look one way, but attend in the opposite direction, as in the aforementioned no-look pass.

Posner (1980) likened attention to a spotlight that we can shine on particular locations in space. In that spotlight, we can process what we see there in a more efficient manner than if the spotlight were not directed there. Much as a spotlight on a stage directs your attention to that location, your internal spotlight makes it easier to process information in that location, while making other locations more difficult to process (see Figure 9.7). On the basis of the experiments described above, Posner also thought the spotlight could be directed away from the region a person is actually looking at. The spotlight metaphor makes a good general model of selective attention in space, but we will see shortly how the spotlight is not always perfect, and we can make errors in processing even when we are attending to a particular location in space.

An interesting extension of Posner's paradigm was conducted by Egly, Driver, and Rafal (1994). As in Posner's paradigm, a cue was given to indicate where a target light would occur. However, the setup was a little different (see Figure 9.8). A target could occur at any of four locations, as seen in Figure 9.8. A cue indicated where the target was likely to occur. The target then occurred most often in the cued location (valid cues) but occasionally in other locations. As in Posner's paradigm, the target was responded to faster in the valid than the invalid locations. However, there was also an advantage for the invalid cue when the target appeared in the same object as the cued location. Notice that in Figure 9.8, locations A and B sit on the same object in the display, even though they are in different spatial locations. That is, in Figure 9.8, we can see that Location B has a faster response time than Location C when it is Location A that is cued. This has been called the same-object advantage. Why? The attentional spotlight is focused on Location A but is big enough to include B as well, and thus response times to Area B also show some enhancement. It is also called the same-object advantage because a location of equal distance from A, but not physically connected to it, would not benefit from the attentional focus. That is, Location C is actually closer to Location A, but it resides a different object.

Thus, Egly et al.'s (1994) experiment extends the concept of spatial attention. Areas in the object we are attending to will benefit even if we are not directly attending that area. Where might this finding apply in the real world? Think about two wrestlers competing with each other. One wrestler may be watching his opponent's eyes for any clue as to what move he will make next. Attending to the wrestler's eyes may allow that wrestler to more quickly sense his opponent's hands moving in a particular way than the hand movements of a spectator sitting nearby. The opponent's hands are attached to his eyes, and thus it makes good sense if the attentional focus spreads to other areas along the same object.

However, unless we are playing competitive sports, engaging in international espionage, or participating in Posner-paradigm experiments, we are usually not engaged in covert attention, but in overt attention. This means that we are looking directly at what we are attending to, or when our attention is shifted, we direct our attention and our gaze to the new stimulus. It is this overt attention that we next examine.

> **TEST YOUR KNOWLEDGE**
>
> How does the Posner paradigm illustrate the difference between overt and covert attention?

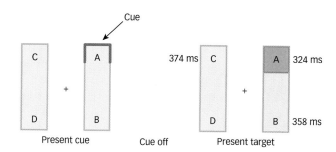

■ FIGURE 9.8   Experimental setup from Egly et al. (1994).

Participants look at the central fixation marker, but the target can occur in any one of four locations. The researchers found that cues to the left or right would have a faster reaction time even when the cue was directed to either the top or the bottom of the same object (same side).

FEATURES OF ATTENTION

9.2   Describe the nature of attentional capture and how it works in our visual system.

Stimulus Salience

Stimulus salience means that some objects in the environment attract our attention. Salience can be any number of features—bright colors, fast movement, personal relevance, or, in the nonvisual domain, a loud or distinctive sound or smell. Think about nodding off during a boring lecture in class, and then the professor calls your name. Hearing your name is a salient stimulus, and you are immediately paying attention—why has she called on me? Another example might be seeing a person streaking by without clothes in your university library. Because this image (positive or negative) is novel, surprising, and potentially important, your attention is immediately diverted from your calculus homework to the sight of the person streaking by. In general, stimuli that are novel or unexpected will act to divert our attention to them. The process by which a stimulus causes us to shift attention is called **attentional capture** (Anderson & Yantis, 2013). In Figure 9.9, we illustrate attentional capture. Here we have a novel situation—a dog wearing reading glasses. Here, your attention is captured by the dog's glasses because this aspect of the photograph is unusual. Most dogs indeed prefer chasing cats and ducks to reading the newspaper.

Brian Anderson and Steven Yantis have explored the notion of attentional capture. They found that one feature that captures our attention is a stimulus that has been previously associated with reward. Rewards are generally considered positive experiences, and we seek them out. Thus, a stimulus associated with a reward ought to attract our attention. Think about those "guns" or launchers that shoot T-shirts at sporting events, which are now nearly ubiquitous at American sporting events. Fans get free T-shirts if they are lucky enough to have one shot

■ FIGURE 9.9   Attentional capture.

A dog wearing reading glasses may attract your attention more so than a less unusual image.

....

Stimulus salience: some objects in the environment attract our attention

Attentional capture: the process whereby a salient stimulus causes us to shift attention to that stimulus

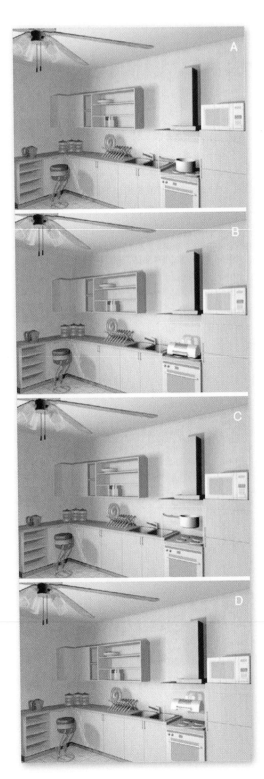

■ FIGURE 9.10 Attentional capture.

Participants' attention was drawn to the printer, and participants spent more time looking at it than when the object was an expected pot. However, when it was presented at the periphery, participants failed to notice the printer miraculously defying gravity and suspended in the air above the stove.

in their direction. Because these T-shirt launchers are associated with rewards, they may capture our attention if we see them in a different context later.

Anderson, Laurent, and Yantis (2013) conducted an experiment in which they paired particular colored stimuli with specific amounts of monetary reward. The participants learned to associate these stimuli with the particular rewards that occurred. Later, participants engaged in a different task using different objects in different colors. However, Anderson et al. periodically presented a nonrelevant stimulus in a color associated with the highest reward in the earlier task. They found that when participants saw this reward-associated object, it captured their attention and slowed their performance on the intended task. Thus, stimuli that have value can also capture our attention.

Semantic meaning may also capture our attention in a visual scene, if that meaning is presented in the fovea. Vō and Henderson (2011) showed participants pictures such as the one seen in Figure 9.10. In one version of the picture, participants saw a kitchen scene with a pot on the stove. In a second version of the scene, participants saw a kitchen scene with a computer printer on the stove. In an earlier experiment, participants could move their eyes freely around the scene (Vō & Henderson, 2009). In this study, they found that participants' attention was drawn to the printer, and that participants spent more time looking at it than when the object was an expected pot. However, in the later study (Vō & Henderson, 2011), participants' ability to move their eyes around the scene was limited by the technology used to present the stimulus. In this study, attentional capture did not work at the periphery. When participants could see the printer only at the periphery, it did attract not attention in the form of eye movements. This was true even when the printer was displayed suspended in space above the stove. Thus, attentional capture works best when the stimulus evoking capture is processed by the fovea.

Consider the situation described by Vō and Henderson (2011). We are looking at a common kitchen scene but fail to notice the printer miraculously defying gravity and suspended in the air above the stove. In real life, of course, we would be moving our eyes about the scene and would pick up this anomaly with our foveal vision. But nonetheless, this failure to detect unusual objects constitutes a failure of attention. It should be adaptive to notice unusual circumstances, as such circumstances may present a threat, especially when we see them only peripherally. This leads us to a discussion of a number of failures of attention, that is, when attention fails to alert us to what should be salient aspects of a scene or changes in a scene. We now consider two of these phenomena, change blindness and inattention blindness.

Change Blindness

Change blindness is the difficulty we experience in detecting differences between two visual stimuli that are identical except for one or more changes to the image. Change blindness is a very counterintuitive effect. We usually think we will notice obvious changes when they occur, but change blindness suggests that we often fail to do so. What is interesting about change blindness is that even when we have engaged our attention and are directing our visual search in a very conscious manner, we may still fail to see the changes in an image. Consider Figure 9.11. Can you find the change? You probably can, but it does not immediately pop out for most people viewing these images.

In a classic demonstration of change blindness, Simons and Levin (1997) conducted a field experiment in the city of Ithaca, New York. Participants were chosen at random on the Cornell University campus. In the experiment, an experimenter posing as a tourist asked a person on

■ FIGURE 9.11   Change blindness.

Can you detect the difference between the photographs? If you cannot find the difference and give up looking, go to the end of the chapter for the answer.

campus for directions. When the participant started giving directions, two other experimenters, posing as construction workers, passed by carrying a detached door. The construction workers passed between the experimenter who had asked for directions and the participant. At this point, Simons and Levin had the first experimenter hide behind the door and exit the scene, while a second experimenter, the same gender and age as the first experimenter, replaced the first. The question was, Would the participant notice that the person to whom he was giving directions had changed? It seems obvious—if you were just talking to one person, and he was replaced by another person, of course you would notice the difference. However, this obvious answer turned out to be wrong, most of the time.

Simons and Levin (1997) asked both professional researchers and undergraduates to predict the outcome of this experiment before the results were made public. Both professionals and students predicted overwhelmingly that almost all people would notice the change. After all, the participant finds himself or herself talking to a different person. When the predictors were asked if they themselves would notice the difference, 95% of people answered in the affirmative. But this is not what Simons and Levin found in the field. In the study, nearly 50% of the participants failed to notice the change from one person to another. Indeed, Simons and Levin have made available video of participants continuing to explain and point without noticing that they are giving directions to a new person. Let us repeat that—nearly half of the participants failed to notice that the people they were talking to had changed from before the workers passed by to after the workers had passed by.

Do these findings generalize to events in the real world? One such situation might be detecting errors of "goofs" in movies. Hollywood has professional staffers who, during postproduction, go through films to detect inconsistencies. However, invariably, some of these inconsistencies get through and make it into the movie. Fans and aficionados look for these errors and catalog them on Web sites, but most of us casual moviegoers never notice them. Of course, nowadays, it is rather easy to look up these goofs online before we go to movies and then annoy our friends by pointing them out, but most of us watch these movies originally without ever noticing these errors. For example, in the movie *Iron Man 3* (2013), the characters of Tony Stark and Colonel Rhodes are talking together via cell phone to the vice president. The vice president's cell phone is different from one shot to the next. Most of us, including the editing staff of the movie, failed to notice this when seeing the movie. Consistent with the concept of change blindness, such errors abound in movies, but we almost always fail to notice them.

Change blindness: the difficulty we experience in detecting differences between two visual stimuli that are identical except for one or more changes to the image

In a more typical experiment on change blindness, Rensink, O'Regan, and Clark (1997) showed photographs of a variety of scenes, one image at a time. After a set period of looking at each photograph, it would disappear and be replaced by a nearly identical image. In this photo, one aspect of the image would be changed, as in Figure 9.11. Participants' task was to identify the nature of the switch. If they could not immediately detect the change, then participants were given a set amount of time to flip between the two images and detect the change. Here too, some participants never found the change between one image and the other.

Thus, particularly if the change from one photograph to the other is not to an important aspect of the meaning of the photograph, we often fail to notice the change. Moreover, the good Samaritan giving directions is not all that concerned with what the lost person looks like. He or she is simply doing the right thing by giving directions and may not really be directing attention at the person inquiring, especially if the directions are complicated and he or she may be focusing on a mental map of the area. Thus, we can think of change blindness as a deficit in attention.

One can ask what is going on at the neural level when we fail to notice these changes. After all, we are looking at different images, but perceiving them as the same. Can we see different patterns of brain activity when we are blind to changes and when we actually recognize the changes? This topic was investigated in an experiment by Busch (2013). Busch showed participants a photograph of a real-world object and then showed a second photograph later in which one of the objects in the photograph had been switched, similar to Figure 9.11. As in all other work on change blindness, many participants failed to recognize the change between the photographs. In Busch's study, the participants did a final recognition task in which they had to identify objects as being part of the study task or new to the study. Some of these were the original object, some were changed objects, and some were entirely novel. This part of the study was done while participants were undergoing electroencephalographic (EEG) recording. Busch found that the EEG patterns were different for old objects and new objects, but also that the EEG patterns were similar for items whose change had been detected and those whose change had not been detected. Thus, some aspect of the change was being encoded, as the changes led to neural changes, even if they did not lead to behavioral changes.

Beck, Muggleton, Walsh, and Lavie (2006) used transcranial magnetic stimulation to examine change blindness. They inhibited the right parietal lobes of some participants and the left parietal lobes of other participants while those participants were doing a change-blindness task, similar to the ones just described. They found that interrupting the function of the right parietal lobe increased change blindness in the sense that participants were less able to detect the differences between photographs. On the other hand, interrupting function of the left parietal lobe had no effect on change blindness. This result suggests that the right parietal lobe may be critical in this form of attention. As we will see later, the right parietal lobe is critical in many aspects of attention in addition to change blindness.

We now turn our attention to another error in attention: inattentional blindness.

Inattentional Blindness

Inattentional blindness refers to a phenomenon in which people fail to perceive an object or event that is visible but not attended to. This refers to situations in which a well-above-threshold event or object is not seen because the person's attention is directed elsewhere. Recently, Dr. Schwartz placed a plastic toy giraffe in the refrigerator, next to the milk and orange juice. It was there for several hours

Inattentional blindness: a phenomenon in which people fail to perceive an object or event that is visible but not attended to

before another family member noticed it, despite frequent openings and closings of the refrigerator door. This demonstrates inattentional blindness, because the giraffe was clearly visible, but family members' attention was elsewhere when opening the refrigerator door. Like change blindness, inattentional blindness is a counterintuitive finding. Most people would not predict it to occur and are quite surprised when they find that they are susceptible to it as well.

Perhaps the most famous demonstration of inattentional blindness comes from a study conducted by Simons and Chabris (1999). Before you continue reading, take a moment to view their video of this demonstration, which can be found at Dr. Simons's Web site (http://www.theinvisiblegorilla.com/videos.html). Like many illusions and phenomena we describe in this book, seeing is believing for this demonstration. On Dr. Simons's Web site, the demonstration we are about to describe is the first video provided.

In the experiment, Simons and Chabris (1999) asked participants to watch a video that shows three young college-age adults wearing white T-shirts, passing a basketball, and three young college-age adults wearing black T-shirts, passing another basketball. The six people are weaving among one another. The participants watching the video are instructed to count the number of times the team with white shirts actually passes the basketball among themselves. Less than a minute into the video, a person wearing a gorilla suit walks into the scene, continues through, and then walks off camera. The "gorilla" is visible at the center of the video for about 5 seconds. Once the video is over, participants are asked how many passes they observed, and then they are asked if they saw the gorilla. As in the change blindness study described earlier, nearly half (46%) of participants failed to notice the "gorilla" walking across the field of view. Simons and Chabris describe the surprise that many participants experienced when they rewatched the video to determine that yes, the "gorilla" was visible and salient while they were attending to the basketball passes.

In Simons and Chabris's (1999) experiment, participants are focused on a challenging perceptual task, counting the white team's basketball passes while ignoring the black team's basketball passes. It is actually quite a difficult task, and many participants were not able to count the number of passes correctly, regardless of whether they noticed the "gorilla." Because of this, their attention was narrowly focused, which then caused them to ignore other stimuli to the extent that they did not even notice the very odd appearance of the "gorilla" (see Figure 9.12).

Inattentional blindness can be demonstrated under more traditional laboratory conditions as well. Mack and Rock (1998), for example, showed that participants were unable to see a perfectly visible stimulus when their attention was drawn to another aspect of the display. Participants maintained fixation on a central point (see Figure 9.13). They then saw a large cross somewhere in the parafoveal region. The participants' task was to determine if the horizontal or vertical lines of the cross were larger. In some trials, but not all, the fixation point transformed into a diamond shape at the exact instant the cross appeared. Remember that the term *fixation point* refers to the point at which participants' eyes were supposed to be focused. In trials in which the fixation point changed, participants were asked if they had seen anything change when the cross appeared on the screen. A majority of the participants did not report seeing the diamond, even though it was being

■ FIGURE 9.12 Inattentional blindness (Simons & Chabris, 1999).

When viewed as a static photograph, it is hard to imagine that participants do not see the gorilla.

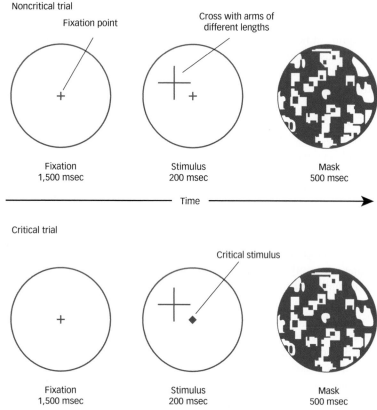

Noncritical trial

Fixation point

Cross with arms of different lengths

Fixation
1,500 msec

Stimulus
200 msec

Mask
500 msec

Time

Critical trial

Critical stimulus

Fixation
1,500 msec

Stimulus
200 msec

Mask
500 msec

Time

■ **FIGURE 9.13**   **Inattentional blindness: stimuli from Mack and Rock (1998).**

In critical trials, the fixation point changed from a cross to a diamond. In many critical trials, participants failed to notice the change.

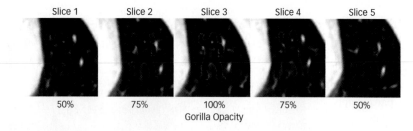

Slice 1   Slice 2   Slice 3   Slice 4   Slice 5

50%   75%   100%   75%   50%

Gorilla Opacity

■ **FIGURE 9.14**   **Inattentional blindness in the real world.**

In this intriguing but frightening study by Drew et al. (2013), most radiologists failed to notice a small image of a gorilla on a CT scan they were asked to inspect for evidence of lung disease.

presented directly onto the foveae. Thus, even when we are looking at something directly, we may not notice a change when our attention is directed elsewhere.

Is it important that people are unable to detect crosses changing to diamonds in simple displays or even fail to see a person dressed up as a gorilla in a contrived video? The question, of course, is, Does inattentional blindness occur in real-world situations? The answer is yes. In a stunning demonstration of this phenomenon, Drew, Võ, and Wolfe (2013) used expert radiologists as their test participants. The stimuli were computed tomographic (CT) scans taken to determine if patients had dangerous nodules on their lungs. The radiologists in the study had many years of experience analyzing CT scans of lungs, looking for these lung nodules. Embedded in one of the CT scans was a small image of a gorilla, about the same size a radiologist would expect a lung nodule to be (see Figure 9.14). Eighty-three percent of the radiologists failed to detect the image of the gorilla, even though eye-tracking software showed that many of them were looking right at the image. The radiologists were better than the nonexperts. Not one of the nonradiologists in the study noticed the gorilla. Nonetheless, even experts, operating within their sphere of expertise, show inattentional blindness.

Visual Search

One of the most important attentional tasks in vision is **visual search**: looking for and finding a particular object amid a background of visual distraction. Think about security personal at the airport. They must examine x-ray screens looking for banned items, such as weapons, among the vast array of objects that people bring onto airplanes. In this case, screeners must distinguish between rifles and golf clubs and between knives and flutes. One can think of few visual searches more important than those airport screeners do countless times every day at airports. But passengers must engage in visual search too when they are at the airport. When you arrive at your destination, you must be able to distinguish the face of your sister among a sea of other faces also waiting for other passengers. In a more peaceful setting, away from the airport, a birdwatcher may be looking for the rare eider duck among a flock of mallard ducks. Finally, young children may spend endless time engaged in visual

Visual search: looking for a specific target in an image with distracting objects

search, trying to see "where's Waldo." In Figure 9.15, you can engage in visual search to look for the dead tree and the satellite dish. How long did it take you to find these objects? We can define visual search as looking for a specific target in an image with distracting objects.

In the laboratory, we can control many aspects of visual search. We can control the size, shape, color, and location of the search item as well as the size, shape, color, location, and number of distracting items. We can then measure how long it takes a participant to find the target under these different circumstances. Consider Figure 9.16a. This figure demonstrates a **feature search**. You are looking for the vertical orange bar amid a mix of different stimuli. Feature searches such as these are very easy. However, in Figure 9.16b, we see a **conjunction search**. Here you are still looking for the vertical orange bar, but now present are horizontal orange bars

■ FIGURE 9.15   Visual search.

Can you find the dead tree and the satellite dish?

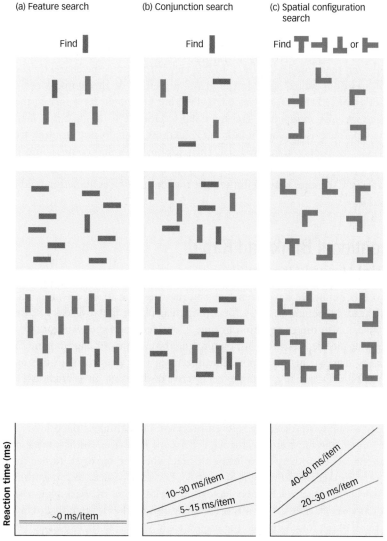

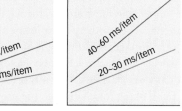

■ FIGURE 9.16   **Visual search tasks.**

In a feature search (a), the participant must identify the object that differs along one dimension (here, color). In a conjunction search (b), the participant must find the unique object among two sets of objects. Finally, in a spatial configuration search (c), the participant must look for a particular shape among numerous related shapes. The feature search takes place in parallel and therefore takes no longer among several distractors than many distractors. However, the conjunction search and the spatial configuration search are done in a serial self-terminating manner, which requires more time the more distractors are present.

Feature search: the search for a target in which the target is specified by a single feature

Conjunction search: the search for a target in which the target is specified by a combination of features

ISLE 9.2 Feature vs. Conjunction Search

and vertical blue bars. Now you are searching for a conjunction between two features—vertical and blue. Because of this, the task gets more difficult with a greater number of distractors. You can vary the set size (number of distractors) and a host of other factors in ISLE 9.2.

The feature search in Figure 9.16a is fast, and the number of distractors is irrelevant. We can pick out the orange bar no matter how many blue bars are shown in the figure. This kind of sudden visual search is called "pop-out," because the target seems to jump out at us from the display. When we are given a feature search, we seem to be able to do the search in parallel (Wolfe, 2012). The conjunction search in Figure 9.16b is different. Here we are looking for the vertical orange bar among some stimuli that are also vertical and some stimuli that are also orange. In this case, we tend not to have a pop-out effect. Instead, we must engage in a serial search, that is, looking at every object until we find the one we are looking for. Because of the conjunctions, we can think of these searches as being less efficient.

Feature Integration Theory

One of the prominent theories advanced to account for visual attention is **feature integration theory** (Treisman & Gelade, 1980). This theory stipulates that some features can be processed in parallel and quickly prior to using attentional resources. Other visual characteristics require us to use attention and are done serially and therefore less quickly. In this view, there are some characteristics that simply pop out at us, such as the gross mispelling of this wird. Most of you instantly noticed that *word* was misspelled, but you might have missed that *misspelling* was also misspelled. Treisman and Gelade (1980) argued that many perceptual characteristics simply pop out, but those that do not require attention. Consider the display in Figure 9.16. The pattern shows that conjunctions require attention. We must actively search in time to determine the mismatched figure. In contrast, the searches that do not require the finding of a conjunction tend to pop out at us.

Attentional Blink and Rapid Serial Visual Presentation

Up to this point, we have been focusing on attending to objects in space. That is, we search through an array for a particular object that we seek to attend to. But we can also direct attention in time. Consider again the overworked airport security agent. He is tasked with monitoring the contents of bags moving through the x-ray detector at the airport. But dozens of bags pass through this machine every minute. Essentially, from the perspective of the agent, he is attending to only a small area of space, but he must maintain this attention to particular objects across time. The agent never knows exactly when the form of a handgun may attempt to slip past. Also along law enforcement lines, think of the role of a SWAT team sniper. She must attend, through the scope of a rifle, to the people passing before her. The job here is to locate in time when the terrorist, rather than the innocent hostage, is in the sight of the rifle. For a less violent example, think of a line worker at a factory. He may have to inspect each set of spark plugs that goes by for any design flaws. As in airport security, this worker is attending to one location but looking for changes in the properties of what is in that space across time.

Attention across time rather than space has been studied with a paradigm called the **rapid serial visual presentation (RSVP) paradigm**. In RSVP, a series of

Feature integration theory: a theory stipulating that some features can be processed in parallel and quickly prior to using attentional resources, whereas other visual characteristics require us to use attention and are done serially and therefore less quickly

Rapid serial visual presentation (RSVP) paradigm: a method of studying attention in which a series of stimuli appear rapidly in time at the same point in visual space

stimuli appear rapidly in time at the same point in visual space. Indeed, the stimuli may appear as fast as 10 items per second. The stimuli are usually letters or photographs (see Figure 9.17). The task of the participant is to determine when a particular stimulus appears and to press a button or key as fast as possible after that stimulus occurs. Thus, the participant might be following a series of letters flashed 10 per second. The participant's task is to press a response button every time the letter *S* occurs. In another version of the RSVP task, photographs might be flashing by at 5 photographs per second. The participant must hit the response button every time a photograph of a guitar player occurs (see Figure 9.17). To try this task yourself, go to ISLE 9.3.

The RSVP paradigm allows various manipulations that can determine what enhances the attentional focus on the stimulus to be responded to, and the paradigm can also allow investigation of what factors can distract our attention. For example, Zivony and Lamy (2014) asked participants to respond when a stimulus was a particular color. The stimuli to be judged were all presented at the point of fixation so that the images would be maintained on the fovea. However, they also presented various distractors at the periphery to determine if these distractors would affect attention and interfere with performance. In their study, they found that distractors at the periphery that were the same color as the intended target attracted attention and reduced accurate performance on the primary task. Irons and Remington (2013) asked participants to track two simultaneous RSVP streams, one on each side of fixation. The participants' task was to respond to a conjunction of color and location. Thus, they might be asked to respond to a red object on the left, but a green object on the right. This made the task quite a bit harder, and therefore, overall errors were relatively high and reaction time was down. But they also found that red objects presented on the right captured attention and slowed participants' responses even further.

If we return to the more simple version of RSVP in which one must track only one stream of letters, we can also vary the time between the presentation of one target and the next target. Thus, if we are following letters and responding to *S*, there might be a lag of 4 letters between one *S* and the next, or there might be a lag of 10 letters between one *S* and the next target (typically another letter). One question we can ask is whether having just seen a target affects the ability to detect the next target. It turns that out it does, if the second stimulus occurs within 500 ms (half a second) of the first stimulus.

This phenomenon is called **attentional blink**, which refers to the tendency to respond more slowly or not at all to the second appearance of a target in an RSVP task. Indeed, in some cases, the participant may not report having seen the second stimulus at all. In a typical study on attentional blink, the first and the second targets may be different. Thus, the participant knows to look for an *S* and then after the *S* to look for a *K*. One can then vary the lag between the *S* and the *K* and determine when and how the participant responds to the *K*. To demonstrate that

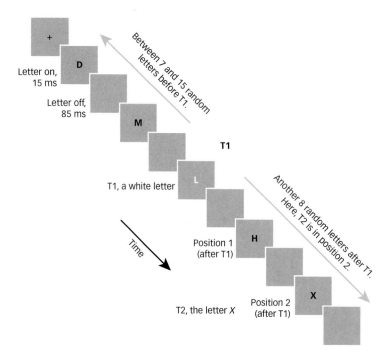

■ FIGURE 9.17   The rapid serial visual presentation (RSVP) paradigm.

In this study, a series of stimuli, here letters, appear rapidly in time at the same point in visual space. The participant presses a button or key as fast as possible after a particular stimulus occurs.

ISLE 9.3 RSVP

Attentional blink: the tendency to respond more slowly or not at all to the second appearance of a target in an RSVP task when the second stimulus occurs within 500 ms of the first stimulus

attentional blink is an issue of attention, we merely have to change the instructions and ask participants to look only for the *K*. Given the same stream of stimuli as with the *S-K* instructions, *K*-only instructions yield faster and more accurate identifications of the *K*. The standard explanation of attentional blink focuses on an inhibition mechanism that dampens responses to other targets while searching for the intended target. When that target is detected, there is a finite amount of time necessary to "reboot" the attentional mechanism for the next target. Variables that slow this disengagement of inhibition can therefore strengthen the blink. For example, simply inducing fatigue in participants increases the intensity and length of the blink period (Kawahara & Sato, 2013). In contrast, there is some evidence to suggest that experienced video game players may show reduced attentional blink because of their training in games that resemble RSVP tasks (Kristjánsson, 2013). Finally, when the second target is the identical stimulus as the first target (e.g., *S-S*) and occurs right after the first target, some participants will fail to see it at all. This phenomenon is called **repetition blindness**. You can see illustrations of both repetition blindness and attentional blink in ISLE 9.4.

ISLE 9.4 Attentional Blink and Repetition Blindness

> **TEST YOUR KNOWLEDGE**
>
> What is rapid serial visual presentation (RSVP), and how has it been used to examine attention and visual search?

THE ANATOMY AND PHYSIOLOGY OF ATTENTION

9.3 Explain the differences between the orienting attention network and the executive attention network.

There are numerous questions that can be asked concerning the interaction of attentional processes in the brain. For example, we could take the standard brain localization approach and ask, What areas of the brain may be involved in the creation of attentional processes? Are there different brain regions for different forms of attention? This standard approach of correlating anatomy and function has yielded numerous successful findings, which we discuss here. But we can also ask other questions, such as, When we are attending to one stimulus, how does that change the neural processing of that stimulus? Put another way, Does attention change the processing of stimuli in sensory areas of the brain, or does attention occur after such processing has occurred? For example, if I am focusing my attention on the pitcher in a baseball game, how does that change the neural processing of the visual image of the pitcher releasing the ball relative to a situation in which I was focusing my attention on the batter? We can also examine what happens to the processing of nonattended visual stimuli. So if I am focusing on the pitcher, does my perceptual processing of the runner on first base change?

We start with the basic anatomy of attention.

The Orienting Attention Network

Much of what we have presented as visual attention in this chapter is a function of a neural system called the **orienting attention network** (also called the **dorsal attention network**), which allows us to engage in visual search and direct

Repetition blindness: the failure to detect the second target in an RSVP task when the second target is identical to the first one; like attentional blink, it occurs when the second target is presented 500 ms or less after the first target

Orienting attention network (dorsal attention network): a neural system, located primarily in the parietal lobe, that allows us to engage in visual search and direct our visual attention to different locations in visual space

our visual attention to different locations in visual space. The orienting attention network is based in circuits in the parietal lobe (Posner & Rothbart, 2013). Damage to this network can cause a number of neuropsychological conditions, most famously unilateral neglect (hemifield neglect), which we consider later in the chapter. Anatomical regions associated with the orienting attention network can be seen in Figure 9.18.

The Executive Attention Network

The **executive attention network** focuses on attention as the inhibition of habitual responses and the top-down control of attention (Posner & Rothbart, 2013). This network allows us to inhibit auditory stimuli so that we can concentrate on visual stimuli, or it can allow us to inhibit visual stimuli so that we can concentrate on auditory stimuli. It also operates on attention directed at memory and higher order cognition. For example, in the context of texting and driving, this is the network that directs our attention to the small screens on our cell phones when we should be attending to the road. It is also the system that must be engaged when we attend to the color of a word (e.g., *green* written in red print) rather than its meaning (the famous Stroop effect). The executive attention network is the product of processes in the prefrontal lobe. In models of memory, the executive attention network is sometimes called the "central executive," because it is the point at which attention is directed to the desired stimulus.

Tamber-Rosenau, Esterman, Chiu, and Yantis (2011) conducted a functional magnetic resonance imaging (fMRI) study with human participants to examine how the executive attention and orienting attention networks allocate attention in a visual attention task. Participants watched an RSVP display, consisting of two streams of letters, one to the left of fixation and one to the right of fixation. The researchers also used a distractor RSVP display above and below fixation to increase the difficulty of the task and to ensure that the participants would need their attentional networks. The above and below streams were not to be attended to, but provided background distraction. However, participants had to monitor both the left and right streams. When the letter *L* occurred, participants were to shift their attention from the left stream to the right stream of letters When the letter *L* occurred again, participants again shifted their attention. The question Tamber-Rosenau et al. were interested in was what areas of the brain would show activity during these attentional shifts. They found that areas of the brain in the prefrontal lobe and in the parietal lobe were active during these attentional shifts. In particular, within the orienting network, the medial parietal lobule was active during shifts of attention. Within the executive attention network, there was activity in the superior frontal sulcus/gyrus (see Figure 9.19). The changes in these areas reflect the attentional mechanism at work. We discuss shortly a similar study that shows how visual areas of the brain change in response to attentional changes.

How Attention Affects the Visual Brain

Think about the Posner paradigm described earlier (Posner, 1980). In this task, people are asked to direct their attention to a spatial location other than the location on which their eyes are fixated. In order to engage in this covert attention,

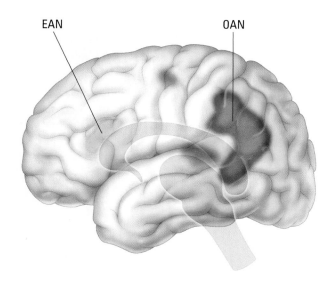

EAN   OAN

■ FIGURE 9.18   Attention networks in the brain.

Executive attention network: a system that focuses on attention as the inhibition of habitual responses and the top-down control of attention; found in the frontal lobe

■ FIGURE 9.19   Results from Tamber-Rosenau et al.'s (2011) study.

These fMRI illustrations show activation in both the prefrontal lobe and the parietal lobe during attentional shifts. Within the orienting attention network, the medial parietal lobule was active during shifts of attention. Within the executive attention network, there was activity in the superior frontal sulcus/gyrus.

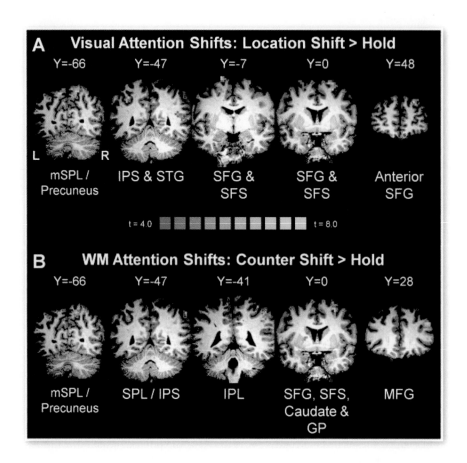

participants must inhibit their tendency to want to move their eyes to the location of the to-be-attended stimuli. They must also inhibit the tendency to remain focused on the point of fixation. Thus, it is likely that this task draws on the executive attention network. But how does this network exert its attentional effect on the task? Attention is useful only if it can alter the efficiency of other cognitive processes. Thus, neutrally, attention must act on other areas of the brain that are otherwise engaged in the visual task at hand—detecting the target and making the response. So attention must show up as both a "command" from an attention network and a change in perceptual processing in visual areas of the brain. This aspect of attention was illustrated elegantly in an experiment by Moran and Desimone (1985).

Moran and Desimone (1985) conducted a single-cell recording experiment with rhesus monkeys. Monkeys were trained to keep their eyes fixated on a central point and then, as in the Posner paradigm, to attend to objects in one of two locations they were not directly looking at (see Figure 9.20). The question the researchers were interested in was how attention would affect the physiological response in cells that were responding to visual characteristics, such as color and orientation. For this reason, they recorded cells in area V4 of the brain, which you will recall is sensitive to both color and orientation.

One of the presented objects was considered the effective stimulus because it elicited a large response, when presented alone, from the receptive field of the V4 neuron they were recording from. The second stimulus was considered ineffective because it did not elicit a strong response when presented alone from the V4 cell being recorded from. Thus, when both stimuli are presented to the visual field, without an attentional manipulation, one would expect a large response driven by the effective stimulus. However, in the study, the monkeys were directed to attend to either the effective or the ineffective stimuli. Note, of course, that there are presumably other cells in V4 that respond to the ineffective stimuli. But the cell being recorded from does not. When attention is directed to the effective

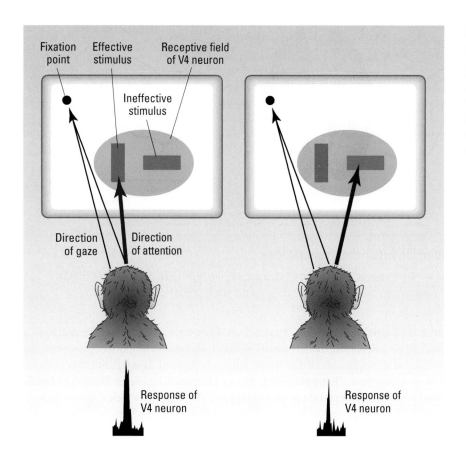

■ FIGURE 9.20 Attentional
networks and V4.

Rhesus macaques fixated on a central
marker but attended to stimuli to the
left or right of that marker. Moran and
Desimone (1985) found that when
attention is directed to the effective
stimuli, the V4 cell responds strongly.

stimuli, the V4 cell responds strongly, in fact, more strongly than when attention is not directed there. However, when attention is directed to the ineffective
stimulus, the cell's response decreased, despite the fact that the effective stimulus
was in the receptive field as well. Because the stimulus was not being attended to,
however, the response of the V4 cell decreased. Thus, this experiment showed that,
at a physiological level, attention can affect the processing of visual information.
Here, attention acts to decrease the activity of a cell when the effective stimulus
for that cell is not being attended to.

We can also see similar patterns of activity in the human brain. Using fMRI,
Chiu and Yantis (2009) examined shifts in activity within the occipital lobe as a
function of attention. In their study, participants fixated on a central marker and
then rapidly shifted attention from stimuli on the left side of fixation and stimuli
on the right side of fixation. The stimuli were either letters or digits. When the letter *R* occurred, it meant to direct attention to the right and keep it there, until participants saw the letter *L*, and then they were supposed to direct their attention to
the left. When attention was directed to the left, there was more activity in areas
of the right occipital lobe, and when attention was directed to the right, there was
more activity in areas of the left occipital lobe (see Figure 9.21). Note that the
point of this study is to demonstrate that directing attention affects neural processing in visual areas of the brain. Thus, attention can affect visual processing.

The Neuropsychology of Attention

One of the most fascinating, albeit tragic, neuropsychological conditions arises
when there is damage to the orienting attention network in the parietal lobe.
When a stroke or some other neurological insult affects the right posterior parietal lobe, a condition called hemifield neglect or unilateral visual neglect may

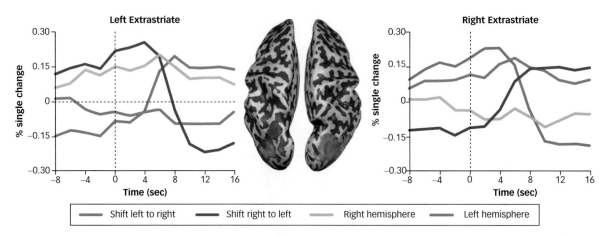

Left Extrastriate

Right Extrastriate

—— Shift left to right ——— Shift right to left ······· Right hemisphere ——— Left hemisphere

■ FIGURE 9.21 **Shifts of attention within the occipital lobe.**

When attention was directed to the left visual world, there was more activity in the right occipital lobe, and when attention was directed to the right visual world, there was more activity in the left occipital lobe

arise. This condition almost always occurs when the right parietal lobe is affected, leading to a deficit in the left visual world. In a handful of patients, one can see neglect of the right side of the world from left parietal damage, but this is much less common than a left-field deficit from right parietal damage. We define **hemifield neglect** or **unilateral visual neglect** as a condition in which a person fails to attend to stimuli on one side of the visual world (usually the left) as a consequence of neurological damage to the posterior parietal lobe.

What are the consequences of not attending to half of the visual world? It may not seem so strange at first, but it has devastating consequences. For example, male patients may shave only one side of their faces. Patients may neglect the care of the left sides of their bodies. In one case described by Sacks (1985), a patient with neglect rejected the fact that the left side of his body belonged to him. In Figure 9.22, you can see bizarre drawings done by patients with this form of neglect.

Sensitive tests can show that these patients have not lost the ability to see in their left visual world, but they no longer attend to stimuli in the left world. When pressed to respond to an item in the left visual world, they may identify it, but under normal circumstances, they simply just ignore it. It is as if they are no longer interested in the left world or, more properly speaking, that they can no longer direct attention to objects in the left visual world.

One of the tests of neglect is to ask patients to copy various drawings. For example, when asked to reproduce a clock face, a patient may put all the numbers of the clock on the right side of the page—the right side of the world from the patient's point of view, though the left side of the clock. When shown a picture of a house, the patient draws only the part of the house on the right side of the paper (see Figure 9.22). When asked to draw her own face, a participant will draw only the side she sees on the right side of the mirror.

One striking demonstration that neglect is an attentional problem and not a visual problem comes from a patient in Italy studied by Bisiach and Luzzatti (1978). Their patient was the editor of a major newspaper in an Italian city and a highly educated man. After his initial hospitalization, he was able to resume his duties with the newspaper. But he continued to visit the lab to be tested by Bisiach and Luzzatti. Asked to imagine himself walking down the main square from north to south in his native city in Italy, the patient described the monuments and buildings only on the west side (his right). When asked to imagine himself walking up the main square from south to north, the patient described the sites only on the east side (now on his right). Thus, there was nothing wrong with

Hemifield neglect (unilateral visual neglect): a condition in which a person fails to attend to stimuli on one side of the visual world (usually the left) as a consequence of neurological damage to the posterior parietal lobe

his visual memory. He successfully retrieved the buildings on each side of the main square during the tests. However, when engaged in this mental walk, he attended only to those buildings that would have been on his right. He consistently ignored the left side of the square, regardless of whether "left" meant east or west. Note that he was doing this in the lab, not actually in the square. Thus, he was showing neglect for the left side of his visual images rather than visual perception. Thus, the imagery deficit mirrored the perceptual deficit.

Left untreated, the symptoms of unilateral visual neglect will persist and can be quite devastating to a patient's long-term health and well-being. However, patients show improvement with intervention and treatment from clinical neuropsychology. One of the more successful treatments is to require patients with hemifield neglect to wear prism glasses, which shift the left visual world into the right visual world, where they will attend to it. In some cases, one can, using a series of prisms with different refractive properties, shift the left visual world leftward and see if the patients continue to attend to it (Jacquin-Cortois et al., 2013). Other treatments have been tested as well. Pavlovian conditioning has been used to increase patients' attention to the left visual world (Domínguez-Borràs, Armony, Maravita, Driver, & Vuilleumier, 2013), and there are studies showing that listening to music can also allow some patients to focus more on the left visual world than if they were not listening to music (Chen, Tsai, Huang, & Lin, 2013). With these treatments, many patients with unilateral neglect will see a diminishment of the symptoms and a chance to resume their normal lives. Actual patients with unilateral visual neglect can be seen in YouTube videos (e.g., http://www.youtube.com/watch?v=ymKvS0XsM4w).

■ FIGURE 9.22   Hemifield neglect or unilateral visual neglect.

Patients with this neurological condition ignore one half of the visual world (usually the left). These pictures show how patients with hemifield neglect interpret the world. They understand that a clock should have 12 numbers, but because they ignore half of the world, they put all 12 numbers on one side of the clock.

Bálint's Syndrome

Bálint's syndrome is a rare condition in which function in both the left and right posterior parietal lobes has been compromised. Patients with this condition have a limited ability to localize objects in space. This results in difficulty grasping for objects, probably its most salient symptom. In addition, patients with Bálint's syndrome seldom move their eyes. As a consequence of this, they have a condition called simultagnosia. **Simultagnosia** is a deficit in perceiving more than one object at a time. Thus, they focus on the one object that is presented directly in front of them and ignore other stimuli. This makes them similar to patients with unilateral neglect, except that patients with Bálint's syndrome ignore both the left and right visual world. Actual patients with Bálint's syndrome can also be seen on YouTube (e.g., http://www.youtube.com/watch?v=4odhSq46vtU).

Bálint's syndrome: a neurological condition caused by damage to both the left and right posterior parietal lobes

Simultagnosia: a deficit in perceiving more than one object at a time

TEST YOUR KNOWLEDGE

What is hemifield neglect? Why is it considered to be an issue of attention?

DEVELOPMENTAL ASPECTS OF VISUAL ATTENTION

9.4   Identify what factors lead to the development of visual attention.

When does the ability to attend develop? Are young infants born with the ability to select locations in space they wish to attend to, or are newborns caught in a world of stimuli without this ability? Is there an age at which we learn to covertly direct attention to a point in space other than the one we are looking at? There are many pertinent questions in the development of visual attention. We just examine a small sample of the possible answers to these questions here.

Attention in very young infants is determined by how long they can maintain a gaze at an interesting stimulus, whether that stimulus is a colorful collage or images of their mothers (see Figure 9.23). As most parents suspect, it turns out that at quite a young age, infants can maintain the direction of gaze for a considerable time, indicative of attentional control (Colombo, 2002).

One means of studying attention in young infants is with a technique called the oddball procedure. In this procedure, an infant is shown a series of related objects (e.g., different kinds of balls). However, after a number of balls have been shown to the infant, a novel object from a different category is shown to the infant (a stuffed animal). In older children, the novel object attracts attention. In infants, such attention would be called stimulus orienting, as the infant focuses on the novel object. This procedure can then be combined with neuroimaging techniques such as using the event-related potential analysis of EEG recording (Richards, Reynolds, & Courage, 2010). Richards et al. (2010) compared infants who were alert and those who were not (i.e., sleepy). They also compared infants at 4, 5, and 7 months of age in an oddball paradigm. Alert babies and older babies showed greater activity as measured by electroencephalography. In addition, alert babies, regardless of age, showed greater EEG activity when presented with the oddball item. Thus, infants as young as 4 months orient toward novel stimuli (Richards et al., 2010).

■ **FIGURE 9.23**   **Infants and attention.**

Do young infants have the ability to direct their attention to specific objects in the environment?

Other recent neuroimaging studies suggest that orientation in the oddball paradigm is accomplished by the same areas of the brain that are associated with selective attention in older children and adults. These brain regions include areas in the extrastriate cortex as well as the posterior parietal lobe. Richards et al. (2010) superimposed the EEG activity discussed above on magnetic resonance images of infant brains to confirm this (see Figure 9.24). If you inspect Figure 9.24, you can see the areas of the brain active in an infant brain during the oddball task.

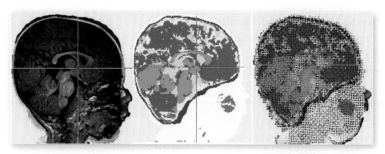

■ **FIGURE 9.24**   **Neuroimaging attention in the infant brain.**

Activity includes brain regions such as the extrastriate cortex and the posterior parietal lobe.

Many adults complain that if a television set is playing, they have difficulty concentrating on their jobs or on their studies. Indeed, we are sure that you have heard professors advise you not to study with the television on. However, infants may function a bit differently in this regard. Setliff and Courage (2011) examined infants at 6 and 12 months of age during play with novel toys. The infants were allowed to play with the toys while a television was either playing or not playing in the background. They found little difference in the attention infants gave to the toys, and very little difference in directed glances at the television during the session. Thus, it is likely that background noise provided by a television is less distracting to infants than it is to adults. In this one regard, we might conclude that infants are better at selective attention than their older family members. Certainly, we know from the literature on aging that older adults have a harder time inhibiting responses to irrelevant stimuli than younger adults, and it looks like the youngest members of our species are even better.

TEST YOUR KNOWLEDGE

What is the oddball paradigm? How can it be used to tell us about the development of visual attention?

IN DEPTH: *Awareness and Visual Consciousness*

For a philosopher, one of the fundamental questions about perception is the following: How can a physical system composed of brain, eyes, and neurons and made of organic materials, such as proteins and fats, produce conscious visual experiences, such as the experience of seeing green or the joy in watching a cat swish its tail when it wakes up from a nap (see Figure 9.25)? Philosophers of mind argue endlessly whether we can account for awareness and consciousness with purely material explanations, even though they acknowledge that without brains and eyes, no seeing would ever occur. This paradox—that the neural processes of seeing do not resemble in any way the subjective experience of seeing—has led neuroscience to examine if we can find the neural correlates of consciousness.

Vision and attention provide a great laboratory for looking at the neural correlates of consciousness, because clearly when you are looking at and attending to an object, such as a cup of chocolate mousse, you are conscious of that object. But as we have seen in this chapter, with phenomena such as change blindness, inattentional blindness, and unilateral visual neglect, that you are conscious of seeing the mousse does not mean that you will consciously perceive the moose and the mouse, approaching from different directions, which just might attempt to eat your mousse. Thus, in this section, we will examine what two phenomenal experiences, perceptual bistability and blindsight, can tell us about awareness and vision.

Perceptual Bistability

Perceptual bistability is one of those phenomena you must see before you can believe, understand, or study. So first go to ISLE 9.5 to see it and experiment with it. You can **ISLE 9.5** Perceptual Bistability

■ FIGURE 9.25   **A sleepy cat.**

Many cat owners will smile at the relaxed pose and poise of the cat in this photo. Why does seeing a cat feel the way it does?

© iStockphoto.com/chictype

also use a pair of three-dimensional (3D) glasses to inspect Figure 9.26. The anaglyph here provides an opportunity to see a bistable image. In examining Figure 9.26, note how first you see the face, and then it fades out and is replaced by the flower, only to have the flower fade out and be replaced by the face again. This is the essence of perceptual bistability.

We can define **perceptual bistability** as the phenomena in which a static visual image leads to alternating perceptions. Perceptual bistability occurs in a number of common illusions, such as the Necker cube, the rabbit-duck image, and the faces-vase image, all of which can be seen in Figure 9.27.

■ FIGURE 9.26   Perceptual bistability and binocular rivalry.

A bistable image anaglyph. Using a pair of anaglyph glasses, you can look at this image. You should sometimes see one image, sometimes the other. However, if you close one eye and then the other, while using the anaglyph glasses, you can clearly see each image.

■ FIGURE 9.27   Famous bistable images.

Each of these drawings has two different interpretations. Most people report seeing one interpretation and then the other but never both simultaneously.

Perceptual bistability: a phenomenon in which a static visual image leads to alternating perceptions

Binocular rivalry: a phenomenon that occurs when a separate image is presented to each eye

Each of these figures creates a paradox for our visual system. For example, in the Necker cube, what we really see are some lines on a two-dimensional surface, namely, the paper of your book or the screen of your computer. However, the lines suggest a 3D cube, and we tend to interpret this figure in three dimensions. However, there are two possible 3D interpretations of this two-dimensional figure. So our perceptual systems may flip back and forth from one to the other. Of interest here is that the exact same physical stimulus creates two separate perceptual experiences.

One of the most striking examples of perceptual bistability comes from a phenomenon known as binocular rivalry. **Binocular rivalry** occurs when a separate image is presented to each eye. Figure 9.26 illustrates the perceptual bistability that arises from binocular rivalry. If you look at the image through just the red filter of a pair of 3D glasses, you see only the "red" image. If you look through only the blue filter of the 3D glasses, you see only the "blue" image. Thus, when you are using both filters, one over each eye, each eye is getting a separate image. Binocular rivalry illustrates a number of important points about awareness in vision. First, our visual system is set up to see a single perception of the world, rather than a separate perception from each eye. Thus, when each eye is seeing a completely different image, rather than creating a double image of the world, it systematically inhibits one perception or the other. Second, it also demonstrates the top-down processing aspect of perception. We usually see the more "important" image more than the less important image. Thus, we usually see a face longer than another stimulus in the display in Figure 9.26 (Sandberg et al., 2013).

In an early study with fMRI, Tong, Nakayama, Vaughan, and Kanwisher (1998) examined two regions of the brain during binocular rivalry. They presented an image that produces binocular rivalry like the one depicted in Figure 9.26. They then focused their fMRI scanner on two regions of the brain, the fusiform face area, which we know is involved in face processing, and another nearby area called the parahippocampal area, which responds well to specific objects such as houses. While participants were being monitored by the fMRI scanner, they indicated whether they were visually conscious of the face or the house. They were asked to press one button to indicate that they were conscious of the face and another button to indicate that they were conscious of the house. Amazingly, when the participants perceived the face, Tong et al. showed that participants had more activity in the fusiform face area, but when participants perceived the house, they had more activity in the parahippocampal region (see Figure 9.28). Other studies since have shown that lower areas in the visual cortex also change responses, depending on which image is being perceived, including V1 and the lateral geniculate nucleus (Meng, Remus, & Tong, 2005). Thus, activity in these areas tracked the participants' visual consciousness rather than the identical nature of the stimuli (see Tong, Meng, & Blake, 2006).

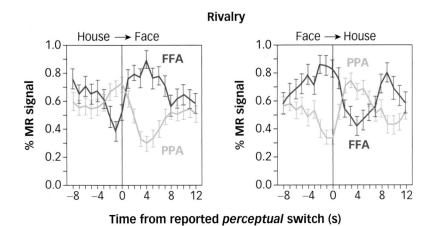

Rivalry

■ **FIGURE 9.28**   Bistability in the brain (Tong, Nakayama, Vaughan, & Kanwisher, 1998).

When participants perceived the face, there was more activity in the fusiform face area, but when participants perceived the house, there was more activity in the parahippocampal region.

Blindsight

One of the most fascinating neuropsychological conditions is known by the odd name of blindsight. **Blindsight** refers to the residual ability to make visual responses when a patient is subjectively blind in certain regions of his or her visual field. This means, paradoxically, that patients with this condition are making visual responses to stimuli they cannot see. This may strike you as very odd—they cannot see, but they are making visual responses? It almost makes no sense. But let us describe a patient who has blindsight, and you will understand what this means.

Patient T.N. is a medical doctor, originally from a nation in Africa, who has been living in Switzerland for many years. Patient T.N. had two strokes less than a month apart in the early 2000s. The strokes caused permanent and complete damage to both the left (first stroke) and right (second stroke) V1 regions of his occipital cortex. The rest of his brain was seemingly intact, and there was no damage to his eyes. There is no other neurological damage, and T.N. has no history of psychiatric problems. He remains an intelligent and interested person. Nonetheless, the damage to V1 left T.N. experiencing complete blindness (Buetti et al., 2013). T.N. reports no visual experience whatsoever, and in most ways, acts as if he is blind. This is confirmed by fMRI studies that show no activity in V1 or indeed in the extrastriate cortex when lights are shined directly into T.N.'s eyes (Buetti et al., 2013).

However, without being consciously aware that he is using vision, T.N. can do a number of tasks solely on the basis of vision alone. For example, when shown an image of an object on either the left side or the right side of a computer, T.N. reports being unable to see anything, but when forced to guess,

he correctly reports the location of the image in over 75% of trials (Buetti et al., 2013). In another study with T.N., Pegna, Khateb, Lazeyras, and Seghier (2005) showed that he could distinguish the emotions of faces presented to him—of course in the absence of any visual experience. As in all studies, T.N. believes that he is guessing, even when his accuracy is quite high. In a fascinating demonstration of T.N.'s blindsight abilities, his doctors made a video of him walking down a hospital corridor, avoiding obstacles as he goes. Take a moment to watch this video (http://www.youtube.com/watch?v=ACkxe_5Ubq8). (see ISLE 9.6) In the test, considerable effort was made to ensure

ISLE 9.6 Video of Navigation in Blindsight

that T.N. could not use sound echoes to navigate. He avoided obstacles strictly on the basis of visual information, despite his experience of complete blindness. In the video, the man who is walking behind T.N. to ensure he does not fall is Lawrence Weiskrantz, one of the pioneers in blindsight research. What you will see in the video is a blind man guiding himself around objects using only visual information. This paradoxical situation results from some interesting features of the human brain.

More than 40 years ago, Weiskrantz initiated the investigation of this phenomenon by studying a young man who had a brain tumor in his right V1 that was removed by surgery (Weiskrantz, Warrington, Sanders, & Marshall, 1974). The surgery cured the patient of seizures he was having and allowed the patient to return to both his job as a computer programmer and his hobbies as an athlete and a musician. The patient, D.B., was left with a scotoma (an area of blindness) in his left visual world, but he was otherwise able to resume his normal life. Unlike T.N., who is completely blind, D.B. has normal vision in his right visual world as well as part of his left visual world. Thus, for practical purposes, his vision is sufficient to allow him to function visually.

But when D.B. keeps his eyes still, he can see little consciously in his left visual world. Thus, Weiskrantz et al. (1974) were able to compare his normal vision on the right with his reports of being blind on the left. Despite his reporting no vision in this scotoma region, D.B. was able to distinguish squares from diamonds, X's from O's, and horizontal lines from vertical lines in the blind field. Of course, DB thought he was guessing, but his guesses were consistently

Blindsight: the presence of visual abilities in the absence of the visual cortex; the patient claims to be blind but make visual responses

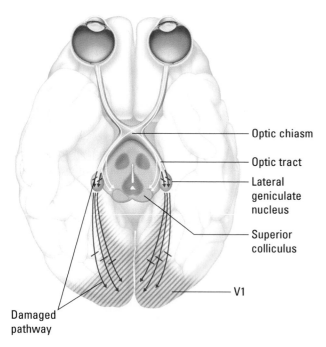

Optic chiasm

Optic tract

Lateral
geniculate
nucleus

Superior
colliculus

V1

Damaged
pathway

■ FIGURE 9.29   The pathways in blindsight.

In people with blindsight, the route from the retinae to the lateral geniculate nucleus to V1 has been damaged. It is this route that supports conscious seeing. However, other routes, such as the link from the retinae to the superior colliculi, may support visual response in the absence of visual consciousness.

above chance. So the question arises, How can someone make visual responses without having the conscious experience of seeing?

At this point, you should be quite familiar with the anatomy of the visual system. You may remember from Chapter 4 that the retinae of the eyes project to many different areas in the brain. The majority of retinal axons project to the lateral geniculate nucleus and from there to the occipital lobe. It is likely that this is the pathway that leads to conscious visual experience. Indeed, it is this pathway that is damaged in T.N., D.B., and others who have blindsight. However, the retinae also project to other areas of the brain. Weiskrantz hypothesized that the responses made by patients with blindsight might be the result of behavior produced by these alternate routes (see Weiskrantz, 2009). In particular, Weiskrantz focused on the route from the retinae to the superior colliculus. The superior colliculus is a region of the brain instrumental in making visually guided head movements as well as eye movements. Weiskrantz hypothesized that because this route is still intact in patients with damage to V1, the superior colliculus can guide their visual responses, even though the route that produces conscious vision, that is, V1, is damaged. Thus, the superior colliculus can allow visual responses in the absence of seeing (see Figure 9.29).

Interestingly, research now shows that the superior colliculus projects axons to higher areas of visual processing in the occipital lobe. So the visual responding seen in patients such as D.B. and T.N. may be the result of this connection between the superior colliculus and the occipital cortex, rather than just the superior colliculus alone. However, even if this is the case, this route, though strong enough to allow visual response, is not sufficient to create a sense of conscious visual experience in these patients.

CHAPTER SUMMARY

9.1   Explain selective and divided attention.

Alertness is a state of vigilance. When alert, we are awake, mindful, and likely scanning our surroundings. Awareness is actively thinking about something, which can be either physically present or just in our imagination. Attention is a set of processes that allow us to select or focus on some stimuli. Attention can also be sustained or temporary. Selective attention can be defined as the processes of attention that allow us to focus on one source when many are present. Divided attention is the process of attending to multiple sources of information. A question we can ask, however, is whether it is possible to attend to spatial locations other than the location we are looking at. Posner and his colleagues investigated this phenomenon. A cue is given that a target will occur in a particular region of space. In most trials, the target does appear in the cued location, but in some it does not. Even though participants cannot look at the cued area, their response times are

faster when the cues are accurate. This tells us that we can devote attention covertly, that is, direct attention to a location in space we are not looking at directly with our foveae.

9.2   Describe the nature of attentional capture and how it works in our visual system.

Stimulus salience means that some objects in the environment attract our attention. Attentional capture occurs when a salient stimulus causes us to shift attention to that stimulus. A history of previous reward and relevant semantic meaning both tend to capture our attention. Change blindness is the difficulty we experience in detecting differences between two visual stimuli that are identical except for one or more changes to the image. In a surprising finding, Simons and Levin (1997) found that participants could even be change blind to the substitution of one person for another. Inattentional blindness is a phenomenon in which people fail to perceive an object or event that is visible but not attended to. Chabris and Simons (1999) conducted the famous gorilla experiment to demonstrate that salient stimuli can actually be missed when the focus of attention is elsewhere. Visual search means looking for a specific target in an image with distracting objects. Feature search means searching for a target in which the target is specified by a single feature. Conjunction search means searching for a target in which the target is specified by a combination of features. Feature integration theory stipulates that some features can be processed in parallel and quickly prior to using attentional resources. Other visual characteristics require us to use attention and are done serially and therefore less quickly. Rapid serial visual presentation (RSVP) is an experimental paradigm in which a series of stimuli appear rapidly in time at the same point in visual space. Participants must direct their attention across the time domain rather than the space domain. Findings show that people can respond quickly to a particular stimulus when it occurs in time. Attentional blink is the tendency to respond more slowly or not at all to the second target in an RSVP task when the second stimulus occurs within 500 ms of the first stimulus. Repetition blindness is the failure to detect the second target in an RSVP task when the second target is identical to the first one. Like attentional blink, it occurs when the second target is presented 500 ms or less after the first target.

9.3 Explain the differences between the orienting attention network and the executive attention network.

The orienting attention network (or dorsal attention network) allows us to engage in visual search and direct our visual attention to different locations in visual space. The orienting attention network is located primarily in the parietal lobe.

The executive attention network focuses on attention as the inhibition of habitual responses and the top-down control of attention. The executive attention network is found in the frontal lobe.

9.4 Identify what factors lead to the development of visual attention.

Moran and Desimone (1985) found that at a physiological level, attention can affect the processing of visual information. Attention acts to decrease the activity of a cell when the effective stimulus for that cell is not being attended to. Hemifield neglect, or unilateral visual neglect, is a condition in which a person fails to attend to stimuli on one side of the visual world (usually the left) as a consequence of neurological damage to the posterior parietal lobe. Bálint's syndrome is a neurological condition caused by damage to both the left and right posterior parietal lobes. Simult-agnosia is a deficit in perceiving more than one object at a time. Perceptual bistability is a phenomenon in which a static visual image leads to alternating perceptions. Binocular rivalry occurs when a separate image is presented to each eye. Binocular rivalry results in perceptual bistability as viewers see the image presented to one eye for a while before the perception shifts to what the other eye is viewing. Blindsight is the residual ability to make visual responses when a patient is subjectively blind in certain regions of his or her visual field. Patients will say that they are blind in regions of their visual fields, but make responses anyway. It is likely that the blindness is caused by damage to area V1 of the occipital cortex but that the residual vision is a function of intact structures, such as the superior colliculus.

REVIEW QUESTIONS

1. What is the difference between selective and divided attention? What function does attention serve in perception?

2. How did Posner and his colleagues study covert attention? Describe their experiment and its results. What do these results tell us about covert attention?

3. What is attentional capture? Describe an experiment reviewed in the textbook that examines features of attentional capture.

4. What is the difference between change blindness and inattentional blindness? Describe an example of each. Why are change blindness and inattentional blindness considered errors of attention?

5. What is feature integration theory? How does it explain feature searches and conjunction searches?

6. What is the rapid serial visual presentation (RSVP) paradigm? How is it conducted in the lab, and what aspect of attention does it measure?

7. What are the orienting attention network and the executive attention network? What area of the brain is each located in? What aspects of attention do they serve?

8. What is unilateral neglect? What are its symptoms? What kind of brain damage causes it?

9. What is binocular rivalry? How is it measured, and what principles of awareness does it demonstrate?

10. What is blindsight? Describe the deficits and preserved function in the patient T.N. What is typically thought of as the neurological basis for the preserved function in blindsight?

KEY TERMS

INTERACTIVE SENSATION LABORATORY EXERCISES (ISLE)

Experience chapter concepts at edge.sagepub.com/schwartz

Sharpen your skills with SAGE edge at edge.sagepub.com/schwartz

SAGE edge for students provides a personalized approach to help you accomplish your coursework goals in an easy-to-use learning environment.

Answer for Figure 9.11: In one image, there are three yellow and gold flowers in the lower left-hand corner. In the other image, there are only two yellow and gold flowers in the lower left-hand corner.

The Auditory System

10

INTRODUCTION

"Friends, Romans, countrymen, lend me your ears." So wrote William Shakespeare in his play *Julius Caesar* (1599). Of course, Caesar meant for his audience to listen to him, not actually allow him to borrow their ears. There was some confusion about this in the mind of one of your authors when he was a young boy and first heard this quotation from the play. But as is often the case with Shakespeare, he summarized quite a bit in one clever line. For all but a small population of sign-language speakers, sound means communication and the ability to talk and listen to others. To lend someone your ears means to listen to the language sounds that he or she is making. Indeed, one of the critical functions of hearing is to perceive and interpret the sound of the human voice. It is hard to imagine a world in which we could not hear one another talk, and for billions of people around the globe, sound and hearing also mean music, which brings us great enjoyment and peace of mind. Indeed, people who have gone deaf after a lifetime of hearing most often miss the ability to hear music.

Think of all the sounds you hear at any given moment. You may hear the whirring of the washing machine, the whining of the air conditioning, the distant buzz of cars on the road, a lawn mower from down the street, and the gentle lapping sounds of your cat drinking from its water bowl. Our ears are always open, and thus we hear these sounds all the time. This contrasts with vision, in that you can close your eyes. In some cases, sounds such as the ones just described may become distracting. In this case, you may create your own world of sound by putting on headphones or ear buds. In this case, listening to your favorite music allows you to concentrate on the sounds you want to hear, not simply those present in the environment. Alternatively, you may put in earplugs to drown out external sound. Although this may succeed in dampening unwanted sound, many people find the silence of this to be strange (see Figure 10.1). Moreover, sound comes at us from all directions. We see only in front of us, but we hear from all 360°. This is likely why wailing sounds, such as a siren, and not flashing lights indicate emergencies that are out of visual range. In sum, we live in a world engulfed in sound.

As with every perceptual system, the essence of hearing is transforming information available in the environment, in this case, sound pressure waves, into a perception we can use to understand the world and guide our actions. As we work through the sensory processes involved in hearing and the perceptual processes involved in speech perception and music perception, you can note both the similarities and the differences between audition and vision. They share similar physiological mechanisms, but these mechanisms must be modified for the specific modality they are responsible for.

LEARNING OBJECTIVES

10.1 Discuss the physical nature of sound and how it correlates with the perceptual nature of sound.

10.2 Describe the basic anatomy of the ear and the difference between the outer, middle, and inner ear.

10.3 Examine the nature of hearing loss and what can be done to improve hearing in hearing-impaired individuals.

SOUND AS STIMULUS

10.1 Discuss the physical nature of sound and how it correlates with the perceptual nature of sound.

In the movie *Alien* (1979), one of the scariest movies ever made, the tag line is "In space, no one can hear you scream." As effective as this is in building tension before you even go into the movie theater (and maybe eliciting screams in the theater), the statement is true, in the sense that there needs to be a medium, such as air or water, to conduct sound. In the absence of such a medium, as in the near vacuum of space, sound cannot exist. So before we can discuss the physiological and psychological processes that allow us to hear, we need to understand a little bit about what sound is.

The **sound stimulus** is the periodic variations in air pressure traveling out from the source of the variations. That is, these periodic variations in pressure are the sound wave, and the source of the variations is the object making the sound. Over time, air pressure will increase and decrease slightly, and these small changes in air pressure constitute sound to our ears if they occur strongly enough and quickly enough. Sound can also be transmitted through other media, such as water, bones, and train tracks—anything that can vibrate. Water transmits sound faster than air does, making it more difficult for a scuba diver to localize a sound underwater than for a person on land. Even someone just swimming in a pool may notice how difficult it is to tell where a sound is coming from. Mostly, humans hear in an air medium, and occasionally in a water medium, but really anything that can reverberate or change in pressure over time can transmit sound. Think of the Old West sheriff listening for the bad guys by putting his ear to the train track. The iron of the rail can also transmit sound, which tells the sheriff when the train is coming and therefore when the train robbers will be coming.

Think of what happens when you clap your hands. The pressure of your hands against each other compresses the air between them, creating the pressure wave. This compression of the air between your hands causes the air molecules to collide with other air molecules in each and every direction around your hands, which then collide with air molecules farther away from your hands, and so on and so forth. As the air molecules are compressed in each area of space, just behind them is a small area in which the air pressure is lower because some of the molecules have been pushed forward. Thus, sound consists of pockets of higher pressure air followed by pockets of lower pressure air. Changes in air pressure propagate outward from the original source of the disturbance, in this case your hands clapping (see Figure 10.2). For a demonstration of this, go to ISLE 10.1a.

When you clap your hands, you disturb the air around your hands and initiate the pattern of high- and low-pressure air movements that move out in all directions from the source. This pattern is called a sound wave. **Sound waves** are the waves of pressure changes that occur in the air as a function of the vibration of a source. Sound waves are like any kind of wave—the wave moves through its medium even though particles within the wave may stay in the same place, just as a standing wave stays put on a river. In the case of sound, the source of the sound is your hands when you clap. The source of the sound could be air blown through a brass instrument or the vibrating of strings on a guitar. Air molecules do not travel very far themselves, as they basically just move back and forth from high-pressure to low-pressure areas, but the wave of pressure change moves across space, causing compression (high pressure) and rarefaction (low pressure)

■ FIGURE 10.1 **Ear protection.**

People who do jobs with a lot of noise nearby are often advised to wear ear protection. Little earplugs like this can block out loud noise.

ISLE 10.1 The Sound Stimulus

Sound stimulus: the periodic variations in air pressure traveling out from the source of the variations

Sound waves: the waves of pressure changes that occur in the air as a function of the vibration of a source

Pressure in small volumes of air molecules

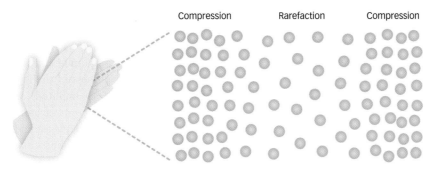

Compression   Rarefaction   Compression

■ **FIGURE 10.2** The propagation of sound through a medium.

When a person claps, air pressure changes are created. The clap creates a compression of air between the hands, which pushes against the air adjacent to it in all directions. The compression creates a rarefaction of air next to it, which alternates with the compression and propagates through the air.

across space, sometimes at great distances, depending on how forceful the original sound was. In this wave, there will be a peak high in air pressure and a peak low in air pressure. Although the physics of light are much more complicated, sound can be measured in an analogous manner, namely, by measuring wavelength and its inverse, frequency. The time between two consecutive high peaks is the cycle of a sound wave. **Cycles** can be measured in their number per second, also known as frequency (see Figure 10.3). Finally, the energy in any sound wave will weaken across time and space. Your clap may sound very loud to you because you are so close to it. But to your friend in another room, it will be audible but not loud. By the time the sound wave gets through the door and out into the street, the energy may have dropped off so much that a person walking by on the sidewalk may not hear it at all. You can see a demonstration of this on ISLE 10.1b.

Under normal conditions, at sea level, sound travels very fast, but much more slowly than light. Sound travels at about 344 m/s (761.2 mph). This is a bit faster than a civilian jet plane (a typical jet on its way from Chicago to New York travels at a peak speed of 550 mph). However, we have planes, mostly used by the military, that can equal and exceed the speed of sound. Indeed, the military has planes that exceed the speed of sound by as much as 3 times ("Mach 3" in military terms means 3 times the speed of sound). Such high speeds are avoided for typical civilian aircraft because they leave a tremendous wake of sound, called a sonic boom, behind them (see Figure 10.4). Interestingly, because the planes themselves are going faster than the sounds they make, pilots and passengers on such supersonic planes experience an incredibly quiet ride.

Although the speed of sound is very high, there are times when we may notice a lag between sound and sight. If the source of a sound is 100 m away, there will be a lag of about 0.3 seconds between when we see the hands clapping and when we hear the sound. Thus, a person watching a sprint race from just behind the finish line will see the gun go off and then hear it a split second later. When we shout across a canyon toward a cliff, the echo is not simultaneous with our shout; it takes time for our shout to reach the distant cliff and for the echo to return. The lag of sound relative to light also accounts for the delay in hearing thunder after we see lightning. Thunder and lightning result from the same event: it is simply that the light reaches your eyes much more quickly than the sound reaches your ears. Interestingly, in water, sound travels about 4 times faster than it does through air (1,483 m/s).

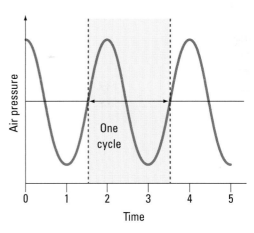

■ **FIGURE 10.3** Frequency or wavelength of sound.

The vibrations coming from an object, such as hands clapping, can be measured by looking at the pattern of increasing and decreasing air pressure. One cycle is the amount of time it takes for air to return to the same state of air pressure at an earlier point in the wave or, more technically, the time between two consecutive high peaks.

Cycle: in a sound wave, the amount of time between one peak of high pressure and the next

REUTERS/Ho New

■ **FIGURE 10.4**

This U.S. Air Force F-22 Raptor is capable of exceeding the speed of sound. Its top speed is Mach 1.8 or nearly twice the speed of sound.

The Relation of Physical and Perceptual Attributes of Sound

If you recall, when examining what light is, we talked about light as a wave. In examining waves, there are two important measures, their amplitude and their wavelength. Amplitude, for light, means the intensity or brightness of the light, and wavelength dictates the color. Sound has similar attributes—amplitude and frequency (the inverse of wavelength). We also consider the concept of waveform, that is, how different frequencies interact with one other to create complex sounds, which also affects our auditory perception. Each of these physical attributes maps onto a perceptual attribute. Amplitude maps onto loudness, frequency maps onto pitch, and waveform maps onto timbre. To start off our discussion, however, we consider **pure tones**, that is, sound waves in which air pressure changes follow the basic sine wave format. A pure tone is heard at a particular pitch but does not have the complexity you would expect when hearing a musical instrument (or a voice) play (or sing) that particular pitch. So we consider each of these attributes now (see Figure 10.5). To listen to a sample of pure tones, go to ISLE 10.1c.

Amplitude and Loudness

The **amplitude** of a sound is expressed as the difference between its maximum and minimum sound pressures. Thus, as with ocean waves, as any surfer will tell you, taller waves are stronger waves. A strong clap produces a bigger change in air pressure than a mild, not-quite-excited clap. Dropping a hammer results in a greater amplitude sound wave than does dropping a feather. Think about the amount of air that gets displaced when an airplane rushes by. This force of the airplane creates large-amplitude sound waves, which can be heard for miles

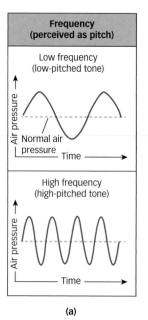
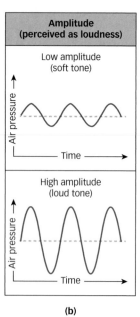
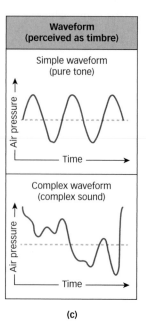

Frequency (perceived as pitch)	**Amplitude** (perceived as loudness)	**Waveform** (perceived as timbre)
Low frequency (low-pitched tone)	Low amplitude (soft tone)	Simple waveform (pure tone)
High frequency (high-pitched tone)	High amplitude (loud tone)	Complex waveform (complex sound)
(a)	(b)	(c)

Pure tone: a sound wave in which changes in air pressure follow a sine wave pattern

Amplitude: the difference between maximum and minimum sound pressures

■ FIGURE 10.5   Amplitude, frequency, and waveform.

(a) Difference between a low- and a high-frequency sound. The perceptual equivalent of frequency is pitch. (b) Difference between a low- and a high-amplitude sound. The perceptual equivalent of amplitude is loudness. (c) Difference between a simple waveform or pure tone and a complex sound. Complex waveforms contribute to our perception of timbre.

in all directions. Amplitude has a very clear psychophysical correlate. **Loudness** is the perceptual experience of amplitude or the intensity of a sound stimulus. High-amplitude (high-intensity) sounds will be heard as loud, and low-amplitude (low-intensity) sounds will be heard as soft. Thus, a person screaming produces greater amplitude of the human voice than does a person whispering.

Amplitude is usually measured in decibels. A **decibel (dB)** is 1/10 of a bel, which is a unit of sound intensity named in honor of Alexander Graham Bell. The decibel scale is a logarithmic scale. This means that the intensity (amplitude) of a sound increases more quickly than the numbers along the decibel scale. With every 6 dB, the sound pressure actually doubles. A decibel level of 120 is nearly 1 million times greater in terms of sound pressure than a decibel level of 10. The formula to determine decibel level is given by (this is one of the few formulas we actually include in this book)

$$dB = 10\log(p^2/p_r^2),$$

in which dB is the sound pressure level, p is the measured sound pressure (in another unit called micropascals), and p_r is an agreed-upon reference sound pressure. Sound measures of decibels are measures of relative intensity, so it is important to know what both sounds are. In this case, p_r derives from the auditory threshold that is being used as the comparison sound. In this case, the measure should be give as dB_{SPL}, where *SPL* stands for "sound pressure level." Figure 10.6 gives the approximate decibel levels of a number of common sounds.

What this means in terms of our loudness perception is that we can hear sounds across a wide range of amplitudes, from really quiet sounds (the proverbial pin dropping) to sounds so loud that they can damage our ears. In addition, we are remarkably good at detecting differences in loudness. Under quiet conditions at average frequencies (e.g., 2,000 Hz), we can discriminate a difference of just 1 dB. For example, if a series of simple pure tones are played one after the other, at the same frequency, we can detect the one tone that is 1 dB stronger than the other tones. We can perform similarly with complex tones as well (see ISLE 10.2).

Loud sounds can be dangerous. Prolonged contact with sounds above 85 dB can cause hearing loss in the long run. That is, people who work around such loud sounds or play loud music frequently run the risk of damaging their hearing. This might include the 90-dB sounds of airplanes taking off from the perspective of a baggage handler. This is why people who work on the tarmac are supposed to wear ear protection, to reduce that 90-dB level to something less harmful.

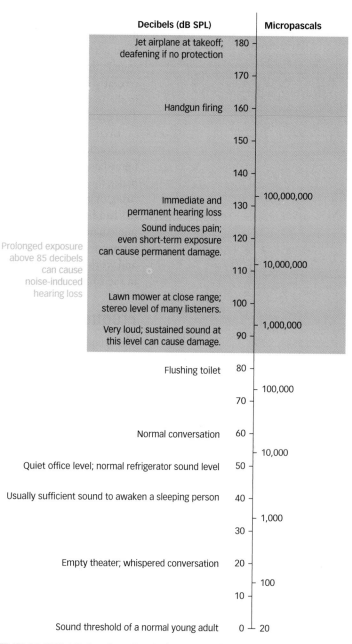

■ FIGURE 10.6   **Amplitude (loudness) of common sounds.**

Sustained exposure to sounds over 85 dB is potentially damaging, and even short 1-second exposures to sounds over 120 dB can result in immediate hearing damage.

ISLE 10.2 The Decibel Scale

Loudness: the perceptual experience of the amplitude or intensity of a sound stimulus

Decibel (dB): a physical unit that measures sound amplitude

Firearms instructors and other people who spend extended time at firing ranges may also experience hearing loss in the long run, even if they wear ear protection. Even with a 30-dB reduction from ear protection, many firearms will still produce sounds that can damage the shooter's ears. Finally, many people listen to car stereos at sound levels that approach or exceed 100 dB, which can lead to damage in the long run. Even a hairdryer at close range can exceed 85 dB, so be careful. There is a moral here—be mindful of your daily exposure to such loud sounds.

Even louder sounds can cause immediate damage. Sounds louder than 120 dB are decidedly painful, and sounds louder than 130 dB will generally result in immediate and permanent hearing loss. A jet airplane at close range may be 140 dB, hence the need for tarmac workers to protect their ears at all times. Similarly, the firing of guns is usually in excess of 160 dB at close range. Even small-caliber bullets can fire at nearly 140 dB. Thus, firing a gun without ear protection can cause immediate damage to one's ears. Most standard ear protection for shooters and tarmac workers results in only a net reduction of 30 dB, which puts the shooters and workers out of the range of pain and immediate damage but leaves them high in the zone of sounds that cause long-term damage.

Frequency and Pitch

The frequency of a sound stimulus refers to the number of cycles in the sound wave that occur in 1 second. The perceptual correlate of frequency is pitch. Tones that have low frequencies are heard as being low in pitch, whereas tones that have high frequencies are heard as high in pitch (see ISLE 10.3). We define **frequency** as the number of cycles in a sound stimulus that occur in 1 second. **Pitch** is the subjective experience of sound that is most closely associated with the frequency of a sound stimulus.

Remember that frequency and wavelength are inverses of each other. Frequency is the number of cycles per second, and wavelength is the time course of one cycle. Thus, as the frequency gets larger, the wavelength gets smaller, and vice versa. For arbitrary reasons, we use a wavelength measure when discussing vision but a frequency measure when discussing sound. This is not done just in this book to confuse you, our readers, but is the convention in all fields that concern themselves with physical measurements of light and sound. Frequency is measured in **hertz (Hz)**, which is a unit of measure indicating the number of cycles per second, named after the German physicist Heinrich Hertz. A sound that has 200 cycles per second (i.e., 200 ups and downs per second) is said to be 200 Hz. A sound that has 20,000 cycles per second (i.e., 20,000 ups and downs per second) is said to be 20,000 Hz.

The psychological equivalent of frequency is pitch. Pitch is the subjective experience of sound that is most closely associated with the frequency of a sound stimulus. Lower frequencies are heard as lower in pitch, and higher frequencies are heard as higher in pitch. Think of the typical man's voice and woman's voice. Typically, women have voices with higher pitches than those of men. You can also think of a piano keyboard. If you play the note farthest to the left, you are playing a note with a low frequency (27 Hz). Play the note farthest to the right, and you are playing a note with a high frequency (4,186 Hz). Middle C is 261 Hz (see Figure 10.7). You can hear how frequency relates to pitch in ISLE 10.3.

Children and young adults can hear over a range from about 20 to 20,000 Hz (Yost, 2007). As we get into our late 20s and beyond, we lose much of our hearing in the highest range. By the time one is 40 years old, it is unlikely that frequencies above 14,000 Hz are heard. By the time one is 50 years old, this upper limit may be down to 12,000 Hz. Dr. Krantz describes an experience in his lab when he was a graduate student in which the students complained to the professor about

ISLE 10.3 Frequency and Pitch on a Piano

Frequency (sound stimulus): in a sound stimulus, the number of cycles that occur in a second

Pitch: the subjective experience of sound that is most closely associated with the frequency of a sound stimulus; related to the experience of whether the sound is high or low, such as the two ends of the keyboard of a piano

Hertz (Hz): a unit of measure indicating the number of cycles per second

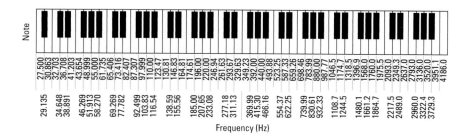

Frequency (Hz)

■ FIGURE 10.7   **Frequency and pitch.**

A piano keyboard nicely illustrates the relation between frequency and pitch. As one moves to the right from the keys farthest to the left on a piano, frequency increases. The lowest key on a piano is 27 Hz, whereas the highest is 4,186 Hz. As one moves from left to right on the piano keyboard, the notes increase from low in pitch to high in pitch.

loud, high-pitched, unpleasant sounds being produced by equipment in the lab. The professor, old enough to be deaf in this range, did not hear the sounds, but they were loud and painful to the younger people in the lab. The loss of high-frequency hearing is inevitable, but it may be exacerbated by exposure to loud sounds when young. The lowest frequencies, however, tend to remain stable with age. To determine your range of frequencies, go to ISLE 10.4.

Above 20,000 Hz and below 20 Hz, humans are simply deaf no matter how loud the sound is. Thus, we could play a sound at 30,000 Hz, and we would not hear it, regardless of the decibel level. However, your dog would hear the 30,000-Hz sound. If it was loud enough, the dog just might complain about it, too. In fact, dogs can hear up to about 50,000 Hz. This is the basis of the dog whistle, which makes a sound inaudible to us but perfectly audible to your dog. This allows you to communicate to your dog without other people being aware. Other animals can hear even higher frequencies than that. Bats and dolphins, for example, can hear frequencies up to about 200,000 Hz. These high frequencies are essential for their biosonar systems, which we discuss in the last section of this chapter. Other animals, such as elephants and humpback whales, can hear much lower frequency sounds than we can. Elephants, for example, use calls as low as 1 Hz for long-distance communication. These low-frequency sounds can travel farther than higher frequency sounds, and whales can make very loud low-frequency sounds that can be heard by other whales many miles away.

Losing these high frequencies has few consequences for understanding speech, as even the highest soprano's frequency is about 1,200 Hz. Similarly, music seldom reaches frequencies higher than 4,186 Hz (the highest note on a piano), which is higher than instruments noted for their high-pitch notes, such as violins and piccolos, can go. Losing the high frequencies does interfere with the perception of timbre, our next topic.

Waveform and Timbre

Imagine the difference between the sounds of a clarinet and a trumpet. A clarinet and trumpet may be playing the same note, such as a B-flat in the same octave (i.e., at the same frequency), and yet they still sound different. A trumpet's sound is pointed and comes right after you, even when played softly. A clarinet seems to have a more subtle sound, which seems to sneak up on you. Composers will call on trumpets often for happy or martial music, whereas the clarinet is often used to express a more sad sound. A piano playing the same note might sound more neutral than either the trumpet or the clarinet. How is it that different instruments playing the same note can sound so different? (To hear the sounds of different musical instruments, you can go to ISLE 10.5.) The difference in sound quality when different instruments play the same note has to do with the concept of harmonics. **Harmonics** are higher frequencies present in a complex sound that are integer multiples of the fundamental frequency (main frequency). There are a lot of terms in that definition that need explaining. So we will now take a step back and explain the concepts of the fundamental frequency, harmonics, and complex sound.

ISLE 10.4 Frequency Response of the Ear

ISLE 10.5 Timbre and Musical Instruments

Harmonics: higher frequencies present in a complex sound that are integer multiples of the fundamental frequency (main frequency)

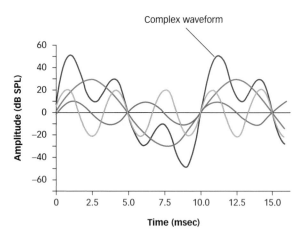

■ FIGURE 10.8   Complex waveforms.

When three notes (green, light blue, and orange) are combined, the result is a complex waveform (dark blue). Fourier analysis can be used to determine how the component waves are combined to create the complex waveform.

ISLE 10.6 Fourier Analysis in Audition

ISLE 10.7 Missing Fundamental

ISLE 10.8 Timbre and Overtones

Complex sound: a sound consisting of a mix of frequencies

Fourier analysis: a mathematical procedure for taking any complex waveform and determining the simpler waveforms that make up that complex pattern; the simpler waves used are sine waves

Fundamental frequency: the lowest frequency in a complex sound, which determines the perceived pitch of that sound

Timbre: the perceived sound differences between sounds with the same pitch but possessing different higher harmonics

Phase: the position in one cycle of a wave; there are 360° in a single cycle of a wave

Pure tones are simple sine waves at single frequencies. However, in nature, pure tones are virtually nonexistent. Almost all sounds are **complex sounds**, which consist of mixes of frequencies. These frequencies combine to form a complex waveform (see Figure 10.8). A complex waveform can be broken down into its composite frequencies through a mathematical formula known as Fourier analysis. **Fourier analysis** is a mathematical procedure for taking any complex waveform and determining the simpler waveforms that make up that complex pattern. The simpler waves used are sine waves. When we do a Fourier analysis, we break down a complex sound into its fundamental frequency and its harmonics. The **fundamental frequency** is the lowest frequency present in the complex sound and the one that determines the perceived pitch of that sound. The harmonics are all frequencies present in the stimulus that are higher in frequency than the fundamental frequency. The fundamental frequency determines the pitch of the sound, but the harmonics provide the timbre that makes the sound of the clarinet different from that of the trumpet or the piano. See ISLE 10.6 for a Fourier analysis of real sound in real time.

So now we continue to unpack this new vocabulary. The fundamental frequency determines the pitch. Thus, if the lowest frequency in a complex sound is 440 Hz, we will hear this note as a pitch at concert-tuning A. However, there may also be frequencies present at 880 Hz, 1,320 Hz, 1,760 Hz, 2,200 Hz, and so on. These additional frequencies represent the harmonics (see Figure 10.9). These harmonics determine the characteristics that give each instrument (or voice, or any sound) a distinct timbre when playing the same note. Observe that the fundamental frequency, though usually louder than its harmonics, need not be the loudest frequency. It is always the lowest frequency present in a sound. Even if the first harmonic is louder than the fundamental frequency, as it is in a clarinet, we still hear the pitch at the fundamental frequency. Indeed, we can remove the fundamental frequency altogether, and we will still hear the pitch at the missing fundamental. We hear the missing fundamental's pitch because the sequence of harmonics implies its presence (Schwartz & Purves, 2004). ISLE 10.7 illustrates pitch both with and without the fundamental frequency.

We hear these differences in the relative strength of harmonics as differences in timbre. **Timbre** is the musical term that refers to the perceived sound differences between sounds with the same pitch but possessing different higher harmonics. Timbre provides the richness in sound we perceive when we hear a good violinist playing on a well-made violin. Well-made violins have a greater array of harmonics than do cheap violins. The relative loudness of different higher harmonics contributes to timbre, but there are other factors that contribute as well; we will wait to consider these factors until Chapter 12. To hear differences in timbre, go to ISLE 10.8.

Phase

The last characteristic of sound stimuli we consider is **phase**. Remember that sound is a change in sound pressure over time and space. Think about that clap again. It creates a wave of high-pressure peaks and low-pressure troughs that propagate

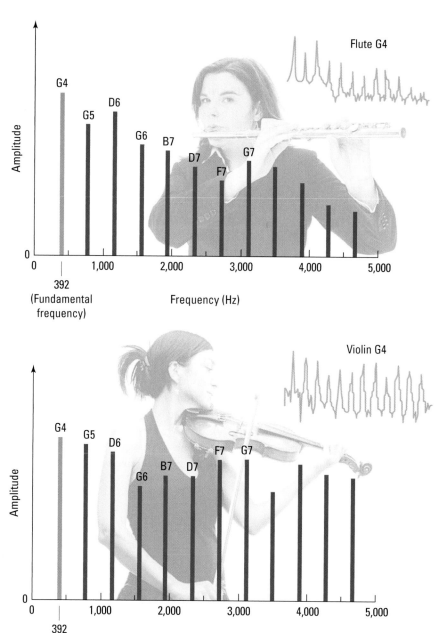

FIGURE 10.9 Fundamental frequency and harmonics of common musical instruments.

The fundamental frequency is the lowest frequency produced when playing a particular note, though it need not be the loudest frequency. The higher harmonics provide overtones that make the sound richer and more complex; that is, they provide timbre.

across space. If you examine Figure 10.10, you see a sound wave with a peak at T1 and a trough at T2. Like any sound, we will hear this wave at the frequency that represents twice the distance from T1 to T2, that is, from one peak to the next one. Now consider Wave B. This wave has the same frequency as Wave A, but it is out of phase by 180°. Thus, when the sound in Wave A is at its peak, the wave in Figure Wave A is at its trough, and when the sound is at its trough, the wave in Figure Wave B is at its peak. In Figure 10.10, we see what happens when we superimpose these sounds on each other: they cancel each other out. That is, when these sound waves are presented at the same time, but 180° out of phase, we hear neither Wave A nor Wave B, as the two sounds cancel out. This is the principle behind noise-canceling headphones, which have become popular among travelers. Some high-end

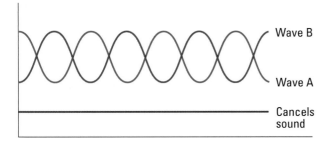

■ FIGURE 10.10   Phase.

Phase refers to the position in one cycle of a wave. The two waves shown here have the same frequency, but are 180° out of phase with each other. If played together, they would cancel each other out, and we would hear nothing.

ISLE 10.9 Phase and Cancellation

cars also have noise-canceling systems to reduce the amount of road noise that one hears inside the car. You can see and hear a demonstration of phase and canceling in ISLE 10.9.

TEST YOUR KNOWLEDGE

What are the physical dimensions of amplitude and frequency, and what perceptual dimensions do they map onto?

ANATOMY OF THE EAR

10.2   Describe the basic anatomy of the ear and the difference between the outer, middle, and inner ear.

We now turn our attention to the anatomy of the ear. Like the eye, the ear is a complex system whose purpose it is to take energy from the external environment and render it into meaningful information. The ear funnels sound waves toward specialized hair cells in the inner ear that transduce the sound from physical sound energy into a neural impulse, which then travels to the auditory regions of the brain. Without transduction of the auditory stimulus, there would be no hearing. So the question for this section is, How does transduction take place? In this section, we start with the entrance of the sound stimulus into the side of the head and follow it until transduction occurs. This process takes us through three distinct anatomical regions. These regions are the outer ear, the middle ear, and the inner ear. Figure 10.11 gives you an overview of the anatomy of the ear.

■ FIGURE 10.11   The anatomy of the human ear.

This illustration shows the outer, middle, and inner ear. Transduction of sound into a neural signal takes place in the inner ear.

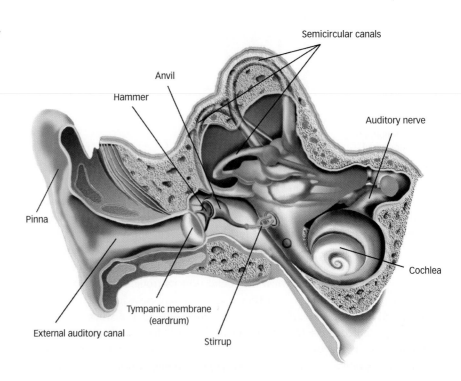

FIGURE 10.12   Pinnae in different mammals.

The Outer Ear

The part of your ear that sticks out on the side of your head is called the pinna (plural *pinnae*). The **pinna** collects sound and funnels it into the external auditory canal. The pinna's fleshy shape helps gather sound waves and channel them to the ear. The shape of the pinna also helps in sound localization, that is, determining the direction a sound is coming from. In other animals, the pinna can be moved in various ways, helping these animals pinpoint sound in space (see Figure 10.12). Think of your dog's ear perking up as it hears someone's car pulling into the driveway. This action helps the dog determine the source of the sound. A select few humans can also wiggle their pinnae, but it is unclear if this gives them an advantage in sound localization, although it may be fun at parties. After sound is collected by the pinna, it is directed into the external auditory canal. The **external auditory canal** (also known as the **external auditory meatus**) conducts sound from the pinna to the tympanic membrane. In all people, regardless of their height, the auditory canal is about 25 mm long (just shy of 1 inch). This length helps amplify certain higher frequencies. The auditory canal also acts to protect the tympanic membrane.

The tympanic membrane is commonly known as the eardrum. The **tympanic membrane** is a thin elastic sheet that vibrates in response to sounds coming through the external auditory canal. Thus, sound moving down the auditory canal hits against the membrane, which vibrates in response to that sound. The tympanic membrane also seals the end of the outer ear.

Damaging the tympanic membrane can result in hearing loss. A common injury in scuba diving is the puncturing of the tympanic membrane due to high pressure in the auditory canal. This injury is very painful but does not cause deafness. Divers may experience temporary hearing loss until the membrane heals. In most cases, the tympanic membrane will repair itself. But repeated injury can result in permanent damage due to scarring, in which case hearing loss will be

Pinna: the structure that collects sound and funnels it into the auditory canal

External auditory canal (external auditory meatus): the channel that conducts sound from the pinna to the tympanic membrane

Tympanic membrane: a thin elastic sheet that vibrates in response to sounds coming through the external auditory canal; commonly known as the eardrum

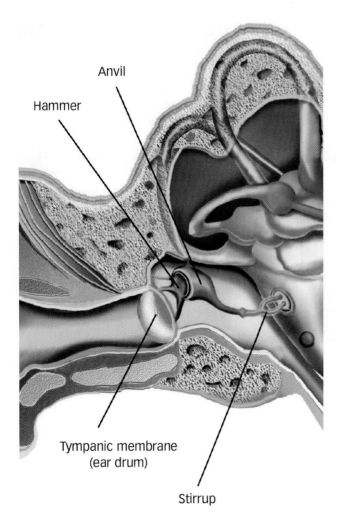

Anvil

Hammer

Tympanic membrane
(ear drum)

Stirrup

■ FIGURE 10.13   Anatomy of the middle ear.

The three bones of the middle ear receive mechanical
stimulation from the tympanic membrane and transmit it to the
oval window. Because the oval window is smaller than the
tympanic membrane, this transmission acts to amplify the sound.

ISLE 10.10 The Middle Ear

....

Ossicles: three small bones in the
middle ear

Malleus: the first ossicle in the
middle ear; receives vibrations
from the tympanic membrane and
transmits them to the incus

Incus: an ossicle in the middle ear;
receives vibrations from the malleus
and transmits them to the stapes

Stapes: an ossicle in the middle
ear; receives vibrations from the
incus and transmits them to the oval
window of the inner ear

permanent. The Bajau people, a traditional diving and sea-faring culture in the Philippines, will intentionally rupture their tympanic membranes as children to reduce pain from free diving (Langenheim, 2010). Not surprisingly, many Bajau people have hearing deficits.

The Middle Ear

The tympanic membrane is the last structure of the outer ear. The next part of the ear is called the middle ear, which consists of three small bones that transmit sound into the inner ear. When the tympanic membrane vibrates, it causes motion in these three small bones, called **ossicles**, which then conduct the sound mechanically. You have probably heard the old (but true) refrain that the ossicles are the smallest bones in the body, but we repeat it here anyway. The three ossicles act to amplify sound waves, although most of the amplification comes from the size of the tympanic membrane relative to the oval window. The tympanic membrane causes sound transmission in the first ossicle, known as the **malleus**. The malleus vibrates and transmits the sound to the next ossicle, known as the **incus**. The incus is then connected to the final ossicle, known as the **stapes**. The stapes then pushes against the oval window of the cochlea, and sound moves into the inner ear. Examine Figure 10.13 to see how these bones are connected inside the ear. For a simulation of how this system works to propagate sound, see ISLE 10.10.

The ossicles are important for the following reason. The cochlea of the inner ear is immersed in liquid, but sound in the auditory canal is in the form of air-based sound waves. Why is this relevant? Sound travels well in water, but it does not cross from air to water very well. In fact, 90% of sound traveling through air will bounce off water rather than penetrate it. This is why that darn party across the lake seems so loud even though it is quite far away. In essence, sound just skips off the surface of the water rather than penetrating it. The sound that heads in the direction of the lake itself echoes off the lake's surface rather than being absorbed by the water, leading it to sound much louder farther away than if the same party were being held at the edge of a field. In contrast, because sound is being transmitted from an air environment to the watery environment of the inner ear, the sound must be amplified as much as possible to overcome the loss of sound due to this transition. In the outer ear, the sound is still traveling through air as it makes its way to the tympanic membrane. Thus, a system is needed to amplify the sound before its intensity is diminished when it hits the liquid medium of the cochlea. The ossicles serve to amplify the sound. Interestingly, this is the reason why fish have no need for an outer and middle ear. Because sound goes directly from the water to their inner ears, they do not need to amplify the sound.

The ossicles amplify sound in the following way. First, they use lever action to increase the amount of pressure change. A small amount of energy at the malleus becomes a larger amount at the stapes. Second, the ossicles transfer energy from a larger surface area, the tympanic membrane, to a smaller surface area, the oval window of the cochlea. Indeed, the tympanic membrane is about 18 times as large as the oval window. Thus, the bones increase the sound pressure 18 times at the oval window, critical in the transmission of sound into the liquid environment of the cochlea. Thus, most of the amplification is due to the difference in size between the tympanic membrane and the oval window.

The middle ear has a number of other important functions. One part of the middle ear is called the Eustachian tube. The **Eustachian tube** is the thin tube that connects the middle ear with the pharynx and serves to equalize air pressure on either side of the tympanic membrane. Normally, the Eustachian tube is closed, but it opens briefly when we swallow or yawn, for example. The brief opening of the Eustachian tube is the technical explanation for the phenomenon of "popping" your ears. When you hold your nose and blow, the Eustachian tubes open to release the pressure. This is also why divers must continually equalize as they descend to deeper depths. Failure to do so during diving brings first intense pain and also potential damage to the tympanic membrane.

The middle ear is filled with air, and except for when the Eustachian tube is open, it is cut off from any changes in air pressure in the outside environment. For optimal operation of the tympanic membrane, it is important for the air pressure on both sides of the tympanic membrane to be equal, but the air pressure outside the tympanic membrane changes regularly due to weather and altitude. The Eustachian tube opens to allow the two air pressures to equalize. Usually the change in air pressure in the middle ear is slight, which is why the Eustachian tube does not open very often under normal circumstances. Yet when you ascend or descend a mountain, especially when you are doing so rapidly in a car, there can be a large change in air pressure, causing your ears to pop, particularly as you descend and the air pressure increases outside your ears relative to inside them. Pressure changes may occur rapidly when ascending or descending in an airplane, and most noticeably when we dive in water, as pressure increases more rapidly as we descend underwater than it does in air. One of the first skills a scuba diver must master is "equalizing," that is, forcibly opening the Eustachian tubes to equalize pressure. If you are ascending a mountain, the air pressure outside your ears decreases with each step up in altitude. If your Eustachian tubes stay closed, you will have much more air pressure on the middle-ear sides of your tympanic membranes than outside, causing them to bow toward the outside of your head. Being pushed out causes the tympanic membrane to move less effectively in response to sound stimuli, and in these cases you might find that your hearing is not quite as good as normal. When you yawn or swallow in these cases there will be a rapid reduction of the air pressure inside your middle ear, which you experience as the popping of your ears.

The ossicles also serve a role in attenuating sustained loud sounds. There is a muscle attached to the malleus called the **tensor tympani** and a second muscle attached to the stapes called the **stapedius**. Like the bones they are attached to, these are the smallest muscles in the body. Their job is to tense in the presence of very loud noises, thus restricting the movements of the ossicles and avoiding damage to the inner ear. This **acoustic reflex** protects somewhat against chronic loud noises, such as car stereos, but it is too slow for sudden loud noises such as the sound of a gun firing (have we mentioned that being around gunfire is not good for your hearing?). Interestingly, these muscles may also tense in response to sounds generated inside the head, such as the sounds generated by chewing or talking.

Eustachian tube: a thin tube that connects the middle ear with the pharynx and serves to equalize air pressure on either side of the eardrum

Tensor tympani: the muscle that is attached to the malleus

Stapedius: the muscle that is attached to the stapes

Acoustic reflex: a reflex that tightens the tensor tympani and the stapedius in response to chronic loud noise

The Inner Ear

The inner ear contains the parts of the ear that transduce sound into a neural signal. In particular, the hair cells situated along the organ of Corti in the cochlea act by taking vibrations and converting them into a neural signal. In this way, the hair cells are equivalent to the rods and cones of the retinae. The inner ear is an amazing accomplishment of evolution, but it has lots of parts with hard-to-remember (and seemingly arbitrary) names, and thus it typically presents a challenge for students learning about it for the first time. So read carefully, study the diagrams, and test yourself repeatedly. For a diagram of the inner ear, examine Figure 10.14. Go to ISLE 10.11 for an interactive model of the workings of the inner ear.

The **cochlea** is the snail-shaped structure of the inner ear that houses the hair cells that transduce sound into a neural signal. The term *cochlea* derives from the Greek word for snail, and if you look at the cochlea depicted in Figure 10.14, you will see that its spiral indeed looks like a snail. The cochlea is a coiled tube, coiled 2.74 times. As a coiled tube, it takes up just about 4 mm of space inside your ear, but if you were to unroll it, it would stretch to about 33 to 35 mm in length (1.3 inches).

Now examine the picture of the cross-section of the cochlea, shown in Figure 10.15. You will see that the cochlea has three liquid-filled chambers, called the **tympanic canal**, the **middle canal** (also called the **cochlear duct**), and the **vestibular canal**. In the apex (the end of the cochlea) is an opening called the helicotrema that allows fluid to flow between the tympanic canal and the vestibular canal. The apex is the part of the cochlea farthest from the oval window if the cochlea were uncoiled. Seated just underneath the oval window is the round window. The **round window** is a soft tissue substance at the base of the tympanic canal. Its function is as an "escape" valve for excess pressure from loud sounds that arrive in the cochlea. This is needed because the oval window cannot be pushed in, and the liquid in the inner ear does not behave like the air in the middle ear. We will return to function shortly, but we need to cover just a bit more anatomy first.

The Basilar Membrane of the Cochlea

Two membranes separate the canals of the cochlea. One is **Reissner's membrane**, which separates the vestibular canal and the middle canal. The other membrane is the **basilar membrane**, which separates the tympanic canal and the middle canal. Lying along the basilar membrane within the middle canal is the **organ of Corti**, which contains the hair cells. The basilar membrane is not really a membrane. Rather, it is composed of harder and thicker material, which allows it to vibrate in response to incoming sound. At the base (nearest to the oval and round windows), the basilar membrane is thicker and stiffer and therefore more responsive to high-frequency sounds. At the apex (the uncoiled opposite end), the basilar membrane is less thick and less stiff and therefore more responsive to low-frequency sounds.

Take a look at Figure 10.16. Notice that the stapes of the middle ear asserts pressure on the oval window. This pressure from the stapes causes a wave in the fluid (**perilymph**) of the middle canal in the inner ear. This pressure wave in the perilymph causes a traveling wave to move down the length of the basilar membrane. *Traveling wave* here simply means that the wave moves from the base to the apex of the basilar membrane (see ISLE 10.12). If the sound being presented

---

ISLE 10.11 The Basilar Membrane and Sound Stimuli

ISLE 10.12 The Traveling Wave

Cochlea: the snail-shaped structure of the inner ear that houses the hair cells that transduce sound into a neural signal

Tympanic canal: one of the three chambers in the cochlea; separated from the middle canal by the basilar membrane

Middle canal (cochlear duct): one of the three chambers in the cochlea; separated from the tympanic canal by the basilar membrane; contains the organ of Corti

Vestibular canal: one of the three chambers in the cochlea; separated from the middle canal by Reissner's membrane

Round window: a soft tissue substance at the base of the tympanic canal whose function is as an "escape" valve for excess pressure from loud sounds that arrive in the cochlea

Reissner's membrane: the membrane that separates the vestibular and middle canals

Basilar membrane: the fibers that separate the tympanic canal from the middle canal; the organ of Corti lies on the basilar membrane

Organ of Corti: a structure on the basilar membrane that houses the hair cells that transduce sound into a neural signal

Perilymph: the fluid that fills the tympanic canal and the vestibular canal

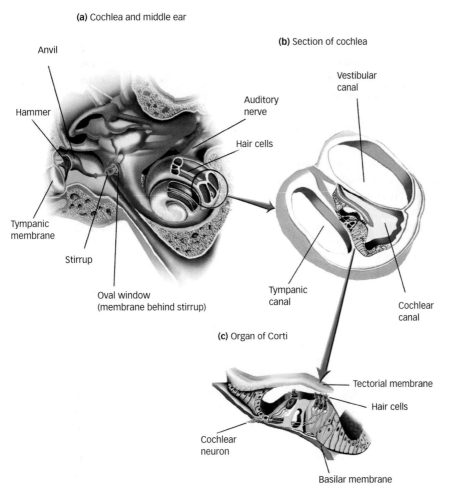

(a) Cochlea and middle ear

Anvil

Hammer

Tympanic
membrane

Stirrup

Oval window
(membrane behind stirrup)

Auditory
nerve

Hair cells

(b) Section of cochlea

Vestibular
canal

Tympanic
canal

Cochlear
canal

(c) Organ of Corti

Tectorial membrane

Hair cells

Cochlear
neuron

Basilar membrane

■ **FIGURE 10.14   The inner ear.**

The inner ear is a very complicated part of the body that contains the hair cells that transduce sound into a neural signal. These hair cells are located along the basilar membrane, which transmits the mechanical input of sound. When sound enters the inner ear, the tectorial membrane causes the basilar membrane to vibrate. These vibrations are detected by the hair cells, starting the neural signal.

is high frequency, the traveling wave will show greater motion toward the base of the basilar membrane. Lower frequency sound will cause more movement farther down the basilar membrane. The lowest frequency sounds we can hear move the basilar membrane near the apex. The movement of this wave is critical to understanding how frequency is coded in the cochlea.

To understand why the thick end of the basilar membrane is conducive to high-frequency sounds and the thinner or "floppy" end to lower frequency sounds, think of stringed instruments. On a violin, for example, lower pitches are produced by the G string, located farthest to the left on the fingerboard. Pull on the G string, and it will feel relatively loose. The highest pitches on a violin are produced by the tightly wound E string, which is farthest to the right on the fingerboard. Pull on this string, and it feels tight. If the E string is out of tune and too flat (too low in pitch), the violinist gets it into tune by tightening the string. Because the E string is so tightly wound to begin with, many novice violinists may snap the string altogether. If the E string is out of tune and too sharp (too high in pitch), the violinist gets it into tune by loosening the string. The basilar membrane is equivalent to this. The base is tightly wound and thus more responsive to high frequencies, whereas the apex is loose and responsive to lower frequencies. For an illustration of how the basilar membrane moves in response to different frequencies, go to ISLE 10.13.

ISLE 10.13 Place Code Theory

■ **FIGURE 10.15**

Cross-section of the cochlea.

You can see Reissner's membrane along the top and the basilar membrane in the middle. Reissner's membrane separates the vestibular canal from the middle canal. The basilar membrane separates the middle canal from the tympanic canal. The organ of Corti rests along the basilar membrane.

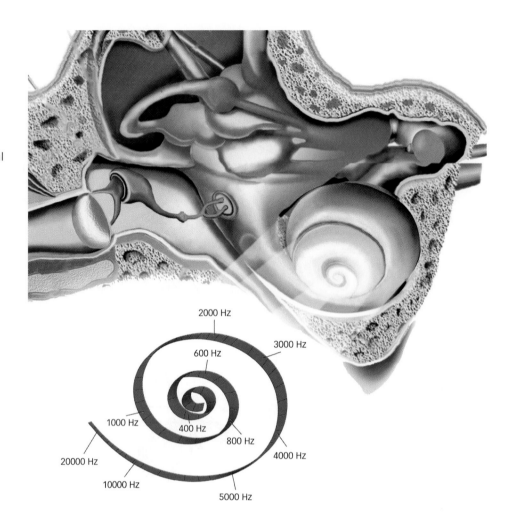

■ **FIGURE 10.16**

Sound waves and changes to the basilar membrane.

Incoming vibrations will cause the basilar membrane to vibrate. The base of the basilar membrane is tightly wound and thus more responsive to high frequencies, whereas the apex of the Basilar membrane is loose and responsive to lower frequencies.

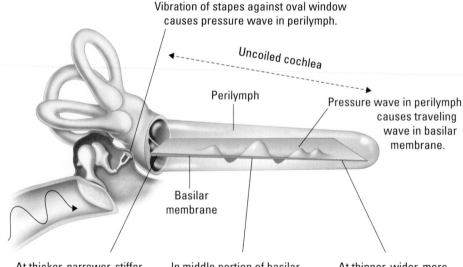

Vibration of stapes against oval window causes pressure wave in perilymph.

Uncoiled cochlea

Perilymph

Pressure wave in perilymph causes traveling wave in basilar membrane.

Basilar membrane

At thicker, narrower, stiffer base of basilar membrane, high-freuence pressure waves cause greatest displacement.

In middle portion of basilar membrane, midfrequency pressure waves cause greatest displacement.

At thinner, wider, more flexible apex of basilar membrane, low-frequency pressure waves cause greatest displacement.

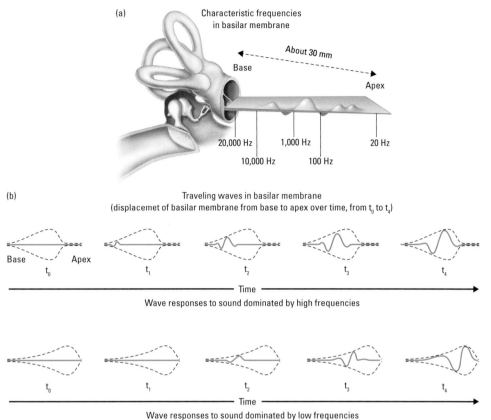

FIGURE 10.17
Frequency and displacement along the basilar membrane.

The basilar membrane is shown here as if it were uncoiled and spread in a line. Each location along the basilar membrane vibrates to the greatest extent in response to one frequency. That is, a sound of a particular frequency will maximally displace the basilar membrane at that location. In (b), we can see characteristic frequencies and their displacement along a schematic basilar membrane. Sounds of high frequency excite locations toward the base of the basilar membrane, whereas sounds of low frequency excite locations toward the apex of the basilar membrane.

Indeed, the displacement of the basilar membrane in response to frequency is quite specific. Each location along the basilar membrane responds to a **characteristic frequency**. Any sound will move the basilar membrane at every location, but a particular location will respond the most, in terms of movement, to its characteristic frequency. In the most common case, in which we hear a number of complex sounds, complete with harmonics, the basilar membrane will reflect these frequencies by moving at various places along its length. In effect, the basilar membrane does a Fourier analysis, breaking down complex sounds into their component frequencies (von Békésy, 1960). To see this visually, look at Figure 10.17. You can also see a demonstration of this on ISLE 10.14.

In essence, the basilar membrane converts the sound energy that beats against the oval window into mechanical movement along its length with any particular location along its length responding to particular frequencies of sound. We are now, finally, ready to begin to discuss how this physical signal gets changed into a neural one.

ISLE 10.14 The Basilar Membrane and Fourier Analysis

The Organ of Corti

The organ of Corti is the structure along the basilar membrane that contains the **hair cells** that transduce sound into a neural signal. The name Corti honors the Italian scientist Alfonso Corti (1822–1876), who experimented on the function of the cochlea in the 1850s. In addition to the hair cells, the organ of Corti also contains the dendrites of the auditory nerve that brings the neural signal to the brain. The critical hair cells in the organ of Corti are specialized cells for

Characteristic frequency: the frequency to which any particular location along the basilar membrane responds best

Hair cells: cells that have stereocilia for transducing the movement of the basilar membrane into a neural signal

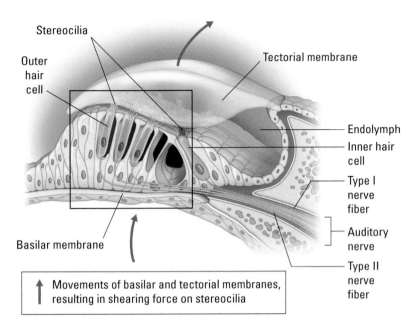

Stereocilia

Outer hair cell

Tectorial membrane

Endolymph

Inner hair cell

Type I nerve fiber

Auditory nerve

Type II nerve fiber

Basilar membrane

↑ Movements of basilar and tectorial membranes, resulting in shearing force on stereocilia

■ **FIGURE 10.18** **The organ of Corti.**

The organ of Corti contains both inner hair cells and outer hair cells, as well as the tectorial membrane. The outer hair cells connect to the auditory nerve.

ISLE 10.15 Transduction and Hair Cells

Stereocilium: the hairlike part of the hair cells on the top of the inner and outer hair cells

Outer hair cells: cells that sharpen and amplify the responses of the inner hair cells

Inner hair cells: cells that are responsible for transducing the neural signal

Tectorial membrane: a membrane that rests above the hair cells within the organ of Corti

Place code theory: the view that different locations along the basilar membrane respond to different frequencies

Temporal code theory: the view that frequency representation occurs because of a match between sound frequency and the firing rates of the auditory nerve

transducing the motion of the basilar membrane into a neural signal. The hair cells have hairlike filaments called **stereocilia** for transducing the movement of the basilar membrane into a neural signal. These stereocilia bend in response to the movement of the basilar membrane, and the bending changes the voltage within the hair cells. There are four layers of hair cells that follow the basilar membrane. The first row is called the **outer hair cells**, and the row that lies inside that is called the **inner hair cells** (see Figure 10.18). There are about 3,500 inner hair cells and about 3 times that many outer hair cells. Each hair cell has anywhere from 50 to 150 stereocilia sticking off its top in order to detect the motion of the basilar membrane. Inner hair cells are responsible for transducing the neural signal, whereas outer hair cells refine and amplify the neural responses of the inner hair cells. The **tectorial membrane** sits above the hair cells within the organ of Corti, helping hold them in place (see ISLE 10.15).

When a vibration of the basilar membrane causes the basilar membrane to move upward, the stereocilia brush against the tectorial membrane. When stereocilia are pushed in this manner, there is a change in the cell's voltage potential. This voltage change causes the release of neurotransmitters, which cause the auditory nerve to send a signal. This process can be seen visually in Figure 10.19. And with the induction of a signal in the auditory nerve, the sound has been transduced and sound information gets conveyed to the brain.

One of the most important scientists in this area was Hungarian-born Georg von Békésy (1899–1972). He did most of his most important work while on the faculty of Harvard University. For his work on the basilar membrane and how it codes for frequency, von Békésy won the 1961 Nobel Prize in Medicine and Physiology. Von Békésy was the first to show that the basilar membrane vibrates more at certain locations along its length in response to different frequencies, thus allowing the auditory system to discriminate among frequencies. Although many of you may find this bizarre, von Békésy did his most famous work by playing really loud sounds into the ears of human cadavers.

Much of the discussion of basilar membrane function in the previous paragraphs is therefore knowledge we learned from von Békésy's work. His view of frequency representation in the cochlea is known as the **place code theory**. The alternative view is known as the **temporal code theory** (Wever & Bray, 1937). This theory states that frequency representation occurs because of a match between sound frequency and the firing rates of the auditory nerve.

The evidence for place code theory rests largely on the observation that the basilar membrane's thickness changes along the cochlea, and this thickness allows it to respond differently to different frequencies along its length. Von Békésy also observed the movement of the basilar membrane in response to loud sounds. In this way, the basilar membrane separates out different frequencies, and the hair

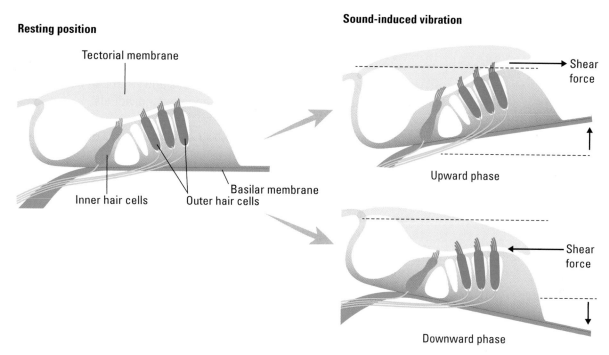

Resting position

Tectorial membrane

Inner hair cells

Outer hair cells

Basilar membrane

Sound-induced vibration

Shear force

Upward phase

Shear force

Downward phase

■ FIGURE 10.19 **Actions of hair cells.**

Vibration causes the tectorial membrane to shear against the hair cells, that is, to move in opposite directions. This movement causes the stereocilia of the hair cells to transduce sound into a neural signal.

cells that lie along the length of the basilar membrane can code for these different frequencies. Thus, when hair cells at a specific position are activated, the auditory system can interpret this as a sound at a particular frequency. This is illustrated in Figure 10.17 as well as in ISLE 10.16.

ISLE 10.16 Temporal Code Theory

As we get older, the basilar membrane gets stiffer. This accounts for the observation that as we age, we lose access to higher frequencies. By the time people reach the age of 50 or so, they cannot hear frequencies above 12,000 Hz or so. This occurs even in the absence of exposure to loud sounds. Even people at 25, by and large, have lost hearing above 16,000 Hz. This age-related hearing loss in the higher frequency range has some amusing consequences. Teenagers can purchase ring tones for their cell phones at very high frequencies that will alert them to incoming messages, but to which their teachers will be deaf. Most adults are not simply impaired when it comes to hearing a 20,000 Hz tone; they are deaf. Thus, a teenager receiving a call or text message has little risk of being detected by anyone other than another teenager. On the other hand, some store owners, in an effort to keep teenagers from "hanging out" in front of their stores, will play very loud high-frequency tones. The store owners and their paying customers are deaf to these sounds and will therefore come and go as they like. But the loud high-frequency sounds will be painful to the loitering teens, who will therefore seek somewhere else to hang out. Tit for tat, we suppose.

TEST YOUR KNOWLEDGE

What is place code theory? How does the displacement of the basilar membrane in response to specific frequencies support this view?

HEARING LOSS, HEARING AIDS, AND COCHLEAR IMPLANTS

10.3 Examine the nature of hearing loss and what can be done to improve hearing in hearing-impaired individuals.

Those who have lost the ability to hear can learn language through sign languages and may often be quite competent at spoken languages by reading lips and inferring contexts. And many deaf people have accomplished great things even without this crucial sensory system. In a beautiful book, Josh Swiller (2007), a profoundly hearing-impaired man, describes his adventures as a Peace Corps volunteer in southern Africa. Swiller does not let his hearing impairment hold him back, helping a town build wells and health clinics. Nonetheless, when his digital hearing aids are stolen while he is thousands of miles away from possible replacements, Swiller begins to understand what it is like to be truly deaf in a world in which hearing is necessary. Upon his return to the United States, Swiller committed himself to becoming fluent in sign language as well as completing this highly recommended book.

We have already mentioned a number of ways the auditory system is vulnerable to damage. In particular, the mechanisms of the ear, while finely tuned to an incredible range of amplitudes and frequencies, are also vulnerable to loud noises and high pressures. And even though each hair cell has a great many stereocilia, there are only so many hair cells, so that damage to hair cells can have grave consequences for hearing also. Luckily, there are many options to improve hearing in those with hearing loss.

In the United States, more than 30 million people have hearing loss, according to the Centers for Disease Control and Prevention (2013). Perhaps three quarters of these people are over the age of 60. *Presbycusis* refers to the loss of hearing associated with aging (Yost, 2007), which is more common in men than women. Presbycusis is also more common in societies such as our own, in which more people are exposed to loud sounds than people are in more traditional societies, where they may not be subjected to all the mechanical sounds people in industrialized societies are (think of how many mornings you have awoken to the sounds of lawn care machines outside your window—and now think of the landscapers' hearing). There are also a number of genetic and acquired hearing loss problems in younger adults. Disease and injury can also cause hearing loss in people of all ages.

Audiologists are doctoral-level specialists who evaluate, diagnose, and treat hearing impairments, provided they do not require immediate medical attention. Audiologists are equivalent to optometrists in the visual domain, in that their specialty is assessing the problem and then helping the patient find the right hearing aid, just as an optometrist evaluates visual problems and then prescribes corrective eyewear. During an audiological exam, an audiologist administers a set of tests using an audiometer. It may be that you have had an audiological exam at some point. The **audiometer** presents pure tones at set frequencies and known amplitudes to either the left or right ear. It is used in the assessment of absolute threshold at each frequency for a patient. The result of this procedure is an **audiogram** (see Figure 10.20). Figure 10.20 shows an audiological report of a patient with a genetic sensorineural hearing impairment (i.e., hearing loss due to congenital damage to hair cells). This patient's peak impairment is around 4,000 Hz in both ears. The patient has mostly normal hearing at lower frequencies. We now consider the various forms of hearing impairment.

Audiometer: a device that can present tones of different frequencies, from low in pitch to high in pitch, at different volumes from soft to loud

Audiogram: a graph that illustrates the thresholds for the frequencies as measured by the audiometer

Conductive Hearing Loss

Conductive hearing loss is characterized by damage to some aspect of sound transmission in the outer or middle ear. Thus, in conductive hearing loss, sound does not properly get to the cochlea for transduction into a neural signal. This can occur because of blockage of the auditory canal, a torn tympanic membrane, or damage to the ossicles. In particular, conductive hearing loss may occur because of otosclerosis. **Otosclerosis** is an inherited bone disease in which the ossicles, particularly the stapes, may calcify and therefore be less conductive of sound. In some cases, hearing loss due to otosclerosis can be improved by replacing the stapes with an artificial bone.

There are also conditions in which hearing loss may occur on a temporary basis. Ruptured tympanic membranes may heal properly, restoring full hearing. Hearing loss may also occur on a temporary basis during an ear infection, if the auditory canal becomes blocked with fluid. Treatment of the infection may be sufficient to return hearing to normal, but in some cases, the middle ear must be drained to allow hearing to return to normal.

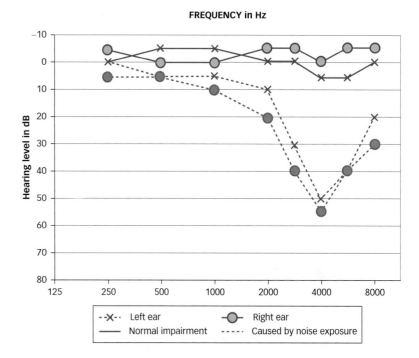

■ FIGURE 10.20   **Audiological report.**

This patient has moderate to severe hearing loss in both ears in the high frequency range. But you can also see that some frequencies are more affected than others.

Source: Reprinted with permission from the *Handbook for Acoustic Ecology*, B. Truax, ed., Cambridge Street Publications, CD-ROM edition, 1999.

Sensorineural Hearing Loss

Sensorineural hearing loss occurs because of damage to the cochlea, the auditory nerve, or the primary auditory cortex. The term *sensorineural hearing loss* can refer to acquired hearing problems or genetic problems, and the condition can range from minor hearing loss to profound hearing deficits. This form of hearing loss is most often precipitated by damage to hair cells, which can occur because of noise exposure or certain drugs. Certain antibiotics and cancer treatments have the side effect of damaging hair cells in the cochlea. These medicines are therefore given only when a patient's life is at stake. Inherited sensorineural hearing loss is rare but may show up at infancy, in childhood, and sometimes not until adulthood. Today, tests are immediately given to a newborn's ear to determine if there is congenital hearing loss. If so, parents can make appropriate decisions for their infant in order to make sure that the infant develops language normally.

Tinnitus

Tinnitus is the condition in which people perceive sounds even when none are present. The perceived sound usually sounds like a pure tone at a particular frequency. Most people experience tinnitus occasionally and for brief periods of time, and for the vast majority of us, tinnitus is seldom a problem. But when it occurs all the time or is subjectively loud, it becomes a problem. It is thought that most cases of tinnitus involve a neural signal being sent to the brain in

Otosclerosis: an inherited bone disease in which the ossicles, particularly the stapes, may calcify and therefore be less conductive of sound

Sensorineural hearing loss: permanent hearing loss caused by damage to the cochlea or auditory nerve or the primary auditory cortex.

Tinnitus: a condition in which people perceive sounds even when none are present

the absence of an actual sound. Thus, tinnitus can interfere with the perception of real sounds in the environment, including speech. Tinnitus is associated with noise-induced hearing loss, but there may be other causes as well (Møller, 2006). A former student of Dr. Schwartz was afflicted with a bad case of tinnitus after being awakened by a loud fire alarm just above his head. The illusory sound was so loud for this young man that it interfered with his ability to study. After several months, the tinnitus decreased and eventually disappeared. In other cases, tinnitus may be the result of damage to the cochlea or damage or infection to the auditory nerve. Treatment may include hearing aids, which can amplify external sounds, such as the frequencies of human voices, while at the same time playing white noise at the same frequency as the tinnitus sound, in hopes of canceling it out. Some attempts to find drugs that reduce tinnitus have also been successful.

(a)

© iStockphoto.com/aerogondo

(b)

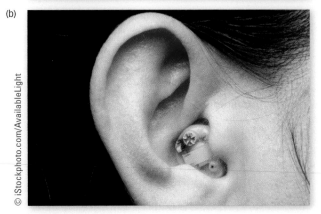

© iStockphoto.com/AvailableLight

■ **FIGURE 10.21 Hearing aids.**

(a) Out-of-the-ear aids. (b) In-the-ear aids. Hearing aids amplify sounds so that the person can hear better. Modern digital hearing aids can be adjusted to amplify only those frequencies at which a person is impaired.

Hearing aids: electronic devices that amplify sound so that people with hearing deficits can hear sounds that otherwise would be below their thresholds

Hearing Aids

Hearing aids are electronic devices that amplify sound so that people with hearing deficits can hear sounds that otherwise would be below their thresholds. Hearing aids can be the "behind the ear" style (see Figure 10.21a) or the "in the ear" style (Figure 10.21b). In-ear hearing aids are smaller and less obtrusive than behind-the-ear aids, but behind-the-ear devices can amplify sounds more and thus are preferable for people with moderate, severe, or profound hearing loss. In-the-ear aids work fine for people with mild to moderate hearing loss. Younger people with hearing loss may also prefer in-the-ear devices because they are less visible.

In the past, hearing aids were analog devices. Analog devices amplify the actual sound present, but because they work with the actual sound, they are limited in what other forms of sound processing they can do. In general, analog hearing aids amplify all sounds the same amount (though many did have volume controls). This is potentially problematic because, as we have just seen, the pattern of hearing loss may be different at different frequencies. Thus, if we amplify all sounds, we may amplify some to a level at which they can be heard, but that may mean that other sounds are too loud and others are still too soft.

In technologically advanced countries, most hearing aids are now digital devices. Digital hearing aids first convert the sound signal into a computer code, which is then reconverted into an analog sound for the wearer. This transformation into a digital signal allows additional processing to the signal in addition to amplification. Digital hearing aids have a number of important advantages over earlier analog aids. First, digital hearing aids can be fitted to a particular individual's pattern of hearing loss. This is important because hearing loss may vary greatly from one patient to another, both in the loudness of sounds required to allow hearing and in the frequency range of the hearing loss. Digital hearing aids can be programmed to amplify some frequencies more than other frequencies. If a patient has nearly normal hearing at 400 Hz, a digital hearing aid can be programmed to amplify not at all or very little at that frequency. But if the same patient has severe hearing loss at 1,000 Hz, the aid can be programmed to amplify much more at that frequency. In this way, the digital aid can restore a pattern of hearing that approximates what a person with normal hearing would experience.

Digital hearing aids can also be programmed to have directionally sensitive microphones. With this feature, a person with hearing loss can amplify sound in front of himself or herself, allowing better hearing of a conversation, and, at the same time, block out irrelevant sounds coming from other directions. This may be useful while trying to have conversations in noisy environments such as in restaurants or cars. In another situation, in which a person does not know the direction from which relevant sounds will be coming, the directional microphone can be switched off. Digital hearing aids can also be programmed to amplify different frequencies at different times. People with digital hearing aids can adjust the programs they are running to suit their needs. For example, a first grade teacher may have a program in her hearing aid that amplifies the frequencies likely to belong to first graders' while she is teaching. She may turn that program off during recess, when the kids are running around on the playground. Later, when she gets home, she can switch to a program that allows her to amplify the deeper voices of adult male relatives.

Hearing aids may also be obtained that have external microphones that can be placed near the desired sound source, and the sound will be electronically transmitted wirelessly into the hearing aid. Consider a student with a hearing deficit. He can request that his professor wear a microphone while teaching the class. The professor need only place the microphone around her neck and speak normally. The sound will be wirelessly sent to the hearing aid, and the student will hear the professor's voice directly from the aid rather than across the room. This aspect of hearing aids can be beneficial in restaurants as well, as the microphone can be placed around the neck of the person being spoken to. Then, despite the noise of the background, the voice will be transmitted directly into the receiver of the hearing aid. Some hearing aids also come equipped with similar systems for watching television. The audio transmission of the television can be transmitted directly into the hearing aid. Such equipment, however, is often expensive and may not be covered by insurance. Thus, many people with insufficient insurance or ability to afford aids may have to settle for less complete systems. In the United States, hearing aids are covered by Medicare, so older adults should have access to quality aids.

Hearing aids require the presence of a minimum of some transmission of a sensorineural signal from the hair cells to the auditory nerve. Hearing aids amplify sound, allowing damaged ears to hear sounds, but they do not replace the need for a functioning cochlea. However, there is another tool that can be used to restore hearing in those who have become clinically deaf because of damage to the cochlea (sensorineural deafness). This is the domain of the cochlear implant, in which a mechanical device essentially replaces the hair cells along the basilar membrane. We turn next to cochlear implants.

Cochlear Implants

Cochlear implants are designed to restore some hearing, typically of spoken voices, to deaf individuals. Cochlear implants stimulate the auditory nerve artificially with an electronic system, replacing the hair cells of the cochlea in the patient receiving the implant. This can restore some hearing to patients who have become deaf. Some parents of deaf children are also electing to have cochlear implants placed in their deaf children's inner ears to allow them to develop the ability to understand spoken language. In order to be eligible for the procedure, one must have profound hearing loss or deafness in both ears, the hearing loss

Cochlear implants: devices that are designed to restore some hearing, typically of spoken voices, to deaf individuals; they stimulate the auditory nerve artificially with an electronic system, replacing the hair cells of the cochlea

must be due to sensorineural problems, but the auditory nerve must be intact. Until recently, the procedure was done in just one ear, but having implants in both ears is now becoming more common. As of 2010, it was estimated that there were more than 200,000 people in the United States with cochlear implants (National Institute on Deafness and Other Communication Disorders, 2010).

To place a cochlear implant into someone's ear requires minor surgery to place components inside the ear. Then it requires anywhere from a few weeks to several months of training and therapy to allow the person to be able to interpret the sounds he or she is now hearing again (or, in children, for the first time). The cochlear implant works by having both external (outside of the ear) components and internal (inside the cochlea) components. The cochlear implant system is illustrated in Figure 10.22.

The first external component is a miniature microphone. The microphone picks up sounds from the environment. The microphone is attached to a small processor, which is essentially a minicomputer. The processor filters out noise and sounds not in the speech range, so that the patient can focus on hearing language-related input. It can be reprogrammed for other purposes as well, such as a person who has gone deaf but wants to experience music again. The processor sends a signal along a small wire to a transmitter. The transmitter sits directly on the surface of the skin, attached to the bone just behind the ear. During surgery, a small magnet is placed on the inside of the skull to keep the transmitter in place. This magnet is barely noticeable but acts to keep the transmitter firmly in place when the implant is being used. The transmitter sends a signal to the internal components of the cochlear implant wirelessly via radio waves.

Underneath the skin are two components that are permanently in place after surgery. First, there is a receiver/stimulator that picks up the radio waves from the external device. The receiver/stimulator converts the radio waves into an electric signal, which then travels by wire into the cochlea. Within the cochlea, set along the length of the basilar membrane, are a series of electrodes, perhaps as many as 30. In the early days of cochlear implants, there may be have been only 4 electrodes, but now up to 30 can be safely placed inside the cochlea. These electrodes, when stimulated by the receiver/stimulator, will induce a neural signal in the auditory nerve fibers that normally would be stimulated by hair cells. The electrodes are placed along the length of the basilar membrane, so when an electrode fires, the person will hear a particular frequency associated with that location on the basilar membrane. Thus, the cochlear implant uses an electric system to induce a normal neural signal in the auditory nerve.

Because thousands of hair cells are being replaced by only a couple dozen electrodes, patients should not expect, nor will they receive, their old hearing back. Sounds will not be perceived as richly with an implant as they were before the person went deaf. Moreover, most patients will not immediately be able to understand speech again once the system is online. Patients will require many hours of training and therapy to basically relearn to hear with their new implants. This may be frustrating at first, but eventually, almost all patients learn to interpret their new hearing abilities. Once this training occurs, many patients can regain their understanding of speech at rather high levels. And some patients may find the sound quality sufficient to enjoy listening to music again.

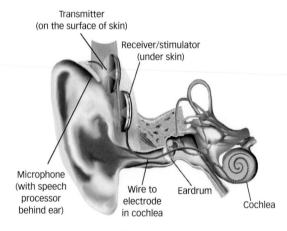

Transmitter
(on the surface of skin)

Receiver/stimulator
(under skin)

Microphone
(with speech
processor
behind ear)

Wire to
electrode
in cochlea

Eardrum

Cochlea

■ FIGURE 10.22   Cochlear implants.

Cochlear implants allow deaf people to hear again by placing electrodes inside the cochlea. These electrodes are connected to an external microphone, which selectively stimulates electrodes depending on what frequencies are present in the sound signal. The electrodes then directly stimulate auditory nerve fibers.

One of the more controversial issues with respect to cochlear implants is whether or not cochlear implants should be placed in infants who are born congenitally deaf. Many in the sign language deaf community object to this practice, as they argue that such children can develop normally and use language appropriately if they start with sign languages from an early age. They argue that forcing these children into the hearing world will actually be a handicap in and of itself, when they could develop language normally through visual sign languages. Nonetheless, many parents, particularly hearing parents, elect to go with cochlear implants. If cochlear

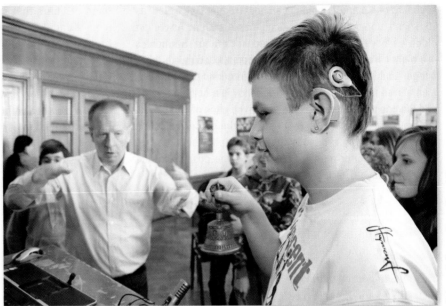

■ **FIGURE 10.23** Cochlear implants. A child born deaf but equipped with cochlear implants can learn to play and appreciate music.

implants are placed in an infant's ears within the first year of life, with proper commitment on the part of the parents and involved professionals, that infant is likely to grow up being able to understand speech and to develop normal speech himself or herself. In some cases, the child may even be able to participate in music activities later on (see Figure 10.23). As you can see in Figure 10.23, the external components of a cochlear implants are not large and look similar to an in-the-ear hearing aid, with the addition of the transmitter. They will not impede a young person from doing other activities.

TEST YOUR KNOWLEDGE

What is the difference between conductive hearing loss and sensorineural hearing loss? How is each treated?

CHAPTER SUMMARY

 10.1 Discuss the physical nature of sound and how it correlates with the perceptual nature of sound.

The sound stimulus consists of the periodic variations in air pressure traveling out from the source of the variations. Sound waves are the waves of pressure changes that occur in the air as a function of the vibration of the source. A cycle is the amount of time between one peak of high pressure and the next. A pure tone is a sound wave in which changes in air pressure follow a sine wave pattern. Complex tones, however, have many different pure tones mixed together, making their waveforms

more complex. The amplitude of a sound is expressed as the difference between its maximum and minimum sound pressure. Amplitude is measured on the decibel scale. Loudness is the perceptual experience of amplitude or the intensity of a sound stimulus. Persistent exposure to sounds over 85 dB can result in hearing loss, and even a one-time exposure to sounds over 135 dB can result in damage to hearing. The frequency of a sound stimulus is the number of cycles that occur in 1 second. Frequency is measured in hertz (Hz). Pitch is the subjective experience of sound that is most closely associated with the frequency of a sound stimulus, related to the experience of whether the sound is high or low (such as the two ends of the keyboard of a piano). Humans can hear frequencies as low as 20 Hz and, depending on age, as high as 20,000 Hz. As we get older, we lose hearing in the high-frequency range. Harmonics are higher frequencies present in a complex sound that are integer multiples of the fundamental frequency. The fundamental frequency is the lowest frequency in a complex sound and the one that determines the perceived pitch of that sound. *Timbre* is the musical term that refers to the perceived sound differences between sounds with the same pitch but possessing different higher harmonics. Phase is the position in one cycle of a wave. There are 360° in a single cycle of a wave.

10.2 Describe the basic anatomy of the ear and the difference between the outer, middle, and inner ear.

The outside portion of the ear is called the pinna and it collects sound and funnels it into the external auditory canal. The external auditory canal conducts sound from the pinna to the tympanic membrane. The tympanic membrane, commonly known as the eardrum, is a thin elastic sheet that vibrates in response to sounds coming through the external auditory canal. The tympanic membrane causes changes in the middle ear. The sound is transmitted by three small bones called ossicles (the malleus, incus, and stapes). The malleus receives vibrations from the tympanic membrane and transmits them to the incus. The incus receives vibrations from the malleus and transmits them to the stapes. The stapes receives vibrations from the incus and transmits them to the oval window of the inner ear. The Eustachian tube is a thin tube that connects the middle ear with the pharynx and serves to equalize air pressure on either side of the eardrum. The stapes beats against the oval window of the inner ear. The cochlea is the snail-shaped structure of the inner ear that houses the hair cells that transduce sound into a neural signal. The basilar membrane is the

band of fibers that separate the tympanic canal from the middle canal. The organ of Corti lies on the basilar membrane. The organ of Corti is a structure that houses the hair cells that transduce sound into a neural signal. Inner hair cells have stereocilia for transducing the movement of the basilar membrane into a neural signal. Place code theory is the view that different locations along the basilar membrane respond to different frequencies.

10.3 Examine the nature of hearing loss and what can be done to improve hearing in hearing-impaired individuals.

Hearing loss affects millions of people. Presbycusis is the loss of hearing associated with aging. An audiometer presents pure tones at set frequencies and known amplitudes to either the left or right ear. An audiogram is a graphical display of the auditory sensitivity of a patient compared with a standard listener. Conductive hearing loss occurs because of structural damage to the outer or inner ear. Otosclerosis is an inherited bone disease in which the ossicles, particularly the stapes, may calcify and therefore be less conductive. Sensorineural hearing loss occurs because of damage to the cochlea, the auditory nerve, or the primary auditory cortex. Tinnitus is the condition in which people perceive sounds even when none are present. Hearing aids are electronic devices that amplify sound so that people with hearing deficits can hear sounds that otherwise would be below their thresholds. Digital hearing aids provide a set of features that can allow a person with hearing loss to function well in the hearing world. Cochlear implants are designed to restore some hearing, typically of spoken voices, to deaf individuals. Cochlear implants stimulate the auditory nerve artificially with an electronic system, replacing the hair cells of the cochlea.

REVIEW QUESTIONS

1. What is sound? How is it transmitted through the environment? How is it measured?

2. What are the relations between amplitude and loudness, frequency and pitch, and waveform and timbre?

3. Why do loud sounds potentially cause damage to hearing? How loud must sound be to cause damage if heard repeatedly? How loud must sound be to cause immediate damage?

4. What are harmonics? How do they relate to the fundamental frequency? What do we hear when the fundamental frequency is deleted from a sound?

5. Describe the anatomy of the outer and middle ear. How does sound get transmitted from the pinna to the oval window?

6. What are the ossicles? How do they transmit sound, and how do they amplify sound? Why is their amplification needed for normal hearing?

7. Describe the anatomy of the inner ear. How does sound get from the oval window to the hair cells of the organ of Corti?

8. What is place code theory? How does it describe the relation of site along the basilar membrane and our perception of pitch?

9. What is the difference between conductive hearing loss and sensorineural hearing loss? How does loud noise cause hearing loss?

10. What is the difference between hearing aids and cochlear implants? How does each improve hearing in the hearing impaired?

KEY TERMS

Acoustic reflex, 272

Amplitude, 262

Audiogram, 278

Audiometer, 278

Basilar membrane, 272

Characteristic frequency, 275

Cochlea, 272

Cochlear implants, 281

Complex sound, 266

Cycle, 261

Decibel (dB), 263

Eustachian tube, 271

External auditory canal (external auditory meatus), 269

Fourier analysis, 266

Frequency (sound stimulus), 264

Fundamental frequency, 266

Hair cells, 275

Harmonics, 265

Hearing aids, 280

Hertz (Hz), 264

Incus, 270

Inner hair cells, 276

Loudness, 263

Malleus, 270

Middle canal (cochlear duct), 272

Organ of Corti, 272

Ossicles, 270

Otosclerosis, 279

Outer hair cells, 276

Perilymph, 272

Phase, 266

Pinna, 269

Pitch, 264

Place code theory, 276

Pure tone, 262

Reissner's membrane, 272

Round window, 272

Sensorineural hearing loss, 279

Sound stimulus, 260

Sound waves, 260

Stapedius, 271

Stapes, 270

Stereocilium, 276

Tectorial membrane, 276

Temporal code theory, 276

Tensor tympani, 271

Timbre, 266

Tinnitus, 279

Tympanic canal, 272

Tympanic membrane, 269

Vestibular canal, 272

INTERACTIVE SENSATION LABORATORY EXERCISES (ISLE)

Experience chapter concepts at edge.sagepub.com/schwartz

ISLE 10.1 The Sound Stimulus, 260

ISLE 10.2 The Decibel Scale, 263

ISLE 10.3 Frequency and Pitch on a Piano, 264

ISLE 10.4 Frequency Response of the Ear, 265

ISLE 10.5 Timbre and Musical Instruments, 265

ISLE 10.6 Fourier Analysis in Audition, 266

ISLE 10.7 Missing Fundamental, 266

ISLE 10.8 Timbre and Overtones, 266

ISLE 10.9 Phase and Cancellation, 268

ISLE 10.10 The Middle Ear, 270

ISLE 10.11 The Basilar Membrane and Sound Stimuli, 272

ISLE 10.12 The Traveling Wave, 272

ISLE 10.13 Place Code Theory, 273

ISLE 10.14 The Basilar Membrane and Fourier Analysis, 275

ISLE 10.15 Transduction and Hair Cells, 276

ISLE 10.16 Temporal Code Theory, 277

⑤SAGE edge™

Sharpen your skills with SAGE edge at edge.sagepub.com/schwartz

SAGE edge for students provides a personalized approach to help you accomplish your coursework goals in an easy-to-use learning environment.

The Auditory Brain and Sound Localization

11

INTRODUCTION

Some of you may know people, perhaps family members, who constantly misplace their cell phones. The routine for finding a missing cell phone is a well-known script. You get someone to call the number of the missing phone. Once you hear it start ringing, it is easy to locate the lost phone, perhaps under a pile of magazines moved out of the way earlier in the day. In this particular situation, we take a simple fact of our auditory system for granted—that we can use sound to localize objects in space. But how do we determine from the sound of the hidden phone exactly where it is located? Few of us reflect on this ability when we dig the phone out from under those magazines. But the localization of objects in space via the auditory system is a very complex process, and one that we discuss at length in this chapter (see Figure 11.1).

At a perceptual level, we use an important cue to home in on the spatial location of the sound, namely, its loudness. The louder the phone sounds, the closer you are to its source. Thus, if the missing phone sounds louder in the kitchen than it did in the living room, you are getting closer. If it is louder still in the pantry, perhaps you left it by the rice when you were cooking and talking on the phone. Interestingly, however, we can localize objects by sound even when we are standing still. In this case, our auditory system does an amazing calculation of differences in loudness and timing between the two ears. Yes. If the cell phone is to your left, the sound will be louder in your left ear than your right ear, and we can use such cues to help us localize sound. However, this requires rather interesting neural machinery.

Our auditory system has developed a mechanism that allows this rapid and precise calculation to be made quickly enough to detect the minute lag between when auditory information reaches one of our ears and the moment it reaches the other, as well as the tiny differences in loudness. These involve incredible neuronal connections called the calyx of Held, named after the German scientist Hans Held, who first discovered these synapses at the end of the 19th century. The calyx of Held is a super-giant synapse that connects two neurons in the auditory primary cortex and has been found to be responsible for spatial localization across a number of mammalian species (Yang & Xu-Friedman, 2013). Because these synapses are so big, they allow the extremely rapid transfer of information from one cell in the network to the next. This extremely rapid transmission of information is necessary for the millisecond-precise timing that is necessary for using the auditory system to detect spatial differences. Thus, you can thank your calyxes of Held for your ability to track down that missing cell phone.

LEARNING OBJECTIVES

11.1 Discuss the ascending neural pathways from the cochlea to the auditory cortex.

11.2 Identify the processes our auditory system uses to localize the sources of sounds in space.

11.3 Explain the concept of auditory scene analysis and how it is achieved by the auditory system.

■ **FIGURE 11.1** Where is the cell phone?

We often have to locate our lost cell phones. We call the number and then use our ability to localize sound to find the phone, as may be the case for this phone left behind in the sand at the beach.

As with vision, the auditory system sends information from the receptor cells to various locations in the brain for processing. As we discuss these brain regions and their responsibilities within the auditory system, think about how these systems are similar to and different from the systems within the visual system.

BRAIN ANATOMY AND THE PATHWAY OF HEARING

11.1   Discuss the ascending neural pathways from the cochlea to the auditory cortex.

Auditory Nerve Fibers

Inner hair cells in the cochlea form synapses with auditory nerve fibers. These nerve fibers are bundled together in the eighth cranial nerve to be sent to the brain. We describe the properties of auditory nerve fibers here. Any particular auditory nerve fiber has a characteristic frequency to which it is most sensitive, consistent with place code theory, discussed in Chapter 10 (see Figure 11.2). If you examine Figure 11.2, you will see that the nerve fibers have characteristic frequencies to

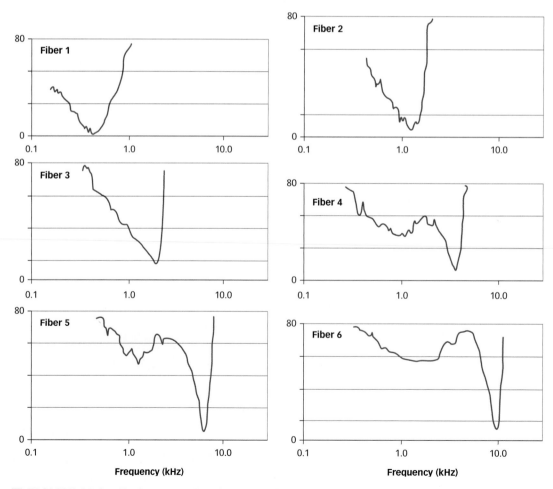

■ FIGURE 11.2   Tuning curve for eighth cranial nerve fibers.

These curves show the maximum sensitivity to frequency for different eighth cranial nerve fibers.

which they respond best, but they also respond to sets of frequencies both higher and lower than these characteristic frequencies. This is referred to as their tuning curve, which consists of the range of tones the cell responds to and its peak characteristic frequency. In Figure 11.2, the graph depicts sensitivity, the lowest sound level that a particular nerve fiber cell will respond to. The lower the curve goes, the more sensitive that nerve fiber is to a particular frequency. Thus, we can see that the auditory system continues to code for frequency in the auditory nerve, similar to the way the optic nerve codes for spatial location.

The auditory nerve fibers form the eighth cranial nerve, which then makes its way to the brain. The eighth cranial nerve takes a complex journey to the auditory cortex. The auditory tract goes through the **cochlear nucleus** first. Attached to the cochlear nucleus is the **trapezoid body**, which is important in determining the direction of sound. The cochlear nucleus also contains subnuclei with specific functions, such as sensitivity to the onset and offset of tones at particular frequencies. Other cells in the cochlear nucleus also serve a lateral inhibition function. These cells sharpen a particular frequency of incoming sound by inhibiting the response to nearby frequencies, either higher or lower.

From the cochlear nucleus and the trapezoid body, the sound signal goes to the **superior olive** in the brain stem. The superior olive receives input from both ears. This early crossover of information from each side of the auditory system is critical for sound localization. From the superior olive, the next synapse in the ascending pathway of auditory information is the **inferior colliculus** (plural *colliculi*). The inferior colliculus then projects to the **medial geniculate nucleus** of the thalamus. The medial geniculate nucleus then projects to the auditory cortex. The medial geniculate nucleus projects to the cortex, but also receives input back from the cortex (He, 2003). Indeed, there are more returning (or efferent) connections from the cortex to the medial geniculate nucleus than there are ascending (or afferent) connections from the medial geniculate nucleus to the cortex. The area in the cortex projected to by the medial geniculate nucleus is called the primary auditory cortex, located in the temporal lobe of the brain. Auditory nerve fibers from each ear go to each side of the temporal lobe, but there are more from the right ear that go to the left temporal lobe, and more from the left ear that go to the right temporal lobe (see Figure 11.3). Because both ears project to both hemispheres, it is often difficult to assess hemispheric specialization in the brain.

Auditory Cortex

The **auditory cortex** is a large multifaceted area located in the temporal lobe. It is located under the lateral sulcus along the top of the temporal cortex (see Figure 11.4). Figure 11.4 shows the complex organization of the auditory cortex. The first area that receives input from the medial geniculate nucleus is known as the **primary auditory cortex** (also known as A1 or Area 41). Cells in the primary auditory cortex show a **tonotopic organization**. That is, cells show a maximal response to specific frequencies, and these cells are organized in maplike patterns. The primary auditory cortex is one of three areas that make up the **auditory core region**. The other two are the **rostral core** and the **rostrotemporal core**. Another area within auditory cortex surrounds the auditory core region. The **belt** and **parabelt** regions essentially wrap around the primary auditory cortex, hence the reference to belts, but are not part of the core region. All of these regions can be seen in Figure 11.4.

Figure 11.4 also shows the tonotopic organization of the auditory cortex. From the basilar membrane on, the auditory system is coded in terms of the

Cochlear nucleus: a structure in the brain stem that receives input from the inner hair cells

Trapezoid body: a structure in the brain stem that plays a role in determining the direction of sounds

Superior olive: a structure in the brain stem that receives input from the cochlear nucleus

Inferior colliculus: a structure in the midbrain that receives input from the superior olive

Medial geniculate nucleus: a structure in the thalamus that receives auditory input from the inferior colliculus and sends output to the auditory cortex

Auditory cortex: the areas in the temporal cortex that process auditory stimuli

Primary auditory cortex: the first area in the auditory cortex, which receives input from the medial geniculate nucleus

Tonotopic organization: the organization of neurons within a region in the brain according to the different frequencies to which they respond

Auditory core region: an area of the auditory cortex, consisting of the primary auditory cortex, the rostral core, and the rostrotemporal core

Rostral core: an area in the auditory core region of the auditory cortex

Rostrotemporal core: an area, in addition to the rostral core, in the auditory core region of the auditory cortex

Belt: a region of the auditory cortex that wraps around the auditory core regions

Parabelt: a region of the auditory cortex, in addition to the belt area, that wraps around the auditory core regions

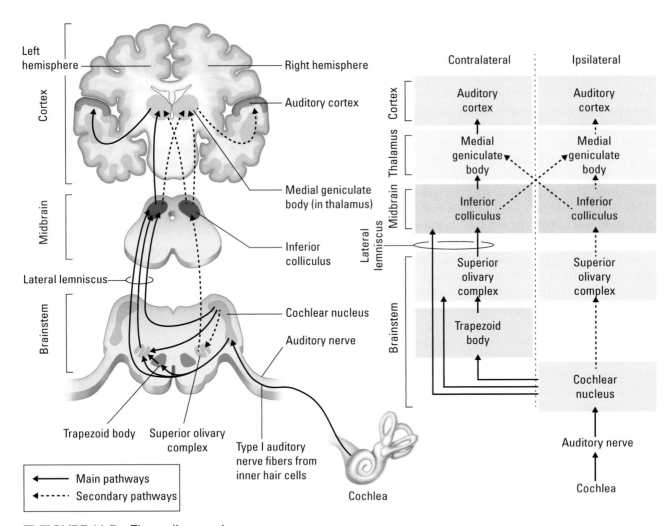

■ FIGURE 11.3   The auditory pathway.

Information goes from the cochleae of the ears up the ascending pathway to the auditory cortex in both the left and right hemispheres.

frequencies of sounds in the environment. Within the auditory core regions, one can find a tonotopic organization of the tissue within this region, gradually moving from high to low frequencies. Thus, just as the visual system is organized by space, we see frequency coding throughout the auditory system. The core region appears to serve the same function as V1, allowing for the primary analysis of frequencies. The belt and parabelt regions seem analogous to the extrastriate cortex, doing more complex analyses of the auditory signal. For example, neurons in these regions are less responsive to pure tones at particular frequencies than they are to complex stimuli consisting of multiple frequencies.

"What" information and "where" information are separated in the auditory system in a manner analogous to the visual system (see Figure 11.5). With respect to audition, the "what" system is involved in using auditory information to identify the identity of a sound. The "what" system forms the basis of both speech perception and music perception, which we consider in Chapters 12 and 13, respectively. The "what" system starts in the core region and then moves to more anterior parts of the temporal lobe. In contrast, the "where" system is responsible for localizing sound in space, a topic for this chapter. It is this system that allows us to determine that the alto saxophone is coming from one side of a jazz band, but the electric bass is coming from the other. The "where" system also begins

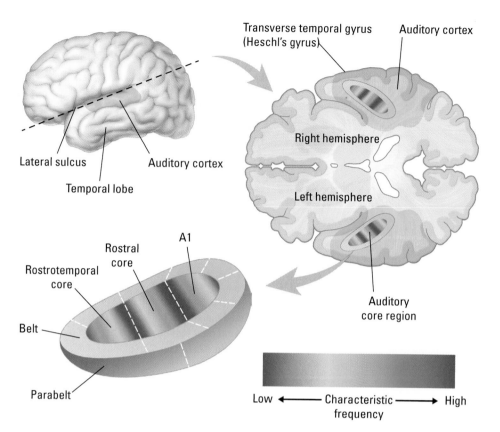

Transverse temporal gyrus (Heschl's gyrus)

Auditory cortex

Lateral sulcus

Auditory cortex

Temporal lobe

Right hemisphere

Left hemisphere

A1

Rostral core

Rostrotemporal core

Belt

Parabelt

Auditory core region

Low ← Characteristic → High
frequency

■ FIGURE 11.4   **Auditory cortex.**

The auditory cortex is located under the lateral sulcus along the top of the temporal cortex. The auditory cortex is composed of the primary auditory cortex as well as the rostral core, the rostrotemporal core, and the belt and parabelt regions.

in the core region of the auditory cortex and then moves to posterior regions of the temporal lobe as well as in the posterior parietal cortex (Rauschecker & Scott, 2009).

> **TEST YOUR KNOWLEDGE**
>
> What is meant by the concept of the "what" and "where" systems in the auditory cortex? How does each contribute to our understanding of the auditory cortex?

LOCALIZING SOUND

 Identify the processes our auditory system uses to localize the sources of sounds in space.

Thousands of people have learned to scuba dive, and they flock to places like Florida and the Bahamas to swim underwater among tropical fish and corals. Scuba diving is a very safe activity, if done correctly and at relatively shallow depths. Perhaps the biggest danger for scuba divers is swimming too close to the surface when motorboats are about. For this reason, scuba divers are taught to listen for the sounds of boats and to associate that sound with danger. The difficulty in hearing while completely immersed is that sound

Frontal lobe

Parietal lobe

Occipital lobe

"Where"

"What"

Auditory core region

Temporal lobe

■ FIGURE 11.5   **The "what" and "where" systems in the auditory cortex.**

The "what" system is responsible for identifying the sources of sounds, whereas the "where" system is responsible for determining where in space those sounds are coming from. The "what" system runs along the dorsal areas in the temporal lobe and then into the frontal lobe. The "where" system heads from the auditory cortex to the parietal lobe.

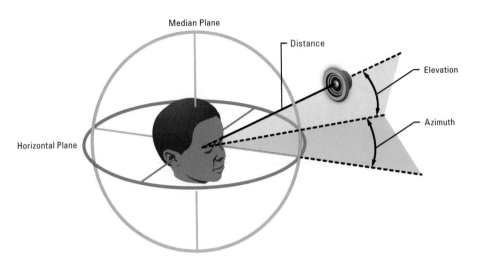

■ FIGURE 11.6 **Sound localization.**

The *azimuth* refers to the left-right or side-to-side position along the horizontal plane. *Elevation* refers to the up-down dimension along the median plane. *Distance* refers to how far a sound is from us and whether it is in front of or behind us. The horizontal plane bisects the head along the left-right dimension, whereas the median plane bisects the head along the vertical axis.

travels much faster in water than it does in air. This creates difficulty in localizing the direction of sound underwater. When a scuba diver hears a boat, it is much harder for him or her to determine if the boat is coming from the left or right relative to his or her position. It is also more difficult to determine if the boat is in front or behind the diver. This is all a direct function of the speed of sound in water, which throws off the mechanisms we use for sound localization, which are based on differences in timing and loudness between the left and right ears. Because underwater, those differences are less, sound is harder to localize in space. On land, however, we can make very clear judgments as to whether a sound is coming from the left or right. To test yourself on this dimension, go to ISLE 11.1. In this section, we take a look at the perceptual and physiological mechanisms necessary for sound localization.

In vision, spatial localization is direct and the main feature of coding in the visual cortex. Spatial position is determined by the retinal position of an image. In the auditory system, the cochlea is organized tonotopically, and spatial localization is done by a number of indirect mechanisms. In the auditory system, sound localization is based on the comparison of sound in the two ears and is thus analogous to stereoscopic vision.

In order to localize an object in space, we must know if it is to the left or right of us, whether it is in front of or behind us, and whether it is above or below us. That is, we must be able to localize sound in three-dimensional space. The **azimuth** refers to the left-right or side-to-side aspect of sound localization. **Elevation** refers to the up-down dimension of sound localization, and **distance** refers to how far a sound is from us, and whether it is in front of or behind us (see Figure 11.6). We discuss how we determine each of these dimensions in this section.

Interaural Time Difference

The **interaural time difference** is the time interval between when a sound enters one ear and when it enters the other ear. In principle, this is a rather straightforward concept. A sound coming to us from the left will enter our left ear a split second before it enters our right ear. A sound coming to us from the right will enter

ISLE 11.1 Sound Localization Experiment

Azimuth: the left-right or side-to-side aspect of sound localization

Elevation: the up-down dimension of sound localization

Distance: how far a sound is from the listener and whether it is in front of or behind the listener

Interaural time difference: the time interval between when a sound enters one ear and when it enters the other ear

our right ear a split second before it enters our left ear. Because our auditory system can detect this millisecond difference in timing, we can use the interaural time difference to determine if a sound is coming from the left or right. Thus, the interaural time difference gives us the location of the object along the azimuth.

To determine the actual interaural time difference is relatively straightforward, although it involves a bit of arithmetic. The speed of sound in air is 343 m/s, and the left ear and right ear are about 10 cm apart. If a sound is coming from a source directly to our right, the sound will reach the right ear 640 microseconds (0.00064 seconds) before it reaches the left ear. That's an amazing 640-millionths-of-a-second difference our ears are detecting. However, not all sounds will be coming directly from the left or the right. Some may be slightly in front on one side or slightly behind (see Figure 11.7). We can think of a big circle around the head and measure the angle of the sound to our head

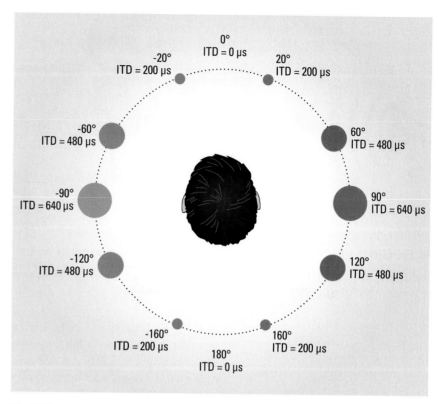

■ FIGURE 11.7   Interaural time differences.

At different angles relative to the head, a sound will reach the left and right ears with different interaural time differences. The auditory system can compute these time differences and use them to determine the direction of a sound.

in degrees. If the sound is coming from 90°, that is, directly to our left or right, the time difference will be 640 microseconds. However, if the angle is only 20° (i.e., coming from in front of us but slightly to the right), the time difference will be only 200 microseconds. Thus, the longer the time lag between the ears, the more toward 90° (or immediately right or left) the sound is coming from. Figure 11.7 shows this point graphically. Research from psychophysical experiments confirms that people do detect such incredibly small time lags (Fedderson, Sandel, Teas, & Jeffress, 1957).

For a region in the brain to compute the interaural time difference, it must have access to information entering the auditory system from both ears. It is likely that for this reason, early crossing over of information from one side of the brain to the other evolved within the auditory system. Physiologically, interaural time differences appear to be computed in the medial superior olives. Yin and Chan (1990) found neurons within the medial superior olives of cats that were sensitive to differences in the interaural time difference, providing support for this region of the brain as being critical for sound localization (see Figure 11.8). Go to ISLE 11.2 to see how interaural time differences influence the direction from which you hear a sound.

ISLE 11.2 Interaural Time Differences

Interaural Level Difference

The **interaural level difference** is the difference in loudness and frequency distribution between the two ears. As sound travels, its strength dissipates. For example, if you are very close to a loud sound, it will sound loud to you. But if you are some distance from the same loud sound, it will not be as loud. Think

Interaural level difference: the difference in loudness and frequency distribution between the two ears

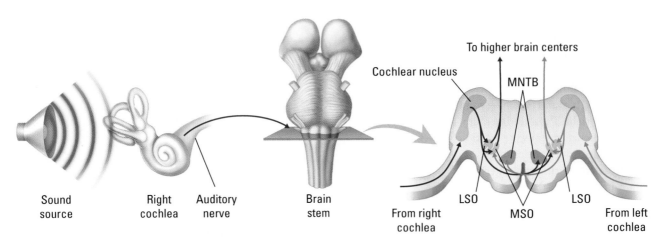

■ FIGURE 11.8   Interaural time difference in the medial superior olives.

Information from the cochlea makes a synapse in the cochlear nucleus and then travels to the medial superior olives, where information from the right and left cochleae is first combined.

ISLE 11.3 Interaural Level Differences

of a dog barking. If it is right in front of you, it will sound loud, but if the same dog barks across a big grassy field, the sound will be much less loud to you. Amazingly, our ears can detect loudness differences between the left and right ears. However, more important for sound localization is that the head casts an acoustic shadow, which changes the loudness and frequency distribution of sound going to each ear. We can define the **acoustic shadow** as the area on the side of the head opposite from the source of a sound in which the loudness of a sound is less because of blocked sound waves. The acoustic shadow is much more prominent for high-frequency sounds than it is for low-frequency sounds (see Figure 11.9 and ISLE 11.3).

Thus, sound coming from the left or right will have a different loudness in each ear and a different frequency composition in each ear. High-frequency sounds will be louder in the closer ear, although low-frequency sounds will be approximately the same loudness in each ear. That is, the ear that is closer to the sound will hear the sound as somewhat louder, and that ear will also detect more of the higher frequency components of the sound. If it is a pure tone, then only the loudness difference will matter, but even with pure tones, the loudness difference will be greater, the higher the frequency of the sound. Psychophysical research shows that people are sensitive to these interaural level differences. Physiological studies suggest that interaural level differences are computed in the lateral superior olive.

The Cone of Confusion

The **cone of confusion** is a region of positions in space in which sounds create the same interaural time and interaural level differences. That is, imagine a sound that is coming from 45° from below you and to the left. This sound will create the same differences as a sound that is coming from 135° above you and to the right. If your head remains still, you cannot tell the difference in spatial position between sounds coming from these sources. This cone of confusion is depicted in Figure 11.10. Although the cone of confusion is real—it is easily demonstrable in psychophysical experiments—it is easily remedied. As soon as the head moves, the ears change position relative to the sources of sound, and sounds from different locations now may have different characteristics. So the cone of confusion seldom bothers a person in motion.

Acoustic shadow: the area on the side of the head opposite from the source of a sound in which the loudness of a sound is less because of blocked sound waves

Cone of confusion: a region of positions in space in which sounds create the same interaural time and interaural level differences

Elevation Perception

Sounds may be coming from above us and below us as well. For spatial localization, identifying this aspect of a sound is as critical as knowing the angle of orientation of our head to that sound. Interestingly, the way our auditory system detects elevation is a function of changes in sound frequency created by the folds in our outer ears, the pinnae (see Figure 11.11). The bumps and folds in the pinnae cause slight reverberations (i.e., echoes). These reverberations amplify some frequencies and dampen others. The **spectral shape cue** is the change in a sound's frequency envelope created by the pinnae. It can be used to provide information about the elevation of a sound source. That the shape of the pinna affects elevation perception has been demonstrated in experiments. When the shape of the pinna is artificially altered, elevation perception is impaired. However, after sufficient time with a newly shaped pinna, elevation perception will be relearned and achieve normal levels (Hoffman, Van Riswick, & Van Opstal, 1998). Thus, one might expect someone with an extreme ear piercing to temporarily lose some ability to localize sound, but that ability should return. Indeed, in Hoffman et al.'s (1998) study, participants with modified pinnae returned to normal localization after approximately 20 days.

Detecting Distance

Detecting the distance of a sound relies on a different set of princi-

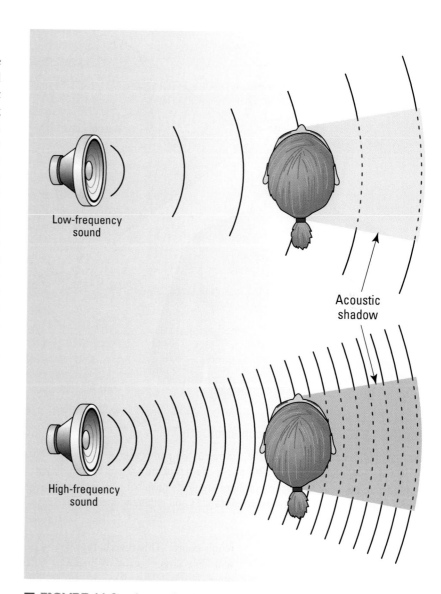

■ FIGURE 11.9   Acoustic shadow.

High-frequency sounds have shorter wavelengths than low-frequency sounds. This causes more reflecting or blocking of the high-frequency waves off the side of the head than occurs with low-frequency waves. Consider how big waves on the ocean roll right past objects such as buoys, but smaller waves break off when encountering such objects. It's the same principle here. When a sound wave encounters objects smaller than its wavelength, the sound wave bends around it, like the low-frequency sound does here. When a sound wave encounters an object bigger than its wavelength, the sound wave does not bend as much around the object. In fact, it may be blocked or distorted, as in the drawing.

ples. One of the chief methods for inferring the distance of sounds relies on our internal knowledge of the loudness of familiar sounds. Thus, when you hear a dog bark, you have knowledge of the approximate loudness of that specific dog's barking, that breed of dog's barking, or dog barking in general. Then, on the basis of the actual loudness of the bark, you can judge its distance as being close or far. Similarly, human voices can be judged as being closer or farther on the basis of their loudness. This, of course, may lead to errors. We may judge an unseen person's voice to be near simply because he is speaking loudly. Frequency also plays

Spectral shape cue: the change in a sound's frequency envelope created by the pinnae; it can be used to provide information about the elevation of a sound source

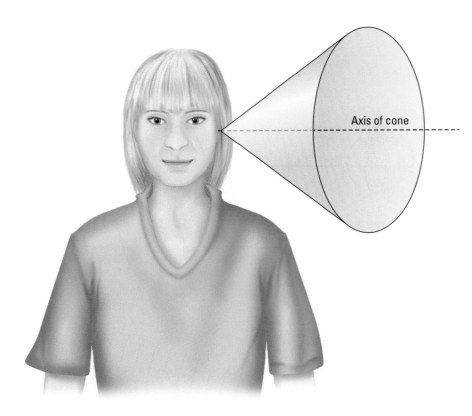

Axis of cone

■ **FIGURE 11.10**   **The cone of confusion.**

Sounds coming from any location on the surface of the cone result in nearly identical interaural time and interaural level differences. Note that the cone is imaginary but exists relative to the sounds present, so there are many possible cones of confusion for different ranges of sounds at different distances and angles to the person.

a role in distance perception. High-frequency sounds show a greater decrease in loudness as a function of distance than do low-frequency sounds. Remember that you can hear the bass line of the music from the party across the lake, but not the voice of the singer. This is also apparent when we hear thunder during a thunderstorm. Thunder nearby has a distinctive "crack" that causes people to look up and cats and dogs to scurry for shelter. Distant thunder lacks the high-frequency component, and we hear it as a less-jarring "boom." So, a diminishment of the high-frequency component of sound also tells us about distance.

Another cue for distance is the proportion of direct sound to reflected sound. When the dog barks across the park from you, some of the sound you pick up travels directly from the dog to your ears. But some of the sound from the dog bounces off objects, such as the ground, the trees, and the wall by the tennis courts. This reverberant sound may also reach your ears. Close-by objects will have larger ratios of direct to reflected sound than faraway objects, under most circumstances. Reverberant sound will have slightly altered frequencies and interaural time differences than direct sound. This allows our auditory systems to compute the ratio, and this gives us information about the relative distances of sound sources.

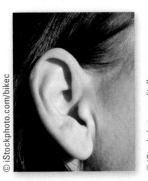
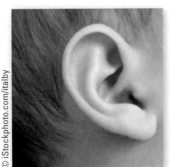
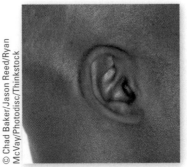
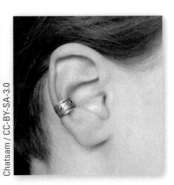

■ **FIGURE 11.11**   **The human pinna.**

Pinnae vary greatly from one person to the next. Each individual learns from birth how his or her pinnae change sound as it enters the ears. The shape of the pinna can provide information about the height of the source of a sound.

We return to the calculation of distance in our discussion of bat echolocation at the end of the chapter. For bats, detecting distance is easier because they can compare their own sound production with the return of echoes, allowing direct computation of distance.

TEST YOUR KNOWLEDGE

Why is the distance between the two ears important in localizing sound? How does having two ears contribute to our perception of localized sound? Might any of the cues to sound localization work in a person with only one functioning ear?

AUDITORY SCENE ANALYSIS

11.3 Explain the concept of auditory scene analysis and how it is achieved by the auditory system.

Stop for a moment right here and listen to all the sounds, however faint, that are currently around you. What do you hear? Even in a quiet room, there are probably half a dozen different sounds you can distinguish. You might be able to hear the slight pulse of the air conditioner, the whirr of the refrigerator, and a car motoring past somewhere outside your window. You might hear the slight chatter from your sister's iPod even though she's wearing headphones, your mother on the telephone in the other room, and the distinct sound of your cat's breathing while it sleeps nearby. Each of these sounds is made up of several frequencies, and in some cases, these frequencies may overlap (see Figure 11.12). They are all hitting your cochlea simultaneously, but seemingly not straining your ability to distinguish the sounds and localize them in space. This ability to distinguish the different sounds in the ambient environment has been called **auditory scene analysis** (Bregman, 2005).

There are only rare situations in which we cannot hear multiple sounds. Being in an environment with multiple sounds is the rule, not the exception. Thus, our auditory systems have evolved to separate and distinguish all these sounds despite the fact that the auditory stream from each sound may have overlapping frequencies as well as overlapping timing. Thus, the auditory system must group together those frequencies coming from common objects rather than simply grouping similar frequencies together. That is, even if the frequency of your whirring refrigerator is the same as that of your gently breathing cat, what is important is that we attribute each sound to its source.

This is a distinctly different problem from the one we face with the visual system. When we look at objects, spatial information about them usually overlaps. Although objects may be occluded, parts of objects do tend to be near to one another. Because our visual system is organized in terms of space, scenes have a more inherent organization. However, given that our auditory system is organized tonotopically, the analysis of scenes is more complex, because any sound-emitting object is probably emitting sounds at multiple frequencies, some of which may overlap in terms of frequency with other sound-emitting objects.

Bregman's (1990, 2005) view of auditory scene analysis is very much akin to the principles of gestalt psychology. That is, the auditory system uses a number of heuristic rules to determine which frequencies go with which other frequencies and which sounds are associated with which objects. These rules are not perfect—they

Auditory scene analysis: the process of identifying specific sound-producing objects from a complex set of sounds from different objects at varying and overlapping frequencies

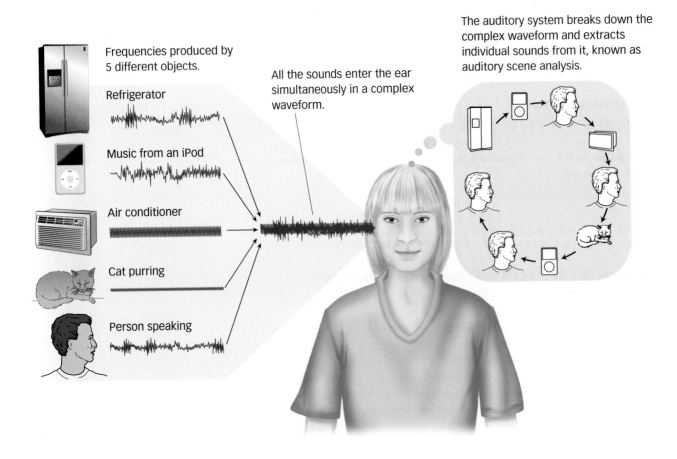

Frequencies produced by 5 different objects.

Refrigerator

Music from an iPod

Air conditioner

Cat purring

Person speaking

All the sounds enter the ear simultaneously in a complex waveform.

The auditory system breaks down the complex waveform and extracts individual sounds from it, known as auditory scene analysis.

■ **FIGURE 11.12**   Auditory scene analysis.

Complex sounds from five different objects enter a person's cochlea at exactly the same time. The person's ability to separate out these inputs and attribute them to the unique objects is known as auditory scene analysis.

sometimes lead to errors in auditory scene analysis—but more often than not, they allow us to correctly parse the auditory landscape. Like the gestalt rules, these processes center on the ability to group different patterns of sounds together. Auditory scene analysis rules fall into three basic types. We group by timing—that is, sounds that are produced at the same time may be grouped together (temporal segregation). We group by space—that is, those sounds that are emanating from the same place in space are grouped together (spatial segregation). We also group by frequency—that is, sounds that are of the same frequency or harmonic pattern are grouped together (spectral segregation). We consider each in turn.

Temporal Segregation

Consider the sound of your washing machine. There might be a relatively loud, high-frequency sound caused by the motor of your machine. At the same time, there might be a lower amplitude and lower frequency sound being produced by the rotation of clothes inside the machine. We group these sounds together because they are linked or correlated in time. When one stops, the other stops, and when the washing machine cycles again, both sounds start anew. In music, we group the violas together because they are all playing the same rhythms at the same time. This is the concept of **temporal segregation**. Sounds that are linked in time are grouped together, whereas sounds that are not correlated with one another are

Temporal segregation: the process whereby sounds that are linked in time are grouped together, whereas sounds that are not correlated with one another are not grouped together

not grouped together. However, in some situations, rapid alternation between two frequencies may be linked in time, but lead to the perception of different streams rather than the same stream (see Figure 11.13). Composers often use this rapid alternation of pitch in time to create the illusion of two sound streams from one musical instrument.

Spatial Segregation

In the section on sound localization, we discussed the mechanisms by which the auditory system can localize sound in space. To review, this involves comparing the loudness, timing, and frequency distribution of sounds reaching our left and right ears. Thus, with **spatial segregation**, we can distinguish where in space sounds are coming from. In auditory scene analysis, we can use this to group sounds together or separate them

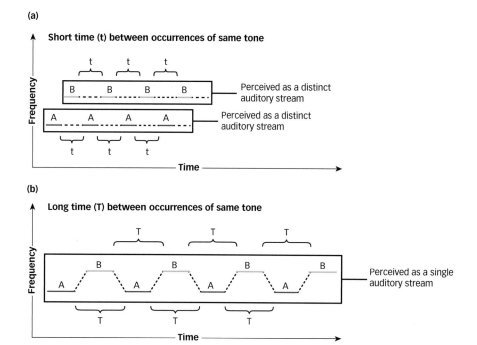

■ **FIGURE 11.13**   Temporal segregation.

In Sequence (a), because the high- and low-frequency tones alternate rapidly, we hear two separate sources of sound. In Sequence (b), when the time between the successive tones gets longer, we join the two tones into a common theme, and tend to hear one sound bouncing between two frequencies.

into different sources. If you can localize one frequency as coming from behind you and slightly to the right and another frequency as coming from above you and to the left, your auditory system will know that these frequencies are associated with different sound sources. However, if both a high frequency and low frequency are coming from the same spot in space, you can assume that those frequencies are linked. Thus, when we hear the revving of the motor and the thumping of the stereo coming from the same source to our right, we associate both sounds with the Ford Mustang waiting to our right for the traffic light to turn. Moreover, when the light does turn green, we hear all of these sounds getting softer together as the Mustang accelerates and drives away.

Spectral Segregation

Spectral segregation refers to a number of separate grouping rules concerning how we use frequency distributions to group sounds together. Note here that a source of sound, such as a person's voice, has multiple frequencies present. You hear a person's voice at its fundamental frequency, but that voice has a number of higher frequency harmonics. Indeed, any complex sound will be composed of multiple frequencies. So consider a person listening to another's voice. The auditory system is detecting multiple frequencies coming from the same location in space. Should the auditory system determine that the multiple frequencies are all coming from the same source, or should the auditory system determine that there are multiple objects in the same location, each emitting a different frequency? Obviously, in most cases, the former will be the case, not the latter. Similarly, consider a person listening to a musical performance. Each musical instrument has a fundamental frequency and a number of higher frequency harmonics. The

Spatial segregation: the process whereby sounds that are coming from the same location are grouped together, whereas sounds that are coming from different locations are not grouped together

Spectral segregation: the process whereby sounds that overlap in harmonic structure are grouped together, whereas sounds that do not overlap in harmonic structure are not grouped together

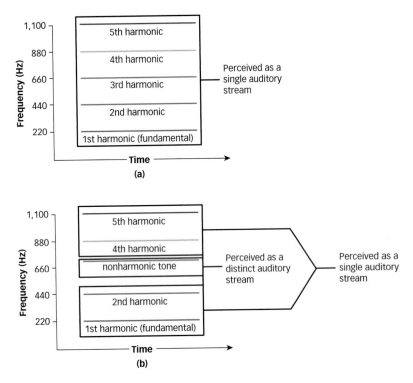

■ FIGURE 11.14   Spectral segregation.

(a) When the fundamental frequency and higher harmonics of a particular sound, such as a voice, are presented together, the auditory system of the listener groups these tones together into a single stream from a single source. (b) When there is a tone present that is not possibly a higher harmonic of the fundamental frequency, that tone is perceived as a separate auditory stream against the background of the grouped frequencies.

listener must associate the fundamental frequency and the harmonics coming from the saxophone and segregate them from the frequencies coming from the piano in order to parse the musical phrases. Thus, a key aspect of spectral segregation is grouping by **harmonic coherence** (see Figure 11.14).

Harmonic coherence is a very strong predictor of what sounds our auditory system will group together. Consider listening to a recording of music. Through headphones or earbuds, you hear a large grouping of frequencies simultaneously. Even though there are only two sound sources—the speakers for your left and right ears—you hear a number of auditory streams, depending on what kind of music you are listening to. For example, if you are listening to a Mozart symphony, you will hear separate auditory streams for the violins, the cellos, the clarinets, the trumpets, and so on. If you are listening to the Beatles, you will hear separate auditory streams for John, Paul, George, and Ringo. This grouping occurs even when some of the frequencies are coming from different sources. That is, harmonic coherence takes precedence over spatial segregation (see Figure 11.15).

TEST YOUR KNOWLEDGE

What is meant by the term *auditory scene analysis*? Why is auditory scene analysis important, and what processes help our auditory system carry it out?

Auditory Development

As most parents now know, the auditory system develops early. Indeed, studies show that shortly after birth, infants will respond differently to sounds they heard in utero and sounds they did not (Partanen et al., 2013). This does not mean that playing Mozart to your unborn child will make that child a genius, but it does suggest that the auditory system develops early. Findings show that the auditory system is functional at about the 25th week of gestation (i.e., the 25th week of pregnancy), long before the visual system is operational (Graven & Browne, 2008). Two-day-old infants can recognize the voices of their own mothers relative to the voices of other mothers (DeCasper & Fifer, 1980), which also suggests early development. However, hair cells and the auditory nerve will continue to change and develop throughout the first few years of a child's life (Graven & Browne, 2008).

In addition, experiments have shown that infants have equivalent thresholds across the frequency range as do young adults. They can detect soft sounds across the frequency range, at least from the age of 3 months, when it becomes possible to test thresholds. An important task for older children and adults is to separate

Harmonic coherence: when frequencies present in the environment resemble the possible pattern of a fundamental frequency and higher harmonics

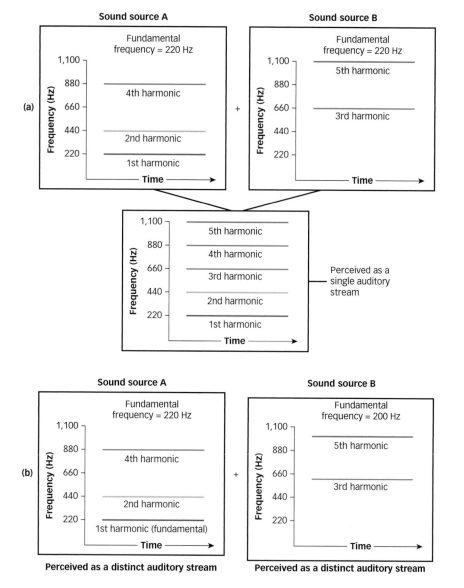

FIGURE 11.15 Spectral sensitivity.

(a) Harmonics of a common fundamental frequency are presented simultaneously but from different spatial sources. In this situation, the listener hears one auditory stream despite the spatial differences. (b) When the harmonic structure from two different sources is not coherent, we hear two separate auditory streams.

concurrent sounds. Moreover, the research suggests that auditory localization of the sources of sounds occurs early. Young infants by the age of 3 months are already tuned to separate the sources of sounds in any auditory input (Grimault et al., 2002).

IN DEPTH: *Biosonar in Bats and Dolphins*

You might not think bats and dolphins would have much in common. Bats are small, nocturnal flying mammals, whereas dolphins are large marine mammals (see Figure 11.16). But they share one very important aspect of their biology together: they both use an active biosonar system. **Biosonar** is a process whereby animals emit sounds and then use comparisons of these emitted

sounds and their returning echoes to sense the world around them. Biosonar has much in common with the electronic sonar systems human technology has developed. The basis of both systems is the determination of the relation of emitted sounds and returning echoes (Simmons, 2012). This contrasts with our own hearing, which involves listening for external sounds but does not involve creating

■ FIGURE 11.16   Bats and dolphins use biosonar.

Bats and dolphins use their auditory system to navigate the world. But bats and dolphins have a biosonar sense. They emit loud, high-frequency sounds and then listen for the echoes. Both species, despite the difference in environments, use this information for hunting. Bats hunt small insects, and dolphins hunt fish.

echoes with our own voices. For this reason, biosonar is really a completely different perceptual system than our auditory system. But because it involves the basic processes of hearing, we include it here. We start with bat sonar and then describe the similarities and differences in dolphins. For those who find this section intriguing, we highly recommend the book *Sensory Exotica* by Howard Hughes (1999), a Dartmouth College professor who discusses biosonar and a host of other nonhuman sensory systems.

Bats hear sounds at much higher frequencies than we do. Most species of bats can hear sounds at over 100,000 Hz, whereas our highest frequency tops out at about 20,000 Hz. Bats can also produce very high-frequency sounds themselves. It is this combination that allows them to use biosonar. Because there is such a short wavelength (remember that frequency and wavelength are inverses), high-frequency sounds will be influenced by small objects that obstruct the wave pattern. For instance, a mosquito flying by would likely not impact a low-frequency wave, but it would deflect a high-frequency wave (see Figure 11.17). That is, the low-frequency wave may miss the insect altogether, but a high-frequency wave will hit the insect and cause an echo to return to the bat. Thus, high-frequency sonar allows bats to detect small prey items, such as mosquitoes, that lower frequencies would not pick up. Dolphins use sonar to hunt for fish. For this reason, they use high frequencies too.

The problem with high frequencies, though, is that they lose energy rapidly. As a consequence of this, their loudness

declines rapidly as the sound moves away from the source. So high frequencies have the advantage of detecting small things, but the disadvantage of losing energy rapidly. We experience this loss of energy in high frequencies ourselves in everyday life when a car with a loud stereo drives by. We hear the bass line (low frequency) from quite far away, but we do not hear the singer's voice (high frequency) until the car is right next to us. This occurs even when the high and low frequencies are equated for loudness at the source of the sound.

This puts an additional requirement on animals using biosonar. Because high frequencies lose volume rapidly, the initial sound must be very loud. Indeed, both bats and dolphins call very loudly. Bat calls are often as loud as 140 dB, and dolphin calls may reach 200 dB. Luckily, we humans are not disturbed by these super loud calls at night. Because

(a)   (b)

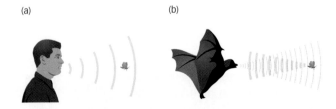

■ FIGURE 11.17   High-frequency waves are better for capturing information.

(a) The low-frequency wave passes right through the small object, which, for a bat, might be a tasty insect. The low-frequency wave will not detect the insect. (b) The high-frequency wave will be deflected by the small object, causing an echo to return toward the source of the sound. It is for this reason that animals equipped with biosonar use high-frequency sounds.

Biosonar: a process whereby animals emit sounds and then use comparisons of the emitted sounds and their returning echoes to sense the world around them

these loud calls are made at frequencies we cannot hear, they can be going on all around us and we will not hear them. In essence, bats and dolphins must call very loudly to give their calls a little more range to strike potential targets. Thus, to summarize what we have discussed so far about bat sonar, bats make loud calls at high frequencies.

Because we cannot hear the sounds made by bats, it took scientists a long time to figure out that bats were using sounds to guide them (Hughes, 1999). For many years, scientists could not determine what sensory mechanism bats were using to hunt in darkness. Many species of bats actually do see quite well and will use vision when there is sufficient light, but early scientists blinded bats and found that they could still hunt. It was not until the 20th century that scientists figured out that bats were using hearing, but at frequencies the scientists could not hear (Hughes, 1999).

It is important to keep in mind that there are many different species of bats, each uniquely adapted to its own natural ecology. Almost all bats use some kind of biosonar system (the exception being Australian flying foxes). Some species of bats live in open spaces, such as the air spaces above deserts, whereas other species of bats live in densely forested areas. This leads to different uses of the biosonar system. Some bats use biosonar to avoid obstacles as well as to hunt, whereas other bats use it for hunting alone. Bats that live in dense forests need to avoid obstacles such as leaves and branches as they fly through the night, but desert bats do not. Desert bats can therefore concentrate on hunting rather than obstacle avoidance. This leads to two different types of calls characteristic of forest and desert bats. The forest bats tend to use what is called a CF-FM call (Hughes, 1999). In these calls, as the bat is flying in the forested environment, it emits a call at a constant high frequency (the CF component). When it detects potential prey, such as a moth, the bat's call sweeps down in frequency (i.e., frequency modulated or FM). This kind of call is depicted in Figure 11.18. This FM component is sometimes called the feeding buzz, as it usually occurs just before the bat catches and eats its prey. In other species, such as those that live in deserts, the CF component may not be present. These FM-only bats emit a series of calls with a downward slope in frequency, which will increase in rate when an insect is detected.

Biosonar systems work by integrating the processing of the call with the processing of the echo. Bats make calls, and then their highly sensitive auditory systems listen for the echoes that bounce off the objects in front of them and return to their ears (see Figure 11.19). This system provides the bat with information about the distance, size, and speed of the target it is tracking. This system allows bats to zoom in on prey and in some cases avoid obstacles and bigger predators. In Figure 11.19, you can see how a bat, once it detects an insect, uses its calls to home in on the insect. We next consider the mechanisms

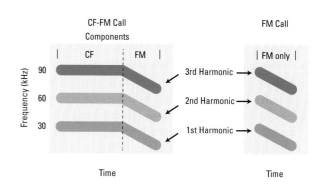

■ **FIGURE 11.18**   Bat biosonar calls.

CF-FM calls involve long calls at a single frequency. When an object is detected, the bat sweeps down in frequency. This is the characteristic pattern of forest bats. FM calls involve just the sweep from high frequency down to relatively lower frequencies. This is the characteristic pattern of desert bats.

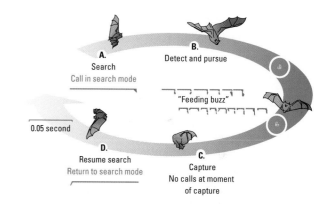

■ **FIGURE 11.19**   How bats use biosonar.

Bat biosonar is used to for the pursuit and capture of insect prey. The bat uses its call and the returning echo to locate food sources.

by which bats use their biosonar to detect objects in their environment.

First, the bat needs to determine the distance from itself to an object. This is important—if the insect is too far away, the bat may not be able to catch up. If the object is close by, the bat may need to begin its capture behaviors. Distance from an object is determined by a calculation of the amount of time it takes for an echo to return to the bat. If the echo returns after a very short lag, the bat knows the object in front of it is very close. If the echo takes longer to return to the bat, the object is farther away. In bat (and military) circles, this aspect is known as the **target range**, how far way the target is. This is a quite remarkable ability when you consider how close bats are likely to be to their targets, and when you consider how

Target range: the distance of a predator from its potential target, determined by timing an echo's return

fast sound moves. Given that sound travels at 343 m/s, it will take only 12 ms between a bat's call and the echo's return from a target 2 m away. Yet bat auditory systems can track such incredibly fast echoes. A target farther away than 2 m will take more than 12 ms, and a target closer will take less time. Thus, by timing the echo, the bat receives a precise estimate of the target range.

Bats also need to know how large an object is. If a bat is following an owl, for example, it may wind up being the meal rather than finding a meal for itself. Thus, bats must be able to infer size information from their biosonar system. This information is also determined by the returning echoes. Larger objects produce bigger echoes. Thus, a bat can infer size from the relative loudness of the echoes. This determination is relative to the distance of the object, which is determined by timing. Thus, closer objects will produce bigger echoes too, but the bat's auditory system can account for distance when using echo loudness to determine the size of the object.

A bat also needs to know if it is gaining on its target or falling behind in its pursuit. If the insect is flying faster than the bat, the bat may need to speed up. If the bat is flying faster than its prey, it may need to moderate its speed to be ready to engage in capturing behaviors. And if the bat is traveling at the same speed as the moth it is pursuing, it will not be able to catch it. This is normally not a problem, as bats fly much faster than most of the insects they prey upon. But the bat still must know how fast it is approaching so that it can initiate its catching behaviors at just the right time. Bats determine approach in an ingenious way. They determine their **rate of approach** by measuring something called the Doppler shift in their calls. Doppler shifts are apparent changes in frequency that occur when there is relative motion between the source of a sound and a detector. In this case, both the source of the sound (the bat's call) and the detector (the bat's detection of echoes) come from the same place. The Doppler shift is an interesting phenomenon in and of itself, so we take a slight digression to explain it here.

If a stationary object is emitting a sound at a particular frequency, a stationary perceiver will hear it at that frequency. However, if the sound-emitting object starts moving away from the perceiver, the object will still be emitting at the same frequency, but each sound wave will be coming from slightly farther away from the perceiver. This creates a perceived frequency somewhat lower than that of the actual sound. Similarly, if the sound-emitting object is moving closer to the perceiver, the sound waves will essentially bunch up together, creating the experience

of a higher frequency sound to the perceiver. This is why an approaching train seems to get higher in pitch, and a receding train appears to get lower in pitch to the stationary observer, waiting for the train to pass. A person on board the train will not hear this shift because he or she is moving with the train and therefore hearing it at the frequency at which the train sounds are emitted. Interestingly, the Doppler shift is important in astronomy as well. It also explains why galaxies moving away from us in space are said to "red-shift," which means that they show a slightly longer wavelength of light than would be expected if the galaxy were not moving away from us.

Now think about one of these bats calling as it flies though the sky. Its calls come at a constant frequency, say 90,000 Hz. First, consider the bat is moving faster than the object, but the bat is moving in the same direction as its calls. Thus, relative to an object in front of the bat, the frequency will appear slightly higher than the frequency the bat is actually calling at because each call comes slightly closer to the previous call. If the object is moving faster than the bat is, it will take longer for the waves to catch up with that object, and the frequency will be perceived as lower than the actual call (see Figure 11.20).

In the case of bats, their auditory system knows exactly what frequency it is emitting. If the returning echo appears to be slightly higher than the frequency of the call, the bat knows that it is gaining on its target. Thus, if it hears the echo at 90,050 Hz, the bat knows that it is approaching the target. If the returning echo appears to be slightly lower in frequency than the frequency of the call, then the bat knows it is losing ground on its target. Thus, if hears the echo at 89,950 Hz, the bat knows that it is falling back from its target.

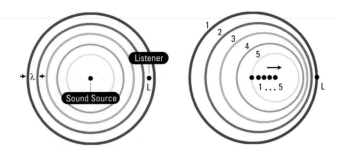

■ FIGURE 11.20   **Doppler shifts.**

If a sound source is approaching you, it will sound slightly higher in frequency to you than it would to an object moving along with it. Similarly, if a sound source is receding from you, it will sound slightly lower in frequency to you than it would to an object moving along with it. Because bats know the frequencies at which they are calling, they can use these Doppler shifts in the echoes to calculate rate of approach.

Rate of approach: the measure of whether a predator is approaching a target or receding from it

Finally, a bat needs to know if its target is moving to the left or right and up or down relative to the bat's position. Left-right determination is done by a comparison of the returning echo to the two ears, similar to the discussion of sound localization earlier in this chapter. If the echo is of equal amplitude in each ear, the bat knows the target is straight ahead. However, a difference in amplitude between the left and right ears indicates that the target is to the left or to the right. If the object is to the left of the bat, the echo will be slightly stronger in the left ear than the right ear, and if the object is to the right, the echo will be slightly stronger in the right ear than the left ear. A bat also needs to know if its target is rising or falling relative to its flight pattern, that is, whether the target is flying higher or lower than the bat. This turns out to be the most complex computation by the bat's auditory system, and it involves comparing sound inputs distributed across its complexly shaped pinnae, similar to the discussion earlier. However, bats have large movable pinnae, so they are much better at elevation determinations than humans are. Studies have shown that blocking a bat's pinnae interferes with its determination of the elevation of its target.

Using this information, a bat uses its auditory system to "see" objects in the external environment (Simmons, 2012). Because it is using its auditory system, a bat can use this system to guide its flight in complete darkness. Biosonar also allows bats to be highly social. It has been shown that they use their sonar systems to avoid bumping into one another in the tight confines of caves, and some bats also use sonar to identify their own offspring (Bohn, Smarsh, & Smotherman, 2013).

What about dolphins? Dolphin sonar is also a call-and-echo system (Hughes, 1999). Although the physiology of the system is very different, functionally, it is very similar. Dolphins also use loud, high-frequency pulses. Indeed, dolphin calls have registered at over 200 dB and nearly 200,000 Hz! It is a good thing we do not hear them. Dolphins compute distance to target, approach to target, size of target, and left-right and up-down differences in the same way as bats. What makes the dolphin's system remarkable is that sound travels 4 times faster through water than it does through air. Thus, the dolphin's brain must be even more sensitive to minute millisecond time differences than that of the bat.

One of the main differences between bat biosonar and dolphin biosonar is that dolphins use neither the sustained CF nor the FM call. Dolphins make pulse calls, like the FM bats, but unlike FM bats, they are at a constant frequency. Dolphins may vary the frequency, but not in the sweeping way bats do. Dolphins appear to change the frequency of their calls when there is "noise" in the area, possibly the result of another dolphin using the same frequency.

Thus, we can see the use of the auditory system for a very different purpose in animals equipped with biosonar. We have not explored the neuroscience of biosonar, though much research is being done in this area (see Simmons, 2012). Biosonar requires modifications to the cochlea and to the auditory nerve, and in both bats and dolphins, one sees an enlargement of the auditory cortex. But as with our auditory and visual systems, we see in bat and dolphin biosonar systems how nature hones incredibly sharp perceptual instruments to allow animals to act in the world.

CHAPTER SUMMARY

| 11.1 | Discuss the ascending neural pathways from the cochlea to the auditory cortex.

Hair cells send signals into the auditory nerve, which then leave the ear and head toward the brain. The cochlear nucleus is a structure in the brain stem that receives input from the inner hair cells. The signal is then sent to the superior olive and from there to the inferior colliculus. The inferior colliculus sends the auditory signal to the medial geniculate nucleus, which then sends its output to the auditory cortex. The primary auditory cortex (and rostral core) is the first area in the auditory cortex that receives input from the medial geniculate nucleus. It is surrounded by the belt and parabelt regions. *Tonotopic organization* means that the auditory cortex is organized by frequency. The auditory cortex develops early in the fetus's neural development.

| 11.2 | Identify the processes our auditory system uses to localize the sources of sounds in space.

To localize an object in space, we must know if it is to the left or right of us, whether it is in front of or behind us, and whether it is above or below us. Sound localization is a very important aspect of the auditory system, as it is often important to pinpoint a sound's source. That is, we must be able to localize sound in three-dimensional space. The interaural time difference is the time interval between when a sound enters one ear and when it enters the other ear. The interaural level difference is the difference in loudness and frequency distribution between the two ears. The acoustic shadow is the area on the side of the head opposite from the source of a sound in which the loudness of a sound is less because of blocked sound waves. The cone of confusion is a region of positions in space in which sounds create the same interaural time and interaural level differences. The shape of the pinna affects elevation perception, which has been demonstrated in experiments. When the shape of the pinna is artificially altered, elevation perception is impaired. This is known as the spectral shape cue.

11.3 Explain the concept of auditory scene analysis and how it is achieved by the auditory system.

Auditory scene analysis is the process of identifying specific sound-producing objects from a complex set of sounds from different objects at varying and overlapping frequencies. The rules of auditory scene analysis fall into three basic types: temporal segregation, spatial segregation, and spectral segregation. The auditory system develops early. Indeed, studies show that shortly after birth, infants will respond differently to sounds they heard in utero and sounds they did not.

REVIEW QUESTIONS

1. List all of the brain regions that make up the ascending auditory pathway. Describe at least one difference of this auditory pathway from the visual pathways to the brain.

2. What are the "what" and "where" systems in auditory perception? What brain regions are involved in each system?

3. What is meant by the term *tonotopic organization* of the auditory cortex?

4. How can the interaural time difference be used to compute the spatial coordinates of a sound in the external world?

5. Why are interaural level differences more useful in localizing high-frequency sounds than low-frequency sounds?

6. What is the cone of confusion? How does it affect sound localization for an unmoving perceiver?

7. What are the mechanisms human auditory systems use to detect the distance of a sound? Why are we better at judging distance for a familiar sound? Why are bats and dolphins better at detecting distance?

8. What is meant by the term *auditory scene analysis*? What mechanisms do we use to group frequencies together from common sources?

9. What is the difference between a call and an echo in bat echolocation? Why does a bat need both to be able to detect objects?

10. How does a bat compute its rate of approach to an object? How might a bat be fooled by an insect equipped with the ability to produce high-frequency sounds, but not able to fly faster than the bat?

KEY TERMS

Acoustic shadow, 294

Auditory core region, 289

Auditory cortex, 289

Auditory scene analysis, 297

Azimuth, 292

Belt, 289

Biosonar, 301

Cochlear nucleus, 289

Cone of confusion, 294

Distance, 292

Elevation, 292

Harmonic coherence, 300

Inferior colliculus, 289

Interaural level difference, 293

Interaural time difference, 292

Medial geniculate nucleus, 289

Parabelt, 289

Primary auditory cortex, 289

Rate of approach, 304

Rostral core, 289

Rostrotemporal core, 289

Spatial segregation, 299

Spectral segregation, 299

Spectral shape cue, 295

Superior olive, 289

Target range, 303

Temporal segregation, 298

Tonotopic organization, 289

Trapezoid body, 289

INTERACTIVE SENSATION LABORATORY EXERCISES (ISLE)

Experience chapter concepts at edge.sagepub.com/schwartz

Sharpen your skills with SAGE edge at edge.sagepub.com/schwartz

SAGE edge for students provides a personalized approach to help you accomplish your coursework goals in an easy-to-use learning environment.

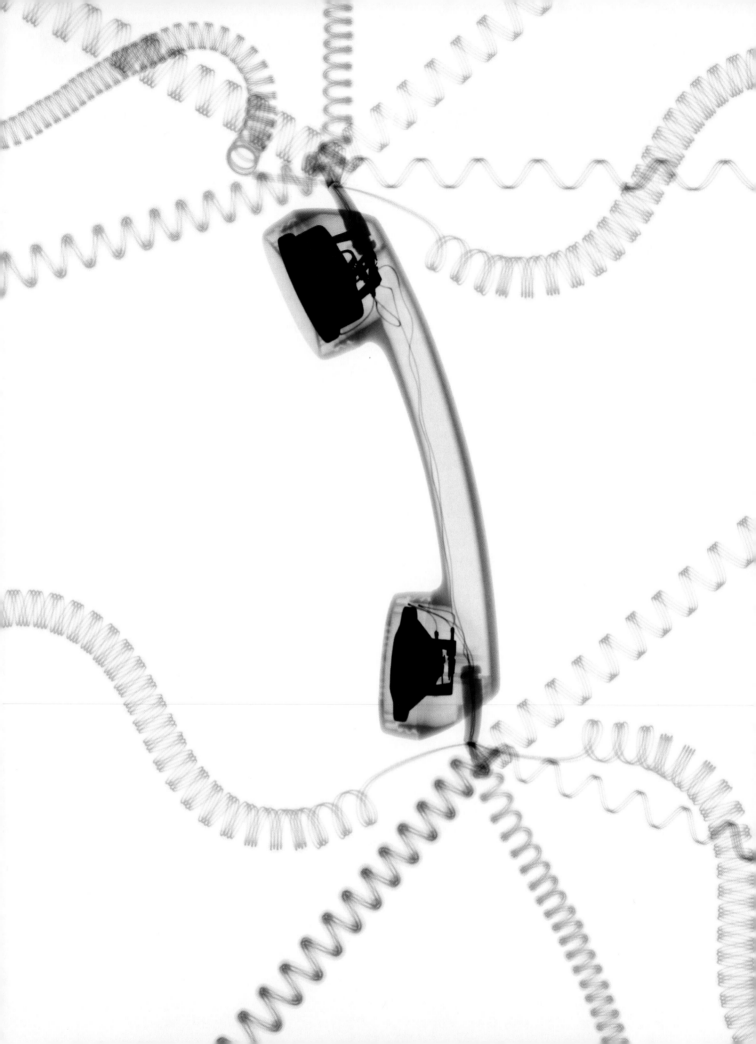

Speech Perception

12

INTRODUCTION

There is no function of our auditory system more vital to human beings than speech perception. Speech perception is critical in interacting and socializing with the people around us. Unless you spend most of your time in your study writing textbooks, you are likely to spend most of your waking hours talking to and listening to other people. Other people constantly surround us, and they communicate with us using speech. You hear "What's your name?" and this sound informs you that the person speaking is asking to interact with you. You hear somebody say, "What's the best restaurant near here?" and you know that she wants your opinion. Speech is everywhere and vital for our everyday life (see Figure 12.1). Moreover, from the auditory signal of a person's voice, we extract not just the information the speaker is conveying, but information about the speaker himself or herself, including gender, age, mood, native language, national background, regional background, educational level, and so on. And all of this information comes from the auditory speech signal.

We need to be able to understand speech rapidly. The average speaker may talk at a rate of roughly four words per second. That is one word every 250 ms. This means our auditory system must convert the sound signal into meaningful language information at very rapid rates to allow us to gather all the information that we do from speech. Our auditory system uses every bit of available information to do this, including using cross-modal information from vision to help us understand speech. It also turns out that the speech signal itself is very complex, which further taxes our speech perception system. This chapter examines some of the processes that allow our auditory systems to quickly interpret very complex speech signals.

A situation many people find themselves in from time to time is a crowded room filled with many conversations all taking place at once. This situation might occur in a busy restaurant, while watching a sporting event, while at a fraternity party, or at an old-fashioned cocktail party. Indeed, in the technical literature, this phenomenon is known as the "cocktail party effect." In the cocktail party effect, you are listening to the speech of one person, but your attention is then distracted by the mention of your name by someone across the room. You may not have even been aware of this conversation, but the mention of your name rivets your attention from across the room (Cherry, 1953). To researchers in the 1950s and 1960s, this suggested that our attentional mechanism does not screen out all perceptual input even when we are focused on one conversation. We covered attention in an earlier chapter, but we mention it here to note that our speech perception systems are capable of monitoring multiple speech inputs at the same time. This requires enormously complex processing in our auditory system to separate out the different voices coming from different directions.

LEARNING OBJECTIVES

12.1 Discuss the complex process of speech perception and speech production.

12.2 Describe the mechanisms our speech perception system uses to extract coherent speech from the speech signal.

12.3 Summarize the general-mechanism theories, special-mechanism theories, and motor theory of speech perception.

12.4 Identify the areas of the brain involved in speech perception and what happens when they are damaged.

■ FIGURE 12.1   Listening to language is critical.

People must listen to and understand others' speech in most aspects of their lives.

From the point of view of your auditory system, all of the voices you hear in different conversations are causing movements along your basilar membrane at the same time. Thus, the auditory system must first be able to separate out the various voices as well as other sounds that are all occurring at the same time. This problem of segmenting the auditory signal into its component parts is called auditory scene analysis (discussed in the last chapter), and it is necessary to determine which particular sounds are coming from which source (Bregman, 1990). Even if no person is speaking to you as you read these words, think of the different sounds you can pick up. You can separate out the sound of the radio playing music in the other room easily from the barking of the dog across the street. Similarly, even when multiple voices are talking at the same time, we can separate out which voice goes with which person and place those voices appropriately in terms of their locations. Recent research shows that an important component of scene analysis for speech is the familiarity of a voice. A familiar voice, such as that of a spouse, a child, or a parent, can be used to mark a particular signal to either be attended to or not. We are better at both with familiar voices relative to unfamiliar voices when listening amid a chatter of conversations (Johnsrude et al., 2013).

Like many perceptual processes, speech perception seems effortless and fluent to adults, in this case, listening to fluent speakers of their native language. However, as with many perceptual processes, what our auditory system must do to achieve this fluent perception is remarkably complex. Indeed, computer speech-processing systems are only now becoming truly workable, and even so, they require enormous computing power.

THE HUMAN VOICE AS STIMULUS

 Discuss the complex process of speech perception and speech production.

Perceptual processes begin with a stimulus in the environment. In the case of human speech perception, that stimulus is a voice. Other people produce speech, which our perceptual apparatus must hear and understand. Therefore, it is necessary to understand just a bit about the acoustics of human voices in order to begin our discussion of speech perception. We are sure you will not be surprised to learn that the human speech organs are quite complex, and many different parts of our anatomy play a role in producing the myriad speech sounds we make.

Speech sounds are produced by movements of the vocal apparatus (see Figure 12.2). Speech sounds are acoustic signals, which start as air pressure changes in the lungs that are then modified by a number of structures in the neck and mouth that create the sounds we use as speech. First, air that produces the sound passes through the **trachea** (or **windpipe**) and into the **larynx** (also known as the **voice box**). The larynx is an important part in the vocal tract, but not the only one necessary for speech. Vocal folds within the larynx open and close to change the pitch of the sound. However, parts of the vocal tract higher up from the trachea are necessary for the array of consonant sounds our voices

Trachea (windpipe): the tube bringing air to and from the mouth

Larynx (voice box): a structure that affects the pitches of sounds being made by the human vocal tract

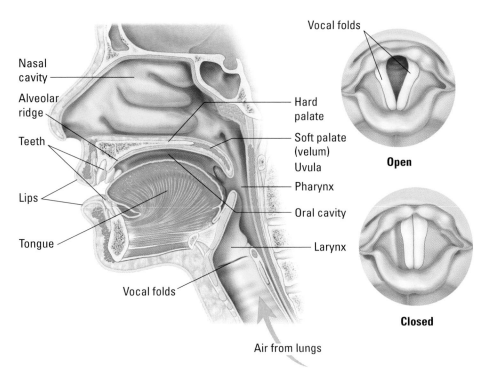

Human beings have a sophisticated anatomical system for producing language sounds. Speech is initiated with air being pushed out of the lungs into the larynx. Vocal folds in the larynx vibrate at different frequencies, producing the different pitches human voices are capable of. Changes in the position of the pharynx, oral cavity, tongue, lips, and teeth can then shape that sound into the particular speech sound the person is saying.

must make. From the larynx, the air passes through the **pharynx** into the mouth and nose, where teeth, tongue, lips, and the **uvula** can affect the sound signal. The pharynx is the top portion of the throat. The uvula is tissue in the back of the mouth attached to the soft palate. Closing the uvula prevents sounds from going up through the nasal cavity, affecting the quality of the sound. The sound signal then exits the vocal apparatus through the mouth and the nose. These articulators are depicted in Figure 12.2.

Vowels and Consonants

Human vocal tracts make two categories of speech sounds: vowels and consonants. These terms are equivalent to the categories one learns when learning to read. **Vowels** are represented in English by the letters *a*, *e*, *i*, *o*, *u*, and sometimes *y*. **Consonants** are the letters that surround these vowels sounds, such as the sounds represented by the letters *b*, *v*, and *p*. Vowels and consonants have different origins within the vocal tract. Vowels are produced by unrestricted airflow through the pharynx and mouth. Changing the shape of the mouth creates different vowel sounds. Restricting the airflow in one place or another along the way up from the larynx produces consonants. For example, movements of the tongue restrict the sound and change the nature of a consonant. Perceptually, as well, vowels and consonants are two distinct categories.

Vowels are produced by vibrations of the vocal cords, and specific vowel sounds ("oo," "ah," "ee," etc.) are made by changes in the position of the oral cavity, particularly the shape of the mouth. If you speak aloud the standard vowel sounds in English, you will feel the shape of your mouth move, as you go through the standard vowel sounds. As we change the shape of our mouth and vocal tract, we change the resonances in the sound. That is, each vowel sound has a characteristic pattern of harmonics. The harmonics that are of highest amplitude are known as formants. **Formants** are the frequency bands with higher amplitudes among the harmonics of a vowel sound. Each individual vowel sound has a specific pattern of formants. Figure 12.3 shows the shapes of the mouth and the

Pharynx: the top portion of the throat

Uvula: a flap of tissue at the top of the throat that can close off the nasal cavity

Vowels: speech sounds made with unrestricted airflow

Consonants: speech sounds made with restricted airflow

Formants: frequency bands with higher amplitudes among the harmonics of a vowel sound; each individual vowel sound has a specific pattern of formants

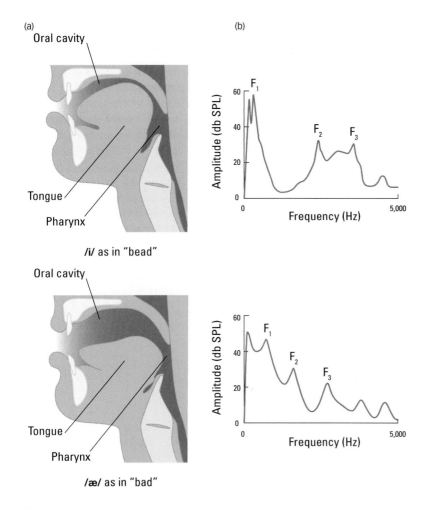

(a)
Oral cavity
Tongue
Pharynx

/i/ as in "bead"

Oral cavity
Tongue
Pharynx

/æ/ as in "bad"

(b)

FIGURE 12.3   **Vowel sound production.**

(a) The mouth producing two different sounds. (b) The frequency spectra for those sounds.

frequency spectra for two different vowel sounds. Note that the fundamental frequency is the same for each vowel. Vowels are distinguished from one another by their formant frequencies.

Consonants are produced by restricting or closing of the flow of air along the vocal tract. In English, the letters, b, d, and f all represent consonant sounds. Some sounds, such as "b" and "v" and "d" and "f," are very similar and are therefore sometimes difficult to distinguish. Other consonant sounds used in English include "m" as in "mom" and "k" as in "kick." In English, we use the consonant sound "sh," though other languages, such as Spanish, do not. In contrast, Spanish uses sounds, such as the "ñ" in "niño," that we do not typically use in English.

Three physical features are important in determining the sound of a consonant. The **place of articulation** refers to the point along the vocal tract at which the airflow is constricted. The place of articulation may include the tongue, the lips, the teeth, and structures at the back of the mouth, such as the soft or hard palate. The **manner of articulation** refers to how that restriction occurs. This involves whether the lips are pushed together, whether the tongue is at the front or back of the mouth, and other variants of the mouth's position. Try saying a few simple words (e.g., "Bring the plate of chocolates, but do not drop it on the floor"), and attend to the positions of your tongue, teeth, and lips as you say each sound, and you will see how each sound is accompanied by different positioning of the vocal tract. Finally, **voicing** refers to whether the vocal cords are vibrating or not. Here, think of the difference between the way we say the sound in the letter p and the sound in the letter b. When you say the letter b, you can feel your vocal cords vibrating immediately as you produce the sound. P, which is voiceless, is not accompanied by vocal cord vibration until after the p has been pronounced. "S" and "z" are also complementary unvoiced and voiced sounds (Figure 12.4 shows what our vocal tract is doing when we speak various sounds).

Speech

The purpose of speech is to convey information. When you tell your friend "I am hungry," you are telling that person how you are feeling and likely implying what you want to do—have lunch. In order for your friend to understand what you are saying and your intentions behind it, she must be able to correctly perceive your utterance. Thus, speech perception involves the process of how we go from the sound signal coming from a speaker to understanding in a listener. This involves complex motor tasks in the speaker, as we just discussed, and complex auditory and cognitive tasks in the listener, which we turn to now. We start with phonemes.

Place of articulation: the point along the vocal tract at which the airflow is constricted

Manner of articulation: how airflow restriction in the vocal tract occurs

Voicing: whether the vocal cords are vibrating or not

Phonemes are the basic units of sound in human language. When a phoneme is changed, the meaning of the utterance is changed. Consider the word *mop*, which consists of three phonemes: "m," "o" or "ə" (the international symbol for the vowel sound in *mop*), and "p." If we change the first phoneme from "m" to "h," we get a new word, *hop*, with a different meaning. If we change the vowel sound in the middle from "ə" to the "æ" sound in *map*, we also get a different word. Finally, we can change the "p" sound at the end of the word to a "b" sound and get *mob*. Thus, in this case, each of the three letters in the word *mop* represents a separate phoneme. It is important to note that phonemes refer to sounds, not letters. We have to represent them with letters in this book, but any particular letter may stand in for multiple phonemes. Think of the letter combination *ch*, which may represent the first sound in *children* and the first sound in *choir*, despite the fact that the two sounds are quite different.

In English, as in many languages, convention in spelling does not match phonemes in a straightforward and direct manner. Users of English must learn by rote what vowel sound to use when pronouncing such words as *mood* and *blood*, *rough* and *through*, and *heard*, *beard*, and *dread*. In other cases, we may have two separate symbols that represent the same phoneme, such as in the "f" sound in *father* and *phoneme*. Thus, spelling and written letters only partially capture the richness of phonemes.

Linguists, in studying phonemes, require a system in which a single symbol represents each sound that people make in a particular language. This alphabet is known as the **International Phonetic Alphabet**, which provides a unique symbol for each and every phoneme in use in human languages. The International Phonetic Alphabet includes symbols for the hundreds of unique sounds that are used across the thousands of languages in use today (MacMahon, 1996). Table 12.1 shows the phonemes used in English and the symbols used to represent them in the International Phonetic Alphabet. Inspect Table 12.1 carefully. You will see that first, in contrast to what you were taught in elementary school, the English language has 15 vowel sounds and 24 consonant sounds. Because we only use 26 symbols in English to represent 39 sounds, many individual letters and letter combinations (e.g., *sh*, *oo*) must be used to represent multiple sounds. For example, using the International Phonetic Alphabet, the word *mop* is spelled "məp," while the word *through* is spelled "θru," and *cash* would be spelled "kæʃ." It takes a while to get comfortable using the International Phonetic Alphabet.

You might well wonder why we do not switch to the International Phonetic Alphabet, as each word's spelling uniquely describes how that word is pronounced, and this might make spelling easier. This is true, except that it would mean that all homophones (e.g., *bear* and *bare*) would be spelled the same, and the meaning

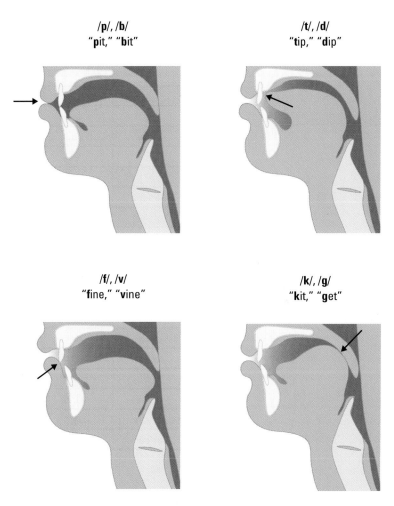

/p/, /b/
"pit," "bit"

/t/, /d/
"tip," "dip"

/f/, /v/
"fine," "vine"

/k/, /g/
"kit," "get"

■ **FIGURE 12.4** **Articulation of consonants.**

Consonant sounds depend on the place of articulation, manner of articulation, and voicing. Several consonant sounds are depicted here.

Phonemes: the basic units of sound in human language

International Phonetic Alphabet: an alphabetic convention that provides a unique symbol for each and every phoneme in use in human languages

Vowel	International Phonetic Alphabet	Example words		Consonant	International Phonetic Alphabet	Example words
a	ə	<u>a</u>ce, st<u>ay</u>		b	b	<u>b</u>at, ja<u>b</u>
a	æ	h<u>a</u>t, c<u>a</u>t		c	k	<u>c</u>ab, blo<u>ck</u>
a	a:	<u>a</u>rt, f<u>a</u>ther		ch	tʃ	<u>ch</u>oke, <u>ch</u>ur<u>ch</u>
ay/ei	e ɪ	pl<u>ay</u>, <u>eigh</u>t		d	d	<u>d</u>o, ba<u>d</u>
e	e	p<u>e</u>t, r<u>e</u>d		f	f	<u>f</u>an, i<u>f</u>
e	i:	h<u>e</u>, k<u>ey</u>		g	g	<u>g</u>ame, lo<u>g</u>
ear/ere	ɪəʳ	f<u>ear</u>, h<u>ere</u>		h	h	<u>h</u>ot, <u>h</u>elp
ere/air	eəʳ	<u>there</u>, p<u>air</u>		j	dʒ	<u>j</u>ump, lar<u>ge</u>
i	ɪ	s<u>i</u>t, m<u>i</u>t		l	ell	<u>l</u>et, <u>l</u>ift
i	ɑɪ	p<u>i</u>pe, l<u>i</u>fe		m	m	<u>m</u>ap, li<u>m</u>e
ow, ou	aʊ	h<u>ow</u>, p<u>ou</u>t		n	n	<u>n</u>ote, pe<u>n</u>
o	oʊ	g<u>o</u>, h<u>o</u>me		n	ŋ	sti<u>ng</u>, fi<u>ng</u>er
o	ɒ	sp<u>o</u>t, l<u>o</u>ck		p	p	<u>p</u>ool, ta<u>p</u>
ou/a	ɔ	t<u>ou</u>r, b<u>a</u>ll		r	r	<u>r</u>est, t<u>r</u>ain
oi/oy	ɔ ɪ	j<u>oi</u>n, t<u>oy</u>		s	s	<u>s</u>oap, ki<u>ss</u>
oul/u	ʊ	c<u>oul</u>d, p<u>u</u>t		s	ʒ	trea<u>s</u>ure, vi<u>s</u>ion
oo/ue	u:	f<u>oo</u>d, bl<u>ue</u>		sh	ʃ	<u>sh</u>irt, tra<u>sh</u>
our/ure	ʊəʳ	t<u>our</u>, p<u>ure</u>		t	t	<u>t</u>ip, se<u>tt</u>ing
ur/ear	ɜːʳ	b<u>ur</u>n, <u>ear</u>n		th	θ	<u>th</u>ought, ba<u>th</u>
				th	ð	<u>th</u>in, bro<u>th</u>er
				v	v	<u>v</u>ote, hi<u>v</u>e
				w	w	<u>w</u>in, <u>w</u>illo<u>w</u>
				y	j	<u>y</u>ell, <u>y</u>et
				z	z	<u>z</u>oom, cra<u>z</u>y

■ TABLE 12.1 Phonemes of American English Using the International Phonetic Alphabet

would depend on context. As it is, our writing system is made more difficult by the complex correspondence between symbol and sound, but also less difficult by this disambiguation of words that have multiple meanings. Using the International Phonetic Alphabet would also mean that regional differences in pronunciation would require different spellings. For example, the word *schedule* would need to be spelled differently in the United States and the United Kingdom, as Americans and Britons use different pronunciations for this word. It would also require that spellings vary as a function of region within any particular English-speaking country. As Harvard linguist Steven Pinker (1994) noted, for native Bostonians, the words *orphan* and *often* would be spelled identically using the International Phonetic Alphabet. Thus, although it may be appealing to come up with a completely phonetic spelling system, it is also not without its problems.

TEST YOUR KNOWLEDGE

Describe the pathway of air as it moves from the lungs and out of the mouth in making speech sounds.

VARIABILITY IN THE ACOUSTICS OF PHONEMES

12.2 Describe the mechanisms our speech perception system uses to extract coherent speech from the speech signal.

When we hear a speaker utter the expression "The boy was resisting arrest," we must engage in some complex auditory processing to go from the sound signal to perceiving phonemes to understanding the sentence. For example, could this sentence really be "The boy was resisting a rest," with far less serious implications? In this case, listeners must use top-down processing using contextual information to parse the words in a sentence. If the sentence is said at a day care center for 5-year-olds, we might gravitate toward the latter interpretation. If it is said by a police officer during a trial, we would opt for the first interpretation. Note that for this sentence, the manner in which most speakers of English would say it aloud gives us no clues. In this case, only the context can disambiguate the speech (see Figure 12.5). We will see in this section that speech perception requires a number of "tricks" that help the auditory system make fast and accurate interpretations of the speech signal.

Coarticulation

Speech perception must take place at very fast rates, as the average speaker can talk at the rate of four words per second. Or, to phrase it another way, the average speaker can produce about 15 phonemes per second. To do this, our articulators (e.g., the parts of our mouth, vocal tract) must do things simultaneously to produce this rapid speech. Indeed, when we speak, we also anticipate what sounds are coming next. In this way, we will say the phoneme "b" in the word *bat* in a slightly different way than we say the phoneme "b" in *bet*, because a different vowel sound follows the "b." Think about the position of your mouth when you say *bat*—it is more rounded right at the start than when you say *bet*. Similarly, the "a" sound in *bat* is said slightly differently than the "a" sound in *back*. This phenomenon is referred to as coarticulation. We can define **coarticulation** as the phenomenon in which one phoneme affects the acoustic properties of subsequent phonemes (see ISLE 12.1).

What this means is that the consonant and vowel sounds in "ba" overlap in when they are said. It also means that the "a" sound is influencing how the "b" is being said. This is a reciprocal process, with the vowel influencing the consonant and the consonant influencing the vowel. We can see this pattern of coarticulation in sound spectrograms of people speaking different consonant-vowel pairs. The physical acoustics of "ba" are different from those of "bə." This is illustrated graphically in Figure 12.6. In Figure 12.6, you can see that the spectrogram looks different right at the beginning for the two different sounds, which both start with the letter *b*.

Coarticulation is an acoustic reality. The acoustic stimuli of "bah," "bee," and "boo" are different, as you can see in Figure 12.6. However, as perceivers of speech, we do not hear the differences in the "b" sounds among "bah," "bee," and "boo." All we hear is the phoneme "b." Thus, even though the signal varies, what we hear is a constant.

We encountered the concept of perceptual constancy in our discussion of visual perception. We discussed how we see the same color regardless of the

■ **FIGURE 12.5   Parsing word boundaries.**

The difference between "resisting arrest" and "resisting a rest."

ISLE 12.1 Coarticulation

....

Coarticulation: the phenomenon in which one phoneme affects the acoustic properties of subsequent phonemes

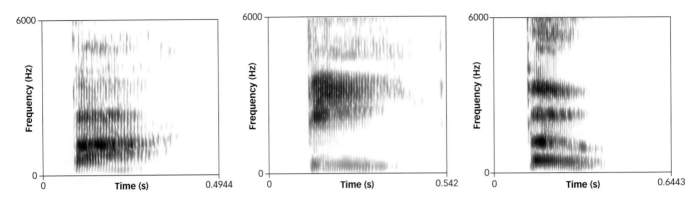

■ FIGURE 12.6 Coarticulation in the pronunciation of consonants.

These spectrograms show the formants for the sounds "bah," "bee," and "boo." You can see that the highest frequency formant is highest for "boo" relative to "bah" and "bee." This is a consequence of coarticulation.

wavelength of illumination in color constancy, and that objects appeared the same size regardless of retinal size. Our perception of coarticulation is an example of an auditory constancy, similar to the concepts of constancy with respect to vision. Because the various "b" sounds refer to the same phoneme, we perceive them as being identical. To reiterate, perception of coarticulation is that two or more different physical sounds are heard as identical phonemes.

What this means for our speech perception systems is that several different sounds must be grouped together to represent a particular phoneme, depending on context. This happens early in auditory processing, such that we do not perceive a difference between the "b" in *bet* and the "b" in *bat*. This can sometimes be a problem when learning a new language. For example, Japanese speakers group together what we English speakers hear as "l" and "r" into a single phoneme. Thus, when learning English, words such as *rail*, and *lair* are difficult to distinguish because the two words sound identical to a native Japanese speaker. It is not simply a matter of not being able to pronounce them. Essentially, native Japanese speakers must unlearn their phoneme groupings in order to perceive ours. Similarly, there are sounds in other languages that English perceivers do not hear. Nonetheless, our speech perception system groups sounds together, such as the "b" in *bet* and *bat*, and the difference between these sounds implicitly allows us to anticipate the sounds that follow each use of the phoneme.

Categorical Perception

As we have seen, being able to distinguish phonemes is critical to speech perception. Thus, our auditory system uses a number of processes to help us hear the right phoneme. Of course, phonemes are categories that represent a range of different physical sounds. In order to help us with phoneme perception, another feature of our perception is categorical perception. **Categorical perception** refers to our perception of different acoustic stimuli as being identical phonemes up to a point at which our perception flips to perceive another phoneme. That is, we do not hear the variation in the signal—we hear only the phoneme. And then, at a certain point, the variation is too much, and we hear a different phoneme altogether. Categorical perception exists in other sensory modalities as well. We see blue across a wide range of the visual spectrum, but then blue abruptly becomes green at about 480 nm. In speech, we may hear the "r" sound across a wide range of acoustics, but it then abruptly becomes "l" at a certain point. In the case of "l" and "r," it is the tongue's position that determines which sound we are making. Sounds with

Categorical perception: the perception of different acoustic stimuli as being identical phonemes up to a point at which perception flips to perceive another phoneme

intermediate tongue positions will be heard as either "l" or "r," and we seldom find these sounds strange.

With respect to phonemes, we hear a particular sound, such as "t," across a range of acoustic stimuli. Then, at a particular point along an acoustic dimension, our perception shifts, and we hear the sound as a different phoneme (e.g., "d"). This is illustrated nicely with a phenomenon called voice-onset time. **Voice-onset time** refers to the production of certain consonants (called stop consonants) in which there is a difference between the first sound of the phoneme and the movement of the vocal cords. The movement of the vocal cords is called voicing. Consider the difference between the phonemes "t" and "d." The phonemes "t" and "d" are similar with respect to the position of the mouth, but "t" is voiceless, and "d" is voiced. That is, the vocal cords do not vibrate when we say "t," but they do when we say "d." In the sound "ta," our vocal cords vibrate 74 ms after the burst of sound for the "t," corresponding to the "a" part of the sound. However, when we say the voiced "da," there is vocal cord vibration within 5 ms of the start of sound. This is illustrated in Figure 12.7. You can see an example on ISLE 12.2.

In normal speech, such as words like *ta-ta* or *da-da*, the voicing will be much different, with "ta" not showing voicing until much later than "da." But what happens when we change the natural voicing? This can be done easily in the lab with sound-processing software. In essence, in the lab, we can create a hybrid sound—something intermediate between the "t" and the "d." Thus, the question becomes, What do we hear when we hear a "t/d"-like sound with voicing halfway in between "ta" and "da"?

This is exactly what Eimas and Corbit (1973) did in a now classic experiment on categorical perception. They presented listeners with sounds in which the voicing varied from 0 ms up to 80 ms for "ta" and "da." At 0 ms, listeners heard the sound as "da," and at 80 ms, listeners heard the sound as "ta." Eimas and Corbit were interested in what listeners would hear when intermediate voicings were presented (e.g., 20-, 40-, and 60-ms voice-onset times). What they found was categorical perception. People heard seemingly normal "ta" and "da" sounds, which abruptly switched from one to the other at a voice-onset time in between the two. That is, we hear the syllable "da" up to about 35 ms, and then our perception abruptly changes, so that at 40 ms, we hear "ta." In only a small zone is the stimulus ambiguous, and once the change of perception is made, we do not hear anything odd about these nonnatural sounds. This transition at 35 ms is the phonemic boundary between "t" and "d." A similar phonemic boundary exists for other voiced-unvoiced pairs, such as "p" and "b," which transition when the voicing occurs at around 30 ms. Figure 12.8 illustrates these results graphically.

Functionally, categorical perception simplifies the category of what makes each letter and allows us to extract relevant phonemic information from individual differences in speech. Thus, for example, we could imagine a speaker whose native language is not English, who may voice the vowel after "p" slightly earlier than we do in English. When this speaker says a word such as *principal* or *poet*,

ISLE 12.2 Voicing Onset Time

(a)

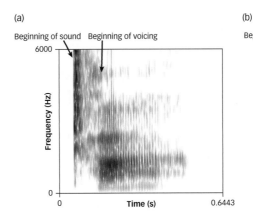

(b)

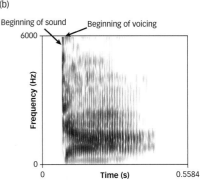

■ FIGURE 12.7   Voice-onset times in voiced and voiceless consonants.

(a) The sound spectrogram for "ta." (b) The sound spectrogram for "da."

Voice-onset time: the production of certain consonants (called stop consonants) in which there is a difference between the first sound of the phoneme and the movement of the vocal cords (called voicing)

(a)

(b)

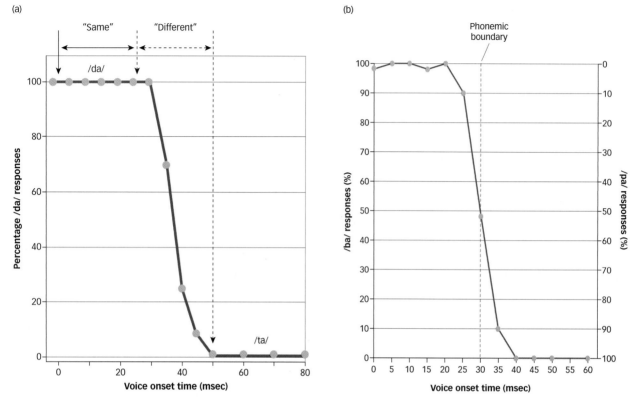

■ FIGURE 12.8   Categorical perception.

In an experiment, Eimas and Corbit (1973) asked participants to classify sounds as either "ta" or "da." They then presented participants with sounds with varying onsets of voicing. They found (a) that almost all sounds with voicing onset lower than 35 ms were classified as "da," but almost all sounds with voicing onset over 35 ms were classified as "ta." (b) The 30-ms phonemic boundary for "p" and "b."

we hear the "p" sound as a "p" because of categorical perception, which translates a wide range of voicing into one phoneme.

The Effect of Vision on Speech Perception and the McGurk Effect

Until the advent of telephones just 135 years ago, almost all speech was done within the range of one speaker seeing the other speaker. Yes, people shouted at a distance back then, but speech without vision was rare, to say the least. Even today, outside of telephone conversations, in most cases, we see the people we are speaking to. We watch as our friends talk to us, we look up toward our teachers when they are addressing the class (and if we are not looking at them, chances are we are not attending to them), and we watch actors move and talk in movies and television shows. Some of us may spend a great bit of time talking to friends and family on the telephone, particularly if we live some distance from those friends and family. But here is a phenomenon you may notice when speaking to a person you do not know via telephone. It is often difficult to distinguish unfamiliar words over the telephone. A customer representative tells you his name, but you cannot tell if it is Denny or Benny. This is less likely to happen in person because of the presence of visual cues we lack when conversing on the phone. In some instances, visual cues can greatly influence our perception of speech. For example, "dubbing" movies requires great skill. If the movements of the mouth do not match up with the sound signal, it can greatly decrease the realism of the movie. Nonetheless, as experimental psychologists, we can ask the question, How much does vision influence speech perception?

A very compelling demonstration of the influence of vision on speech perception was developed by McGurk and MacDonald (1976) and has come to be known as the **McGurk effect**. To demonstrate the McGurk effect, participants are shown a video of a person's mouth saying monosyllabic sounds, such as "ba," "da," and "tha." However, the audio component does not always match what the speaker's mouth was saying when the syllables were recorded. That is, the video has been dubbed, and the sound track is simply "ba" over and over again. To be clear, the sound is "ba" but the movement of the mouth may signal "ga." The question is, What would the participants hear? Would they hear what they heard or what they saw? Thus, the question McGurk and MacDonald were interested in was whether people would hear the sound track or what the mouth was doing. Strangely, but compellingly, when participants watch the video, they perceive the sounds as being different from what they actually hear (see Figure 12.9). In Figure 12.9, the observer is watching a mouth say "ga," but the sound track is "ba." However, the observer's perceptual experience is that of hearing "da," a perception different from the actual sound. In order to really understand the McGurk effect, though, you have to hear it and see it for yourself. You can see an example on ISLE 12.3, or view it on YouTube (https://www.youtube.com/watch?v=aFPtc8BVdJk). Watch the video once and think about what you hear. Then play the video again and keep your eyes closed. You will be surprised to find out that initially, you heard what you saw. The McGurk effect is a very compelling illusion that affects virtually all people.

The McGurk effect is surprisingly robust, given that it is fundamentally an error in perception. It works when participants can see only the mouth and when they can see the entire face saying the syllables. It works with people of all ages and language backgrounds, and it works on faces so degraded that they are scarcely recognizable as faces. Indeed, one study found that there was a McGurk effect for touch (Fowler & Dekle, 1991). In this study, participants felt a mouth saying one set of syllables, while a sound track played another set. Fowler and Dekle found that the participants heard what they felt. Szycik, Stadler, Tempelmann, and Münte (2012) examined the McGurk effect while participants were

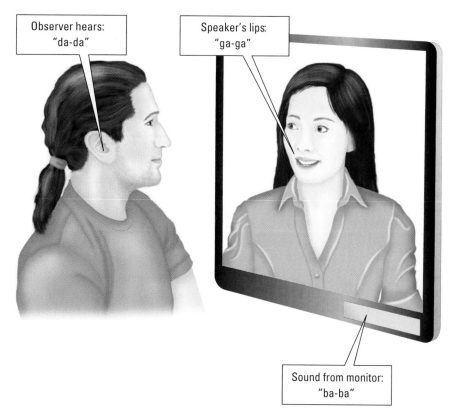

■ FIGURE 12.9   The McGurk effect.

An observer is watching a mouth. The mouth is saying "ga," but the sound track plays the syllable "ba." The observer does not hear what the actual sound is. Rather, the observer hears a "da" sound.

ISLE 12.3 McGurk Effect

McGurk effect: a phenomenon in which vision influences the sounds participants report hearing

undergoing functional magnetic resonance imaging (fMRI). They found an area of the brain that was active during McGurk effect illusions, that is, when there was a mismatch between audition and vision. This area was not active when participants only heard the sounds or when the sounds and visuals were compatible. This integrative area that drives the McGurk effect seems to rest along the superior temporal sulcus.

Top-Down Processing and Speech Perception

ISLE 12.4 Familiar vs. Unfamiliar Languages

Think about listening to someone speaking in English (presumably a language you are fluent in, if you are reading these words) and about listening to someone speak in a language with which you are not familiar (e.g., Telugu, Yalunka, or Sorani). When listening to English, we hear distinct words, pauses in between words, and then more words again (see ISLE 12.4). When listening to an unfamiliar language, it often sounds like a continuous cascade of sound. In a language you are learning, there may be a flip between the word-pause-word perception and the continuous sound. At some points, you may be able to parse the speech correctly into words, but in other cases, you may not. Why does this perception occur? It turns out that speech perception is dependent on a number of top-down processes. That is, knowledge about language influences how we perceive speech. For example, because we know where the boundaries between English words are, we are likely to hear pauses between individual English words. Earlier we pointed out the difference between "The boy was resisting arrest," and "The boy was resisting a rest." To hear the difference between these two sentences, we must use top-down processes to determine where the word boundary goes between *a* and *rest*. Because we may not be familiar with Telugu (a language spoken in India), we do not hear these word boundaries when we are listening to a person speaking Telugu. To be more specific, evidence for top-down processing in speech perception comes from knowledge of specific combinations of phonemes within a language, and knowledge of the context of speech. For example, we know in English that "s" sounds may be followed by "p" sounds, but not by "f" sounds. Thus, if we hear someone say "sfecial," we may assume that what he or she meant to say was "special." Or, if the context is different and we know that the person is talking informally about a man or "fellow," the person may have said "this fella," but we heard the "s" in "this" run into the "f" in "fella" (also see Figure 12.10).

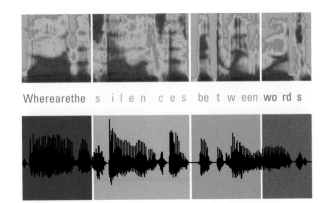

Whererarethe s i l e n c e s be t w een wo rd s

■ **FIGURE 12.10** **Parsing word boundaries.**

The physical boundaries in sound among syllables do not always correspond to the boundaries between one word and the next.

Word segmentation is the ability of speakers of a language to correctly perceive boundaries between words. This means that we use knowledge of our language to draw boundaries as to where one word ends and the next word begins. Consider the following sentences:

How to wreck a nice peach.

How to recognize speech.

In these sentences, we must determine, depending on context, whether the speaker is intending to say three words, *wreck a nice*, or simply one, *recognize*. Examining a sound spectrogram will reveal no differences in the pauses between the syllables of the three words and the one word. As a fluent speaker of English, one immediately uses context to determine which of these two utterances is

Word segmentation: the ability of speakers of a language to correctly perceive boundaries between words

intended. If you are in sensation and perception class at 8 a.m., you are likely to opt for the second sentence, but if you are at a juice bar, and the person making your smoothie accidentally drops a piece of fruit on the floor, you might think the word boundaries correspond to the first sentence. If you are not a fluent speaker of English, you will probably not be able to distinguish these utterances, and therefore not even know how many words the speaker intended to say. Context, which is provided by existing knowledge, is therefore an important aspect of speech perception.

The Phonemic Restoration Effect

We have seen with the McGurk effect that it is possible to induce an illusion of one speech sound even though the actual sound in the environment is another speech sound. In this case, processing of the visual information overrides the input from the cochlea. In the **phonemic restoration effect**, top-down processing of what one expects to hear overrides input from the cochlea. Like the McGurk effect, phonemic restoration is a very strong subjective effect, and we encourage all readers to go to ISLE 12.5 and listen to it. The phonemic restoration effect refers to an illusion that illustrates the importance of top-down processing for speech perception.

ISLE 12.5 Phonemic Restoration Effect

In the phonemic restoration effect, an experimenter uses a computer to delete or mask a particular sound in a sentence in which the context clearly indicates what the missing sound should be (Warren, 1970). The experimenter then asks the participant what he or she just heard. For example, the sentence might be

> British viewers flocked to the opening **ight performance of *Doctor Who*.

In this sentence, the "n" sound in *night* has been replaced by white noise, represented here by the double asterisk. Thus, the "n" sound is not actually present, but listeners are asked what they heard. Indeed, listeners report hearing the word *night*, complete with the "n" sound that is not physically present. It is not merely that they infer that the word must be *night*; participants actually hear the missing sound. To sample the phonemic restoration effect for yourself, go to ISLE 12.5.

What is particularly striking about the phonemic restoration effect is that it works even when the context of the missing sound occurs after the missing sound. Consider the following sentence:

> It was found that the **eel was on the axle.

In this sentence, the context clearly suggests that the missing sound is "wh," as in *wheel*. However, at the time the participant hears "**eel," he or she has not yet heard the context. We do not learn about the axle until after the missing sound. Nonetheless, when participants heard this sentence (actually used in Warren's research), they reported hearing the missing "wh" sound. This was not a fluke of this particular sentence. Warren found the same thing when participants listened to this sentence:

> It was found that the **eel was on the orange.

Note that here, the sentence is identical to the previous sentence with the exception of the last word. As in the "wheel" sentence, the context occurs about a third of a second after the missing sound. Nonetheless, here too, participants reported hearing the correct word, in this case *peel*. For this reason, the phonemic restoration effect has intrigued philosophers as well as psychologists, because speech perception essentially goes back in time and supplies a perceptual experience after the

Phonemic restoration effect: an illusion in which participants hear sounds that are masked by white noise, but context makes the missing sound apparent

stimulus has been past for almost half a second. It speaks to the strong power of expectations, or what we call here top-down processing, to influence perceptual experience, even when that experience occurred a split second earlier.

Some recent research suggests strongly that the phonemic restoration effect occurs early in information processing, certainly before conscious control, despite the nature of the top-down processing. Mattys, Barden, and Samuel (2014) showed that the perception of the missing sound became more pronounced as a secondary task became more difficult. That is, when participants had to devote more attention to a secondary visual task they were doing in addition to the phonemic listening task, the illusion of hearing the missing sound grew stronger. Thus, the phonemic restoration effect must occur at a preattention stage in speech perception processing. This emphasizes how critical the understanding of context is to understanding fluent speech.

We can ask what neural mechanisms allow us to unconsciously infer the missing sound even when it occurs before the context is supplied. Sunami et al. (2013) used magnetoencephalography to examine the neurological correlates of the phonemic restoration effect. They found that areas within the auditory cortex in the temporal lobe were involved with the phonemic restoration effect, presumably the areas responsible for the "hearing" of the missing sound. But just prior to that activation, they found areas in the left prefrontal lobe that responded more strongly to context for missing sounds than for sounds that were actually present. It is likely that this area of the brain houses the processes that make the top-down inference about context and then what the sound must be. It then transmits this information to the temporal lobe, which "hears" the missing sound.

> **TEST YOUR KNOWLEDGE**
>
> How does our speech production system create different consonant sounds?

THEORIES OF SPEECH PERCEPTION

12.3 Summarize the general-mechanism theories, special-mechanism theories, and motor theory of speech perception.

What should be clear from the discussion so far is that our sensory systems engage in complex processing to transform a complex speech signal into meaning, and they do so amazingly quickly. We have introduced a number of features the human speech perception system uses to allow this rapid processing. We attend to coarticulation; that is, that the sound being heard in the present informs us as to what to expect in the future. Our perceptual systems also benefit from categorical perception, which allows us to quickly distinguish among similar phonemes. Furthermore, we use the visual signal of the movements of the mouth to help us understand speech. And we fill in missing sounds when the context suggests what they should be. But are there overall rules that guide speech perception? That is, are there theories that can explain the overall process of speech perception?

Such theories can be divided into two general classes. First, some theorists argue that speech is no different than any other sound and that we use the same mechanism with speech that we do with other sounds. These theories are called **general-mechanism theories**. By contrast, other theorists argue that because of the importance of language to humans, special mechanisms have evolved that are specific to speech and are not used in the processing of other kinds of sound. Not surprisingly, these theories are called **special-mechanism theories** (Diehl et al., 2004).

General-mechanism theories: theories of speech perception that claim that the mechanisms for speech perception are the same as the mechanisms for auditory perception in general

Special-mechanism theories: theories of speech perception that claim that the mechanisms for speech perception are distinct and unique relative to the mechanisms for auditory perception in general

Special-mechanism theories start with the premise that there is a unique neurocognitive system for speech perception that is distinct from other kinds of auditory perception. One influential version of the special mechanism is the **motor theory of speech perception** (Liberman & Mattingly, 1985). This view contends that we have a special mechanism that allows us to detect speech as unique and then relate the sounds to the presumed speech movements (i.e., talking) of the speaker (Galantucci, Fowler, & Turvey, 2006). The goal of speech perception is to infer the movements of the speaker's mouth. This may sound crazy, but it was developed with the observation in mind that there is seemingly nothing constant about the auditory signal—remember that "b" is a different sound depending on whether it is followed by an "ah" sound or an "eh" sound. In the motor theory view, what is constant across individual phonemes is the speech articulations that produce that sound. Evidence for this view certainly comes from the McGurk effect, in which the speech sound we perceive is what we are seeing, not what is coming in on the sound track.

In contrast, the general-mechanism approach argues that speech perception occurs through the same neurocognitive processes as other forms of auditory perception. In this view, what makes speech perception unique is its importance, which is learned rather than based on an innate neural mechanism. In terms of theories, scientists tend to prefer a simpler theory unless there is compelling evidence to support a more complex theory. In this case, the general-mechanism theory is less complex than the special-mechanism theory because the general-mechanism theory requires only one neurocognitive system. Thus, this theory should be considered the default until proponents of the special-mechanism theory can definitively demonstrate that speech perception requires its own unique mechanism.

One general-mechanism approach includes the view that speech perception involves top-down mechanisms of categorization. Thus, any sound is analyzed by processes that categorize sound in general. When we hear speech, we immediately classify it as such. If we hear the creaking of a door, we do not invest any meaning into that sound other than that someone or something is pushing on that door. If the sound is something like "meow," we classify it as a nonspeech sound, although, in this case, one that might contain information (see Figure 12.11). Any cat owner knows the difference between his or her cat's meow that means "feed me" and the one that means "open the door." However, when we hear a stimulus that sounds like "Open the door, please" (I'm not a cat, so of course I say please)," we immediately classify many features of the utterance, such as the speaker's gender, regional dialect, age, emotional state, and identity. It is this act of classification that represents what makes speech perception unique (Holt & Lotto, 2010).

■ FIGURE 12.11   Do we know what cats are saying?

Cat owners know the messages their cats are sending when they listen to their meows. Cats use a different meow to indicate "feed me" than they do for "scratch my ears."

Holt and Lotto (2010) pointed out that in many cases, nonspeech sounds can influence our perception of speech sounds, consistent with the general-mechanism approach. For example, in one study (Holt, 2005), a speech sound such as "ga" or "da" was preceded by a series of 21 nonspeech sounds. Each series created a different history of sound perception intended to influence the perception of the speech sounds presented at the end. If speech perception occurs by a unique and special mechanism, the pattern of preceding nonspeech sounds should have no effect on the perception of speech. However, if the general-mechanism approach is correct, then there is the possibility that nonspeech sounds influence speech perception. And this is what Holt found.

Motor theory of speech perception: the theory that the core of speech perception is that the system infers the sound from the movements of the vocal tract

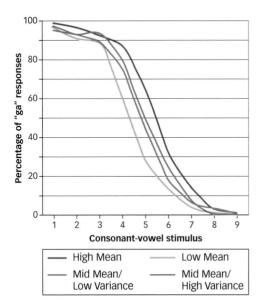

■ FIGURE 12.12   Perception of speech is influenced by nonspeech sounds (Hoot, 2005).

The more repetitions of the nonword stimulus, the less likely the test stimulus was heard as a speech sound.

The pattern of the 21 nonspeech sounds influenced the likelihood of hearing the speech sound as "ga" or "da," consistent with the general-mechanism view (see Figure 12.12).

Because of studies such as Holt's (2005) and others, most researchers today think of speech perception as a form of auditory perception in general. The tricky part, however, is still how we extract speech signals, such as phonemes, from complex and variable stimuli. Thus, many speech perception researchers have moved away from the special mechanism model but still think the goal of speech perception is to connect sound to the source of that sound, namely, the movements of the vocal tract (Fowler & Thompson, 2010). Fowler's view is a direct perception view (e.g., Gibson, 1979). She argues that the goal of perception is to guide us through the environment. In the case of speech perception, Fowler argues that it is the movement of the vocal tract that is the invariant in the word, and that the perceptual apparatus is tuned to that invariant. In other words, our speech perception is really about figuring out what the vocal tracts of others are doing. Thus, it is no wonder that our speech perception is sometimes fooled by sounds, if our goal is to infer how somebody's vocal tract works rather than to perceive sounds per se.

The Development of Phoneme Perception

Infants are born into the world with a remarkable aptitude for acquiring language, but no genetic penchant for learning one language or another. The language learned is, of course, determined by the linguistic environment the infant finds himself or herself in. An infant raised by an English-speaking mother will learn English, and an infant raised by a Sorani-speaking mother will learn Sorani (Kurdish). However, languages vary in the phonemes they use, and even when they use the same phonemes, there may be subtle differences among them. For example, the English "p" sound is more explosive than the Spanish "p" sound. During the first year of life, infants are engaged in an intensive learning of the rules of speech perception in the language or languages that surround them. In the United States, monolingualism is the norm, but in many other countries, children are bilingual or multilingual from a very early age.

During the first 6 months of life, an infant can distinguish among all of the phonemes used in a language and can discern subtle differences in sound among equivalent phonemes across languages (Harley, 2014). We may think of infants at this age as not being linguistic in nature, as they cannot speak yet and do not understand meaning, but these infants are paying very close attention to sound. Indeed, they are paying closer attention to sound than are the adults around them. Consider the difference between the English "p" and the Spanish "p." When we hear a person who is a native speaker of Spanish speak in English, we may note that he has an accent, but when we listen to his speech, we are attending to meaning, not subtle differences in sound. The difference between saying "Harry Potter" with an explosive English "p" or "Harry Potter" with a soft Spanish "p" is irrelevant. Either way, we are talking about a fictional wizard. However, young infants are attending to just these differences (Harley, 2014). And, just in case you do not know, Harry Potter should not go back to Hogwarts.

Consider a study done by Janet Werker and her colleagues (e.g., Maurer & Werker, 2014). They compared infants and adults in their perceptions of the two ways of saying the "t" sound in Hindi, a language widely spoken in India and throughout the Indian diaspora. In Hindi, there is a "t" sound spoken with the tongue at the back of the mouth, and a "t" spoken with the tongue at the front of the mouth, as it is in English. Because the sounds may be associated with different meanings in Hindi, Hindi adults recognize the difference between these two sounds. To English-speaking adults, however, they both sound like "t," and we do not hear the difference.

In one of her seminal studies, Werker looked at whether infants being raised in English-speaking homes would hear the sound difference between the two Hindi "t" sounds (see Werker, 2012). Werker found that at 6 months of age, these infants were able to distinguish the two sounds with nearly 100% accuracy. However, by the time these infants were 10 months old, their accuracy had dropped to about 20%. In contrast, Indian babies (being raised in a Hindi-speaking environment) maintained this 100% accuracy at 10 months and beyond. Thus, because the sound difference is relevant in Hindi, Hindi babies maintain the distinction, but because it is irrelevant in English, English babies no longer perceive the difference.

These results illustrate something that Werker calls perceptual narrowing (Werker & Gervain, 2013). **Perceptual narrowing** refers to the developmental process whereby regularly experienced phonemes are homed in on, as well as the simultaneous diminishing of the ability to discriminate unfamiliar phonemes. That is, as infants get older, they focus their attention on stimuli that are relevant to them, rather than attending to all stimuli out there. This is advantageous in learning one's first language, though it makes it more difficult to acquire a native-sounding accent in a second language later on. We have focused here on the experiments comparing Hindi-language infants and English-language infants, but one can see these perceptual narrowing differences across many language pairs (Harley, 2014). Because speech signals are so complex, it benefits young children (and, later, adults) to ignore irrelevant differences in sound and focus only on those sound differences that are meaningful in the language that they speak.

> **TEST YOUR KNOWLEDGE**
>
> What are the general-mechanism theories of speech perception and the special-mechanism theories of speech perception? What differences do they anticipate?

SPEECH PERCEPTION AND THE BRAIN

 Identify the areas of the brain involved in speech perception and what happens when they are damaged.

Understanding language is an extremely important aspect of being a human being. Therefore, we should expect to see complex neural systems involved in the processing of the human speech signal. And this is exactly what we find in the human brain. Although we focus on perceptual aspects of language, equally important to language is producing speech. Indeed, there is close integration of the perception and comprehension networks for language and the brain regions responsible for producing speech.

Two 19th-century neurologists, Pierre Broca and Carl Wernicke, were instrumental in beginning our understanding of the neuroanatomy of speech and language. For their work, each has an area in the brain named after him: **Broca's area** and **Wernicke's area**. Interestingly, the patient Broca studied had damage in an area different from the one now named after him, but Broca is given credit for being one of the first to associate specific areas of the brain with unique language

---

Perceptual narrowing: the developmental process whereby regularly experienced phonemes are homed in on, with simultaneous diminishing of the ability to discriminate unfamiliar phonemes

Broca's area: an important area in the production of speech, located in the left frontal lobe

Wernicke's area: an important area in speech comprehension, located in the left temporal lobe

■ FIGURE 12.13 Broca's and Wernicke's areas.

Broca's area is in the frontal lobe, and Wernicke's area is in the temporal lobe.

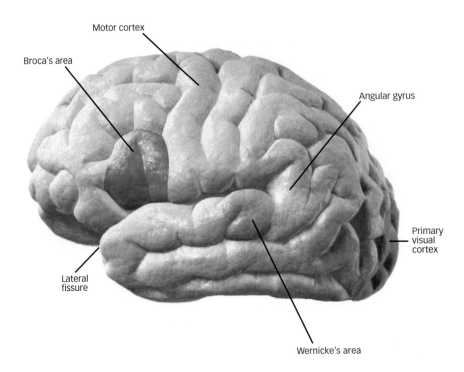

functions. Wernicke correctly identified the areas for the production of language and for the comprehension of language. For this reason, some anatomists call Broca's area Broca-Wernicke's area to honor the better scientist but still distinguish it from Wernicke's area proper. We use the term *Broca's area*, despite Broca's own misidentification of the area. It is also important to note that Broca's and Wernicke's areas are not the only areas in the brain associated with language, and there is even some debate as to the role of these two areas in language function. Broca's area and Wernicke's area are depicted in Figure 12.13.

Broca's area is in the left frontal lobe and is an important area in the production of speech. Wernicke's area is in the left temporal lobe and is critical in understanding language. In the vast majority of people, Broca's and Wernicke's areas are localized in the left hemisphere, although a very small minority, most of them left-handers, may have these areas localized in the right hemisphere.

Aphasia is an impairment in language production or comprehension brought about by neurological damage. In **Broca's aphasia**, the damage is to Broca's area of the brain. Broca's aphasia is characterized by nonfluent speech. However, by and large, speech perception is not affected, and language comprehension is normal. Broca's aphasics have a halted speech pattern and have difficulty speaking sentences. There is also some evidence that Broca's aphasics have deficits in understanding complex grammar relative to controls, even though their word comprehension shows no such deficit. A video of a patient with Broca's aphasia is available on YouTube (https://www.youtube.com/watch?v=gocIUW3E-go).

Wernicke's area is located in areas of the brain associated with the auditory system in the temporal lobe. Anatomically, it is located in the posterior section of the superior temporal gyrus. This area is also known as Brodmann Area 22. Damage to Wernicke's area results in deficits in the comprehension of language, a condition called **Wernicke's aphasia**. Severe Wernicke's aphasia may result in a complete absence of understanding language. Speech is, by and large, fluent, but it may appear to not make sense to listeners, as the patients themselves cannot understand what they are saying. This meaningless speech is sometimes called jargon aphasia. A video of a patient with Wernicke's aphasia can be found on YouTube (https://www.youtube.com/watch?v=dKTdMV6cOZw).

Aphasia: an impairment in language production or comprehension brought about by neurological damage

Broca's aphasia: a form of aphasia resulting from damage to Broca's area, causing a deficit in language production

Wernicke's aphasia: a form of aphasia resulting from damage to Wernicke's area, causing a deficit in language comprehension

Interestingly, although Wernicke's area clearly emerges from auditory processing parts of the brain, its role in language is comprehension. There are cases in which sign language speakers have developed brain damage in Wernicke's area. These sign language speakers have a deficit in understanding sign language equivalent to the deficit in comprehension seen in Wernicke's aphasia for spoken language (Bellugi, Klima, & Hickok, 2010). Thus, in people whose language is visual-manual instead of auditory, it is the auditory cortex that is interpreting language.

As with any neurological damage, the extent of the brain damage may vary from patient to patient. Thus, a patient with a relatively small lesion in Wernicke's area may be able to produce sensible speech and understand some elements of others' speech. However, a patient with a large lesion may not understand speech at all.

As you have probably guessed by now, nothing having to do with perception is simple. This is true for the neurological basis for speech perception as well. Although Wernicke's area is critical for speech perception, there are many other areas of the cortex also involved in this process. This includes auditory perception areas in the temporal lobes as well as monitoring areas in the left prefrontal cortex. Studies with neuroimaging techniques have delineated some of the connections and links between these areas. In particular, many neuroscientists now think that the distinction between "what" and "where" is applicable to speech perception. That is, our auditory cortex has pathways for identifying the "what" of the signal, namely, recognizing meaning in speech, and a "where" system, which processes where the speech signal is coming from (Hickok & Poeppel, 2007). Figure 12.14 shows these areas associated with the two streams.

Some other neuroscience evidence is relevant to the topic of whether speech perception constitutes a special mechanism or is best thought of as a function of a general auditory perception mechanism. This research concerns the discovery of a **voice area** in the superior temporal sulcus. Research shows that this area becomes more active in response to human voices than it does to nonspeech sounds (Belin, Bestelmeyer, Latinus, & Watson, 2011). Indeed, fMRI studies show that an area Belin et al. (2011) called the temporal voice area, located in the superior temporal

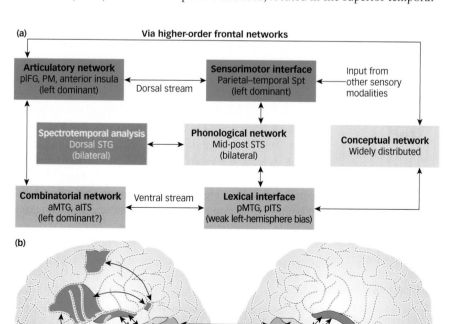

■ FIGURE 12.14   The dual-stream model of speech perception (Hickok & Poeppel, 2007).

The dual-stream model of speech perception involves a ventral pathway that recognizes speech as speech and a dorsal stream that links that speech to the movements of individual speakers.

Voice area: an area located in the superior temporal sulcus that responds to the sound of the human voice, but less so to other stimuli

■ FIGURE 12.15 The temporal voice area (Belin et al., 2011).

The temporal voice area is located in the superior temporal sulcus, shown here. It responds more to voice than to nonvoice sounds.

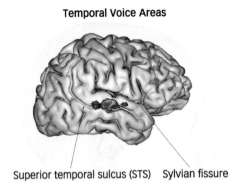

Temporal Voice Areas

Superior temporal sulcus (STS)   Sylvian fissure

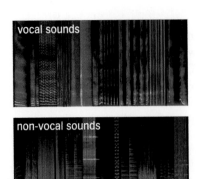

vocal sounds

non-vocal sounds

sulcus, shows greater responses to voices than to natural nonvoice sounds or to unidentifiable noise (see Figure 12.15).

One of the questions that has always fascinated neuroscientists and laypersons alike is whether we can tell what a person is thinking on the basis of the observable activity of his or her brain. Many science fiction movies and novels involve fancy electronic equipment that can determine exactly what someone is thinking. With the advent of neuroimaging, perhaps we can ask whether a neuroscientist watching the activity of your brain in real time with fMRI might be able to know that you are thinking about the time you were looking over the rim at the Grand Canyon, or about how much Descartes's religious beliefs informed his philosophy. Or perhaps you were thinking about something you would prefer the neuroscientist not know about and that we will not mention here. This kind of research is still in its infancy, but some fascinating research has been able to infer what words a person is listening to based on the activity in his or her auditory cortex (Pasley et al., 2012).

In this unique and fascinating study, Pasley et al. (2012) recruited patients who were soon to undergo surgery on their temporal lobes as a treatment for epilepsy or brain tumors. All of the participants had normal language abilities. Because of the impending neurosurgery, the patients had been fitted with intracranial electrodes, that is, sensitive electrodes fitted on the temporal lobe underneath the skull, thus allowing fine spatial and temporal resolution of ongoing human brain activity. While these electrodes were actively recording brain activity, the patients heard recordings of words and sentences from a variety of speakers. This is interesting enough as it is, but what Pasley et al. did then was feed the pattern of brain activity into a computer programmed to decode what those words and sentences were. This program did not originally know what the stimuli were, so it allowed Pasley et al. to determine if it was possible to infer what the speech areas of the brain were listening to by observing activity in the auditory cortex alone. In essence, their program serves as a speech decoder, taking the brain's output to re-create the input.

So here is the goal of the algorithm built into the computer program: Based only on the pattern of activity seen in the temporal lobe, can the program extract the original auditory signal? In this way, an experimenter will know what word was spoken to the patient without actually having heard the word, but only seeing the output of the computer program. Although not perfect, the algorithm in the computer program was able to re-create the auditory

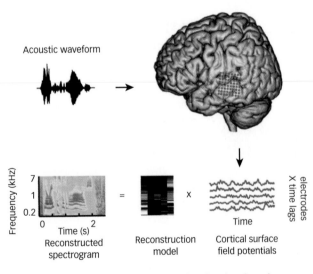

■ FIGURE 12.16   Reinterpreting brain signals (Pasley et al., 2012).

This figure shows how the original signal is recorded in the brain and then re-created via the algorithm that interprets the electrical activity in the temporal lobe.

signal on the basis of the pattern of activity in the auditory cortex, and it did so particularly well for words, though less well for sentences. You can see both the process and the results in Figure 12.16. In the words of Pasley et al. (2012), "The results provide insights into higher order neural speech processing and suggest it may be possible to read out intended speech directly from brain activity" (p. 2). We think this is an important and bold step not just in the understanding of speech perception but in the way in which neuroscience is heading.

TEST YOUR KNOWLEDGE
What is aphasia? What is Broca's aphasia?

IN DEPTH: *Hearing Loss and Speech Perception*

Taylor Monroe is a fictional 45-year-old woman. She has a graduate degree in education and has been teaching high school social studies for 20 years, and she is one of the more popular teachers among the students. Ms. Monroe has been wearing hearing aids to compensate for sensorineural hearing loss since she was in college. Ms. Monroe's hairstyles tend to cover her ears, so most of her students do not know that she has a hearing impairment. Ms. Monroe uses the latest technology in hearing aids, but she still complains that it is often difficult for her to understand her students' questions when there is more than one person talking or if there is construction noise outside. Ms. Monroe's complaint is typical of many hearing-impaired people. Even with amplification, speech comprehension may still be difficult, especially when other sounds are present. Although Ms. Monroe has had her whole life to adjust to her hearing loss, this problem is even more pervasive in older adults who experience hearing loss late in life.

As we discussed in the previous chapter, today's digital hearing aids are amazing apparatuses that use complex engineering to help people hear (see Figure 12.17). As recently as 20 years ago, hearing aids merely amplified sound. But now they have complex programs to help individuals with hearing loss, especially with the problem of speech perception. Nonetheless, the major goal of hearing aids still is the selective amplification of frequencies in order to compensate for higher thresholds at those frequencies (Kochkin, 2005).

Amplification of speech brings sounds for which an individual is hearing impaired above threshold, so that he or she can hear them, but the same amplification may also amplify sounds the person can hear normally, resulting in their being too loud. As we know, any voice has multiple harmonics (formants), some of which may not be amplified and some of which may be amplified too much. These frequency

© iStockphoto.com/snapphoto

■ FIGURE 12.17   **Hearing aids.**

Hearing aids are small and easily concealable, but they help people with hearing disabilities in tremendous ways.

components that are too loud introduce a new kind of distortion. Many of the latest tricks in hearing aids are designed to compensate for this aspect of hearing. But because one can never be certain of what a new person's voice will sound like, in practice, this is very difficult. To summarize the problem, when hearing aids compensate for loss of sensitivity, they may introduce distortion by amplifying irrelevant aspects of the signal.

Imagine a speaker saying an unexpected sentence, such as "The Jade Rabbit landed on the moon." Unless you have been following the Chinese space agency's moon exploration program, this sentence might not make sense to you at first. In the case of our hypothetical teacher, context may not lend much of a hand to help Ms. Monroe figure out what her student just said about a jade rabbit. As we have emphasized in this chapter, speech takes place over time. It takes a small amount of time to say the word *rabbit*, and coarticulation helps listeners decode sounds. However, if there is noise, either natural or distortion produced by hearing aids, comprehension of the words and sentence may be slowed to a point at which the person cannot make intelligible sense of the words. Amid noise, hearing-impaired individuals have more difficulty following the stream of speech, because they are missing cues that are present when there is less noise or that are always available to those with normal hearing. The noise may interfere with the signal such that syllables within words are less clearly separated in time. Thus, people with hearing loss have difficulty understanding speech in noise (Henry, Turner, & Behrens, 2005). That is, because speech perception is so complex, and the processes must be achieved so quickly, those with hearing loss may not have sufficient time to process speech stimuli, even when they are hearing sounds amplified with their hearing aids. This problem may be even more profound in older adults who develop hearing loss later in life (Anderson, White-Schwoch, Parbery-Clark, & Kraus, 2013).

To summarize, individuals with hearing impairments choose to wear hearing aids in order to help them understand speech. However, evidence suggests that some difficulties in speech perception are actually introduced by the pattern of amplification and suppression from the hearing aids themselves. In essence, the combination of the hearing aid and the impaired cochlea results in a number of ways in which speech perception can be affected adversely. Because the signal going into the auditory nerve is impaired, it requires the auditory cortex to work harder to decode the signal, leading to impaired perception amid noise or if the individual is distracted (Leek & Molis, 2009).

The solution is to design hearing aids with faster and more efficient processing. But the exact nature of that processing will require research to determine what features of the human auditory system need tweaking in each individual patient. Although appropriate amplification may address the problem of impaired hearing in general, it may not be enough to compensate for the slowed temporal processing and distortion prevalent in people with moderate sensorineural hearing loss (Leek & Molis, 2009). As the science of hearing aids continues to improve, patients can expect to find hearing aids with a greater range of internal programs that adjust the acoustics of the situation automatically depending on ambient conditions. Thus, in a noisy environment, hearing aids will focus on amplifying sounds in the frequencies commonly heard in speech. In addition, loud sounds will generate a quick attenuation of the amplification of those sounds, such that coughs or squeaking chairs lead to less interference with speech perception. When the person moves to another environment, say a quiet room at home, the hearing aid will adjust to that room and inhibit only some high-frequency sounds, such as the hum of an air conditioner or the buzz of a refrigerator, leaving the person maximally able to converse with his or her family. Even with hearing aids, Ms. Monroe may never be able to pick up speech in a noisy classroom as well as her nonimpaired colleagues, but hearing aids are evolving quickly to maximize speech perception.

CHAPTER SUMMARY

 12.1   **Discuss the complex process of speech perception and speech production.**

Speech perception is the most critical aspect of auditory perception for human beings. Perceptual processes begin with a stimulus in the environment. In the case of human speech perception, that stimulus is a voice. The human vocal tract produces both consonant and vowel sounds, which are the bases of the sounds used in human language. Formants are the frequency bands with higher amplitudes among the harmonics of a vowel sound. Each individual vowel sound has a specific pattern of formants. The place of articulation is the point along the vocal tract at which the airflow is constricted. The manner of articulation is how that restriction occurs. *Voicing* refers to whether the vocal cords are vibrating or not. Phonemes are the basic units of sound in human language. The International Phonetic Alphabet is an alphabetic convention that provides a unique symbol for each and every phoneme in use in human languages.

12.2   **Describe the mechanisms our speech perception system uses to extract coherent speech from the speech signal.**

A problem for our speech perception systems is to identify what is constant in the speech signal. Our auditory system uses a number of mechanisms to identify phonemes and understand speech. Coarticulation is the phenomenon in which one phoneme affects the acoustic properties of subsequent phonemes. Our auditory systems pick up on coarticulation and use it to understand speech. Categorical perception is our perception of different acoustic stimuli as being identical phonemes, up to a point at which our perception flips to perceive another phoneme. Voice-onset time is the production of certain consonants (called stop consonants) in which there is a difference between the first sound of the phoneme and the movement of the vocal cords. The movement of the vocal cords is called voicing. In the McGurk effect, participants are shown a video of a person's mouth saying monosyllabic sounds, such as "ba," "da," and "tha." However, the audio component does not always match what the speaker's mouth was saying when the syllables were recorded. The results show that the visual input affects what people report hearing. Word segmentation is the ability of speakers of a language to correctly perceive boundaries between words. The phonemic restoration effect is an illusion in which participants hear sounds that are masked by white noise, but context makes the missing sounds apparent.

12.3 Summarize the general-mechanism theories, special-mechanism theories, and motor theory of speech perception.

General-mechanism theories of speech perception claim that the mechanisms for speech perception are the same as the mechanisms for auditory perception in general. Special-mechanism theories claim that the mechanisms for speech perception are distinct and unique relative to the mechanisms for auditory perception in general. The motor theory of speech perception argues for a special mechanism that makes attributes about sound from the movements of the vocal tract.

12.4 Identify the areas of the brain involved in speech perception and what happens when they are damaged.

Perceptual narrowing is the developmental process whereby regularly experienced phonemes are homed in on, with the simultaneous diminishing of the ability to discriminate unfamiliar phonemes. Broca's area is in the left frontal lobe and is an important area in the production of speech. Wernicke's area is located in areas of the brain associated with the auditory system in the temporal lobe. Aphasia is an impairment in language production or comprehension brought about by neurological damage. Broca's aphasia is a form of aphasia resulting from damage to Broca's area. In Broca's aphasia, the deficit is in language production. Wernicke's aphasia is a form of aphasia resulting from damage to Wernicke's area. In Wernicke's aphasia, the deficit is in language comprehension. The voice area is located in the superior temporal sulcus and responds to the sound of the human voice. In a fascinating study by Pasley et al. (2012), a computer program was able to determine what a speaker was saying based only on the activity of the speaker's auditory cortex. Speech perception in hearing-impaired individuals may be a particularly difficult problem for hearing aids to address. Amplification of higher harmonics may distort the speech signal, requiring the auditory systems of hearing-impaired people to slow down in their interpretation of human speech signals. Future hearing aids need to be designed with this problem in mind.

REVIEW QUESTIONS

1. What are the important parts of the vocal tract? How are consonants and vowels produced in our vocal tract?

2. What is meant by the terms *place of articulation*, *manner of articulation*, and *voicing*?

3. What is coarticulation? How does its perception affect our understanding of speech?

4. What is categorical perception? How does it affect our perception of speech? What is its likely function?

5. What is the McGurk effect? How does it show the relation between vision and audition with respect to speech perception?

6. What is phonemic restoration? How does it demonstrate top-down processing in speech perception?

7. What is the difference between general-mechanism theories of speech perception and special-mechanism theories of speech perception? Which theory offers a better explanation of speech perception? What is the motor theory of speech perception?

8. What is perceptual narrowing? How does it help infants improve their speech perception? What problems can develop from it?

9. What areas of the brain are associated with speech production and language comprehension? What other areas of the brain may be involved in speech perception?

10. Why is speech perception difficult for those who wear hearing aids? What aspect of hearing-aid technology needs to be improved to help those with mild to medium hearing impairments?

KEY TERMS

Aphasia, 326

Broca's aphasia, 326

Broca's area, 325

Categorical perception, 316

Coarticulation, 315

Consonants, 311

Formants, 311

General-mechanism theories, 322

International Phonetic
    Alphabet, 313

Larynx (voice box), 310

Manner of articulation, 312

McGurk effect, 319

Motor theory of speech
    perception, 323

Perceptual narrowing, 325

Pharynx, 311

Phonemes, 313

Phonemic restoration effect, 321

Place of articulation, 312

Special-mechanism theories, 322

Trachea (windpipe), 310

Uvula, 311

Voice area, 327

Voice-onset time, 317

Voicing, 312

Vowels, 311

Wernicke's aphasia, 326

Wernicke's area, 325

Word segmentation, 320

INTERACTIVE SENSATION LABORATORY EXERCISES (ISLE)

Experience chapter concepts at edge.sagepub.com/schwartz

ISLE 12.1 Coarticulation, 315

ISLE 12.2 Voicing Onset Time, 317

ISLE 12.3 McGurk Effect, 319

ISLE 12.4 Familiar vs. Unfamiliar
    Languages, 320

ISLE 12.5 Phonemic
    Restoration Effect, 321

Sharpen your skills with SAGE edge at edge.sagepub.com/schwartz

SAGE edge for students provides a personalized approach to help you accomplish
your coursework goals in an easy-to-use learning environment.

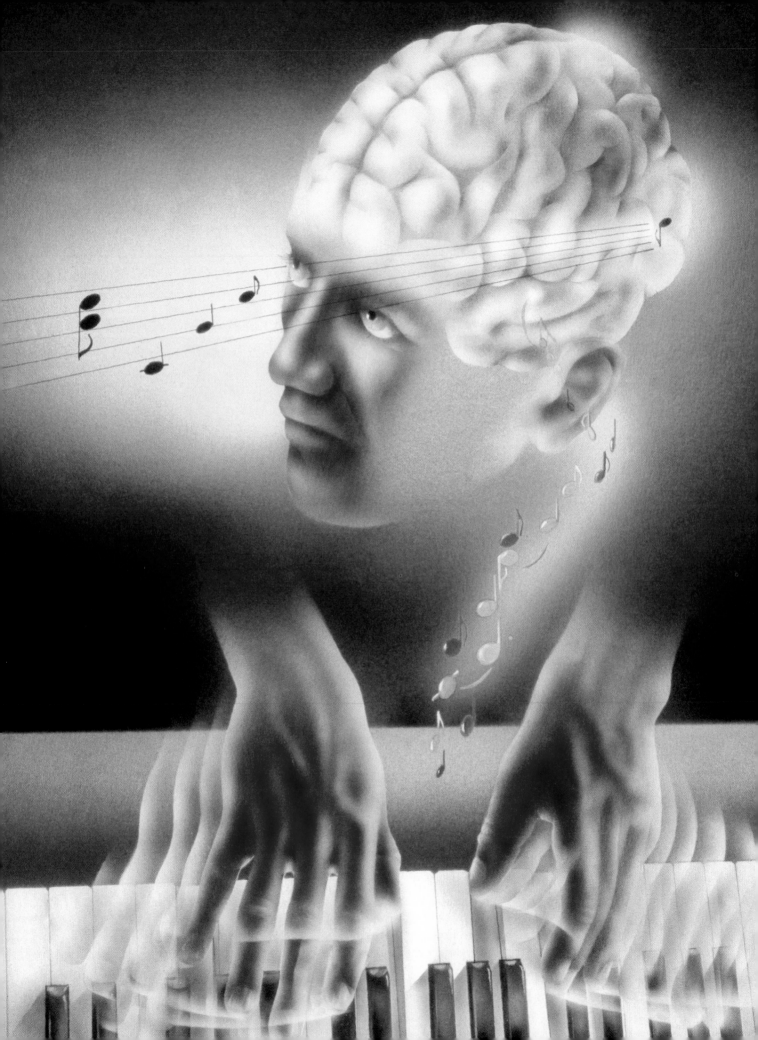

Music Perception

13

INTRODUCTION

Wherever you travel, you will find music. It may sound very different from the music you are accustomed to hearing, but you will recognize it instantly as music. In Kurdistan, we find a unique culture of music featuring such instruments as the tanbur (a fretted string instrument), the qernête (a double-reed wind instrument), and the şimşal (a flutelike instrument) (see Figure 13.1). Although most of you may never have heard of these instruments and may never have heard Kurdish music before, you would instantly recognize them as musical instruments, and you might even like Kurdish music (see ISLE 13.1 for an example of Kurdish music).

More well known in the United States, though further from our own musical tradition, is Javanese gamelan. Gamelan music uses a very different scale system from our own, so it sounds very different. The slendro scale is a pentatonic (five-note) scale using intervals not used in Western music. Despite this difference, we certainly recognize gamelan as music (listen to ISLE 13.2 for examples of Javanese gamelan music). Figure 13.2 shows the xylophone-like instruments that are used in gamelan music.

Within our own culture, we make the most of differences in musical tradition—many of you may debate the relative merits of East Coast hip-hop and snap music, or funk metal versus nu metal (see Figure 13.3). There is, however, continuity in our Western music tradition. All of these varieties of music, from classical to jazz to country to gangsta rap, use the basic Western music system, even if the performers violate Western norms of dress and body art. In this manner, most variants of rock music have more in common with the classical music tradition than fans of either style might care to admit. For example, both Mozart and gangsta rap use the same basic Western scale system, playing the same notes, and in mostly the same keys. One can contrast either style of music with the aforementioned gamelan music, which uses a completely different scale system.

Music also has a long history. Wherever we find written records of past civilizations, we find descriptions of musical events. For example, the ancient Greeks left numerous written descriptions of music, as well as many illustrations of musical instruments. The story of Orpheus is as poignant today as it was then, because we can relate to the longing power of music, just as the Greeks did when the story was new. In the story, Orpheus uses music to win his love back from the dead, only to lose her again. However, we do not know what ancient Greek music

LEARNING OBJECTIVES

13.1 Explain how frequency is related to pitch, chroma, and the octave.

13.2 Summarize the basic neuroscience of music, including how training and experience can affect the representation of music in the brain.

13.3 Discuss how learning and culture affect music perception.

ISLE 13.1 Kurdish Music

ISLE 13.2 Javenese Gamelan Music

© Aurora Photos / Alamy

■ FIGURE 13.1   A Tanbur.

Man playing a tanbur, a traditional Kurdish instrument.

actually sounded like. Although there are some records of musical notation from the time of Plato, archaeologists have not been able to decipher what it means, and therefore we do not know what ancient Greek music sounded like. We can speculate, given the Greek academic tradition and its discovery of the relation of string length and the musical octave, that there may have been some similarities between ancient Greek music and the music of today, but that is about all we know at present.

Traveling millennia further back in time, there are no written records of music notation. But there is a fine archaeological record that demonstrates musical instruments being made far back into the Stone Age. Wind, percussion, and string instruments all date back this far into antiquity. The oldest known instruments are flutes made from the bones of birds, some of which date back as far as 35,000 years (Conard, Malina, & Münzel, 2009). Figure 13.4 shows such flutes. We can wonder what a prehistoric man or woman might have played on one of these flutes, looking across a primordial forest landscape from the mouth of a cave, but we will never know. However, reconstructions of these flutes show that notes representing octave equivalence were present. This suggests that music has been a part of human culture for as long as humans have had culture.

■ FIGURE 13.2   **Different musical cultures.**

Gamelan musical instruments.

■ FIGURE 13.3   **Popular music.**

Rock music is popular throughout the world.

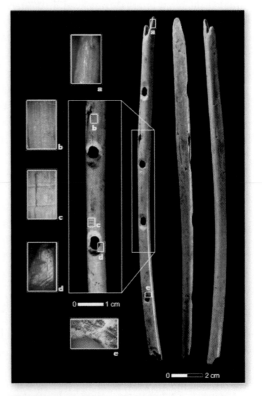

■ FIGURE 13.4   **Paleolithic musical instruments (Conrad, Malina, & Münzel, 2009).**

Bone flutes dating to at least 30,000 years ago.

We can also ask this question: What is music? A dictionary definition might define music as an art form based on sound. But how do we know what sounds are art and what sounds are, well, just sounds? On one hand, when we hear Paramore singing "Ain't It Fun" or the Cleveland Orchestra playing Schubert's Symphony Number 2, there is no disagreement—we are hearing music. And when we hear the sound of a washing machine whirring or the sound of landscapers mowing lawns, we know that such sounds are not music. However, some artists stretch the limits of music. For example, in John Cage's famous piece *4'33"*, audiences "listen" to a performer doing absolutely nothing for 4½ minutes. The music is the rustle of people in their seats and the occasional embarrassed cough. Is this music? That depends on your perspective. Certainly, Cage wanted us to think of music in a whole new way. And what about the following? The Melbourne Symphony Orchestra played a piece of music in which every member of the orchestra was playing beer bottles instead of his or her normal musical instrument (http://www .youtube.com/watch?v=pUru7nSyKxQ). Many of you may have also heard the typewriter symphony, which went viral on YouTube in 2012 (http://www.youtube .com/watch?v=wZCh4EY_kug). Are these pieces satire, or are they actually music? Finally, we can also consider whether natural sounds are music. We may find many natural sounds beautiful, from birds singing to waves lapping to the wind whistling. But is birdsong music? What about the sounds of waves lapping on the sand on a peaceful beach? Most of us would hesitate to classify this as music, even though the sounds may be decidedly pleasing to listen to. Thus, it may actually be difficult to come up with a definition of music that satisfies all of its boundary conditions. But we will try to define music as follows: **Music** is ordered sound made and perceived by human beings, created in meaningful patterns (Tan, Pfordresher, & Harre, 2010).

The last introductory question concerns the function of music. Why do we do it? Many scholars from many different disciplines have sought to determine the function of music for human beings, given the universality of music to the human species. Some have argued that this implies that music evolved, in the biological sense of the word, and therefore must have a function. What function might music serve in evolution? Some have argued that it served a sexual selection function. A highly musical person was likely fit, with musical ability signaling both good health and intelligence. In this view, music is something of a peacock's tail—only a fit bird can afford such an extravagant tail. By analogy, only a fit person has the time to develop musical talent. Another evolutionary view is that music serves to bind people together in coherent groups. Singing and dancing brought people together and helped them find common purpose. Of course, it is also possible that music served no evolutionary function and is just a happy by-product of the evolution of auditory processing in humans in general. The answers to these questions are beyond the scope of this book. We now turn to issues in sensation and perception.

THE ACOUSTICS OF MUSIC

 Explain how frequency is related to pitch, chroma, and the octave.

Pitch, Chroma, and the Octave

In Chapter 10, we described the relation between **pitch** and frequency. As frequency increases, we hear sounds at higher and higher pitches. As frequency decreases, we hear sounds at lower and lower pitches. Human beings can hear

Music: ordered sound made and perceived by human beings, created in meaningful patterns

Pitch: the subjective experience of sound that is most closely associated with the frequency of a sound stimulus; related to the experience of whether the sound is high or low, such as two ends of the keyboard of a piano

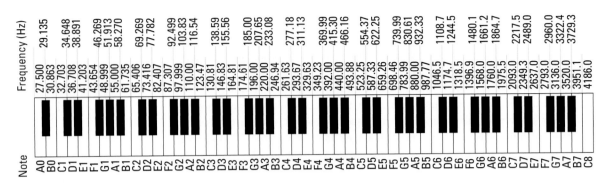

FIGURE 13.5 Piano keyboard.

A piano's notes start at 27.5 Hz at the far left and go up to 4,186 Hz at the far right. Most music is played within this range.

sounds between 20 and 20,000 Hz, but the range that is used in music is more restricted. Indeed, music is generally played in the range of only up to about 5,000 Hz. A piano, for example, has its lowest note tuned at 27.5 Hz and its highest note tuned at 4,186 Hz (see Figure 13.5). No Western instruments play lower than 27.5 Hz, and only a few Western instruments play higher than the piano does (e.g., the piccolo). In terms of the range at which humans can sing, the range is even more restricted. A human bass voice may get as low as 75 Hz, and a human soprano may get as high as 1,300 Hz. Thus, the notes used in music fall within a subrange of the full range of human hearing.

Although the fundamental frequency of musical notes seldom exceeds 5,000 Hz, harmonics typically range higher than this. Therefore, higher frequencies are important for music perception. Remember that natural sounds, including those of all voices and musical instruments, have higher harmonics. That means that in addition to the pitch we hear, there are other sounds present at higher frequencies. These higher harmonics contribute to the experience of timbre. Thus, having recording equipment that records at higher frequencies will preserve the timbre (to be reviewed shortly) of voices and instruments. Even then, we seldom use the very high frequencies for music—a good thing, as most of us lose our hearing above 10,000 Hz anyway by middle age.

The Western orchestra uses a range of instruments, some of which are designed to play lower notes and others designed to play higher notes. Among the string instruments, double basses play at the lower end of the musical range of pitches, whereas violins reach to some of the highest pitches used in music. Thus, in a string orchestra, without wind or brass instruments, the violins will play the higher notes, the violas and cellos will play intermediate pitches, and the double basses will play the low notes. Among the brass instruments, tubas and trombones play at lower pitches, whereas trumpets play at higher pitches. Among woodwinds, bassoons play at the lower end of the pitch range, whereas the piccolo has the highest notes of any instrument used in Western music. Figure 13.6 shows the frequency ranges of many common Western musical instruments.

The Octave

Pitches get higher as frequencies go up, but there is another important dimension of pitch that is highly relevant to music: the octave. The **octave** is the interval between one note and a note with either double the frequency or half the frequency of that note. This is a physical definition: A frequency of 200 Hz has octaves of 100 Hz below it and 400 Hz above it. Psychologically, we hear similarities between these doubled or halved frequencies. In musical terms, we refer to them by the same note name, but at different octaves. Thus, even though notes

Octave: the interval between one note and a note with either double the frequency or half the frequency of that note

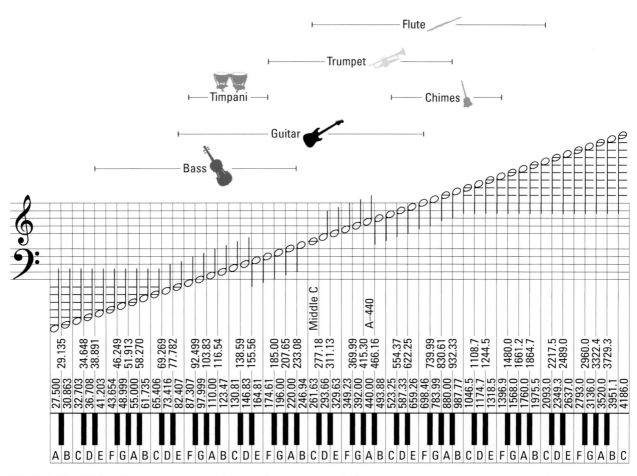

■ FIGURE 13.6   The symphony orchestra: frequency and pitch.

This diagram shows several instruments and their frequency ranges.

at 200 and 220 Hz are more similar in pitch, we hear notes at 200 and 400 Hz as being alike in a way that notes at 200 and 220 Hz are not (to hear this for yourself, go to ISLE 13.3).

ISLE 13.3 The Octave and Tone Similarity

We hear notes that are an octave apart as similar in a fundamental way. That is, there are perceived similarities between sounds that are an octave apart from one another. Notes that are one octave apart are said to be of the same **chroma**. This concept of an octave is present in all Western and non-Western musical traditions, including, as we mentioned earlier, in the functioning of prehistoric musical instruments. When we hear two notes that are an octave apart, they sound similar to us, despite their difference in pitch. On a piano keyboard, we label notes an octave apart with the same name. Thus, middle C has a frequency of 261.6 Hz, and the C one octave above it has a frequency of 523.3 Hz, or approximately double that frequency. The next C is at 1,046.5 Hz. Any musician recognizes that a scale begins at one note and continues to the same note at the next octave.

Think now about a piano keyboard and examine the illustration in Figure 13.5. We see a pattern of white and black keys. You will see the white keys labeled as being one of seven chromas of notes, C, D, E, F, G, A, and B, and then the pattern repeats back to C. This pattern repeats across the piano keyboard. Each C shares a feature of sound in common with other C's, but not with other notes. Similarly, each G shares a feature of sound in common with other G's, but not with other notes. This feature that these notes share in common is that they sound similar to us, and we call this feature chroma. For example, middle C (262 Hz) is closer in

Chroma: the subjective quality of a pitch; we judge sounds an octave apart to be of the same chroma

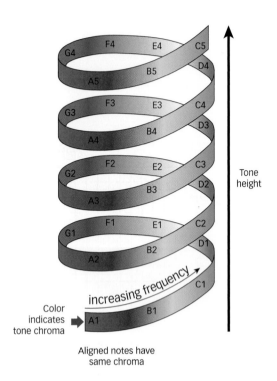

Color indicates tone chroma

Aligned notes have same chroma

Tone height

increasing frequency

■ **FIGURE 13.7**   **Pitch helix (Shepard, 1982).**

The pitch helix shows the relation of both pitch and frequency and of pitch similarity across octaves.

frequency to the D just above it (294 Hz), but it sounds more similar to the C in the next octave (523 Hz). This similarity of chroma from one octave to the next is represented by the pitch helix shown in Figure 13.7. As one goes up the helix, pitches get progressively higher, but the twists in the helix indicate the octave equivalence across similar notes.

Returning to the piano keyboard, we also have the black keys, which represent "sharps" and "flats" in musical terms. These keys are at frequencies between the white keys to either side. Thus, the black key between middle C and the D next to it plays at a frequency of 277 Hz, approximately halfway between the frequencies of the C and the D. In musical notation, this black key can be called either C-sharp or D-flat. The black key between the D and the E can be called either D-sharp or E-flat. Whether the note is called by its sharp name or its flat name depends on the musical context, but the sound is the same. When we add the sharps and flats to our musical hierarchy, we have 12 notes in an octave, as we ascend from one note to the same note an octave higher. Each adjacent note is sometimes called a **semitone**. There are 12 semitones in an octave in Western music. In music, when every note, including the sharps and flats, is played between one octave and the next (i.e., every semitone), this is called the chromatic scale. This would mean playing a 13-note scale, starting, for example, with C and including and ending with the C one octave above it. Almost all Western instruments allow musicians to play all 12 notes of the octave. Exceptions include some kinds of harps and recorders.

The other feature of the Western musical tradition is the use of an **equal-temperament scale**. This means that every adjacent note has an identical frequency ratio. The absolute difference between adjacent notes increases as one gets higher in frequency, but the ratio matters for perception. In this way, we perceive the difference between each successive semitone as equivalent in terms of difference in pitch to the one before it. This demonstrates Weber's law. What matters in perception is the ratio, not the absolute difference. One advantage of the equal-temperament system is that any melody can be played starting on any particular note.

In most Western music, the differences in frequency between each note are well established and do not vary (this may change in some music, such as a cappella choirs). When musicians tune their instruments, they tune them so that their C's (or, usually, A above middle C) all match at the same pitch or frequency. A piano or tuning whistle often provides this frequency. This organization has become standardized across Western music. Thus, a violinist in California and a cello player in Zurich, Switzerland, will usually agree that the A above middle C is tuned to 440 Hz (as long as they are not specifically tuning to standards from centuries past, as some orchestras do).

Traditional Chinese music uses a different scale system. Instead of the diatonic (eight-note) scale used in Western music (C, D, E, F, G, A, B, and C), Chinese music uses only a five-note (pentatonic) scale. In addition, the notes are not tuned according to an equal-temperament system, so that one cannot play the same melody starting on a different note, because the ratios between successive notes are not the same. Some early 20th century classical music, in trying to defy convention, essentially used pentatonic scales as well. Figure 13.8 shows a woman playing a guqin, a traditional Chinese instrument. The guqin is a

Semitones: the 12 equivalent intervals or notes within each octave

Equal-temperament scale: a tuning system in which the difference between each successive semitone is constant both in pitch and in frequency

seven-string instrument similar to a zither. Traditionally, it was tuned to the Chinese scale known as zheng diao, a pentatonic scale, although most instrumentalists use Western-based notes today.

Westerners typically find traditional Chinese music a bit odd because the notes do not map directly onto the notes in our scale, which we have become so accustomed to hearing. Some Western forms of music use pentatonic scales, but versions using the notes or pitches used in the equal-temperament scale system. These pentatonic traditions include Celtic folk music, some forms of West African music, and the American blues tradition. The five-note tradition makes improvisation, a hallmark of both Celtic music and American blues, easier. ISLE 13.4 gives examples of both Celtic music and improvisation in the American blues tradition.

To summarize, pitch is the psychological experience of frequency. As frequency gets higher, we hear the sound at a higher pitch. Musical notes are set at particular frequencies, and the relations between notes in Western music follow an equal-temperament system.

Consonance and Dissonance

In most music, more than one note is played at the same time. This is true in any musical style. Even a lonely folk singer and his or her guitar is playing at least two notes (one in voice, one on guitar) at the same time. A piano player has 10 fingers, and thus can play at least 10 notes at the same time, though this is very rare. A symphony orchestra may have many instruments playing several different notes at the same time. Jazz bands may have a number of different musical instruments playing at once. Rock bands tend to have singing, guitar playing, and percussion simultaneously. How do composers know which notes will sound good to listeners when played at the same time as other notes?

The concept of **harmony** in music refers to which pitches sound pleasing when played together. In technical terms, **consonance** refers the perception of pleasantness or harmony when two or more notes are played; that is, the notes fit with each other. In contrast, **dissonance** refers to the perception of unpleasantness or disharmony when two or more notes do not fit together. Why some notes are consonant when played together whereas others are dissonant has been the subject of much debate within Western culture, with theories going back all the way to the time of the ancient Greeks. The Greeks were impressed that two tones that could be expressed as a simple ratio of each other tended to sound consonant, whereas those that were more complex tended to sound dissonant. They did not know about frequency, but they measured these ratios in terms of the lengths of vibrating strings. Thus, the Greeks knew that a vibrating string twice the length of another would produce a consonant octave sound. We now know that two notes separated by an octave have approximately a 2:1 ratio of frequency. For example, concert A is 440 Hz, and the A above it is 880 Hz. Similarly, intervals of a major third (e.g., C and E) and a perfect fourth (e.g., C and F) sound consonant, but adjacent notes (e.g., C and D, a major second) sound dissonant. Major thirds and perfect fourths are easy to express as ratios, whereas adjacent notes are not.

When more than two notes are played at the same time, the result is called a chord. Chords are often played on the piano with the left hand, while the right hand plays a melody. Fundamental training in music allows musicians to learn which chords are consonant and which are dissonant. In many pieces of music, chords are selected to be harmonious or consonant with the melody line. We will discuss melody later in this section.

■ FIGURE 13.8   **A guqin.**

A woman playing a guqin, a traditional Chinese instrument.

ISLE 13.4 Pentatonic Music

Harmony: the pleasant sound that results when two or more notes are played together

Consonance: the perception of pleasantness or harmony when two or more notes are played; that is, the notes fit with each other

Dissonance: the perception of unpleasantness or disharmony when two or more notes do not fit together

Musical context also plays a role in our perception of consonance and dissonance. There may be some musical situations in which adjacent notes go together and would sound consonant, so consonance goes beyond simple ratios. In addition, culture plays a role in our perception of consonance and dissonance. What we find consonant in Western culture might be dissonant in traditional Chinese music, and what traditional Chinese music deems consonant we might find dissonant. In addition, norms within a culture change over time. This is true of the major third in Western music. Prior to Bach's time, the major third was avoided, as it was considered dissonant. It is now considered the most consonant interval in Western music after the octave itself.

Dynamics and Rhythm

Music is not just a series of pitches. Equally important in the production and appreciation of music are dynamics and rhythm. Indeed, drum music may not vary at all in pitch—the differences are in the complex rhythms. We start by defining the relevant terms in this section. **Dynamics** refers to the relative loudness and how loudness changes across a composition. That is, a piece may start off very loud, then grow softer, and then finish loud again. Changing from loud to soft may be important in transmitting the meaning and emotion in any piece of music. In musical notation, soft is indicated by a *p* for *piano*, and loud is indicated by an *f* for *forte* (these are the Italian terms for "soft" and "loud"). In physics terms, *dynamics* refers to amplitude, measured in decibels. Forte means more decibels, whereas piano means fewer decibels.

Rhythm refers to the temporal patterning of the music, including the tempo, the beat, and the meter. **Tempo** refers to how fast or slow a piece of music is played, that is, the speed of the music. For example, a beginning musician may elect to play a piece at a slower tempo so as not to make mistakes, whereas a more experienced musician may play the piece faster. Tempo can also change within a piece. Usually brisk or fast tempos are used to express joy, whereas slower tempos render a more sad feeling. Think of Christmas music. "Rudolf, the Red-Nosed Reindeer" is played quickly to express joy, whereas "Silent Night" is a slow piece that reflects a more thoughtful or religious approach to the holiday. **Meter** refers to the temporal pattern of sound across time, which usually repeats itself across the piece. Meter is completely intertwined with beat. **Beat** refers to spaced pulses that indicate if a piece is fast or slow. Thus, meter tells you how many beats occur per musical measure (the repeating temporal pattern), and beat tells you which notes to emphasize. In rock music, drums usually "keep the beat" by pulsing throughout each measure. In traditional classical music, instruments such as the double bass are responsible for keeping the beat. In most popular music, as well as in marches and many other styles of music, the meter is called 4/4, meaning that there are four beats per measure. In this meter, there is usually an emphasis, often indicated by relative loudness, on the first beat out of every four and a secondary emphasis on the third beat in each measure. Waltzes are played in 3/4 time, with the emphasis placed on the first beat out of every three in a measure. The characteristic feature of Jamaican reggae music is that instead of the first beat getting the emphasis in a 4/4 measure, the second and the fourth beats out of every four get the emphasis in each measure. If you hum the melody to such nearly universally known tunes as Bob Marley's "Jammin," you can feel the pulses on those second and fourth beats (see ISLE 13.5 for some examples of meter and beat).

Rhythm is therefore a complicated feature of music. It refers to tempo, meter, and beat. In any given piece of music, each note or pitch may also be maintained for either a short period of time or a long period of time. That is, a note, such

ISLE 13.5 Meter and Beat

Dynamics: relative loudness and how loudness changes across a composition

Rhythm: the temporal patterning of music, including the tempo, the beat, and the meter

Tempo: the pace at which a piece of music is played

Meter: the temporal pattern of sound across time

Beat: spaced pulses that indicate if a piece is fast or slow

as B-flat, may be played for just one beat, or it may be sustained across four or more beats. The pattern of notes across these beats also contributes to rhythm. In jazz, for example, a common motif is a tendency to have a slightly longer note is followed by a slightly shorter note, typically eighth notes. These eighth notes are indicated by the same musical notation, but a jazz musician automatically gives the note on Beat 1 a bit longer and shortens the note on Beat 2. This pattern gives jazz its characteristic rhythm. Waltzes usually contrast a note played on the one beat with notes played on the other two notes, to give waltzes their particular 3-count rhythm, which also makes them easy to dance to.

Timbre

Timbre refers to the complex sound created by harmonics (see Chapter 10 if this definition does not make sense). For example, a violin and a flute may be playing a note with the same pitch, but it sounds different on each instrument. The harmonics, as well as attack and decay characteristics, give each voice and each instrument its own distinct sound. Composers will select specific musical instruments because of their timbres. Depending on context, specific timbres of different instruments will convey particular meanings or emotions. The oboe, for example, is often used to express sadness, bittersweet emotion, and perhaps puzzlement, whereas a flute is more likely to express joy. In his famous piece *Bolero* (1928), Ravel has different instruments play the same theme repeatedly. Each instrument gives the theme a different feel, as Ravel builds up to finally having all the strings play the theme together and then the entire orchestra (you can hear this piece on ISLE 13.6). Ravel's *Bolero* also neatly illustrates a number of other principles. It is written in 3/4 meter, and you can hear the emphasis on the first beat of every measure. Moreover, as the piece progresses, the dynamics change, and the piece gradually builds from very soft to very loud.

As stated earlier, the fundamental frequencies of music predominantly fall below 5,000 Hz. Only the piccolo and piano even come close to that frequency. However, the harmonics of musical notes often exceed 5,000 Hz, and these harmonics contribute to the timbre of a voice or instrument. For this reason, recording equipment should be able to record frequencies well in excess of 5,000 Hz in order to capture the full complexity and musicality of any musical piece, even though we do not perceive these high-frequency harmonics as actual pitches (see Figure 13.10).

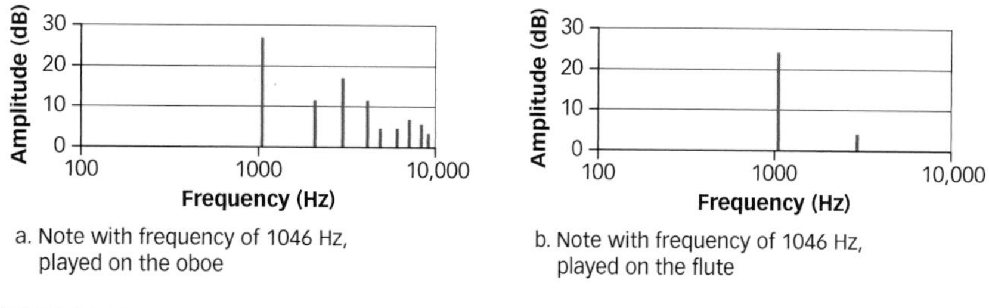

Timbre is also important in distinguishing between well-made and poorly made instruments. The materials and craftsmanship that go into a well-made instrument allow harmonics to be created, each at the right level of loudness. Thus, well-made instruments sound better than poorly made ones, assuming the musician playing each one is of equal ability. That is, the same good musician playing on a fine violin relative to a cheap violin will sound much better on the fine violin. The well-made violin has a rich and deep timbre, even when high notes are being played, whereas the cheap violin will sound shrill on higher notes, even when played by an expert. It is for this reason that violinists favor well-made violins, including such famous antique violins such as the legendary Stradivarius violins. Because of differences in timbre from instrument to instrument, the price

■ **FIGURE 13.9 Louis Armstrong.**

Louis Armstrong (1901–1971) was a famous trumpet player and singer in the jazz tradition. Jazz has roots in Western art music, popular music, and West African musical traditions.

ISLE 13.6 Bolero Clip

■ FIGURE 13.10

a. Note with frequency of 1046 Hz, played on the oboe

b. Note with frequency of 1046 Hz, played on the flute

Sound spectrograms of two different instruments, an oboe and a flute, playing the same note.

Timbre: the perceived sound differences between sounds with the same pitch but possessing different higher harmonics

differences between well-made and poorly made instruments can be shocking. A beginner's violin might cost as little as U.S. $80, whereas violins made for professionals usually run higher than U.S. $20,000 (and even higher; some violins cost millions). Similarly, a student's saxophone may cost as little as U.S. $200, whereas a professional one may cost over U.S. $8,000.

It is also clear that harmonics are not the only factor that affects timbre. Two other important features of timbre are attack and decay. **Attack** refers to the beginning buildup of a note. This means how quickly the instrument expresses all of its frequencies and if there are any differences in the onset of harmonics. **Decay** refers to how long the fundamental frequency and harmonics remain at their peak loudness until they start to disappear. For example, a trumpet has a very fast attack, leading to the sharp sound we associate with trumpets. In electronic instruments, attack and decay can be altered to mimic the sounds of other instruments or to create timbres that are not possible using string or wind instruments. You can hear differences in attack and decay by going to ISLE 13.7.

That gives us the basic building blocks of music—pitch, loudness, rhythm, and timbre. Musicians combine these building blocks in infinite ways to create music of all kinds. But to understand the perception of music requires more than a description of the building blocks—it also requires a more gestalt approach, as music transpires over time. For this reason, melody is of the utmost importance. We turn to melody in the next section.

Melody

Most people can hum a variety of melodies, from tunes learned in childhood, such as "Mary Had a Little Lamb," to Christmas songs to famous classical melodies, such as Beethoven's *Ode to Joy*, to the melody of the current hot songs on the Top 40. If you think about these tunes, you may realize that melody is essentially a series of pitches joined together with rhythm created by different lengths of each note (see Figure 13.10). Thus, we can define **melody** as a rhythmically organized sequence of notes, which we perceive as a single musical unit or idea. What carries melody beyond pitch and rhythm is that the sequence forms a unit with properties that transcend the individual pitches and lengths of notes. A melody coheres in time to create an experience in its listeners. Thus, the two melodies in Figure 13.10 are very similar in terms of the notes used and the rhythms used, but anyone brought up in Western culture would never confuse these two melodies (also see ISLE 13.8). Most music, in any tradition, starts with a melody, usually sung by a voice, played on the piano or with other instruments, which is then augmented by various musical accompaniments. Untrained listeners focus first on the melody.

Scales and Keys and Their Relation to Melody

Consider the piano keyboard again (see Figure 13.5). If we start on middle C and play every white note to the next C, we have played a C major scale. A **scale** is a set of ordered notes starting at one note and ending at the same note one octave higher. In this way, a scale is a very simple melody. In Western music, major scales refer to sequences of notes with the following pattern of semitones: 2, 2, 1, 2, 2, 2, 1. The numeral 2 means that we go up two semitones, whereas the numeral 1 means that we go up one semitone. Thus, a G major scale starting on G will include one black note (F-sharp). One can start a major scale on any note on the piano and follow this sequence. For example, the C-sharp major scale will have the following notes: C-sharp, D-sharp, F (E-sharp), F-sharp, G-sharp, A-sharp, C (B-sharp), and C-sharp. In essence, you can start a major scale on any note

ISLE 13.7 Attack and Decay

ISLE 13.8 Examples of Melody

Attack: the beginning buildup of a note

Decay: how long the fundamental frequency and harmonics remain at their peak loudness until they start to disappear

Melody: a rhythmically organized sequence of notes, which we perceive as a single musical unit or idea

Scale: a set of ordered notes starting at one note and ending at the same note one octave higher if you follow the pattern of 2, 2, 1, 2, 2, 2, 1 on your piano keyboard or any other instrument. Major scales are among the first melodies any instrumentalist learns when first starting to learn to play an instrument, and the major scale is the most common kind of scale in Western music. (You can hear an assortment of scales in ISLE 13.9.)

Major scales can be contrasted with the chromatic scale, in which every step is one semitone. Thus, the chromatic scale cannot be divided into keys, because it does not matter where you start or stop—the sequence is always the same. Each note is one semitone higher or lower than the previous one. On a piano, a chromatic scale means playing every key, including all of the black keys (again, see ISLE 13.9).

There are also a number of different types of minor scales, which have different sequences of semitones as one moves from one octave to the next. For example, the natural minor scale has the following sequence: 2, 1, 2, 2, 1, 2, 2. The natural minor scale is relatively simple in both its sequence and its relation to the major scale. However, more commonly used in music is the harmonic minor scale, with the following sequence: 2, 1, 2, 2, 1, 3, 1. The harmonic minor scale is often used in Western music to express sadness. It is also commonly used in Middle Eastern music. Other minor scales exist, but they are seldom used in music today. If you have taken a course in music theory, however, you are familiar with the whole family of minor scales.

Any particular melody can be expressed in terms of its key signature, which relates the melody to the pattern of scales described above. That is, every melody is played in a particular key, which refers to the main scale pattern. If we are playing "Mary Had a Little Lamb" in the key of C major, this means that the tonic is C, and we are not likely to have any sharps or flats (that is, no black keys on the piano). Thus, **key** refers to the tonic note (e.g., C in a C major or minor scale) that gives a subjective sense of arrival and rest in a musical piece. Because melodies are defined in terms of the pattern of notes relative to other notes, any melody can be played in any key. Thus, "Mary Had a Little Lamb" can be played in the key of C, the key of G, or any other key. If you hum the piece, its last note is the tonic of that key. If you are singing it in the key of C major, the tonic will be C. If you switch to another key, the name of that key will be the tonic. Composers will make deviations from the key. Thus, when a G-sharp is called for in a melody played in the key of C, the G-sharp is called an "accidental" by musicians. Thus, for musicians, the term *accidental* refers to a note that requires a special mark to remind the musician to play the sharp or flat not present in that key.

In most cases, what defines a melody is the relation of pitches within a piece rather than the absolute pitches. For example, it really does not matter what note we start "Mary Had a Little Lamb" on, as long as the remaining notes show the same relation to that note as in the original version. For example, "Mary Had a Little Lamb" is shown in the key of G in Figure 13.11. In this key, the first note is B, the second is A, and the third is G. Each of these notes is one step (or interval or two semitones) higher than the next note in the sequence. If we switch the key to F, the first three notes will be A, G, and F. Although there is no overlap in actual notes, we hear these sequences as being the same, and both can create the melody of "Mary Had a Little Lamb." That there can be two or more versions of a melody,

■ FIGURE 13.11   (a) The musical notation for "Mary Had a Little Lamb" and (b) the musical notation for Beethoven's *Ode to Joy*. These pieces are seldom grouped together because of their different histories, but they are quite similar in terms of their melodies.

ISLE 13.9 Types of Scales

Key: the tonic note (e.g., C in a C major or minor scale) that gives a subjective sense of arrival and rest in a musical piece

each starting on a different note, is known as a **transposition** in music. Trained musicians may be able to detect what key a simple melody is being played in, but most listeners hear the melody as such but do not register the key or starting note.

Our perception of melody across transpositions starts very early in life. Plantinga and Trainor (2005) examined melody perception in 6-month-old infants. In the study, Plantinga and Trainor played particular melodies to infants numerous times over a 7-day period. On the next day, the infants either heard the same melody, but transposed into another key, or a novel melody. If the transposed melody was heard as the same melody as the original, the infant would not consider it novel and would look toward the source of the novel melody. If, however, the infant heard the transposed melody as novel, he or she would show no difference in looking time toward the source of the transposed melody or the new melody. The results showed that the infants looked more often toward the source of the novel melody, rather than the transposed melody, indicating that they perceived the transposed melody as being similar to something heard earlier. In this way, we can assert that even young infants hear melodies across transpositions of key.

Gestalt Principles of Melody

Because of the importance to melody of the relation among notes rather than absolute pitch, and because the perception of melody is qualitatively different than the perception of a string of pitches, melody perception lends itself to the use of gestalt principles. If you remember from Chapter 5, gestalt psychology approaches perception by examining emergent properties that can be seen across a perceptual array but may not be obvious in any particular single element of that stimulus. That is, the motto of gestalt psychology is that the "whole is bigger than the sum of the parts." The gestalt principles described in Chapter 5 are certainly applicable to melody perception (Tan et al., 2010). We review these principles and then apply them to music (also see ISLE 13.10).

The four principles are as follows:

1. Proximity: elements near each other are seen as a group.
2. Similarity: elements that are similar are seen as a group.
3. Closure: an incomplete pattern is seen as whole when the completion occurs.
4. Good continuation: smooth continuity is preferred over changes in direction.

These principles are applied in melody processing over time processing rather than space (e.g., visual processing). Indeed, music transpires over time—a melody is a sequence of notes in time. Of course, other aspects of music involve space—the source of a voice or instrumental sound is often critical—but the time dimension comes first. For example, we tend to hear notes that are close in chroma as grouped together, even when they come from different instruments or different locations, a source of the music illusions described at the end of the chapter. Space does play a role in music perception, as anyone who has heard an old monophonic record can attest. The old monophonic recordings lack the depth provided by modern recordings, which allow listeners to imagine where different instruments' sounds are coming from. But returning to the gestalt principles, we start with proximity. We then consider similarity and closure.

Proximity In music, *proximity* may refer to elements' being close together in pitch, time, or space (Tan et al., 2010). For example, notes that are similar in pitch may be grouped together. Notes are also grouped together if they are played together in time or if they come from the same instrument or section of a larger musical group. To get a sense for the idea of proximity, imagine a person playing

ISLE 13.10 Gestalt Principles Review

Transposition: the process through which one can create multiple versions of a melody that start on different notes but contain the same intervals or sequence of changes in notes

a piano. Typically, the right hand plays notes that are higher in pitch than the left hand. Also, most often, it is the right hand that plays the melody, while the left hand plays the bass line or accompaniment. Even though all of the notes are played in close spatial proximity and at approximately the same time, we hear the notes from the right hand emerging as melody because they are grouped together with respect to pitch (see Figure 13.12). Similarly, in some of Bach's famous solo music for violin, the violinist essentially creates two streams of music by simultaneously playing both high and lower notes. Perceptually, we group the high notes together and group the low notes together, so we hear it as polyphonic or as two lines of music (for an example, go to ISLE 13.11 to hear Bach's Partita No. 3 in E major).

ISLE 13.11 Gestalt Principle: Proximity: Bach's Partita #3

Similarity Think of listening to your favorite music. Chances are your favorite music is created by a group of musicians, playing different parts. From hometown garage bands to the Vienna Philharmonic, most music consists of multiple parts. A rock band may have a drummer, a guitar player, a bass player, and one or more singers. An orchestra may consist of more than 100 musicians playing 16 different instruments. Composers will use our perception of similarity to create seamless perceptions of melody even when the melody crosses from one voice or one instrument to another. Similarity plays out at several levels. We may hear similar timbres grouped together. A modern orchestra may have 16 violinists all playing the same part. Because these musicians are playing the same notes with the same approximate timbre, we hear them as grouped together. Moreover, once a melody has been established, we may follow the melody because of its similarity across changes in instruments. In Ravel's *Bolero*, the instruments playing the melody constantly change, but we have no difficulty distinguishing the melody from the bass line, drum rhythms, and harmony (hear this in ISLE 13.6).

C D   C B

■ **FIGURE 13.12** Notes grouped together by proximity.

Because C and D are close in pitch, they are grouped together. Because C and B in a higher octave are not close in pitch, we think of them as separate.

Principle of Closure In music, this means that a melody should end on the tonic note of any particular scale or another note implied by the progression of the melody. Typically, if the melody is played in the key of C, the last note will be C. Occasionally, the note might be G, but seldom any other note in the key of C. To illustrate this point, think of the very short melody of the song "Shave and a Haircut." If you do not know the melody, but can read music, see Figure 13.13 (you can hear it in ISLE 13.11c). If you simply play the notes or sing the words "shave and a haircut," most people experience a strong longing to hear or sing the last two notes ("two bits"). Try it yourself: most people cannot stop themselves from singing the last two notes of the sequence. In the 1988 movie *Who Framed Roger Rabbit?* the character of Roger Rabbit is lured out of hiding because he cannot stop himself from completing this melody.

Experimentally, the importance of closure in melody perception was demonstrated in an experiment by DeWitt and Samuel (1990). Their experiment was a musical demonstration of the phonemic restoration effect we discussed in the last chapter, except instead of hearing a missing phoneme, participants heard an implied but missing note. In this perceptual restoration effect, participants heard a major scale plus the next two notes, for a total of 10 notes, each predictable from the note played before it. One note of the 10 was replaced by white noise. Under these conditions, many participants reported hearing the missing note. This effect was greater when the note was later in the scale, allowing

Shave and a hair-cut   two bits

■ **FIGURE 13.13** Principle of closure.

It is hard not to want closure of this famous, albeit very short, piece of music.

more time for expectations to build up. The effect did not occur if the notes were randomly arranged rather than in a melody-like scale. Thus, our expectation of what to hear in a particular sequence can actually create the perception of that note.

> **TEST YOUR KNOWLEDGE**
>
> Describe the difference between frequency, pitch, and chroma. How does the concept of the octave relate to each of these terms?

THE NEUROSCIENCE OF MUSIC

 Summarize the basic neuroscience of music, including how training and experience can affect the representation of music in the brain.

One of the central tenets of modern psychology is that perceptual and cognitive processes arise in the brain. Even if these processes are about objects in the world and perceived through sensory organs, the brain's role is still considered central. Implicit in this view is that all human brains are organized in similar ways. This turns out to be supported over and over again. For example, regardless of gender, age, ethnic background, racial identification, native language, and any other feature that distinguishes one human from another, brain regions serve the same functions across these distinctions. For example, the occipital lobe processes visual information for all sighted persons (indeed, all sighted mammals). Wernicke's area and Broca's area are language areas in all human brains. The primary auditory cortex processes input from the cochlea in all human brains. Neurosurgeons may need to be aware of slight deviations in individual human brains—one region may be shifted a few millimeters forward or backward relative to other individuals—but by and large, this rule of brain universalism has been upheld in modern science.

The Neuroanatomy of Music

The neuroanatomy of music is a bit different because music is in some ways an optional feature of human cognition. Although all cultures have music (including those that forbid it), people vary greatly in their interest in music, the time spent listening to music, their individual training in music, and the musical traditions they are exposed to. As a result, there are greater individual differences in the regions responsible for music perception and in the way these regions function than there are for many other functions of the brain. Nonetheless, we can make some generalizations about how music perception occurs in the brain.

First, we start with a quick review of information covered in Chapters 10 and 11. Recall that from the cochlea to the auditory cortex, the auditory signal has a tonotopic organization. This means that the auditory nerve preserves a representation of the frequency of sound, which we perceive in music as the pitch of a particular note. Loudness is represented by the strength of the signal at any particular frequency. We also see tonotopic organization throughout the primary auditory cortex. Music perception is certainly a variant of sound perception, but not all sounds are music. So we can ask if there are common areas of the brain that process musical stimuli, independent of other sounds, in all human beings. We find these areas starting in the secondary auditory cortex in the temporal lobe (Overy, Peretz, Zatorre, Lopez, & Majno, 2012).

One of the clear findings is that music perception usually causes greater activation in the right temporal lobe than the left temporal lobe (Overy et al., 2012). It seems that the right hemisphere is more sensitive to small changes in pitch, which are likely relevant to music, but less relevant to speech. For example, Hyde, Peretz, and Zatorre (2008) used functional magnetic resonance imaging (fMRI) to examine the function of the right and left auditory cortical regions in frequency processing of melodic sequences. They found that better behavioral pitch resolution was associated with activity in the right secondary auditory cortex. More specifically, these areas included the planum temporale as well as some areas within the primary auditory cortex (see Figure 13.14). Indeed, many neuroimaging studies have now shown the importance of the right secondary auditory cortex in pitch perception in music (Janata, Birk, Van Horn, Leman, Tillmann, & Bharucha, 2002; Overy et al., 2012). However, the greater the musical training, the more left-hemisphere involvement one sees in music perception (Habibi, Wirantana, & Starr, 2013). That is, musical training forces the brain to devote more networks to music, and perhaps requires the brain to involve meaning and language circuits to help with music perception and cognition.

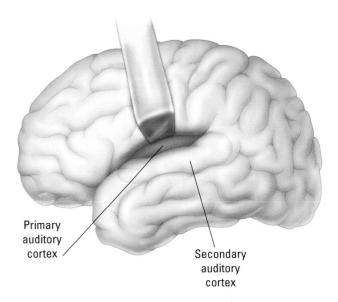

Primary auditory cortex

Secondary auditory cortex

■ FIGURE 13.14   Secondary auditory cortex.

Secondary auditory cortex areas with specialization in fine pitch perception are important in music perception.

Other neuroimaging studies have focused on harmonic expectations. For example, Seger et al. (2013) played small samples of Western classical music to participants while they were being monitored by fMRI. Compared with when participants were not listening to music, Seger et al. found activity in the bilateral superior temporal gyrus and the right inferior frontal gyrus. These areas also became even more active when the experimenters changed the music to violate expected patterns.

Another important component of music, as previously discussed, is rhythm. Rhythm appears to be processed in areas of the primary auditory cortex, and more noticeably in the right hemisphere as well. In particular, the belt and parabelt areas are important in the processing of rhythm (Snyder & Large, 2005; Tramo, 2001). Moreover, when people are producing rhythm, we also see some more prominent activity in the left hemisphere, including areas of both the left prefrontal cortex and the left parietal cortex. Because people producing rhythm are also engaged in action, we also see activity in the cerebellum (Tramo, 2001).

Most of the studies reviewed above have been conducted with participants who were college students, but who did not have specific musical training. Most college students have spent many hours over the course of their lives listening and attending to music. But we can also ask how musical training affects the networks in the brain for music perception. Although there are a great many similarities between the brains of nonmusicians and musicians, we can find some important differences as a function of musical training. For example, the organization of the motor cortex changes in response to the demands of the complex motor movements needed to play many instruments. In particular, Krings et al. (2000) examined the brain areas used by professional piano players and a control group. Piano players must use complex movements of both hands, and in many cases, the movements of each hand may follow very different patterns simultaneously. Using fMRI, they found that the professional piano players required lower levels of cortical activation in motor areas of the brain relative to controls while doing the same task. That is, musical training allowed greater control of the hands in piano players, meaning that they needed to recruit fewer neurons to do an easy manual task relative to controls. In essence, musical training also recruits motor networks to allow musicians to engage in the complex motor movements necessary to play music.

Recent neuroimaging studies show that visual areas of the brain are activated when people are listening to music, consistent with a number of studies linking auditory and visual cortices (Liang, Mouraux, Hu, & Iannetti, 2013). It may be that listening to music invokes thoughts that invoke visual images, which we know are produced in the visual areas of the brain. Certainly, this is often the goal of some composers, that is, to cause us to bring to mind a particular image. If this is the case, then we may find more interactions between vision and music that might be intuitive. To test this view, Landry, Shiller, and Champoux (2013) compared listeners under normal conditions with those who had been deprived of visual stimulation for 90 minutes. The listeners who had been kept in the dark showed a temporary improvement in their perception of harmonicity, that is, whether a chord was in tune or slightly out of tune. The participants who had been visually deprived performed better at this task for up to 5 minutes after the visual deprivation ended. Landry et al. interpreted this to mean that the visual system may play a role in music perception, as there was an observed interaction.

Synesthesia

The interaction between music and the visual system is even more pronounced in people with color-music synesthesia. **Synesthesia** is defined as a condition in which a stimulus in one modality consistently triggers a response in another modality. Estimates of the incidence of synesthesia suggest that it occurs in approximately 1% to 4% of the population (Simner et al., 2006). Synesthesia includes a number of different kinds of cross-modality experiences. For some people with synesthesia, particular words or letters may elicit particular colors, whereas for others, visual stimuli may trigger a taste experience. **Color-music synesthesia** occurs when particular pitches, notes, or chords elicit experiences of particular visual colors. Whereas most of us do not have synesthesia, we can do cross-modality matching with some degree of consistency and accuracy. That is, most people will use similar principles to match pitch to color or loudness to temperature (you can try this for vision-audition comparisons in ISLE 13.12). Although normal people may make similar judgments, we seldom experience color while listening to music. The interesting aspect of synesthesia is that these people do experience a sensation in another modality. Note that people with synesthesia are not hallucinating—they are well aware that the secondary experience is illusory. Nonetheless, the experience in the second modality may be very vivid and strong. Color-music synesthesia has been described by many musicians and composers, including classical composers Leonard Bernstein and Nikolai Rimsky-Korsakov and jazz pianist Marian McPartland.

Recent neuroimaging studies confirm that people with synesthesia have different brain organization than those who do not have synesthesia (Hubbard, Brang, & Ramachandran, 2011; Loui, Zamm, & Schlaug, 2012). These studies show that people with synesthesia tend to have stronger connections between one sensory area and another sensory area than do people without synesthesia. To be more specific, this means that the white matter (axons) between one perceptual area and another is stronger in those with synesthesia. Zamm, Schlaug, and Eagleman (2013) examined the brains of people with color-music synesthesia. They found that relative to controls, people with color-music synesthesia had stronger connections between the

ISLE 13.12 Cross Modal Matchings as a Simulation of Synesthesia

Synesthesia: a condition in which a stimulus in one modality consistently triggers a response in another modality

Color-music synesthesia: a form of synesthesia that occurs when particular pitches, notes, or chords elicit experiences of particular visual colors

visual and auditory cortices and areas in the frontal lobe. They found that a tract from the sensory areas to the frontal lobe called the inferior fronto-occipital fasciculus was enlarged in people with synesthesia (see Figure 13.15). Zamm et al. showed that connections between visual areas in the occipital lobe and auditory association regions in the temporal lobe may be differently structured in people with color-music synesthesia.

The Neuropsychology of Music

Amusia is a condition in which brain damage interferes with the perception of music, but does not otherwise interfere with other aspects of auditory processing. Amusia usually is acquired after brain damage, but there is also a form called **congenital amusia**, in which individuals are seemingly born with an impairment in music percep-

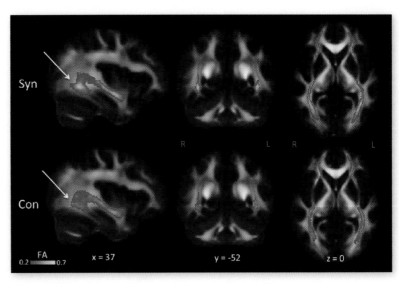

■ **FIGURE 13.15**   The brain in synesthesia (Zamm, Shlaug, and Eagleman, 2013).

People with color-music synesthesia have stronger connections between the visual and auditory cortices and areas in the frontal lobe. This is demonstrated in these functional magnetic resonance images.

tion. The critical deficit in most forms of amusia, including congenital amusia, is that people with this condition have an impaired ability to discriminate pitches, which affects their music perception but, in most cases, leaves speech perception intact. This is likely the case because pitch is less critical in phoneme perception, but the condition interferes with their ability to perceive and therefore appreciate music (Peretz & Hyde, 2003). Amusia has recently garnered public attention because of the publication of Oliver Sacks's bestselling 2007 book *Musicophilia*, which describes a number of fascinating cases of amusia and also describes its opposite, that is, cases of people who have become intensely musical after brain damage.

Isabelle Peretz and her colleagues at the University of Montreal have been conducting extensive studies on congenital amusia (e.g., Moreau, Jolicoeur, & Peretz, 2013). People with congenital amusia show deficits in music perception as well as production (e.g., they cannot sing in tune and have difficulty learning to play musical instruments). Although it is extremely rare, Peretz estimates that as many as 4% of the population may suffer from some form of amusia. You may know some of these people as the people who cannot sing even a simple tune and who have no interest in going to concerts with you. Congenital amusia seems to be related to impaired pitch discrimination, so people with congenital amusia will not show deficits in speech perception or in most other aspects of auditory perception.

As indicated above, it is likely that poor pitch perception lies at the heart of congenital amusia. However, Peretz (2013) was concerned that an initial deficit in pitch perception may spiral in people with amusia. Because they cannot appreciate melodies like normal individuals, they may avoid listening to music. Because of this lack of exposure, their musical impairment will grow with lack of exposure. To remedy this potential in the real world, Peretz conducted experiments in which people diagnosed with amusia agreed to listen to music for an hour per day over a series of weeks. Peretz showed that patients with congenital amusia who are exposed to music over a long period of time do not show any improvement in pitch perception or in musical understanding (Mignault-Goulet, Moreau, Robitaille, & Peretz, 2012). Thus, mere exposure to music does not "treat" amusia.

Amusia: a condition in which brain damage interferes with the perception of music, but does not otherwise interfere with other aspects of auditory processing

Congenital amusia: a condition in which people are inherently poor at music perception

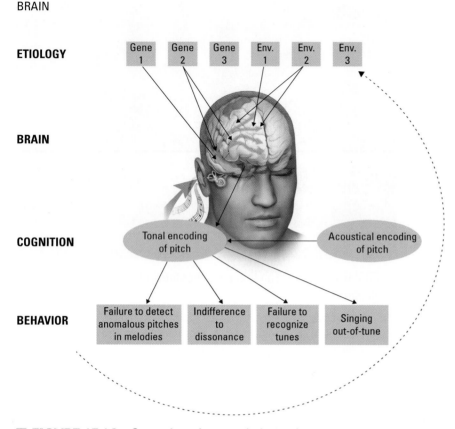

BRAIN

ETIOLOGY

BRAIN

COGNITION

BEHAVIOR

■ FIGURE 13.16   Causation of congenital amusia.

This diagram illustrates the potential causes of amusia.

Because of this, Peretz (2013) is convinced that congenital amusia is a genetically linked syndrome that occurs in some people. Indeed, Peretz (2008) described research that shows that congenital amusia occurs within families more than chance would predict, thus pointing to a genetic component. She argues for a neuroanatomical pathway that might be suppressed or impaired in people with congenital amusia. For example, she argued that research shows that there may be deficits in the transmission of information from the auditory associative cortex, that is, those areas that surround the primary auditory cortex, to areas in the frontal lobe, such as the inferior frontal gyrus (see Figure 13.16).

We will cover one last interesting aspect of congenital amusia. We have seen that one of the primary deficits is an inability to distinguish close pitches. Because of this pitch confusion, it may be hard for individuals to distinguish music that is in tune from music that is out of tune, and music that is consonant from music that is dissonant. Thus, most individuals with congenital amusia tend to shy away from music. However, what happens to individuals with congenital amusia when they attempt to learn a language such as Mandarin (Chinese) or Vietnamese, in which the pitch with which a word is said is important to meaning? Early studies suggest these are extremely difficult languages for congenital amusia individuals to learn as second languages, but we do not know if native Mandarin speakers with congenital amusia have a deficit in understanding semantics conveyed by pitch (see Peretz, 2008). Future research will hopefully tease these issues out.

TEST YOUR KNOWLEDGE

What changes in the brain occur when people acquire musical training?

LEARNING, CULTURE, AND MUSIC PERCEPTION

13.3   Discuss how learning and culture affect music perception.

Music and Language

One of the ongoing debates in the field of music perception is the extent of the metaphor between language and music. Is music a form of language in which the ideas transmitted are not words and semantic meaning but notes and emotions?

Are there special parallels in the processes that allow us to understand language and appreciate music? Some researchers argue that language and music are very similar processes, whereas other researchers argue for little overlap between the two. We briefly address some of the arguments for both views here.

One of the most passionate spokespeople for the idea that language and music share similar neurocognitive systems is noted music neuroscientist Aniruddh Patel (Patel, 2008, 2013). Patel asserts that language and music have much in common at the behavioral level. First, music and language are both perceptive (listening) and productive (singing, talking) systems in which perceiving and producing are equally important (if only to sing in the shower). Moreover, both involve the perception of novel and complex sounds that unfold rapidly over time. Subjectively, hearing a melody is different from hearing a sentence, but both are sound stimuli that transmit meaning, so it is not unrealistic to expect some overlap. Patel (2013) also argues that both music and language have structure that must be followed for the sounds to make sense to listeners. For example, language has syntax that governs which words can be joined together to make a coherent sentence. Patel argues that music theory describes a syntax that serves a similar function in music, namely, limiting those notes that can be joined together to form consonant music. Similarly, words have specific meanings, but that meaning can depend on context. For example, the word *bugger* may be a term of affection in one situation, but a vile insult in another. Meaning can also vary in music as a function of context. In many situations, minor keys denote sadness, but there are also a great many wedding celebration songs written in minor keys.

On a neural level, there are also some striking parallels between music and language. First, both use the same basic auditory machinery. Whereas language uses more neural space in the left hemisphere, music perception and production appear to be housed in the analogous regions of the right hemisphere. Moreover, the better someone becomes at language, the more right hemisphere involvement we see. Similarly, many studies have shown the acquisition of musical expertise is accompanied by greater left-hemisphere involvement in music (Patel, 2013).

Nonetheless, there are also important differences between music perception and language perception that must be acknowledged, which cloud the analogy between music and language. First, speech perception is based on the inference of subtle differences in the patterns that produce different vowels and consonants, whereas music focuses on pitch and pitch contrasts. We can say a sentence without varying the pitch; the movements of the mouth create different sounds that carry phoneme information. Similarly, music can be sung using different phonemes, but as long as the pitch remains, we recognize the music as such. For example, think of the conventional way of singing Henry Mancini's "Pink Panther" (1963)—"dead ant, dead ant, dead ant, dead ant, dead ant, dead ant, dead . . . ant." We could certainly change the semantic content from dearly departed insects to anything we like and still represent the melody of this song. Indeed, when humming the melody, we may think of the Pink Panther's bumbling French detectives or cool jazz, but seldom do we think of it as a dirge for the *Formicidae*. Thus, the meaning in music extends beyond what is sung. Finally, it is also possible to interpret the neural evidence as suggesting differences between language and music. That is, language predominates in the left hemisphere, whereas music predominates in the right hemisphere. What could be a more basic difference than that?

Culture and Music Perception

An obvious truism about music is that it varies so much—from culture to culture, from generation to generation, from "pop" traditions to "highbrow" traditions. Given this incredible diversity of music, are we justified in making the generalizations about music perception that we have been making throughout this chapter? Our assertion here is that despite the differences in music across cultures, there are some universalities that allow us to talk about music and not just "varieties of music." We have already discussed, for example, the universality of the octave, which all music traditions respect. All cultures use pitch and rhythm to express emotion in their music, either with or without singing. So we now briefly consider some rules that may be universal and some that may be specific to our own Western traditions.

A brief reminder of the context of the term *Western music*: Our use of the term refers to a huge gamut of music, including what most of us would commonly call "classical" music and "pop" music, as well as jazz, hip-hop, rap, reggae, southern rock, rock 'n' roll, country, grunge, and so on. All of these styles follow the Western music tradition. However passionately you may love one form (e.g., reggae) and hate another (e.g., country), they all share the Western music tradition and therefore have more in common with one another than they do with non-Western forms of music. Western musical styles use the same scale structure, the same relations among notes within the octave, a common means of notating written music, a common set of assumptions about what is consonant and what is dissonant. Indeed, they use many of the same musical instruments. Although from where most of us sit, the tattooed and nose-ringed fans of a heavy metal group may have little to do with the tuxedoed and gowned attendees of an opera, they are both engaging with music that derives clearly and directly from Western music traditions.

But outside the Western music tradition, we find music that is organized by radically different principles. For example, the Indian rag (or raga) scales that govern much traditional Indian music are very different from Western scales. First, in much Indian music, there are 22 notes within each octave, far more than the traditional Western 12. In addition, few of these notes fall exactly at the same frequencies as Western notes (see Figure 13.17). Thus, at a very basic level, Indian music is using notes that would fall between the notes of the Western music scale. Thus, it would be impossible to play raga music on a Western instrument, such as a piano or any woodwind instrument. Moreover, in traditional Indian music, different scales are associated with different times of year, different moods, and even different times of day (Tan et al., 2010). Research shows that the networks in the brain react differently to daily exposure to Indian music as opposed to Western music (Ambady & Bharucha, 2009).

Similarly, Javanese gamelan music uses different scale systems, called slendro, which is a five-tone scale, and pelog, which is a seven-tone scale. These scales bear a rough correspondence to Western scales, but the notes are distributed at different intervals relative to the octave of each scale. Perlman and Krumhansl (1996) found that Western listeners were impaired in their ability to detect aspects of Javanese music relative to those who were more familiar with it.

Performance may also vary across musical traditions. In the Western tradition—from art and classical music on one hand to garage rock bands on the other—we have performers, and we have listeners. Listeners may dance and shout in less formal venues (but do not try that in a symphony concert hall), but they are not part of the musical performance. This history of performers and listeners goes back centuries in our musical traditions. In many non-Western music traditions, it is expected that all present will be part of the act of making music as well as listening to it.

Musical traditions differ in their approaches to rhythm as well. In particular, research has focused

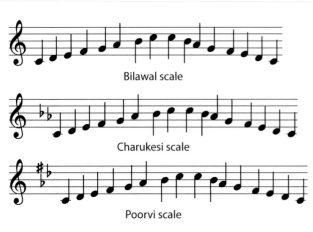

■ FIGURE 13.17   Indian raga scales.
The Bilawal scale is identical to our major scale, but the other ragas are quite different from the scales used in Western music.

on differences between Western musical approaches to rhythm and those of traditional West African drumming (Temperley, 2000). Temperley argues that syncopation (varying the emphasized beat in a musical piece) is usually more pronounced in West African traditions. However, syncopation became very much a part of the Western tradition in jazz and in classical music in the 20th century, perhaps borrowing from African traditions. So differences in rhythm may be quantitative changes among similar traditions rather than markers of completely different musical traditions, as we see in the case of different notes within a scale.

An interesting pattern that may be universal across musical traditions is the relation between music and the experience of emotion. Seemingly, in all cultures, music is used to convey emotion ranging from sadness and anger to joy and ecstasy. Most of us know this experience firsthand. A song comes on the radio and reminds us of a particularly romantic night with our significant other; another song reminds us of a particularly unpleasant breakup. The composer Johann Sebastian Bach wrote the sarabande of his Violin Partita No. 2 in D minor (Opus 1004) in the weeks after the death of his wife. Even today, more than 300 years later, we can hear the inconsolable sadness in the piece (you can hear a sample of this piece on ISLE 13.13). Even if you have never listened to classical music, you should be able to determine the sadness conveyed by the minor chords and the haunting melody.

ISLE 13.13 Bach Violin Partita #2

However, moving across cultures, it may be difficult to detect the intended emotion in a musical composition. In the Western music tradition, minor scales often convey sadness, as certainly Bach's Violin Partita No. 2 in D minor does. However, in Middle Eastern music, those same minor scales may be used to express joy. The research, however, suggests that listeners can detect the intended emotion across musical traditions, supporting the idea of the universality of emotion in music. For example, Balkwill and Thompson (1999) found that Western listeners could accurately identify the intended emotion in Indian raga music. Listeners attended to pitch (lower is sadder, higher is happier) and tempo (slower is sadder, faster is happier) to find the intended emotion, and these features appear to be universal. Meyer, Palmer, and Mazo (1998) showed that Western listeners could identify the emotional content of traditional Russian laments by listening for timbre cues in the singers' voices. Thus, it may be that the expression of emotion in music transcends musical traditions.

TEST YOUR KNOWLEDGE

What are minor scales? What do they represent in different cultures?

IN DEPTH: *Musical Illusions*

Our perceptual systems are designed to detect stimuli in the environment, but also to extract meaning from those sensory stimuli. In a sense, this is what music is—the extraction of patterns and emotional meaning out of a stream of patterned auditory stimuli. As we have seen throughout this chapter, what creates music is a pattern in melody, in harmony, or in rhythm. And as you have seen throughout this book, when our perceptual systems attend to patterns, they can be tricked into perceiving patterns even when elements of those patterns are missing. Music is no exception. Music perception researchers have identified and created a number of engaging musical illusions. These illusions are fun to listen to, but they also tell us about the underlying structures and functions of musical perception. We will start with one of the more compelling and frustrating musical illusions, called Shepard tones after the researcher who first designed this illusion (Shepard, 1964).

Shepard Tones

In Shepard tones, one hears a scale that sounds like it increases in pitch continually. (The illusion can also be designed so that one hears a scale that sounds like it is decreasing in pitch.) Each sound in the scale seems a bit higher than the one preceding it, but the listener eventually realizes that the tone one is hearing is back at the pitch at which the scale started, although all one hears is increasing pitches (the example on ISLE 13.14, is a must-hear). That is, the pitches sound like they are getting continually higher, but in fact, the sound frequencies return back to lower frequencies without our noticing it in any change from one note to the next. The illusion can also be run in reverse, with the perception being that the notes get lower and lower, when actually they do not. Again, please listen to the demonstration—in this case, hearing is believing. How did Shepard do this?

ISLE 13.14 Shepard Tones

The illusion is created by simultaneously sweeping different pure tones that are an octave apart. By *sweeping*, we mean starting at one note and sliding through all the intermediate frequencies to another note. Thus, the scale may start with an A at 220 Hz, and the tone slowly slides up to an A at 440 Hz. At the same time, there is another A starting at 880 Hz and sliding down to 440 Hz. This creates the illusion of a rising pitch, even though there is no difference in the frequencies being presented (Figure 13.18). In essence, this is an auditory version of the barber pole illusion, in which the color pattern looks like it is continually going up or going down, despite the obvious fact that this cannot be occurring (see Figure 13.19).

The Octave Illusion

Deutsch (1974) described the octave illusion, a phenomenon she had been studying in her laboratory. You can listen to the octave illusion in ISLE 13.15. It is a stereo illusion, so please make sure that you listen to it with headphones on. If you do not, the illusion will not work properly. In the octave illusion, one tone is presented to one ear while another tone, exactly one octave higher or lower, is presented simultaneously to the other ear. However, the next note combination is of the same two notes, but to the opposite ears. That is, if a middle G is presented to the left ear, and the G an octave lower is presented to the right ear, the next notes will be a middle G presented to the right ear and the G an octave lower presented to the left ear (see Figure 13.20).

ISLE 13.15 Octave Illusion

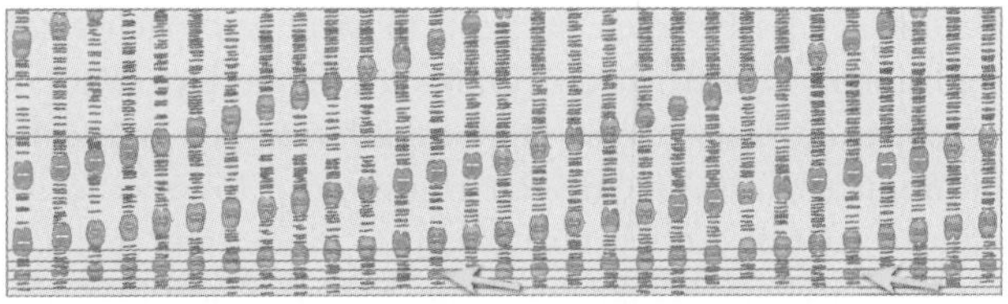

■ **FIGURE 13.18**   Spectrogram of Shepard tones.

The spectrogram shows that the interlacing of rising tones along with an octave shift down (indicated by yellow arrows) causes the perception of a gradually increasing sequence in pitch, even though the actual sequence does not rise in pitch.

This is an illusion, so think first about what you should hear: the same note, alternating between ears, and another note also alternating between ears. It should sound the same, as the stimuli are the same for both notes, just presented to different ears. But listen to it on ISLE again. What do you actually hear? What most people report hearing is the following: You hear a single note (the middle G) in your right ear followed by a single note an octave lower in your left ear. And then a continuous alternation between the two occurs, regardless of which ear the higher G is actually being presented to. So what you hear differs from what is actually being presented—hence the term *illusion*. If you reverse your headphones, you get the feeling not that the sounds are coming from different ears, but that the order of notes reverses (Deutsch, 1975). Some left-handers may hear

■ **FIGURE 13.19**   The barber pole illusion.

When this barber pole is set in motion, it looks as if it continually rises (or falls), when it actually just circles back to the same place.

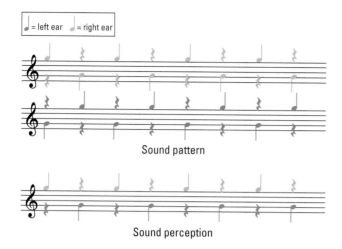

= left ear   = right ear

Sound pattern

Sound perception

■ **FIGURE 13.20   The octave illusion.**

Deutsch (1974) presented one tone to one ear and another tone, exactly one octave higher or lower, simultaneously to the other ear. However, the next note combination was of the same two notes, but to the opposite ears. You hear a single note (middle G) in your right ear, followed by a single note an octave lower in your left ear.

the pattern in reverse, that is, the higher note in the left ear. This illusion is likely due to differences in pitch processing between the left and right auditory cortices (see Deutsch, 2013). You can also go to Dr. Deutsch's Web site to hear a number of variants of this illusion.

The Tritone Paradox

This illusion was also discovered by Deutsch (1986). In music, *tritone* refers to the half octave, or the interval spanning six semitones. Thus, in the key of C major, there is one tritone: If you start on F, you can go up six semitones to B. Similarly, E and A-sharp are tritones (see Figure 13.21). In the tritone paradox, Deutsch presents stimuli generated similar to the way Shepard generated his paradoxical scale, that is, each note is an envelope of sound sweeping from one octave to the next, but with a heard pitch equivalent to the lower note. Thus, in the tritone paradox, Deutsch played a note with a perceived pitch of C and one with a perceived pitch of F-sharp, a tritone away (You can hear this illusion in ISLE 13.16). Here's the paradox: Some people hear the notes as ascending, as in a lower C to a higher F-sharp, whereas other people hear the notes descending, as in a higher C to a lower F-sharp. Deutsch even tested musicians and found the same result. Thus, it is good to do this

demonstration in a group, because people will disagree on what they just heard.

What is the explanation of the individual differences in the perception of these tritones? Deutsch and her colleagues have studied it extensively (Deutsch, 2013). It turns out that there are regional differences in the perception of the tritone paradox. One sees a different distribution of hearing the tritone paradox as ascending or descending whether one is examining Americans in California or English in England. Vietnamese who emigrated to the United States at an early age show a different distribution of perceptions of the tritone paradox than do Vietnamese who emigrated later. Deutsch thinks these differences have to do with the pitches typically heard in speech for different communities. Vietnamese and English show greater variance in their pitch patterns in speech than do Americans. Thus, this illusion potentially shows a relation between music perception and speech perception. For more on Deutsch's work, you can visit her Web site or listen to a number of other of her illusions at http://www.radiolab .org/story/292109-musical-illusions/.

ISLE 13.16 Tritone Paradox

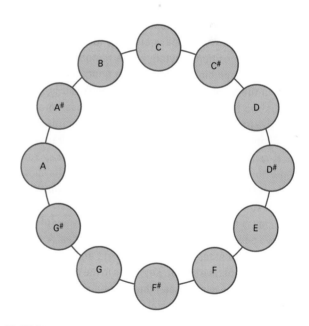

■ **FIGURE 13.21   The pitch class circle.**

As you move to the left on the circle, notes sound higher in pitch. As you move to the right, notes sound lower in pitch. From Deutsch (1986).

CHAPTER SUMMARY

13.1 Explain how frequency is related to pitch, chroma, and the octave.

Music is ordered sound made and perceived by human beings created in meaningful patterns. Humans have been making music since at least the Stone Age. Pitch is the subjective experience of sound that is most closely associated with the frequency of a sound stimulus. Pitch is related to the experience of whether a sound is high or low, such as the notes at the far right and far left of a piano. The octave is the interval between one note and a note with either double the frequency or half the frequency of that note. Chroma is the subjective quality of a pitch. We judge sounds an octave apart to be of the same chroma. In Western music, there are 12 semitones or 12 equivalent intervals or notes within each octave. Western music also uses an equal-temperament scale in which the difference between each successive semitone is constant in pitch and a constant ratio in frequency. Harmony occurs when two or more notes sound pleasant when played together. In musical terms, consonance is the perception of pleasantness or harmony when two or more notes are played; that is, the notes fit with each other. In contrast, dissonance is the perception of unpleasantness or disharmony when two or more notes do not fit together.

Pitch is not the only critical aspect of music. *Dynamics* refers to the relative loudness and how loudness changes across a composition. Rhythm is the temporal patterning of the music, including the tempo, the beat, and the meter. Tempo is the speed at which a piece of music is played. Meter is the temporal pattern of sound across time. *Beat* refers to spaced pulses that indicate if a piece is fast or slow. Timbre is the complex sound created by harmonics. Attack is the beginning buildup of a note. *Decay* refers to how long the fundamental frequency and harmonics remain at their peak loudness until they start to disappear. All of these factors are critical to music.

Melody is the rhythmically organized sequence of notes, which we perceive as a single musical unit or idea. A scale is a set of ordered notes starting at one note and ending at the same note one octave higher. *Key* refers to the tonic note (e.g., C in a C major or minor scale) that gives a subjective sense of arrival and rest in a musical piece. Transposition allows more than one version of the same melody, beginning on different notes but containing the same intervals or sequences of changes in notes. Gestalt principles predict many of the patterns that determine melody in musical compositions.

13.2 Summarize the basic neuroscience of music, including how training and experience can affect the representation of music in the brain.

The neuroanatomy of music is a bit different because music is in some ways an optional feature of human cognition. Most prominent are areas in the right temporal cortex, adjacent to the right auditory regions. One clear finding is that music perception usually causes greater activation in the right temporal lobe than the left temporal lobe, but we also see activity in the left temporal lobes and the frontal lobes when perceiving music. In trained musicians, it has been found that the level of activation of the left hemisphere increase when listening to music. Synesthesia is a condition in which a stimulus in one modality consistently triggers a response in another modality. Color-music synesthesia occurs when particular pitches, notes, or chords elicit experiences of particular visual colors. People with color-music synesthesia show a greater activation of the tract that connects the frontal lobes to the auditory cortex. Amusia is a condition in which brain damage interferes with the perception of music but does not otherwise interfere with other aspects of auditory processing. Congenital amusia is a condition in which people are inherently poor at music perception. There is some research that suggests connections between music and language.

13.3 Discuss how learning and culture affect music perception.

Music is seen in all cultures, but the music of other cultures differs in systematic ways from Western music. For example, ragas from India use a 22-note scale instead of the Western 12-note scale. Moreover, the notes of the raga scale fall at different frequencies than Western notes. Shepard tones, the octave illusion, and the tritone paradox are all illusions that illustrate how listeners extract musical meaning from stimuli, even when it is not an accurate description of the physical stimuli.

REVIEW QUESTIONS

1. Provide a definition of music. How is musical perception different from other forms of perception, and how is it similar?

2. What is the relation of pitch to chroma? What is the octave? And what evidence is there that the octave is a musical universal?

3. What is meant by *consonance* and *dissonance*? How do they relate to chroma and octaves?

4. What are the differences between tempo, meter, and beat? How does each one contribute to musical perception?

5. What is timbre? What defines the physical differences that make up timbre? How is timbre used by musicians to convey meaning or mood?

6. What is a scale? How does it differ from culture to culture? What starts and ends a scale? What is meant by *transposition*?

7. What areas of the brain are critical to perceiving music? What other areas are needed for musicians? How does the brain change with musical training?

8. What is synesthesia? What is color-music synesthesia? What is amusia?

9. How does music differ from culture to culture? In particular, how does the scale system differ between Western music and ragas from India?

10. Describe two musical illusions. What are the physical stimuli? How are those stimuli perceived?

KEY TERMS

Amusia, 351

Attack, 344

Beat, 342

Chroma, 339

Color-music synesthesia, 350

Congenital amusia, 351

Consonance, 341

Decay, 344

Dissonance, 341

Dynamics, 342

Equal-temperament scale, 340

Harmony, 341

Key, 345

Melody, 344

Meter, 342

Music, 337

Octave, 338

Pitch, 337

Rhythm, 342

Scale, 344

Semitones, 340

Synesthesia, 350

Tempo, 342

Timbre, 343

Transposition, 346

INTERACTIVE SENSATION LABORATORY EXERCISES (ISLE)

Experience chapter concepts at edge.sagepub.com/schwartz

ISLE 13.1 Kurdish Music, 335

ISLE 13.2 Javenese Gamelan Music, 335

ISLE 13.3 The Octave and Tone Similarity, 339

ISLE 13.4 Pentatonic Music, 341

ISLE 13.5 Meter and Beat, 342

ISLE 13.6 Bolero Clip, 343

ISLE 13.7 Attack and Decay, 344

ISLE 13.8 Examples of Melody, 344

ISLE 13.9 Types of Scales, 345

ISLE 13.10 Gestalt Principles Review, 346

ISLE 13.11 Gestalt Principle: Proximity: Bach's Partita #3, 347

ISLE 13.12 Cross Modal Matchings as a Simulation of Synesthesia, 350

ISLE 13.13 Bach Violin Partita #2, 355

ISLE 13.14 Shepard Tones, 356

ISLE 13.15 Octave Illusion, 356

ISLE 13.16 Tritone Paradox, 357

Sharpen your skills with SAGE edge at edge.sagepub.com/schwartz

SAGE edge for students provides a personalized approach to help you accomplish your coursework goals in an easy-to-use learning environment.

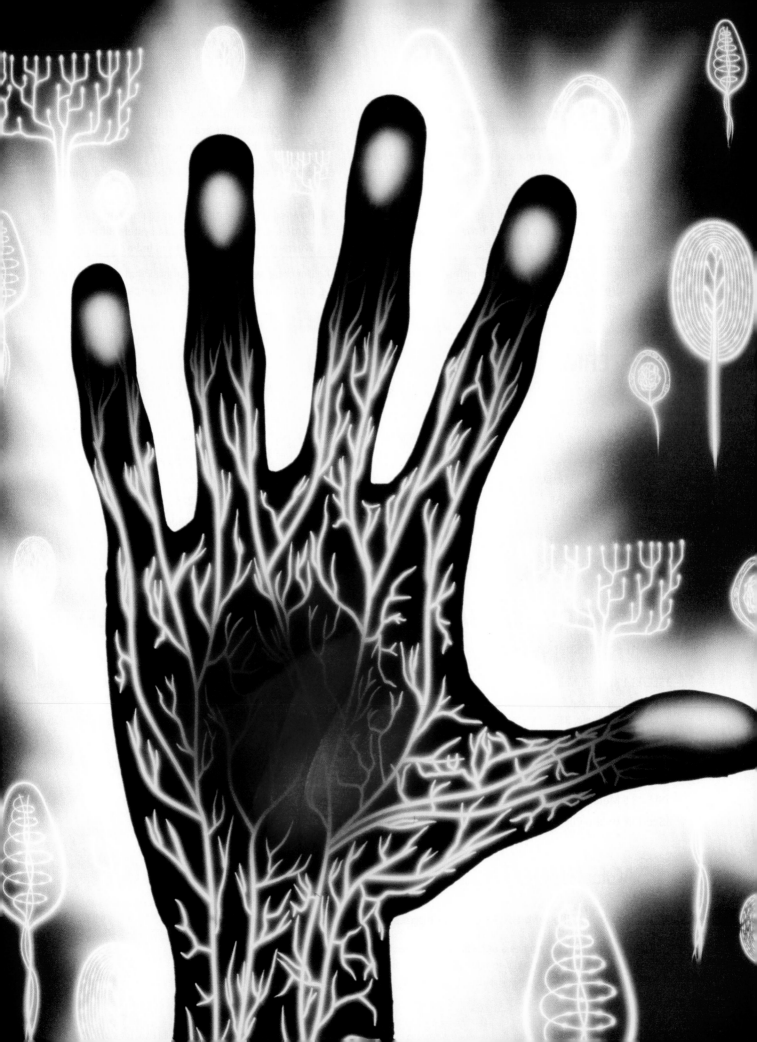

14

Touch and Pain

INTRODUCTION

Think of many of the things that bring us the most pleasure and the most discomfort. Think of the relaxation brought by stroking the fur of a sleepy cat. Think of the feeling of the joy of life when the cool water of a pool rushes around your face as you dive in. Think of the thrill and the excitement as your lips meet those of your romantic partner. You will note that all of these desirable experiences occur through our senses of touch. Similarly, think of unpleasant sensations, the throbbing pain of a toothache, the quick pain when you cut yourself while shaving, or the maddening itchiness of a mosquito bite. You will note here that many of the experiences we deem to be most negative also occur through the skin senses, mainly the skin sense we know as pain. We often take our senses of touch for granted, but in reality, they are essential in many ways. Take a look at Figure 14.1 and see if you can imagine how these various surfaces would feel to your skin. Luckily, we have very poor imagery for pain, so it is hard to conjure up the experience of a toothache without actually having one.

The touch senses are different in an important way from the already discussed vision and audition. Vision, audition, and olfaction can work at a distance. For example, I can see the boat on the lake even though it is a half mile away, I can

LEARNING OBJECTIVES

14.1 Explain how touch perception is actually a number of senses served by a number of receptor systems.

14.2 Discuss the role of proprioception in allowing us to know the position and movements of our limbs and joints.

14.3 Describe how the skin registers changes in temperature at the skin.

14.4 Discuss the role of nociceptors in the perception of pain and how pain is modified by gate control theory.

14.5 Identify the pathways from receptors in the skin to the somatosensory cortex in the brain.

14.6 Examine the role of endogenous opioids in controlling pain perception.

14.7 Explain the difference between pain and itch and how they interact.

14.8 Describe the role movement plays in creating the perception of active touch.

14.9 Explain how the vestibular system operates to aid in the perception of balance and acceleration.

14.10 Explain how our somatosensory system is used in the reading of Braille.

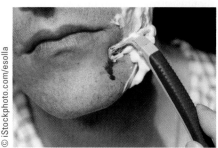

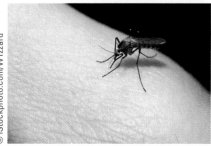

© iStockphoto.com/haveseen

© iStockphoto.com/esolla

© iStockphoto.com/CPaulussen

© iStockphoto.com/W1zzard

■ **FIGURE 14.1** **Somatosensory experiences.**

Imagine what each of these would feel like on your skin. Some of these may be touch experiences we long for, whereas others may be perceptions we would prefer to avoid.

hear the barking of the dogs even though they are across the street, and I can smell the cookies baking in the other room. Touch is more intimate; it requires direct bodily contact and preferably contact and bodily motion. As such, it is interactive. It is often quite difficult to detect whether a surface is smooth or rough using a nonmoving finger. We move our fingers and the rest of our skin to sense surfaces. Thus, from the very beginning of our discussion of the touch senses, we will need to consider movement of the body as well.

Here is another thought about the importance of our touch systems. Think about waking up in the middle of the night and feeling very hungry. You do not want to wake anyone else up, so you decide not to turn the lights on. Without visual or auditory cues, you can feel your way from your bedroom into the kitchen, find the cutlery drawer and remove a fork, feel the piece of cake that was left on the counter from dessert earlier in the evening, and enjoy your midnight snack alone in the dark. You do all these tasks that you might normally do with visual guidance by using your touch senses alone. You may move about the house a bit more slowly as you feel your way along the wall, but you can probably do this without stumbling. If you have midnight snacks too often, you may need to go on a diet, but the point is, we can feel our way around familiar environments without the use of sight.

Before we begin our discussion of the details of our touch senses, we will note we are using the plural to describe these senses. Properly speaking, there is not a single sense of touch, but several somatosensory senses, that is, those sensations that arise from the skin, muscles, and other interior senses. There are different kinds of receptors in our skin to detect light pressure, deep pressure, pain, coldness, and heat. There are also receptors within our muscles that help us regulate the position of our body, which we also consider in this chapter. This chapter also considers the vestibular system, which is not a somatosensory system, but we examine it here to ensure that we cover all the sensory systems in this book. The vestibular system is rather unique, so we include it here for convenience, not because it is related to the somatosensory senses. We also include a diversion into the realm of nonhuman animal senses in this chapter. The "in-depth" section is about electroreception in fish.

THE SKIN AND ITS RECEPTORS

14.1 Explain how touch perception is actually a number of senses served by a number of receptor systems.

If you are ever on a game show, and you are asked the following question, you will now get it right and win thousands of dollars: What is the heaviest organ of the body? The answer is the skin, which weighs in at over 4 kg (9 lb). The skin can be considered the sense organ of touch, much as the eyes house the visual system receptors and the ears house the auditory receptors. Touch receptors exist everywhere on the surface of the skin, though not necessarily in a uniform fashion. Touch receptors are closely grouped on your fingers and lips and less closely grouped on your upper back, legs, and arms. There are also touch receptors inside your mouth and on your tongue.

The skin is a complex organ, despite its familiar surface features. Many touch receptors are located just below the outer layer of skin, called the **epidermis**. The epidermis is interestingly avascular, as it draws oxygen directly from the air rather than from the bloodstream. The epidermis is thickest on our palms and the soles our feet, and it is thinnest on our eyelids. The epidermis functions to keep out

Epidermis: the outer layer of the skin

pathogens and keep in fluids, in addition to its sensory functions. Indeed, it is composed mainly of dead cells that protect the dermis below. Below the epidermis is the **dermis**, which houses most of our touch receptors. The dermis also holds the connective tissue and has a blood supply. Skin can also be divided into hairy skin, that is, skin with hair growing on it, and glabrous skin, which is hairless skin. Glabrous skin can be found on the palms and fingertips and the soles of our feet and bottoms of our toes. The anatomy of the skin is depicted in Figure 14.2.

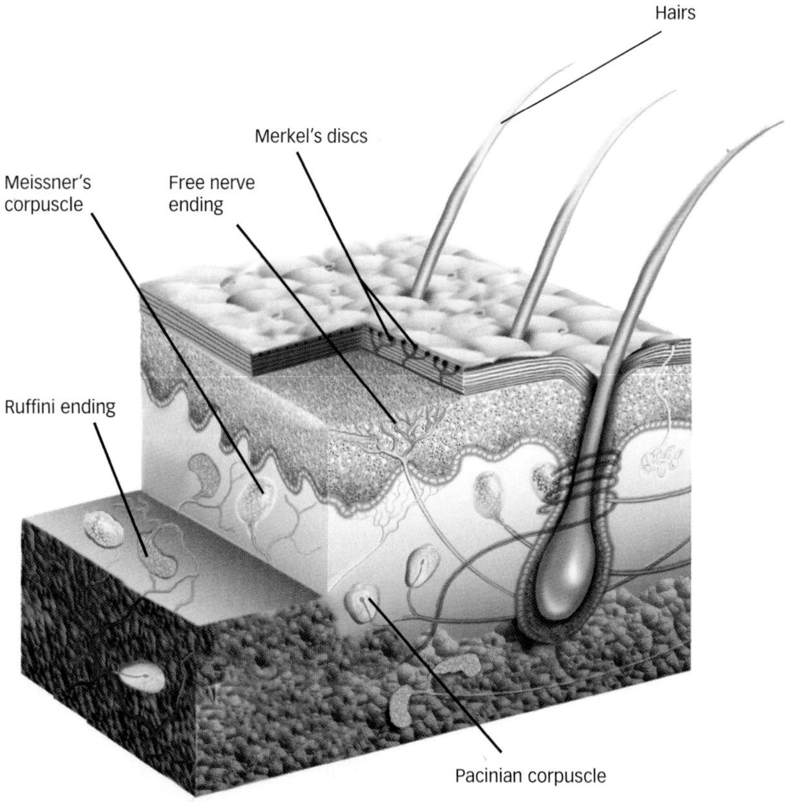

Touch perception occurs when the skin is moved or touched. This includes indentation, such as when a finger presses against your skin; vibration, such as when you touch an active electric toothbrush; and stretching, such as when someone scratches your back or pulls on your skin. Such mechanical stimulation of the skin activates one or more of the four types of mechanoreceptors in your skin. **Mechanoreceptors** are sensory receptors in the skin that transduce physical movement on the skin into neural signals, which are sent to the brain.

■ FIGURE 14.2   Touch receptors in a cross-section of skin.

This illustration shows the dermis, the epidermis, and the different types of nerve endings found in the skin.

Now, take a deep breath, as we need to get a bit technical and introduce a bit of jargon. There is no avoiding it—touch perception is complex, with multiple kinds of receptors, each with a multisyllabic name.

The four types of mechanoreceptors are called **SAI mechanoreceptors**, **SAII mechanoreceptors**, **FAI mechanoreceptors**, and **FAII mechanoreceptors**. Each mechanoreceptor differs on a number of relevant dimensions, which are important to producing a complex touch response. The mechanoreceptors are distinguishable anatomically and also in terms of their functional capacities. *SA* stands for "slow-adapting," whereas *FA* stands for "fast-adapting." The mechanoreceptors labeled with a Roman numeral I have small receptive fields, whereas the II receptors have larger receptive fields. As you read through these distinctions, think about how they map onto other sensory distinctions, such as the differences between the magnocellular tract and the parvocellular tract in vision.

The slow-adapting mechanoreceptors (SAI and SAII) produce a steady stream of neural response when the skin is deformed, that is, a sustained response that continues for as long as the skin is stimulated. This is important because we want to know if there is continued pressure on our skin, such as when someone is holding your arm. The fast-adapting mechanoreceptors (FAI and FAII) respond vigorously when the skin is first touched and then again when the stimulus ends. This is important because it gives us information about changes on our skin—when something contacts us and when it is no longer in contact with us. However, if the pressure continues, FA mechanoreceptor responses lessen and do not increase until the stimulus is over. Thus, the SA mechanoreceptors tell us about continued pressure on the skin, such as the constant contact between our skin and our shirts.

Dermis: the inner layer of the skin, which also houses touch receptors

Mechanoreceptors: the sensory receptors in the skin that transduce physical movement on the skin into neural signals, which are sent to the brain

SAI mechanoreceptors: slow-adapting receptors using Merkel cells, with small receptive fields, densely packed near the surface of the skin

SAII mechanoreceptors: slow-adapting receptors using Ruffini endings, with large receptive fields, more widely distributed, deeper in the skin

FAI mechanoreceptors: fast-adapting receptors, with Meissner corpuscle endings and small receptive fields, densely packed near the surface of the skin

FAII mechanoreceptors: fast-adapting receptors with Pacinian corpuscle endings and large receptive fields, more widely distributed, deeper in the skin

The FA receptors give us information about temporary stimulation of the skin, such as when that annoying mosquito lands on our arm.

The SAI and FAI receptors have relatively small receptive fields with densely packed receptors. This gives them high spatial resolution, allowing us to detect exactly where on the skin a stimulation occurs. That is, SAI and FAI fibers help us detect small objects and pinpoint objects in space. Again, this is useful for detecting the location of the mosquito on the skin and for fine manipulation of objects, such as when we thread a needle. Both SAI and FAI mechanoreceptors are also close to the skin's surface.

In contrast, the SAII and FAII mechanoreceptors are deeper in the skin. The SAII and FAII receptors have larger receptive fields with more dispersed mechanoreceptors. This means that their spatial resolution is not as good as the SAI and FAI mechanoreceptors, but that they have a lower threshold or higher sensitivity to light touch. Thus, they help us feel very light touches, as they sum across space, but are not as precise as determining where on the skin these touches occur. Thus, when an entire hand brushes against our arm, the SAII and FAII mechanoreceptors let us know that our arm is being moved. These differences are summarized in Table 14.1. You can see a video of the actions of the mechanoreceptors on ISLE 14.1. We now review each mechanoreceptor's structure and function.

ISLE 14.1 Action of Mechanoreceptors

SAI Mechanoreceptors

SAI mechanoreceptors have a sustained response to continued pressure, giving them maximum response to steady pressure. They have small receptive fields and thus have high spatial sensitivity. They respond best to vibrations at low frequencies. They are important for the touch perceptions of pattern and texture. Because of their high spatial sensitivity, SAI mechanoreceptors are responsible for two-point thresholds, that is, the minimum distance at which a person can detect two touches instead of just one (see Figure 14.3). Thus, these cells are important when we need fine manual control, especially without visual feedback. SAI mechanoreceptors are also critical for blind individuals reading Braille. Two-point threshold responses vary across the skin's surface. Where it is most sensitive, such as on the fingertips and lips, we find the highest density of SAI mechanoreceptors. Where it is least sensitive, such as on the back and legs, we find the lowest density of SAI

Meissner corpuscles: specialized transduction cells in FAI mechanoreceptors

Pacinian corpuscles: specialized transduction cells in FAII mechanoreceptors

Merkel cells: specialized transduction cells in SAI mechanoreceptors

Ruffini endings: specialized transduction cells in SAII mechanoreceptors

Fast Adapting		Slow Adapting	
Small receptive field	Larger receptive field	Small receptive field	Larger receptive field
FAI	FAII	SAI	SAII
Meissner corpuscles	**Pacinian corpuscles**	**Merkel cells**	**Ruffini endings**
High spatial resolution	Low spatial resolution	High spatial resolution	Low spatial resolution
Upper dermis	Lower dermis	Upper dermis	Dermis
Medium sensitivity to temperature variation	High	Low	Low
Perceiving change	Fine texture	Patterns	Stretch/feedback

■ TABLE 14.1 **Mechanoreceptors: Types and Response Properties**

mechanoreceptors. For a discussion and illustration of the relation of SAI mechanoreceptors and the Aristotle illusion, see ISLE 14.2.

SAII Mechanoreceptors

SAII mechanoreceptors have a sustained response to continued pressure, also giving them maximum response to steady pressure. However, they are also good at stretching from side to side, making them crucial for object grasping. Thus, when you pick up your spoon to eat your soup, your SAII mechanoreceptors will be critical. SAII mechanoreceptors have much larger receptive fields than SAI mechanoreceptors, and so are more vital for detecting touch than for pinpointing where it occurs.

FAI Mechanoreceptors

FAI mechanoreceptors respond to the onset and offset of a stimulus. These mechanoreceptors also have small receptive fields for good spatial accuracy. They also respond well to low-frequency vibrations. They are especially good at detecting "slip," that is, when an object is sliding across the surface of the skin. As such, they are useful in avoiding dropping objects, as they detect an object as it begins to slip away from your hands. These mechanoreceptors are also critical in maintaining grip for sports. For example, when a baseball hits a bat, the force causes slippage of the grip. FAI mechanoreceptors detect this slip and cause us to tighten our grip on the bat.

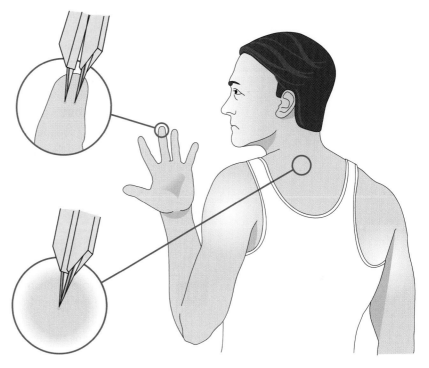

■ FIGURE 14.3   A model of the body's two-point threshold response.

In this diagram, a person is touched at two points on the skin or one point on the skin. The person must determine if there is one point or two points of touch. Sensitivity to two-point touch is better in parts of the body with higher densities of SAI mechanoreceptors. Two-point thresholds are better on the fingers than on the back.

ISLE 14.2 Mechanoreceptors and Aristotle's Illusion

FAII Mechanoreceptors

FAII mechanoreceptors also respond to the onset and offset of a stimulus. They have larger receptive fields, as they are less densely packed in the skin. They are also more sensitive to higher frequency vibrations. Experientially, when FAII mechanoreceptors are firing, what we feel is more of a buzz than for the other mechanoreceptors. Because of their high sensitivity to touch, they are helpful in feeling small pressure on the skin, such as when an insect lands on our skin. These mechanoreceptors are also used when we use fine motor control, such as when writing with a pen or tightening a screw with a small screwdriver.

The names of the receptive cells in each of these mechanoreceptors are given in Table 14.1. In all of the above types of mechanoreceptors, the mechanical movement of the ending of the receptor induces a neural signal, which is sent first to the spinal column and then to the brain. The nerve fibers from the mechanoreceptors are myelinated, which allows fast transmission of these signals. Interestingly, a new kind of unmyelinated mechanoreceptor has been discovered (Olausson, Wessberg, Morrison, McGlone, & Valbo, 2010). This new fifth mechanoreceptor is known as the C-tactile mechanoreceptor. C-tactile mechanoreceptors are present only in hairy skin and respond to slow gentle movements on the skin. When stimulated, C-tactile mechanoreceptors induce a pleasant feeling. C-tactile fibers project to the insular cortex, which also receives input from pleasant tastes and odors.

TEST YOUR KNOWLEDGE

Describe the difference between slow-adapting and fast-adapting mechanoreceptors. How is each important for perceiving different aspects of the perceptual world?

PROPRIOCEPTION: PERCEIVING LIMB POSITION

14.2 Discuss the role of proprioception in allowing us to know the position and movements of our limbs and joints.

Proprioception is perhaps our most unique sense, as it is designed to monitor not the external world but the internal world. The mechanoreceptors, the rods and cones of our retinae, and the hair cells of our cochleae in our auditory system are all designed to pick up features external to us, whereas proprioception gives us our awareness of how our own bodies are positioned. Thus, you do not have to see your arms to know that they are in front of your torso, extended outward (doing what you normally do—tapping on your laptop). You also do not need to see or even feel your feet touching the floor to know that your legs are below you and that you are in a sitting position. We define **proprioception** as the perception of the movements and position of our limbs. You may also see the term *kinesthesis*, which refers to our awareness or perception of bodily movements.

There are three different kinds of sensory receptors in our bodies that provide us with information about limb movement and position. They are the muscle spindles, joint receptors, and Golgi tendon organs. We consider each in turn. **Muscle spindles** are muscle cells that have receptors embedded in them that sense information about muscle length and therefore muscle action. As muscles contract and lengthen, different neural signals are transduced in the spindles, giving the brain information on muscle position. **Joint receptors** are receptors found in each joint that sense information about the angle of the joint. This provides the brain with information about how far the limb is stretched and whether it can be stretched any farther before it must be contracted. **Golgi tendon organs** are receptors in the tendons that measure the force of a muscle's contraction. Because force will be a function of how many muscle fibers are used, Golgi tendon organs can provide feedback as to how much more force has been applied by that muscle (see Figure 14.4).

Because proprioception is directed inward, we seldom consciously focus on it. Rather, we are take it for granted that we are aware of the position of our body, how much force we are asserting, and what muscles are moving. However, if we did not have Golgi tendon organs, we might not be able to gauge whether we are applying enough muscle strength to lift weights at the gym or if we are applying too much muscle strength when we intend to be gently patting a friend on the back. We can be thankful for these receptors when we do not break any bones in the fingers of our friends as we shake their hands. When a limb is under physical

Proprioception: the perception of the movements and position of our limbs

Muscle spindles: receptors embedded in the muscles that sense information about muscle length and therefore muscle action

Joint receptors: receptors found in each joint that sense information about the angle of the joint

Golgi tendon organs: receptors in the tendons that measure the force of a muscle's contraction

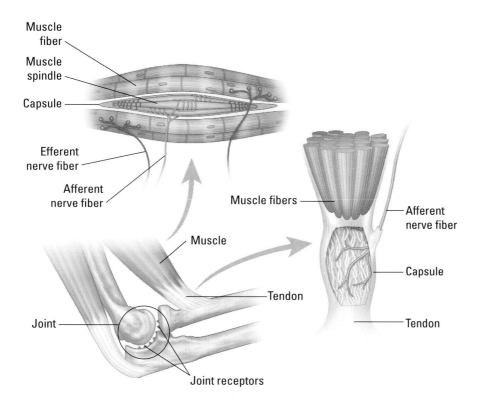

Muscle fiber

Muscle spindle

Capsule

Efferent nerve fiber

Afferent nerve fiber

Muscle

Joint

Joint receptors

Muscle fibers

Afferent nerve fiber

Capsule

Tendon

Tendon

■ FIGURE 14.4   Sensory receptors for proprioception.

This anatomical drawing shows where one can find muscle spindles, joint receptors, and Golgi tendon organs.

pressure and blood is temporarily cut off, we may have the experience of an arm or leg "going to sleep." This feeling is caused by a temporary inability of the proprioception system to detect limb position.

Alcohol consumption affects our proprioception system, making it harder for our sensory receptors to give feedback on limb position. It is for this reason that one of the main tests police administer for sobriety is a proprioception test. When a driver is suspected of driving under the influence of alcohol, a field sobriety test is given. One of these tests is to ask the driver to touch his or her nose with eyes closed. Inaccuracy in this test suggests that alcohol consumption has compromised the functioning of the proprioception system.

In people who have lost limbs through accidents or surgery, false proprioception may still occur, in a condition known as phantom limb syndrome. **Phantom limb syndrome** refers to continued but illusory sensory reception in a missing appendage. Some amputees have the sense that they feel the position of a missing limb. That is, an amputee may feel as if his arm is resting at his side, in much the way we know our arm is resting at our side even if our eyes are closed. Phantom limb syndrome is likely the result of continued activity in the regions of the brain that would have responded to sensory input from the missing limb. Later in this chapter, we discuss a darker side of phantom limb syndrome, namely, phantom pain. However, phantom limb proprioception is useful in helping an amputee adjust to life with a prosthetic (Weeks, Anderson-Barnes, & Tsao, 2010).

TEST YOUR KNOWLEDGE

What is meant by proprioception? What deficits would a person have if that person lost his or her proprioception systems?

Phantom limb syndrome: continued but illusory sensory reception in a missing appendage

THERMORECEPTION

14.3 Describe how the skin registers changes in temperature at the skin.

If you live in a part of the world that has cold winters, think about stepping outside when you leave your home for school or work. The wind and cold seem to bind to your face, you shiver, and you pull your coat a little tighter around your body. Compare this with the feeling of leaving your air-conditioned hotel on a summer visit to Phoenix, Las Vegas, or some other very hot and very dry climate. Here, it is the heat that stings you. Few people would mistake one experience for the other.

Thermoreception is the ability to sense changes in temperature on the skin. This can be passive, as when cold air blows against your face on a winter's morning, or it can be active, as when we touch another's forehead to determine if that person has a fever. Obviously, thermoreception has an important function—being able to sense temperature is critical for survival. Imagine not being able to sense cold and going out into an Arctic blizzard in a swimsuit. Or imagine not being able to sense how hot it is in the Nevada desert in July and wearing a winter coat. In each case, the lack of thermoreception could have deadly consequences.

Thermoreceptors are the sensory receptors in the skin that signal information about the temperature as measured on the skin. Thermoreceptors respond to a range of skin temperatures, from 17°C (63°F) to 43°C (109°F). This is the range of temperatures experienced by our skin, not the actual ambient temperature. Thus, the weather may be colder than 17°C or hotter than 43°C, but our bodies are designed to regulate the conditions in and on our bodies. Skin temperature above 43°C and below 17°C are experienced as pain. In general, our skin maintains a surface temperature between 30°C and 36°C (86°F and 97°F). At these temperatures, our thermoreceptors are mostly inactive. However, when the temperature goes below 30°C, our cold fibers become active, and when the temperature rises above 36°C, our warm fibers become active. If you are inside wearing a thick sweater and sitting by a warm open fire, your skin temperature will increase, and your warm fibers will start firing. If you take off your sweater and go out into the blizzard, your skin will rapidly decrease in temperature, and your cold fibers will start increasing their firing rate. **Cold fibers** are thermoreceptors that fire in response to colder (30°C and below) temperatures as measured on the skin. **Warm fibers** are different thermoreceptors that fire in response to warmer temperatures (above 36°C) as measured on the skin. At intermediate temperatures, both fibers show a steady firing rate. They differ when the temperature rises above 36°C or falls below 30°C (see Figure 14.5).

Thermoreception: the ability to sense changes in temperature on the skin

Thermoreceptors: the sensory receptors in the skin that signal information about the temperature as measured on the skin

Cold fibers: thermoreceptors that fire in response to colder (30°C and below) temperatures as measured on the skin

Warm fibers: thermoreceptors that fire in response to warmer temperatures (above 36°C) as measured on the skin

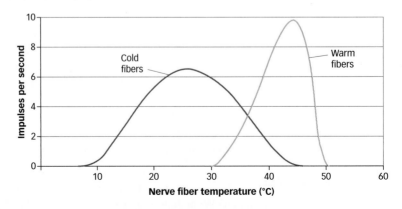

■ FIGURE 14.5 Rate of firing in response to skin temperature.

Graph of firing rates of cold and warm nerve fibers. From Guyton (1991).

Cold and warm fibers also respond when you touch objects that are either colder or warmer than the temperature of your skin. For example, when you remove the ice cream container from the freezer, the surface of the ice cream container will feel cold because the temperature of the container is lower than that of your fingers, causing your cold fibers to fire. When you pick up your hot mug of coffee, the mug feels hot because it is causing warm fibers to fire. Both cold and warm fibers also adapt to new temperatures. Thus, when you first jump into a pool, the water, which is colder than your skin, triggers responses in the cold fibers. But after a couple of minutes, your cold fibers adapt, and the pool no longer feels quite so cold.

Interestingly, your warm fibers have a secondary peak in sensitivity when they are exposed to very low temperatures. This is also known as a paradoxical heat experience because it is brought about by contact with extremely cold temperatures. The temperatures are so low that they also induce pain responses. Nonetheless, some of you may have experienced this during minor medical treatment. If you have ever had a skin abnormality, such as a wart, treated with liquid nitrogen, you know the experience of paradoxical heat. Liquid nitrogen is kept at about –200°C (–328°F). When it is applied to our skin, however, we feel pain and heat, not coldness, because of this secondary peak for the warm fibers. Some Antarctic explorers have also described feeling paradoxical heat when being buffeted by 160 km/h winds in –60°C cold. See ISLE 14.3 for instructions on a safe way to demonstrate this to yourself.

ISLE 14.3 Heat Grille

TEST YOUR KNOWLEDGE

Why is it likely that animals, such as ourselves, evolved to have two separate systems, one for detecting cold and one for detecting heat? What advantages does this have over a single-receptor system that simply detects temperature, much as a thermometer might?

NOCICEPTION AND THE PERCEPTION OF PAIN

14.4 Discuss the role of nociceptors in the perception of pain and how pain is modified by gate control theory.

Pain is the perception and the unpleasant experience of actual or threatened tissue damage. Thus, pain is the result of activation of receptors in our skin and elsewhere, as well as the unpleasant subjective feeling associated with it. As we will see in this chapter, pain can arise from a number of different causes and may be accompanied by emotional distress that may act to increase the experience of pain. In this section, we focus on the sensory receptors in the skin that transduce a neural signal, causing an experience of pain in the affected area. This type of pain is called nociceptive pain. **Nociceptive pain** is the pain that develops from tissue damage that causes nociceptors in the skin to fire. This type of pain occurs from direct trauma to the skin, such as from cutting, puncturing, pinching, heating, freezing, or coming in contact with toxic chemicals (ouch!). These types of events cause nociceptors in the skin to fire, leading to a signal to the brain. **Nociceptors** are sensory receptors in the skin that, when activated, cause us to feel pain. They are found in both the epidermis and dermis. Although we focus on the nociceptors in the skin, there are nociceptors in many other areas of the body, including muscle, bone, and the digestive system. There are also

Pain: the perception and unpleasant experience of actual or threatened tissue damage

Nociceptive pain: pain that develops from tissue damage that causes nociceptors in the skin to fire

Nociceptors: sensory receptors in the skin that, when activated, cause us to feel pain; they are found in both the epidermis and dermis

Nociceptors

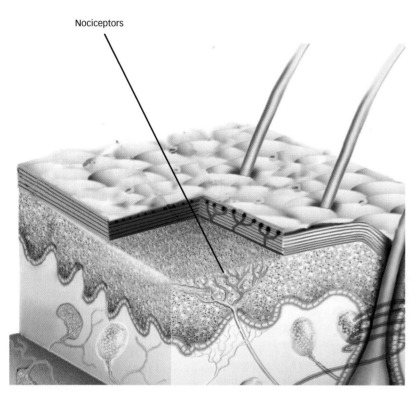

■ **FIGURE 14.6   Nociceptors in the skin.**

Nociceptors are located just below the epidermis, in the dermis. Nociceptors are activated when tissue is damaged, leading to the experience of pain.

other forms of pain, such as inflammatory pain, in which an inflamed or swollen region causes changes in nearby nociceptors. Neuropathic pain occurs when the nervous system itself is damaged. Nociceptors are anatomically distinguishable from other skin receptors. Nociceptors are often referred to as free nerve endings because of their anatomical appearance (see Figure 14.6).

Nociceptors are divided into two main types: **A-delta fibers** and **C-fibers**. A-delta fibers are myelinated, so they conduct signals rapidly and respond to both heat and pressure, both of which can induce pain. C-fibers are nonmyelinated and hence slower, and they respond to pressure, extreme degrees of either heat or cold, and toxic chemicals. The signals from both of these free nerve endings are experienced as pain. A-delta fibers are associated with the stinging feeling of pain. This stinging pain is often what we experience first when we are injured. C-fibers are associated with the more chronic experience of throbbing pain (Williams & Purves, 2001). This pain may be a bit delayed from the actual accident. Think about touching a hot stovetop. You first get a searing pain, and you quickly move your hand away from the hot surface. This searing pain is the result of the fast action of the A-delta fibers. After you start treating your injury, you start to feel continued dull throbbing in your finger, which is the result of the C-fiber response (see Figure 14.6 for a figure showing the nociceptors).

It probably has crossed every human being's mind at one time or another how much better life would be if we did not experience pain at all. Certainly, anyone who has experienced serious pain can identify with the wish not to have pain at all. Something as seemingly simple as an infected tooth can cause excruciating and debilitating pain, as anyone who has ever gone through a root canal can tell you. However, the argument can be made that pain serves an important evolutionary function, by alerting an organism to tissue damage, allowing it to take steps to minimize or repair the tissue damage or move away from the source of that damage. Through evolution, pain evolved presumably because organisms that moved away from sources of pain were more likely to survive than those that did not. When we do not experience pain, we might not act to avoid these consequences. Indeed, Melzack and Wall (1988) described a case of a human patient lacking in nociceptors. This woman experienced numerous avoidable injuries because she lacked pain perception. These injuries included burns from not removing her hand from a stovetop, biting her own tongue, early joint problems, and ultimately death from curable infections.

A-delta fibers: myelinated nociceptors that conduct signals rapidly and respond to both heat and pressure

C-fibers: nonmyelinated nociceptors that are slower and respond to pressure, extreme degrees of either heat or cold, and toxic chemicals

TEST YOUR KNOWLEDGE

What are the differences between A-delta fibers and C-fibers? How do they each contribute to the perception of pain?

NEURAL PATHWAYS

14.5 Identify the pathways from receptors in the skin to the somatosensory cortex in the brain.

In May, off the coast of the Dominican Republic, boats can take you out to go free diving with the humpback whales that migrate close to the shores of that country. Diving with some magnificent creatures is an amazing experience, as humans are dwarfed by the incredible size of these whales, which can exceed 16 m (52 ft). You can swim right up to these creatures, which do not see divers as a threat and are sometimes curious about their presence. You are not supposed to touch the animals at all, but what would happen if you brushed against the tail of the whale (see Figure 14.7)? Given the distance involved between the whale's tail and the whale's brain, it would take upward of a second for the whale to feel your touch. That is, if instead of a gentle brush, you pricked the tail with a pin, it would be nearly a second before the whale experienced pain (Hof & van der Gucht, 2007). Of course, reflex circuits would cause the whale to swish its tail away from you much earlier, hopefully filling your mouth and mask with seawater (after all, you pricked the whale's tail). In this section, we consider the areas in the somatosensory cortex responsible for the experience of pain.

In humans, the distance nerve fibers must travel is much less than in whales, but it is still much farther for touch and pain than it is for sensory systems already arranged in the head (vision, audition). For a tall person, it may still be 2 m (6 ft 6 in.) from toes to somatosensory cortex. Thus, when you stub your toe, the neural message has a greater distance to travel than when someone yanks your ear or when light hits your retinae. As a function of this, we see some major differences too in the pathways for the pain. All right, now, get your attention in gear, as we start with the complex anatomy involved in transmitting the neural signal for pain from the skin to the brain.

Consider a nerve ending in the skin of the palm of your hand. This nerve ending sends its axon into a nerve bundle, where it is joined by many other axons from adjacent nerve fibers. These nerve bundles then enter the spinal column and form synapses with bipolar cells at a **dorsal root ganglion** (the ventral root ganglion transmits information to the muscles). The dorsal root ganglia surround the vertebrae of the spinal column, on both the left and the right sides (see Figure 14.8). The axons of the cells within the dorsal root ganglion enter the dorsal part of the spinal column (you can see an interactive model of the dorsal root ganglion in ISLE 14.4).

Once in the spinal column, information is divided into two parallel tracts, which head up the spinal column to the brain. It is important to keep these two tracts distinct, as they serve different functions. But the anatomy and terminology are both tricky. So stay with the text and review the text and figures often. One tract is called the **dorsal column–medial lemniscal pathway**. The dorsal column–medial lemniscal pathway carries information from the mechanoreceptors (i.e., tactile perception) and from the proprioceptors (i.e., muscle position perception). The **spinothalamic pathway** carries information from the nociceptors

■ **FIGURE 14.7**   A whale's tail.

A humpback whale's tail may be as far as 16 m from its brain. Thus, the neural signal that occurs when the diver touches the tail may take nearly a second to reach the somatosensory cortex of the whale.

© iStockphoto.com/ShaneGross

ISLE 14.4 Somatosensory Pathways

Dorsal root ganglion: a node on the spine where one finds nerve cells carrying signals from sensory organs toward the somatosensory areas of the brain

Dorsal column–medial lemniscal pathway: a pathway for the mechanoreceptors (tactile perception) and proprioceptors (muscle position) that travels up the spinal column on the ipsilateral side and crosses to the contralateral side in the medulla

Spinothalamic pathway: a pathway for the nociceptors (pain) and thermoreceptors (temperature) that travels up the contralateral side of the spinal column; does not synapse in the brain until the ventral posterior nucleus of the thalamus

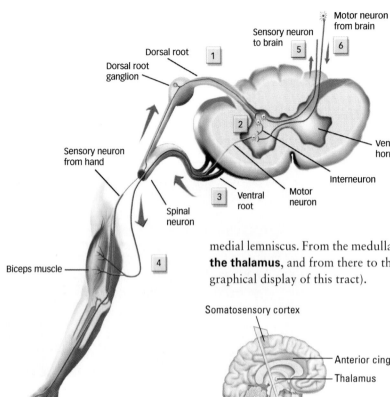

(pain) and the thermoreceptors (temperature). The names are a mouthful, but the anatomy is tricky too. The dorsal column–medial lemniscal pathway travels on the dorsal side of the spinal column and on the ipsilateral side of input from the skin (the same side as the input from the body). The dorsal column–medial lemniscal pathway makes a synapse in the medulla of the brain, where it crosses over to the contralateral side (the opposite side of the input from the body). It then ascends into the brain as the medial lemniscus. From the medulla, it travels to the **ventral posterior nucleus of the thalamus**, and from there to the somatosensory cortex (see Figure 14.9 for a graphical display of this tract).

■ **FIGURE 14.8   The dorsal root ganglion.**

Nerve fibers from nociceptors enter the dorsal root ganglion. In this illustration, you can see the anatomy of the ganglion and its exit route into the spinal column.

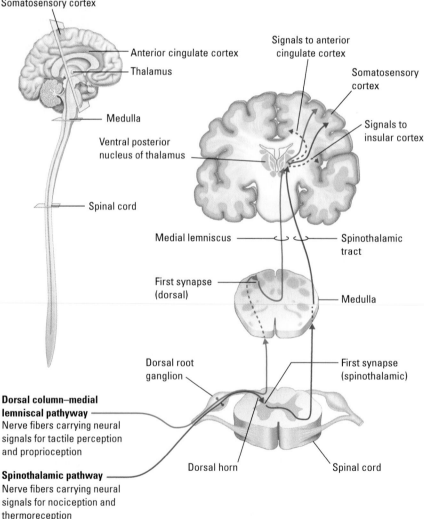

■ **FIGURE 14.9   The two pathways to the brain.**

This anatomical diagram shows the dorsal column–medial lemniscal pathway and the spinothalamic pathway.

Ventral posterior nucleus of the thalamus: an area in the thalamus that receives input from both the dorsal column–medial lemniscal pathway and the spinothalamic pathway

The spinothalamic pathway's fibers cross over to the contralateral side within the spinal column and then ascend toward the brain. That is, information from the left side of the body travels up the right side of the spinothalamic pathway, and information from the right side of the body travels up the left side of the spinothalamic pathway. Then, without any additional synapses, the spinothalamic pathway goes directly to the ventral posterior nucleus of the thalamus and from there to the somatosensory cortex. This anatomy is also depicted in Figure 14.9.

The goal of these pathways is to get information to the brain for processing. There are also reflex channels in the spinal cord that take the information and send it right back to the muscles to allow fast reaction to dangerous situations. In order to experience the feeling, though, the information must be sent to the somatosensory cortex. You may have experienced this at one time or another. If you ever accidentally (or on purpose) placed your hand on a hot stovetop, you may have noticed that you jerked your hand away before you actually felt the acute pain. Like the whale's tail, it takes a bit longer for the information to get to your brain for you to experience pain than it does for the reflex arc to allow you to remove your hand quickly.

Somatosensory Cortex

The **somatosensory cortex** is an area in the parietal lobe of the cerebral cortex devoted to processing the information coming from the skin senses. The somatosensory cortex is in the anterior (front) of the parietal lobe, just behind the central sulcus, which divides the parietal lobe from the frontal lobe. The most anterior area is called the primary somatosensory cortex (S1), and just posterior to it is the secondary somatosensory cortex (S2) (see Figure 14.10). The primary somatosensory cortex receives input from the ventral posterior nucleus of the thalamus and thus receives input from both the dorsal column–medial lemniscal pathway and the spinothalamic pathway. Directly across the central sulcus lies an area in the frontal lobe devoted to the control of movement. The movement area in the frontal lobe maps mostly onto the primary somatosensory cortex. This means that if the primary somatosensory cortex receives input from the left thumb, the area adjacent to it in the frontal lobe motor cortex will be involved in movement of this area.

A brief historical interlude is called for here. Much of what we know of the function of the somatosensory cortex comes from pioneering studies by Canadian neurosurgeon Wilder Penfield (1891–1976). Penfield was interested in surgical ways to relieve the agony of epilepsy. He reasoned that if damaged brain tissue was surgically removed, patients with severe epilepsy might improve. However, it was important to know the function of the brain areas in question before they were surgically removed. Therefore, Penfield pioneered a technique of directly stimulating areas of the brain with an electrical probe and observing the behavior of the patient. This required only local anesthetic to the skull and skin, as the brain itself has no nociceptors. When probing

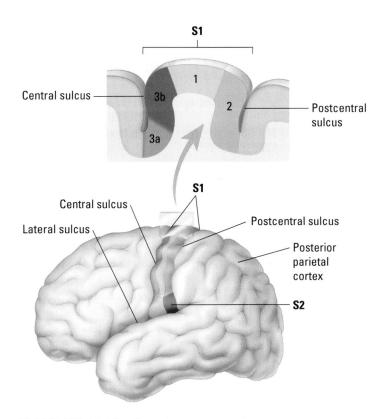

■ FIGURE 14.10 Somatosensory cortex.

Regions S1 and S2 are both important in somatosensory perception, from touch to pain.

Somatosensory cortex: an area in the parietal lobe of the cerebral cortex devoted to processing the information coming from the skin senses

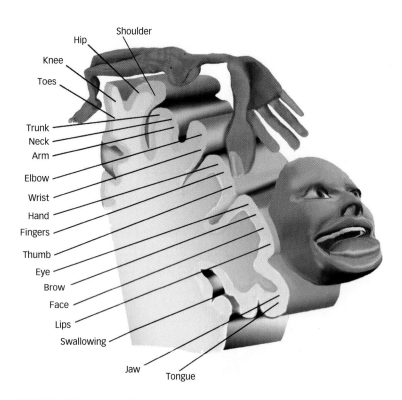

Shoulder
Hip
Knee
Toes
Trunk
Neck
Arm
Elbow
Wrist
Hand
Fingers
Thumb
Eye
Brow
Face
Lips
Swallowing
Jaw   Tongue

■ FIGURE 14.11   The somatosensory cortex.

A homunculus drawing of the somatosensory cortex as conceived by Penfield and Rasmussen (1950). Note the larger areas in the somatosensory cortex devoted to the fingers and mouth and the relatively smaller areas devoted to the back and the legs.

along the primary somatosensory cortex, Penfield found that if he stimulated one area, the patient felt a tingling in a specific area of the body. Moving to an adjacent area of the somatosensory cortex, the tingling would occur in an adjacent area of skin. In this way, Penfield was able to map out the relation between the primary somatosensory cortex and a map of the skin's surface (Penfield & Rasmussen, 1950). You can see this map in Figure 14.11.

The primary somatosensory cortex maintains a **somatotopic map** of the body. In the somatotopic map, the skin of the body maps onto the surface of the primary somatosensory cortex in a systematic way. When you scratch your chin, this stimulates an area in the primary somatosensory cortex responsible for perceiving sensations on your chin. Scratch the tip of your nose, and an area slightly higher in the somatotopic map will be stimulated. Rub your forehead, and an adjacent area to that in somatosensory cortex becomes active. In fact, as Figure 14.12 demonstrates, the somatosensory cortex actually holds multiple maps of the skin surface. But throughout these maps, you can see the feature Penfield originally noted. The maps are distorted—areas of the body for which we need greater sensitivity (e.g., hands, mouth) have a greater representation in the somatosensory cortex maps than do areas of the body for which we do not need as high sensitivity (e.g., back, legs). It is for this reason that the homunculus drawing (Figure 14.11) looks so odd. Penfield and Rasmussen enlarged those areas that receive greater space in the somatosensory cortex and shrank those areas that receive less space in the somatosensory cortex.

If you examine Figure 14.12, you will see that the representation of the face is very close to the representation of the hands. This turned out to be very important in determining some of the mysteries associated with phantom limb syndrome. Patients with phantom limb syndrome may experience sensation in a missing hand when they are touched on the face. They may also experience sensation in a missing hand when touched on what remains of their arm. Ramachandran and Hirstein (1999) hypothesized that this is because of the proximity of the regions in the somatosensory cortex responsible for the missing hand and the face. In their view, the area normally responsible for feeling on the face starts to draw on areas that are otherwise dormant because they are not receiving signals from a hand no longer present. However, because the rest of the brain is functioning on the assumption that the area responsible for the hand is perceiving sensation from the hand, the touching of the face causes the experience of having one's missing hand touched. Initially, this sensation may be disturbing initially to patients, but then they get used to it. In most cases, however, patients may continue to have illusions of feeling in their missing hands. Real problems with phantom limbs occur when people experience pain in missing limbs.

Somatotopic map: a feature whereby the skin of the body maps onto the surface of the primary somatosensory cortex in a systematic way

Suborganization of the Somatosensory Cortex

The primary somatosensory cortex is divided into three distinct neuroanatomical regions. One of these regions is then divided again into two regions. These regions are called Area 1, Area 2, Area 3A, and Area 3B. Each area has a distinct map of the body's surface. In addition, each area receives input from a particular tract in the somatosensory system. Area 1 receives input from mechanoreceptors and is therefore the primary area for tactile perception. Area 2 receives input from proprioceptors in the muscles and tendons (as does Area 3A). Area 3A receives input from nociceptors. Area 3B also receives input from nociceptors, along with input from the mechanoreceptors. These areas then send information to S2 (the secondary somatosensory cortex), which is the somatosensory system's "what" channel for identifying the nature of the touched object (Hsiao, 2008). That is, this channel, sometimes called the ventral system, is critical for using touch information to identify both the shape of an object and the identity of that object. Thus, this area allows us to discriminate softballs from grapefruits (see Figure 14.13).

There is also a "where" channel or dorsal system in the somatosensory system. The dorsal system allows us to control guided movements on the basis of input from the somatosensory system. For example, we use feedback from this system to adjust our grip on a large textbook when it starts slipping away from our hands. When we feel that the barbell we are about to lift is heavy, feedback from the somatosensory system tightens our grip. The "where" channel continues from areas in S1 to the posterior parietal cortex, an area involved in the control of action, to the premotor cortex in the frontal lobe (Hsiao, 2008).

Left out of the above description is the pathway for temperature information. It turns out that temperature information takes a slightly different pathway when it makes its way to the cortex. Thermoreceptors send axons up the spinothalamic pathway that travel to the ventral posterior nucleus of the thalamus and from there to S1. In contrast to other somatosensory systems, temperature

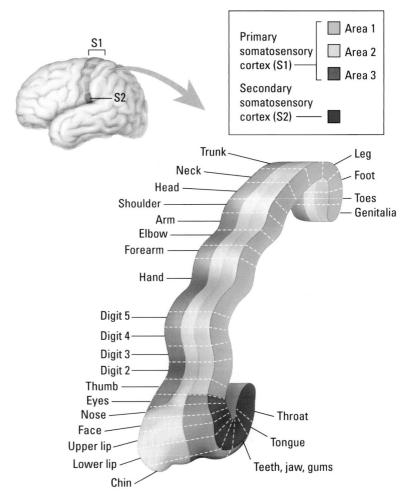

■ FIGURE 14.12   The somatotopic map.

A more modern view of the somatotopic map, showing multiple regions of the somatosensory cortex and both S1 and S2.

■ FIGURE 14.13   Shape and texture.

The "what" channel allows us to discriminate and identify objects that have similar shapes and sizes, such as this softball and this grapefruit.

information then goes to areas of the frontal lobe, including the insular cortex and the anterior cingulate cortex (Hua, Strigo, Baxter, Johnson, & Craig, 2005). The insular cortex and anterior cingulate cortex have complex roles in cognition and are not typically associated with sensory perception. Thus, their roles in perceiving temperature remain to be determined. But given that both areas are associated with emotion, it may explain why some people feel so passionate about the weather.

Pathways for Pain

When we touch a hot stove, or prick a finger with a sewing needle, or feel the injection of Novocain into our gums at the dentist's office, we feel pain. Much to our regret, nothing could be more real than the uncomfortable, distracting, and unpleasant experience of pain. We may try to avoid it, we may dread it, we may develop ways of coping with it, but from time to time, human beings experience pain, almost invariably unpleasant. However, it turns out that the experience of pain arises from interactions among multiple systems, not just the nociceptors. Pain can also be modified by emotion and cognition, which act to change the pain experience in very real ways. For example, we describe in the next chapter how the experience of pain can enhance the perception of flavor in spicy foods, a rare situation in which pain is perceived as a positive. The neuroscience of pain is therefore a fascinating story of the complex interactions of bottom-up (nociceptive) and top-down (cognitive and emotional) processes.

As we discussed earlier, nociceptors in the skin detect damage or trauma at the skin and transmit that information up the spinothalamic pathway. However, there is also a downward pathway, leading from higher centers in the brain and heading down into the spinal column. The information coming from the brain can inhibit the flow of information upward toward the brain from the nociceptors. When it does so, the experience of pain is inhibited. When the downward signals are excitatory, the transmission of pain information continues unabated. This view of pain perception has been called the **gate control theory** (Melzack & Wall, 1988). It is depicted in Figure 14.14 and can be seen in ISLE 14.5. We also know where gate control occurs. The nociceptors first synapse in the spinal cord in an area called the **substantia gelatinosa** of the **dorsal horn**. It is here that neural signals from the brain can inhibit the upward flow of pain information.

Think of the implications of the gate control model. Think, if you will for just a moment, of a prisoner being tortured. The fear a prisoner may experience in this circumstance may ensure that the gate control is wide open, and all pain signals are heading upstream unchecked. Indeed, a small pinprick may cause enormous pain under these circumstances. Contrast that with a visit to the dentist. The dentist is not your enemy, but your doctor. You know your dentist is not out to maim you, but rather to make sure your teeth are healthy. The comfort of that knowledge may be enough to activate the gate control mechanism and effectively lower the experience of pain. Visits to the dentist may still involve pain, but because we know the reasons behind this pain, our gate control mechanism may mute the pain.

This leads us to the role of the **anterior cingulate cortex** in emotional pain (Davis, Taylor, Crawley, Wood, & Mikulis, 1997). The anterior cingulate cortex receives input from the primary and secondary somatosensory cortices (S1 and S2) and responds to pain caused by pinches, pricks, and extreme heat and cold. Indeed, in one study, patients undergoing neurosurgery showed strong activity in their anterior cingulate cortices when experiencing pain (Hutchinson, Davis, Lozano,

ISLE 14.5 Melzack and Wall's Gate Control Theory

Gate control theory: a model that allows for top-down control of the pain signal coming up the spinal cord

Substantia gelatinosa: the region in the dorsal horn where neurons meet

Dorsal horn: an area of the spinal cord that receives input from nociceptors and feedback from the brain

Anterior cingulate cortex: a region in the prefrontal lobe of the brain associated with the emotional experience of unpleasantness during pain perception

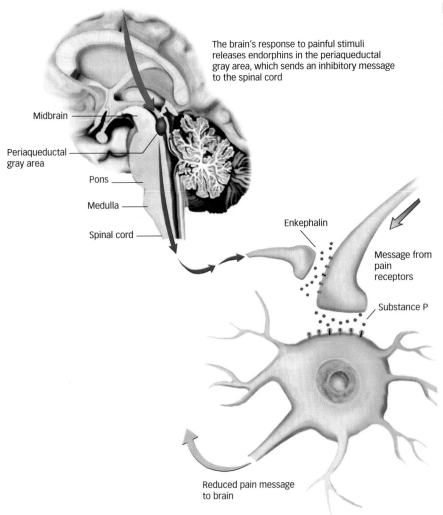

Midbrain

Periaqueductal gray area

Pons

Medulla

Spinal cord

The brain's response to painful stimuli releases endorphins in the periaqueductal gray area, which sends an inhibitory message to the spinal cord

Enkephalin

Message from pain receptors

Substance P

Reduced pain message to brain

■ FIGURE 14.14   Gate control theory.

This model shows both how pain arises in the nociceptors and how it is transmitted to the brain. It also depicts top-down control of the pain signal coming down from the brain through the spinal column.

Tasker, & Dostrovsky, 1999). In another study (Rainville, Duncan, Price, Carrier, & Bushnell, 1997), participants were hypnotized and then had their hands placed in either painfully hot water or tepid water. S1 and S2 were activated regardless of hypnotic suggestions given to participants, but the activity in the anterior cingulate cortex varied as a function of hypnosis condition. When participants were led to believe that more pain was coming, more activity was seen in the anterior cingulate cortex than when people were led to believe that pain was diminishing. Another study has shown that people show activity in the anterior cingulate cortex when other people are experiencing pain (Singer et al., 2004). In this way, the anterior cingulate cortex is seen as an area important to the emotional component of pain perception. It regulates pain and likely can initiate the gate control mechanism to inhibit pain.

TEST YOUR KNOWLEDGE

What is the difference between the dorsal column–medial lemniscal pathway and the spinothalamic pathway? Where is each located, and what somatosensory systems is each responsible for?

THE NEUROCHEMISTRY OF PAIN: ENDOGENOUS OPIOIDS

14.6 Examine the role of endogenous opioids in controlling pain perception.

As we have described, pain is useful because it alerts an organism to the potential of trauma to the body. This is useful because it allows the organism to move away from or reduce the potential for further injury. However, there may be some situations in which an organism must continue to put itself in harm's way. For example, think of the pain an antelope may feel from a thorn in its foot as it runs away from a cheetah. In other circumstances, this pain might be a signal to slow down and see if the antelope can shake out the thorn, but with the cheetah in pursuit, the pain must be ignored because a greater danger needs to be confronted. Similarly, think of a human mountain climber battling the steep slope she must descend to return from the mountain and the pain she is experiencing from a twisted ankle. Giving in to the pain of the ankle means death, so the climber must ignore the pain to continue her descent. Humans may also mimic some of these situations in athletic contests. Consider the marathon runner, whose muscles are exhausted and overheated, and whose nociceptors are firing at high rates by the middle of a race, even in the best of conditioned athletes. In order to complete the 26.2 miles, the marathon runner must continue to run despite his pain. It turns out that the brain has a mechanism to reduce pain in these circumstances. The brain can release chemicals known as **endogenous opioids** into the bloodstream, which act as analgesics to reduce pain. Endogenous opioids are chemicals produced by the body that reduce pain, via **analgesia**, throughout the body. Thus, the marathon runner will begin to feel the "runner's high" when these opioids kick in. The pain associated with muscle fatigue seems to lessen, and the runner can even speed up at the finish. Stories abound of lost hikers who overcame pain and injury to make it to safety. Endogenous opioids may have contributed to many of these self-rescues.

Opioids are naturally produced opiates. Opiates include many drugs, both legal and illegal, that people take externally to reduce pain. Opiates include medically used painkillers, such as codeine, and illegal drugs, such as heroin. Endorphins are a class of opioids produced by the body, which inhibit pain responses in the central nervous system and thus reduce pain perception. Because artificial opiates mimic the effects of these natural painkillers, they can be effective at reducing pain, although in many cases, the risk for addition is high as well. For this reason, the use of opiates as painkillers is by prescription only.

> **TEST YOUR KNOWLEDGE**
>
> What are endogenous opiates? How do they work to control pain?

THE PERCEPTION OF ITCH

14.7 Explain the difference between pain and itch and how they interact.

Itchiness is usually a minor inconvenience. Dry skin feels itchy, and you give it a quick scratch and move on. A single mosquito bite annoys you with

---

Endogenous opioids: chemicals produced by the body that reduce pain throughout the body

Analgesia: processes that act to reduce pain perception

its itchiness, but it is easily ignored. But itchiness can also be tremendously debilitating. Jellyfish stings can itch all over one's skin with an incredible intensity. This itchiness can lead to self-induced wounds that may get infected. Itchiness can also disrupt sleep patterns and distract attention from necessary tasks. There is a disease called river blindness (technically, onchocerciasis). This disease is a major problem in tropical regions of Africa. The disease may affect tissue in the eye, causing partial or complete blindness, but it also causes a terrible itching sensation all over the body. People with river blindness have been known to throw themselves into water, even when crocodiles may be swimming about in that water, just to relieve the itching.

If you think about it subjectively, itch is different from pain, even though both may be considered negative sensory experiences. Itchiness causes us to want to scratch the affected skin, a response not usually caused by pain (see Figure 14.15). Pain induces a withdrawal response—we move away from pain. Thus, behaviorally, they have different consequences as well. Other animals use itch perception in other ways. Think of your cat and her notorious itchy ears. Cats' faces and ears are loaded with itch receptors in order to induce them to rub against landmarks and leave their scents for other cats to detect. Other animals may feel itchy for similar reasons.

Recent research shows that itch perception is caused by a different class of receptors in our skin. These receptors have been labeled **pruriceptors** (*pruri* is a Latin root meaning "itch"). Pruriceptors respond mostly to chemical irritants on the skin rather than tissue damage (LaMotte, Shimada, Green, & Zelterman, 2009). Like nociceptors, pruriceptors also send their axons up the spinothalamic tract, where they eventually synapse in the somatosensory cortex. Pruriceptors have been less well studied than other forms of skin perception, but there is now strong evidence that pruriceptors are anatomically different than nociceptors.

The function of the relation of itching and scratching has undergone some scrutiny. One hypothesis is that we scratch to remove the possible irritant that may be bothering us. Thus, a landing mosquito causes our skin to itch, and our scratch removes the insect from our skin. Another hypothesis is that itching causes us to scratch, which then induces actual, albeit minor, tissue damage. That is, the goal of the itchy sensation is to induce us to cause minor tissue damage. This tissue damage initiates an autoimmune response, which acts to reduce the risk caused by the original irritant (LaMotte et al., 2009). Consistent with this view is the finding that pain inhibits itch. That is, when you scratch an irritant on your skin, it may induce mild pain, which causes the itch to decrease as well as possibly an immune response (Ward, Wright, & McMahon, 1996). Thus, for most people, having one's back scratched feels good at first, but if the scratching is too hard, pain perception takes over. So the next time you get a mosquito bite, you can feel a bit more comfortable scratching your itch, knowing that in small doses, it may help your body react to the irritant.

■ FIGURE 14.15 **The perception of itch.**

Skin irritations cause itching, and itching induces us to scratch.

© iStockphoto.com/offstocker

TEST YOUR KNOWLEDGE

What are the anatomical and functional differences between pain and itch?
What evolutionary purpose is itch supposed to be related to?

Pruriceptors: receptors in our skin that respond to mild irritants by producing itch sensations

HAPTIC PERCEPTION

14.8 Describe the role movement plays in creating the perception of active touch.

Think about finding your way around in a dark room. You reach out and touch objects to determine what they are, but you do not just touch them—you pick them up and put your hands around them. Indeed, the determination of shape and identity from touch involves a dynamic process of perception, motor control, and feedback. We cannot do this on ISLE, but try having a friend blindfold you and then give you common objects to identify by touch. When given a small rectangular wafer-shaped metallic object, you feel it, you move it around, and you see if it has moving parts before you confidently declare that it is a flash drive. This dynamic process of object identification by touch is called haptic perception. **Haptic perception** refers to the active use of touch to identify objects. Haptic perception includes integrating information from mechanoreceptors, proprioceptors, thermoreceptors, and perhaps nociceptors as well.

Normally, we are not blindfolded, but haptic perception is important in many situations as well. For example, you may need to find a quarter (25-cent piece) in your pocket. You do not need to take out every coin and examine them visually to determine the right coin. Rather, you feel the shapes of the coins in your pocket and use your haptic perception to determine the correct coin. Men who must wear ties for work become so accustomed to putting on ties that they may be able to do so without looking in the mirror. Cooks know when their batter is ready to go in the oven not because it looks right but because they feel it with their hands and know when the texture is correct. And perhaps most important, surgeons may often be required to perform operations by touch, as that information is more readily available than visual information. Thus, haptic perception is relevant in many different situations.

Think again about identifying objects while blindfolded. There have been experiments examining exactly that ability in people. For example, Klatzky (see Lederman & Klatzky, 2009) gave participants 100 common objects to touch and identify. These objects included eyeglasses, keys, spoons, and coffee cups. Not only were the participants highly accurate (nearly 100%); they did so very quickly. Klatzky, Loomis, Lederman, Wake, and Fujita (1993) showed that wearing a glove while attempting to identify objects haptically interfered with the perception and lowered accuracy. They hypothesized that the glove prevented the receptors from picking up vital information from the objects, thus reducing the accuracy of the judgments. Thus, we can identify objects via touch, and factors that interfere with efficient touch can interfere with object identification.

To identify objects, participants make a number of discrete movements, such as lateral motion, applying pressure, following the edges, supporting the object to determine approximate weight, and several others (see Figure 14.16). These motions are called exploratory procedures. **Exploratory procedures** are hand movements we make in order to identify an object. Thus, for example, we can determine the texture of an object by lateral motion, or moving our hands along its surface. A smooth object will result in a very different pattern on our mechanoreceptors than will a bumpy object. You can tell the difference between your cat and your dog without looking at them by feeling the differences in the shape of their heads.

Think about moving your fingers across a rough surface, perhaps sandpaper. As you move your fingers across the sandpaper, the pattern registers in unique ways on the mechanoreceptors of your fingers. And depending on the grain of the sandpaper,

Haptic perception: the active use of touch to identify objects

Exploratory procedures: hand movements made in order to identify an object

different patterns of high and low activity will occur in the FA and SA receptors. This pattern allows the somatosensory cortex to develop a spatial map of what the surface is. This conjecture was put to the experimental test in a clever experiment conducted by Hollins, Bensmaia, and Washburn (2001), who compared the responses of mechanoreceptor fibers across different surfaces.

Hollins et al. (2001) did this by inducing a tactile illusion. They started with the assumption that FAII (fast-adapting, large receptive fields) mechanoreceptors would be important in determining the identities of objects with fine texture (e.g., the least scratchy sandpaper). They fatigued these receptors by presenting to participants a high-frequency vibration. The idea here was that the high-frequency vibration would tire or cause adaptation in the FAII receptors. After exposure to these vibrations, participants found the surfaces of objects less "rough" than when they were not preadapted to these vibrations. A low-frequency vibration did not have these effects. Thus, this experiment supports the idea that our different mechanoreceptors contribute to different aspects of haptic perception (Pei, Hsiao, Craig, & Bensmaia, 2011).

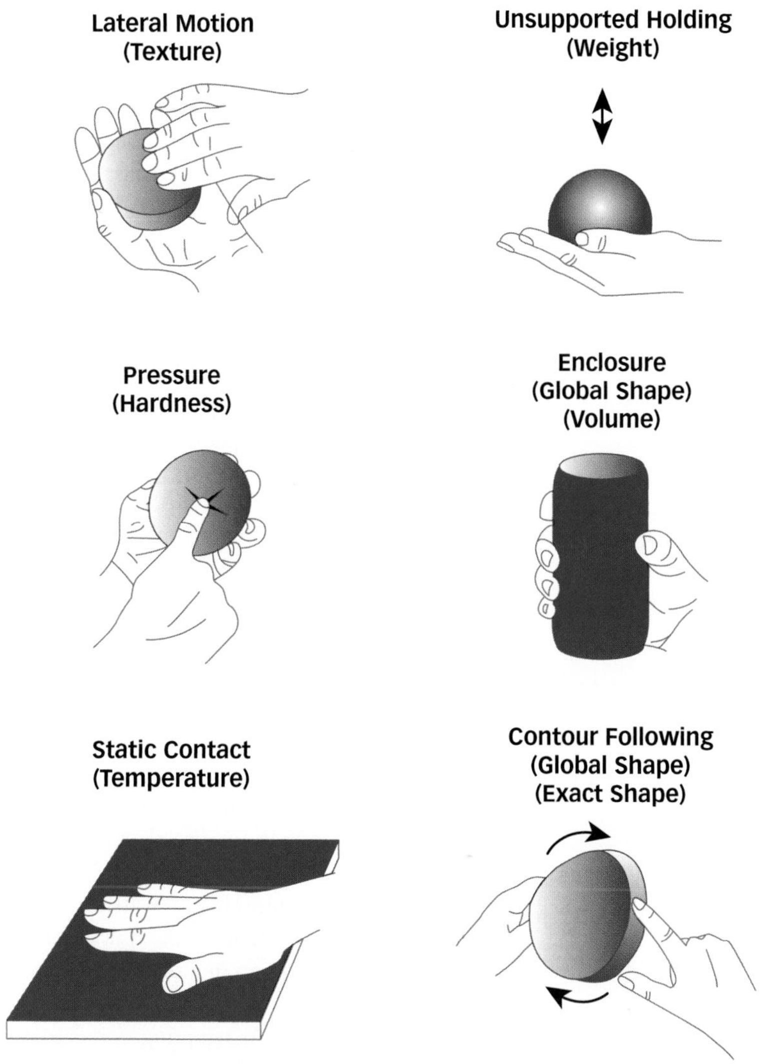

Tactile Agnosia

Tactile agnosia is a neurological condition caused by damage to the somatosensory areas of the parietal lobe. **Tactile agnosia** is defined as an inability to identify objects by touch. In order for a patient to be diagnosed with tactile agnosia, he or she must show normal perception of texture, temperature, and pain and must show no deficits in motion. For example, a patient should be able to tell you that a surface is smooth and cold, but not be able to identify it as an icepack. That is, the neurological problem must be one of identification rather the perception (Reed, Caselli, & Farah, 1996).

An important characteristic of most patients with tactile agnosia is that only one hand is affected, but the other hand is spared. This is because the left hemisphere receives input from the right hand, and the right hemisphere receives input from the left hand. Thus, tactile agnosia is typically seen in only one hand. If the damage is to the left somatosensory cortex, tactile agnosia will be seen with the right hand, but not the left hand. If both hands show agnosia, a different neural cause is suspected (Gerstmann, 2001).

Reed et al. (1996) studied a patient with tactile agnosia. E.C. was a 65-year-old woman who had tactile agnosia only in her right hand because of a left hemisphere lesion caused by a stroke in that area. The patient had no difficulty identifying objects visually or with her left hand. However, when identifying objects by using

FIGURE 14.16 Exploratory procedures (Lederman & Klatzky, 2009). We use our hands to explore objects and determine their shapes and identities.

Tactile agnosia: an inability to identify objects by touch

only her right hand, she showed a massive deficit in object identification, though she could still identify textures, shapes, and characteristics such as smoothness. The patient also had cognitive knowledge of the shapes of objects. That is, she could describe the differences in textures among objects. However, when she felt objects with only her right hand (and could not see what they were), she was unable to identify most objects. The tactile agnosia, however, was not the only problem she had with her somatosensory system. She reported general numbness in her right hand, though thresholds and temperature sensitivity appeared normal. Thus, although her perception of objects was not affected, her ability to identify objects was specifically impaired, thus classifying the diagnosis as agnosia.

TEST YOUR KNOWLEDGE

What are exploratory procedures? How do they contribute to haptic perception?

THE VESTIBULAR SYSTEM: THE PERCEPTION OF BALANCE

14.9 Explain how the vestibular system operates to aid in the perception of balance and acceleration.

We are including the vestibular system in this chapter, although the vestibular system is not directly related to the somatosensory systems. The vestibular system may be most linked to the auditory system, with which it shares a number of anatomical features. Its inclusion here does not diminish its importance to proper sensory functioning. But for the sake of time and brevity, we have included it here rather than in a separate chapter.

Movement is essential to any animal, including humans. We are constantly in motion. As tempting as it is to remain in bed when your alarm clock goes off at 6 a.m., you must stand up and leave your bedroom. Once in the kitchen, you may need to bend down to pick up the coffee beans from the bottom shelf to brew yourself some coffee. After that, you may have to reach up to get a coffee cup from the top shelf. All of these ordinary daily activities require balance. Your weight shifts as you perform each of these tasks, and your ability to counter gravity changes as well. Balance is even more important in the sports we play. Consider a downhill skier who must keep herself upright on thin strips of carbon fiber while hurtling down a steep and slippery mountain at 85 mph (137 km/h). Balance here is the critical difference between winning a gold medal and spending the next 6 months recovering from serious injuries in the hospital. Nothing is worse for a skier than a compromised vestibular system!

The **vestibular system** is the sensory system responsible for the perception of balance and acceleration and it is housed in the **semicircular canals** and **otolith organs**, both located adjacent to the inner ear. The semicircular canals are three tubes located in the inner ear responsible for the signaling of head rotation. The semicircular canals are filled with a fluid called endolymph. The otolith organs are responsible for detecting acceleration of the head and identifying when the head is being held at a tilted angle. Hair cells within the semicircular canals signal information about balance, and hair cells within the otolith organs signal information about acceleration. The anatomy of the vestibular system is depicted in Figure 14.17. Note the proximity of the vestibular system to the

Vestibular system: the sensory system responsible for the perception of balance and acceleration, housed in the semicircular canals and otolith organs, both located adjacent to the inner ear

Semicircular canals: three tubes located in the inner ear responsible for the signaling of head rotation

Otolith organs: organs responsible for detecting acceleration of the head and identifying when the head is being held at a tilted angle

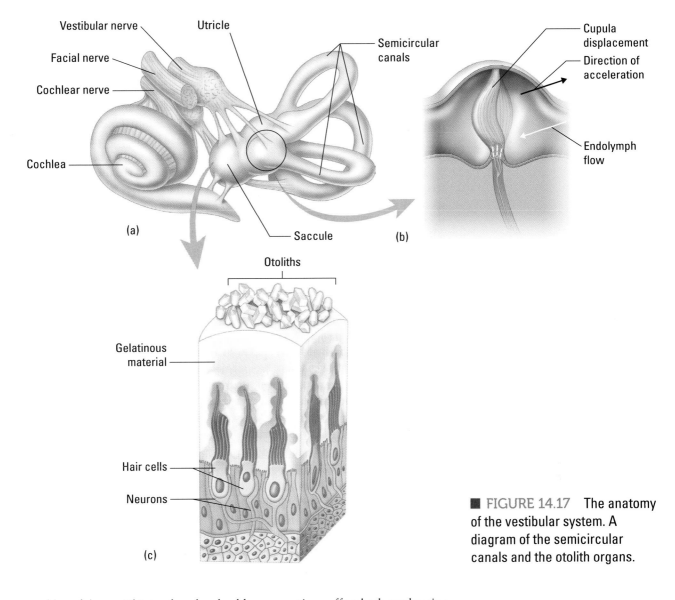

Vestibular nerve

Facial nerve

Cochlear nerve

Utricle

Semicircular canals

Cochlea

(a)

Saccule

(b)

Cupula displacement

Direction of acceleration

Endolymph flow

Otoliths

Gelatinous material

Hair cells

Neurons

(c)

■ FIGURE 14.17 **The anatomy of the vestibular system. A diagram of the semicircular canals and the otolith organs.**

cochlea of the ear. This is why a head cold can sometimes affect both our hearing and our sense of balance, as both of these areas may be clogged.

The semicircular canals are tubes aligned in a perpendicular way to one another. Each semicircular canal is filled with a liquid called **endolymph**. At the bottom of each canal is a chamber called the ampulla, which contains a structure called the crista. Inside the crista are the hair cells. Similarly, in the otolith organs is a structure called the macula, which houses the hair cells that respond to changes in head orientation.

When our head moves in any particular direction, the endolymph sloshes from one direction to another. Think of holding up a glass. If you hold it straight, the water level is aligned with the glass. However, if you tilt the glass to the left, the water moves to stay aligned with gravity, but no longer appears aligned with the glass. That is, it piles up against the left side of the glass. Similarly, if you move your head, the endolymph shifts with it. If you move your head left, the endolymph piles up along that side, triggering a neural response. When the endolymph shifts, the hair cells bend, transducing a neural signal, which informs the brain about head position. Because the three semicircular canals are perpendicular to one another, each transmits information about head movement along

Endolymph: fluid that fills the semicircular canals

a different axis. That is, by comparing the movement in each canal, the brain can make inferences about movements to the left or right (yaw), in front or behind (roll), and up or down (pitch). Thus, the movement of endolymph in each canal can provide information about relative head movement in great detail.

Meanwhile, the otolith organs are responsible for detecting acceleration. When you start sprinting down the track, hair cells in the otolith organs bend, transducing a neural signal, thus providing you with information about motion and acceleration. Similarly, when you move your head to one side or another, the hair cells in the otolith will bend, thus giving you information on head tilt.

If you have ever spent extended time at sea—sometimes even a relatively short ferry ride will do it—you may have experienced the following illusion created by the vestibular system. After you return to dry land after your 7-day cruise through the Caribbean, you may continue to experience a sensation of rocking or swaying while on what you know to be terra firma, such as in your own home. In the vast majority of people, these symptoms disappear after a few hours, though in some very rare cases, they may persist for years. It is likely that these symptoms are caused by adaptation—after a day or two at sea, you adapt to the constant motion caused by the rocking boat, but then when you return to land, it takes a while to readapt to land, leading to the temporary disorientation.

The nerve fibers from the semicircular canals and the otolith come together in the vestibular nerve that then synapses in a brain stem area called the **vestibular complex**. The vestibular complex projects to several areas, including the **parietal insular vestibular cortex**, located in the parietal lobe. This area of the brain is thought to maintain a representation of head angle, critical for maintaining balance. Patients with damage to this area of the cortex may experience distortions of orientation, including vertigo, a sense of the world spinning when it is not, and illusory tilt; that is, they may feel that their heads are tilted when they are not. Indeed, some patients with damage in the parietal insular vestibular cortex may hold their heads at odd angles because it feels like proper orientation to them.

Thus, the vestibular system is an important sensory system in its own right and quite different from the more widely known and studied systems. Damage to it can have severe consequences, but we seldom attend to it unless there is something wrong, such as in the case of seasickness. We include it in this chapter because of the diverse number of systems covered in this chapter, not because it is a somatosensory system.

TEST YOUR KNOWLEDGE

What is the function of the vestibular system? Briefly describe the anatomy of the vestibular system and how its anatomy is related to its function.

APPLICATION: READING BRAILLE

14.10 Explain how our somatosensory system is used in the reading of Braille.

Braille is an alphabet system using easy-to-feel tactile letters instead of visual letters. It was developed by Louis Braille (1809–1852). Braille was a young boy in France when an accident robbed of him of his sight. He struggled to use raised letters to read, which are very difficult to tell apart. Finding that this was the case for most blind individuals, Braille set out to develop a writing system that would be easier to read via touch. The system he developed

Vestibular complex: a brainstem area that receives input from the vestibular nerve and sends the information to the forebrain

Parietal insular vestibular cortex: an area in the parietal lobe that receives input from the vestibular nerve and is responsible for the perception of balance and orientation

nearly 200 years ago is still a critical system for the blind today (see Figure 14.18 for an illustration of the Braille system). Interestingly, Braille was based on a night-writing system developed so that military orders could be given by the French army at night without having to alert enemies to their position. Braille is usually read using the index figure, which feels the dots raised about the surface of the page. Blind readers can now read Braille off the surface of a computer (see Figure 14.19). It should be noted that in recent years, there has been a slight decline in the use of Braille, as computer technology allows text-to-voice translation, allowing blind individuals to hear instead of feel what they need to read.

In order to read Braille, one must feel the dots raised above the page and perceive the number of dots. As you can see in Figure 14.18, small differences in the number of dots indicate different letters. Thus, Braille is dependent on fine touch and the "what" system in the somatosensory cortex. Fluent visual readers may perceive many letters at the same time, but research shows that Braille readers feel fewer letters per unit of time than do visual readers seeing letters. On average, a competent Braille reader can read about 100 words per minute, somewhat less than the 250 words per minute sighted people can read (Mountcastle, 2005). As such, Braille reading tends to be slower than visual reading. In general, because our index fingers have the greatest number of mechanoreceptors, even compared with other fingers, Braille readers are able to read fastest by using their two index fingers together. Fluent Braille readers will also move the left hand down to the next line of text, even as the right hand continues to finish the line above (Lowenfield & Able, 1977). This research also suggests that natural left-handers can read Braille faster.

Neuroimaging studies have revealed interesting reorganization of the brain in congenitally blind individuals compared with individuals who became blind later in life (Voss & Zatorre, 2012). First, we see more white-matter fibers in the area of the somatosensory cortex for congenitally blind individuals than for individuals who become blind later in life. Moreover, the occipital lobe reorganizes and receives input from the somatosensory cortex (and from the auditory cortex) in congenitally blind individuals. It is thought that this reorganization allows blind people greater area to devote to spatial processing deriving from nonvisual spatial modalities. Moreover, Braille readers show activity in the occipital lobe when reading (Voss & Zatorre, 2012). Although people who become blind later in life will show activity in the occipital lobe when touching objects, the earlier one becomes blind, the more the occipital lobe is co-opted by other senses (Collignon et al., 2013).

This research speaks to the relation of behavioral adaptation and neural reorganization in the face of disruption of normal sensory systems. Thus, the brain does not waste the visual cortex when a person loses sight (due to damage to the eyes). Rather, the visual cortex is co-opted for spatial perception through other modalities. Reading by touch allows blind individuals the same opportunities in reading as does sight in normal individuals. It also gives blind people a distinct advantage—they can read in total darkness, without making a sound.

a	b	c	d	e	f	g	h	i	j	k
l	m	n	o	p	q	r	s	t	u	v
			w	x	y	z				

■ FIGURE 14.18 **The Braille alphabet.**

These letters are raised off the page, so that blind readers can feel them. A fluent Braille reader can read almost half as fast as a sighted individual can read text.

© iStockphoto.com/portokalis

■ FIGURE 4.19 **A person reading Braille.**

IN DEPTH: *Electroreception in Fish*

The bodies of all animals generate electricity. Think about the billions of neurons in our brains and throughout our nervous systems sending electric signals among one another. We have seen how neurons work embedded in muscle tissue as well. In the terrestrial environment, the electric fields generated by animals are incredibly weak, because air is such a poor conductor of electricity. This is why we need to put electrodes directly on the scalp to record electroencephalograms. No known land animal has a sensory system that picks up electric output, all claims of extrasensory perception notwithstanding.

However, as every worrying mother knows, water is much better at conducting electricity than air (at the first sign of lightning, every parent considers it a sacred duty to get every child out of the pool at once). Thus, the electric output of the nervous systems of fish is detectable by other fish if they are in relatively close proximity if those fish have evolved special electroreceptors. It turns out that many species of fish have sensory organs that allow them to detect the electric fields of other fish. Many sharks and rays, for example, are able to detect prey in complete darkness by homing in on their electric fields (Hughes, 1999). Think of Jaws closing in on you as you swim at night simply because you are deep in thought. Now you might not really want to go back to the beach.

Electroreception in fish can be considered either passive or active. **Passive electroreception** means simply that an organism can detect the electric fields generated by other animals. It is analogous to our hearing—we hear the sound generated by objects in our environment. **Active electroreception** means that the fish generates its own electric field around itself and then senses disturbances to that electric field. This is analogous to the biosonar systems of bats and dolphins, animals that listen for echoes from their own calls.

Electroreception involves detecting electric fields, but a number of electric fish have also evolved the ability to generate strong electric fields for the purpose of hunting and predation avoidance. The vaunted Amazonian electric eel

(*Electrophorus electricus*) has been measured at generated shocks at 600 volts, enough to knock out a horse (Hughes, 1999) (see Figure 14.20). Another species, the Nile catfish, can produce more than 300 volts. It is likely that these weapons developed from organs already being used for sensory purposes. There are also fish that cloak their own electric signals to avoid such fierce predators (Stoddard & Markham, 2008). But our attention focuses on electroreception. Electroreception has evolved multiple times among many species of fishes. So our discussion includes much generalization, but interestingly, there is a great deal of similarity even across whole Linnaean classes of fish. Electroreception has also been discovered in at least one species of aquatic mammals, the platypus (Pettigrew, 1999).

The electroreceptors are located inside the scales along the surface of most fish. In some species, the electroreceptors are kept under the surface of the skin, but in other species they extend outward into the water. Electroreceptors are also found in the lateral line—a long row of mechanoreceptors that stretch along the backs of many fish, which allow them to coordinate their rapid swimming movements. But the electroreceptors are quite distinct from the mechanoreceptors of the lateral line. The lateral line mechanoreceptors respond to movement of the water, whereas electroreceptors respond to electric

Electroreception: the ability to detect electric fields, seen in many species of fish

Passive electroreception: the ability only to detect electric fields

Active electroreception: the ability to generate electric fields and then detect disturbances or changes to those electric fields caused by external events

■ FIGURE 14.20 **An electric eel.**

The electric eel (*Electrophorus electricus*) is not really an eel at all. It is classified with knifefish. Do not let its bland appearance lull you—this fish is loaded with juice.

© iStockphoto.com/Richelle_67

fields. The electroreceptors are known as **ampullae of Lorenzini**, after the Italian anatomist who first identified them. The ampullae are used for passive electroreception. A second class of receptors, called the **tuberous receptors**, are used for active electroreception in those fish that use active electroreception. These receptors are shown in Figure 14.21. In Figure 14.22, we see the mouth and teeth of a tiger shark (*Galeocerdo cuvier*). The pits or dots along its snout are ampullae of Lorenzini.

The ampullae of Lorenzini and the tuberous receptors are tuned to electric fields of different frequencies. In terms of electricity, *frequency* means variations in voltage across time. We use variations in voltage in our appliances. Batteries, for example, produce DC—direct current, in which voltage does not vary across time. However, the electricity in our houses and offices is AC—alternating current, in which the voltage varies in a predictable manner across time. Biological organisms tend to produce alternating current but with much smaller variations in voltage than produced by human-made sources. Fish electroreceptors are tuned to this. The ampullae of Lorenzini are tuned to DC and to very low frequency AC, whereas tuberous receptors are tuned to much higher AC frequencies (Fields, 2007; Hughes, 1999). As such, the two types of receptors are tuned to very different kinds of electrical events in the water. The ampullae of Lorenzini are tuned to detect the weak voltage produced by the movements and body functions of other nearby fish. The tuberous receptors, however, are tuned by evolution to detect the fields generated by specific electric discharges by that fish. That is, just as bats listen for their own echoes, the tuberous receptors sense the changes in the AC produced by the fish itself. Fish equipped with tuberous receptors can then detect the differences between smaller fish, which might mean food,

■ FIGURE 14.22   **Tiger shark.**

The mouth and teeth of a tiger shark (*Galeocerdo cuvier*). The pits or dots along its snout are ampullae of Lorenzini. We probably do not want to mess with this guy.

and bigger fish, which they want to avoid. In general, these electric fields are not that powerful and would give a human hand only a mild shock. This distinguishes them from other fish, such as the electric eel and the Nile catfish, which use their electric organs to deliver a knockout blow rather than as sensory organs.

Until quite recently (the 1950s), scientists did not know that fish had this electric sense and puzzled over the purpose of these obvious sense receptors. Because electric senses are not feasible in land animals such as ourselves, it was hard to imagine that animals such as tiger sharks could be so dependent on this completely alien sense. This is not to say that humans were unaware of the electric abilities of fish. Egyptian fisherman have feared the Nile catfish for thousands of years, and Amazonian peoples have feared the electric eel for presumably at least as long. But it really was not until the 20th century that we determined the relation between these sensory receptors and electricity.

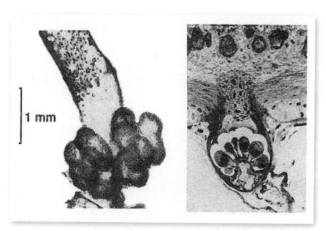

■ FIGURE 14.21   **Electroreception (Hughes, 1999).**

The ampullae of Lorenzini and the tuberous receptors.

Ampullae of Lorenzini: the organ that contains the hair cells that detect electric fields, used in passive electroreception

Tuberous receptors: the organ that contains the hair cells that detect electric fields, used in active electroreception

CHAPTER SUMMARY

14.1 Explain how touch perception is actually a number of senses served by a number of receptor systems.

Our somatosensory system starts with receptors embedded in the skin as well as in our muscles, joints, and tendons. Unlike audition and vision, touch requires direct physical contact with the object to be perceived. The somatosensory system is also composed of several distinct senses. Mechanoreceptors are embedded in our skin. The epidermis is the outer layer of the skin, housing touch receptors, and the dermis is the inner layer of skin, also housing touch receptors. Mechanoreceptors are sensory receptors in the skin that transduce physical movement on the skin into neural signals, which are sent to the brain. They tell us what we are touching and how to respond to it. Mechanoreceptors are divided into four types: SAI mechanoreceptors, SAII mechanoreceptors, FAI mechanoreceptors, and FAII mechanoreceptors. *SA* refers to slow-adapting, whereas *FA* refers to fast-adapting. "I" mechanoreceptors have small receptive fields, whereas "II" mechanoreceptors have larger receptive fields.

14.2 Discuss the role of proprioception in allowing us to know the position and movements of our limbs and joints.

Proprioception is the perception of the movements and position of our limbs. Proprioception gives us important information about the placement of our bodies. Proprioception is subserved by three kinds of receptors, muscle spindles, joint receptors, and Golgi tendon organs. Interestingly, an illusion of proprioception may occur in amputees. When this occurs, they are said to have phantom limb syndrome.

14.3 Describe how the skin registers changes in temperature at the skin.

Thermoreceptors are the sensory receptors in the skin that signal information about the temperature as measured on the skin. Cold fibers are thermoreceptors that fire in response to colder (30°C and below) temperatures as measured on the skin. Warm fibers are different thermoreceptors that fire in response to warmer temperatures (above 36°C) as measured on the skin. When the temperature is abnormally cold, such as when liquid nitrogen is placed on the skin, this extremely cold stimulus will also activate the warm fibers, leading to a perception of heat (and pain).

14.4 Discuss the role of nociceptors in the perception of pain and how pain is modified by gate control theory.

Pain is the perception and the unpleasant experience of actual or threatened tissue damage. As unpleasant as it is, pain is a warning to avoid dangerous objects and protect oneself against greater damage. Nociceptors are sensory receptors in the epidermis and dermis that, when activated, cause us to feel pain. Nociceptors are divided into A-delta fibers, which conduct signals rapidly and respond to both heat and pressure, and C-fibers, which react more slowly and respond to pressure, extreme degrees of either heat or cold, and toxic chemicals.

14.5 Identify the pathways from receptors in the skin to the somatosensory cortex in the brain.

The dorsal column–medial lemniscal pathway is the pathway for the mechanoreceptors (tactile perception) and the proprioceptors (muscle position). It travels up the spinal column on the ipsilateral side and crosses to the contralateral side in the medulla. The other tract for the somatosensory system is the spinothalamic pathway, which conducts information from the nociceptors (pain) and the thermoreceptors (temperature). It travels up the contralateral side of the spinal column. The somatosensory cortex is an area in the parietal lobe of the cerebral cortex devoted to processing the information coming from the skin senses. It houses maps of the skin for the different skin senses. Thus, a touch to an area of the body will cause activation in these areas of the cortex. The maps are also scaled for the number of receptors. Thus, there is more space in the somatosensory cortex devoted to the fingers than to the upper back.

Gate control theory is a model that allows for top-down control of the pain signal coming up the spinal cord. Indeed, activation in the anterior cingulate cortex of the frontal lobe may initiate a sequence that reduces pain via the gate control mechanism.

14.6 Examine the role of endogenous opioids in controlling pain perception.

Pain may also be inhibited by endogenous opioids, which are chemicals produced by the body that reduce pain throughout the body.

14.7 Explain the difference between pain and itch and how they interact.

Finally, recent research suggests that itch perception is separate from pain perception. Itch induces scratching, whereas pain induces movement away from the source of pain. Pruriceptors are receptors in our skin that respond to mild irritants by producing itch sensations.

14.8 Describe the role movement plays in creating the perception of active touch.

Haptic perception is the active use of touch to identify objects. Haptic perception includes integrating information from mechanoreceptors, proprioceptors, thermoreceptors, and perhaps nociceptors as well. Haptic perception integrates movement and touch to determine the shapes and identities of objects, known as exploratory procedures. Tactile agnosia may occur after brain damage to the somatosensory cortex. People with tactile agnosia can still feel texture and shape, but cannot identify objects by touch.

14.9 Explain how the vestibular system operates to aid in the perception of balance and acceleration.

The vestibular system is the sensory system responsible for the perception of balance and acceleration. It is housed in the semicircular canals and otolith organs, both located adjacent to the inner ear. The semicircular canals are three tubes located in the inner ear responsible for the signaling of head rotation. Otolith organs are responsible for detecting acceleration of the head and identifying when the head is being held at a tilted angle. Both project to the parietal insular vestibular cortex.

14.10 Explain how our somatosensory system is used in the reading of Braille.

Braille reading uses tactile perception of raised dots rather than visual letters. It allows completely blind individuals to read. Braille readers have been shown to have more area in the occipital lobe devoted to spatial and somatosensory touch.

REVIEW QUESTIONS

1. What are mechanoreceptors? What are the four kinds of mechanoreceptors, and what kinds of stimuli do they respond to?

2. What is proprioception? Where do we find the receptors for proprioception?

3. What is phantom limb syndrome? How does it manifest itself in both proprioception and the pain domain?

4. What is thermoreception? What two fibers project thermoreception information? What is the difference between them?

5. What are nociceptors? What is the difference between A-delta fibers and C-fibers? How do nociceptors differ from pruriceptors?

6. What is a homunculus? What does it tell us about the organization of the somatosensory cortex? What are the subareas of S1 (the primary somatosensory cortex)?

7. What is gate control theory? What anatomical regions are associated with it? How does it differ from regulating pain with opioids?

8. What are exploratory procedures? What do they tell us about haptic perception?

9. What is the vestibular system? What are the important anatomical correlates of the perception of balance in the vestibular system?

10. What is electroreception? What species use it? What is the difference between passive and active electroreception?

KEY TERMS

INTERACTIVE SENSATION LABORATORY EXERCISES (ISLE)

Experience chapter concepts at edge.sagepub.com/schwartz

Sharpen your skills with SAGE edge at edge.sagepub.com/schwartz

SAGE edge for students provides a personalized approach to help you accomplish your coursework goals in an easy-to-use learning environment.

© J. Daugherty 92

Olfaction and Taste

15

INTRODUCTION

Karen is a guidance counselor and a swim coach at a local high school. She was a competitive swimmer herself and still likes to get into the pool and demonstrate good form to her athletes. She's happily married to a science teacher and track coach, and they have a 14-year-old daughter who excels at playing the flute. Karen and her family are certainly a successful family, happy and secure. However, Karen suffers from migraines. Migraines are terrible headaches that bring pain, nausea, and discomfort and can incapacitate someone for days. Migraines can be triggered by stress, changes in weather patterns, pollution, and, critically here, some odors. Karen seldom gets migraines anymore, as she has been able to remove most of the triggers from her daily life. However, when her husband and daughter took her out to dinner for her 50th birthday, a perfume being worn by a woman at a nearby table triggered a migraine, ruining her 50th birthday party. We can wonder why certain odors, particularly fragrant perfumes, induce migraines in some, whereas for others, the smell is pleasant enough to swath one's body in. Perfume-induced migraines have become such a problem for some people that they have attempted to use the Americans With Disabilities Act to prevent coworkers from wearing strong, migraine-inducing perfumes (Oltman, 2009).

In contrast, think of the smell of one of your favorite foods or drinks—the aroma of coffee, the flavor of chocolate melting in your mouth, the smell of bananas wafting off a frying pan. In contrast to Karen, you might also find some perfumes to be very pleasing. Think of the perfume your girlfriend wears or the cologne your boyfriend wears. Even mentioning these odors and flavors in a textbook may induce some of you to take a break from reading and head to the kitchen for a snack. Indeed, odors may induce cravings for particular foods (Herz, 2007). Cravings may often seemingly force people to desperately search for an open pizzeria, regardless of the time of day. And for many of us, nothing is more pleasurable than eating our favorite foods.

In this chapter, we examine the sensory apparatus underlying our senses of **olfaction** (smell) and **gustation** (taste), how they interact, and what functions they serve. We also discuss the trigeminal nerve system, which is important to both smell and taste and also receives input from the somatosensory system.

Together olfaction and gustation are considered chemical senses because their role is to detect chemicals in the environment. Olfaction brings to our attention airborne chemicals, whereas gustation alerts us to the chemical compositions of substances brought into our mouths. Similar to vision and audition, olfaction is a distal sense, detecting objects that may be some distance from a person. However, gustation is similar to the somatosensory systems, in that the taste must be

LEARNING OBJECTIVES

15.1 Examine the role of the olfactory system in detecting harmful and helpful substances.

15.2 Describe the anatomical and physiological basis for olfaction.

15.3 Describe the nature of olfactory perception, olfactory imagery, and olfactory illusions.

15.4 Explain the anatomical and physiological basis for taste perception.

Olfaction: the sense of smell

Gustation: the sense of taste

in direct contact with the taste receptors in the mouth for gustation to detect it. Thus, when we encounter coffee, our olfaction system detects the chemicals emanating from the beverage before we ingest it, and our sense of taste samples it as it passes through our mouth. The chemical senses may be the oldest senses in an evolutionary framework. Many unicellular organisms have evolved to detect chemicals, either food or toxins, in their environment.

OLFACTION

15.1 Examine the role of the olfactory system in detecting harmful and helpful substances.

Olfaction refers to our ability to detect odors. **Odors** are the perceptual experiences that derive from the detection of **odorants**, which are airborne chemical molecules. Odorants are volatile chemicals; that is, in order to be smelled, an odorant must be able to float through the air and thus pass into our nose. Odorants must be repellant to water and relatively small molecules in order to be detected by our olfactory systems. In this way, our sense of smell is an early warning system, allowing us to detect potentially harmful or helpful substances before we come into direct contact with them.

Our olfactory system does not respond to all airborne chemicals. Think of carbon monoxide, a toxic chemical produced by car engines. We cannot smell this odor, so we are unaware of the buildup of carbon monoxide. This is why sitting in a car in the garage with its engine running is dangerous. The engine produces carbon monoxide, which cannot escape because of the enclosed condition. Because we do not smell the carbon monoxide, it can build up to lethal levels without any warning. Natural gas is also odorless. But when it is used to heat homes, a chemical is added to give it a strong, unpleasant odor. Why would you want to make something smell bad? Well, a natural gas leak can be dangerous, but if the gas is odorless, it will not be detected. With the additive, a leak will smell like rotten eggs, something that surely gets a person's attention. Other unpleasant odors allow us to avoid dangerous situations. Rotting meat may contain toxic bacteria that can make us very sick. Thus, we evolved to find this smell putrid and unpleasant. In some cases, however, cultures may find ways to treat rotting meat to avoid sickness, in which case people learn to appreciate the smell rather than be repulsed by it (Herz, 2007).

Many plants and animals emit molecules into the air, some of which are intended to be detected by themselves, other members of their own species, or other species (see Figure 15.1). Many animals emit pheromones, which may indicate their mating status to other members of their species. In other cases, animals may use odorants to mark their territory. Furthermore, in some cases, plants and animals may deliberately produce odorants for self-defense. Think of the characteristic odor of skunks. Skunks deliberately produce these odorants to deter predators, which are repelled by skunks' smell (see Figure 15.1).

Odors: the perceptual experience of odorants, which are airborne chemical stimuli

Odorants: molecules our olfactory system responds to when we detect them in the air

TEST YOUR KNOWLEDGE

What is the difference between an odor and an odorant? How might animals use the to communicate with other members of their species or other species?

■ FIGURE 15.1   Odors.

Examine these photographs. Each is associated with a characteristic odor. Consider each object and think about the odor of that object. Is it pleasant or unpleasant? Is it weak or strong?

THE ANATOMY AND PHYSIOLOGY OF THE OLFACTORY SYSTEM

15.2   Describe the anatomical and physiological basis for olfaction.

The Nose

We have two nostrils in our nose, which serve as the entranceway into the nasal cavities. The nostrils are separated by a wall of cartilage called the **nasal septum**. Damage to the nose, such as from a punch or a hard fall, can cause a deviated septum, in which the wall of cartilage is no longer straight. A deviated septum can interfere with both proper breathing and the sense of smell. The nasal septum may also be punctured or perforated. For example, chronic cocaine use can cause holes to form in the septum, which can also interfere with breathing and olfaction. In human beings, the two nasal cavities are extremely close to each other, so they are essentially sampling the same air. Thus, there is no real analogy to the binocular vision our two eyes can achieve or the ability of our auditory system to integrate across ears, such as in sound localization.

Inside the nasal cavity, turbinates serve to disperse air. **Turbinates** are bony knots of tissue. Turbinates ensure that some air will be passed upward through a

Nasal septum: the wall of cartilage that separates the nostrils

Turbinates: bony knots of tissue that serve to disperse air within the nasal cavity

space called the **olfactory cleft** and land on an area of tissue called the **olfactory epithelium**. **Olfactory receptor neurons** are located inside the olfactory epithelium, and these neurons serve as the transducers of the olfactory system. The olfactory receptor neurons are pretty far up into the nasal cavity; indeed, they are just a couple of centimeters behind each eye. The air passes through the cleft and then rejoins the air being sent through the pharynx toward the lungs. Odorants from food find their way to the olfactory epithelium through a passage in the oral cavity in the back of the mouth. This is illustrated in Figure 15.2.

The olfactory epithelium serves as the organ of transduction, taking chemical stimulation and transforming it into a neural signal. There is an olfactory epithelium at the top of each nostril, measuring about 1 to 2 cm². In addition to the olfactory receptor neurons, the olfactory epithelium contains supporting cells and basal cells. **Supporting cells** provide metabolic supplies to the olfactory receptor neurons. **Basal cells** create olfactory receptor neurons. Interestingly, olfactory receptor neurons die out after about a month, so basal cells are continually resupplying the olfactory epithelium with olfactory receptor neurons. It is estimated that olfactory receptor neurons are completely regenerated every 28 days. The anatomy of the olfactory epithelium is shown in Figure 15.3.

■ FIGURE 15.2   **Gross anatomy (no pun intended) of the human nose.**

Odorants enter the nasal cavity and make their way up to the olfactory epithelium. The turbinates, which are bones covered with epithelial tissue, keep the air circulating up toward the olfactory epithelium.

Olfactory cleft: the channel at the back of the nasal cavity that funnels air up toward the olfactory epithelium

Olfactory epithelium: a mucous membrane inside each nostril of the nose that contains the receptor cells for the olfactory system

Olfactory receptor neurons: receptor cells located in the olfactory epithelium that detect specific chemicals in the air and transduce them into a neural signal

Supporting cells: cells that provide metabolic supplies to the olfactory receptor neurons

Basal cells: cells that create olfactory receptor neurons

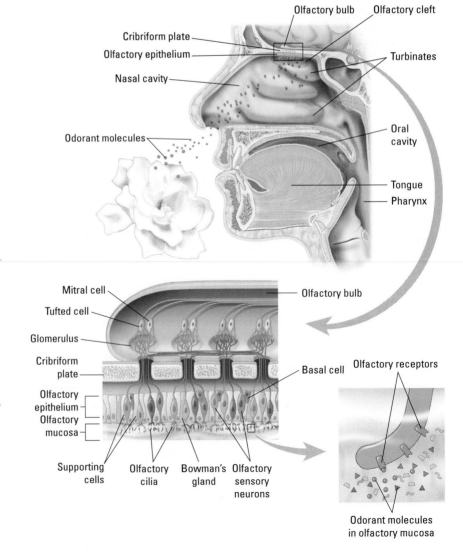

(a)

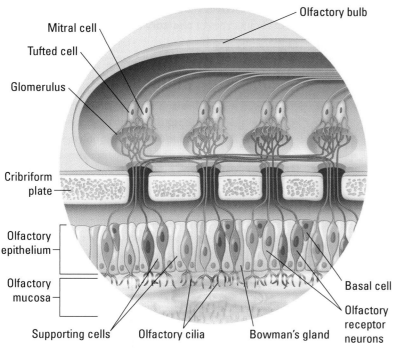

Olfactory bulb

Mitral cell

Tufted cell

Glomerulus

Cribriform plate

Olfactory epithelium

Olfactory mucosa

Supporting cells   Olfactory cilia   Bowman's gland

Basal cell

Olfactory receptor neurons

(b)

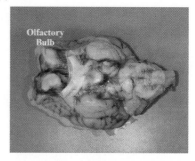

■ **FIGURE 15.3**   **The anatomy of the olfactory epithelium.**

(a) The olfactory receptor neurons are located beneath the mucous layer of the epithelium. The olfactory epithelium houses three types of cells, olfactory receptor neurons, basal cells, and supporting cells. The olfactory receptor neurons are found beneath the olfactory epithelium. (b) The location of the olfactory bulbs on the bottom of the sheep brain. They are much larger in sheep than human brains but lie in very similar locations in the brain. Use your anaglyph glasses to view this image.

The olfactory receptor neurons have cilia extending into the mucus covering of the olfactory epithelium. These cilia contain the transducing elements of the cell on their tips. As a particular molecule of a particular odorant comes into contact with the tip of the cilium of the olfactory receptor neuron, a chain of chemical events is initiated, ending with an action potential leaving the olfactory receptor neuron along an axon heading toward the olfactory bulb. That is, the chemical triggers the cilia, causing a neural signal to begin. As few as seven molecules of the same odorant can trigger an action potential in an olfactory receptor neuron.

There are approximately 20 million olfactory receptor neurons in the human nose. Although this is more sensory neurons than for any other human sensory modality, it is much fewer olfactory receptor neurons than seen in other species. Dogs, such as bloodhounds and Basset hounds, have as many as 10 times more olfactory receptor neurons than we do. Grizzly bears may even have more olfactory receptor neurons than dogs. Pigs also have large concentrations of olfactory receptor neurons. The density of the olfactory receptor neurons in these species gives these animals enormously sensitive senses of smell. Grizzly bears can detect the aroma of meat from nearly 20 miles away (see Figure 15.4). Bloodhounds can detect the presence of a specific animal even if it passed by a location several days earlier. Pigs are trained to detect truffles buried underground and are still better than mechanical detectors. Species, such as pigs, bears, and dogs, that depend heavily on smell are called **macrosmatic**. Humans, who are more dependent on vision and audition, are considered **microsmatic**, regardless of the importance of olfaction. You can see some illustrations of different animals' brains and the space devoted to olfaction on ISLE 15.1.

It is estimated that humans have about 350 different kinds of olfactory receptor neurons. Each kind of olfactory receptor neuron responds to a relatively small class of odorants. When we compare the olfactory system with the visual system, we find that the 350 types of olfactory receptor neurons roughly correspond to the three cones and one rod in the visual system. Thus, the function of identifying

ISLE 15.1 Brain Area for Olfactory Bulbs

Macrosmatic: species that are heavily dependent on their olfactory system

Microsmatic: species that are less dependent on their olfactory system

■ FIGURE 15.4   Grizzly bear.

Grizzly bears have tremendously sensitive senses of smell.

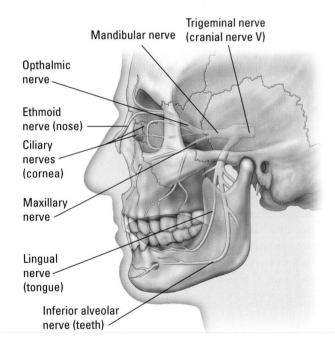

■ FIGURE 15.5   The anatomy of the trigeminal nerve.

The trigeminal nerve carries information from somatosensory receptors in the nose to the thalamus. The experience of "heat" when eating chili peppers is caused by activation of the trigeminal nerve.

Trigeminal nerve: a nerve that is associated with the feel of odorants; also known as the fifth cranial nerve

Cribriform plate: a perforated section of skull bone that separates the nose from the brain; axons from olfactory receptor neurons pass through to allow olfactory information to enter regions in the brain

smells is a very different process than how we identify color. Macrosmatic species may have as many as 1,000 different types of olfactory receptor neurons.

Genes and Olfaction

In 2004, neuroscientists Linda Buck and Richard Axel received a Nobel Prize for their groundbreaking work on the genetics of transduction of olfactory receptor neurons. In 1991, Buck and Axel published an important paper that described their discovery of a collection of genes that regulate the expression of different olfactory receptor neurons (Buck & Axel, 1991). They described a family of about 1,000 genes across mammalian species that are involved in genetic coding for olfactory transduction. However, in human beings, the majority of these genes are inactive. Indeed, it is estimated that only about 350 of these genes actually code for olfactory reception in humans (Malnic, Godfrey, & Buck, 2004). In other species, such as the macrosmatic species (e.g., dogs, bears) just described, far fewer of these genes will be inactive. In humans, the number of active genes is a predictor of individual differences in olfaction. Research suggests that when a person has more copies of a particular gene active, he or she may be more sensitive to the odorant that the gene maps onto. Moreover, if a gene is absent that allows people to detect a pleasant odor, foods with that odor may not be as appealing to those in whom the gene is not expressed relative to those in whom it is (Menashe, Man, Lancet, & Gilad, 2003). Thus, for example, if you lack a gene that codes for lavender, you may not like certain perfumes.

The Trigeminal Nerve

Many odorants also have a second sensory component to them, which often may be described as a feeling. Some odors burn, whereas others soothe. Indeed, odorants such as ammonia (burning) and menthol (cooling) also cause reactions in the somatosensory system. This aspect of olfaction is mediated by the **trigeminal nerve**, which transmits information about the feel of an odorant (see Figure 15.5). Trigeminal stimulation accounts for a number of the experiences associated with eating food as well. For example, the burning sensation of chili peppers is the result of trigeminal stimulation. It is also trigeminal stimulation that induces tears when we eat or cut fresh onions.

The Pathway to the Brain

The olfactory receptor neurons project axons through little holes in the base of the skull called the **cribriform plate**, a bone of the skull that separates the nose from the brain. Because of its location and its perforated surface, the cribriform plate is susceptible to injury when the head receives a hard blow. Even a human punch can cause the cribriform plate to become fractured. When it is fractured, it may sever the axons coming from the olfactory receptor neurons, causing impairment to the sense of smell. In some cases, anosmia may develop. **Anosmia (or smell blindness)** is the inability to smell, usually caused by cribriform plate damage. Despite the regeneration of olfactory receptor neurons, a fractured cribriform plate may scar over, preventing the new neurons from projecting through it to the brain. Figure 15.6 shows the passage of axons from the olfactory receptor neurons to the first areas of olfactory processing in the brain. Sinus infection may also cause anosmia, either temporarily or permanently. We return later, in the "In Depth" section of this chapter, to the causes and consequences of anosmia.

The axons of the olfactory receptor neurons converge to form the olfactory nerve, which exits through the cribriform plate. The **olfactory nerve** (also known as the **first cranial nerve**) consists of the axons of the olfactory receptor neurons that leave the nose and enter the olfactory bulb. The **olfactory bulb** is a part of the brain just behind the nose. It is the first place in the brain where olfactory information is processed. Once inside the olfactory bulb, the axons from the olfactory receptor neurons enter and synapse with dendrites in spherical structures called **glomeruli**. There are two types of dendrites in the glomeruli. One of the dendrites is from **mitral cells**, whereas the other is from **tufted cells**. These two types of cells form the **olfactory tract**, which projects olfactory information from the olfactory bulb to other regions of the brain.

The olfactory bulb is one of the most forward parts of the human brain. It is found in humans just above the nose and just behind the eyes. It is also a primitive part of the brain, in the sense that our olfactory bulbs do not differ greatly from other mammalian olfactory bulbs. The beginning of olfactory processing occurs in the glomeruli. The cells in the glomeruli form an odorant map, organizing similarly structured odorants together. This means that odorants from chemicals with similar structures are processed adjacent to one another. This map is analogous to frequency coding in the auditory cortex or spatial mapping in the visual brain. It is worth noting here that odorants with similar chemical structures may not have similar subjective odors. Nonetheless, processing in the olfactory bulb is organized by chemical structure. Information passes from the glomeruli to the mitral and tufted cells, which then project to structures beyond the olfactory bulb.

The axons of the mitral cells and the tufted cells project further into the brain and synapse in a variety of locations in the brain. Chief among these projections are connections to the **amygdala** (an emotion area), the **entorhinal cortex** of the temporal lobe (a memory area), and the **piriform cortex**, also in the temporal lobe (see Figure 15.7). Of particular interest is the piriform cortex, which is often considered the primary olfactory cortex. The piriform cortex is devoted exclusively to olfaction, but the entorhinal cortex is an important memory area of the brain, and the amygdala is an important emotion area of the brain.

The fact that the olfactory bulb directly projects to these areas is critical in two aspects of olfaction—its association with memory and its association with

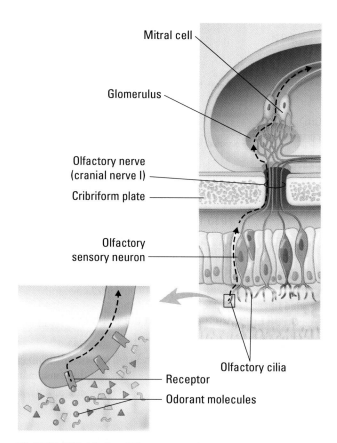

■ FIGURE 15.6   **Olfactory pathway.**

The pathway of odors from the olfactory receptor neurons to the brain.

Anosmia (smell blindness): the inability to smell, usually caused by cribriform plate damage

Olfactory nerve (first cranial nerve): the axons of the olfactory receptor neurons that leave the nose and enter the olfactory bulb

Olfactory bulb: a part of the brain just behind the nose; it is the first place in the brain where olfactory information is processed

Glomeruli: spherical structures within the olfactory bulb where the olfactory tract forms synapses with mitral cells and tufted cells

Mitral cells: neurons that start in the glomeruli of the olfactory bulb and project to other areas of the brain

Tufted cells: neurons that start in the glomeruli of the olfactory bulb and project to other areas of the brain

Olfactory tract: the pathway leading from the olfactory bulb to other regions of the brain

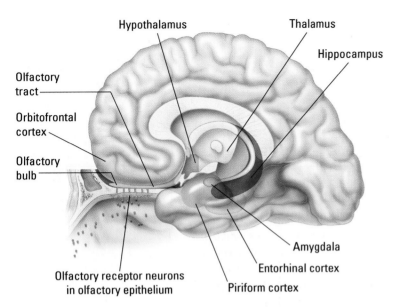

Hypothalamus

Thalamus

Hippocampus

Olfactory
tract

Orbitofrontal
cortex

Olfactory
bulb

Olfactory receptor neurons
in olfactory epithelium

Amygdala

Entorhinal cortex

Piriform cortex

■ **FIGURE 15.7** **The areas of the brain receiving input from the olfactory bulb.**

The olfactory bulb is located just behind the nose itself. It sends information to the piriform cortex, located in the temporal lobe, the entorhinal cortex, and the amygdala. The piriform cortex projects to the orbitofrontal cortex.

emotion. The direct connection between the olfactory bulb and the entorhinal cortex is likely why a particular odor can elicit an involuntary autobiographical memory so quickly. The entorhinal cortex is deeply connected to the hippocampus, also a known memory area of the brain. Many people will report that a particular smell will evoke strong memories, often of childhood, with striking regularity. For example, the smell of naphthalene (or mothballs) always reminds one of your authors of his grandmother's apartment from when he was a child.

Moreover, the direct connection between the olfactory bulb and the amygdala is most likely pivotal in the rapid negative associations that occur when we smell an odor in a negative situation. Even in microsmatic humans, one up-close interaction with an angry skunk will leave you disliking the musk of skunk for life. Similarly, one very positive experience with a particular perfume or cologne, and you may find that odor pleasant for life as well. The amygdala projects directly to the hypothalamus, which is critical in the regulation of activities such as hunger, thirst, and sexual desire.

Amygdala: an area of the brain in the limbic system, associated with the experience of emotion, particularly fear

Entorhinal cortex: an area in the medial temporal lobe, associated with a number of memory functions

Piriform cortex: an area in the anterior region of the temporal lobe that receives input from the olfactory bulb and is involved in olfactory processing; often considered the primary olfactory cortex

Anterior piriform cortex: a structure located in the front portion of the piriform cortex that is associated with representing the chemical structures of odorants

Posterior piriform cortex: a structure located in the back portion of the piriform cortex that is associated with an odor's quality, regardless of its chemical composition

Representation Within the Piriform Cortex

The piriform cortex is found in the temporal lobe. It is adjacent to areas of the brain known as the limbic system, which are critical in such functions as emotion and memory. The piriform cortex has two main anatomical subdivisions, the anterior piriform cortex and the posterior piriform cortex (Kadohisa & Wilson, 2006). As the names suggest, the anterior piriform cortex is located in the front portion of the piriform cortex, and the posterior piriform cortex is located in the back portion of the piriform cortex. The **anterior piriform cortex** is associated with representing the chemical structures of odorants. That is, like the olfactory bulb, the anterior piriform cortex creates a map of odorants organized by their chemical structure. Moreover, neurons within the anterior region are narrowly tuned, responding to a very small range of odorant molecules and not others. In contrast, the **posterior piriform cortex** is associated with an odor's quality, regardless of its chemical composition. That is, the posterior piriform cortex groups together odors that smell similar to us, regardless of chemical origin. You can see the location of the piriform cortex in Figure 15.7. You can see an interesting simulation of the posterior piriform on ISLE 15.2.

The posterior piriform cortex represents the subjective qualities of odors rather than their chemical compositions. In the posterior piriform cortex, neurons are grouped by subjective similarities between odors. For example, odors that smell "smoky" are grouped together, regardless of the types of molecules that elicit them. Moreover, chemicals that are similar in their molecular structures may be represented in different areas of the posterior piriform cortex if they elicit different olfactory experiences. In this way, the posterior piriform cortex serves a similar function to the extrastriate cortex in vision, processing the identities of odorants in the environment, just as areas such as V2 and V4 process the identity of visual stimuli.

An interesting study by Howard, Plailly, Grueschow, Haynes, and Gottfried (2009) neatly illustrates the difference between the anterior piriform cortex and the posterior piriform cortex. Howard et al. recorded brain activity via functional magnetic resonance imaging while participants were sampling three different odor categories (minty, woody, and citrus). The odors within each category (e.g., minty) were subjectively similar but had different chemical structures. The pattern of brain activity showed that the posterior piriform cortex was similarly activated for odors that were subjectively similar, that is, they all smelled minty. However, when looking at other regions of the brain responding to odors, such as the anterior piriform cortex, this pattern was not seen. Therefore, Howard et al. concluded that the posterior piriform cortex must be involved in identifying the qualities of odorants.

The Orbitofrontal Cortex

Another important region of the brain that has an olfactory function is the **orbitofrontal cortex**, particularly the right orbitofrontal cortex. This area receives projections from both the piriform cortex and the limbic system. It is thought that this area of the brain is critical in establishing the emotional nature of odors. Odors are also fundamentally an emotional and affective experience (Herz, Eliassen, Beland, & Souza, 2004). Certain odors (e.g., coffee, chocolate, certain perfumes) may elicit very positive emotions, whereas others (e.g., skunk, rotting garbage, excrement) may elicit very negative emotions. Thus, the affective values of odors are important, as positive odors elicit approach and negative odors afford distancing. Much of this cognition appears to be occurring in the orbitofrontal cortex. The orbitofrontal cortex is located just behind and above our eyes, in the very most frontal part of the frontal cortex. This area of the cortex appears to be critical in integrating olfaction and taste perception of foods, allowing us to enjoy some foods and reject others. The right orbitofrontal cortex is critical to the actual experience of an odor, that is, the "feeling" we get when we smell an odor, or what philosophers call its qualia (Li, Lopez, Osher, & Howard, 2010).

> **TEST YOUR KNOWLEDGE**
>
> What is the trigeminal nerve? How does it bridge the gap between olfaction and the somatosensory system?

OLFACTORY PERCEPTION

 15.3 Describe the nature of olfactory perception, olfactory imagery, and olfactory illusions.

Detection

We reviewed the physiology of olfaction in the last section. Now we cover olfactory psychophysics. Here, the questions concern exactly what our sense of smell can do. In detection, we want to know how much of an odorant must be in the air for people to detect that odorant. It turns out that the answer to this question depends on what the molecule is. Some odors can be detected in much smaller quantities than others. Of course, as concentrations of a particular odorant increase, so will the likelihood of detection. Thus, just as the amount of light necessary to see depends on which wavelength of light is available, different odorants require different concentrations for olfactory detection. So, although our

Orbitofrontal cortex: a part of the prefrontal cortex that appears to be critical in the emotional experience of odors and integrating olfaction and taste perception, among other functions

■ FIGURE 15.8   Vanilla ice cream.

The extract known as vanillin that creates the vanilla smell and taste is an odorant we are very sensitive to.

■ FIGURE 15.9   Would you recognize the aromas of these dishes?

detection varies greatly from odor to odor, we can still make some generalizations about odor detection.

The amount of odorant in the environment is typically measured as a function of the number of molecules of that odorant per 1 million molecules of air. This is known as parts per million, or ppm for short. If you recall from Chapter 2, thresholds will vary depending on a number of characteristics. However, averaging over these characteristics, we can discuss the mean ppm required to detect a particular odor. To refresh the concept, an absolute threshold is the minimum amount of stimulus intensity required to elicit a perception of that stimulus. Different odorants require different concentrations to be detected. For example, we are extremely sensitive to the sweet smell of vanilla; it requires only 0.000035 ppm to detect vanilla (see Figure 15.8). However, the smell of acetone, which many of us know as nail polish remover, requires 15 ppm to detect (Devos, Patte, Rouault, Laffort, & Van Gemert, 1990). We can also look at the JND (just noticeable difference) for any particular odorant, that is, how much more odor we must add to the air for us to detect a stronger concentration of that odor. This will also vary among odors.

Identifying Odors

Imagine the following scenario. You arrive at a friend's house and smell a beautiful aroma of something cooking in the kitchen. It smells wonderful, and you are sure you know the aroma, but you cannot name it. What is that smell? It is familiar to you, but you cannot put a name to it. This altogether common phenomenon has been called the **tip-of-the-nose phenomenon** (Jönsson & Olsson, 2012; Jönsson & Stevenson, 2014), and it occurs when a person is familiar with an odor but cannot recall its name, despite feeling as if he or she can. If your host tells you that she is cooking a curry, you instantly recognize the aroma as being that of curry and wonder why you did not identify the aroma yourself in the first place (see Figure 15.9). You can even try this out with friends. Open up spice bottles for them and see if they can name the spices by sniffing. You will be amazed at how few smells they will be able to name. But if you give them multiple choices, they will be very accurate (Jönsson & Olsson, 2012; Jönsson & Stevenson, 2014).

As we have discussed, there is an intimate connection between olfaction and emotion. Odors elicit emotions, both positive and negative. There is also a close connection between olfaction and memory—some odors elicit very specific memories. However, there seems to be a disconnect between olfaction and language, rendering it difficult to identify the names of certain odors, especially when these odorants are encountered in an unusual context (Cain, 1979; Herz, 2007).

Research shows that when people are given odors to sniff in a lab, they are very poor at naming these odors. Indeed, in most experiments, most participants seldom approach naming even half of the odors (Jönsson & Olsson, 2012). However, this does not mean the odors are not familiar and known to the

Tip-of-the-nose phenomenon: a phenomenon that occurs when a person is familiar with an odor but cannot recall its name, despite feeling as if he or she can

participants—the problem is in labeling them. This point is easy to demonstrate by giving participants a recognition test in which they must identify the correct name of an odor from among a list of alternatives. Under these circumstances, odor identification increases tremendously. In one study, de Wijk and Cain (1994) found that young adults' odor naming was just about 40% correct, but performance increased to above 80% correct when the participants were permitted to choose from a list of possible names.

Discrimination in psychophysics means distinguishing between two stimuli. In most psychophysics experiments, the two stimuli to be discriminated will be closely related in frequency or some other variable. We are good at discriminating odors even when we cannot name them. It is estimated that we can distinguish more than a thousand different aromas, and that professionals (e.g., wine tasters and perfumists) can discriminate as many as 100,000 different odors (Herz, 2007). There is some debate as to the advantages experts have in the sense domain, but the ability to discriminate is clearly demonstrable. Research shows that experts are better able to identify odors by name and identify subcomponents within an odor. However, whether wine experts can reliably predict which wines are of higher quality has been an issue of some debate, often showing results quite embarrassing to those experts.

Odor Imagery

A fascinating question in olfaction is why so few people are able to experience olfactory imagery. By olfactory imagery, we mean the ability to experience the "smell" of a particular odor when that odor is not physically present. Imagery is different from hallucination because the person generates the imagery himself or herself and knows that the image is present only internally. In the visual domain and the auditory domain, it is easy to experience a sensory experience known to be not actually present. Just sitting there reading this text, you can image what a Sicilian pizza looks like, and without so much as moving your lips or vibrating your vocal chords, you can imagine your favorite song. But try coming up with an olfactory image of the smell of that pizza or what your significant other's perfume smells like. Most people report being unable to experience olfactory images (Djordjevic et al., 2008). Thus, unlike the senses of vision and audition, olfactory imagery is difficult for most of us. However, there is some research that supports the idea that some people are able to make olfactory images. One study showed that people who reported olfactory imagery showed brain activity in the piriform cortex when engaged in olfactory imagery. Control participants asked to make olfactory images did not show this activity (Djordjevic, Zatorre, Petrides, Boyle, & Jones-Gotman, 2005).

Olfactory Illusions

Our chapters on vision and audition abound with the concept of illusions. Illusions are situations in which what we perceive is not what is physically present. For example, after staring at a waterfall, we see the world moving in the opposite direction, even though we know this is not so. We hear scales continually becoming higher pitched even though the frequencies do not get higher. Olfactory illusions exist, though unlike visual and auditory illusions, we are seldom conscious of the dissociation of stimulus and perception (Stevenson, 2011). Because we are seldom aware of these olfactory illusions, they get less attention than visual and auditory illusions. Nonetheless, we consider a few olfactory illusions here.

There are a number of illusions that arise from context effects. That is, the olfactory environment that surrounds a particular odorant changes the way that odorant is perceived. Lawless (1991), for example, used the odorant chemical called dihydromyrcenol. When this chemical is surrounded by woody-smelling odors, it is perceived as smelling like citrus. However, when it is surrounded by citrus smells, it is perceived as being woody in character. This is like some of the center-surround illusions in vision, in which the border of an image influences the perception of lightness or color of the image inside that border. In Lawless's illusion, the surrounding odor influences the perception of a target odor. In a number of other cases, surrounding odors can affect the perception of a target odor (Stevenson, 2011).

Verbal labeling can also cause olfactory illusions. In particular, the label for a perceived odor will often affect whether the odor elicits a positive or negative emotion. Imagine being presented with an odor and being told it was "aged parmesan cheese." It is likely that your reaction might be positive. But if you were told the same odor was "vomit," you might have a very different reaction. Indeed, in this case, the two substances have odorants in common, so it is likely in this case that you would be influenced by the verbal label. This was put to the empirical test by Herz and von Clef (2001), who presented odors with both a positive label and a negative label, but examined the influence of which label was presented first. In this case, participants read both the positive and negative labels, but Herz and von Clef reasoned that the first label would have a bigger impact on emotional reaction to the odor. For example, the odor of pine trees was presented with either the label "Christmas tree" first or the label "toilet cleaner" first. The independent variable was which label occurred first. Herz and von Clef found an outsized role for the first label. If the "Christmas tree" label was given first, the odor was rated more positively than if the "toilet cleaner" label was given first. Thus, the same odor with the same labels received a different pleasantness judgment depending on the order of the labeling. For this reason, Stevenson (2011) classified this effect as an olfactory illusion.

Other sensory modalities can also influence the perception of odor. For example, Engen (1972) showed participants colored or noncolored liquids. Participants were more likely to report smelling something in the colored liquids even when there were no odorants present in the liquids. In effect, the visual perception of a colored liquid induced an olfactory illusion of an odor even though the liquid had no odorants in it. Certainly, this is as much an illusion as any visual illusion.

The final olfactory illusion we consider is olfactory rivalry (Stevenson & Mahmut, 2013). Olfactory rivalry is analogous to binocular rivalry, the illusion created by presenting one image to the left eye and a very different image to the right eye. In vision, we see only one of the images at any one time, but the perception of which image it is may vary seemingly randomly across time. In olfactory rivalry, one odorant is presented to one nostril, and a different odor is presented to the other nostril. For example, the left nostril might receive the smell of roses (phenylethyl alcohol), whereas the right nostril might receive the smell of "permanent markers" (butanol). Using this procedure, Zhou and Chen (2009) found an analog to binocular rivalry. There was a seeming randomized likelihood that people would smell the roses or the markers. People reported smelling one and then the other, but not both at the same time. As with binocular rivalry, the perception of odor would switch over time from one to the other, also in a seemingly random fashion. Stevenson and Mahmut showed that this illusion can occur even when both nostrils are receiving both odors.

TEST YOUR KNOWLEDGE

What is the tip-of-the-nose phenomenon? What does it tell us about the relation of olfaction to other functions in the brain?

TASTE PERCEPTION

15.4 Explain the anatomical and physiological basis for taste perception.

M.F.K. Fisher wrote a number of books about both cooking and eating throughout her illustrious career as a writer. Born in Michigan, Fisher lived in France and California and wrote some of the most delectable writing about eating. Cunning and clever, her essays were equally about food and life. Even a passage about cauliflower from more than 70 years ago may still stop your reading in your tracks and send you off to the kitchen. She wrote, "There in Dijon, the cauliflowers were very small and succulent, grown in that ancient soil. I separated the flowerlets and dropped them in boiling water for just a few minutes. Then I drained them and put them in a wide shallow casserole, and covered them with heavy cream, and a thick sprinkling of freshly grated Gruyere, the nice rubbery kind that didn't come from Switzerland at all, but from the Jura. It was called râpé in the market, and was grated while you watched, in a soft cloudy pile, onto your piece of paper" (Fisher, 1943). Most people eat cauliflower only because it is healthy, but that description may cause you to look up a recipe for a cauliflower casserole. See Figure 15.10.

What we can see in Fisher is the eloquent way in which she expresses the pleasure and joy food brings to us. Pick your favorite food—a slice of pepperoni pizza, poutine, sushi, Belgian chocolate, hot and sour soup, chana masala, or a breakfast omelet loaded with cheese and mushrooms—many foods bring us distinct joy.

In this section, we discuss both the anatomy of the receptors that transduce chemicals in the mouth into taste sensations and the neural circuitry in the brain responsible for the sense of taste. We also discuss the term *flavor* (a technical term here) that is used to describe the combination of taste and olfactory sensations into a combined perception, which is often what we are appreciating when enjoying good food.

Like the sense of smell, the sense of taste is a chemical detection system that probably evolved to help us sort edible foodstuffs from toxins. We want to bring into our bodies only foods that are not toxic. So we have evolved to enjoy foods that bring nourishment and reject foods that do not. Our tongues therefore serve as both a gateway to nutrition and to warn us of toxic chemicals. And that food brings us pleasure reinforces the need to eat and supply our body with nutrition.

There are basic similarities between the two chemical senses of olfaction and gustation (taste). Both respond to molecules, but for the sense of taste, we respond to molecules called **tastants**, which dissolve when in contact with our saliva. Like odorants, tastants initiate a transduction response in the receptors in our tongues. **Tastes** therefore are the perception of the transduction of tastants along the surface of the tongue. There are also taste buds in other areas of the mouth that detect taste. However, what we typically crave when we think of our favorite food is its flavor. **Flavor** refers to the combined sensory experience of a food, which combines its taste, its odor, and its effect on the trigeminal nerve. If we think of the flavor of coffee, the smell of coffee is more instrumental to the flavor of this beverage than is its taste. If we think of the flavor of pizza, the smell of that pizza

■ **FIGURE 15.10** **Cauliflower casserole.**

© iStockphoto.com/Elena_Danileiko

Tastants: molecules recognized by taste receptors that induce responses in taste receptors on the tongue

Taste: the perception of the transduction of tastants along the surface of the tongue

Flavor: the total perceptual experience that occurs during eating, which combines taste and olfaction, but also somatosensory experience and visual experience

slice is as critical to flavor as is its taste. Tastes can be broken down into five basic tastes, which correspond to specific receptors along the surface of the tongue. The basic tastes are sweet, salty, sour, bitter, and umami (savory).

Sweet, salty, and umami tastes alert us to foods with needed nutrients. Sweet means sugar and therefore carbohydrates, which we need to survive. Salty foods obviously contain salt, which our bodies require as well, and umami (a Japanese word meaning "savory") is associated with the taste of proteins, which our bodies need to break down into amino acids in order to build our own proteins. In contrast, though we may like sour and bitter foods in small doses, it is likely that sour and bitter tastes evolved as warnings about foods to avoid because they may be inedible or toxic. Young children tend to avoid very sour and bitter foods because of this innate reaction to them. This is why young children invariably reject bitter foods such as broccoli or coffee. Try giving a 3-year-old an endive and kale salad, and you will have a tantrum on your hands. We slowly acquire the pleasure of bitter foods, usually as we combine them with sweet, salty, and savory tastes. We also find that many of the bitter foods others eat do not make us sick after all and thus acquire a taste for them. Even so, an adult eating an endive and kale salad probably puts a dressing on that salad that adds sweetness, saltiness, or umami to it.

Sugars are the tastant molecules that give food its sweet taste. These include sucrose (the sugar commonly used as table sugar), fructose (the sugar found in fruits and used in many processed foods), and glucose (which is used as an energy source in the body). Artificial sweeteners, such as aspartame, are built from amino acids but mimic the actions of sugars along the tongue. The salty taste is elicited by foods that contain the chemical associated with common table salt, sodium chloride (NaCl). The sodium part of salt is necessary for a number of bodily functions, so a desire for salty foods pushes us to seek out and eat salty foods. Sour tastes are caused by acids and may be pleasurable at low concentrations. Many of us like sour foods such as grapefruits and other citrus fruits, pickles, kimchi, and yogurt. Bitter tastes are elicited by a number of different kinds of molecules—usually, bitter tastes arise from plant substances that are used to discourage animals from eating their leaves and other parts of the plants. Some salad greens, such as endive and kale, have a bitter taste because those plants evolved to deter would-be eaters by tasting bad. Ironically, these plants now thrive because humans like their bitter taste.

Umami is now considered a basic taste, though its inclusion in that group is relatively recent (Yasuo, Kusuhara, Yasumatsu, & Ninomiya, 2008). There is evidence that umami receptors exist on the tongue that are anatomically distinct from other receptors. These are activated by amino acids found in foods such as meats and mushrooms, as well as by the chemical MSG (monosodium glutamate). Umami is thought to signal the presence of amino acids, which we need in our diet to synthesize proteins. Traditionally, these amino acids come from meat or dairy products, although many plant foods also contain amino acids. These plant-based amino acids, such as in tomatoes and mushrooms, also trigger umami responses.

Anatomy of the Tongue and Taste Coding

Tastants are detected by receptors, located mostly on the tongue but also on other surfaces within the mouth. Most taste buds are on the tongue, but about 33% of taste buds can be found on the epiglottis, the soft palate, and the upper esophagus. These receptors, then, as we have seen with other sensory systems, transmit a neural signal to the brain, which then interprets the signal and integrates it with

Taste buds: small structures located along the surface of the tongue or mouth that contain the receptor cells

Papillae: small structures that contain the taste buds

other sensory information. So we again start with the anatomy that supports transduction and then follow the neural signal.

The human mouth contains approximately 10,000 taste buds (Bartoshuk, 1971), most of which are found on the tongue (see Figure 15.11). **Taste buds** are small structures located along the surface of the tongue or mouth that contain the receptor cells. Taste buds are found within **papillae**, which line the surface of the tongue and mouth. There are four different kinds of papillae, three of which contain the taste buds. The four different kinds of papillae are referred to as **fungiform papillae, foliate papillae, circumvallate papillae**, and **filiform papillae**. The fungiform papillae are located mostly along the edges and top of the tongue. The foliate papillae are found along the side of the tongue. The circumvallate papillae are found along the very back of the tongue, aligned seemingly along a row. The filiform papillae are found all over the tongue. But rather than taste buds, these papillae contain somatosensory receptors. See Figure 15.12 for the anatomy of the tongue.

Each taste bud contains anywhere from 40 to just more than 100 taste receptor cells, which are elongated neurons with cilia at the end. **Taste receptor cells** are the cells within the taste buds that transduce tastants into a neural signal. As with the olfactory receptors, taste receptor cells die off after about a week and are replaced by new taste receptor cells that develop within the taste bud. Tastants come into contact with the surface of the tongue, where they are felt by the cilia and transduction may occur.

Our tongues contain two kinds of taste receptor cells. One type is simply called receptor cells. **Receptor cells** transduce sweet tastes, umami tastes, and bitter tastes. Anatomically distinct **presynaptic cells** are also receptor cells, but they transduce salty and sour tastes. In receptor cells, the cilia contain receptors that respond to one and only one kind of taste, but unlike earlier conceptions, the different tastes are mixed across the surface of the tongue (Chandrashekar, Hoon, Ryba, & Zuker, 2006). Each presynaptic cell can transduce both salty and sour tastes. Presynaptic cells are connected to cranial nerve fibers, which transmit the signal to the brain. Receptor cells appear to have specific responses they transmit to presynaptic cells, which then transmit the signal to the brain, although this idea is still quite controversial (Yoshida & Ninomiya, 2010).

Information leaves the taste buds through the 7th, 9th, and 10th cranial nerves and heads to the brain. It then synapses in the nucleus of the solitary tract in the medulla and then travels to the ventral posterior medial nucleus of the thalamus before heading to the cortex. The first area of the cortex that receives input from the taste system is the **anterior insular cortex** (part of the area known as the **insula**), located in the frontal lobe. The insular cortex has a variety of functions in addition to taste perception, but it is sometimes called the gustatory cortex for its functions in taste perception. The insular cortex also projects to the orbitofrontal cortex, where taste and olfaction mix to create flavor perception. The orbitofrontal cortex also has a number of other functions, including a role in emotion and emotional control. Figure 15.13 shows an anatomical drawing of the brain's network for taste.

Some interesting work has been done on how taste perception centers in the orbitofrontal cortex. When rats eat food, we can see activity in the anterior insular cortex, regardless of whether the rats are hungry or not. However, in the orbitofrontal cortex, there is activity only when the rats are hungry (Rolls, 2006). Thus, it is thought that the orbitofrontal cortex is largely responsible for the pleasure involved in the eating of food. This is compounded by the fact that the orbitofrontal cortex also responds to a number of other sensory modalities that process the quality of food.

Richard Hutchings / Photo Researchers, Inc.

■ **FIGURE 15.11   An actual human tongue.**

The little bumps are the papillae, which contain the taste buds.

Fungiform papillae: located mostly along the edges and top of the tongue; they respond to all five basic tastes

Foliate papillae: found along the side of the tongue; they respond to all five basic tastes

Circumvallate papillae: found along the very back of the tongue in a virtual row; they respond to all five basic tastes

Filiform papillae: found all over the tongue; contain somatosensory receptors rather than taste buds, so that they feel food rather than taste it

Taste receptor cells: cells within the taste buds that transduce tastants into a neural signal

Receptor cells: taste receptor cells that transduce sweet tastes, umami tastes, and bitter tastes

Presynaptic cells: taste receptor cells that transduce salty and sour tastes

Anterior insular cortex (insula): a part of the frontal lobe that serves as the primary taste cortex

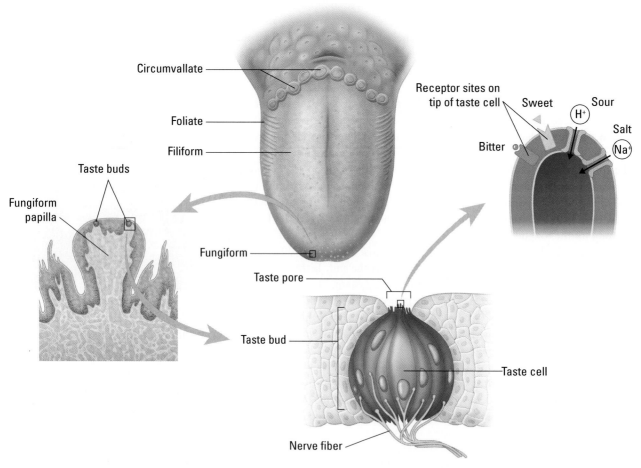

■ FIGURE 15.12   **The anatomy of the tongue.**

The human tongue contains four kinds of papillae, three of which contain taste buds. Circumvallate papillae are located in a line along the back of the tongue. Foliate papillae are located along the sides of the tongue. Fungiform papillae are widely distributed but more concentrated toward the front of the tongue.

Taste and Flavor

We have mentioned throughout this chapter how important the interaction is between our two chemical senses, taste and olfaction. Indeed, the concept of flavor refers to the combination of both of these senses and others as well in determining the basic pleasantness of foods. Thus, we define flavor as the total perceptual experience that occurs during eating, which combines taste and olfaction, but also somatosensory experience and visual experience. For example, think about drinking a cup of hot chocolate. Flavor is composed of olfactory sensations—the smells wafting up to the olfactory epithelium. It is also composed of the response along the tongue, in particular the interesting combination of sweetness and bitterness evoked by chocolate. Also important to flavor is the action of the somatosensory system. In this case, the hotness of the hot chocolate is registered by thermoreceptors in the mouth and thus contributes to flavor as well. If there is a minty taste to your hot chocolate, the trigeminal nerve contributes to flavor as well. Finally, even vision and audition contribute to flavor. The sight of the chocolaty liquid with the marshmallows and cinnamon flakes on top is part of the delight as well. Audition can also contribute to flavor as well. The sound of crunchiness may be an important part of flavor for some foods (though not hot chocolate). We eat potato chips

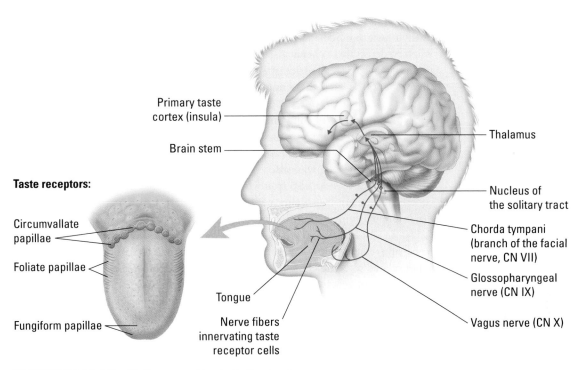

■ FIGURE 15.13   Pathways of taste to the brain.

Information from the tongue is sent through the cranial nerves to the nucleus of the solitary tract, then to the ventral posterior medial nucleus of the thalamus, then to the insula, and from there to the orbitofrontal cortex as well as areas in the limbic system.

because we crave salt, but the crunch they make in our mouth is important to flavor. Much of this integration takes place in the orbitofrontal lobe (see Figure 15.14).

Individual Differences in Taste Perception

As with other sensory modalities, there are individual differences in our ability to taste. We probably notice these differences whenever we eat with friends and family. Some may require more salt to make their food taste the way they want it, and some may drown their food in chili pepper sauce. Some of these individual differences have a genetic basis. Just as most of us have a three-cone visual system, but some of us have a two-cone (or fewer) visual system, genetic differences affect taste perception as well. By far the most widespread of these genetic differences is differences in our ability to taste bitter foods. There is a particular gene, known as *TAS2R38*, that codes for bitter-taste receptors. The *TAS2R38* gene comes in two forms, the PAV form and the AVI form. Most of us have the PAV form, which allows us to

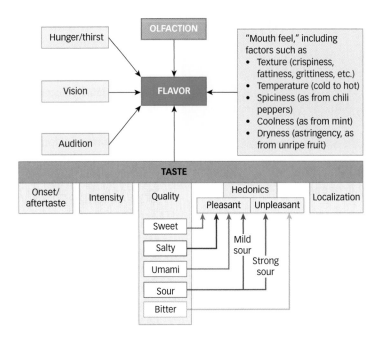

■ FIGURE 15.14   The perception of flavor.

Taste and olfaction, as well as vision, audition, and the somatosensory system, all contribute to our perception of flavor. Sweet, salty, and umami tastes alert us to foods with needed nutrients. Sweet means sugar and therefore carbohydrates, which we need to survive. Salty foods obviously contain salt, which our bodies require, and umami (a Japanese word meaning "savory") is associated with the taste of proteins, which our bodies need to break down into amino acids in order to build our own proteins.

detect bitter tastes, especially those that derive from two chemicals known as phenylthiocarbamide and propylthiouracil. People with the PAV form of the gene who can detect these chemicals are called simply **tasters**. Most of us are just plain tasters. However, a minority of about 25% of people, who have the AVI form of the gene, are referred to as **nontasters** because they require much higher doses of these chemicals in order to detect a bitter taste (Bartoshuk, Duffy, & Miller, 1994). Nontasters will enjoy many bitter foods not because they sense the bitter taste but rather because other tastes are more salient to them.

There is also a class of people known as **supertasters**, who have the PAV form of the gene but who also have more fungiform papillae on their tongues than normal tasters do, also from genetic causes. Because of the genetic origins of supertasters, there is a higher percentage of supertasters among non-European-origin populations. Asians, for example, are more likely to be supertasters than Europeans. In addition, there is a sex difference. Women are more likely than men to be supertasters. However, recent data suggest that fungiform papillae density is not related to being classified as a supertaster (Garneau et al., 2014). Thus, the neural, but not genetic, basis of supertasters is now in some doubt.

Because of their high concentration of fungiform papillae, supertasters are highly sensitive to bitter tastes and usually avoid them, as they find bitter tastes overwhelming. Thus, supertasters tend to avoid bitter beverages, including beer, green tea, and coffee, which contain many bitter compounds. In addition, supertasters may avoid bitter foods, such as Brussels sprouts, kale, cabbage, olives, some soy products, and some citrus fruit, such as grapefruits. Supertasters may also avoid spicy foods because the fungiform papillae are innervated by the nerve fibers that send information about burn and touch sensations on the tongue. Thus, supertasters may also avoid foods containing chili peppers (Delwiche, Buletic, & Breslin, 2001). To summarize, there are individual differences in the detection of tastes, some of which derive from genetic differences among individuals.

Some research shows that these distinctions have health implications. Supertasters avoid some healthy foods because they just taste too bitter. In support of this view, Duffy, Lucchina, and Bartoshuk (2004) found that older supertasters had more colon polyps (a precursor to colon cancer) than did control participants because they avoided vegetables that lower the risk for these colon polyps. However, they also found that because supertasters avoid fatty foods as well, they show lower risk for cardiovascular disease.

■ FIGURE 15.15   **The joys of chili peppers.**

Tasters: people who can detect bitter compounds

Nontasters: people who cannot detect bitter compounds except at very high concentrations

Supertasters: people who are extremely sensitive to bitter tastes; they usually do not like foods with many bitter compounds

The Wonderful World of Chili Peppers

In Chapter 2, we introduced the effect of chili peppers on taste perception as an example of how psychophysics works in the real world. We discussed the Scoville scale and how it measures our perception of capsaicin, the active ingredient in chili peppers that causes them to be experienced as piquant or "spicy hot." In this section, we briefly describe the process by which we taste the capsaicin in chili peppers (see Figure 15.15). Capsaicin content varies in different peppers, from relatively small amounts in a banana pepper to enough to cause a "heat" response in a habanero pepper to the specially bred chili peppers of today with very high capsaicin content, such as the Trinidad Moruga Scorpion. Dr. Schwartz has tried a sauce made from Trinidad Moruga Scorpion and found it painful far beyond any possible enjoyment of spicy foods, though a friend of his wife's downed some of the sauce, and she seemingly had no ill effects.

The painful or burning sensation caused by capsaicin in chili peppers is caused by its activation of activity in the trigeminal nerve, which codes for heat in the mouth. Capsaicin also stimulates taste receptors in the fungiform papillae, which contribute to the sensation of heat on the tongue. It is the action along the fungiform papillae that make supertasters more sensitive to capsaicin than are normal tasters. Despite the feeling of pain that eating a very hot chili pepper may bring, it causes no actual physical damage. There may be slight swelling or inflammation, but this is caused by the actions of the nerves themselves, not the capsaicin. Interestingly, exposure to capsaicin causes the receptors to desensitize to the chemical. Thus, if you accidentally eat a hot chili pepper and wait until the burn subsides, you will find yourself curiously able to handle another one (and impress your friends). This desensitization ironically allows capsaicin to be used as a painkiller in some medical applications.

Development of Taste Perception

Infants are seemingly born with an attraction to foods that are sugary and foods that are salty (Herz, 2007). As any parent knows, sweet foods will elicit smiles in young infants (see Figure 15.16). Virtually every family has a photograph of a happy baby whose face is covered in chocolate cake.

However, many of our taste preferences are conditioned responses that develop as a function of experience and reinforcement. For example, most infants and young children avoid coffee, as it is too bitter for their tastes. We acquire a liking for the taste of coffee as we associate it with the sugar we put in it and the milk we put in it, as well as the wakefulness that the caffeine in coffee causes. Thus, by the time we reach adulthood, many of us enjoy both the aroma and the taste of coffee, even when not combined with milk or sugar. Similarly, most young children will reject alcoholic beverages unless they are paired with large concentrations of sugar. This is true for some adults as well. Beverages such as rum and tequila are popular because they are very sweet as well as highly alcoholic. And, of course, few parents would subject their infants to Scotch bonnet peppers. This taste preference develops later in life.

■ FIGURE 15.16   **Young children crave sugary foods.**

© iStockphoto.com/bloodstone

Some research shows how a person's early environment can affect taste perception. For example, an early deficiency in salt intake can cause later cravings for and higher intake of salts (Stein et al., 1996). Even when pregnant mothers do not receive adequate salt in their diet, their offspring will show later salt cravings (Crystal & Bernstein, 1995). Similarly, our desire for fatty foods may also be influenced by early developmental experiences.

TEST YOUR KNOWLEDGE

What does the term *umami* mean? How do taste perceptions interact with olfaction to create flavor?

IN DEPTH: *Anosmia*

Carl is a young man in his late teens. He attends the local community college, where he made the dean's list in his first year. Carl is athletic, outgoing, and a big dog enthusiast. He never misses walking his family's four dogs every morning. Carl's father was a champion professional boxer and has trained Carl to box. Although Carl's career ambitions lie elsewhere, he frequently spars at the local boxing gym with other young men. While sparring, Carl was punched in the nose, breaking the cartilage and forcing some of the cartilage up through his olfactory tract, fracturing the cribriform plate and shearing the olfactory nerve. Since then, Carl has had a condition called anosmia, the inability to perceive odor because of malfunctioning olfactory perception. Carl has since complained that food does not taste as good, and he has lost a bit of weight. But he now seeks out more high-calorie food to compensate for his loss of appetite. Interestingly, he regrets not being able to smell his dogs, but in general, he has adjusted to his condition.

Anosmia such as this may be only temporary, or it may be permanent, depending on the damage to the cribriform plate and whether the olfactory nerve was just damaged or completely cut. In some cases, as long as the olfactory nerve is not severed, olfaction may eventually come back. In addition to head trauma, anosmia may be caused by inflammation in the nasal cavities, blockage of the nasal passageways (in which case the anosmia may be temporary), or damage to the areas of the brain responsible for olfactory perception (in which case the anosmia is likely permanent). Temporary anosmia may also develop in depressed patients receiving electroconvulsive shock therapy. Anosmia may occur in progressive neurological disorders such as Parkinson's disease and Alzheimer's disease (Attems, Walker, & Jellinger, 2014). Indeed, patients' awareness of their anosmia may be one of the early clues that lead doctors to make these more serious diagnoses. There are also people who are born with an extremely rare condition known as congenital anosmia. Such individuals do not develop a normal sense of smell or any sense of smell at all (Frasnelli, Fark, Lehmann, Gerber, & Hummel, 2013). Most people with congenital anosmia may not realize it until well into adulthood, as in most situations, they may compensate for it with their other senses.

Anosmia may result from traumatic brain injury to areas of the brain receiving input from the olfactory bulb as well. In particular, given its location near the front of the skull and behind the eyes, the orbitofrontal cortex may often be damaged in accidents, such as car crashes. Damage to the orbitofrontal cortex can result in anosmic symptoms (Caminiti, Ciurleo, Bramanti, & Marino, 2013). Until recently, the different causes of anosmia were grouped together. But recently, researchers have begun to notice differences in the etiology resulting from damage to different sections along the olfactory tract.

Think back to our discussion of different forms of visual impairment. Damage to the eyes can cause blindness. However, damage to the visual areas of the brain is more complex. Damage to V1 causes blindness (except for areas of blindsight), but damage to higher areas of the extrastriate cortex can cause complex agnosias, such as the inability to identify objects, even though a patient can see them and describe them. A similar situation exists in the olfactory system, though it is just being acknowledged and investigated. Shearing of the olfactory nerve causes a loss of olfactory sensation. People who, like Carl, have severed olfactory nerves can no longer detect odors. Thus, they are unable to recognize them, but it is likely that if they possessed olfactory imagery, it might still exist. However, recent research on anosmia in people with orbitofrontal damage suggests that these people can still detect odors, but they are extremely impaired in recognizing them relative to controls (Caminiti et al., 2013).

Thus, damage to the orbitofrontal cortex may be more similar to a form of olfactory agnosia than anosmia. That is, damage to the nose itself and the olfactory bulb produces deficits in the detection of odors, whereas damage to the piriform cortex and orbitofrontal cortex produces deficits in odor recognition and discrimination. For example, Tranel and Welsh-Bohmer (2012) identified a patient with extensive damage to his limbic system and orbitofrontal cortex and found intact detection of odors but severely impaired naming, recognition, and discrimination of odors.

Anosmia may also occur in the normal process of aging. It is estimated that by the age of 80 years, nearly half of the population has experienced some deficit in their sense of smell (Herz, 2007). Because this loss is gradual, many older adults may not be aware that their senses of smell have diminished. Although we cannot compensate for olfactory loss (i.e., there is no such invention yet as a smelling aid), awareness of the effects of anosmia might help some older adults cope with the problems caused by anosmia. For example, if the sense of smell is compromised, food may not be as appealing, leading to declines in caloric intake and proper nutrition. In fact, Herz reported that older adults have fewer "cravings" for specific foods than do younger adults, which may be due partially to reduced olfactory abilities. Older adults may also add more salt to their food, which in some cases can result in increased blood pressure. Adding salt may compensate for the loss of flavor due to lost olfactory sensitivity. We can experience something akin to this form of anosmia when we have a very stuffed nose. When we have such a cold, food does not have the same flavor, because we are not getting the same olfactory input. With a cold, you may find that you avoid foods that rely on olfaction for their flavor, such as coffee, and prefer foods with heavy salt content (e.g., chicken soup).

Anosmia is also linked with depression. The higher areas of the olfactory system are closely linked to the limbic system, which is involved in the regulation of emotions. Many brain regions associated with olfaction, such as the orbitofrontal cortex, are considered part of the limbic system. Thus, the loss of smell may affect emotion (Herz, 2007). It is likely that there is a causal direction between anosmia and depression because brain areas associated with olfaction and emotion are connected, such that damage to the olfactory regions also impairs emotional responding. Some studies suggest that depression may develop gradually after the onset of anosmia.

There also exists a neurological condition called phantosmia (Landis, Croy, & Haehner, 2012). **Phantosmia** is a condition in which people smell odors that are not physically present. In this sense, phantosmia is essentially an olfactory hallucination, which can be quite distracting to patients who have it. It differs from olfactory imagery because the person is not in control of olfactory experience, nor is he or she aware that the experience is different from real odor perception. Phantosmic smells occur without any conscious control over them. Phantosmia may occur during early Parkinson's disease and in other neurological disorders. Phantosmia may also occur as a precursor to an epileptic seizure. Similarly, phantosmia may also occur as part of an "aura" just before a patient experiences a migraine. Fortunately, though, most bouts of phantosmia tend to dissipate over time (Landis et al., 2012). Thus, in most cases, phantosmia is not permanent (though if the smell is of chocolate, one might want it to be so). Phantosmia is an interesting area, but one that awaits further study. And in case you were wondering, **ageusia** is the term that describes a person who has lost the ability to taste. It is an extremely rare condition, especially for all tastes.

....

Phantosmia: hallucinatory perception of odors

Ageusia: loss of the ability to taste

CHAPTER SUMMARY

 15.1 Examine the role of the olfactory system in detecting harmful and helpful substances.

The chemical senses allow us to detect molecules either in the air or in our mouths. Olfaction is the sense of smell, whereas gustation is the sense of taste. Olfaction detects odorants, volatile chemicals in the air, that enter our nose. Odors are the perceptual experience of odorants, which are airborne chemical stimuli. Odorants enter our noses, where they head up the two nostrils, which are separated from each other by the nasal septum. Turbinates then disperse air within the nasal cavity. The odorants rise to the olfactory cleft, the channel at the back of the nasal cavity that funnels air up toward the olfactory epithelium. The olfactory epithelium is a mucous membrane inside each nostril of the nose that contains the receptor cells for the olfactory system. The olfactory receptor neurons are the receptor cells located in the olfactory epithelium. When they detect specific chemicals in the air, they transduce them into a neural signal. The signal is then sent to brain structures associated with the olfactory system. The olfactory receptor neurons are replaced frequently by the generation of new ones from the basal cells. We have about 350 different kinds of olfactory receptors, depending on how many genes we have activated to code for different forms of olfactory receptors. Just internal to the nose is the trigeminal nerve, also known as the fifth cranial nerve, which is associated with the feel of odorants, such as the burn of chili peppers.

15.2 Describe the anatomical and physiological basis for olfaction.

The olfactory receptor neurons project axons through little holes through the cribriform plate, which travel to the olfactory bulb. If the olfactory tract is severed, anosmia, a deficit in olfactory perception, may result. The olfactory nerve starts with olfactory receptor neurons that leave the nose and enter the olfactory bulb. The olfactory bulb is a part of the brain just behind the nose. It is the first place in the brain where olfactory information is processed. The olfactory tract leaves the olfactory bulb to other regions of the brain, including the amygdala, entorhinal cortex, and piriform cortex. The piriform cortex is considered the primary olfactory cortex. The piriform cortex is divided into two sections. The anterior piriform cortex is located in the front portion of the piriform cortex and is associated with representing the chemical structure of odorants. The posterior piriform cortex is located in the back portion of the piriform cortex and is associated with an odor's quality, regardless of its chemical composition. The piriform cortex projects to the orbitofrontal cortex. The orbitofrontal cortex is critical in the emotional experience of odors and integrating olfaction and taste perception, among other functions.

15.3 Describe the nature of olfactory perception, olfactory imagery, and olfactory illusions.

Detection thresholds vary across odorants, though in general it does not take too many odorants to elicit an odor. We are also good at discriminating odors, that is, telling one from another. However, we appear not to be good at naming odors. The tip-of-the-nose phenomenon occurs when a person is familiar with an odor but cannot recall its name, despite feeling as if he or she can. This experience of finding an odor familiar but being unable to name it is quite common. Most individuals do not have olfactory imagery, although a minority of people do. Those who do have olfactory imagery show activity in the piriform cortex when engaging in olfactory imagery. Olfactory illusions occur when our perceptions of odorants change depending on the external conditions. In one illusion, olfactory rivalry, one odorant is presented to one nostril, and a different odor is presented to the other nostril. In olfactory rivalry, we experience only one odor at a time, even though both are present.

15.4 Explain the anatomical and physiological basis for taste perception.

Taste perception (gustation) is also a chemical system designed to make nutritious foods appealing and to make us withdraw from potentially toxic foods. The term *tastant* refers to molecules recognized by taste receptors that induce responses in taste receptors on the tongue. Taste is the perception of the transduction of tastants along the surface of the tongue, whereas flavor is the combined sensory experience of a food, which combines its taste, its odor, and its effect on the trigeminal nerve. Sweet, salty, and umami tastes alert us to foods with needed nutrients. Sour and bitter tastes evolved as warnings about foods to avoid because they may be inedible or toxic. However, in many cultural contexts, we have learned to enjoy sour and bitter foods as well. Taste buds are located along the surface of the tongue or mouth and contain the receptor cells that transduce the chemicals in foods into neural signals. The papillae are small structures that house the taste buds. There are four different kinds of papillae, distinguishable by their shapes, the kinds of taste buds they contain, and where along the tongue they are. Taste receptor cells are the cells within the taste buds that transduce tastants into a neural signal. There are two kinds of taste receptor cells. Receptor cells transduce sweet tastes, umami tastes, and bitter tastes, whereas presynaptic cells transduce salty and sour tastes. Information leaves the taste buds through the 7th, 9th, and 10th cranial nerves and then synapses in the nucleus of the solitary tract in the medulla and then travels to the ventral posterior medial nucleus of the thalamus. The first area of the cortex that receives input from the taste system is the anterior insular cortex located in the frontal lobe. The anterior insular cortex is known as the primary gustatory cortex because of its functions in taste perception. The anterior insular cortex also projects to the orbitofrontal cortex, where taste and olfaction mix to create flavor perception.

There are individual differences in taste perception, some of which are genetic in origin. One of the more well studied ones concerns the genes that code for the perception of bitter tastes. People can be divided into normal tasters, who can detect bitter compounds; nontasters, who cannot detect bitter compounds except at very high concentrations; and supertasters, who are extremely sensitive to and repelled by bitter tastes. Anosmia is a deficit in the detection or perception of odors. This condition can occur from damage to both the nasal pathway and the brain regions involved in olfaction. Phantosmia is the hallucinatory perception of odors. Ageusia is a loss of the ability to taste.

REVIEW QUESTIONS

1. What are odorants? How do they differ from other molecules? Why do we have chemical detection systems?

2. What is the trigeminal nerve? How does it interact with olfaction and gustation? What basic sensations does it detect?

3. Describe the pathway from when an odorant enters the nose to when it is processed in the frontal lobes of the brain. Describe each step along the pathway.

4. What is the piriform cortex? What are the different functions of the anterior and posterior anterior piriform cortices?

5. What is an olfactory illusion? Describe two olfactory illusions and what they tell us about olfaction in general.

6. Describe the gustatory pathway from when food is felt on the tongue to when it is processed in the frontal lobes of the brain. Describe each step along the pathway.

7. What is the difference between taste perception and flavor perception? What area of the brain seems to be responsible for flavor perception?

8. What are the five basic tastes? How are they processed on the tongue? Why is information about each basic taste essential for survival?

9. Describe the differences in genetics, anatomy, and behavior among tasters, nontasters, and supertasters.

10. What is anosmia? What causes anosmia to occur? How does anosmia brought about by damage to the nose differ from anosmia brought about by damage to the piriform cortex? What is phantosmia? How does it differ from olfactory illusions?

KEY TERMS

Ageusia, 413

Amygdala, 399

Anosmia (smell blindness), 399

Anterior insular cortex (insula), 407

Anterior piriform cortex, 400

Basal cells, 396

Circumvallate papillae, 407

Cribriform plate, 398

Entorhinal cortex, 399

Filiform papillae, 407

Flavor, 405

Foliate papillae, 407

Fungiform papillae, 407

Glomeruli, 399

Gustation, 393

Macrosmatic, 397

Microsmatic, 397

Mitral cells, 399

Nasal septum, 395

Nontasters, 410

Odorants, 394

Odors, 394

Olfaction, 393

Olfactory bulb, 399

Olfactory cleft, 396

Olfactory epithelium, 396

Olfactory nerve (first cranial nerve), 399

Olfactory receptor neurons, 396

Olfactory tract, 399

Orbitofrontal cortex, 401

Papillae, 407

Phantosmia, 413

Piriform cortex, 399

Posterior piriform cortex, 400

Presynaptic cells, 407

Receptor cells, 407

Supertasters, 410

Supporting cells, 396

Tastants, 405

Taste, 405

Taste buds, 407

Taste receptor cells, 407

Tasters, 410

Tip-of-the-nose phenomenon, 402

Trigeminal nerve, 398

Tufted cells, 399

Turbinates, 395

INTERACTIVE SENSATION LABORATORY EXERCISES (ISLE)

Experience chapter concepts at edge.sagepub.com/schwartz

ISLE 15.1 Brain Area for Olfactory Bulbs, 397

ISLE 15.2 Posterior Piriform Cortex, 400

Sharpen your skills with SAGE edge at edge.sagepub.com/schwartz

SAGE edge for students provides a personalized approach to help you accomplish your coursework goals in an easy-to-use learning environment.

GLOSSARY

Absolute threshold: the smallest amount of a stimulus necessary to allow an observer to detect its presence

Accommodation: the process of adjusting the lens of the eye so that both near and far objects can be seen clearly

Accretion: the gradual reappearance of a moving object as it emerges from behind another object

Action: any motor activity

Active electroreception: the ability to generate electric fields and then detect disturbances or changes to those electric fields caused by external events

Acoustic reflex: a reflex that tightens the tensor tympani and the stapedius in response to chronic loud noise

Acoustic shadow: the area on the side of the head opposite from the source of a sound in which the loudness of a sound is less because of blocked sound waves

Additive color mixing: the creation of a new color by a process that adds one set of wavelengths to another set of wavelengths

A-delta fibers: myelinated nociceptors that conduct signals rapidly and respond to both heat and pressure

Affordance: information in the visual world that specifies how that information can be used

Aftereffect: a sensory experience that occurs after prolonged experience of visual motion in one particular direction

Afterimages: visual images that are seen after an actual visual stimulus has been removed

Ageusia: loss of the ability to taste

Agnosia: a deficit in some aspect of perception as a result of brain damage

Akinetopsia (motion blindness): a rare condition in which a patient is unable to detect motion despite intact visual perception of stationary stimuli, caused by damage to Area MT

Amplitude: the difference between maximum and minimum sound pressures

Ampullae of Lorenzini: the organ that contains the hair cells that detect electric fields, used in passive electroreception

Amusia: a condition in which brain damage interferes with the perception of music, but does not interfere with other aspects of auditory processing

Amygdala: an area of the brain in the limbic system, associated with the experience of emotion, particularly fear

Analgesia: processes that act to reduce pain perception

Anomalous trichromacy: a condition in which all three cone systems are intact, but one or more has an altered absorption pattern, leading to different metameric matches than in normal individuals

Anosmia (smell blindness): the inability to smell, usually caused by cribriform plate damage

Anterior chamber: the fluid-filled space between the cornea and the iris

Anterior cingulate cortex: a region in the prefrontal lobe of the brain associated with the emotional experience of unpleasantness during pain perception

Anterior insular cortex (insula): a part of the frontal lobe that serves as the primary taste cortex

Anterior intraparietal (AIP) area: a region of the posterior parietal lobe involved in the act of grasping

Anterior piriform cortex: a structure located in the front portion of the piriform cortex that is associated with representing the chemical structures of odorants

Aphasia: an impairment in language production or comprehension brought about by neurological damage

Apparent motion: the appearance of real motion from a sequence of still images

Ascending series: a series in which a stimulus gets increasingly larger along a physical dimension

Astigmatism: a condition that develops from an irregular shape of the cornea or the lens, which makes it impossible for the lens to accommodate a fully focused image

Atmospheric perspective: a pictorial depth cue that arises from the fact that objects in the distance appear blurred and tinged with blue

Attack: the beginning buildup of a note in music

Attention: a set of processes that allow us to select or focus on some stimuli

Attentional blink: the tendency to respond more slowly or not at all to the second appearance of a target in an RSVP task when the second stimulus occurs within 500 ms of the first stimulus

Attentional capture: the process whereby a salient stimulus causes us to shift attention to that stimulus

Audiogram: a graph that illustrates the thresholds for the frequencies as measured by the audiometer

Audiologist: a trained professional who specializes in diagnosing hearing impairments

Audiometer: a device that can present tones of different frequencies, from low in pitch to high in pitch, at different volumes from soft to loud

Auditory core region: an area of the auditory cortex, consisting of the primary auditory cortex, the rostral core, and the rostrotemporal core

Auditory cortex: the areas in the temporal cortex that process auditory stimuli

Auditory scene analysis: the process of identifying specific sound-producing objects from a complex set of sounds from different objects at varying and overlapping frequencies

Azimuth: the left-right or side-to-side aspect of sound localization

Bálint's syndrome: a neurological condition caused by damage to both the left and right posterior parietal lobes

Basal cells: cells that create olfactory receptor neurons

Basilar membrane: the fibers that separate the tympanic canal from the middle canal; the organ of Corti lies on the basilar membrane

Beat: spaced pulses that indicate if a musical piece is fast or slow

Belt: a region of the auditory cortex that wraps around the auditory core regions

Binocular disparity: the binocular depth cue that arises from the fact that the images of most objects that are in the visual scene do not fall on the same location of the retinae of the two eyes; disparity is actually the measure of this difference in the position of the images on the two retinae

Binocular rivalry: a phenomenon that occurs when a separate image is presented to each eye

Biosonar: a process whereby animals emit sounds and then use comparisons of the emitted sounds and their returning echoes to sense the world around them

Bistratified retinal ganglion cells (K cells): retinal ganglion cells that project to the koniocellular layer of the LGN; they represent 10% of ganglion cells, possess low sensitivity to light, and are sensitive to wavelength

Blindsight: the presence of visual abilities in the absence of the visual cortex; the patient claims to be blind but makes visual responses

Blobs: groups of neurons within V1 that are sensitive to color

Bottom-up processing: a process whereby physical stimuli influence how we perceive them

Brightness: the amount of light present

Broca's aphasia: a form of aphasia resulting from damage to Broca's area, causing a deficit in language production

Broca's area: an important area in the production of speech, located in the left frontal lobe

Capsaicin: the active ingredient in chili peppers that provides the experience of hotness, piquancy, or spiciness

Cataracts: a condition that results from a darkening of the lens

Catch trial: a trial in which the stimulus is not presented

Categorical perception: the perception of different acoustic stimuli as being identical phonemes up to a point at which perception flips to perceive another phoneme

Center-surround receptive field: a receptive field in which the center of the receptive field responds opposite to how the surround of the receptive field responds; if the center responds with an increase of activity to light in its area, the surround responds with a decrease in activity to light in its area

C-fibers: nonmyelinated nociceptors that are slower and respond to pressure, extreme degrees of either heat or cold, and toxic chemicals

Change blindness: the difficulty we experience in detecting differences between two visual stimuli that are identical except for one or more changes to the image

Characteristic frequency: the frequency to which any particular location along the basilar membrane responds best

Chroma: the subjective quality of a pitch; we judge sounds an octave apart to be of the same chroma

Ciliary muscles: the small muscles that change the curvature of the lens, allowing accommodation

Circumvallate papillae: found along the very back of the tongue in a virtual row

Coarticulation: the phenomenon in which one phoneme affects the acoustic properties of subsequent phonemes

Cochlea: the snail-shaped structure of the inner ear that houses the hair cells that transduce sound into a neural signal

Cochlear implants: devices that are designed to restore some hearing, typically of spoken voices, to deaf individuals; they stimulate the auditory nerve artificially with an electronic system, replacing the hair cells of the cochlea

Cochlear nucleus: a structure in the brain stem that receives input from inner hair cells

Cold fibers: thermoreceptors that fire in response to colder (30°C and below) temperatures as measured on the skin

Color constancy: the ability to perceive the color of an object despite changes in the amount and nature of illumination

Color deficiency: the condition of individuals who are missing one or more of their cone systems

Color-music synesthesia: a form of synesthesia that occurs when particular pitches, notes, or chords elicit experiences of particular visual colors

Color-opponent cells: neurons that are excited by one color in the center and inhibited by another color in the surround, or neurons that are inhibited by one color in the center and excited by another color in the surround

Complex cells: neurons in V1 that respond optimally to stimuli with particular orientations; unlike simple cells, they respond to a variety of stimuli across different locations, particularly to moving stimuli

Complex sound: a sound consisting of a mix of frequencies

Computational approach: an approach to the study of perception in which the necessary computations the brain would need to carry out to perceive the world are specified

Conductive hearing loss: the inability of sound to be transmitted to the cochlea

Cone of confusion: a region of positions in space in which sounds create the same interaural time and interaural level differences

Cone-opponent cells: neurons that are excited by the input from one cone type in the center, but inhibited by the input from another cone type in the surround

Cones: photoreceptors in the fovea of the retina; they are responsible for color vision and our high visual acuity

Congenital amusia: a condition in which people are inherently poor at music perception

Conjunction search: the search for a target in which the target is specified by a combination of features

Consonance: the perception of pleasantness or harmony when two or more musical notes are played; that is, the notes fit with each other

Consonants: speech sounds made with restricted airflow

Constancy: the ability to perceive an object as the same under different conditions

Constructivist approach: the idea that perceptions are constructed

using information from our senses and cognitive processes

Contralateral organization: the process whereby the signal from each half of the visual world goes to the opposite side of the brain; more generally, any neural organization in which stimuli from one side of the body are sent to the opposite side of the brain

Contralateral representation of visual space: the arrangement whereby the left visual world goes to the right side of the brain, and the right visual world goes to the left side of the brain

Convergence: the number of photoreceptors that connect to each ganglion cell; more convergence occurs for rods than for cones

Cornea: the clear front surface of the eye that allows light in; it also is a major focusing element of the eye

Corollary discharge theory: the theory that the feedback we get from our eye muscles as our eyes track an object is important to the perception of motion

Correct rejection: in signal detection analysis, a correct rejection occurs when a nonsignal is dismissed as not present

Correspondence problem (depth perception): the problem of determining which image in one eye matches the correct image in the other eye

Correspondence problem (motion perception): how the visual system knows if an object seen at Time 1 is the same object at Time 2

Cortical achromatopsia: loss of color vision due to damage to the occipital lobe

Cortical magnification: the allocation of more space in the cortex to some sensory receptors than to others; the fovea has a larger cortical area than the periphery

Cribriform plate: a perforated section of skull bone that separates

the nose from the brain; axons from olfactory receptor neurons pass through to allow olfactory information to enter regions in the brain

Criterion: a bias that can affect the rate of hits and false alarms

Crossed disparity: the direction of disparity for objects in front of the horopter (the image in the left eye is to the right of the image of the object in the right eye)

Crossover point: the point at which a person changes from detecting to not detecting a stimulus or vice versa

Cue approach to depth perception: the system whereby depth perception results from three sources of information, monocular cues to depth present in the image, binocular cues from the comparison of images in each eye, and cues from focusing the eyes, such as vergence and accommodation

Cycle: in a sound wave, the amount of time between one peak of high pressure and the next

d' (d-prime): a mathematical measure of sensitivity

Dark adaptation: the process in the visual system whereby its sensitivity to low light levels is increased

Decay: how long the fundamental frequency and harmonics remain at their peak loudness until they start to disappear

Decibel (dB): a physical unit that measures sound amplitude

Deletion: the gradual occlusion of a moving object as it passes behind another object

Dermis: the inner layer of the skin, which also houses touch receptors

Descending series: a series in which a stimulus gets increasingly smaller along a physical dimension

Deuteranopia: a lack of M-cones, leading to red-green deficiency; this trait is sex linked and thus more common in men

Difference threshold (JND): the smallest difference between two stimuli that can be detected

Diplopia: double images, or seeing two copies of the same image; usually results from the images of an object having too much disparity to lead to fusion

Direct perception (Gibsonian approach): the approach to perception that claims that information in the sensory world is complex and abundant, and therefore the perceptual systems need only directly perceive such complexity

Dissonance: the perception of unpleasantness or disharmony when two or more musical notes do not fit together

Distance: how far a sound is from the listener and whether it is in front of or behind the listener

Divided attention: the process of attending to multiple sources of information

Doctrine of specific nerve energies: the argument that it is the specific neurons activated that determine the particular type of experience

Dorsal column–medial lemniscal pathway: a pathway for the mechanoreceptors (tactile perception) and proprioceptors (muscle position) that travels up the spinal column on the ipsilateral side and crosses to the contralateral side in the medulla

Dorsal horn: an area of the spinal cord that receives input from nociceptors and feedback from the brain

Dorsal pathway: starts with parasol retinal ganglion cells and continues through the visual cortex into the parietal lobe; often called the "where" pathway, as it codes for the locations of objects and their movement

Dorsal root ganglion: a node on the spine where one finds nerve cells carrying signals

from sensory organs toward the somatosensory areas of the brain

Double-opponent cells: cells that have a center, which is excited by one color and inhibited by the other; in the surround, the pattern is reversed

Duplex theory of vision: the doctrine that there are functionally two distinct ways in which our eyes work, the photopic, associated with the cones, and the scotopic, associated with the rods

Dynamics: relative loudness and how loudness changes across a composition

Ecological approach to perception: another name for the direct perception view

Edge completion: the perception of a physically absent but inferred edge, allowing us to complete the perception of a partially hidden object

Edge detection: the process of distinguishing where one object ends and the next begins, making edges as clear as possible

Electromagnetic energy: a form of energy that includes light that is simultaneously both a wave and a particle

Electromagnetic spectrum: the complete range of wavelengths of light and other electromagnetic energy

Electroreception: the ability to detect electric fields, seen in many species of fish

Elevation: the up-down dimension of sound localization

Endogenous opioids: chemicals produced by the body that reduce pain throughout the body

Endolymph: fluid that fills the semicircular canals

End-stopped neurons: neurons that respond to stimuli that end within the cell's receptive field

Entorhinal cortex: an area in the medial temporal lobe, associated with a number of memory functions

Epidermis: the outer layer of the skin

Equal-temperament scale: a tuning system in which the difference between each successive semitone is constant both in pitch and in frequency

Eustachian tube: a thin tube that connects the middle ear with the pharynx and serves to equalize air pressure on either side of the eardrum

Executive attention network: a system that focuses on attention as the inhibition of habitual responses and the top-down control of attention; found in the frontal lobe

Exploratory procedures: hand movements made in order to identify an object

External auditory canal (external auditory meatus): the channel that conducts sound from the pinna to the tympanic membrane

Extrastriate body area: an area within the inferotemporal cortex that is activated when its cells view bodies or body parts, but not faces

Extrastriate cortex (secondary visual cortex): the collective term for visual areas in the occipital lobe other than V1

FAI mechanoreceptors: fast-adapting receptors, with Meissner corpuscle endings and small receptive fields, densely packed near the surface of the skin

FAII mechanoreceptors: fast-adapting receptors with Pacinian corpuscle endings and large receptive fields, more widely distributed, deeper in the skin

False alarm: in signal detection analysis, a false alarm is an error that occurs when a nonsignal is mistaken for a target signal

Familiar size: the cue whereby knowing the retinal size of a familiar object at a familiar distance allows us to use that retinal size to infer distance

Feature integration theory: a theory stipulating that some features can be processed in parallel and quickly prior to using attentional resources, whereas other visual characteristics require us to use attention and are done serially and therefore less quickly

Feature search: the search for a target in which the target is specified by a single feature

Field of view: the part of the world you can see without eye movements

Figure-ground organization: the experience viewers have as to which part of an image is in front and which part of an image is in the background of a particular scene

Filiform papillae: found all over the tongue; contain somatosensory receptors rather than taste buds

Flavor: the combined sensory experience of a food, which combines its taste, its odor, and its effect on the trigeminal nerve

Focus of expansion: the destination point in an optic flow display, from which point perceived motion derives

Foliate papillae: found along the side of the tongue

Forced-choice method: a psychophysical method in which a participant is required to report when or where a stimulus occurs instead of whether it was perceived

Formants: frequency bands with higher amplitudes among the harmonics of a vowel sound; each individual vowel sound has a specific pattern of formants

Fourier analysis: a mathematical procedure for taking any complex waveform and determining the simpler waveforms that make up that complex pattern; the simpler waves used are sine waves

Fovea: an area on the retina that is dense in cones but lacks rods; when we look directly at an object, its image falls on the fovea (also referred to as the macula)

Frequency: the number of waves per unit of time; frequency is the inverse of wavelength

Frequency (sound stimulus): the number of cycles that occur in a second

Functional magnetic resonance imaging (fMRI): a neuroimaging technique that generates an image of the brain on the basis of the blood levels in different areas of the brain, which correlate with activity levels in those regions

Fundamental frequency: the lowest frequency in a complex sound, which determines the perceived pitch of that sound

Fungiform papillae: located mostly along the edges and top of the tongue

Fusiform face area: an area in the inferotemporal area of the temporal lobe that specializes in recognizing familiar faces

Gate control theory: a model that allows for top-down control of the pain signal coming up the spinal cord

Gelb effect: a phenomenon whereby an intensely lit black object appears to be gray or white in a homogeneously dark space

General-mechanism theories: theories of speech perception that claim that the mechanisms for speech perception are the same as the mechanisms for auditory perception in general

Geons: the basic units of objects, consisting of simple shapes such as cylinders and pyramids

Gestalt psychology: a school of thought claiming that we view the world in terms of general patterns and well-organized structures rather than separable individual elements

Glomeruli: spherical structures within the olfactory bulb where the olfactory tract forms synapses with mitral cells and tufted cells

Golgi tendon organs: receptors in the tendons that measure the force of a muscle's contraction

Gradient of flow: the difference in the perception of the speeds of objects moving past us in an optic flow display

Grouping: the process by which elements in a figure are brought together into a common unit or object

Gustation: the sense of taste

Hair cells: cells that have stereocilia for transducing the movement of the basilar membrane into a neural signal

Haptic perception: the active use of touch to identify objects

Harmonic coherence: when frequencies present in the environment resemble the possible pattern of a fundamental frequency and higher harmonics

Harmonics: higher frequencies present in a complex sound that are integer multiples of the fundamental frequency (main frequency)

Harmony: the pleasant sound that results when two or more musical notes are played together

Hearing aids: electronic devices that amplify sound so that people with hearing deficits can hear sounds that otherwise would be below their thresholds

Hemifield neglect (unilateral visual neglect): a condition in which a person fails to attend to stimuli on one side of the visual world (usually the left) as a consequence of neurological damage to the posterior parietal lobe

Hertz (Hz): a unit of measure indicating the number of cycles per second

Heterochromatic light: white light, consisting of many wavelengths

Heterochromia: a condition in which a person has irises of two different colors

Hit: in signal detection analysis, a hit occurs when a signal is detected when the signal is present

Horopter: the region in space where the two images from an object fall on corresponding locations on the two retinae

Hue: the color quality of light, corresponding to the color names we use, such as orange, green, indigo, and cyan; hue is the quality of color

Hue cancellation: an experiment in which observers cancel out the perception of a particular color by adding light of the opponent color

Hypercolumn: a 1-mm block of V1 containing both the ocular dominance and orientation columns for a particular region in visual space

Hyperopia: a condition causing an inability to focus on near objects, also called farsightedness; occurs because accommodation cannot make the lens thick enough

Hyperpolarization: a change in the voltage of a neuron whereby the inside of the cell becomes more negative than it is in its resting state

Illusory contours: perceptual edges that exist because of edge completion but are not actually physically present

Inattentional blindness: a phenomenon in which people fail to perceive an object or event that is visible but not attended to

Incus: an ossicle in the middle ear; receives vibrations from the malleus and transmits them to the stapes

Induced motion: an illusion whereby one moving object may cause another object to look like it is moving

Inferior colliculus: a structure in the midbrain that receives input from the superior olive

Inferotemporal (IT) area: the area of the temporal lobe involved in object perception; it receives input from V4 and other areas in the occipital lobe

Inferotemporal cortex: the region in the temporal lobe that receives input from the ventral visual pathway; one of its functions is object identification

Information-processing approach: the view that perceptual and cognitive systems can be viewed as the flow of information from one process to another

Inner hair cells: cells that are responsible for transducing the neural signal

Intensity: when referring to waves, the height of a wave

Interaural level difference: the difference in loudness and frequency distribution between the two ears

Interaural time difference: the time interval between when a sound enters one ear and when it enters the other ear

Interblobs: groups of neurons that are sensitive to orientation in vision

International Phonetic Alphabet: an alphabetic convention that provides a unique symbol for each and every phoneme in use in human languages

Ipsilateral organization: same-side organization; in the visual system, the nasal retina projects to the same side of the brain

Iris: the colored part of the eye; it is really a muscle that controls the amount of light entering through the pupil

Joint receptors: receptors found in each joint that sense information about the angle of the joint

Key: the tonic note (e.g., C in a C major or minor scale) that gives a subjective sense of arrival and rest in a musical piece

Koniocellular layers: layers of the lateral geniculate nucleus with very small cells that receive input from K ganglion cells

Koniocellular pathway (K pathway): a pathway that starts with bistratified retinal ganglion cells and projects to the koniocellular layers of the lateral geniculate nucleus

Larynx (voice box): a structure that affects the pitches of sounds being made by the human vocal tract

Lateral geniculate nucleus: a bilateral structure (one is present in each hemisphere) in the thalamus that relays information from the optic nerve to the visual cortex

Lateral inhibition: the reduction of a response of the eye to light stimulating one receptor by stimulation of nearby receptors, caused by inhibitory signals in horizontal cells

Lateral intraparietal (LIP) area: an area of the primate parietal cortex involved in the control of eye movements

Law of common fate: the gestalt grouping law that states that elements that are moving together tend to be perceived as a unified group

Law of good continuation: the gestalt grouping law stating that edges that are smooth are more likely to be seen as continuous than edges that have abrupt or sharp angles

Law of proximity: the gestalt grouping law stating that elements that are close together tend to be perceived as a unified group

Law of similarity: the gestalt grouping law stating that elements that are similar to one another tend to be perceived as a unified group

Law of symmetry: the gestalt grouping law that states that elements that are symmetrical to each other tend to be perceived as a unified group

L-cone: the cone with its peak sensitivity to long-wavelength light, around 565 nm (yellow)

Lens: the adjustable focusing element of the eye, located right behind the iris of the eye; also called the crystalline lens

Light adaptation: the process whereby the visual system's sensitivity is reduced so that it can operate in higher light levels

Lightness: the amount of light that gets reflected by a surface

Lightness constancy: the ability to perceive the relative reflectance of objects despite changes in illumination

Linear perspective: the pictorial depth cue that arises from the fact that parallel lines appear to converge as they recede into the distance

Loudness: the perceptual experience of the amplitude or intensity of a sound stimulus

Macrosmatic: species that are heavily dependent on their olfactory system

Macula: the center of the retina; the macula includes the fovea but is larger than it

Macular degeneration: a disease that destroys the fovea and the area around it

Magnitude estimation: a psychophysical method in which participants judge and assign numerical estimates to the perceived strength of a stimulus

Magnocellular layers: layers of the lateral geniculate nucleus with large cells that receive input from M ganglion cells

Magnocellular pathway (M pathway): a pathway that starts with the parasol retinal ganglion cells and projects to the magnocellular layers of the lateral geniculate nucleus

Malleus: the first ossicle in the middle ear; receives vibrations from the tympanic membrane and transmits them to the incus

Manner of articulation: how airflow restriction in the vocal tract occurs

M-cone: the cone with its peak sensitivity to medium-wavelength light, around 535 nm (green)

McGurk effect: a phenomenon in which vision influences the sounds participants report hearing

Mechanoreceptors: the sensory receptors in the skin that transduce physical movement on the skin into neural signals, which are sent to the brain

Medial geniculate nucleus: a structure in the thalamus that receives auditory input from the inferior colliculus and sends output to the auditory cortex

Medial intraparietal (MIP) area: an area of the posterior parietal lobe involved in the planning and control of reaching movements of the arms

Meissner corpuscles: specialized transduction cells in FAI mechanoreceptors

Melody: a rhythmically organized sequence of notes, which we perceive as a single musical unit or idea

Merkel cells: specialized transduction cells in SAI mechanoreceptors

Metamer: a psychophysical color match between two patches of light that have different sets of wavelengths

Meter: the temporal pattern of sound across time

Method of adjustment: a method whereby the observer controls the level of the stimulus and "adjusts" it to be at the perceptual threshold

Method of constant stimuli: a method whereby the threshold is determined by presenting the observer with a set of stimuli, some above the threshold and some below it, in a random order

Method of limits: stimuli are presented in a graduated scale, and participants must judge the stimuli along a certain property that goes up or down

Microelectrode: a device so small that it can penetrate a single neuron in the mammalian central nervous system without destroying the cell

Microsmatic: species that are less dependent on their olfactory system

Middle canal (cochlear duct): one of the three chambers in the cochlea; separated from the tympanic canal by the basilar membrane; contains the organs of Corti

Midget retinal ganglion cells (P cells): retinal ganglion cells that project to the parvocellular layer of the LGN; they represent 80% of ganglion cells, possess low sensitivity to light, and are sensitive to wavelength

Miss: in signal detection analysis, a miss is an error that occurs when an incoming signal is not detected

Mitral cells: neurons that start in the glomeruli of the optic bulb and project to other areas of the brain

Monochromatic light: light consisting of one wavelength

Monocular depth cues: depth cues that require only one eye

Motion: a change in position over time

Motion aftereffect: a motion-based visual illusion in which a stationary object is seen as moving in the opposite direction of real or apparent motion just observed

Motion parallax: a monocular depth cue arising from the relative velocities of objects moving across the retinae of a moving person

Motor theory of speech perception: the theory that the core of speech perception is that the system infers the sound from the movements of the vocal tract

Movement-based cues: cues about depth that can be seen with a single eye in which the inference of distance comes from motion

MT (V5): an area of the occipital lobe in the dorsal pathway, specific to motion detection and perception

Muscle spindles: receptors embedded in the muscles that sense information about muscle length and therefore muscle action

Music: ordered sound made and perceived by human beings, created in meaningful patterns

Myopia: a condition causing an inability to focus clearly on far objects, also called nearsightedness; occurs because accommodation cannot make the lens thin enough

Nasal septum: the wall of cartilage that separates the nostrils

Near point: the closest distance at which an eye can focus

Neural response: the signal produced by receptor cells that can then be sent to the brain

Neuroimaging: technologies that allow us to map living intact brains as they engage in ongoing tasks

Neuropsychology: the study of the relation of brain damage to changes in behavior

Neuroscience: the study of the structures and processes in the nervous system and brain

Nociceptive pain: pain that develops from tissue damage that causes nociceptors in the skin to fire

Nociceptors: sensory receptors in the skin that, when activated, cause us to feel pain; they are found in both the epidermis and dermis

Nontasters: people who cannot detect bitter compounds except at very high concentrations

Object agnosia: an acquired deficit in identifying and recognizing objects even though vision remains intact

Occipital face area: an area of the brain in the occipital lobe, associated with recognizing faces as distinct from other objects

Occlusion: a visual cue that occurs when one object partially hides or obstructs the view of a second object; we infer that the hidden object is farther away from us than the object that obstructs it

Octave: the interval between one musical note and a note with either double the frequency or half the frequency of that note

Ocular dominance column: a column within V1 that is made up of neurons that receive input from only the left eye or only the right eye

Odorants: molecules our olfactory system responds to when we detect them in the air

Odors: the perceptual experience of odorants, which are airborne chemical stimuli

Off-center receptive fields: retinal ganglion cells that decrease their firing rate (inhibition) when light is presented in the middle of the receptive field and increase (excitation) their firing rate when light is presented in the outside or surround of the receptive field

Olfaction: the sense of smell

Olfactory bulb: a part of the brain just behind the nose; it is the first place in the brain where olfactory information is processed

Olfactory cleft: the channel at the back of the nasal cavity that funnels air up toward the olfactory epithelium

Olfactory epithelium: a mucous membrane inside each nostril of the nose that contains the receptor cells for the olfactory system

Olfactory nerve (first cranial nerve): the axons of the olfactory receptor neurons that leave the nose and enter the olfactory bulb

Olfactory receptor neurons: receptor cells located in the olfactory epithelium that detect specific chemicals in the air and transduce them into a neural signal

Olfactory tract: the pathway leading from the olfactory bulb to other regions of the brain

On-center receptive fields: retinal ganglion cells that increase their firing rate (excitation) when light is presented in the middle of the receptive field and decrease (inhibition) their firing rate when light is presented in the outside or surround of the receptive field

Opponent theory of color perception: the theory that color perception arises from three opponent mechanisms, for red-green, blue-yellow, and black-white

Opsin: the protein portion of a photopigment that captures the photon of light and begins the process of transduction; it is the variation in opsin that determines the type of visual receptor

Optic chiasm: the location in the optic tract where the optic nerve from each eye splits in half, with nasal retinae crossing over and temporal retinae staying on the same side of the optic tract

Optic disc: the part of the retina where the optic nerve leaves the eye and heads to the brain; along the optic disc, there are no receptor cells

Optic flow (Chapter 7): a motion depth cue that involves the relative motion of objects as an observer moves forward or backward in a scene

Optic flow (Chapter 8): the relative motions of objects as an observer moves forward or backward in a scene

Optic tract: the optic nerve starting at the optic chiasm and continuing into the brain

Optometrist: a trained professional who specializes in diagnosing visual impairments and diseases

Orbitofrontal cortex: a part of the prefrontal cortex that appears to be critical in the emotional experience of odors and integrating olfaction and taste perception, among other functions

Organ of Corti: a structure on the basilar membrane that houses the hair cells that transduce sound into a neural signal

Orientation column: a column within V1 that is made up of neurons with similar responses to the orientation of a shape presented to those neurons

Orienting attention network (dorsal attention network): a neural system, located primarily in the parietal lobe, that allows us to engage in visual search and direct our visual attention to different locations in visual space

Orienting tuning curve: a graph that demonstrates the typical response of a simple cell to stimuli or different orientations

Ossicles: three small bones in the middle ear

Otolith organs: organs responsible for detecting acceleration of the head and identifying when the head is being held at a tilted angle

Otosclerosis: an inherited bone disease in which the ossicles, particularly the stapes, may calcify and therefore be less conductive of sound

Outer hair cells: cells that sharpen and amplify the responses of the inner hair cells

Pacinian corpuscles: specialized transduction cells in FAII mechanoreceptors

Pain: the perception and unpleasant experience of actual or threatened tissue damage

Panum's area of fusion: the region of small disparity around the horopter where the two images can be fused into a single perception

Papillae: small structures that contain the taste buds

Parabelt: a region of the auditory cortex, in addition to the belt area, that wraps around the auditory core regions

Parahippocampal place area (PPA): an area within the inferotemporal cortex that appears to have the specific function of scene recognition

Parasol retinal ganglion cells (M cells): retinal ganglion cells that project to the magnocellular layer of the LGN; they represent 10% of ganglion cells and possess high sensitivity to light

Parietal insular vestibular cortex: an area in the parietal lobe that receives input from the vestibular nerve and is responsible for the perception of balance and orientation

Parvocellular layers: layers of the lateral geniculate nucleus with small cells that receive input from P ganglion cells

Parvocellular pathway (P pathway): a pathway characterized by the retinal ganglion cells known as midget retinal ganglion cells

Passive electroreception: the ability only to detect electric fields

Perception: the process of creating conscious perceptual experience from sensory input

Perceptual bistability: a phenomenon in which a static visual image leads to alternating perceptions

Perceptual narrowing: the developmental process whereby regularly experienced phonemes are homed in on, with simultaneous diminishing of the ability to discriminate unfamiliar phonemes

Perceptual organization: the process by which multiple objects in the environment are grouped, allowing us to identify multiple objects in complex scenes

Perilymph: the fluid that fills the tympanic canal and the vestibular canal

Phantom limb syndrome: continued but illusory sensory reception in a missing appendage

Phantosmia: hallucinatory perception of odors

Pharynx: the top portion of the throat

Phase: the position in one cycle of a wave; there are 360° in a single cycle of a wave

Phenomenology: our subjective experience of perception

Phonemes: the basic units of sound in human language

Phonemic restoration effect: an illusion in which participants hear sounds that are masked by white noise, but context makes the missing sound apparent

Photon: a single particle of light

Photopic vision: the vision associated with the cones; it is used in the daytime, has good acuity in the fovea, and has color vision

Photopigment: a molecule that absorbs light and by doing so releases an electric potential by altering the voltage in the cell

Pictorial cues: information about depth that can be inferred from a static picture

Pinna: the structure that collects sound and funnels it into the auditory canal

Piriform cortex: an area in the anterior region of the temporal lobe that receives input from the olfactory bulb and is involved in olfactory processing; often considered the primary olfactory cortex

Pitch: the subjective experience of sound that is most closely associated with the frequency of a sound stimulus; related to the experience of whether the sound is high or low, such as the two ends of the keyboard of a piano

Place code theory: the view that different locations along the basilar membrane respond to different frequencies

Place of articulation: the point along the vocal tract at which the airflow is constricted

Point-light walker display: an experiment in which small lights are attached to the body of a person or an animal, which is then filmed moving in an otherwise completely dark environment

Point of subjective equality (PSE): the settings of two stimuli at which the observer experiences them as identical

Posterior chamber: the space between the iris and the lens; it is also filled with fluid, known as aqueous humor

Posterior piriform cortex: a structure located in the back portion of the piriform cortex that is associated with an odor's quality, regardless of its chemical composition

Presbyopia: a condition in which incoming light focuses behind the retina, leading to difficulty focusing on close-up objects; common in older adults, in whom the lens becomes less elastic

Presynaptic cells: taste receptor cells that transduce salty and sour tastes

Primary auditory cortex: the first area in the auditory cortex, which receives input from the medial geniculate nucleus

Primary visual cortex (V1): the area of the cerebral cortex that receives input from the LGN, located in the occipital lobe and responsible for early visual processing

Proprioception: the perception of the movements and position of our limbs

Prosopagnosia: face agnosia, resulting in a deficit in perceiving faces

Protanopia: a lack of L-cones, leading to red-green deficiency; this trait is sex linked and thus more common in men

Pruriceptors: receptors in our skin that respond to mild irritants by producing itch sensations

Psychophysical scale: a scale on which people rate their psychological experiences as a function of the level of a physical stimulus

Psychophysics: the study of the relation between physical stimuli and perception events

Pupil: an opening in the middle of the iris

Pupillary reflex: an automatic process by which the iris contracts or relaxes in response to the amount of light entering the eye; the reflex controls the size of the pupil

Pure tone: a sound wave in which changes in air pressure follow a sine wave pattern

Purkinje shift: the observation that short wavelengths tend to be relatively brighter than long wavelengths in scotopic vision versus photopic vision

Quality: a value that changes but does not make the value larger or smaller

Random-dot stereograms: stereograms in which the images consist of a randomly arranged set of black and white dots, with the left-eye and right-eye images arranged identically except that some of the dots are moved to the left or the right in one of the images, creating either a crossed or an uncrossed disparity

Rapid serial visual presentation (RSVP) paradigm: a method of studying attention in which a series of stimuli appear rapidly in time at the same point in visual space

Rate of approach: the measure of whether a predator is approaching a target or receding from it

Real motion: motion in the world created by continual change in the position of an object relative to some frame of reference

Receiver-operating characteristic (ROC) curve: in signal detection theory, a plot of false alarms versus hits for any given sensitivity, indicating all possible outcomes for a given sensitivity

Receptive field: a region of adjacent receptors that will alter the firing rate of a cell that is higher up in the sensory system; the term can also apply to the region of space in the world to which a particular neuron responds

Receptor cells: taste receptor cells that transduce sweet tastes, umami tastes, and bitter tastes

Receptors: specialized sensory neurons that convert physical stimuli into neural responses

Recognition: the ability to match a presented item with an item in memory

Recognition by components: a theory stating that object recognition occurs by representing each object as a combination of basic units (geons) that make up that object; we recognize an object by the relation of its geons

Reichardt detectors: neural circuits that enable the determination of direction and speed of motion by delaying input from one receptive field, to determine speed, to match the input of another receptive field, to determine direction

Reissner's membrane: the membrane that separates the vestibular and middle canals

Relative height: a visual cue in which objects closer to the horizon are seen as more distant

Relative size: the fact that the more distant an object, the smaller the image will be on the retina

Repetition blindness: the failure to detect the second target in an RSVP task when the second target is identical to the first one; like attentional blink, it occurs when the second target is presented 500 ms or less after the first target

Representation: the storage and/or reconstruction of information in memory when that information is not in use

Response compression: as the strength of a stimulus increases, so does the perceptual response, but the perceptual response does not increase by as much as the stimulus increases

Response expansion: as the strength of a stimulus increases, the perceptual response increases even more

Retina: the paper-thin layer of cells at the back of the eye where transduction takes place

Retinal: a derivative of vitamin A that is part of a photopigment

Retinal image: the light projected onto the retina

Retinitis pigmentosa: an inherited progressive degenerative disease of the retina that may lead to blindness

Retinotopic map: a point-by-point relation between the retina and V1

Rhythm: the temporal patterning of music, including the tempo, the beat, and the meter

Rods: photoreceptors at the periphery of the retina; they are very light sensitive and specialized for night vision

Rostral core: an area in the auditory core region of the auditory cortex

Rostrotemporal core: an area, in addition to the rostral core, in the auditory core region of the auditory cortex

Round window: a soft tissue substance at the base of the tympanic canal whose function is as an "escape" valve for excess pressure from loud sounds that arrive in the cochlea

Ruffini endings: specialized transduction cells in SAII mechanoreceptors

Saccades: the most common and rapid of eye movements; they are sudden eye movements and are used to look from one object to another

SAI mechanoreceptors: slow-adapting receptors using Merkel cells, with small receptive fields, densely packed near the surface of skin

SAII mechanoreceptors: slow-adapting receptors using Ruffini endings, with large receptive fields, more widely distributed, deeper in the skin

Saturation: the purity of light

Scale: a set of ordered notes starting at one note and ending at the same note one octave higher

Sclera: the outside surface of the eye; it is a protective membrane covering the eye that gives the eye its characteristic white appearance

S-cone: the cone with its peak sensitivity to short-wavelength light, around 420 nm (blue)

Scotoma: an area of partially or completely destroyed cells, resulting in a blind spot in a particular region of the visual field

Scotopic vision: the operation of the visual system associated with the rods; it has relatively poor acuity and no color ability but is very sensitive to light

Scoville scale: a measure of our detection of the amount of an ingredient called capsaicin in chili peppers

Segregation: the process of distinguishing two objects as being distinct or discrete

Selective attention: the processes of attention that allow us to focus on one source when many are present

Semicircular canals: three tubes located in the inner ear responsible for the signaling of head rotation

Semitones: the 12 equivalent intervals or notes within each octave

Sensation: the registration of physical stimuli on sensory receptors

Sensitivity: the ability to perceive a particular stimulus; it is inversely related to threshold

Sensitivity (signal detection theory): the ease or difficulty with which an observer can distinguish signal from noise

Sensorineural hearing loss: permanent hearing loss caused by damage to the cochlea or auditory nerve

Shadows: a depth cue arising because an object is in front of its shadow, and the angle of the shadow can provide some information about how far the object is in front of the background

Signal detection theory: the theory that in every sensory detection or discrimination, there is both sensory sensitivity to the stimulus and a criterion used to make a cognitive decision

Simple cells: V1 neurons that respond to stimuli with particular orientations to objects within their receptive field; the preferred orientation of a simple cell is the stimulus orientation that produces the strongest response

Simultagnosia: a deficit in perceiving more than one object at a time

Simultaneous color contrast: a phenomenon that occurs when our perception of one color is affected by a color that surrounds it

Size-arrival effect: bigger approaching objects are seen as being more likely to collide with the viewer than smaller approaching objects

Size constancy: the perception of an object as having a fixed size, despite the change in the size of the visual angle that accompanies changes in distance

Size-distance invariance: the relation between perceived size and perceived distance, whereby the perceived size of an object depends on its perceived distance, and the perceived distance of an object may depend on its perceived size

Smooth-pursuit eye movements: voluntary tracking eye movements

Somatosensory cortex: an area in the parietal lobe of the cerebral cortex devoted to processing the information coming from the skin senses

Somatotopic map: a feature whereby the skin of the body maps onto the surface of the primary somatosensory cortex in a systematic way

Sound stimulus: the periodic variations in air pressure traveling out from the source of the variations

Sound waves: the waves of pressure changes that occur in the air as a function of the vibration of a source

Spatial segregation: the process whereby sounds that are coming from the same location are grouped together, whereas sounds that are coming from different locations are not grouped together

Special-mechanism theories: theories of speech perception that claim that the mechanisms for speech perception are distinct and unique relative to the mechanisms for auditory perception in general

Spectral reflectance: the ratio of light reflected by an object at each wavelength

Spectral segregation: the process whereby sounds that overlap in harmonic structure are grouped together, whereas sounds that do not overlap in harmonic structure are not grouped together

Spectral shape cue: the change in a sound's frequency envelope created by the pinnae; it can be used to provide information about the elevation of a sound source

Spinothalamic pathway: a pathway for the nociceptors (pain) and thermoreceptors (temperature) that travels up the contralateral side of the spinal column; it does not synapse in the brain until the ventral posterior nucleus of the thalamus

Stapedius: the muscle that is attached to the stapes

Stapes: an ossicle in the middle ear; it receives vibrations from the incus and transmits them to the oval window of the inner ear

Stereocilium: the hairlike part of the hair cells on the top of the inner and outer hair cells

Stereopsis: the sense of depth we perceive from the visual system's processing of the comparison of the two different images from each retina

Stevens' power law: a mathematical formula that describes the relationship between stimulus intensity and our perception; it allows for both response compression and expansion

Stimulus: an element of the world around us that impinges on our sensory systems

Stimulus onset asynchrony: the difference in time between the occurrence of one stimulus and the occurrence of another, in this case, the cue and the target

Stimulus salience: some objects in the environment attract our attention

Substantia gelatinosa: the region in the dorsal horn where neurons meet

Subtractive color mixing: color mixing in which a new color is made by the removal of wavelengths from a light with a broad spectrum of wavelengths

Superior colliculus: a structure located at the top of the brainstem, just beneath the thalamus, whose main function in mammals (including humans) is the control of rapid eye movements

Superior olive: a structure in the brain stem that receives input from the inner hair cells and from the cochlear nucleus

Supertasters: people who are extremely sensitive to bitter tastes; they usually do not like foods with many bitter compounds

Supporting cells: cells that provide metabolic supplies to the olfactory receptor neurons

Synesthesia: a condition in which a stimulus in one modality consistently triggers a response in another modality

Tactile agnosia: an inability to identify objects by touch

Target range: the distance of a predator from its potential target, determined by timing an echo's return

Tastants: molecules recognized by taste receptors that induce responses in taste receptors on the tongue

Taste: the perception of the transduction of tastants along the surface of the tongue

Taste buds: small structures located along the surface of the tongue or mouth that contain the receptor cells

Taste receptor cells: cells within the taste buds that transduce tastants into a neural signal

Tasters: people who can detect bitter compounds

Tectorial membrane: a membrane that rests above the hair cells within the organ of Corti

Tempo: the pace at which a piece of music is played

Temporal code theory: the view that frequency representation occurs because of a match between sound frequency and the firing rates of the auditory nerve

Temporal segregation: the process whereby sounds that are linked in time are grouped together, whereas sounds that are not correlated with one another are not grouped together

Tensor tympani: the muscle that is attached to the malleus

Texture gradient: a monocular depth cue that occurs because textures become finer as they recede in the distance

Thermoreception: the ability to sense changes in temperature on the skin

Thermoreceptors: the sensory receptors in the skin that signal information about the temperature as measured on the skin

Timbre: the perceived sound differences between sounds with the same pitch but possessing different higher harmonics

Time to collision: the estimate that an approaching object will contact another

Tinnitus: a condition in which people perceive sounds even when none are present

Tip-of-the-nose phenomenon: a phenomenon that occurs when a person is familiar with an odor but cannot recall its name, despite feeling as if he or she can

Tonotopic organization: the organization of neurons within a region in the brain according to the different frequencies to which they respond

Top-down processing: a process whereby our existing knowledge of objects influences how we perceive them

Topographic agnosia: a deficit in recognizing spatial landscapes, related to damage to the parahippocampal place area

Trachea (windpipe): the tube bringing air to and from the mouth

Transduction: the process of converting a physical stimulus into an electrochemical signal

Transposition: the process through which one can create multiple versions of a melody that start on different notes but contain the same intervals or sequence of changes in notes

Trapezoid body: a structure in the brain stem that plays a role in determining the direction of sounds

Trichromatic theory of color vision: the theory that the color of any light is determined by the output of the three cone systems in our retinae

Trigeminal nerve: a nerve that is associated with the feel of odorants; also known as the fifth cranial nerve

Tritanopia: a lack of S-cones, leading to blue-yellow color deficiency; this trait is much rarer and is not sex-linked

Tuberous receptors: the organ that contains the hair cells that detect electric fields, used in active electroreception

Tufted cells: neurons that start in the glomeruli of the optic bulb and project to other areas of the brain

Turbinates: bony knots of tissue that serve to disperse air within the nasal cavity

Two-point touch threshold: the minimum distance at which two touches are perceived as two touches and not one

Tympanic canal: one of the three chambers in the cochlea; separated from the middle canal by the basilar membrane

Tympanic membrane: a thin elastic sheet that vibrates in response to sounds coming through the external auditory canal; commonly known as the eardrum

Unconscious inference: perception is not adequately determined by sensory information, so an inference or educated guess is part of the process; this inference is not the result of active problem solving but rather a nonconscious cognitive process

Uncrossed disparity: the direction of disparity for objects that are behind the horopter (the image of the object in the left eye is to the left of the position of the image of the object in the right eye)

Unilateral dichromacy: the presence of dichromacy in one eye but normal trichromatic vision in the other

Unique colors: colors that can be described only with a single color term—red, green, blue, and yellow

Univariance: the principle whereby any single cone system is colorblind, in the sense that different combinations of wavelength and intensity can result in the same response from the cone system

Uvula: a flap of tissue at the top of the throat that can close off the nasal cavity

Ventral pathway: starts with midget and bistratified retinal ganglion cells and continues through the visual cortex into the inferotemporal cortex in the temporal lobe; often called the "what" pathway, as it codes for object identification as well as color vision

Ventral posterior nucleus of the thalamus: an area in the thalamus that receives input from both the dorsal column–medial lemniscal pathway and the spinothalamic pathway

Vergence: the inward bending of the eyes when looking at closer objects

Vestibular canal: one of the three chambers in the cochlea; separated from the middle canal by Reissner's membrane

Vestibular complex: a brainstem area that receives input from the vestibular nerve and sends the information to the forebrain

Vestibular system: the sensory system responsible for the perception of balance and acceleration, housed in the semicircular canals and otolith organs, both located adjacent to the inner ear

V4: an area of the occipital lobe involved in both color vision and shape perception

Viewpoint invariance: the perception that an object does not change when an observer sees the object from a new vantage point

Visual angle: the angle of an object relative to the observer's eye

Visual search: looking for a specific target in an image with distracting objects

Visual spectrum (visible spectrum): the band of wavelengths from 400 to 700 nm that people with normal vision can detect

Voice area: an area located in the superior temporal sulcus that responds to the sound of the human voice, but less so to other stimuli

Voice-onset time: the production of certain consonants (called stop consonants) in which there is a difference between the first sound of the phoneme and the movement of the vocal cords (called voicing)

Voicing: whether the vocal cords are vibrating or not

Vowels: speech sounds made with unrestricted airflow

V2: the second area in the visual cortex that receives input; often considered the area that starts with visual associations rather than processing the input (sometimes called the prestriate cortex)

Warm fibers: thermoreceptors that fire in response to warmer temperatures (above 36°C) as measured on the skin

Wavelength: the distance between two adjacent peaks in a repeating wave; different forms of electromagnetic energy are classified by their wavelengths

Weber's law: a just-noticeable difference between two stimuli is related to the magnitude or strength of the stimuli

Wernicke's aphasia: a form of aphasia resulting from damage to Wernicke's area, causing a deficit in language comprehension

Wernicke's area: an important area in speech comprehension, located in the left temporal lobe

Word segmentation: the ability of speakers of a language to correctly perceive boundaries between words

Zero disparity: the situation in which retinal images fall along corresponding points, which means that the object is along the horopter

Zonule fibers: fibers that connect the lens to the choroid membrane

REFERENCES

Adelson, E. H. (1993). Perceptual organization and the judgment of brightness. *Science, 262*, 2042–2044.

Albright, T. D. (1984). Direction and orientation selectivity of neurons in visual area MT of the macaque. *Journal of Neurophysiology, 52*, 1106–1130.

Alpern, M., Kitahara, K., & Krantz, D. H. (1983). Perception of color in unilateral tritanopia. *Journal of Physiology, 335*, 683–697.

Alpern, M., Lee, G. B., Maaseidvaag, F., & Miller, S. S. (1971). Colour vision in blue-cone "monochromacy." *Journal of Physiology, 212*, 211–233.

Alvarado, J. C., Vaughan, J. W., Stanford, T. R., & Stein, B. E. (2007). Multisensory versus unisensory integration: Contrasting modes in the superior colliculus. *Journal of Neurophysiology, 97*, 3193–3205.

Ambady, N., & Bharucha, J. J. (2009). Culture and the brain. *Current Directions in Psychological Science, 18*, 342–345.

Anderson, B. A., Laurent, P. A., & Yantis, S. (2013). Reward predictions bias attentional selection. *Frontiers in Human Neuroscience, 7*, 262.

Anderson, B. A., & Yantis, S. (2013). Persistence of value-driven attentional capture. *Journal of Experimental Psychology: Human Perception & Performance, 39*, 6–9.

Anderson, S., White-Schwoch, T., Parbery-Clark, A., & Kraus, N. (2013). A dynamic auditory-cognitive system supports speech-in-noise perception in older adults. *Hearing Research, 300*, 18–32.

Anstis, S. (2012). The furrow illusion: Peripheral motion becomes aligned with stationary contours. *Journal of Vision, 12*, 1–11.

Anstis, S., & Rogers, B. (2011). Illusory rotation of a spoked wheel. *i-Perception, 2*, 720–723.

Arroyo, J. G. (2006). A 76-year-old man with macular degeneration. *JAMA, 295*, 2394–2406.

Arthur, C. (2013, February 14). New self-driving car system tested on UK roads. *The Guardian*. Retrieved from http://www.guardian.co.uk/technology/2013/feb/14/self-driving-car-system-uk

Attems, J., Walker, L., & Jellinger, K. A. (2014). Olfactory bulb involvement in neurodegenerative diseases. *Acta Neuropathologica, 127*, 459–475.

Babadi, B., Casti, A., Xiao, Y., Kaplan, E., & Paninski, L. (2010). A generalized linear model of the impact of direct and indirect inputs to the lateral geniculate nucleus. *Journal of Vision, 10*, 22.

Balkwill, L.-L., & Thompson, W. F. (1999). A cross-cultural investigation of the perception of emotion in music: Psychophysical and cultural cues. *Music Perception, 17*, 43–64.

Barlow, H. B. (1953). Summation and inhibition in the frog's retina. *Journal of Physiology, 119*, 69–88.

Barlow, H. B. (1995). The neuron in perception. In M. S. Gazzaniga (Ed.), *The cognitive neurosciences* (pp. 415–434). Cambridge, MA: MIT Press.

Barlow, H. B., Blakemore, C., & Pettigrew, J. D. (1967). The neural mechanism of binocular depth discrimination. *Journal of Physiology, 193*, 327–342.

Bartoshuk, L. M. (1971). The chemical senses: I. Taste. In J. W. Kling & L. A. Riggs (Eds.), *Experimental psychology* (3rd ed.). New York: Holt, Rinehart & Winston.

Bartoshuk L., Duffy, V. B., & Miller, I. J. (1994). PTC/PROP tasting: Anatomy, psychophysics, and sex effects. *Physiology & Behavior, 56*, 1165–1171.

Beck, D. M., Muggleton, N., Walsh, V., & Lavie, N. (2006). Right parietal cortex plays a critical role in change blindness. *Cerebral Cortex, 16*, 712–717.

Beckers, G., & Zeki, S. (1995). The consequences of inactivating areas V1 and V5 on visual motion perception. *Brain, 118*, 49–60.

Belin, P., Bestelmeyer, P.E.G., Latinus, M., & Watson, R. (2011). Understanding voice perception. *British Journal of Psychology, 102*, 711–725.

Bellugi, U., Klima, E. S., & Hickok, G. (2010). *Brain organization: Clues from deaf signers with left or right hemisphere lesions*. In L. Clara (Ed)., *Gesture and word* (pp. 2–17). Lisbon, Portugal: Editorial Caminho.

Benedetti, F. (1985). Processing of tactile spatial information with crossed fingers. *Journal of Experimental Psychology: Human Perception and Performance, 11*, 517–525.

Bennett, C. M., Wolford, G. L., & Miller, M. B. (2009). The principled control of false positives in neuroimaging. *Social, Cognitive, and Affective Neuroscience, 4*, 417–422.

Beran, M. J. (2012). We cannot know what it is like to be a bat, but we can know better what it is like to see like a bat. *PsychCRITIQUES, 57*, 38.

Biederman, I. (1987). Recognition-by-components: A theory of human image understanding. *Psychological Review, 94*, 115–147.

Birch, E. E. (1993). Introduction to binocular vision. In K. Simons (Ed.), *Early visual development: Normal and abnormal*. New York: Oxford University Press.

Birch, J. (2001). *Diagnosis of defective colour vision* (2nd ed.). New York: Elsevier.

Bisiach, E., & Luzzatti, C. (1978). Unilateral neglect of representational space. *Cortex, 14*, 129–133.

Blackwell, H. R. (1953). *Psychophysical thresholds: Experimental studies of methods of measurement* (Bulletin No. 36). Ann Arbor: University of Michigan Engineering Research Institute.

Blake, R., & Shiffrar, M. (2007). Perception of human motion. *Annual Review of Psychology, 58*, 47–73.

Bohn, K. M., Smarsh, G. C., & Smotherman, M. S. (2013). Social context evokes rapid changes in bat song syntax. *Animal Behavior, 85,* 1485–1491.

Born, R. T., & Bradley, D. C. (2005). Structure and function of visual area MT. *Annual Review of Neuroscience, 28,* 157–189.

Bowmaker, J. K. (1998). Visual pigments and molecular genetics of color blindness. *News in Physiological Science, 13,* 63–69.

Bregman, A. S. (1990). *Auditory scene analysis: The perceptual organization of sound.* Cambridge, MA: Bradford.

Bregman, A. S. (2005). Auditory scene analysis and the role of phenomenology in experimental psychology. *Canadian Psychology, 46,* 32–40.

Brendel, E., DeLucia, P. R., Hecht, H., Stacy, R. L., & Larsen, J. T. (2012). Threatening pictures induce shortened time-to-contact estimates. *Attention, Perception & Psychophysics, 74,* 979–987.

Bressler, N. M. (2004). Age-related macular degeneration is the leading cause of blindness. *JAMA, 291,* 1900–1901.

Bridgeman, B., & Stark, L. (1991). Ocular proprioception and efference copy in registering visual direction. *Vision Research, 31,* 1903–1913.

Brincat, S., & Connor, C. E. (2004). Underlying principles of visual shape selectivity in posterior inferotemporal cortex. *Nature Neuroscience, 7,* 880–886.

Bruce, C., Desimone, R., & Gross, C. G. (1981). Visual properties of neurons in a polysensory area in superior temporal sulcus of the macaque. *Journal of Neurophysiology, 46,* 369–384.

Bryan, S. M. (2012, February 16). Trinidad Scorpion Moruga blend wins hottest pepper title. *USA Today.* Retrieved from http://usatoday30.usatoday.com/news/health/wellness/fitness-food/story/2012-02-16/Trinidad-Moruga-Scorpion-wins-hottest-pepper-title/53113826/1

Buck, L. B., & Axel, R. (1991). A novel multigene family may encode odorant receptors: A molecular basis for odor recognition. *Cell, 65,* 175–187.

Buetti, S., Tamietto, M., Hervais-Adelman, A., Kerzel, D., de Gelder, B., & Pegna, A. J. (2013). Dissociation between goal-directed and discrete response localization in a patient with bilateral cortical blindness. *Journal of Cognitive Neuroscience, 25,* 1769–1775.

Busch, N. A. (2013). The fate of object memory traces under change detection and change blindness. *Brain Research, 1520,* 107–115.

Busigny, T., & Rossion, B. (2011). Holistic processing impairment can be restricted to faces in acquired prosopagnosia: Evidence from the global/local Navon effect. *Journal of Neuropsychology, 5,* 1–14.

Buzás, P., Kóbor, P., Petykó, Z., Telkes, I., Martin, P. R., & Lénárd, L. (2013). Receptive field properties of color opponent neurons in the cat lateral geniculate nucleus. *Journal of Neuroscience, 33,* 1451–1461.

Cain, W. S. (1979). To know with the nose: Keys to odor identification. *Science, 203,* 467–470.

Cain Miller, C., & Wald, M. L. (2013, May 30). Self-driving cars for testing are supported by the U.S. *The New York Times.* Retrieved from http://www.nytimes.com/2013/05/31/technology/self-driving-cars-for-testing-are-supported-by-us.html?pagewanted=all&_r=0

Caminiti, F., Ciurleo, R., Bramanti, P., & Marino, S. (2013). Persistent anosmia in a traumatic brain injury patient: Role of orbitofrontal cortex. *Brain Injury, 27,* 1715–1718.

Carroll, J., Neitz, M., Hofer, H., Neitz, J., & Williams, D. R. (2004). Functional photoreceptor loss revealed with adaptive optics: An alternate cause of color blindness. *Proceedings of the National Academy of Sciences of the United States of America, 101,* 8461–8466.

Centers for Disease Control and Prevention. (2013). *Hearing loss in children: Data and statistics.* Retrieved from http://www.cdc.gov/ncbddd/hearingloss/data.html

Chabris, C., & Simons, D. (2009). *The invisible gorilla.* New York: Broadway.

Chandrashekar, J., Hoon, M. A., Ryba, N.J.P., & Zuker, C. S. (2006). The receptors and cells for mammalian taste. *Nature, 444,* 288–294.

Chen, M.-C., Tsai, P.-L., Huang, Y.-T., & Lin, K. (2013). Pleasant music improves visual attention in patients with unilateral neglect after stroke. *Brain Injury, 27,* 75–82.

Cherry, E. C. (1953). Some experiments on the recognition of speech, with one and with two ears. *Journal of the Acoustical Society of America, 25,* 975–979.

Chino, Y. M., Smith, E. L., III., Hatta, S., & Cheng, H. (1997). Postnatal development of binocular disparity sensitivity in neurons of the primate visual cortex. *Journal of Neuroscience, 17,* 296–307.

Chiu, Y.-C., & Yantis, S. (2009). A domain-independent source of cognitive control for task sets: Shifting spatial attention and switching categorization rules. *Journal of Neuroscience, 29,* 3930–3938.

Chow, A., Chow, V., Packo, K., Pollack, J., Peyman, G., & Schuchard, R. (2004). The artificial silicone retina microchip for the treatment of vision loss from retinitis pigmentosa. *Archives of Ophthalmology, 122,* 1156–1157.

Chrastil, E. R. (2013). Neural evidence supports a novel framework for spatial navigation. *Psychonomic Bulletin & Review, 20,* 208–227.

Chun, M. M., Golomb, J. D., & Turke-Browne, N. B. (2011). A taxonomy of external and internal attention. *Annual Review of Psychology, 62,* 73–101.

Colby, C. L., Duhamel, J.-R., & Goldberg, M. E. (1996). Visual, pre-saccadic, and cognitive activation of single neurons in monkey lateral intraparietal area. *Journal of Neurophysiology, 76,* 2841–2851.

Collignon, O., Dormal, G., Albouy, G., Vandewalle, G., Voss, P., Phillips, C., & Lepore, F. (2013). Impact of blindness onset on the functional organization and the connectivity of the occipital cortex. *Brain, 136,* 2769–2783.

Colombo, J. (2002). Infant attention grows up: The emergence of a developmental cognitive neuroscience perspective. *Current Directions in Psychological Science, 11,* 196–200.

Conard, N. J., Malina, M., & Münzel, S. C. (2009). New flutes document the earliest musical tradition in southwestern Germany. *Nature, 460,* 737–740.

Coren, S., & Girgus, J. S. (1978). *Seeing is deceiving: The psychology of visual illusions.* Hillsdale, NJ: Lawrence Erlbaum.

Cornsweet, T. N. (1970). *Visual perception.* New York: Academic Press.

Crystal, S. R., & Bernstein, I. L. (1995). Morning sickness: Impact on offspring salt preference. *Appetite, 25,* 231–240.

Culham, J. C., Cavina-Pratesi, C., & Singhal, A. (2006). The role of parietal cortex in visuomotor control: What have we learned from neuroimaging? *Neuropsychologia, 44,* 2668–2884.

Curcio, C. A., Sloan, K. R., Kalina, R. E., & Hendrickson, A. E. (1990). Human photoreceptor topography. *Journal of Comparative Neurology, 292,* 497–523.

Davis, K. D., Taylor, S. J., Crawley, A. P., Wood, M. L., & Mikulis, D. J. (1997). Functional MRI of pain- and attention-related activations in the human cingulate cortex. *Journal of Neurophysiology, 77,* 3370–3380.

Daw, N. (2009). The foundations of development and deprivation in the visual system. *Journal of Physiology, 587,* 2769–2773.

Day, R. H. (1990). The Bourdon illusion in haptic space. *Perception and Psychophysics, 47,* 400–404.

DeCasper, A. J., & Fifer, W. P. (1980). Of human bonding: Newborns prefer their mothers' voices. *Science, 208,* 1174–1176.

de Gelder, B. (2010). Uncanny sight in the blind. *Scientific American, 302,* 60–65.

de Gelder, B., Tamietto, M., van Boxtel, G., Goebel, R., Sahraie, A., Van den Stock, J., . . . Pegna, A. (2008). Intact navigation skills after bilateral loss of striate cortex. *Current Biology, 18,* R1128–R1129.

DeLucia, P. R. (Ed.). (2011). *Reviews of human factors and ergonomics* (Vol. 7). Santa Monica, CA: Human Factors and Ergonomics Society.

DeLucia, P. R. (2013). Effects of size on collision perception and implications for perceptual theory and transportation safety. *Current Directions in Psychological Science, 22,* 199–204.

Delwiche, J. F., Buletic, Z., & Breslin, P.A.S. (2001). Covariation in individuals' sensitivities to bitter compounds: Evidence supporting multiple receptor/transduction mechanisms. *Perception and Psychophysics, 63,* 761–776.

DeMarco, P. J., Jr., Yarbrough, G. L., Yee, C. W., McLean, G. Y., Sagdullaev, B. T., Ball, S. L., & McCall, M. A. (2007). Stimulation via a subretinally placed prosthetic elicits central activity and induces a trophic effect on visual responses. *Investigative Ophthalmology & Visual Science, 48,* 916–926.

Dennett, D. C. (1991). *Consciousness explained.* Boston: Little, Brown.

Deutsch, D. (1974). An auditory illusion. *Nature, 251,* 307–309.

Deutsch, D. (1975). Musical illusions. *Scientific American, 233,* 92–104.

Deutsch, D. (1986). A musical paradox. *Music Perception, 3,* 275–280.

Deutsch, D. (2013). *The psychology of music* (3rd ed.). San Diego, CA: Elsevier.

DeValois, R. L. (1960). Color vision mechanisms in the monkey. *Journal of General Physiology, 43,* 115–128.

DeValois, R. L. (1965). Behavioral and electrophysiological studies of primate vision. In W. D. Ness (Ed.), *Contributions to sensory physiology* (Vol. 1). New York: Academic Press.

DeValois, R. L. (2004). Neural coding of color. In L. M. Chalupa & J. S. Werner (Eds.), *The visual neurosciences* (Vol. 2, pp. 1003–1016). Cambridge, MA: MIT Press.

DeValois, R. L., Abramov, I., & Jacobs, G. H. (1966). Analysis of response patterns of LGN cells. *Journal of the Optical Society of America, 56,* 966–977.

Devos, M., Patte, F., Rouault, J., Laffort, P., & Van Gemert, L. J. (1990). *Standardized human olfactory thresholds.* Oxford, UK: Oxford University Press.

Dewald, A. D., Sinnett, S., & Leonidas, A. A. (2013). A window of perception when diverting attention? Enhancing recognition for explicitly presented, unattended, and irrelevant stimuli by target alignment. *Journal of Experimental Psychology: Human Perception and Performance, 39,* 1304–1311.

de Wijk, R. A., & Cain, W. S. (1994). Odor quality: Discrimination versus free and cued identification. *Perception and Psychophysics, 56,* 12–18.

DeWitt, L. A., & Samuel, A. G. (1990). The role of knowledge-based expectation in music perception: Evidence for musical restoration. *Journal of Experimental Psychology: General, 119,* 123–144.

DeYoe, E. A., & Van Essen, D. C. (1988). Concurrent processing streams in monkey visual cortex. *Trends in Neurosciences, 11,* 219–226.

Diehl, R. L., Lotto, A. J., & Holt, L. L. (2004). Speech perception. *Annual Review of Psychology, 55,* 149–179.

Djordjevic, J., Lundstrom, J. N., Clement, F., Boyle, J. A., Pouliot, S., & Jones-Gotman, M. (2008). A rose by any other name: Would it smell as sweet? *Journal of Neurophysiology, 99,* 386–393.

Djordjevic, J., Zatorre, R. J., Petrides, M., Boyle, J., & Jones-Gotman, M. (2005). Functional neuroimaging of odor imagery. *NeuroImage, 24*, 791–801.

Doerschner, K., Kersten, D., & Schrater, P. (2009). Rapid classification of surface reflectance from image velocities. *Computer Analysis of Images and Patterns, Lecture Notes in Computer Science, 5702*, 856–864.

Domínguez-Borràs, J., Armony, J. L., Maravita, A., Driver, J., & Vuilleumier, P. (2013). Partial recovery of visual extinction by Pavlovian conditioning in a patient with hemispatial neglect. *Cortex, 49*, 891–898.

Downing, P. E., Jiang, Y., Shuman, M., & Kanwisher, N. (2001). Cortical area selective for visual processing of the human body. *Science, 293*, 2470–2473.

Drew, T., Võ, M.L.-H., & Wolfe, J. M. (2013). The invisible gorilla strikes again: Sustained inattentional blindness in expert observers. *Psychological Science, 24*, 1848–1853.

Duchaine, B. C., & Nakayama, K. (2006). Developmental prosopagnosia: A window to content-specific face processing. *Current Opinion in Neurobiology, 16*, 166–173.

Duffy, V. B., Lucchina, L. A., & Bartoshuk, L. M. (2004). Genetic variation in taste: Potential biomarker for cardiovascular disease risk? In J. Prescott & B. J. Tepper (Eds.), *Genetic variation in taste sensitivity: Measurement, significance, and implications* (pp. 195–228). New York: Marcel Dekker.

Egly, R., Driver, J., & Rafal, R. D. (1994). Shifting visual attention between objects and locations: Evidence from normal and parietal lesion subjects. *Journal of Experimental Psychology: General, 123*, 161–177.

Eimas, P. D., & Corbit, J. D. (1973). Selective adaptation of linguistic feature detectors. *Cognitive Psychology, 4*, 99–109.

Engen, T. (1972). The effect of expectation on judgments of odor. *Acta Psychologica, 36*, 450–458.

Epstein, R., & Kanwisher, N. (1998). A cortical representation of the local visual environment. *Nature, 392*, 598–601.

Epstein, R. A. (2005). The cortical basis of visual scene processing. *Visual Cognition, 12*, 954–978.

Fain, G. L. (2003). *Sensory transduction*. Sunderland, MA: Sinauer.

Farah, M. J. (2006). Visual perception and visual imagery. In M. J. Farah & T. E. Feinberg (Eds.), *Patient-based approaches to cognitive neuroscience* (2nd ed., pp. 111–116). Cambridge, MA: MIT Press.

Fechner, G. T. (1860). *Elements of psychophysics* (H. E. Adler, Trans., D. H. Howes & E. G. Boring, Eds.). New York: Holt, Rinehart. (Original work published 1966)

Fedderson, W. E., Sandel, T. T., Teas, D. C., & Jeffress, L. A. (1957). Localization of high frequency tones. *Journal of the Acoustical Society of America, 28*, 988–991.

Feynman, R. P. (1985). *QED: The strange theory of light and matter*. Princeton, NJ: Princeton University Press.

Feynman, R. P. (1995). *Six easy pieces: Essentials of physics explained by its most brilliant teacher*. Reading, MA: Perseus.

Fields, R. D. (2007). The shark's electric sense. *Scientific American, 297*, 74–81.

Fisher, M.F.K. (1943). *The gastronomical me*. New York: Duell, Sloan & Pearce.

Foster, D. H. (2011). Color constancy. *Vision Research, 51*, 674–700.

Fowler, C. A., & Dekle, D. J. (1991). Listening with eye and hand: Cross-modal contributions to speech perception. *Journal of Experimental Psychology: Human Perception and Performance, 17*, 816–828.

Fowler, C. A., & Thompson, J. M. (2010). Listeners' perception of "compensatory shortening." *Attention, Perception & Psychophysics, 72*, 481–491.

Fraser, A., & Wilcox, K. J. (1979). Perception of illusory movement. *Nature, 281*, 565–566.

Frasnelli, J., Fark, T., Lehmann, J., Gerber, J., & Hummel, T. (2013). Brain structure is changed in congenital anosmia. *Neuroimage, 83*, 1074–1080.

Furl, N., Garrido, L., Dolan, R. J., Driver, J., & Duchaine, B. (2011). Fusiform gyrus face selectivity relates to individual differences in facial recognition ability. *Journal of Cognitive Neuroscience, 23*, 1723–1740.

Galanter, E. (1962). Direct measurement of utility and subjective probability. *American Journal of Psychology, 75*, 208–220.

Galantucci, B., Fowler, C. A., & Turvey, M. T. (2006). The motor theory of speech perception reviewed. *Psychonomic Bulletin & Review, 13*, 361–377.

Galletti, C., & Fattori, P. (2003). Neuronal mechanisms for detection of motion in the field of view. *Neuropsychologia, 41*, 1717–1727.

Gallivan, J. P., McLean, D. A., Flanagan, J. R., & Culham, J. C. (2013). Where one hand meets the other: Limb-specific and goal-dependent movement plans decoded from preparatory signals in single human parieto-frontal brain areas. *Journal of Neuroscience, 33*, 1991–2008.

Garneau, N. L., Nuessle, T. M., Sloan, M. M. Santorico, S. A., Coughlin, B. C., & Hayes J. E. (2014, May 27). Crowdsourcing taste research: Genetic and phenotypic predictors of bitter taste perception as a model. *Frontiers in Integrative Neuroscience*. Retrieved from http://journal.frontiersin.org/Journal/10.3389/fnint.2014.00033/abstract

Gelbard-Sagiv, H., Mukamel, R., Harel, M., Malach, R., & Fried, I. (2008). Internally generated reactivation of single neurons in human hippocampus during free recall. *Science, 322*, 96–101.

Gelfand, S. A. (2009). *Essentials of audiology* (3rd ed.). New York: Thieme Medical.

Gerstmann, J. (2001). Pure tactile agnosia. *Cognitive Neuropsychology, 18*, 267–274.

Gibson, J. J. (1950). *The perception of the visual world*. Boston: Houghton Mifflin.

Gibson, J. J. (1979). *The ecological approach to visual perception*. Hillsdale, NJ: Lawrence Erlbaum.

Gibson, E. J. (2001). *Perceiving the affordances: A portrait of two psychologists*. Hillsdale, NJ: Lawrence Erlbaum.

Gilchrist, A., Kossyfidis, C., Bonato, F., Agostini, T., Cataliotti, J., Li, X., . . . Economou, E. (1999). An anchoring theory of lightness perception. *Psychological Review, 106*, 795–834.

Goodale, M. A., Milner, A. D., Jakobsen, L. S., & Carey, D. P. (1991). A neurological dissociation between perceiving objects and grasping them. *Nature, 349*, 154–156.

Graham, C. H., & Hsia, Y. (1958). Color defect and color theory. *Science, 127*, 675–682.

Graven, S. N., & Browne, J. V. (2008). Auditory development in the fetus and infant. *Newborn and Infant Nursing Review, 8*, 187–193.

Green, D. M., & Swets, J. (1966). *Signal detection theory and psychophysics*. New York: John Wiley.

Greenwood, V. (2012, July–August). The humans with super human vision. *Discover*. Retrieved from http://discovermagazine.com/2012/jul-aug/06-humans-with-super-human-vision

Gregory, R. L. (1966). *Eye and brain*. New York: McGraw-Hill.

Grill-Spector, K., Knouf, N., & Kanwisher, N. (2004). The fusiform face area subserves face perception, not generic within-category identification. *Nature Neuroscience, 7*, 555–562.

Grimault, N., Bacon, S. P., & Micheyl, C. (2002). Auditory stream segregation on the basis of amplitude-modulation rate. *Journal of the Acoustical Society of America, 113*, 1340–1348.

Grossman, E. D., Battelli, L., & Pascual-Leone, A. (2005). Repetitive TMS over STSp disrupts perception of biological motion. *Vision Research, 45*, 2847–2853.

Grüsser, O.-J. (1993). The discovery of the psychophysical power law by Tobias Mayer in 1754 and the psychophysical hyperbolic law by Ewald Hering in 1874. *Behavioral and Brain Sciences, 16*, 142–144.

Guyton, A. C. (1991). *Textbook of medical physiology* (8th ed.). Philadelphia, PA: Saunders.

Habibi, A., Wirantana, V., & Starr, A. (2013). Cortical activity during perception of musical pitch: Comparing musicians and nonmusicians. *Music Perception, 30*, 463–479.

Hahnel, U.J.J., & Hecht, H. (2012). The impact of rear-view mirror distance and curvature on judgements relevant to road safety. *Ergonomics, 55*, 23–26.

Harley, T. A. (2014). *The psychology of language: From data to theory* (4th ed.). New York: Psychology Press.

Hartline, H. K., & Ratliff, F. (1958). Spatial summation of inhibitory influences in the eye of Limulus and the mutual interaction of receptor units. *Journal of General Physiology, 41*, 1049–1066.

Hartong, D. T., Berson, E. L., & Dryja, T. P. (2006). Retinitis pigmentosa. *Lancet, 368*, 1795–1809.

Hastorf, A. H., & Cantril, H. (1954). They saw a game: A case study. *Journal of Abnormal and Social Psychology, 49*, 129–134.

He, J. (2003). Corticofugal modulation of the auditory thalamus. *Experimental Brain Research, 153*, 579–590.

Hecht, H., & Savelsbergh, G.J.P. (2004). *Advances in psychology: Vol. 135. Time-to-contact*. Amsterdam, The Netherlands: Elsevier.

Hecht, S., Schlaer, S., & Pirenne, M. H. (1942). Energy, quanta, and vision. *Journal of General Physiology, 39*, 651–673.

Hedges, J. H., Gartshteyn, Y., Kohn, A., Rust, N. C., Shadlen, M. N., Newsome, W. T., & Movshon, J. A. (2011). Dissociation of neuronal and psychophysical responses to local and global motion. *Current Biology, 21*, 2023–2028.

Held, R. (1965). Plasticity in sensory-motor systems. *Scientific American, 213*, 84–94.

Held, R. (1980). The rediscovery of adaptability in the visual system: Effects of extrinsic and intrinsic chromatic dispersion. In C. S. Harris (Ed.), *Visual coding and adaptability* (pp. 69–94). Hillsdale, NJ: Lawrence Erlbaum.

Held, R., & Hein, A. (1963). Movement-produced stimulation in the development of visually guided behavior. *Journal of Comparative and Physiological Psychology, 56*, 872–876.

Hendry, S.H.C., & Reid, R. C. (2000). The koniocellular pathway in primate vision. *Annual Review of Neuroscience, 23*, 127–153.

Henry, B. A., Turner, C. W., & Behrens, A. (2005). Spectral peak resolution and speech recognition in quiet: Normal hearing, hearing impaired, and cochlear implant listeners. *Journal of the Acoustical Society of America, 118*, 1111–1121.

Herz, R. (2007). *The scent of desire*. New York: HarperCollins.

Herz, R., Eliassen, J. C., Beland, S. L., & Souza, T. (2004). Neuroimaging evidence for the emotional potency of odor-evoked memory. *Neuropsychologia, 42*, 371–378.

Herz, R. S., & von Clef, J. (2001). The influence of verbal labelling on the perception of odors: Evidence for olfactory illusions? *Perception, 30*, 381–391.

Hickok, G., & Poeppel, D. (2007). The cortical organization of speech processing. *Nature Reviews Neuroscience, 8*, 393–401.

Hof, P. R., & van der Gucht, E. (2007). Structure of the cerebral cortex of the humpback whale, *Megaptera novaeangliae* (Cetacea, Mysticeti, Balaenopteridae). *Anatomical Record, 290*, 1–31.

Hofeldt, A. J., & Hoefle, F. B. (1993). Stereophotometric testing for Pulfrich's phenomenon in professional baseball players. *Perceptual and Motor Skills, 77*, 407–416.

Hofeldt, A. J., Hoefle, F. B., & Bonafede, B. (1996). Baseball hitting, binocular vision, and the Pulfrich phenomenon. *Archives of Ophthalmology, 114*, 1490–1494.

Hoffman, P. M., Van Riswick, J. G., & Van Opstal, A. J. (1998). Relearning sound localization with new ears. *Nature Neuroscience, 1*, 417–421.

Hollins, M., Bensmaia, S., & Washburn, S. (2001). Vibrotactile adaptation impairs discrimination of fine, but not coarse, textures. *Somatosensory and Motor Research, 18*, 253–262.

Holt, L. L. (2005). Temporally non-adjacent non-linguistic sounds affect speech categorization. *Psychological Science, 16*, 305–312.

Holt, L. L., & Lotto, A. J. (2010). Speech perception as categorization. *Attention, Perception & Psychophysics, 72*, 1218–1227.

Holway, A. H., & Boring, E. G. (1941). Determinants of apparent visual size with distance variant. *American Journal of Psychology, 54*, 21–37.

Horridge, A. (2012). Visual discrimination by the honeybee (*Apis mellijera*). In O. F. Lazareva, T. Shimizu, & E. A. Wasserman (Eds.), *How animals see the world: Comparative behavior, biology, and evolution of vision* (pp. 165–190). New York: Oxford University Press.

Horswill, M., Helman, S., Ardiles, P., & Wann, J. P. (2005). Motorcycle accident risk could be inflated by a time to arrival illusion. *Optometry and Vision Science, 82*, 740–746.

Howard, I. P., & Rogers, B. J. (2002). *Seeing in depth: Vol. 2. Depth perception.* Toronto, Canada: Porteus.

Howard, J. D., Plailly, J., Grueschow, M., Haynes, J. D., & Gottfried, J. A. (2009). Odor quality coding and categorization in human posterior piriform cortex. *Nature Neuroscience, 12*, 932–938.

Hsiao, S. (2008). Central mechanisms of tactile shape perception. *Current Opinion in Neurobiology, 18*, 418–424.

Hua, L. H., Strigo, I. A., Baxter, L. C., Johnson, S. C., & Craig, A. D. (2005). Anteroposterior somatotopy of innocuous cooling activation focus in human dorsal posterior insular cortex. *American Journal of Physiology: Regulatory, Integrative, and Comparative Physiology, 289*, R319–R325.

Hubbard, E. M., Brang, D., & Ramachandran, V. S. (2011). The cross-activation theory at 10. *Journal of Neuropsychology, 5*, 155–177.

Hubel, D. H., & Wiesel, T. N. (1959). Receptive fields of single neurons in the cat's striate cortex. *Journal of Physiology, 148*, 574–591.

Hubel, D. H., & Wiesel, T. N. (1962). Receptive fields, binocular interaction and functional architecture in the cat's visual cortex. *Journal of Physiology, 160*, 106–154.

Hubel, D. H., & Wiesel, T. N. (1965). Receptive fields and functional architecture in two nonstriate visual areas (18 and 19) of the cat. *Journal of Neurophysiology, 28*, 229–289.

Hubel, D. H., & Wiesel, T. N. (1979). Brain mechanisms and vision. *Scientific American, 241*, 150–162.

Hubel, D. H., & Wiesel, T. N. (2005). *Brain and visual perception: The story of a 25-year collaboration.* New York: Oxford University Press.

Hughes, H. C. (1999). *Sensory exotica: A world beyond experience.* Cambridge, MA: MIT Press.

Hughes, H. C., & Zimba, L. D. (1985). Spatial maps of directed visual attention. *Journal of Experimental Psychology: Human Perception and Performance, 11*, 409–430.

Humayun, M. S., Dorn, J. D., da Cruz, L., Dagnelie, G., Sahel, J. A., Stanga, P. E., . . . Greenberg, R. J. Argus II Study Group. (2012). Interim results from the international trial of Second Sight's visual prosthesis. *Ophthalmology, 119*, 779–788.

Hurvich, L. M., & Jameson, D. (1957). An opponent-process theory of color vision. *Psychological Review, 64*, 384–404.

Hutchinson, W. D., Davis, K. D., Lozano, A. M., Tasker, R. R., & Dostrovsky, J. O. (1999). Pain-related neurons in the human cingulate cortex. *Nature Neuroscience, 2*, 403–405.

Huttenlocher, P. R., & de Courten, C. (1987). The development of synapses in striate cortex of man. *Human Neurobiology, 6*, 1–9.

Hyde, K., Peretz, I., & Zatorre, R. (2008). Evidence for the role of the right auditory cortex in fine pitch resolution. *Neuropsychologia, 46*, 632–639.

Irons, J., & Remington, R. (2013). Can attentional control settings be maintained for two color-location conjunctions? Evidence from an RSVP task. *Attention, Perception & Psychophysics, 75*, 862–875.

Isaacs, L. D. (1981). Relationship between depth perception and basketball-shooting performance over a competitive season. *Perceptual and Motor Skills, 53*, 554.

Jacquin-Cortois, S., O'Shea, J., Luaté, J., Pisella, L., Revol, P., . . . Rossetti, Y. (2013). Rehabilitation of spatial neglect by prism adaptation: A peculiar expansion of sensorimotor after-effects to spatial cognition. *Neuroscience and Biobehavioral Reviews, 37*, 594–609.

Jameson, K. A., Highnote, S., & Wasserman, L. (2001). Richer color experience in observers with multiple photopigment opsin genes. *Psychonomic Bulletin & Review, 8*, 244–261.

Janata, P., Birk, J. L., Van Horn, J. D., Leman, M., Tillmann, B., & Bharucha, J. J. (2002). The cortical topography of tonal structures underlying Western music. *Science, 298*, 2167–2170.

Johansson, G. (1973). Visual perception of biological motion and a model for its analysis. *Perception and Psychophysics, 14*, 195–204.

Johnson, E. N., Hawken, M. J., & Shapley, R. (2001). The spatial transformation of color in the primary visual cortex of the macaque monkey. *Nature Neuroscience, 4*, 409–413.

Johnsrude, I. S., Mackey, A., Hakyemez, H., Alexander, E., Trang, H. P., & Carylon, R. P. (2013). Swinging at a cocktail party: Voice familiarity aids speech perception in the presence of a competing voice. *Psychological Science, 24,* 1995–2004.

Jones, F. N. (1956). A forced-choice method of limits. *American Journal of Psychology, 69,* 672–673.

Jönsson, F. U., & Olsson, M. J. (2012). Knowing what we smell. In G. M. Zucco, R. S. Herz, & B. Schaal (Eds.), *Olfactory cognition: From perception and memory to environmental odours and neuroscience* (pp. 115–136). Amsterdam, The Netherlands: John Benjamins.

Jönsson, F. U., & Stevenson, R. J. (2014). Odor knowledge, odor naming and the "tip of the nose" experience. In B. L. Schwartz & A. S. Brown (Eds.), *Tip-of-the-tongue states and related phenomena* (pp. 305–326). Cambridge, UK: Cambridge University Press.

Jordan, G., Deeb, S. S., Bosten, J. M., & Mollon, J. D. (2010). The dimensionality of color vision in carriers of anomalous trichromacy. *Journal of Vision, 10,* 1–19.

Julesz, B. (1971). *Foundations of cyclopean perception.* Chicago: University of Chicago Press.

Kaas, A., Weigelt, S., Roebroeck, A., Kohler, A., & Muckli, L. (2010). Imagery of a moving object: The role of occipital cortex and human MT/V5+. *Neuroimage, 49,* 794–804.

Kadohisa, M., & Wilson, D. A. (2006). Separate encoding of identity and similarity of complex familiar odors in piriform cortex. *Proceedings of the National Academy of Sciences of the United States of America, 103,* 15206–15211.

Kandil, F. I., Rotter, A., & Lappe, M. (2010). Car drivers attend to different gaze targets when negotiating closed vs. open bends. *Journal of Vision, 10,* 1–11.

Kanizsa, G. (1979). *Organization in vision: Essays on gestalt perception.* New York: Praeger.

Kanwisher, N., & Dilks, D. (2013). The functional organization of the ventral visual pathway in humans. In L. Chalupa & J. Werner (Eds.), *The new visual neurosciences* (pp. 733–748). Cambridge, MA: MIT Press.

Kanwisher, N., McDermott, J., & Chun, M. M. (1997). The fusiform face area: A module in human extrastriate cortex specialized for face perception. *Journal of Neuroscience, 17,* 4302–4311.

Kanwisher, N., & Yovel, G. (2006). The fusiform face area: A cortical region specialized for the perception of faces. *Philosophical Transactions of the Royal Society of London, 361,* 2109–2128.

Kau, S., Strumpf, H., Merkel, C., Stoppel, C. M., Heinze, H. J., Hopf, J. M., & Schoenfeld, M. A. (2013). Distinct neural correlates of attending speed vs. coherence of motion. *Neuroimage, 64,* 299–307.

Kawahara, J. I., & Sato, H. (2013). The effect of fatigue on the attentional blink. *Attention, Perception & Psychophysics, 75,* 1096–1102.

Keane, A. G. (2011, December 8). U.S. highway deaths decline for a fifth year, longest streak since 1899. *Bloomberg News.* Retrieved from http://mobile .bloomberg.com/news/2011-12-08/u-s-highway-deaths-decline-2-9-falling-for-fifth-year-1-

Kirchhof, H. (1950). A method for the objective measurement of accommodation speed of the human eye. *American Journal of Optometry, 27,* 163–178.

Kitaoka, A. (2005). *Trick eyes graphics.* Tokyo, Japan: Kanzen.

Klatzky, R. L., Loomis, J. M., Lederman, S. J., Wake, H., & Fujita, N. (1993). Haptic identification of objects and their depictions. *Perception and Psychophysics, 54,* 170–178.

Klüver, H., & Bucy, P. C. (1939). Preliminary analysis of function of the temporal lobes in monkeys. *Archives of Neurology and Psychiatry, 42,* 979–1000.

Kochkin, S. (2005). MarkeTrak VII: Customer satisfaction with hearing instruments in the digital age. *Hearing Journal, 58,* 30–44.

Krantz, J. H., Silverstein, L. D., & Yeh, Y.-Y. (1992). Visibility of transmissive liquid crystal displays under dynamic lighting conditions. *Human Factors, 34,* 615–632.

Krings, T., Töpper, R., Foltys, H., Erberich, S., Sparing, R., Willmes, K., & Thron, A. (2000). Cortical activation patterns during complex motor tasks in piano players and control subjects: A functional magnetic resonance imaging study. *Neuroscience Letters, 278,* 189–193.

Kristjánsson, A. (2013). The case for causal influences of action videogame play upon vision and attention. *Attention, Perception & Psychophysics, 75,* 667–672.

Kuffler, S. W. (1953). Discharge patterns and functional organization of mammalian retina. *Journal of Neurophysiology, 16,* 37–68.

LaMotte, R. H., Shimada, S. G., Green, B. G., & Zelterman, D. (2009). Pruritic and nociceptive sensations and dysesthesias from a spicule of cowhage. *Journal of Neurophysiology, 101,* 1430–1443.

Land, E. H. (1977). The retinex theory of color vision. *Scientific American, 237,* 108–128.

Landis, B. N., Croy, I., & Haehner, A. (2012). Long lasting phantosmia treated with venlafaxine. *Neurocase, 18,* 112–114.

Landry, S. P., Shiller, D. M., & Champoux, F. (2013). Short-term visual deprivation improves the perception of harmonicity. *Journal of Experimental Psychology: Human Perception and Performance, 39,* 1503–1507.

Langenheim, J. (2010, September 17). The last of the sea nomads. *The Guardian.* Retrieved from http://www .theguardian.com/environment/2010/sep/18/last-sea-nomads

Larsen, A., Madsen, K. H., Lund, T. E., & Bundesen, C. (2006). Images of illusory motion in primary visual cortex. *Journal of Cognitive Neuroscience, 18,* 1174–1180.

Lawless, H. T. (1991). A sequential contrast effect in odor perception. *Bulletin of the Psychonomic Society, 29,* 317–319.

Lederman, S. J., & Klatzky, R. L. (2009). Haptic perception: A tutorial. *Attention, Perception & Psychophysics, 71,* 1439–1459.

Leek, M. R., & Molis, M. R. (2009). Beyond audibility: Hearing loss and the perception of speech. *ASHA Leader, 14,* 14–17.

Lettvin, J. Y., Maturana, H. R., McCulloch, W. S., & Pitts, W. H. (1968). What the frog's eye tells the frog's brain. In W. C. Corning & M. Baladan (Eds.), *The mind: Biological approaches to its functions* (pp. 233–258). New York: Interscience.

Li, W., Lopez, L., Osher, J., & Howard, J. D. (2010). Right orbitofrontal cortex mediates conscious olfactory perception. *Psychological Science, 21,* 1454–1463.

Liang, M., Mouraux, A., Hu, L., & Iannetti, G. D. (2013). Primary sensory cortices contain distinguishable spatial patterns of activity for each sense. *Nature Communications, 4,* 1979.

Liberman, A. M., & Mattingly, I. G. (1985). The motor theory of speech perception. *Cognition, 21,* 1–36.

Liu, J., Harris, A., & Kanwisher, N. (2010). Perception of face parts and face configurations: An fMRI study. *Journal of Cognitive Neuroscience, 22,* 203–211.

Livingstone, M. (2002). *Vision and art: The biology of seeing.* New York: Abrams.

Livingstone, M. S., & Hubel, D. H. (1984). Anatomy and physiology of a color system in the primate visual cortex. *Journal of Neuroscience, 4,* 309–356.

Looser, C. E., & Wheatley, T. (2010). The tipping point of animacy: How, when, and where we perceive life in a face. *Psychological Science, 21,* 1854–1862.

Loui, P., Zamm, A., & Schlaug, G. (2012). *Absolute pitch and synesthesia: Two sides of the same coin? Shared and distinct neural substrates of music listening.* Paper presented at the 12th International Conference for Music Perception and Cognition, Thessaloniki, Greece.

Lowenfield, B., & Abel, G. L. (1977). *Methods of teaching Braille reading efficiency of children in lower senior classes.* Birmingham, UK: Research Centre for the Education of the Visually Handicapped.

Mack, A., & Rock, I. (1998). *Inattentional blindness.* Cambridge, MA: MIT Press.

MacMahon, M.K.C. (1996). Phonetic notation. In P. T. Daniels & W. Bright (Eds.), *The world's writing systems* (pp. 821–846). New York: Oxford University Press.

Maertens, M., & Pollmann, S. (2005). fMRI reveals a common neural substrate of illusory and real contours in V1 after perceptual learning. *Journal of Cognitive Neuroscience, 17,* 1553–1564.

Malnic, B., Godfrey, P. A., & Buck, L. B. (2004). The human olfactory receptor gene family. *Proceedings of the National Academy of Sciences of the United States of America, 101,* 2584–2589.

Marr, D. (1982). *Vision.* San Francisco, CA: W. H. Freeman.

Masland, R. H. (2012). The tasks of amacrine cells. *Visual Neuroscience, 29,* 3–9.

Mason, C., & Kandel, E. R. (1991). Central visual pathways. In E. R. Kandel, J. H. Schwartz, & T. M. Jessel (Eds.), *Principles of neural science* (3rd ed., pp. 420–439). Norwalk, CT: Appleton & Lange.

Matthews, G., Warm, J., Reinerman-Jones, L., Langheim, L., Washburn, D., & Tripp, L. (2010). Task engagement, cerebral blood flow velocity, and diagnostic monitoring for sustained attention. *Journal of Experimental Psychology: Applied, 16,* 187–203.

Mattys, S. L., Barden, K., & Samuel, A. G. (2014). Extrinsic cognitive load impairs low-level speech perception. *Psychonomic Bulletin & Review, 21,* 748–754.

Maurer, D., & Werker, J. F. (2014). Perceptual narrowing during infancy: A comparison of language and faces. *Developmental Psychobiology, 56,* 154–178.

May, P. J. (2006). The mammalian superior colliculus: Laminar structure and connections. *Progress in Brain Research, 151,* 321–378.

Mazyn, L.I.N., Lenoir, M., Montagne, G., & Savelsbergh, G. J. (2004). The contribution of stereo vision to one-handed catching. *Experimental Brain Research, 157,* 383–390.

McGurk, H., & MacDonald, T. (1976). Hearing lips and seeing voices. *Nature, 264,* 746–748.

McKeegan, N. (2013). Argus II becomes first "bionic eye" to gain approval for sale in the U.S. *Gizmag.* Retrieved April 11, 2013, from http://www.gizmag.com/argus-ii-becomes-first-bionic-eye-to-gain-approval-for-sale-in-us/26295/

Melzack, R., & Wall, P. D. (1988). *The challenge of pain* (2nd ed.). New York: Penguin.

Menashe, I., Man, O., Lancet, D., & Gilad, Y. (2003). Different noses for different people. *Nature Genetics, 34,* 143–144.

Mendez, M. F., & Cherrier, M. M. (2003). Agnosia for scenes in topographagnosia. *Neuropsychologia, 41,* 1387–1395.

Meng, M., Remus, D. R., & Tong, F. (2005). Filling-in of visual phantoms in the human brain. *Nature Neuroscience, 8,* 1248–1254.

Meyer, R., Palmer, C., & Mazo, M. (1998). Affective and coherence responses to Russian laments. *Music Perception, 16,* 135–150.

Mignault-Goulet, G., Moreau, P., Robitaille, N., & Peretz, I. (2012). Congenital amusia persists in the developing brain after daily music listening. *PLoS ONE, 7,* e36860.

Mishkin, M., Ungerleider, L. G., & Macko, K. A. (1983). Object vision and spatial vision: Two cortical pathways. *Trends in Neurosciences, 6,* 414–417.

Møller, J. (2006). *Hearing: Anatomy, physiology, and disorders of the auditory system* (2nd ed.). Amsterdam, The Netherlands: Elsevier.

Mollon, J. (1992). Worlds of difference. *Nature, 356*, 378–379.

Monnier, P. (2008). Standard definitions of chromatic induction fail to describe induction with S-cone patterned backgrounds. *Vision Research, 48*, 2708–2714.

Moran, J., & Desimone, R. (1985). Selective attention gates visual processing in extrastriate cortex. *Science, 229*, 782–784.

Moreau, P., Jolicoeur, P., & Peretz, I. (2013). Pitch discrimination without awareness in congenital amusia: Evidence from event-related potentials. *Brain and Cognition, 81*, 337–344.

Moscovitch, M., & Moscovitch, D. (2000). Super face inversion effects for isolated internal or external features, and for fractured faces. *Cognitive Neuropsychology, 17*, 201–219.

Mountcastle, V. B. (2005). *The sensory hand: Neural mechanisms of somatic sensation.* Cambridge, MA: Harvard University Press.

Murphy, G., & Kovach, J. K. (1972). *Historical introduction to modern psychology* (3rd ed.). New York: Harcourt Brace.

Nagata, T., Koyanagi, M., Tsukamoto, H., Saeki, S., Isono, K., Shichida, Y., . . . Terakita, A. (2012). Depth perception from image defocus in a jumping spider. *Science, 335*, 469–471.

Nassi, J. J., & Callaway, E. M. (2009). Parallel processing strategies of the primate visual system. *Nature Reviews Neuroscience, 10*, 360–372.

Nathans, J., Piantanida, T., Eddy, R., Shows, T., & Hogness, D. (1986). Molecular genetics of inherited variation in human color vision. *Science, 232*, 203–210.

National Institutes of Health. (n.d.). *Hearing loss.* NIH Senior Health. Retrieved from http://nihseniorhealth.gov/hearingloss/hearinglossdefined/01.html

National Institute on Deafness and Other Communication Disorders. (2011). *Cochlear implants* (NIH Publication No. 11-4798). Bethesda, MD: Author.

Neitz, J., & Jacobs, G. (1986). Polymorphism of the long-wavelength cone in normal human colour vision. *Nature, 323*, 623–625.

Neitz, J., & Jacobs, G. (1990). Polymorphism in normal human color vision and its mechanism. *Vision Research, 30*, 620–636.

Newsome, W. T., Britten, K. H., & Movshon, J. A. (1989). Neuronal correlates of a perceptual decision. *Nature, 341*, 52–54.

Newsome, W. T., & Paré, E. B. (1988). A selective impairment of motion perception following lesions of the middle temporal visual area (MT). *Journal of Neuroscience, 8*, 2201–2211.

Newsome, W. T., Shadlen, M. N., Zohary, E., Britten, K. H., & Movshon, J. A. (1995). Visual motion: Linking neuronal activity to psychophysical performance. In M. S. Gazzaniga (Ed.), *The cognitive neurosciences* (pp. 401–414). Cambridge, MA: MIT Press.

Olausson, H., Wessberg, J., Morrison, I., McGlone, F., & Valbo, A. (2010). The neurophysiology of unmyelinated tactile afferents. *Neuroscience and Behavioral Reviews, 34*, 185–191.

Oltman, M. (2009). *Migraines, perfume, and the Americans with Disabilities Act.* Retrieved from http://www.healthcentral.com/migraine/c/11175/67623/disabilities-act/

Orban, G. A., Kennedy, H., & Butler, J. (1986). Velocity sensitivity and direction sensitivity of neurons in areas V1 and V2 of monkeys: Influence of eccentricity. *Journal of Neurophysiology, 56*, 462–480.

Otero-Millan, J., Macknik, S. L., & Martinez-Conde, S. (2012). Microsaccades and blinks trigger illusory rotation in the "rotating snakes illusion." *Journal of Neuroscience, 32*, 6043–6051.

Overy, K., Peretz, I., Zatorre, R., Lopez, L., & Majno, M. (Eds.). (2012, April). *The neurosciences and music IV: Learning and memory* [Entire issue]. *Annals of the New York Academy of Sciences, 1252.*

Parker, A. J. (2007). Binocular depth perception and the cerebral cortex. *Nature Reviews Neuroscience, 8*, 379–391.

Partanen, E., Kujalaa, T., Näätänen, R., Litola, A., Sambeth, A., & Huotilainen, M. (2013). Learning-induced neural plasticity of speech processing before birth. *Proceedings of the National Academy of Sciences of the United States of America, 110*, 15145–15150.

Pasley, B., David, S. V., Mesgarani, N., Flinker, A., Shamma, S. A., Crone, N. E., . . . Chang, E. F. (2012). Reconstructing speech from human auditory cortex. *PLoS Biology, 10*, 1–13.

Pasternak, T., Bisley, J. W., & Calkins, D. (2003). Visual processing in the primate brain. In M. Gallagher & R. J. Nelson (Eds.), *Handbook of psychology: Biological psychology* (Vol. 3, pp. 139–185). Hoboken, NJ: Wiley & Sons.

Pasupathy, A., & Connor, C. E. (2002). Population coding of shape in V4. *Nature Neuroscience, 5*, 1332–1338.

Patel, A. D. (2008). *Music, language, and the brain.* New York: Oxford University Press.

Patel, A. D. (2013). Sharing and nonsharing of brain resources for language and music. In M. Arbib (Ed.), *Language, music, and the brain* (pp. 329–355). Cambridge, MA: MIT Press.

Pegna, A. J., Khateb, A., Lazeyras, F., & Seghier, M. (2005). Discriminating emotional faces without the primary visual cortices involves the right amygdala. *Nature Neuroscience, 8*, 24–25.

Pei, Y. C., Hsiao, S. S., Craig, J. C., & Bensmaia, S. J. (2011). Neural mechanisms of tactile motion integration in somatosensory cortex. *Neuron, 69*, 536–547.

Penfield, W., & Rasmussen, T. (1950). *The cerebral cortex of man: A clinical study of localization and function.* New York: Macmillan.

Peretz, I. (2008). Musical disorders: From behavior to genes. *Current Directions in Psychological Science, 17*, 329–333.

Peretz, I. (2013). The biological foundations of music: Insights from congenital amusia. In D. Deutsch (Ed.), *The psychology of music* (pp. 551–564). New York: Elsevier.

Peretz, I., & Hyde, K. L. (2003). What is specific to music processing? Insights from congenital amusia. *Trends in Cognitive Sciences, 7*, 362–367.

Perlman, M., & Krumhansl, C. L. (1996). An experimental study of internal interval standards in Javanese and Western musicians. *Music Perception, 14*, 95–116.

Peterson, M. A., & Salvagio, E. (2008). Inhibitory competition in figure-ground perception: Context and convexity. *Journal of Vision, 8*, 1–13.

Petry, S., & Meyer, G. E. (1987). *The perception of illusory contours*. New York: Springer Verlag.

Pettigrew, J. D. (1999). Electroreception in monotremes. *Journal of Experimental Biology, 202*, 1447–1454.

Plantinga, J., & Trainor, L. J. (2005). Memory for melody: Infants use a relative pitch code. *Cognition, 98*, 1–11.

Posner, M. I. (1980). Orienting of attention. *Quarterly Journal of Experimental Psychology, 32*, 3–25.

Posner, M. I., & Rothbart, M. K. (2013). Development of attention networks. In B. R. Kar (Ed.), *Cognition and brain development: Converging evidence from various methodologies* (pp. 61–83). Washington, DC: American Psychological Association.

Ptito, A., & Leh, S. E. (2007). Neural substrates of blindsight after hemispherectomy. *Neuroscientist, 13*, 506–518.

Quiroga, R. Q., Reddy, L., Kreiman, G., Koch, C., & Fried, I. (2005). Invariant visual representation by single neurons in the human brain. *Nature, 435*, 1102–1107.

Quiroga, R. Q., Reddy, L., Kreiman, G., Koch, C., & Fried, I. (2008). Sparse but not "grandmother-cell" coding in the medial temporal lobe. *Trends in Cognitive Sciences, 12*, 87–91.

Quiroga, R. Q., Snyder, L. H., Batista, A. P., Qui, H., & Andersen, R. A. (2006). Movement intention is better predicted than attention in the posterior parietal cortex. *Journal of Neuroscience, 26*, 3615–3620.

Radtke, N. D., Aramant, R. B., Petry, H. M., Green, P. T., Pidwell, D. J., & Seiler, M. J. (2008). Vision improvement in retinal degeneration patients by implantation of retina together with retinal pigment epithelium. *American Journal of Ophthalmology, 146*, 177–182.

Rainville, P., Duncan, G. H., Price, D. D., Carrier, B., & Bushnell, M. C. (1997). Pain affect encoded in human anterior cingulate, but not somatosensory cortex. *Science, 277*, 968–971.

Ramachandran, V. S. (1992). Filling in the blind spot. *Nature, 356*, 115.

Ramachandran, V. S., & Hirstein, W. (1998). The perception of phantom limbs: The D. O. Hebb lecture. *Brain, 121*, 1603–1630.

Rauschecker, J. P., & Scott, S. K. (2009). Maps and streams in the auditory cortex: Nonhuman primates illuminate human speech processing. *Nature Neurosciences, 12*, 718–724.

Read, J.C.A. (2005). Early computational processing in binocular vision and depth perception. *Progress in Biophysics and Molecular Biology, 87*, 77–108.

Reed, C. L., Caselli, R. J., & Farah, M. J. (1996). Tactile agnosia: Underlying impairment and implications for normal tactile object recognition. *Brain, 119*, 875–888.

Reichardt, W. (1969). Movement perception in insects. In W. Reichardt (Ed.), *Processing of optical data by organisms and by machines*. New York: Academic Press.

Rensink, R. A., O'Regan, J. K., & Clark, J. (1997). To see or not to see: The need for attention to perceive changes in scenes. *Psychological Science, 8*, 368–373.

Richards, J. E., Reynolds, G. D., & Courage, M. L. (2010). The neural bases of infant attention. *Current Directions in Psychological Science, 19*, 41–46.

Rodieck, R. W. (1998). *The first steps in seeing*. Sunderland, MA: Sinauer.

Rolls, E. T. (2006). Brain mechanisms underlying flavour and appetite. *Philosophical Transactions of the Royal Society of London, Series B: Biological Sciences, 361*, 1123–1136.

Rolls, E. T., & Tovee, M. J. (1995). Sparseness of the neuronal representation of stimuli in the primate temporal visual cortex. *Journal of Neurophysiology, 73*, 713–726.

Rosch, E. H. (1973). Natural categories. *Cognitive Psychology, 4*, 328–350.

Ruggeri, M., Major, J. C., Jr., McKeown, C., Knighton, R. W., Puliafito, C. A., & Jiao, S. (2010). Retinal structure of birds of prey revealed by ultra-high resolution spectral-domain optical coherence tomography. *Investigative Ophthalmology & Visual Science, 51*, 5789–5795.

Rushton, W. A. (1965). Visual adaptation. *Proceedings of the Royal Society of London, Series B: Biological Sciences, 162*, 20–46.

Rutstein, R. P., & Daum, K. M. (1998). *Anomalies of binocular vision: Diagnosis & management*. St. Louis, MO: Mosby.

Sacks, O. (1985). *The man who mistook his wife for a hat and other clinical tales*. New York: HarperPerennial.

Sacks, O. (2007). *Musicophilia: Tales of music and the brain*. New York: Knopf.

Sacks, O. (2010). *The mind's eye*. New York: Knopf.

Sakurai, K., Kurita, T., Takeda, Y., Shiraishi, H., & Kusumi, I. (2013). Akinetopsia as epileptic seizure. *Epilepsy & Behavior Case Reports, 1*, 74–76.

Sandberg, K., Bahrami, B., Kanai, R., Barnes, G. R., Overgaard, M., & Rees, G. (2013). Early visual responses predict conscious face perception within and between subjects during binocular rivalry. *Journal of Cognitive Neuroscience, 25,* 969–985.

Schachar, R. A. (2006). The mechanism of accommodation and presbyopia. *International Ophthalmology Clinics, 46,* 39–61.

Schacter, D. L. (2001). *Forgotten ideas, neglected pioneers: Richard Semon and the story of memory.* Philadelphia, PA: Psychology Press.

Schenk, T., Ellison, A., Rice, N., & Milner, A. D. (2005). The role of V5/MT+ in the control of catching movements: An rTMS study. *Neuropsychologia, 43,* 189–198.

Schenk, T., Mai, N., Ditterich, J., & Zihl, J. (2000). Can a motion-blind patient reach for moving objects? *European Journal of Neuroscience, 12,* 3351–3360.

Schiells, R. A., & Falk, G. (1987). Joro spider venom: Glutamate agonist and antagonist on the rod retina of the dogfish. *Neuroscience Letters, 77,* 221–225.

Schoenlein, R. W., Peteanu, L. A., Mathies, R. A., & Shank, C. V. (1991). The first step in vision: Femtosecond isomerization of rhodopsin. *Science, 254,* 412–415.

Schultz, D. P., & Schultz, S. E. (1992). *A history of modern psychology* (5th ed.). New York: Harcourt Brace.

Schwartz, B. L. (2014). Memory for people: Integration of face, voice, name, and biographical information. In T. Perfect & S. Lindsay (Eds.), *Sage handbook of applied memory* (pp. 3–19). Thousand Oaks, CA: Sage.

Schwartz, D. A., & Purves, D. (2004). Pitch is determined by naturally occurring periodic sounds. *Hearing Research, 194,* 31–46.

Scott, M. A., van der Kamp, J., Savelsbergh, G. J., Oudejans, R.R.D., & Davids, K. (2004). Object rotation effects on the timing of a hitting action. *Research Quarterly for Exercise and Sport, 75,* 130–137.

Seger, C. A., Spiering, B. J., Sares, A. G., Quraini, S. I., Alpeter, C., David, J., & Thaut, M. H. (2013). Corticostriatal contributions to musical expectancy perception. *Journal of Cognitive Neuroscience, 25,* 1062–1077.

Setliff, A. E., & Courage, M. L. (2011). Background television and infants' allocation of their attention during toy play. *Infancy, 16,* 611–639.

Shepard, R. N. (1964). Circularity in judgements of relative pitch. *Journal of the Acoustical Society of America, 36,* 2346–2353.

Shepard, R. N. (1982). Geometrical approximations to the structure of musical pitch. *Psychological Review, 89,* 305–333.

Silverstein, L. D., & Merrifield, R. M. (1985). *The development and evaluation of color systems for airborne applications* (DOT/FAA Technical Report No. DOT/FAA/PM-85-19). Washington, DC: U.S. Department of Transportation.

Simmons, J. A. (2012). Bats use a neuronally implemented computational acoustic model to form sonar images. *Current Opinion in Neurobiology, 22,* 311–319.

Simner, J., Mulvenna, C., Sagiv, N., Tsakanikos, E., Witherby, S. A., Fraser, C., . . . Ward, J. (2006). Synaesthesia: The prevalence of atypical cross-modal experiences. *Perception, 35,* 1024–1033.

Simons, D. J., & Chabris, C. F. (1999). Gorillas in our midst: Sustained inattentional blindness for dynamic events. *Perception, 28,* 1059–1074.

Simons, D. J., & Levin, D. T. (1997). Change blindness. *Trends in Cognitive Science, 1,* 261–267.

Singer, T., Seymour, B., O'Doherty, J., Kaube, H., Dolan, R. J., & Frith, C. D. (2004). Empathy for pain involves the affective but not sensory components of pain. *Science, 303,* 1157–1162.

Smith, V. C., & Pokorny, J. (2003). Color matching and color discrimination. In S. K. Shevell (Ed.), *The science of color* (pp. 103–148). New York: Elsevier.

Snyder, J. S., & Large, E. W. (2005). Gamma-band activity reflects the metric structure of rhythmic tone sequences. *Cognitive Brain Research, 24,* 117–126.

Snyder, L. H., Batista, A. P., & Anderson, R. A. (2000). Intention-related activity in the posterior parietal cortex: A review. *Vision Research, 40,* 1433–1441.

Sommer, M. A., & Wurtz, R. H. (2008). Brain circuits for the internal monitoring of movements. *Annual Review of Neuroscience, 31,* 317–338.

Stein, B. E., & Meredith, M. A. (1993). *The merging of the senses.* Cambridge, MA: MIT Press.

Stein, L. J., Cowart, B. J., Epstein, A. N., Pilot, L. J., Laskin, C. R., & Beauchamp, G. K. (1996). Increased liking for salty foods in adolescents exposed during infancy to a chloride-deficient feeding formula. *Appetite, 27,* 65–77.

Stevens, K. A., & Brookes, A. (1988). The concave cusp as a determiner of figure-ground. *Perception, 17,* 35–42.

Stevens, S. S. (1956). The direct estimation of sensory magnitudes—loudness. *American Journal of Psychology, 69,* 1–25.

Stevens, S. S. (1957). On the psychophysical law. *Psychological Review, 64,* 153–181.

Stevens, S. S. (1961). To honor Fechner and repeal his law. *Science, 133,* 80–86.

Stevenson, R. J. (2011). Olfactory illusions: Where are they? *Consciousness and Cognition, 20,* 1887–1898.

Stevenson, R. J., & Mahmut, M. K. (2013). Detecting olfactory rivalry. *Consciousness and Cognition, 22,* 504–516.

Stoddard, P. K., & Markham, M. R. (2008). Signal cloaking in electric fish. *Bioscience, 58,* 415–442.

Stone, E. M. (2007). Macular degeneration. *Annual Review of Medicine, 58,* 477–490.

Strayer, D. L., Watson, J. M., & Drews, F. A. (2011). Cognitive distraction while multitasking in the automobile. In B. H. Ross (Ed.), *The psychology of learning and motivation: Advances in research and theory* (Vol. 54, pp. 29–58). San Diego, CA: Academic Press.

Sunami, K., Ishii, A., Takano, S., Yamamoto, H., Sakashita, T., Tanaka, M., . . .Yamane, H. (2013). Neural mechanisms of phonemic restoration for speech comprehension revealed by magnetoencephalography. *Brain Research, 1537*, 164–173.

Susilo, T., & Duchaine, B. (2013). Advances in developmental prosopagnosia research. *Current Opinion in Neurobiology, 23*, 423–429.

Swaminathan, S. K., Masse, N. Y., & Freedman, D. J. (2013). A comparison of lateral and medial intraparietal areas during a visual categorization task. *Journal of Neuroscience, 33*, 13157–13170.

Swettenham, J., Remington, A., Laing, K., Fletcher, R., Coleman, M., & Gomez, J. C. (2013). Perception of pointing from biological motion point-light displays in typically developing children and children with autism spectrum disorder. *Journal of Autism and Developmental Disorders, 43*, 1437–1446.

Swiller, J. (2007). *The unheard: A memoir of deafness and Africa.* New York: Henry Holt.

Szycik, G. R., Stadler, J., Tempelmann, C., & Münte, T. F. (2012). Examining the McGurk illusion using high-field 7 tesla functional MRI. *Frontiers in Human Neuroscience, 6*, 95.

Tamber-Rosenau, B. J., Esterman, M., Chiu, Y.-C., & Yantis, S. (2011). Cortical mechanism of cognitive control for shifting attention in vision and working memory. *Journal of Cognitive Neuroscience, 23*, 2905–2919.

Tamietto, M., Cauda, F., Corazzini, L. L., Savazzi, S., Marzi, C. A., Goebel, R., . . . de Gelder, B. (2010). Collicular vision guides non-conscious behavior. *Journal of Cognitive Neuroscience, 22*, 888–902.

Tan, S.-L., Pfordresher, P., & Harre, R. (2010). *Psychology of music: From sound to significance.* New York: Psychology Press.

Tapia, E., & Breitmeyer, B. G. (2011). Visual consciousness revisited: Magnocellular and parvocellular contributions to conscious and nonconscious vision. *Psychological Science, 22*, 934–942.

Teller, D. Y. (1983). Scotopic vision, color vision, and stereopsis in infants. *Current Eye Research, 2*, 199–210.

Temperley, D. (2000). Meter and grouping in African music: A view from music theory. *Ethnomusicology, 44*, 65–96.

Tomita, T. (1970). Electrical activity of vertebrate photoreceptors. *Quarterly Review of Biophysiology, 3*, 179–222.

Tramo, M. J. (2001). Biology and music: Enhanced: Music of the hemispheres. *Science, 291*, 54–56.

Tranel, D., & Welsh-Bohmer, K. A. (2012). Pervasive olfactory impairment after bilateral limbic system destruction. *Journal of Clinical and Experimental Neuropsychology, 34*, 117–125.

Treisman, A., & Gelade, G. (1980). A feature-integration theory of attention. *Cognitive Psychology, 12*, 97–136.

Tremblay, P., Dick, A. S., & Small, S. L. (2011). New insights into the neurobiology of language from functional brain imaging. In H. Duffau (Ed.), *Brain mapping: From neural basis of cognition to surgical applications* (pp. 131–144). New York: Springer.

Troje, N. F. (2013). What is biological motion? Definition, stimuli and paradigms. In M. D. Rutherford & V. A. Kuhlmeier (Eds.), *Social perception: Detection and interpretation of animacy, agency, and intention* (pp. 13–36). Cambridge, MA: MIT Press.

Troje, N. F., & Westhoff, C. (2006). The inversion effect in biological motion perception: Evidence for a "life detector"? *Current Biology, 16*, 821–824.

Troncoso, X. G., Macknik, S. L., & Martinez-Conde, S. (2008). Microsaccades counteract perceptual filling-in. *Journal of Vision, 8*, 151–159.

Tong, F., Meng, M., & Blake, R. (2006). Neural bases of binocular rivalry. *Trends in Cognitive Science, 10*, 502–511.

Tong, F., Nakayama, K., Vaughan, J. T., & Kanwisher, N. (1998). Binocular rivalry and visual awareness in human extrastriate cortex. *Neuron, 21*, 753–759.

Turner, R. S. (1977). Hermann von Helmholtz and the empiricist vision. *Journal of the History of the Behavioral Sciences, 13*, 48–58.

Turner, R. S. (1993). Vision studies in Germany: Helmholtz versus Hering. *Osiris, 8*, 80–103.

Vasterling, J. J., Proctor, S. P., Amoroso, P., Kane, R., Heeren, T., & White, R. F. (2006). Neuropsychological outcomes of army personnel following deployment to the Iraq war. *JAMA, 206*, 519–529.

Venrooij, J., Mulder, M., Abbink, D. A., van Paassen, M. M., van der Helm, F.C.T., & Bülthoff, H. H. (2013). A new view on biodynamic feedthrough analysis: Unifying the effects on forces and positions. *IEEE Transactions on Systems, Man, and Cybernetics, Part B: Cybernetics, 43*, 129–142.

Verstraten, F.A.J. (1996). On the ancient history of the direction of the motion aftereffect. *Perception, 25*, 1177–1187.

Võ, M. L., & Henderson, J. M. (2009). Does gravity matter? Effects of semantic and syntactic inconsistencies on the allocation of attention during scene perception. *Journal of Vision, 9*, 1–15.

Võ, M. L., & Henderson, J. M. (2011). Object-scene inconsistencies do not capture gaze: Evidence from the flash-preview moving-window paradigm. *Attention, Perception & Psychophysics, 73*, 1742–1753.

von Arx, S. W., Müri, R. M., Heinemann, D., Hess, C. W., & Nyffeler, T. (2010). Anosognosia for cerebral achromatopsia: A longitudinal case study. *Neuropsychologia, 48*, 970–977.

von Békésy, G. (1960). Vibratory pattern of the basilar membrane. In E. G. Wever (Trans., Ed.), *Experiments in hearing* (pp. 404–429). New York: McGraw-Hill.

von der Heydt, R., Peterhans, E., & Baumgartner, G. (1984). Illusory contours and cortical neuron responses. *Science*, *244*, 1260–1262.

Voss, P., & Zatorre, R. J. (2012). Organization and reorganization of sensory-deprived cortex. *Current Biology*, *22*, R168–R173.

Wade, A., Augath, M., Logothetis, N., & Wandell, B. (2008). fMRI measurements of color in macaque and human. *Journal of Vision*, *8*, 1–19.

Wade, N. J. (1996). Descriptions of visual phenomena from Aristotle to Wheatstone. *Perception*, *25*, 1137–1175.

Wald, G. (1968). The molecular basis of visual excitation. *Nature*, *219*, 800–807.

Walls, G. L. (1963). *The vertebrate eye and its adaptive radiation*. Bloomfield Hills, MI: Cranbrook Institute of Science.

Wang, C., & Yao, H. (2011). Sensitivity of V1 neurons to direction of spectral motion. *Cerebral Cortex*, *21*, 964–973.

Wang, Q., Schoenlein, R. W., Peteanu, L. A., Mathies, R. A., & Shank, C. V. (1994). Vibrationally coherent photochemistry in the femtosecond primary event of vision. *Science*, *266*, 422–424.

Ward, L., Wright, E., & McMahon, S. B. (1996). A comparison of the effects of noxious and innocuous counterstimuli on experimentally induced itch and pain. *Pain*, *64*, 129–138.

Warren, R. M. (1970). Perceptual restoration of missing speech sounds. *Science*, *167*, 392–393.

Warren, W. H., Kay, B. A., Zosh, W. D., Duchon, A. P., & Sahuc, S. (2001). Optic flow is used to control human walking. *Nature Neuroscience*, *4*, 213–216.

Watanabe, M., & Rodieck, R. W. (1989). Parasol and midget ganglion cells in the primate retina. *Journal of Comparative Neurology*, *289*, 434–454.

Weeks, S. R., Anderson-Barnes, V. C., & Tsao, J. (2010). Phantom limb pain: Theories and therapies. *Neurologist*, *16*, 277–286.

Weigelt, S., Singer, W., & Kohler, A. (2013). Feature-based attention affects direction-selective fMRI adaptation in hMT+. *Cerebral Cortex*, *23*, 2169–2178.

Weiskrantz, L. (1986). *Blindsight: A case study and implications*. Oxford, UK: Clarendon.

Weiskrantz, L. (1996). Blindsight revisited. *Current Opinion in Neurobiology*, *6*, 215–220.

Weiskrantz, L. (2009). *Blindsight: A case study spanning 35 years and new developments*. Oxford, UK: Oxford University Press.

Weiskrantz, L., Warrington, E. K., Sanders, M. D., & Marshall, J. (1974). Visual capacity in the hemianopic field following a restricted occipital ablation. *Brain*, *97*, 709–728.

Weitzmann, K. (1970). *Illustrations in roll and codex*. Princeton, NJ: Princeton University Press.

Werker, J. (2012). Perceptual foundations of bilingual acquisition in infancy. *Annals of the New York Academy of Sciences: The Year in Cognitive Neuroscience*, *1251*, 50–61.

Werker, J. F., & Gervain, J. (2013). Language acquisition: Perceptual foundations in infancy. In P. Zelazo (Ed.), *The Oxford handbook of developmental psychology* (pp. 909–925). Oxford, UK: Oxford University Press.

Wert, K. J., Davis, R. J., Sancho-Pelluz, J., Nishina, P. M., & Tsang, S. H. (2013). Gene therapy provides long-term visual function in a pre-clinical model of retinitis pigmentosa. *Human Molecular Genetics*, *22*, 558–567.

Wertheimer, M. (1938). Laws of organization in perceptual forms. In W. Ellis (Ed.), *A source book of gestalt psychology* (pp. 71–88). London: Routledge & Kegan Paul. (Original work published 1923)

Westhoff, C., & Troje, N. F. (2007). Kinematic cues for person identification from biological motion. *Perception and Psychophysics*, *69*, 241–253.

Wever, E. G., & Bray, C. W. (1937). The perception of low tones and the resonance-volley theory. *Journal of Psychology*, *3*, 101–114.

Wheatley, T., Weinberg, A., Looser, C. E., Moran, T., & Hajcak, G. (2011). Mind perception: Real but not artificial faces sustain neural activity beyond the N170/VPP. *PLoS ONE*, *6*, e17960.

Wiesel, T. N., & Hubel, D. H. (1963). Single cell responses in striate cortex of kittens deprived of vision in one eye. *Journal of Neurophysiology*, *26*, 1003–1017.

Wiesel, T. N., & Hubel, D. H. (1965). Comparison of the effects of unilateral and bilateral eye closure on cortical unit responses in kittens. *Journal of Neurophysiology*, *28*, 1029–1040.

Williams, S. J., & Purves, D. (2001). *Neuroscience*. Sunderland, MA: Sinauer Associates.

Wolfe, J. M. (2012). Saved by a log: How do humans perform hybrid visual and memory search? *Psychological Science*, *23*, 698–703.

Wong-Riley, M. T. (1979). Changes in the visual system of monocularly sutured or enucleated cats demonstrable with cytochrome oxidase histochemistry. *Brain Research*, *171*, 11–28.

Woods, C. B., & Krantz, J. H. (2001). Sensation and perception: A window into the brain and mind. In J. S. Halonen & S. F. Davis (Eds.), *The many faces of psychological research in the 21st century* (chap. 5). Retrieved from http://teachpsych.org/Resources/Documents/ebooks/faces2001.pdf

Xu, X., Bonds, A. B., & Casagrande, V. A. (2002). Modeling receptive-field structure of koniocellular, magnocellular, and parvocellular LGN cells in the owl monkey (*Aotus trivigatus*). *Visual Neuroscience*, *19*, 703–711.

Xue, J., Peng, G., Yang, J. S., Ding, Q., & Cheng, J. (2013). Predictive factors of brain metastasis in patients with breast cancer. *Medical Oncology, 30*, 337.

Yabuta, N. H., & Callaway, E. M. (1998). Functional streams and local connections of layer 4C neurons in primary visual cortex of the macaque monkey. *Journal of Neuroscience, 11*, 1352–1360.

Yang, H., & Xu-Friedman, M. A. (2013). Stochastic properties of neurotransmitter release expand the dynamic range of synapses. *Journal of Neuroscience, 33*, 14406–14416.

Yasuo, T., Kusuhara, Y., Yasumatsu, K., & Ninomiya, Y. (2008). Multiple receptor systems for glutamate detection in the taste organ. *Biological & Pharmaceutical Bulletin, 31*, 1833–1837.

Yin, T. C., & Chan, J. C. (1990). Interaural time sensitivity in medial superior olive of cat. *Journal of Neurophysiology, 65*, 465–488.

Yoshida, R., & Ninomiya, Y. (2010). New insights into the signal transmission from taste cells to gustatory nerve fibers. *International Review of Cell and Molecular Biology, 279*, 101–134.

Yost, W. A. (2007). *Fundamentals of hearing: An introduction* (5th ed.). New York: Academic Press.

Zamm, A., Schlaug, G., & Eagleman, D. M. (2013). Pathways to seeing music: Enhanced structural connectivity in colored-music synesthesia. *Neuroimage, 74*, 359–366.

Zeki, S. (1993). *A vision of the brain*. Oxford, UK: Blackwell.

Zheng, J., Zhang, B., Bi, H., Maruko, I., Watanabe, I., Nakasata, C., . . . Chino, Y. M. (2007). Development of temporal response properties and contrast sensitivity of V1 and V2 neurons in macaque monkeys. *Journal of Neurophysiology, 97*, 3905–3916.

Zhou, W., & Chen, D. (2009). Binaral rivalry between the nostrils and in the cortex. *Current Biology, 19*, 1561–1565.

Zihl, J., von Cramon, J. D., & Mai, N. (1983). Selective disturbance of movement vision after bilateral brain damage. *Brain, 106*, 313–340.

Zivony, A., & Lamy, D. (2014). Attentional engagement is not sufficient to prevent spatial capture. *Attention, Perception & Psychophysics, 76*, 19–31.

Zokoll, M. A., Wagener, K. C., Brand, T., Buschermöhle, M., & Kollmeier, B. (2012). Internationally comparable screening tests for listening in noise in several European languages: The German digit triplet test as an optimization prototype. *International Journal of Audiology, 51*, 697–707.

AUTHOR INDEX

SUBJECT INDEX

⑤SAGE researchmethods

The essential online tool for researchers from the world's leading methods publisher

Find exactly what you are looking for, from basic explanations to advanced discussion

More content and new features added this year!

"I have never really seen anything like this product before, and I think it is really valuable."

John Creswell, University of Nebraska–Lincoln

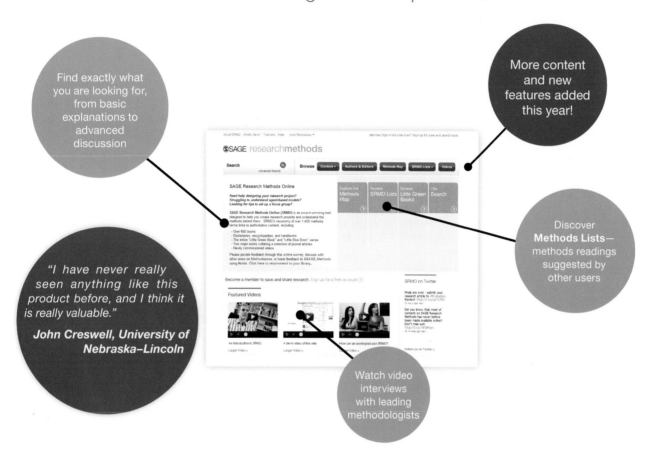

Discover **Methods Lists**—methods readings suggested by other users

Watch video interviews with leading methodologists

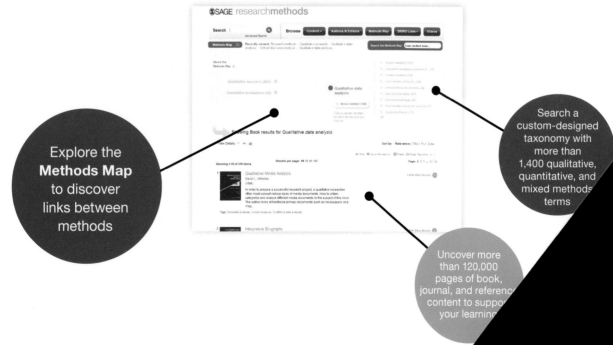

Explore the **Methods Map** to discover links between methods

Search a custom-designed taxonomy with more than 1,400 qualitative, quantitative, and mixed methods terms

Uncover more than 120,000 pages of book, journal, and reference content to support your learning

Find out more at
www.sageresearchmethods.com